We Are
Your
Sisters

**By Dorothy Sterling
in Norton Paperback**

Ahead of Her Time
Abby Kelley and the Politics of Antislavery

(Editor) *We Are Your Sisters*
Black Women in the Nineteenth Century

We Are Your Sisters

Black Women in the Nineteenth Century

We are thy sisters . . .
Our skins may differ, but from thee we claim
A sister's privilege and a sister's name.

— Sarah L. Forten, 1837

Edited by Dorothy Sterling

W · W · NORTON & COMPANY

NEW YORK · LONDON

Reissued in a Norton paperback 1997

Book design by Marjorie J. Flock

Grateful acknowledgment is made to the following for permission to reprint previously published material:

Association for the Study of Afro-American Life and History, Inc., for excerpts from *The Journal of Negro History*, July 1935 and Fall 1980, and from *The Mind of the Negro*, edited by Carter G. Woodson, copyright 1926.

Jim Bearden, Linda Butler, and N. C. Press for excerpts from *Shadd* by Jim Bearden and Linda Butler, copyright 1977.

Beehive Press for excerpts from *Slavery Time When I Was Chillun Down on Marster's Plantation*, edited by Ronald Killion and Charles Waller, copyright 1973.

Greenwood Press for excerpts from *The American Slave* by George P. Rawick.

Hastings House, Publishers, for excerpts from *The Negro in Virginia* by the Virginia Works Progress Administration, copyright 1940.

Holt, Rinehart and Winston for excerpts from *Voices From Slavery* by Norman Yetman, copyright 1970.

Houghton Mifflin Company for an excerpt from *Gumbo Ya-Ya* by Lyle Saxon, copyright 1945 and © renewed 1973 by the Louisiana State Library.

Annie May Hunt and Ruthe Winegarten for an excerpt from "I Am Annie May," edited by Ruthe Winegarten and published in *Chrysalis*, 1980.

Alfred A. Knopf, Inc. for excerpts from *Memorials of a Southern Planter* by Susan Dabney Smedes, copyright 1965.

Randall M. Miller and Cornell University Press for excerpts from *"Dear Master" Letters of a Slave Family*, edited by Randall M. Miller, copyright 1978.

Temple University Press for excerpts from *The Black Worker*, edited by Philip Foner and Ronald Lewis, copyright 1978, and for an excerpt from *Children of Strangers* by Kathryn L. Morgan, copyright 1980.

University of Chicago Press for excerpts from *Lay My Burden Down* by Benjamin A. Botkin, copyright 1945.

University of Illinois Press for an excerpt from *Sinful Tunes and Spirituals* by Dena J. Epstein, copyright 1977.

University of Massachusetts Press for excerpts from *Lydia Maria Child Selected Letters, 1817–1880*, edited by Milton Meltzer and Patricia G. Holland, copyright 1982, and for excerpts from *Race Relations in Virginia and Miscegenation in the South, 1776–1860* by James Hugo Johnston, copyright 1970.

University Press of Virginia for excerpts from *Weevils in the Wheat*, edited by Charles Perdue, Thomas E. Barden, and Robert K. Phillips, copyright 1976.

Vanderbilt University Press for excerpts from *Dear Ones at Home*, edited by Henry L. Swint, copyright 1966.

Many thanks are also due to the libraries and individuals listed below for the use of manuscripts in their collections:

American Antiquarian Society, Worcester, Mass.; Amistad Research Center; Trustees of the Boston Public Library; Carole Bovoso; Clarke Historical Library, Central Michigan University; Department of Manuscripts and University Archives, Cornell University Libraries; Fisk University Library; the Houghton Library, Harvard University; Historical Society of Pennsylvania; Kansas State Historical Society; Library of Congress; Massachusetts Historical Society; Medical College of Pennsylvania; Moorland-Spingarn Research Center; National Archives; Oberlin College Archives; Ohio Historical Society; William Phillips, Jr.; Schomburg Center for Research in Black Culture; Sophia Smith Collection, Smith College; George Arents Research Library at Syracuse University; Tulane University Library; Joseph Regenstein Library, University of Chicago; King Library North, University of Kentucky; William L. Clements Library, University of Michigan; University of Rochester Library; Manuscripts Department, University of Virginia Library.

Library of Congress Cataloging in Publication Data
Sterling, Dorothy, 1913–
  We are your sisters.
  Bibliography: p.
  Includes index.
  1. Afro-American women—History—19th century.
I. Title.
E185.86.S75 1984   973'.0496   83-11469

ISBN 0-393-31629-7

W. W. Norton & Company, Inc., 500 Fifth Avenue, New York, NY 10110
W. W. Norton & Company Ltd., 10 Coptic Street, London WC1A 1PU

4 5 6 7 8 9 0

For
Septima P. Clark, Ruby Cornwell, Jean B. Hutson,
Sara D. Jackson, Dorothy B. Porter, Orial Redd,
and in memory of
Vivian Alston, Carol C. Bowie, Georgia Britto, Annette S. Lee—
all strong and loving black women.

Contents

Foreword

READING WE ARE YOUR SISTERS for the first time in the spring of 1995, 1 felt elated and triumphant to discover the rich and compelling story of our American foremothers that is woven together in this remarkable documentary of nineteenth-century African-American women. But I also felt sorrow and anger that these stories of faith, courage, and resistance, an entire century of black women's physical and intellectual labor, had for so long been absent from the historical record. *We Are Your Sisters* gives us, finally, black women speaking—*in their own words*—as mothers, wives, slaves, ex-slaves, entrepreneurs, newspaper correspondents, teachers, artists, farmers, washerwomen, and physicians. In this history, African-American women, so often the objects of other people's observations, become subjects, the centers of their own consciousness, their own lives, their own communities, their own histories. What is perhaps the most striking about *We Are Your Sisters* is that the diversity of voices in these documents reveals the multiplicity, the particularity, the heterogeneity of black women's stories. In hundreds of primary sources—letters, diaries, court testimony, newspaper articles, autobiographies, and oral interviews—each section and chapter present a marvelous set of revelations. Listen to this story of a former slave recounting her courting days like any lover recalling her first love affair: "They say I was a pretty gal then, face shiny like a ginger cake, and hair straight and black as a crow. One springtime de flowers get be blooming, de hens to cackling, and de guineas to patarocking. Sam come along when I was out in de yard wid de [white] baby. He fust talk to de baby, and I asked him if de baby wasn't pretty? He say, 'Yes, but not as pretty as you is, Louisa.' I looks at Sam, and dat kind of foolishness wind up in a weddin.'"(33)

Every page of this documentary contains such revelations—stories that make us revise old assumptions and stereotypes about black women. We learn about black women after slavery starting businesses and going to school, or about others who worked in the fields in order to send their husbands and children to get "edicated." One woman, who had to learn clandestinely what white folks meant by "the market," figured out how to amass enough capital to buy fifteen acres and to pay for the property on time doing sewing and farming. Certainly these women were subjected to overwhelming injustices and cruelties, but *We Are Your Sisters* also tells us about Reconstruction women defying the authority of ex-slave holders and risking severe retaliation. Some were even bold enough to file official complaints against their former owners with the Freedmen's Bureau. In spite of the terrorism of the Ku Klux Klan later in the century, black women fought back, refused to submit, and sometimes overcame. In Atlanta in 1881, washerwomen, joined by cooks, nurses, and other servants, organized a strike and wrote to the mayor of Atlanta, declaring, "We will have full control of the city's washing at our own prices, as the city has control of our husbands' work at their price....We mean business this week or no washing." (357)

No matter how successful they were at combating the overwhelming odds against them, black women of this century did their work as "daughters of a despised race." Whether they were the wives and daughters of black politicians living in a social world of elegance and luxury, or scholars educated at prestigious schools like Oberlin and Fisk, all were subjected to the casual indignities and routine injustices of Jim Crow. They were ejected forcibly from the "ladies" rooms of train stations, slapped in the mouth by white men, segregated in and thrown out of white churches, pushed off sidewalks, and stoned. In the face of the growing hostility from whites and more deeply entrenched racism, black women throughout the nineteenth century show a persistent concern for the "the welfare of the race." Writer and lecturer Frances Harper said that "when it was a question of race, she let the lesser question of sex go." In spite of the primacy of race issues, many of these women were activists for women's rights. Harper herself preached against husbands' ill-treating their wives and was one of the first black women to support the American Woman Suffrage Association. Newspaperwoman Mary Ann Shadd Cary courageously published an account of an attempted rape of a "respectable colored lady" by a white man, though rape was a taboo subject in both the black and white abolitionist press. Rejecting both gender and racial oppression, former slave Lucy Skipworth said she intended to use her new freedom to leave her husband and her master, both of whom she said tried to control her.

What is perhaps most compelling about Sterling's text are the intimate, private revelations: Sarah Douglass's fear of sexual intercourse; Edmonia Highgate's interracial love affair, which ends with her death from an abortion; Sara Stanley's angry response to the prejudice she encounters among white missionaries in the antebellum south; Emma Brown's decision to shave off all her hair to try to cure her headaches; Mary Cuffe's letter to a lawyer trying to get child support from her famous husband after he deserts her. Rosetta Douglass Sprague's letters to her father, Frederick Douglass, which expose the deteriorating relations between her husband and her father, tell us a great deal about the difficulties of life with the great and famous.

Dorothy Sterling has been preparing for many years for the task of editing this prodigious volume. As a self-taught historian she trained by reading the pioneers of modern black history—Benjamin Quarles, John Hope Franklin, Herbert Aptheker, and W. E. B. DuBois. In the 1930s and 40s she worked as a researcher for *Life* magazine and on the Federal Writers Project, where she learned to gather information on every conceivable subject and to sort through historical records. In 1953, on the eve of the modern civil rights movement, Sterling began what was to become for her "the living work," publishing *Freedom Train: The Story of Harriet Tubman* and five more books of black history for young people. This early work established Sterling's methods and practices as an historian: she is always the unobtrusive presence, amassing the painstakingly researched facts that cumulatively become the persuasive evidence, the political document. Throughout *We Are Your Sisters* Sterling provides the textual commentary that knits these documentary fragments into a coherent and dramatic narrative. Here in this powerful and eloquent documentary is the untold story of nineteenth-century America, told now by the eyewitnesses. In its faithfulness to these voices, to the truth(s) of black women's lives, *We Are Your Sisters* is indeed a "living work."

Mary Helen Washington

Introduction

My grandmothers were strong.
They followed plows and bent to toil.
They moved through fields sowing seed.
They touched earth and grain grew.
They were full of sturdiness and singing.

— *Margaret Walker*

To be a black woman in nineteenth-century America was to live in the double jeopardy of belonging to the "inferior" sex of an "inferior" race. Yet 2 million slave and 200,000 free women of that time possessed a tenacity of spirit, a gift of endurance, a steadfastness of aspiration that helped a whole population to survive.

This book is a documentary portrayal of the black women who lived between 1800 and the 1880s. Portions of it are oral history—selections from more than a thousand interviews with ex-slaves and first-person testimony found in government records. It also includes hundreds of letters, excerpts from diaries and autobiographies, and newspaper accounts. The language of the documents is necessarily uneven, ranging from the folk speech of the untutored slave to the flowery Victorian prose of the free woman. Although the voices may seem dissimilar, they serve to corroborate and complement one another and to round out the whole picture. The participants in the great drama of slavery and freedom who talk of themselves and their world in these pages speak for tens of thousands of their sisters with whom they shared a common history, common daily experiences, and a common future.

I have searched for the expressions of the women at the bottom as well as the top, for reports from washerwomen and domestics as well as those of teachers, lecturers, writers. A rich but fragmentary record made it impossible to maintain a numerically precise balance, but in the mobile society of black nineteenth-century America, the working-class woman and the superachiever often encountered the same problems. In selecting documents, I have chosen those that represent the intimate and the personal, which best portray the black woman's interior world. The letters to family and friends, which were never intended for publication, illuminate the women's feelings, their goals for themselves and their people, and their relations with white contemporaries.

The book contains no formal writings, no sermons, few speeches; it omits material that is available elsewhere and skips whole categories of women—the preachers, for example—for whom no private writings were found. *We Are Your Sisters* is not a definitive history of black women, or, indeed of slavery and emancipation. Rather, it is a sourcebook, a sampler, which may lead others to compile a complete history.*

As I reread the documents, I see that some general observations can be made. The difference between the experiences of most black and white women is striking. While white women were hampered by the bonds of "true womanhood" and told that their sphere was the home, the black woman was enslaved. Her job was to work and to produce workers. Her master owned her in a literal sense. He could beat her, sell her away from her family, and keep her at backbreaking labor. Within the framework of slavery she was forced to be submissive, but within the slave community—the Afro-American culture that developed in the quarters—the black woman had a status that was not accorded to her white sister. To survive the harsh system, and many did not, she did a man's work in the fields. Perhaps she took pride in the dexterity with which she filled her basket with bolls of cotton or the strength with which she swung a heavy hoe. Perhaps she defied authority by putting stones in her basket before weighing-in time or by napping in the shade of the corn tassels after the overseer drove by.

At dusk the slave woman returned to her cabin to cook, sew, and tend to her children. All decisions then made around the hearth were ones in which she participated equally with her husband. If the master did not interfere in the selection, slave marriages were based on genuine affection, because a husband was not chosen for his wealth or position or a wife for her dowry or blue blood. Interviews with ex-slaves tell tender tales of courtship and young love, and their letters testify to the heartbreak of separation and the joy of reunion.

Emancipation found the freedwoman emptyhanded, without home or land or mule for plowing. But under the stress of slavery she

---

*While this book has been in press, two books with fresh documentary material on black women have appeared. *Our Nig, or Sketches from the Life of a Free Black* (N.Y., 1983) was written by Harriet E. Wilson in 1858; *The Black Military Experience*, edited by I. Berlin, J. Reidy, and L. Rowland, is the first of five volumes from the National Archives.

had developed tools for survival. One was an understanding of the people in power. As if she were looking through a one-way window, she could observe the behavior of Mister Charlie and Miss Ann. In her dealings with them she wore a mask that concealed her own feelings. The ability to empathize and please has always been expected of women. An old slave who said, "If your head is in the lion's mouth, it's best to pat him a little," had learned her lesson in a hard school.

Beyond this, the freedwoman had acquired not so much independence as self-dependence. *If I am not for myself, who will be for me?* After the day of jubilee, she gathered her children, sought missing family members, and went to work. Contracting with a planter, often her former owner, she toiled in the fields for a small wage or a share of the crop. If her marriage had survived slavery and war, she worked together with her husband; sometimes they hired themselves out, sometimes they worked as tenant farmers, dreaming of the day when they could purchase their own land.

Ironically, the egalitarian slave marriage, which might have served as a model for northern feminists who were by then seeking greater freedom for themselves, quickly came under attack. The freedpeople's best friends—Union soldiers, Freedmen's Bureau officers, missionaries and teachers from the North—all agreed that the ex-slaves should formally marry. There must be no more living together without benefit of clergy. Further, sex roles must change. "Be a man!" the bureau officers lectured. "Husband, you are the head of your family. You must provide for their wants." "Wives," they counseled, "stay home with your children. Sew curtains for your windows, carpets for your floors. Greet your husband with a kiss when he comes home at night." This advice was reinforced when freedmen, but not women, were given the vote. They attended political rallies, made speeches, organized militia companies, and were on their way to becoming full-fledged members of the patriarchal society, except for one thing. The vast majority could not earn enough to support their families. The pittance that they were paid was eaten up by "deducts"; each season found them deeper in debt. Furthermore, planters would not agree to freedwomen "playing the lady, being supported by their husbands like white folks." When a freedman contracted for a year's labor, his boss insisted on the services of his wife as well. Even Freedmen's Bureau officers deplored "the evils of female loaferism."

It is difficult to guess what might have happened if freedmen's earnings had been higher. Certainly the women longed to spend more time with their children, to educate them, and to go to school themselves. They wanted curtains and carpets and the other comforts they saw in white homes. But would they have been willing to accept a subordinate position in exchange for financial support? The choice was never theirs to make. Putting their shoulders to the plow, bending over a washtub, the freedwomen worked alongside their husbands as they had done in the past.

When the slave marriage became the two-income union of freedom, frictions developed. It is not surprising that a slave suddenly released into the "free" labor market and endowed with a voice and a vote in the polity would wish to dominate his home. Reports of wife beatings, infidelity, and desertion appeared frequently in the records of the Freedmen's Bureau. The freedman who beat his wife was only imitating the patriarchal family model presented to him by white society.* No quantitative study has been made to determine how widespread this practice was in postbellum black families, but my conjecture is that some of the conflicts between modern black men and women date from this period when sex roles were in transition.

It is not, however, the purpose of this book to discuss black men. Women's letters and first-person accounts make it clear that despite encounters with white culture after the war, black women still remembered the lessons learned in adversity: They had to depend on themselves. Ida B. Wells, the daughter of slaves, was sixteen years old when she went to work to support herself and her younger siblings. On her twenty-fifth birthday, she thanked God, not so much for taking care of her, but because "I have always been provided with the means to make an honest living." "Having been a black woman," Lena Horne said almost a century later, "You learn not to depend on anything. You get into the habit of surviving."

The free women of the North had somewhat different experiences from the slaves. In the black communities, men were the acknowledged leaders—ministers, newspaper editors, political spokesmen, even voters in a few states. However, because segregation barred the majority from all but the most menial jobs, the women, too, were breadwinners. In addition to working, they organized their own societies for mutual relief, self-education, and against slavery. In 1821 the Daughters of Africa, washerwomen and domestics of Philadelphia, were pooling their pennies to pay sick and death benefits to needy members. A decade later, and several steps up the social ladder, there were Colored Ladies' Literary Societies in major cities of the North-

---

*An 1868 editorial in the *Nation* noted that working-class families remained intact because husbands enforced obedience "by blows and abuse."

east. The nation's first Female Anti-Slavery Society was organized by the black women of Salem, Massachusetts, in 1832.

In the abolitionist movement, in the organizations for freedpeople's relief during and after the war, and in the struggle for woman's rights, black women worked with the most progressive white women of the country, sometimes forging lasting friendships. Sojourner Truth, Frances Ellen Watkins and Sarah Remond were employed as antislavery speakers; Mary Ann Shadd became the first black "editress." When schoolmarms traveled to the South at war's end, blacks were members of the crusading band and often the most effective teachers. Although no black women were present at Seneca Falls in 1848, they participated in similar woman's rights meetings thereafter, until the turn of the century when the need of southern support for a woman suffrage amendment made them unwelcome.

The black women who worked with whites were caught between two worlds. Only a generation or two removed from slavery themselves, hemmed in by the same discriminatory laws that poor blacks faced, they nevertheless strove to live up to the standards of their white associates. No one's curtains were as starched, gloves as white, or behavior as correct as black women's in the antislavery societies. Yet the pinch of poverty was almost always there. Light-skinned Susan Paul, an officer of the Boston Female Anti-Slavery Society and a welcome guest in white homes, did not tell her white friends of her desperate struggle to support her mother and four orphaned children until she was on the verge of eviction from her home.

As educational opportunities widened, a second generation of black Puritans pushed themselves to excel, determined to demonstrate their people's capabilities. "I never rose to recite in my classes at Oberlin but I felt that I had the honor of the whole African race upon my shoulders," said Fannie Jackson Coppin. Letters from other college students and from the schoolmarms in the South reflect the intensity of their struggle to win acceptance from whites and, at the same time, hold on to their own identity. Blinding headaches and mental breakdowns were part of the price paid for being black and a woman at coeducational Oberlin or in a "family" of missionary-teachers in the postwar South. A few were quickly burned out, but most persisted, bringing literacy to millions and initiating a tradition that led to such dedicated women educators as Mary McCleod Bethune.

Little is known about the romantic attachments of the free women. The fact that marriage offered few material advantages may explain why so many of the women achievers married late or not at all. Some may have shared Elleanor Eldridge's belief that marriage was a waste of time for, she pointed out, while her mistress was courting she had knitted five pairs of stockings! Others, doubtless, longed for love and companionship, although the Victorian code prevented them from mentioning or perhaps even admitting to sexual feelings. The letters of wives and husbands that have survived—Nancy Ruffin's and Mary Ann Shadd Cary's, for instance—and the autobiographies indicate that marriages were based on mutual affection, with the husband taking pride in his wife's achievements.

My introduction to black women came three decades ago when I wrote a young people's biography of Harriet Tubman. Moved by Tubman's heroic life, I wanted to know and write more about black history. During several research trips to the South—the segregated South of the 1950s—I met people who were as impressive, and as new to me, as the historical figures I was pursuing: the school principal who had to go to the back door of the Beaufort, South Carolina, public library while I entered at the front, and who shrugged off the humiliation with quiet humor; the dean of a North Carolina state college who flattered legislators into appropriating money for auditorium draperies, money that she then spent for additional classrooms; the ten-year-old girl in Kentucky who braved threats and name-calling to attend a newly desegregated school and explained, "I wanted to show that I could do the same work they did. And I can."

Nor were these capable and courageous women only to be found in the South. For the first time I made black friends—librarians, writers, teachers, political activists. My white neighbors, caught up in the feminine mystique, were decorating cakes and hooking rugs to conceal their longing for meaningful occupations, while these black women were juggling work, family, and community responsibilities with extraordinary grace and self-possession. I observed the same combination of strength and charm in public figures. Mary Church Terrell, in her ninetieth year, dressed in her best fur coat and Queen Mary hat as she led the picket lines that ended segregation in Washington, D.C.; dignified Rosa Parks whose refusal to give up her bus seat sparked the civil rights revolution of the 1960s. And following them, Fanny Lou Hamer and Coretta Scott King, Barbara Jordan, Shirley Chisholm, and a host of others. Why did they seem more able and resilient then the women I had grown up with? I had always accepted the liberal shibboleth of the day: black women were just like whites, except that their skins were darker. Later I realized that this was untrue. The strengths and skills that black women were forced to develop had been transmitted to their descendants. My black friends were different because their history and culture were different.

I did not come to this insight overnight. I had long been collecting documents by and about black women, but more than a decade passed before I was able to devote full time to an investigation of primary sources. After I read the wealth of material that went into the making of this book, the key to the women's personalities became clear. Thrown on their own resources ("Nobody ever helps me over mudpuddles," Sojourner Truth had said), they had learned the art of survival, acquiring a vitality and independence that made them unique. They were full of sturdiness and singing.

Throughout *We Are Your Sisters*, I have tried to be unobtrusive, offering only enough historical background to make the documents clear. I make no effort, however, to conceal my admiration and respect for the women who speak in the succeeding pages.

EDITORIAL METHOD

To UNDERLINE the authenticity of the documents, original spellings and capitalizations have been retained. I have, however, added periods at the ends of sentences, and started new ones with capitals. I have also made the salutations, datelines, and signatures of the letters uniform, using square brackets when a place or date was added.

Almost all the documents are excerpts from longer originals. Although I have been careful to preserve the writer's meaning, I have deleted extraneous phrases and tedious repetition. Except where they are essential to continuity or clarity, I have not used ellipses. Scholars who wish to read the full texts will find the sources of all documents listed on pages 504–14.

Part I
Slavery Time

Mammy Prater, an ex-slave, was 115 years old when this photograph was taken. *(Library of Congress)*

SINCE THE BEGINNING OF the nineteenth century there has been an endless flow—at times a trickle, at times a torrent—of books about slavery in the United States. Yet few have been written from the point of view of the slave, and fewer still have permitted us to hear from the female slave. This omission has not been for lack of source material. During the nineteenth century, journalists, schoolteachers, and local historians interviewed slave women; a small number of women also wrote their own accounts of slave life. In the 1920s and '30s, more than two thousand former slaves were interviewed by the Works Progress Administration (WPA) Federal Writers' Project and by researchers at Fisk and Southern universities. Some of the Fisk interviews were published in the university's Unwritten History of Slavery and God Struck Me Dead. A sampling of the WPA interviews appeared in Benjamin A. Botkin's moving Lay My Burden Down, in Negro in Virginia and in Gumbo Ya-Ya, but the bulk of the Slave Narrative Collection remained in typescript in the Rare Book Room of the Library of Congress for almost forty years.

Historians knew about this collection of eyewitness testimony but questioned its validity. Critics said the ex-slaves had been too young before emancipation for their recollections to be meaningful and were too old when interviewed for their memories to be reliable. They also claimed the informants did not represent a scientific sample of the ex-slave population; besides, the interviewers had been untrained, biased, and insensitive. Only after the civil rights struggles of the 1960s stimulated interest in black history and in history "from the bottom up" did scholars begin to examine these interviews. Norman R. Yetman published 100 of them in his Life Under the 'Peculiar Institution': Selections from the Slave Narrative Collection*. Two years later, George P. Rawick edited The American Slave: A Composite Autobiography. This eighteen-volume collection reproduced the original typescripts of the Writers' Project and Fisk University interviews. Since then Slavery Time When I was Chillun Down on Marster's Plantation and Weevils in the Wheat, additional WPA interviews with Georgia and Virginia ex-slaves, have been published, and in

---

*Later titled Voices from Slavery.

1978–79 Rawick added twenty-two supplementary volumes to The American Slave.

Reading more than a thousand interviews with former slave women is a stirring experience. One can overlook the women's muddled dates, ignore their conventional bows to white interviewers, skim over the repetitions and rambling. Here are the genuine voices of slave women. "I wanna tell you all I kin, but I wants to tell it right", one says. "This is what I know. I see dis myself," says another. In folk idiom rich in metaphor, they recall the minutiae of a slave woman's life: her work in field and kitchen, child care and child loss, sexual assault and loving family life. Regardless of technical flaws, these interviews have the ring of truth. Does a story sound exaggerated or unbelievable? Read on, and women from Georgia, Mississippi, Virginia, Texas will describe a similar incident in almost the same words. And a young woman in South Carolina in 1866 and an octogenarian in Arkansas seventy years later will confirm their testimony.

Slavery Time, the opening section of this book, consists of excerpts from nineteenth- and twentieth-century interviews with slave women, selections from written narratives, testimony from wills and court cases, and more than twenty letters from slaves. To guard against the women's biases, and my own, I have included primarily those incidents that were reported three, four, five times; once or twice, when this rule has been broken, I have so indicated in the text.

Few of the interviewers were linguists. They transcribed the ex-slaves' speech as they heard it, as they thought they heard it, or as they thought it should have been said—and sometimes, the whiter the interviewer's skin, the heavier the dialect and the more erratic the spelling. A number of the interviews also went through an editorial process in which dialect was cleaned up or exaggerated, depending on the editor's judgment. To attempt to make the language of the interviews consistent or to "translate" them into standard English would add still another change. Therefore, each selection is printed as it appeared in the original source.

ONE

Childhood

"YOU WANTS TO KNOW ALL 'bout de slavery time? I could tell
you a trunk full of good and easy, bad and hard," the old woman said.
She had been one of 2 million girls and women enslaved in the American South in the decades before the Civil War. Her earliest memory
was of the "nuss house" where her mother left her when she went to
the fields each morning. On large plantations, these primitive day-care
centers might house as many as 100 children, from month-old babies
to four- and five-year-olds. Usually, the nurse was an old woman who
had a child or two as helpers. On smaller places, an older girl might
act as babysitter; sometimes mistress herself took on the job. The
women explained:

Dey had a nuss house whar dey put all de young chillun 'till dey
wuz old enough to work. Dey had one old 'oman to look atter us and
our some'p'm t'eat wuz brought to dis house. Our milk wuz put on de
floor in a big wooden tray and dey give us oyster shells to eat wid. All
de chillun would gather 'round dis tray and eat.

I was Ant Hannah's helper, and each mornin' mama would drap
me past Ant Hannah's house. Guess dey was 'bout fo'teen chillun she
had to look arter. Deed, chile, you ain't gonna believe dis but it's de
gospel truf. Ant Hannah had a trough in her back yard jus' like you
put in a pig pen. Well, Ant Hannah would just po' dat trough full of
milk an' drag dem chillun up to it. Chillun slop dat milk jus' like pigs.

Sometimes they's as many as fifty cradle with little nigger babies
in 'em and the mistus, she look after them. She turn them and dry
them herself. I'd blow the horn for the mudders of the little babies to
come in from the fields and nurse 'em, in mornin' and afternoon.
Mistus feed them what was old enough to eat victuals.

We children had no supper, and only a little piece of bread or
something of the kind in the morning. Our dishes consisted of one
wooden bowl, and oyster shells were our spoons. This bowl served for
about fifteen children, and often the dogs and the ducks and the
peafowl had a dip in it. Sometimes we had buttermilk and bread in our
bowl, sometimes greens or bones.

I stayed with my ma every night but my mistress raised me. Ev'y ev'nin'* at three 'clock ol' mistress would call all us litsy bitsy chillun in an we would lay down on pallets an have to go to sleep. I can hear her now singin':

> Hush-a-bye, bye, mammy's piccaninnies
> Way beneath the silver shining moon
> Hush-a-bye, bye, mammy's piccaninnies
> Daddy's little Carolina coons
> Now go to sleep yo' little piccaninnies.

Diapers were rarely mentioned in plantation records, although one Mississippi planter ruled that the babies were to be kept "as dry and cleanly as possible, under the circumstances." Older children were bathed and spruced up at least once a week.

They took all the children to the spring and set them in a row. They had a tubful of water and they washed them and dried them and put on their clean clothes. They used homemade lye soap and greased them with tallow and mutton suet. That made them shine.

Chillen was just as lousy as pigs. They had these combs that was just like cards you card cotton with, and they would comb your head with them. That wouldn't get the lice out, but it would make it feel better. They had to use larkspur to get 'em out; that would always get lice out of your head.

Slave girls were put to work earlier than the boys. When they were four or five they took care of babies.

They had cradles for the little nigger babies, and long before the War I was big enough to rock them. I'd get tired and make like I was asleep, and would ease the cradle over and throw the baby out. I never would throw mammy's out, though. The white folks was crazy 'bout their nigger babies, 'cause that's where they got their profit.

I was just a little small girl when Miss Earlie Hatchel bought me en she wouldn't let me hold de baby cause she was 'fraid I would drop it. I just sat dere on de floor en set de baby 'tween my legs. Father an mother belong to de old Bill Greggs en dat whe' Miss Earlie Hatchel buy me from. After dat I didn't never live wid my parents any more, but I went back to see dem every two weeks. Miss Hatchel want a nurse en dat how-come she buys me.

*Many southerners used *evening* to mean the hours between noon and sunset.

When the colored women has to cut cane all day till midnight come and after, I has to nurse the babies for them and tend the white children too. Some them babies so fat and big I had to tote the feet while 'nother gal tote the head. The big folks leave some toddy for colic and crying, and I done drink the toddy and let the children have the milk. I don't know no better. Lawsey me, it a wonder I ain't the biggest drunker in this here country, counting all the toddy I done put in my young belly!

I 'member dat big ole joggling board dere on de front piazza dat I use 'er ge' de chillun to sleep on eve'y evenin'. I be dere singin' one uv dem baby song to de child en it make me hu't lak in me bosom to be wid my ole mammy back up dere in de quarter. I wuz jes uh child den en yuh know it uh child happiness to be raise up wid dey mammy.

As they grew older, the girls were put to work full time in the house or were sent to the fields.

When I is about six years old they take me into the big house to learn to be a house woman, and they show me how to cook and clean up and take care of babies. I didn't have to work very hard. Just had to help the cooks and peel the potatoes and pick the guineas and chickens and do things like that. Sometimes I had to watch the baby. I had to git up way before daylight and make the fire in the kitchen fireplace and bring in some fresh water, and go get the milk what been down in the spring all night, and do things like that until breakfast ready. Old Master and Old Mistress come in the big hall to eat in the summer, and I stand behind them and shoo off the flies.

When I was nine years old, dey took me from my mother an' sol' me. Massa Tinsley made me de house girl. I had to make de beds, clean de house an' odder things. After I finished my reg'ler work, I would go to de mistress' room, bow to her, an' stand dere 'till she noticed me. Den she would say, "Martha, is you thew wid yo' wuk?" I say "Yes mam." She say, "No you ain'; you isn't lowed de shades." I'd den lower de shades, fill de water pitcher, 'range de towels on de washstand an' anything else mistress wants me to do. Den she'd tell me dat was 'bout all to do in dere. Den I would go in de odder rooms in de house an' do de same things. We wasn't 'lowed to sit down. We had to be doing something all day. Whenebber we was in de presence of any of de white folks, we had to stand up.

When I was a little bitty girl dey used to make a scarecrow outen me. Dey'd make me git up fo' daybreak an' go out into de cornfields an' set dere till way pas' dark so's to keep de crows from diggin' up de young corn that was just poppin' hits head 'bove de ground. A heap of mornin's de fros'bit my feet, an' when hit come time to go back to de cabin I could hardly walk.

In de mornin' when de bell ring, I am gap tender. De cattle am 'lowed to run where dey wants, here, there and all over. Fences am 'round de fields and there am gates to go through, but us calls dem gaps. It am my job to open and close dem, 'cause somebody allus wantin' to drive or walk through dem gaps.

My sis am de fly chaser. She has de big fan make from de tail feathers of a peacock. 'Twas awful purty thing. She stands 'round de white folks and shoo off de flies.

Guess I was a girl 'bout five or six when I was put wid de other chillun pickin' de bugs off de terbaccy leaves.* Crissy kep' whisperin' to me to pick em all off. Didn' pay no 'tention to her, any dat fell off I jus' let lay dere. Purty soon old Masser come long, an' see dat I done been missin' some of dem worms. Picked up a hand full of worms, he did, an' stuffed 'em inter my mouth. Lordy knows how many of dem shiny things I done swallered, but I sho picked em off careful arter dat.

I held a hoe handle mighty unsteady when they put a old woman to larn me and some other children to scrape the fields. That old woman would be in a frantic. She'd show me and then turn 'bout to show some other little nigger and I'd have the young corn cut clean as the grass. She say, "For the love of God, you better larn it right, or Solomon will beat the breath out you body." Old Man Solomon was the nigger driver.

Although they were performing the work of adults, the youngsters still longed for playtime and lusted after forbidden sweets.

De worstest whippin' I ever got was for playin' with a doll what belonged to one of marse's chillen. I 'members it yet and I ain't never seed a doll purty as dat doll was to me. It was made out of a corncob with arms and legs that moved and a real head, with eyes and hair and mouth painted on. It had a dress out o' silk cloth, jist like one my

*Many ex-slaves remembered picking tobacco hornworms. The insect *(Protoparce sexta)* is a fearsome four-inch-long caterpillar with a red horn at its rear. It is closely related to the gardener's enemy, the tomato hornworm.

missus weared when she went to meetin'. Dat li'l gal done leave de doll under de tree, but missus found me playin' with it and whipped me hard.

I recollects once when I was trying to clean the house like Old Miss tell me I finds a biscuit, and I's so hongry I et it, 'cause we never see such a thing as a biscuit only sometimes on Sunday morning. We just have corn bread and syrup and sometimes fat bacon, but when I et that biscuit and she comes in and say, "Where that biscuit?" I say, "Miss, I et it 'cause I'm so hungry." Then she grab that broom and start to beating me over the head with it and calling me low-down nigger, and I guess I just clean lost my head 'cause I knowed better than to fight her if I knowed anything 't all, but I start to fight her, and the driver, he comes in and he grabs me and starts beating me with that cat-o'-nine-tails, and he beats me till I fall to the floor nearly dead. He cut my back all to pieces, then they rubs salt in the cuts for more punishment. Lord, Lord, honey! Them was awful days.

They didn't 'low you to eat watermelons and cantaloupes then. I went through the patch one day and pulled a muskmellon and throwed it way over the weeds, but they found it and measured that melon against my mouth, and measured my feet in the dust, and I sure did get a beating for taking that melon.

Interviewed after the war, Harriet Tubman, the legendary Underground Railroad conductor, described the first time she ran away.

I was only seven years old when I was sent away to take car' of a baby. One mornin' after breakfast I stood by de table waitin' till I was to take it; just by me was a bowl of lumps of white sugar. Now you know, Missus, I never had nothing good; no sweet, no sugar, an' dat sugar, right by me, did look so nice, an' my Missus's back was turned to me so I jes' put my fingers in de sugar bowl to take one lump, an' she turned an' saw me. De nex' minute she had de raw hide down; I give one jump out of de do', an' I saw dey came after me, but I jes' flew, and dey didn't catch me. I run, an' I run, an' I run. By an' by, when I was clar tuckered out, I come to a great big pig-pen. Dar was an ole sow dar, an' perhaps eight or ten little pigs. I was too little to climb into it, but I tumbled ober de high board, an' fell in on de ground; I was so beat out I couldn't stir.

An' dere, Missus, I stayed from Friday till de nex' Chuesday, fightin' wid dose little pigs for de potato peelin's an' oder scraps dat came down in de trough. De ole sow would push me away when I tried to git her chillen's food, an' I was awful afeard of her. By Chuesday I was so starved I knowed I'd got to go back to my Missus, I hadn't got no whar else to go.

The sadism described in the following recollection was not common. Nevertheless, the slave system permitted owners to mistreat slaves almost with impunity.

Marsa was a well-meanin' man, but ole Missus was a common dog. She put a piece of candy on her washstan' one day. I was 'bout eight or nine years ole, an' it was my task to empty the slop ev'y mornin' I seed dat candy layin' dere, an' I was hungry. Ain't had a father workin' in de fiel' like some of de chillun to bring me eats—had jes' little pieces of scrapback each mornin' throwed at me from de kitchen. I seed dat peppermint stick layin' dere, an' I ain't dared go near it 'cause I knew ole Missus jus' waitin' for me to take it. Den one mornin I was so hungry dat I cain't resist. I went straight in dere an' grab dat stick of candy an' stuffed it in my mouf an' chew it down quick so ole Missus never fin' me wid it. Next mornin' ole Missus say: "Henrietta, you take dat piece o'candy out of my room?" "No mam, ain't seed no candy." "Chile, you lyin' to me an' I'm gonna whip you. Come here." Well, she got her rawhide down from de nail by de fire place, an' she grabbed me by the arm an' she try to turn me 'cross her knees whilst she set in de rocker so's she could hol' me. I twisted an' turned till finally she called her daughter. De gal took dat strap like her mother tole her and commence to lay it on real hard whilst Missus holt me. I twisted 'way so dere warn't no chance o' her gittin' in no solid lick. Den ole Missus lif' me up by de legs, an' she stuck my haid under de bottom of her rocker, an' she must of whupped me near a hour wid dat rocker leg a-pressin' down on my haid. Nex' thing I knew de ole Doctor was dere, an' he was a-pushin' an diggin' at my face, but he couldn't do nothin' at all wid it. Seem like dat rocker pressin' on my young bones had crushed 'em all into soft pulp. I couldn' open my mouf an' dey warn't no bone in de lef' side. I ain't never growed no mo' teef on dat side. Ain't never been able to chaw nothin' good since. Been eatin' liquid, stews, an' soup ever since dat day, an' dat was eighty-six years ago.

Far more frequent was the mental cruelty that took children from their parents. "Babies was snatched from deir mother's breasts and sold to speculators. Chillens was separated from sisters and brothers and never saw each other again. I could tell you about it all day, but even den you couldn't guess de awfulness of it," a woman said.

Most folks can't remember many things happened to 'em when they only eight years old, but one of my biggest tribulations come about that time and I never will forget it! That was when I was took away from my mammy and pappy and sent 'way off two-three hundred miles from where I live. And that's the last time I ever see either one of them, or any my own kinfolks!

Where I was born was at Hazlehurst, Mississippi. One evening 'long come a man and eat supper at the house and stay all night. The next morning I hear him ask Old Doctor what is my name, and Old Doctor start in to try to sell me to that man. I run away from the house and went out to the cabin where my mammy and pappy was, but they tell me to go on back to the big house 'cause maybe I am just scared. But Old Doctor and the man come, and Old Doctor make me go with the man. We go in his buggy a long ways off to his house. I ask him how far it is back home, and he say about a hundred miles or more, and laugh.

In 1860 I wuz a happy chile. I had a good ma and a good pa; one older bruther an one older suster, an a little bruther an a baby suster, too. All my fambly wucked in de fields, 'ceptin me an de two little uns, which I stayed at home to mind.

It was durin' cotton chopping time dat year, a day I'll never fergit, when de speculataws bought me. Ma come home from de fiel' 'bout haf atter 'leven dat day an cooked a good dinner, I hopin her. O, I never has forgot dat last dinner wid my folks! Bout de middle of the even' up ride my young Marster an' two strange white mens. Dey hitch dere hosses an' cum in de house. Den one o' de strangers said, "git yo clothers, Mary; we has bought you from Mr. Shorter." I c'menced cryin' an' beggin' Mr. Shorter to not let 'em take me away. But he say, "yes, Mary, I has sole yer, an' yer must go wid em."

Den dese strange mens driv off wid me, me hollerin' at de top o' my voice an' callin' my Ma! Den dem speculataws begin to sing loud —jes to drown out my hollerin. We passed de very field whar paw an' all my fokes wuz wuckin, an' I calt out as loud as I could an' as long as I could see 'em, "good-bye, Ma! good-bye Ma!" But she never heard me. I ain't never seed nor heared tell o' my Ma an' Paw, an' bruthers, an' susters from dat day to dis.

Among the earliest lessons that slave children had to learn were the commandments governing relations between the two races. "Thou shall be submissive to Master" was as important as "Thou shall work." Some slave owners used whips to teach the children their inferior status; others used gentler means. But the most significant teaching

took place in the quarters where worried mothers knew that sparing
the rod could mean trouble for their youngsters.

Old Master sure thought more of his little nigger children. He used
to ride in the quarters 'cause he like to see 'em come running. The
cook, she was a old woman name Forney, and she had to see after
feeding the children. She holler, "tee, tee, t-e-e," and all us little
niggers just come running. Old Master he ride up and say, "Forney,
call up them little pickaninnies," and Old Forney she lift up her voice
and holler, "Tee, t-e-e, t-e-e," and Old Master just set up on the hoss
and laugh and laugh to see us come running. He like to count up how
many little niggers he did have. That was fun for us, too.

Miss Cornelia was the finest woman in the world. Come Sunday
morning she done put a bucket of dimes on the front gallery and stand
there and throw dimes to the nigger children just like feeding chickens.
I sure right here to testify, 'cause I's right there helping grab.

Yes, ma'am, my white folks was proud of dey niggers. Um, yessum,
when they used to have company to the big house, Miss Ross would
bring them to the door to show them us children. And, my blessed,
the yard would be black with us children, all string up there next the
doorstep looking up in they eyes. Old Missus would say, "Ain't I got
a pretty crop of little niggers coming on?"

Mah mammy, she wuz cook at duh big house, an Ah wuz raised
in de kitchen en de back yahd. Ah mus' not a been mo' en thee uh
fo' yeahs ole when Miss Millie cum out in de kitchen one day, en 'gin
tuh scold my mammy 'bout de sorry way mammy done clean de
chitlins. Ah ain' nebber heard nobuddy fuss et my mammy befo'. Little
ez Ah wuz, Ah swell up en rar' back, en I sez tuh Miss Millie, "Doan
you no' Mammy is boss ob dis hyar kitchen. You cyan' cum a fussin'
in hyar." Miss Millie, she jus laff, but Mammy grab a switch an 'gin
ticklin' my laigs.

TWO

Work

By the time she was ten years old, a slave girl was classified as a half-hand. At puberty she was doing the work of a woman, and woman's work was scarcely distinguishable from man's.

I had to do everythin' dey was to do on de outside. Work in de field, chop wood, hoe corn, till sometime I feels like my back surely break. I done everythin' 'cept split rails. I never did split no rails.

This race coming up now don't know nothing 'bout hard work. Over there, see a road all turned up and you would see men and women both throwing up dirt and rocks; the men would haul it off and the women would take picks and things and get it up. You could, any day see a woman, a whole lot of 'em making on a road. Could look up and see ten women up over dar on the hill plowing and look over the other way and see ten more. I have done ever thing on a farm what a man done 'cept cut wheat.

I split rails like man. I used a iron wedge drove into the wood with a maul.

I drive the gin, what was run by two mules.

My mama could hunt good as any man. Ustuh be a coup'la pedluh men come 'round. My mammy'd a'ways have a pile o'hides tuh trade with 'em fo' calico prints. She'd have coon hides'n' mink, 'n' beavers, lawd!

Marster Boles didn't have many slave on de farm, but lots in brickyard. I toted bricks and put 'em down where dey had to be. Six bricks each load all day. I fired de furnace for three years. Standin' front wid hot fire on my face. Hard work, but God was with me.

There was little division of labor between the sexes except on the largest plantations, but some jobs were always assigned to women:

On wash days the neighbors would send several of their women to the creek to do the family wash. They would wash and spread the clothes on the bushes and low branches of the trees to dry. They had no tubs or wash boards. They had a large flat block of wood and a wooden paddle. They'd spread the wet garment on the block, spread soap on it and paddle the garment till it was clean. They would rinse the clothes in the creek.

We had a washing house. Dere wuz five women who done de washing an' ironing. Dey had to make de soap. Dat wuz done by letting water drip over oak ashes. After de clothes had soaked in dis lye-soap and water, dey put de clothes on tables and beat 'em 'till dey wuz white.

At night de men chops wood and hauls poles to build fences and de women folks has to spin four cuts of thread and make all de clothes. Some has to card cotton to make quilts and some weave and knits stockin's. Marse give each one a chore to do at night and iffen it warn't did when we went to bed, we's whipped. One time I fells plumb asleep befo' I finished shellin' some corn.

In the fields the white overseers and the black drivers saw to it that everyone maintained the pace set by the lead workers.

It don't make no dif'ence is you big or l'il, you better keep up or de drivers burn you up with de whip, sho'nough. Sometime I gits so tired come night, I draps right in de row and gone to sleep. Den de driver come 'long and, wham, dey cuts you 'cross de back with de whip and you wakes up when it lights on you, yes, suh! Bout nine o'clock dey hollers, "cotton up" and dat de quittin' signal. We goes to de quarters and jes' drap on de bunk and go to sleep with nothin' to eat.

When the pace was not too fast, the girls enjoyed the camaraderie of the fields and took pleasure in their strength and dexterity. During the cotton harvest planters encouraged competition by offering prizes for the best workers, and women often won them.

I nursed and cooked sometimes, but I liked the field work better than I did the housework. We could talk and do anything we wanted to, just so we picked the cotton; we used to sing and have lots of fun. I couldn't pick fast like some of 'em.

I used to pick 150 pounds of cotton every day. We would pick cotton and sing, pick and sing all day. A girl would wet in the basket to make her cotton heavier, and she would put rocks in the bottom of it. I told on her, for I didn't want her to beat me.

Us pick 'bout 100 pound cotton in one basket. I didn't mind pickin' cotton, 'cause I never did have de backache. I pick two and three hunnert pounds a day and one day I picked 400.* Sometimes I win de prize give by massa to de slave what pick de most. De prize am a big cake or some clothes. Pickin' cotton not so bad, 'cause us used to it and have de fine time of it. I gits a dress one day and a pair shoes 'nother day for pickin' most. I so fast I take two rows at de time.

Susan Dabney Smedes, a planter's daughter, told of Nelly who won the annual prize for picking cotton:

To get five hundred pounds a picker had to use both hands at once. Those who went into the cotton-fields after they were grown only knew how to pull out cotton by holding on to the stalk with one hand and picking it out with the other. Two hundred pounds a day would be a liberal estimate of what the most industrious could do in this manner. A very tall and lithe young woman was the best cotton-picker at Burleigh. She picked two rows at a time, going down the middle with both arms extended and grasping the cotton bolls with each hand. At Christmas Nelly's share of the prize-money was something over seventeen dollars.

The line between field hand and house slave was not as rigid as tradition has led us to believe. Lady's maids represented less than 5 percent of the total slave population.

Cook? No, ma'am. I never cooked until after I was married, and I never washed, never washed so much as a rag. All I washed was the babies and maybe my mistress's feet. I was a lady's maid. I'd wait on my mistress and I'd knit sox for all the folks. When they would sleep it was our duty—us maids—to fan them with turkey feathers—feather fans.

My young mistress name Catherine. When her marry, I was give to them for a housemaid, 'cause I was trim and light complected lak you see I is dis very day. Young missie say, "You come in my room Delia, I wants to see if I can put up wid you." I goes in dat room, winter time mind you, and Miss Charlotte sets down befo' de fire. Well, she

*A cotton picker walked down the row dragging a bag somewhat longer than a pillow case. When the bag was filled with cotton, she emptied it into a basket. At day's end, the baskets were weighed and a record kept of each individual's productivity.

allowed to me, "Delia, put kettle water on de fire." So I does in a jiffy. Her next command was: "Would you please be so kind as to sweep and tidy up de room?" I do all dat, then she say, "You is goin' to make maid, a good one!" She give a silvery giggle and says "I just had you put on dat water for to see if you was goin' to make any slop. No, No! You didn't spill a drop, you ain't goin' to make no sloppy maid, you just fine." Then her call her mother in. "See how pretty Delia's made dis room, look at them curtains, draw back just right, observe de pitcher, and de towels on de rack of de washstand, my I'm proud of her!" She give old mistress a hug and a kiss and thank her for de present. Dat present was me. De happiness of dat minute is on me to dis day.

Far more typical was the maid-of-all work:

I worked in de house for old Miss, and we had plenty to do and plenty to eat. When de white folks was through eatin', I got a pan and got de grub, and set on de floor and et it. Oh Lordee, but I worked hard since I was twelve years old.

I washed and cooked for all of us. And ironed too. I het de irons, great big old irons, in de fireplace. I ironed on a quilt spread out on de floor, and I ironed jes' as nice as anybody. I lived right in de house with de white folks. In summer we slept, my brother Henry and me, in a trundle bed in the kitchen; and in de winter made a pallet beside de fireplace.

"House servants 'bove de field servants, them days. If you didn't get better rations and things to eat in de house, it was your own fault," one ex-slave said. But when the privileges of the big house (the master's house) were weighed against the long hours and lack of privacy, women often opted for the fields. Susan Dabney Smedes told how Alcey managed to change jobs:

[Alcey] systematically disobeyed orders and stole or destroyed the greater part of the provisions given to her for the table. No special notice was taken, so she resolved to show more plainly that she was tired of the kitchen. Instead of getting the chickens for dinner from the coop, as usual, she unearthed from some corner an old hen that had been sitting for six weeks, and served her up as a fricassee! We had company to dinner that day; that would have deterred most of the servants, but not Alcey. She achieved her object, for she was sent to the field next day. We were very sorry, for she was the most accomplished cook whom we had had in Mississippi.

On large plantations, women developed special skills.

Dey was a big weavin' room where de blankets was wove, and cloth for de winter clothes. Linda Herndon and Milla Edwards was de head weavers; dey looked after de weavin' of de fancy blankets. De cardin' and spinnin' room was full of niggers. I can hear dem spinnin' wheels now turnin' round and saying hum-m-m-m, hum-m-m-m.

Mammy Rachel stayed in de dyein' room. She knew every kind of root, bark, leaf, and berry dat made red, blue, green, or whatever color she wanted. Dey had a big shelter where de dye pots set over de coals. Mammy Rachel would fill de pots with water, den she put in de roots, bark and stuff and boil de juice out. Den she strain it and put in de salt and vinegar to set de color. After de wool and cotton done been carded and spun to thread, Mammy take de hanks and drop dem in de pot of boilin' dye. She stir dem round and lift dem up an down with a stick, and when she hang dem up on de line in de sun, dey was every color of de rainbow. When dey dripped dry dey was sent to de weavin' room.

Patience work to de loom house. She help do aw de weaving fa de plantation. Weave aw t'rough de winter en aw t'rough de summer. She make aw kinder uv pretty streak in de cloth outer de yarn dat dey dye wid t'ing dat dey ge' outer de woods lak walnut wha' make brown, en cedar en sweet gum wha' make purple. Den dey make de blue cloth outer dat t'ing dat dey raise right dere on de plantation call indigo.

Women trained to be midwives earned substantial sums for their owners.

When I was 13 years old my ol' mistress put me wid a doctor who learned me how to be a midwife. Dat was 'cause so many women on de plantation was catchin' babies. I stayed wid dat doctor, Dr. McGill his name was, for 5 years. I got to be good. Got so he'd sit down an' I'd do all de work.

When I come home, I made a lot o' money for old miss. Lots of times, didn't sleep regular or git my meals on time for three–four days. Cause when dey call, I always went. Brought as many white as culled children. I's brought lots of 'em an' I ain't never lost a case. You know why. It's cause I used my haid. When I'd go in, I'd take a look at de woman, an' if it was beyond me, I'd say, "Dis is a doctor case. Dis ain't no case for a midwife. You git a doctor." An' dey'd have to get one. I'd jes' stan' before de lookin' glass, an I wouldn't budge. Dey couldn't make me.

THREE

Seduction, Rape, Concubinage

THE POIGNANT DAGUERROTYPE *on this page, perhaps the earliest photograph of an adolescent slave girl, was made in Columbia, South Carolina, in 1850. Delia, a slave belonging to B. F. Taylor, was ordered to pose in the nude for the benefit of Louis Agassiz's scientific*

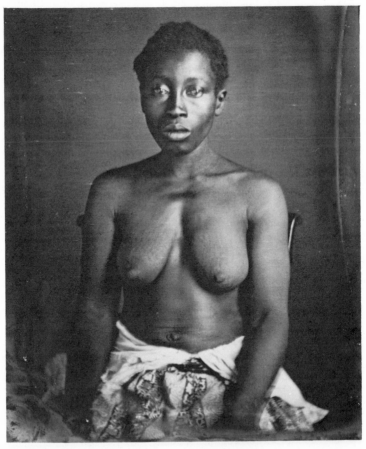

This daguerrotype of Delia was made in Columbia, South Carolina, in March 1850. *(Peabody Museum)*

studies. Surely the experience was humiliating, yet she seems inno-
cently unaware of any sexual interest that she might arouse.*

*The puberty rites that introduced girls to the menarche and
defined the role of women's sexuality in African culture did not survive
transplantation to the American South. Cut off from their ancestral
traditions, slave mothers tended to shy away from discussing sex with
their daughters. Perhaps it was a reticence developed to protect their
own privacy in the too-public sleeping quarters that a whole family
shared. Perhaps they hoped beyond all reason that ignorance would
buy a few extra months of childhood for their daughters. In a score of
interviews, the women recalled their mothers' gruff yet loving evasion
when asked, "Whe' us come from?"*

My ma say, no stork bird never fetch me but de fust railroad train
dat come up de railroad track, when they built de line, fetched me. She
say I was a baby, settin' on de cow-ketcher, and she see me and say
to pa: "Reuben, run out dere and get our baby befo' her falls off and
gets hurt under them wheels!" Do you know I believed dat tale 'til I
was a big girl? Sure did, 'til white folks laugh me out of it!

They didn't tell you a thing. I was a great big girl twelve or thirteen
years old, I reckon, and a girl two or three years older than that and
we'd be going 'round to the parsley bed looking for babies; and looking
in hollow logs. It's a wonder a snake hadn't bitten us. The woman that
would wait on my mother would come back and tell us here's her baby;
and that was all we knew. We thought she brought it because it was
hers. I was twenty years old when my first baby came, and I didn't
know nothing then. I didn't know how long I had to carry my baby.
We never saw nothing when we were children.

Only one woman mentioned her first menstruation.

When that happened, mother didn't tell us. I didn't know
what happened to me. I went running to the branch and washed myself. I come on up the road, just as naked. It never did hurt me,
though.

*At a time when white women were thought immodest if they so
much as showed their feet, slave girls, scantily clad at best, were
required to strip for inspection by would-be purchasers.*

**Agassiz, a Harvard University professor, wanted to study anatomical details of "the
African race" to bolster his theory that blacks were a separate species, separately created.
Glad to have scientific backing for his own belief in black inferiority, a slave owner
obliged him with fifteen daguerrotypes of South Carolina slaves.*

Us didn't have no clothes for goin' round. I never had a undershirt until just before my first child was borned. I never had nothin' but a shimmy and a slip for a dress, and it was made outen de cheapest cloth dat could be bought, unbleached cloth, coarse, but made to last.

We was all chained and dey strips all our clothes off and de folks what gwine buys us comes round and feels us all over. Iffen any de niggers don't want to take dere clothes off, de man gets a long, black whip and cuts dem up hard. When Marse Jones seed me on de block, he say "Dat's a whale of a woman."

Some conscientious slave owners applied the Victorian moral code to the quarters as well as to the big house, but the majority—and their sons, neighbors, overseers—held to a double standard that coupled veneration for white womanhood with disrespect for black. House servants were particularly susceptible to sexual exploitation. Harriet Brent Jacobs (c. 1815–97) grew up in the small town of Edenton, North Carolina, with a kindly mistress who taught her to read and a concerned grandmother who was a respected member of the free black community. Her life changed abruptly when her mistress died and she was willed to the family of "Dr. Flint."* After her escape to the North and introduction to the antislavery movement (pp. 73–84), she wrote of "Flint's" attempts to seduce her. Although she told her story in literary English, it is nevertheless authentic, corroborating reports from other slaves who were forced into long-term relationships with their masters.

I now entered on my fifteen year—a sad epoch in the life of a slave girl. My master began to whisper foul words in my ear. Young as I was, I could not remain ignorant of their import. I turned from him with disgust and hatred. But he was my master. I was compelled to live under the same roof with him.

I would have given the world to have laid my head on my grandmother's bosom, and told her all my troubles. But although my grandmother was all to me, I feared as well as loved her. I felt shamefaced about telling her such impure things. Though I did not confide in my grandmother, her presence in the neighborhood was some protection. Though she had been a slave, Dr. Flint dreaded her scorching rebukes —and he did not wish to have his villainy made public. It was lucky for me that I did not live on a distant plantation, but in a town not so large that the inhabitants were ignorant of each other's affairs.

*Dr. Flint was Jacobs's pseudonym for James Norcom, a prominent Edenton physician.

Mrs. Flint might have used [her] knowledge to counsel and to screen the young and innocent among her slaves; but for them she had no sympathy. She watched her husband with unceasing vigilance; but he was well practised in means to evade it.

Sometimes he would complain of the heat of the tea room, and order his supper to be placed on a small table in the piazza. He would seat himself there with a well-satisfied smile, and tell me to stand by and brush away the flies. These intervals were employed in describing the happiness I was so foolishly throwing away, and in threatening me with the penalty that finally awaited my stubborn disobedience.

When I succeeded in avoiding opportunities for him to talk to me at home, I was ordered to come to his office, to do some errand. When there, I was obliged to stand and listen to such language as he saw fit to address to me.

I had entered my sixteenth year, and every day it became more apparent that my presence was intolerable to Mrs. Flint. After repeated quarrels between the doctor and his wife, he announced his intention to take his youngest daughter, then four years, to sleep in his apartment. It was necessary that a servant should sleep in the same room, to be on hand if the child stirred. I was selected for that office. Mrs. Flint heard of this new arrangement, and a storm followed. She now took me to sleep in a room adjoining her own.

Dr. Flint contrived a new plan. He told me that he was going to build a small house for me, in a secluded place, four miles away from the town. I was constrained to listen while he talked of his intention to give me a home of my own, and to make a lady of me. I soon heard that the house was actually begun. What *could* I do?

Louisa Picquet, a Georgia slave, had a similar experience. Her master, Mr. Cook, took her to Mobile, Alabama, in order to escape his creditors. There she worked for Mrs. Bachelor, landlady of the boarding house where Cook stayed. She told the following story years later after reaching the North.

I was a little girl, not fourteen years old. One day Mr. Cook told me I must come to his room that night and take care of him. He said he was sick. I told Mrs. Bachelor what Mr. Cook said. Then she whispered with her sister, and told me I need not go. At breakfast-time I had to take his breakfast up to his room, on a waiter. He had not got up yet. Then he order me to shut the door. At the same time, he was kind of raisin' up out of bed. Before I had time to shut the door, a gentleman walks out of another room close by. Then Mr. Cook said,

"What you stand there for, you dam' fool? Go'long downstairs, and get me some more salt." Mrs. Bachelor caught my look, and said, "Louisa, one of the boys will take that salt up, I want you for a minute." He call out of the window for me to bring him up a pitcher of water. Then he told me I must come to his room that night; if I didn't he'd give me hell in the mornin'. I promised him I would, for I was afraid to say anything else. Then I came to the conclusion that he could not do anything but whip me so I didn't go.

In the mornin' he want to know why I didn't come up, and I told him I forget. So he whip me, so that I won't forget another time. I told Mrs. Bachelor that I guess I'd have to go up stairs that night; and ask her what I should do. She said the best plan would be to keep out of his way.

Well, about tea-time, he wanted water. That was sent up. Then he wanted a button sewed on his wristband. Mrs. Bachelor sent him word to send the shirt down, and her sister would put a button on for him. Then he sent word that I must come up and get his boots and black them. About bedtime, he call one of the boys to know if they told me about the boots; and they said they hadn't seen me.

In the mornin' he came to the ironin'-room, downstairs, where I was, and whip me with the cowhide, naked, so I 'spect I'll take some of the marks with me to the grave.

When he was whippin' me so awfully, I made up my mind 'twas of no use, and I'd go, and not be whipped any more. That very day, we was taken by the sheriff, and was sold the next mornin'. I tell you I was glad when I was taken off to be sold, but I jump out of the fryin' pan into the fire.

Fifteen-year-old Harriet Jacobs and fourteen-year-old Louisa Picquet fought off their masters only to say "yes" to the next white men who approached them. In Incidents in the Life of a Slave Girl, *which was published in 1861, Jacobs recalled the reasons that led to her fall.*

Now I come to a period which I would gladly forget if I could. I will not try to screen myself behind the pleas of compulsion from a master; for it was not so. Neither can I plead ignorance. I knew what I did and I did it with deliberate calculation.

Dr. Flint's persecutions and his wife's jealousy had given rise to some gossip in the neighborhood. A white unmarried gentleman knew my grandmother and often spoke to me in the street. He expressed a great deal of sympathy, and wrote to me frequently. I was only fifteen years old. So much attention from a superior person was, of course,

flattering. I also felt grateful for his sympathy. It seemed to me a great
thing to have such a friend. By degrees, a more tender feeling crept
into my heart. I knew the impassable gulf between us but to be an
object of interest to a man who is not married and not her master is
agreeable to the pride and feelings of a slave. It seems less degrading
to give one's self, than to submit to compulsion.

When I found that my master had actually begun to build the
lonely cottage, other feelings mixed with those I have described. I
knew nothing would enrage Dr. Flint so much as to know that I
favored another. I thought he would revenge himself by selling me, and
I was sure Mr. Sands* would buy me. With all these thoughts revolving
in my mind, and seeing no other way of escaping the doom I so much
dreaded, I made a headlong plunge.

At last [Dr. Flint] told me the cottage was completed, and ordered
me to go to it. I replied, "I will never go there. In a few months I shall
be a mother." He looked at me in dumb amazement, and left the house
without a word. I thought I should be happy in my triumph. But now
that the truth was out, and my relatives would hear of it, I felt
wretched.

I went to my grandmother. My lips moved to make confession, but
the words stuck in my throat. I think she saw something unusual was
the matter with me. The mother of slaves is very watchful. After they
have entered their teens she lives in daily expectation of troubles.
Presently, in came my mistress, like a mad woman, and accused me
concerning her husband. My grandmother believed what she said.
She exclaimed, "Has it come to this? I had rather see you dead than
to see you as you now are. Go away! and never come to my house
again."

How I longed to throw myself at her feet, and tell her all the truth!
But she had ordered me to go, and never to come there again. I walked
to the house of a woman who had been a friend of my mother. When
I told her why I was there, she spoke soothingly to me; but I could not
be comforted. I thought I could bear my shame if I could only be
reconciled to my grandmother.

My friend advised me to send for her. Days of agonizing suspense
passed before she came. I knelt before her, and told her things that

*Mr. Sands, Jacobs's pseudonym for her lover, was probably Samuel Tredwell Sawyer,
a lawyer who was a member of the North Carolina legislature from 1829 to 1832 and
a U.S. congressman from 1837 to 1839. The only Edentonian to be elected to Congress
in the first decades of the century, Sawyer lived a short distance from Jacobs's grandmother's house. Their relationship ended when he married a white woman. Although
he purchased their two children, he never bought Jacobs.

had poisoned my life. She listened in silence. I told her I would bear anything if I had hopes of obtaining her forgiveness. She did not say, "I forgive you" but she looked at me lovingly with her eyes full of tears and murmured, "Poor child! Poor child!"

Louisa Picquet had even less choice. Interviewed after she was set free, she recalled:

Mr. Williams told me what he bought me for soon as we started for New Orleans. He said if I behave myself he'd treat me well; but, if not, he'd whip me almost to death. He was over forty; I guess pretty near fifty.

Q. Had you any children while in New Orleans?

A. Yes; I had four.

Q. Who was their father?

A. Mr. Williams.

Q. Was it known that he was living with you?

A. Everybody knew I was housekeeper, but he never let on that he was the father of my children. I did all the work in his house—nobody there but me and the children. When he had company, gentlemen folks, he took them to the hotel.

When Mr. Williams told me what he bought me for I thought, now I shall be committin' adultery, and there's no chance for me, and I'll have to die and be lost. I had this trouble with my soul the whole time. I begin to pray that he might die, so that I might get religion. It was some time before he got sick. He said that if I would promise him that I would go to New York, he would leave me and the children free. In about a month, he died. I didn't cry nor nothin', for I was glad he was dead. I was left *free,* and that made me so glad I could hardly believe it myself.

When Fanny Kemble* reproached a slave for her "sinfulness," the woman replied, "When he make me follow him into de bush, what use me tell him no? He have strength to make me." Rape, white on black, was not a crime under slave law. Even today many scholarly histories of slavery do not mention the word. This reluctance to give the deed its name may have stemmed from the centuries-old legend that black women were more passionate than white and, hence, more willing. The bitter recollection of ex-slaves and their descendants belie this.

*Frances Anne Kemble (1809–93), noted British actress, married Pierce Butler without realizing that he was the coowner of a Georgia plantation with some 700 slaves. Her *Journal* of her stay in Georgia gave an unusually sensitive report of the plight of slave women.

Ma mama said that a nigger 'oman couldn't help herself, fo' she had to do what de marster say. Ef he come to de field whar de women workin' an' tell gal to come on, she had to go. He would take one down in de woods an' use her all de time he wanted to, den send her on back to work. Times nigger 'omen had chillun for de marster an' his sons and some times it was fo' de ovah seer.

Aunt Jane Peterson told me things took place in slavery times. She said no chance to run off, you had to stay and take what come. She was the cook. Old master say, "Jane, go to the lot and get the eggs." She was scared to go and scared not to go. He'd beat her out there, put her head between the slip gap where they let the hogs into the pasture from the lot down back of the barn. She say "Old missis whip me. This ain't right." He'd laugh. She was scared to death of him.

Grandma say that she were near thirteen year old, behind the house tee-teein when young marster came up behind her. She didn't see him, but he put his hand up under her dress and said, "Lay down, Tildy." They called her Tildy, but her actual name was Matilda. And so this thing happened, and her stomach began to get big.

One day, grandma and old mistress, they was putting up clean clothes. Old mistress had a pair of socks in her hand. She said, "Tildy, who been messin wit you down there?" Grandma say, "Young marster." Old mistress run to her and crammed these socks in her mouth and say, "Don't you ever tell nobody. If you do, I'll skin you alive."

Although gang rapes, like the following, were not often reported, many women described the beatings their mothers suffered if they resisted white men's advances.

My sister was given away when she was a girl. She told me and ma that they'd make her go out and lay on a table and two or three white men would have sex with her before they'd let her up. She was just a small girl. She died when she was still in her young days, still a girl.

I don't like to talk 'bout dem times, 'cause my mother did suffer misery. You know dar was an overseer who use to tie mother up in the barn wid a rope aroun' her arms up over her head, while she stood on a block. Soon as dey got her tied, dis block was moved an' her feet dangled, you know, couldn't tech de flo'. Dis ole man, now would start beatin' her nekked 'til the blood run down her back to her heels.

I asked mother "what she done fer 'em to beat and do her so?" She said, "Nothin 'tother dan 'fuse to be wife to dis man."

A vivid account of attempted rape comes from testimony in a Georgia divorce case. After witnesses reported that James Odom had had sexual relations with two slaves, Louisa, his wife's maid, told how she had managed to evade him.

LOUISA, (colored) sworn over defendant's objection, said Odom used to come into witness' bed-room and try to have intercourse with her, offered her one time two dollars to feel her titties; on one occasion, to avoid Odom, she went up stairs and carried the children to sleep with her and locked the door; she nailed up the windows of her house to keep Odom out; he made these offers to her when Mrs. Odom was from home. Odom got into witness' window one night, and tried to throw her on to the bed; she told him if he did she'd halloo. She blew up the light to keep him off of her, and he would blow it out. She said that Odom never had connexion with her.

Records from other divorce cases show men using slave women as weapons in an unpleasant game with their wives. In numerous petitions for divorce, the wife charged that her husband had brought his slave to "his own wife's bed and there carried out his licentious designs"; in some instances these were carried out in her presence.

Your petitioner states that shortly after her marriage with her present husband she discovered that he had taken up with one of his female slaves who acted as cook and waited about the house. So regardless was her husband of her feelings, that he would before her eyes and in the very room in which your petitioner slept go to bed to the said slave or cause the said slave to come in and go to bed with him. Your petitioner states that without complaint, she submitted in silence to her husband's infidelity, and attempted to reclaim him by caresses and obedience but in vain.

Women who were strong enough sometimes fought off their attackers. In the Louisiana cane fields, the cutters sang, "Rains come wet me/Sun come dry me/Stay back, boss man/ Don't come nigh me." In Tennessee Cherry Logue swung a club at a man who made "insulting advances." In Virginia Sukie used her fists.

She used to cook for Miss Sarah Ann, but ole Marsa was always tryin' to make Sukie his gal. One day Sukie was in the kitchen makin' soap. Had three gra' big pots o' lye jus' comin' to a bile when ole Marsa come in. He tell Sukie to take off her dress. She tole him no. Den he grabbed her an' pull it down off'n her shoulders an' try to pull her down on de flo'. Den dat black gal got mad. She took an' punch ole Marsa an' made him break loose an' den she gave him a shove an' push his hindparts down in de hot pot o' soap. It burnt him near to death. He ran from de kitchen, not darin' to yell, 'cause he didn't want Miss Sarah Ann to know 'bout it.

Well, few days later he took Sukie off an' sol' her to de nigger traders. De traders 'zamined her an' pinched her an' den dey open her mouf, an' stuck dey fingers in to see how her teeth was. Den Sukie got awful mad, and she pult up her dress an' tole old nigger traders to look an' see if dey could fin' any teef down there.

Slaves selected for their grace, beauty and light skins were shipped to the "fancy-girl markets" of New Orleans and other cities. At a time when prime field hands sold for $1,600, a "fancy girl" brought $5,000. Some ended up in bordellos,* but the majority became the mistresses of wealthy planters, gamblers, or businessmen.

New Orleans also had a unique tradition of plaçage *(literally, placing), which originated during the French colonial era when male settlers depended on their female slaves for domestic companionship. The* gens de couleur libres *(free people of color) who emerged from these relationships were a caste apart from other blacks in the antebellum United States. Although some had stable families, the predominance of women (100 women to 57 men in 1850) made marriage impossible for large numbers. Because intermarriage was illegal and marriage to a slave unthinkable,* plaçage *developed. A* plaçée, *light skinned, well educated, chaste, was introduced to society at one of the famed quadroon balls, where attendance was limited to white gentlemen and free women of color. When her charms attracted a "protector," a period of courtship followed. Then* maman *and protector signed a formal contract stipulating the support she and her future children could expect. A* plaçage *might last for several years, occasionally for a lifetime. When the relationship ended, the* plaçée, *left in reasonably comfortable circumstances, made a living as a fashionable hairdresser, dressmaker, or boarding-house keeper. Her sons were taught a trade, while her daughters were trained to be the belles of future quadroon balls.*

---

*Although Aunt Henney, a black woman, owned a flourishing brothel in St. Louis, most prostitutes in the antebellum South were white.

Most slave owners settled for less formal arrangements. Two ex-slaves recalled their masters' "yaller girls":

Mr. Mordicia had his yaller gals in one quarter to dere selves and dese gals belongs to de Mordicia men, dere friends an' de overseers. When a baby was born in dat quarter dey'd sen' it over to de black quarter at birth. Some of dese gal babies got grown an' after goin' back to de yaller quarter had chilluns for her own dad or brother. De yaller women was highfalutin'. Dey thought they was better dan black ones.

Once Massa goes to Baton Rouge and brung back a yaller girl dressed in fine style. She was a seamster nigger. He builds her a house 'way from the quarters, and she done fine sewing for the whites. This yaller girl breeds fast and gits a mess of white young-uns. She larnt them fine manners and combs out they hair.

Oncet two of them goes down the hill to the dollhouse, where the Missy's children am playing. They wants to go in the dollhouse and one the Missy's boys say, "That's for white children." They say, "We ain't no niggers, 'cause we got the same daddy you has, and he comes to see us near every day." They is fussing, and Missy is listening out her chamber window. She heard them white niggers say, "We call him daddy when he comes to our house to see our mama."

When Massa come home that evening, his wife hardly say nothing to him, and he asks her what the matter and she tells him, "I'm studying in my mind 'bout them white young-uns of that yaller nigger wench from Baton Rouge. He say, "Now, honey, I fotches that gal just for you, 'cause she a fine seamster." She say, "It look kind of funny they got the same kind of hair and eyes as my children, and they got a nose like yours." She say, "Over in Mississippi I got a home and plenty with my daddy."

Well, she didn't never leave, and Massa bought her a fine, new span of surrey hosses. But she don't never have no more children. That yaller gal has more white young-uns, but they don't never go down the hill no more to the big house.

A bachelor could rent a wife, buy or borrow one without any legal or romantic entanglements. Former slaves reminisced.

Lots o' white men had culled wives. Ole man Tom Greene what lived very near us comes over to ole Marse Berry one day an' wants to buy mama. He wants mama but he don' want we uns kids, you see? Mama jes' sits roun' jes' as sad an' cried all de time. She was always nice lookin' an' we all knew what de old Marse Greene want. But ole

Marse Berry swear he be damn if he sell her. He say if old man Greene take de chillun he kin have mama. Ole man Greene say he don't want de chillun, so ole Marse Berry sell him nuffin. Well, ole Marse Greene, he buys a nigger 'oman name Betsy f'om some whar. He was a bachluh you know an' he need a 'oman. Dat 'oman had three chillun and I 'clare if ole man Greene didn't think much o' dem chillun o' Betsy's as if dey was by a white 'oman.

My mother had two children by my father. My father never married. He loved my mother, and he said if he could not marry Mary he did not want any other woman. My father would give me anything I asked for. Mother would make me ask him for things for her. She said it was no harm for me to ask him for things which she could not get unless I asked him for them. When the surrender came my mother told my father she was tired of living that kind of life, that if she could not be his legal wife she wouldn't be anything to him, so she left and went to Leavenworth, Kansas.

Records of wills attest to large numbers of stable interracial unions in which genuine affection and loyalty were felt on both sides. In the following, selected from almost 100 similar documents, the testator attempted to provide for his dark-skinned family despite increasingly stringent laws against manumission.

I, Walter Robertson, late of Virginia, but now of New Bern, North Carolina—do make this my last will and testament. It is my will that my bosom friend, Ann Rose, for her long and faithful services, be immediately after my death put in possession of all my lands, slaves, household furniture, plate, stocks of horses, cattle, and every kind of real and personal estate which may belong to me, which real and personal estate I lend to the said Ann to enable her to support herself and to maintain and educate my daughter Margaret by the said Ann, as also a child with which she is now pregnant, provided the said child be born within nine months from the date of these presents.

I Thomas Wright give and bequeath to Sylvia, a woman of color, formerly my slave but since emancipated and with whom I have had children, the sole and exclusive enjoyment of the house or tenement on my plantation, also all the household furniture therein, also all the monies of which I die possessed; secondly I give and bequeath to my natural son, Robert Wright, by the said Sylvia who I have duly emancipated all that tract of land on which I now live with its appertenances.

I, Philip Stanislas Noisette, of the City of Charleston, South Carolina, do make this my last Will and testament. I do hereby recognize
& declare that the issue of my slave & housekeeper, Celestine, are my
children, and I will order and direct that my executors send the said
woman Celestine and all her said issue my children, out of this State
to some other State, Territory or Country, where they can severally be
made free and their liberty secured to them. I request the Eldest of
my children to support their mother in her old age and also the younger
children till these be able to earn their livelihood. The whole of my
furniture shall be divided among Celestine and her children above
mentioned. My collection of living exotic plants shall be sold at public
auction together with my house, kitchen & hot house: the proceeds of
the sale shall belong to to the said Celestine & children.

*Further insights into the relationship between master and concu-
bine can be found in contested will cases. In* Farr v. Thompson, *South
Carolina, witnesses* testified:*

The testator was never married. He had lived for many years in a
state of illicit intercourse with [Fan] a mulatto woman, his own slave
who assumed the position of a wife and controlled, at least, all the
domestic arrangements of the family. Fan had the influence over him
of a white woman and a wife. He bargained for a negro, but would not
buy till her pleasure was consulted; sold a negro girl at her desire, and
made titles to another one that she offered for sale as her own. Fan
refused to let a servant come to him when he called; they quarreled
about it—she shook a fist in his face and threatened to knock his teeth
down his throat; witness heard them quarrel in the night; heard her
call Hannah, a servant, to bring her the whip and she'd beat his skin
off. They would get drunk together.

In Jolliffe v. Fanning, *South Carolina, testimony showed that Eli-
jah Willis treated his concubine, Amy, as if she were his wife.*

The deceased was often under gloomy depression of spirits avoiding society on account of his connection with Amy; that he permitted
her to act as the mistress of his house; to use saucy and improper
language; that she was drunken and probably unfaithful to him; and
that she exercised great influence over him in his domestic affairs and
in taking slaves from his business to make wheels for little wagons for

*The witnesses, usually relatives seeking to break the will, were not, of course, unpreju-
diced.

his mulatto children, and in inducing him to take off for sale the negro man who was her husband.

No matter how assertive Fan or Amy or the others may have been at home, they were at the mercy of the white world after their protectors died. In almost all instances, they lost the legacies that had been left to them. Some won freedom and a chance to educate their children; many, perhaps the majority, remained in slavery.

FOUR

Courtship and Family Life

WHEN AN OVERSEER ASKED FOR *"a negro woman, young and likely, and be sertin that she is sound," he was taking the first step toward becoming a man of property. A slave woman was both the nucleus of a labor force and the producer of wealth that increased rapidly. In the decade before the Civil War, her child was worth $100 at birth, $500 at the age of five. The dollar-and-cents value of a good "breed woman" was well known in the quarters. Tempie Herndon, who had nine children before freedom, said:*

I was worth a heap to Marse George 'cause I had so many chillen. De more chillen a slave had de more day was worth. Lucy Carter was de only nigger on de plantation dat had more chillen den I had, but her chillen was sickly and mine was muley strong.

Most slave owners did not care who fathered the children, as long as they kept on coming. A minority employed studs or forced couples to mate "just like cattle":

Dr. Ware had a man he bred his colored house women to. He was hostler, looked after the stock and got the wood. The women hated him, and the men on the place hated him too.

[Master] would never allow the men to be single after they were eighteen, nor the women after they were fifteen. I remember one day, when he had returned from town with about twenty-five heads of slaves, he called out all those who had no wives or husbands on the place. Said he, "Well, boys, I've gotten a fine set of girls for you, and I am going to put you all together; likewise you, girls, I've got these fine boys, and I am going to put you all together, so that there will be no reason for any of you to have wives and husbands off the place." So then he gave each one his wife or husband; he chose them out himself.

On the Blackshear place, they took all the fine looking boys and girls that was thirteen years old or older and put them in a big barn. They used to strip them naked and put them in a big barn every Sunday and leave them there until Monday morning. Out of that came sixty babies.

The majority of planters utilized the carrot rather than the stick to increase their stock. A "good breeder" was given a pig, a calico dress, or better rations. One planter ruled that "women with six children alive are allowed Saturday to themselves"; another promised his house servant her freedom after she bore five children, one for each of his sons and daughters. Lulu Wilson was persuaded by a white dress.

Missus told me I had ought to marry. She said if I'd marry she'd togger me up in a white dress and give me a weddin' supper. She made the dress and Wash Hodges married me out'n the Bible to a nigger 'longin' to a nephew of his' n. I was 'bout thirteen or fourteen. It warn't long after that when Missus Hodges got a doctor to me. The doctor told me less'n I had a baby, old as I was and married, I'd start in on spasms. So it warn't long till I had a baby.

The quarters had its own moral code, accepting premarital intercourse but frowning on promiscuity. A resident of a Georgia coastal village remembered community sanctions that originated in Africa.

I heard many times 'bout how in Africa when a girl don't ack jis lak dey should, dey drum her outuh town. Dey jis beat de drum, and call her name on de drum an de drum say 'bout all de tings she done. Girls hab to be careful den. In Africa dey gits punished. Sometimes when dey ben bad, dey put 'em on de banjo in dis country. When dey play dat night, dey sing bout dat girl and dey tell all 'bout her. Den everybody know an dat girl sho better change her ways.

Under planter law, there was no such thing as an illegitimate slave child. "The unmarried woman who becomes a mother has not materially lowered her character, or her station in society. Her offspring is not a burden but an acquisition to her owner," a South Carolina jurist wrote. Although a so-called outside child was accepted in the quarters, mothers and grandmothers preferred their daughters to marry, and they tried to exercise close maternal supervision.

I walk with Jim to de gate and stood under de honeysuckle dat was smelling so sweet. I heard de big ol' bullfrogs a' croakin' by de river and de whippoorwills a-hollerin' in de woods. Dere was a big yellow moon, and I reckon Jim did love me. Anyhow he said so and asked me to marry him and he squeezed my hand. I told him I'd think it over and I did and de next Sunday I told him dat I'd have him.

He ain't kissed me yet but he asked my mammy for me. She says dat she'll have to have a talk to me and let him know. Well all dat week she talks to me, tellin' me how serious gettin' married is and dat it last a powerful long time. I tells her dat I knows it but dat I am ready.

On Sunday night Mammy tells Jim dat he can have me and you ought to seed dat black boy grin. He comes to me without a word and he picks me up out dat chair and dere in de moonlight he kisses me right before my mammy who am a-cryin'.

I married when I was 14 years old. So help me God, I didn't know what marriage meant. I had an idea when you loved de man, you an' he could be married an' his wife had to cook, clean up, wash an' iron for him was all. I slept in bed he on his side an' I on mine for three months an' dis aint no lie. He never got close to me 'cause mama had sed, "Don't let no body bother yo' principle, 'caus dat wuz all yo' had." I 'bey my mama, an' tol' him so, and I said to go an' ask mama an' ef she sed he could get close to me hit was alright. An' he an' I went together to see and ask mama. Den mama said "Come here chillun," and she began telling me to please my husband, an' 'twas my duty as a wife, dat he had married a pu'fect lady.

Former slaves recalled their courting days with tenderness.

I was a housemaid and my mammy run de kitchen. They say I was a pretty gal then, face shiny like a ginger cake, and hair straight and black as a crow. One springtime de flowers git be blooming, de hens to cackling, and de guineas to patarocking. Sam come along when I was out in de yard wid de [white] baby. He fust talk to de baby, and I asked him if de baby wasn't pretty. He say, "Yes, but not as pretty as you is, Louisa." I looks at Sam, and dat kind of foolishness wind up in a weddin'.

My mammy stay on wid de same marster 'til I was grown, dat is fifteen, and Thad got to lookin' at me, meek as a sheep and dumb as a calf. I had to ask dat nigger, right out, what his 'tentions was, befo' I get him to bleat out dat he love me. Him name Thad Guntharpe. I glance at him one day at de pigpen when I was sloppin' de hogs, I say: "Mr. Guntharpe, you follow me night and mornin' to dis pigpen; do you happen to be in love wid one of these pigs? If so, I'd like to know which one 'tis; then sometime I come down here by myself and tell dat pig 'bout your 'fections." Thad didn't say nothin; but just grin. Him took de slop bucket out of my hand and look at it, put upside down on de ground, and set me down on it; then he fall down dere on de grass by me and warm my fingers in his hands. I just took pity on him and told him mighty plain dat he must limber up his tongue and say what he mean, wantin' to visit them pigs so often. Us carry on foolishness 'bout de little boar shoat pig and de little sow pig, then I squeal in laughter over how he scrouge so close; de slop bucket tipple over and I lost my seat. Dat ever remain de happiest minute of my eighty-two years.

Violet told a northern woman who was visiting in South Carolina how she was finally persuaded to marry.

My first husband—nice man; den he sold off to Florida—neber hear from him 'gain. Den I sold up here. Massa want me to breed; so he say "Violet you must take some nigger here."

Den I say, "No, Massa, I can't take any here." Well den, Missis, he go down Virginia, and he bring up two niggers—and Missis say, "One ob dem's for you Violet;" but I say, "No, Missis, I can't take one ob dem, 'cause I don't lub 'em." By-and-by, Massa he buy tree more, and den Missis say, "Now, Violet, ones dem is for you." I say "I do' no—maybe I can't lub one dem neider;" but she say "You must hab one ob dese." Well, so Sam and I we lib along two year—he watchin my ways and I watchin his ways. At last, one night, we was standin' by de wood-pile togeder, and de moon bery shine, and I do' no how 'twas, Missis, he answer me, he want a wife, but he didn't know where he get one. I say, "Plenty girls in G." He say, "Yes—but maybe I shan't find any I like so well as you." Den I say maybe he wouldn't like my ways, 'cause I'se an ole woman, and I hab four children; and anybody marry me must be jest kind to dem children as dey was to me, else I couldn't lub him. Well, so we went on from one ting to anoder, till at last we say we'd take one anoder, and so we've libed togeder eber since—and I's had four children by him—and he never slip away from me nor I from him.

When Violet's interviewer asked how she and Sam were married, the slave explained.

We just takes one anoder—we asks de white folks' leave, and den takes one anoder. Some folks dey's married by de book; but den, what's de use? Dere's my fus husband, we'se married by de book, and he sold way off to Florida, and I's here. Dey do what dey please wid us, so we jest make money for dem.

Slave weddings ranged from a so-called Parson Blanket marriage in which "he bring his blanket and lay it down beside mine" to a full-scale ceremony with white dress, bridesmaids, and minister. There was never a license or certificate. The marriage did not exist in a legal sense, and could be terminated at will by the master. When a white minister married a couple "by de book," he routinely omitted the phrases "till death do you part" and "Those whom God hath joined together, let no man put asunder." "Dey just puts black folks together in de sight of man and not in de sight of God, and dey puts dem asunder too," a woman said.

Because there was no prescribed civil or religious ritual, the slave community developed rituals of its own. The commonest of these was "jumping the broomstick";* that is, the couple sealed their vows by jumping or stepping over a broomstick.

We didn't have no preacher when we married. My Marster said, "Now you and Lewis wants to marry and there ain't no objections so go on and jump over the broom stick together and you is married." That was all there was to it. I lived on with my white folks and he lived on with his and kept comin' to see me jest like he had done when he was a courtin'. He never brought me any presents 'cause he didn't have no money to buy them with, but he was good to me and that was what counted.

On some plantations, an older woman performed the ceremony.

My mother an' dad went down to de quarters an' tole Ant Lucky dat' Marsa say it was all right fo' 'em to git married. So she went outside—was Sunday, mind you, an' all de slaves was lyin' roun' slee-

---

*The origin of the broomstick ritual is obscure. The practice existed throughout the antebellum South; it has also been reported in England and New England.

pin' an restin'. She called 'em together an' right den an' dere married 'em. Dey all form a ring 'roundst my mother an' dad, an' Ant Lucky read sumpin from de Bible, an' den she put de broomstick down an' dey locked dey arms together an' jumped over it. Den dey was married.

A favorite house servant might be married in the big house, with both white people and slaves in attendance.

Your pa gib me a head-weddin—kilt a mutton—a round o' beef—tukkeys—cakes, one on t'other—trifle. I had all de chany off de sideboard, cups an' saucers, de table, de white table-cloth. I had on your pa's wife's weddin' gloves and slippers an' veil. De slippers was too small, but I put my toes in. Marster brought out a milk-pail o'toddy an more in bottles. De gentlemans an' marster stand up on de tables. Nobody else didn't hab sich a weddin'. De whole day 'fore I was to be married Miss Mary kep' me shut up in a room. "A bride must not be seen," she said. An' she wouldn't lemme come out to dinner, but she sent my dinner in to me on a plate. De nex' mornin' I went to marster's an' Miss Mary's room 'fore dey was up. "Who is that?" she say. I say, "Harriet." "Good morning, Mrs. Bride. I wish you joy, and every year a son or a daughter."

These lavish big house weddings had different meanings for master and slave. Few owners were as cynical as Aunt Mary Jane's who contrived a comic spectacle when his concubine married, but even the most generous master had "to have his little fun."

[Aunt Mary Jane] was her young marster's woman and he let her marry because he could get her anyhow if he wanted her. He dressed her up all in red—red dress, red band and rosette around her head, and a red sash with a big red bow. She was so black that when we saw a person who was real black, we would say "black as Aunt Mary Jane," and you can imagine all that black and all that red; but they had a little ceremony and all the young white folks were there looking at them get married. It was the funniest looking sight I ever did see, and she married a yellow man and had two yellow girls to wait on her! After the ceremony, there was a dance, and the white men and women were standing 'round looking at them dance all night.

Uncle Edmond Kirby married us. He was de nigger preacher dat preached at de plantation church. After Uncle Edmond said de last words over me and Exter, Marse George got to have his little fun. He say, "Come on, Exter, you and Tempie got to jump over de broom stick backwards to see which one gwine be boss of your household." Marse George hold de broom about a foot high off de floor. De one dat jump over it backwards, and never touch handle, gwine boss de house. If both of dem jump over without touchin' it, dey won't gwine be no bossin', dey just gwine be congenial. I jumped first, and I sailed right over dat broom stick same as a cricket. But when Exter jump he done had a big dram and his feets was so big and clumsy dat dey got all tangled up and he fell headlong. Marse George he laugh, and told Exter he gwine be bossed 'twell he scared to speak. After de weddin' we went down to de cabin Mis' Betty done all dressed up, but Exter couldn't stay no longer den dat night 'cause he belonged to Marse Snipes Durham and he had to go back home.

Despite Marse George's prediction, it is unlikely that Tempie bossed Exter. At the age of 103, she described an enduring marriage in which husband and wife shared responsibilities.

I was glad when de War stopped 'cause den me and Exter could be together all de time. After we was free we rented land, den after while we bought a farm. We paid three hundred dollars we done saved. We had a hoss, a steer, a cow, and two pigs besides some chickens and four geese. Den we hitched up de wagon and throwed in de passel of chillen and moved to our new farm.

Ironically, a slave woman had a potential for marital happiness that was denied to most of her white contemporaries. For one thing, unless her master refused permission she could marry the man of her choice without concern about property settlements or improving her status in the community. For another, when she and her husband crossed the threshold of the cabin assigned to them, they were roughly equal. As working partners, both contributed to the rude comforts of their home. Neither was boss.

Although the law defined slave families as matrilineal, that is, the children's status was determined by the mother's, a slave woman was by no means a matriarch. Matriarchy implies power. The slave woman had no power over husband, children, or even her own body. All power flowed from her master and his male deputies, the overseer and the driver. The rules that they laid down to govern life in the quarters reflected the attitudes of their patriarchal society. Moreover, most residents of the quarters agreed with these attitudes, as the following folktale with African roots illustrates. This tale was recorded in the

*1890s in the South Carolina Sea Islands where residents spoke Gullah,
a dialect with many Africanisms.*

Dere was a beautiful nyung [young] lady, an' she said she wouldn't
married a man what got a scratch on 'e back. Well, de Tiger 'e tu'n
himself to a man an' dressed himself up bery nice, an' drove up ter de
nyung lady house in a buggy. So de nyung lady came out an' saw him
an' say "Mudder, dis is de man dat I'll married."

An' de Tiger did married de nyung lady an' carried her right off
in 'e buggy. An' dey went 'way down in de swamp where de Tiger hab
lib, an' 'e tell her to stay dere tel him come back. Nuttin' she had to
eat, nuttin' she had to look on but ole carcass an' ol' bone de Tiger
done leabe. [When the Tiger returned he said] "I only married um for
le'um know dat a woman isn't more dan a man, for de word dat she
say, dat she "wouldn't married a man what gots a scratch on him
back." An' straightway dey tuk dey journey back home to de mudder.
Den de mudder say, "Daughter, I tol' you dat you always speak too
venomous. God had nebber made a woman for be head of a man."

*No matter how much traditional male labor a woman performed
all day, when she returned to her cabin at night, she took up the typical
duties of wife and mother.*

When slaves come in from de fields de womans cleant up deir
houses atter dey et, and den washed and got up early next mornin' to
put de clothes out to dry. Mens would eat, set 'round talkin' to other
mens and den go to bed.

Mammy and pappy and us twelve chillen lives in one cabin, so
mammy has to cook for fourteen people, 'sides her field work. She am
up way befo' daylight fixin' breakfast and supper after dark with de
pine knot torch to make de light. She cook on de fireplace in winter
and in de yard in summer.

*Pregnancy brought added strains. On well-ordered plantations
"lusty women" were assigned lighter tasks in their last months but were
required to work until the day of their confinement. Three to four
weeks after childbirth, they were sent back to the fields. Some ex-slaves
remembered this period as pleasant; others told of beatings and inadequate prenatal care.*

When the women had babies they was treated kind and they let
them stay in. We didn't go to no hospitals. We just had our babies
and had a granny to catch them. The granny would put a rust piece
of tin or an axe under the straw tick, and this would ease the pains.

Us didn't have no mattresses in them days but filled a bed tick with fresh straw after the wheat was thrashed, and it was good sleeping, too. We'd set up the fifth day and after the "layin-in" time was up they told us to walk around the house just once and come in. This was to keep us from taking a relapse.

When women was with child they'd dig a hole in the groun' and put their stomach in the hole, and then beat 'em. They'd allus whop us.

Dere was uh young woman named Lucy dat was in chile birth an' in de moanin's was so sick she couldn't go tuh de field. Well, dey thought dat she was jes' stallin' so as tuh git outa wukkin'. Fin'lly de overseer comes tuh huh cabin one moanin' when she don' line up wid de other field niggers an' he dragged huh out. He laid huh 'cross uh big tabaccy barrell an' he tuk his rawhide an' whupt huh somepin terrible. Well suh, dat woman dragged huhse'f back tuh de cabin an' de next day she give birth tuh uh baby girl. An' dis ain't no lie, 'cause ah seed et, dat chile's back was streaked wid raid marks all criss-cross lak. De nex' day Lucy died.

When my little brother was borned, I members dat day. Mammy and I wuz working out in the corn patch. She wuz coverin corn, and she jes had about three or four more rows to cover, then she ran to de house. Dey wuz jes one room en she tried to made de udder children go outside but dey wouldn' go, so she ran outside in de chimney corner, en soon dey heard a baby holler. Dey called me to cum quick cause Mammy found a baby. No, mammy diden have nobody to help tend to her.

Those Amazonian women who had their babies in the fields or returned to work a day after childbirth were few and far between. Slave women were far less healthy than their mistresses, suffering from a host of gynecological problems, hernias and back and joint diseases. When Fanny Kemble visited her husband's Georgia plantation, she found "every other woman" with a prolapsed uterus or similar disorder. Singly and in delegations, the women begged her to speak in favor of a longer lying-in period.

One poor woman, named Molly, came to beg that I would, if possible, get an extension of their exemption from work after child-bearing. The close of her argument was concise and forcible. "Missis, we hab um pickanniny—tree weeks in de ospital, and den right out upon the hoe again, *can we strong* dat way, missis? No!" And truly I do not see that they can. This poor creature has had eight children and two miscarriages. All her children were dead but one.

An 1862 interview with a South Carolina woman also told of frequent miscarriage and high infant mortality.

"How many children have you?"

"Six, Missus. But I'se lost five."

"My poor woman! What was the disease?"

"Oh, no disease, Missus, strainin' and workin' so hard in de fiel', sometimes dead born, all mash! sometimes lib little while, neber ober tree or four weeks scarcely. You neber 'lowed to drop you hoe till labor 'pon you, neber! no matter how bad you feel, you neber 'lowed to stop till you go in bed, neber!"

So many pregnancies ended in miscarriage that slave women were suspected of deliberately aborting. Undoubtedly, many tried decoctions of roots and seeds to prevent conception or bring about abortion. In "An Essay on the Causes of the Production of Abortion among our Negro Population," a paper read before a Tennessee Medical Society in 1860, Dr. John S. Morgan listed "tansy, rue, roots and seed of the cotton plant, pennyroyal, cedar berries and camphor" as "remedies mostly used by the negroes to produce abortion." Morgan and his colleagues agreed, however, that medicines alone would not effect an abortion in a healthy woman. Slaves miscarried because they were overworked and poorly cared for, he said.

The functions of menstruation and pregnancy being so peculiarly delicate, negroes suffer seriously during those periods from hard labor and exposure in bad weather, frequently being badly fed and badly clothed; consequently catamenial derangements, with various uterine diseases, often follow, which may prevent conception, and if it does take place, very often the uterine irritability or disease causes the embryo to be thrown off. Under these circumstances abortion may take place from very slight causes referable either to the mother, or to the foetus.

Although planters blamed careless mothers for the high rate of infant deaths, most babies died because of poor maternal nutrition and unsanitary, inadequate care. Tetanus from improperly dressed umbilical cords, for instance, was frequent in the quarters but rarely seen in white households. After their lying-in periods, mothers were obliged to leave their infants.

My master would make me leave my child before day to go to the canefield; and he would not allow me to come back till ten o'clock in the morning to nurse my child. When I did go I could hear my poor child crying long before I got to it. And la, me! my poor child would be so hungry! Sometimes I would have to walk more than a mile to get to my child, and when I did get there I would be so tired I'd fall asleep while my baby was sucking.

Mother tole me de overseer would come ter her when she had a young child an' tell her ter go home and suckle dat thing, and she better be back in de field at work in 15 minutes. Mother said she knowed she could not go home and suckle dat child and git back in 15 minutes so she would go somewhere an' sit down an' pray de child would die.

On small places where there was no nurse house, the mother would have to leave the child alone, a woman explained to an interviewer during the Civil War.

"Have you no children?"

"No, Missus, had to leab baby 'e in house all day while gone to work."

"Not alone?"

"Yes, Missus, 'lone, couldn't help it, 'bliged to do it."

"Why how did you fix it?"

"Hang it up dere in de basket, an' boil some flou' for it. It cry all day an' I cry all day, an' he died, 'cause he cry so."

Older children also suffered from the enforced neglect.

My mammy grieve lots over brother George, who die with de fever. Granny she doctor him as best she could, every time she get ways from de white folks' kitchen. My mammy never get chance to see him, 'cept when she get home in de evenin'. George, he just lie. One day I look at him and he had such a peaceful look on his face, I think he sleep, but he was dead. Mammy never know till she come at night. Poor Mammy she kneel by de bed and cry her heart out. Old Uncle Allen, he make pine box for him and carry him to de graveyard over de hill. My mammy just plow and cry as she watch 'em put George in de ground.

Although child care was a job for Mamma and Granny, fathers and brothers played a role in the household too. They built furniture for the cheerless cabins, supplied firewood, and brought home fish and

game to add to the sparse diet. Lullabies, as well as reminiscences,
attest to the masculine role in the slave family.

> Bye baby buntin'
> Daddy's gone a-huntin'
> Ter fetch a little rabbit skin
> Ter wrap de baby buntin' in.

> Kink head, wherefore you skeered?
> Old snake crawled off, 'cause he's a-feared.
> Papa will smite on de back
> With a great big club—ker whack! Ker whack!

On de cold winter night de boys and old men was allus whittlin'
and it wasn't jes foolishment. Dey whittles traps and wooden spoons
and needles to make seine nets and checkers and sleds. We all sits
workin' and singin' and smokin' pipes.

My father had a garden of his own and he also had some chickens.
Mr. Dodge who owned the hotel was pa's regular customer. He would
buy anything my pa brought to him,; and many times he was buying
his own stuff. I have seen pa go out at night with a big sack and come
back with it full. He'd bring sweet potatoes, watermelons, chickens and
turkeys. We were fond of pig roast and sweet potatoes, and the only
way to have pig roast was for pa to go out on one of his hunting trips.

Despite the crushing burdens that both partners bore, slave mar-
riages succeeded when they were allowed to remain intact. Unfortu-
nately, large numbers of them were part time from their inception. On
farms worked by only two or three slave families, the women had to
marry men from other places. Even on large plantations, they some-
times chose to marry off the place. Their " 'broad husbands" were
permitted to visit them once or twice a week. A white Georgian
remembered that "Saturday night the roads were filled with men on
their way to the 'wife house,' each bearing in his bag his soiled clothes
and all the good things he could collect during the week for the
delectation of the household." Former slaves recalled.

My Pa uster come evy Sadday evenin' to chop wood out uv de wood
lot and pile up plenty fur Ma tell he come agin. On We'nsday evenin',
Pa uster come after he been huntin' and bring in possum and coon.
He sho could get 'em a plenty.

My Pa b'longin' to one man and my mammy b'longin' to another,
four or five miles apart, caused some confusion, mix-up, and heart-

aches. My pa have to git a pass to come to see my mammy. He come sometimes widout de pass. Patrollers catch him way up de chimney hidin' one night; they stripped him right befo' mammy and give him thirty-nine lashes, wid her cryin' and a hollerin' louder than he did.

Difficult as these " 'broad" marriages could be, their "mixups and heartaches" were mild compared to the anguish of permanent separation. A plaintive work song told of being sold to Georgia:

> Farewell, fellow servants! Oho!
> I'm gwine way to leabe you, Oho!
> I'm gwine to leabe de ole country, Oho!
> I'm sold off to Georgy! Oho!
>
> My dear wife un one chile, Oho!
> My poor heart is breaking, Oho!
> No more shall I see you, Oho!
> Oh! no more foreber! Oho!

A slave owner who broke up a family was not heartless by his lights. The kindliest of masters saw nothing wrong in giving a slave child to his son or daughter when they married. An economically pressed planter might regret that husbands and wives would be separated if he moved to the Southwest, but what could he do? Sometimes debts mounted and slaves were seized by the sheriff or owners died and estates were divided.

O, dat was a terrible time! All de slaves be in de field, plowin', hoein', and singin' in de boilin' sun. Old Marse, he comes through de field with a man call de speculator. Dey walked round just lookin', just lookin'. All de darkies know what dis mean. Dey didn't dare look up, just work right on. Den de speculator he see who he want. He talk to old Marse, den dey slaps de handcuffs on him and take him away to de cotton country.

When de darkies went to dinner de ole nigger mammy she ask where am such and such. None of de others want to tell her. But when she see dem look down to de ground she just say: "De speculator, de speculator." Den de tears roll down her cheeks, cause maybe it her son or husband and she knows she never see 'em again.

No slave marriage was secure. Every family lived with the possibility of separation.

FIVE

Letters from Slave Women

*WATCHING A WHITE WOMAN write a letter, a slave said "O!
dat be great comfort, Missis. You can write to your friends all 'bout
ebery ting, and so hab dem write to you. Our people can't do so.
Wheder dey be 'live or dead, we can't neber know—only sometimes
we hears dey be dead." The vast majority of slaves lost contact with
one another when they were separated, but a small number who had
learned to write* or who had white friends willing to write for them
communicated with distant family members. Letters from slave women, preserved by their descendants or by former owners, offer further
testimony to the strength and endurance of family ties. In one group
of letters, wives begged their husbands to save them from slave traders.*

Dear Husband: Richmond, Virginia, October 27, 1840
    This is the third letter that I have written to you, and have not
received any from you. I think very hard of it. The trader has been here
three times to look at me. I wish that you would try to see if you can
get any one to buy me. If you don't come down here this Sunday,
perhaps you wont see me any more. Give my love to them all, and to
your mother in particular, and to aunt Betsey, and all the children, tell
Jane and Mother they must come down a fortnight before Christmas.
I wish to see you all, but I expect I never shall—never no more.
                    I remain your Dear and affectionate Wife,
                                Sargry Brown

*Sargry Brown's husband never received her appeal; it was found in
the Dead Letter Office in Washington, D.C. Louisa and Archer Alexander had better luck. Both slaves belonging to the Hollman family,
they had been married for thirty years when Archer ran away during
the Civil War. He kept in touch with his wife until he was able to
engineer her escape.*

                                Naylor's Store [Missouri]
Dear Husband: November 16, 1863
    I received your letter yesterday, and lost no time in asking Mr. Jim
if he would sell me, and what he would take for me. He flew at me,
and said I would never get free only at the point of the Baynot, and

*Perhaps 5 percent of the slaves knew how to read and write by 1860.

there was no use in my ever speaking to him any more about it. I don't see how I can ever get away except you get soldiers to take me from the house, as he is watching me night and day. He is always abusing Lincoln, and calls him an old Rascoll. He is the greatest rebel under heaven. It is a sin to have him loose. He says if he had hold of Lincoln he would chop him up into mincemeat. I had good courage all along until now but now I am almost heart broken. Answer this letter as soon as possible.

I am your affectionate wife,
Louisa Alexander

Harriet Newby, a Virginia slave, was about forty years old when she wrote to her husband, Dangerfield Newby. Freed by his white father, he was working in the North and trying to raise money to buy Harriet and their six children.

Dear Husband: Brentville, [Virginia,] April 22d, 1859
I received your letter today, and it gives much pleasure to here from you, but was sorry to [hear] of your sikeness; hope you may be well when you receive this. I wrote to you several weeks ago, and directed my letter to Bridge Port, but I fear you did not receive it, as you said nothing about it in yours. I wrote in my last letter that Miss Virginia had a baby—a little girl. I had to nurse her day and night. Dear Dangerfield, you cannot imagine how much I want to see you. Com as soon as you can for nothing would give more pleasure than to see you. It is the greatest Comfort I have is thinking of the promist time when you will be here. The baby commenced to crall to-day it is very delicate. Nothing more at present, but remain

your affectionate wife
Harriet Newby

Dear Husband: Brentville, [Virginia,] August 16, 1859
Your letter came duly to hand and it gave me much pleasure to here from you, and especely to here you are better of your rhumatism. I want you to buy me as soon as possible, for if you do not get me some body else will. Dear Husband you [know] not the trouble I see; the last two years has been like a trouble dream. It is said Master is in want of money. If so, I know not what time he may sell me, and then all my bright hopes of the futer are blasted, for their has been one bright hope to cheer me in all my troubles, that is to be with you. If I thought I shoul never see you this earth would have no charms for me. Do all you can for me, witch I have no doubt you will. The children are all well. The baby cannot walk yet. It can step around everything by

holding on. I must bring my letter to a Close as I have no newes to write. You mus write soon and say when you think you can come.

Your affectionate wife,

Harriet Newby.

Two months after the above letter was written, Dangerfield Newby returned to Virginia with John Brown and his men. He was killed in the attack on Harpers Ferry. After Harriet Newby's letters were found on his body, she was sold to the Deep South.

When Emily Saunders (1815–76) married Adam Plummer (1819–1905) in 1841, they were Maryland house servants belonging to different masters. Every Saturday night Adam walked eight miles to see his wife, returning to his owner in time for work on Monday. After Emily's owner died in 1851, she and their older children were purchased by residents of Washington, D.C., fifteen miles from Adam's home. Adam was able to visit his family every second week until 1855 when Emily's owner moved to a farm near Baltimore. After that, he was seldom permitted to visit more than twice a year, at Christmas and Easter. It was then that husband and wife began to correspond. Emily dictated her letters to her mistress or to a white seamstress in the household. A selection from her letters follows.

Ellicott Mills, Maryland,

My Dear Plummer: April 20, 1856

I want you to let me know why you wrote me so troubled a letter. I was very sorry to hear that you should say you and I are parted for life, and am very troubled at it. I don't think I can stand it long. What do you mean? Does your master say he will not let you come any more? Or what is the reason you say we are parted for life? I can't think it is your wish to give me up for another wife.

I want you to write me about my two children, if they are well and comfortable, and how mother is.* Saunders said today "My Pappy is coming to bring me a hat and a pair of boots to go to church with." I want to have the baby baptized and I want to know if you can come, when you will be able to do so, and I will wait until you come.

The baby has her chills come back on her now and then. The other children are all well, and Henry sends his love to his father. I have been quite well, and have no trouble but the one great trouble, the want to see you sometimes. God bless and keep you!

Your affectionate wife,

Emily Plummer

*The older Plummer children and other family members were in Washington where Adam was able to keep in touch with them.

Ellicott Mills, Maryland,
My Deare Husband: September 18, 1860
    I recived you kind letter and was very much oblige to you for what
you sent me. The fridy night after i rote to you i was confined with
too babys* one was a boy and the other a girl every body that see them
says they are the fines chrilden they every sar. When mother came and
scene them she was delited. I am as well as can bee expected. The
chrilden ar all well and join me in love to you from your wife
                    Emily Plummer

Ellicott City, Maryland,
My ever dear Husband: August 19, 1861
    I have been hoping each day to hear from you. We are all well. The
babies grow and improve rapidly. They can almost walk. And Papa,
Saunders is not with me, he is hired to Miss Eliza Dorsey, as house
servant, is doing very well. He and all the children are so anxious to
see you.
    I think each day I cannot longer wait for a visit from you. My heart
aches at the thought of this long and painful separation. I dream of
you and think you are once more with me, but wake to find myself
alone and so wretchedly unhappy.
    Could you come up early some Sunday morning to breakfast? Do
try this plan, my dear husband, and let me hear from you soon, that
you will come, but under any circumstances write very frequently. It
is our next great pleasure to seeing your kind face, and hearing your
voice of affection.
                    Your truly affectionate wife,
                    Emily Plummer

*Set free in 1863, Emily Plummer joined her husband, to live with
him for the rest of her life. Their happiness was marred only by the
absence of their oldest daughter, Sarah Miranda. Sold South in 1861,
she had last written to them from New Orleans.*

Dear Mother: New Orleans, Louisiana, May 24, 1861
    I write with much grief to say that I was in Alexandria† two
months, and could not hear from any of you. I do not blame you
because you could not come to see me, I think it very hard that father
did not come as he was nearer than you were. Though I may hear from
you, I never expect to see you again. You will please write to Grandma.
Give my love to her, and tell her I am sorry I did not come to see her.

*Forty-five-year-old Emily Plummer had given birth to twins.
†She was in the slave pen in Alexandria, Virginia, awaiting a purchaser.

I have been low spirited since I left you all, but I will try to do the best I can. I hope that you will not forget that I am still alive. Remember me to my brother, and tell him I hope he has not forgotten to write to me as he promised to do. Though you will be sorry to hear I am so far yet you will be glad to hear that I met with my aunt Sarah. She did not know me until I made myself known unto her. She said when I wrote to give her love to sister and all the children. I suppose you will answer my letter as soon as you can because I want to hear from you as bad as you do from me.

I remain as ever your affec daughter

S. M. Plummer

The war put a stop to all correspondence, but in 1866 the Plummers pooled their savings and sent their son to Louisiana to look for his sister. He returned with her for a grand family reunion in October 1866.

The owners of slave pens in Alexandria permitted their prisoners to write to relatives in the hope that they could raise money to buy them. Nancy Cartwright who had bought her own freedom was working as a washerwoman in New York when she received the following plea from her daughter.

My Dear Mother: Alexandria, [Virginia,] January 22, 1850

I take this opportunity of writing you a few lines, to inform you that I am in Bruin's Jail, and Aunt Sally and all of her children, and Aunt Hagar and all her children, and grandmother is almost crazy. My dear mother, will you please to come on as soon as you can? I expect to go away very shortly. O mother! my dear mother! come now and see your distressed and heart-broken daughter once more. Mother! my dear mother! do not forsake me, for I feel desolate! Please to come now.

Your daughter,

Emily Russell.

P.S. If you do not come as far as Alexandria, come to Washington, and do what you can.

Appealing to abolitionists in Washington and New York for help, Cartwright learned that Bruin & Hill, the slave traders, were asking $5,300 for her sisters and their children and $1,800 for Emily who, they wrote, "is said to be the finest-looking woman in the country." When Cartwright was unable to ransom her, Emily Russell was sent to the fancy-girl market in New Orleans. She died during the overland trip.

Born in Virginia, Lucy Tucker was a slave in Alabama for more than a decade before she had an opportunity to send a letter to her mother. Although a white amanuensis was undoubtedly responsible for much of the language of the letter, the sentiments were Tucker's.

Dear Mother: Huntsville, Alabama, May 20, 1845
I have never heard from you but once since I left. I received a letter some year or two after I came to this country. I wish I had written to you & kept up a continual correspondence for I know not whether you all still live or whether many have not since passed from the stage of human existence. This may is eleven years since I have professed religion & trusted the helm of my shattered bark to the Saviour of mankind. I desire to know from you who of all the family have embraced the cause of Christ Since I left & whom mournfull death has taken away. I also wish to know how many have taken consorts those companions on whom depend the future condition whether happy or the reverse & if those who are married are married well or not & to whom. Give my affectionate love to all my kind friends not one or two but all. My son Burrel has also enlisted on the side of the saints some two or three years. He has been absent from me nine years. He is now grown but I have not seen him since he was a boy though I hear from him now & then. Mary Ann the child which I brought with me died as also Susanna who was born after I came to this country in their fifth year. I have seen a great deal of trouble since I came to Alabama but by the grace of God I have overcome it all. I cant inform you anything about those that came with me for I have not heard from them since the second year after I came to this country. Moses was drowened some years ago in Kentucky drunk as usual. Scipio is in Nashville doing very well. All he desires is to hear from his wife & children.
I have been very sick for the las two or three years But now am doing well. Have a good husband & give the white people 25 cts a day.* I follow washing ironing &c. I send this letter by kindness of Mrs Burr and hope to receive an answer when she comes back. This is from your daughter

Lucy Tucker

After a twenty-year separation, Louisa Picquet learned that her mother, Elizabeth Ramsey, was in Wharton County, Texas, the slave of Colonel A. C. Horton. Mother and daughter corresponded for many months while Picquet and her husband tried to raise the purchase

*Lucy Tucker was hiring her own time, that is, supporting herself and paying her owner twenty-five cents a day for the privilege.

money that Horton demanded. Two of Ramsey's letters to her daughter:

My Dear Daughter: Wharton, [Texas,] March 8, 1859
    I have written you twice, but I hav not yet received an answer from you. I can not imagin why you do not writ. I feel very much troubel. I fear you hav not recived my letters or you would hav written. I sent to my little grand children a ring also a button in my first letter. I want you to writ to me on recept of this letter, whether you hav ever received the letters and presents or not. I said in my letter to you that Col. Horton would let you have me for 1000 dol. or a woman that could fill my place. I think you could get one cheaper where you are than to pay him the money. I am anxios to hav you to make this trade. You have no Idea what my feelings are. I hav not spent one happy moment since I received your kind letter. I was more than rejoyest to hear from you my Dear child; but my feelings on this subject are in Expressible. In regard to your Brother John Col. Horton is willing for you to hav him for a boy fifteen years old or fifteen hundred dol. I think that 1000 dollars is too much for me. You must writ very kind to Col Horton and try to Get me for less money. I think you can change his Price by writing Kindly to him. I think you can soften his heart and he will let you hav me for less than he has offered me to you for.
    You Brother John sends his love to you and 100 kisses to your little son. Kiss my Dear little children 100 times for me particuler Elizabeth. Say to her that she must writ to her grand mar ofton. I want you to hav your ambrotipe* taken also your children and send them to me. I would giv this world to see you and my sweet little children; may God bless you my Dear child and protect you is my prayer.
                          Your affectionate mother,
                          Elizabeth Ramsey

Dear Daughter: Matagorda, [Texas,] April 21, 1860
    I received your kind & affectionate letter, & was glad to hear that you was well, & getting along very well. I was sorry to learn that you were disappointed in raising the amount of money required to purchase me. In a conversation with my master he says he is willing to take a woman in exchange for me, of my age, and capasity or he will under the circumstances take nine hundred dollars in *cash* for me. He also says that money cannot buy John. He is a training John to take charge of one of his Plantations & will not part with him untel death parts

*An ambrotype was a photograph made with a glass negative.

them. I should be very happy to see you My Dear Daughter as well as my Grandchildren. I hope there will be a way provided for us to meet on earth once more before we die. Cant you come and see us. Your Brother John is well and desires to be very kindly remembered to you. Farewell My Dear Daughter. May God protect you from All evil, is the prayer of your affectionate Mother.

Elizabeth Ramsey

With the help of abolitionists in Ohio and elsewhere, Louisa Picquet was able to raise $900 and purchase her mother's freedom. In October 1860 Elizabeth Ramsey at last met her grandchildren.

Sometimes the best way to obtain news of one's family was to write to mistress or master. Gooley had remained in Virginia when her sister and several of her children were taken to Kentucky. She wrote to her former mistress to check on some disturbing rumors.

Dear Mistress: Port Royal, [Virginia] November 30, 1807
I have heard that Mr. Bhoon is likely to loose all his Negroes and I assure you it has given me much uneasiness. You will therefore be good enough to write me by the first opportunity Respecting it. I likewise heard you were going to be married again. Is that true. If it is I Hope it is to one of your Likeing. I have further more heard you have lost some of your Small Negroes by death. Do when you write me inform me which of them are dead. I have to inform you that I have had one child since I saw you. You will please to tell my Sister Clary not to let my poor children Suffer & tell her She must allso write me & inform me how she & my children are.

Mr. Miller is now on the brink of death & is about to Sell 40 of his Negroes and it likely Joshua may be one. I woud wish to stay with him as long as possible as you must know its very bad to part man & wife. Mr. Miller has been very good to me & I am now liveing with his daughter Mrs. Gray. I should Be glad to no what sort of a life Clary leads. Be pleased to inform me how my little daughter Judith is & if she is now injoying health. I have no more at present only my best wishes to all my friends & relations and Except my Warmest Love & friendship for your Self Dear Mistress from your Most Affectionate Servant.

Gooley

Not all of the expressions of affection in letters to master or mistress were self-serving. Most of the slave-to-owner correspondence that has survived comes from privileged house servants who undoubtedly *were fond of their masters, although not, as the old stereotype would have it, at the expense of their own families. In rare instances, however, a slave dared to express anger at her owner. Forty-seven-year-old Phoebe and her forty-five-year-old husband, Cassius, had spent their lives on the south Georgia plantation of the Reverend Charles Colcock Jones.* Although Jones described Phoebe as "an accomplished servant, good cook, washer and ironer and fine seamstress," she was also a strong-minded woman who quarreled with Cato, the black driver. After one of Phoebe's daughters ran away, Jones decided to sell Phoebe, Cassius, and five of their children. Jones's agent was instructed to sell them to an upstate planter rather than a speculator, but instead they were sent to the slave mart in New Orleans. While awaiting a purchaser, Phoebe sent messages back home through Mr. Lyons, a white man who lived near the Joneses. Although she directed her anger only at Cato, she was reasonably sure that her letter would reach the Reverend Jones.*

Mr Delions: New Orleans, [Louisiana,] March 17, 1857
     Pleas tell my daughter Clairissa and Nancy a heap how a doo for me. We left Savanah the first of Jany we are now in New Orleans. Please tell them that their sister Janet† died the first of Feby. We did not know what was the matter with her some of the doctors said that she had the Plurisly and some thought that she had the Consumption.
     Although we were sold for spite I hope that it is for our own good. We cannot be doing any better than we are doing. Mr Delions will please tell Cato that what [food] we have got to t[h]row away now it would be anough to furnish your Plantation for one season. Mr Delions will please answer this Letter for Clairssa and Let me know all that has hapened since i left. Please tell them that the Children were all sick with the measles but they are all well now. Clairssa your affectionate mother and Father sends a heap of Love to you and your Husband and my Grand Children my aunt and all of their Children. Give our Love to Cashes Brother Porter and his wife Patience.
     I have no more to say untill i get a home. I remain your affectionate Mother and Father
                              Pheobia and Cash

---

*Charles Colcock Jones, considered an enlightened slave owner, was the leading advocate of teaching Christianity to slaves and the author of *Suggestions on the Religious Instruction of the Negroes in the Southern States.* His correspondence about the sale of Phoebe and her family appears in *The Children of Pride,* a collection of Jones family letters, edited by Robert Manson Myers. However, the book does not report on Phoebe's angry reaction to her sale.
†Jane was Phoebe's runaway daughter.

The Reverend Jones did indeed see Phoebe's letter. It was preserved with his other papers after his death.

The most extensive collection of letters from a slave woman are those from Lucy Skipwith to her master, John Hartwell Cocke.* Cocke, a pious Virginian, planned to free his slaves and send them to Liberia after they became "civilized." To speed up that process, he bought Hopewell, a plantation in Alabama where selected slaves were sent to be trained for freedom. In 1840, Lucy Skipwith, then a teenager, went to Hopewell with her parents. Although she fell into disfavor when she had a child by an overseer, Cocke later spoke of her as his "Christian Matron" who was teaching a "school for Liberian freedom." A widower by then, he visited Hopewell only during the winter months. For the rest of the year, Lucy Skipwith was virtual mistress of the plantation. Overseers supervised the field hands, while she bossed "the house gang" and taught the children Cocke's special brand of evangelical Protestantism. In monthly reports to her master, she formally acknowledged his superior knowledge and power: "It is my desire to do whatever you commands me to do"; she then proceeded to manipulate him in order to gain favors for friends and punishment for enemies. In the following selections from her letters, Skipwith seeks approval for herself and her daughters, Maria and Betsey, snipes at her husband, Armistead Hewitt, with whom she did not get along, and slyly criticises the white overseers and their wives.

My Dear Master: Hopewell, Alabama, October 13, 1856
     Since I wrote to you last, their has been missbehaviour with some of the people. Armstead has had another falling out with mr Carter,† and master John has been put to the truble to come here to have him corrected for his behaviour to mr C.
     Another thing makes me backward in writeing, I am not as far ahead with my winter Clothes as I wanted to get before writeing to you. Sister Etter has been very unwell of late, and I haves her business to attend to which is a great pullback to mine. As no one can weave on the new loom but me, I have yet 200 yrd to weave before my winter Clothes will be compleeted. We keeps up family Prayers every morning. I does the best I can teaching the Children but I can never get more than two and sometime three little ones of week days. My little

---

*Fifty-five letters from Lucy Skipwith to John Hartwell Cocke can be found in *"Dear Master" Letters of a Slave Family*, edited by Randall M. Miller.
†J. Willie Carter was overseer at Hopewell for three years. Lucy Skipwith disliked his wife who kept nine-year-old Maria busy with household tasks when Lucy wanted her to 'study.

girl maria is begining to write very well and is very anxious to write to you. I haves a very little chance to teach her as she stays in the house with mrs Carter. My little girl at master Joes* is learning but a very little as miss Fanny has been staying at her mothers ever since July, and the girl left at home to do mostly as she please. She cannot write atall, but reads very well. I will now come to a close hopeing soon to hear from you. I remane your servant

Lucy Skipwith

My Dear Master: Hopewell, Alabama, June 9, 1859
    I knoe that you will be mortified to hear of the troble that my little girl Betsey has got into at mr Joe Bordens by being perswaded by one of their servants to steal money for him, and I learned that this is the second time that he has made her do it. He saw that she did not dress up like the other girls did and he tempted her with such things as he knew she wanted. Her mistress has taken very little pains to bring her up right. The girl has had the raising of her self up. She has been left down there among those people four and six weeks at a time with not as much as a little sewing to do, and now they complains of her being so lazy.
    It seems to be almost Imposeing upon you to ask the faver of you to let the Child come home, but I would thank you a thousand times If you would do so. I want to give her religious instructions and try to be the means of saving her soul from death. Let me hear from you on the Subject by the first of July. If it was not for the grace of god I would sink beneath such a load as this, but I have a preasant help in the time of troble. I have not seen the girl but once in twelve months.
    I will write to you again soon. The people Joines me in love to you. Nothing more at preasant from your servant

Lucy Skipwith

Experienced in plantation politics, Skipwith made no secret of her distaste for Mrs. Lawrence, another overseer's wife. Her frankness paid off when Cocke discharged the Lawrences on his next visit to Hopewell.

My Dear master: Hopewell, [Alabama,] July 28, 1859
    Every thing seem to be going on very well. Mr. Lawrence has had no fuss with his hands attall. We all think a great deal of him for we can see in his conversation that he is a Child of god. The habits of his

*Betsey had been apprenticed to Joseph and Frances Borden when she was seven years old.

wife are the same as when you was here. She still uses the snuff and the Laudanum, by night and by day. Her Children are spoilt as bad as ever. She whips them to day and humours them to morrow and so her whiping them does them no good atall. I never saw such Children in my life. It is a pitty for such a good man as mr L is to have such a family as he is got for they all imposes upon him. Our garden is still very good. We have a plenty of greens, and thousands of Tomatoes. There is five of the Chessnuts up at preasant. None of the Japan plum seed have come up as yet. Write to me soon and believe as ever your servant

LS

During the war, Cocke was no longer able to visit Hopewell. When a Confederate manpower shortage made it impossible to hire white overseers, he depended to an increasing extent on Lucy Skipwith's reports. Aware of the changes that the end of the war might bring, she expressed a new assertiveness. Although Cocke offered to free her and Maria if they would go to Liberia, she postponed a decision. Six months later when Richard D. Powell, Cocke's steward, who had his own plantation in Mississippi, tried to buy Maria, she barely pretended to be submissive.

Dear master: Hopewell, [Alabama,] August 15, 1863

I received your last letter & have carefully considered its contents. The white people who have stayed on the plantation are always opposed to my writeing to you & always want to see my letters and that has been the reason why my letters has been short, but there is no white person here at preasant.

The Cotton is opening very fast. It will soon be open enough to commence picking it out. The weather at preasant is quite rainy & has been for the last two or three days which maekes it bad on the fodder. There is three mulberry trees that has had fruit besides the old tree. The Scuppernong grapes are full of fruit. We have 60 Hogs, 32 Pigs, & 9 Sows, 53 Sheep, 21 Lambs, 5 Cows, 4 young Calves, 4 old Goats 1 kid. The provision lots for their support is very good.

We have our morning prayers regularly. I have not kept up the sabbath school. Some white people in the neighborhood has said that they would punish me if they caught me at it, and I have been afraid to carry it on unless some grown white man was liveing here, but I will commence Teaching again as soon as this talk dies out.

I Thank you a thousand times for what you purpose doing for Maria & myself & I hope that we may both walk sattisfactory before you while you live. I cannot tell at preasent what will be best for me to do, but I will keep the subject upon my mind & try to deside what will be best. Maria is growing very fast and is learning to write very fast. She is a great comfort to me & to every one about her.

                              Lucy Skipwith

Dear master: [Hopewell, Alabama,] March 28, 1864
    Mr. Powell asked my consent to buy Maria from you, & I [told] him that he could perpose the thing to you & see what you say about it.
    I do not wish Maria sold to him, for she is a child after my own heart & I hate to part from her. If you think propper to hire her to him I will try to make up my mind to that, but it goes hard with me to think of parting with her. If he must have her I would rather be hired to him & go myself rather than be parted from her.
    My other poor child came very near being ruined while liveing away from me. There is nothing like a Mothers watchful eye over a child. I hope that you will look into the matter & do what you think best. Let me hear from you on the subject. Your servant

                              Lucy Skipwith

Maria was permitted to remain with her mother until the Union victory brought them freedom. Lucy Skipwith's last letter to John Hartwell Cocke appears on page 310.

SIX

Resistance

"FIGHT, and if you can't fight, kick; if you can't kick, then bite," one slave advised her daughter. A sizable minority of "fighting, mule-headed" women refused to "take foolishness" from anybody.

[My mother's] boss went off deer hunting. While he was gone, the overseer tried to whip her. She knocked him down and tore his face up so that the doctor had to 'tend to him. When Pennington came

back the overseer told him that he went down to the field to whip the
hands and that he just thought he would hit Lucy a few licks, but she
jumped on him and like to tore him up. Old Pennington said to him,
"Well, if that is the best you could do with her, damned if you won't
just have to take it." She could do more work than any two men. There
wasn't no use for no one man to try to do nothing with her. No overseer
never downed her.

The white folks said I was the meanest nigger that ever wuz. One
day my Mistress Lydia called for me to come in the house, but no, I
wouldn't go. She walks out and says she is gwine make me go. So she
takes and drags me in the house. Then I grabs that white woman and
shook her until she begged for mercy. When the master comes in, I
wuz given a terrible beating but I didn't care for I give the mistress
a good un too.

[Mistress] set me to scrubbing up the bar-room. I felt a little grum,
and didn't do it to suit her; she scolded me about it, and I sassed her;
she struck me with her hand. Thinks I, it's a good time now to dress
you out, and damned if I won't do it. I set down my tools and squared
for a fight. The first whack, I struck her a hell of a blow with my fist.
I didn't knock her entirely through the panels of the door, but her
landing against the door made a terrible smash, and I hurt her so badly
that all were frightened out of their wits and I didn't know myself but
what I'd killed the old devil.

*Not many slave women killed their mistresses. The few who tried
usually resorted to poison or arson, putting jimsonweed seeds in the
coffee pot or torching the barn. Others, driven to desperation by ill
treatment, turned their anger on themselves or their children.*

I knew a woman who could not be conquered by her mistress, and
so her master threatened to sell her to New Orleans Negro traders. She
took her right hand, laid it down on a meat block and cut off three
fingers, and thus made the sale impossible.

He owned a woman who was the mother of several children, and
when her babies would get about a year or two of age he'd sell them,
and it would break her heart. She never got to keep them. When her
fourth baby was about two months old, she just studied all the time
about how she would have to give it up, and one day she said "I'm not
going to let Old Master sell this baby; he just ain't going to do it." She

got up and give it something out of a bottle, and pretty soon it was
dead.

*Lewis Hayden who became a leader of Boston's black community
after his escape told of his mother's "crazy turns."*

She married my father when he was working near by. After a while
my father's owner moved off and took my father with him, which broke
up the marriage. She was a very handsome woman. My master kept
a large dairy, and she was the milkwoman. A man who saw my mother
when she was about her work made proposals of a base nature to her.
When she would have nothing to say to him, he told her that she need
not be so independent, for if money could buy her, he would have her.
My mother told old mistress, and begged that master might not sell
her. But he did sell her. My mother had a high spirit, being part Indian.
She would not consent to live with this man, as he wished; and he sent
her to prison, and had her flogged, and punished her in various ways,
so that at last she began to have crazy turns. She tried to kill herself
several times, once with a knife and once by hanging. When she had
her raving turns, she always talked about her children. The jailer told
the owner that if he would let her go to her children, perhaps she would
get quiet. They let her out one time, and she came to the place where
we were. I might have been seven or eight years old—don't know my
age exactly. I came in and found her in one of the cabins near the
kitchen. She caught my arms, and seemed going to break them, and
then said, "I'll fix you so they'll never get you!" I screamed, for I
thought she was going to kill me. They tied her, and carried her off.
At last her owner sold her, for a small sum, to a man named Lackey.
While with him she had another husband and several children. After
a while this husband either died or was sold. The man then sold her
to another person. My father's owner now came and lived in the
neighbourhood of this man, and brought my [father] with him. He and
my mother came together again, and finished their days together. My
mother almost recovered her mind in her last days.

*Women tried every way they could to keep their children from
being sold.*

My mother often hid us all in the woods, to prevent master selling
us. When we wanted water, she sought for it in any hole or puddle
formed by falling trees or otherwise. It was often full of tadpoles and
insects. She strained it, and gave it round to each of us in the hollow

of her hand. For food, she gathered berries in the woods, got potatoes, raw corn &c. After a time, the master would send word to her to come in, promising he would not sell us.

Harriet Tubman's mother, Harriet Ross*, saved her youngest son from a Georgia trader. An older brother reported the incident during an interview in 1863.

A Georgia man came and bought my brother; and after he had bought him, the master calls to him to come to the house & catch the gentleman's horse, but instead of his coming to catch the horse, my mother who was out in the field, and knew what the master was doing, comes in. She says, "What do you want of the boy?" He wouldn't tell her, but says to her, "Go and bring a pitcher of water"; and after she brought the pitcher of water he makes another excuse, & hollers to the boy to come & put the horse into the carriage. But the mother comes again. Then he says, "What did you come for? I hollared for the boy." And she up & swore, and said he wanted the boy for that (ripping out an oath) Georgia man. He called three times, but the boy did not come; and the third time, he came to look for the boy, but the mother had him hid. The master still kept the money and told the Georgia man, "Before you get ready to make up your flock, I will try to catch the boy someway." Late at night [master] came to the door, and asked the mother to let him come in, but she was suspicious and she says, "What do you want?" Says he, "Mr. Scott wants to come in to light a segar." She ripped out an oath, and said; "You are after my son; but the first man that comes into my house, I will split his head open." That frightened them, and they would not come in. So she kept the boy hid until the Georgia man went away.

Finally, when life became insupportable, women ran away.

[My mother] worked so long and so often that once she went to sleep at the loom. Her master's boy saw her and told his mother. His mother told him to take a whip and wear her out. He took a stick and went out to beat her awake. When she woke up, she took a pole out of the loom and beat him nearly to death with it. She said, "I'm going to kill you. These black titties sucked you, and then you come out here to beat me." And when she left him he wasn't able to walk.

*Biographers of Harriet Tubman have portrayed her father as a strong character, and her mother as ineffectual and somewhat of a scold. This anecdote casts new light on Harriet Ross.

And that was the last I seen of her until after freedom. She went out and got on an old cow that she used to milk—Dolly, she called it. She rode away from the plantation.

Most runaways remained in the neighborhood of their homes so that they could keep in touch with their families and perhaps strike a bargain that would permit them to return.

My mammy was de cook. Old Master had some purty strict rules and one of 'em was iffen you burnt de bread you had to eat it. One day mammy burnt de bread. She knowed dat old Master would be mad and she'd be punished so she got some grub and her bonnet and she lit out. She hid in de woods and cane brake for two weeks and dey couldn't find her either. One of de women slipped food out to her. Finally she came home and old Master give her a whipping but he didn't hurt her none. She told us dat she could'a slipped off to de North but she didn't want to leave us children.

Occasionally, a woman remained in hiding for years, living a Swiss Family Robinson kind of existence.

I had to pick one hundred and fifty pounds of cotton every day or get a whipping. One night I got up just before day and run away. I stayed in the woods. Sometimes I'd go so far off from the plantation I could not hear the cows low or the roosters crow. I slept on logs. I had moss for a pillow; and I tell you, child, I wasn't scare of nothing. I could hear bears, wild-cats, panthers, and every thing. I would come across all kinds of snakes—moccasin, blue runner, and rattlesnakes— and got used to them. One night a mighty storm came up; and the winds blowed, the rain poured down, the hail fell, the trees was torn up by the roots and broken limbs fell in every direction; but not a hair on my head was injured, but I got as wet as a drowned rat. Next day was a beautiful Sunday, and I dried myself like a buzzard.

Many times I'd find out where the hands on the place were working, and if the overseer was away I'd get something from them. I had a flint-rock and piece of steel, and I could begin a fire any time I wanted. Sometimes I'd get a chicken and would broil it on the coals and would bake ash-cake.

The weather was beginning to turn cold, and I made me a moss bed just like a hog, and I kept warm at night. But many times I used to sleep in the chimney-corners on a plantation next to my marster's.

Stories of slave women who lived in caves were told in many parts of the South.

My sister Tamar had children very fast. As soon as each of the children became big enough, it was sold away from her. After parting thus with five, she was sold along with the sixth to the speculators. After travelling with them more than one hundred miles, she made her escape. On her journey homeward she travelled by night and hid herself in thick woods by day. She reached the woods near us. I, my mother, and her husband knew where she was. She lived in a den she made for herself. She sometimes ventured down to my mother's hut, where she hid in a hollow under the floor. Her husband would sometimes spend part of the night with her, and get back before sunrise; sometimes he would spend Sunday with her. We all supplied her with such provisions as we could save. It was necessary to be very careful in visiting her; we tied pieces of wood or bundles of rags to our feet, that no track might be made.

In the woods she had three children born; one of them died. She had not recovered from the birth of the youngest when she was discovered and taken to the house of her old master.

One of the slaves married a young gal, and they put her in the Big House to work. One day Mistess jumped on her about something and the gal hit her back. Mistess said she was going to have master put her in the stock and beat her. When the gal told her husband about it, he told her where to go 'till he got there. That night he carried her to a cave and hauled pine straw and put in there for her to sleep on. He fixed that cave up just like a house for her, put a stove in there and run the pipe out through the ground into a swamp. Everybody always wondered how he fixed that pipe. Of course, they didn't cook on it until night when nobody could see the smoke. He sealed the house with pine logs, made beds and tables out of pine poles, and they lived in this cave seven years. During this time, they had three chillun. Nobody was with her when these chillun was born but her husband. He waited on her with each child. The chillun didn't wear no clothes except a piece tied round their waists. They was wild. When they come out of that cave they would run every time they seed a person.

The seven years she lived in the cave, different folks helped keep them in food. Her husband would take it to a certain place, and she would go and get it. Our Marster didn't know where she was, and it was freedom before she come out of that cave for good.

Women were reluctant to leave their families, and, therefore, a much smaller number of women than men escaped to the free states. To a field hand in Mississippi, the North was as remote as Mars.

The runaways from the Deep South who made their way across the Mason-Dixon line were usually urban slaves with a modicum of education and money. Ellen Craft, who had been fathered by her master and given to her half-sister as a child, worked as a seamstress in Macon, Georgia. Her husband, William Craft, was a cabinetmaker who moonlighted as a hotel waiter to earn extra money. Although neither was badly treated, their marriage was strained by Ellen's fear of having a child who could be sold away from her.* Shortly before Christmas 1848, they matured a bold scheme for an escape. The following account, written by Josephine Brown, a free woman, was based on conversations she had with Ellen Craft in the 1850s.

"Now William," said Ellen, "listen to me and take my advice, and we shall be free in less than a month." "Let me hear your plans, then," said William. "Take part of your money and purchase me a good suit of gentlemen's apparel, and when the white people give us our holiday, let us go off to the North. I am white enough to go as the master, and you can pass as my servant." "But you are not tall enough for a man," said the husband. "Get me a pair of very high-heeled boots, and they will bring me up more than an inch, and get me a very high hat, then I'll do," rejoined the wife. "But then, my dear, you would make a very boyish looking man, with no whiskers or moustache," remarked William. "I could bind up my face in a handkerchief," said Ellen, "as if I was suffering dreadfully from the toothache, and then no one would discover the want of beard." "What if you were called upon to write your name in the books at hotels?" "I would also bind up my right hand and put it in a sling, and that would be an excuse for not writing." "I fear you could not carry out the deception for so long a time, for it must be several hundred miles to the free States," said William. "Come William," entreated his wife, "Don't be a coward! Get me the clothes, and I promise you we shall both be free in a few days. You have money enough to fit me out and to pay our passage to the North."

The improbable masquerade succeeded. A passenger on the steamer General Clinch *that sailed from Savannah to Charleston on*

---

*Although little is known about slaves' use of birth control, it is interesting to note that the Crafts, who married in 1846, did not have their first child until 1852, after they had been living free in England for more than a year.

Ellen Craft wearing the male attire in which she escaped from slavery. From *London Illustrated News,* April 19, 1851. *(Harvard University Library)*

December 21, 1848, described the couple in a letter to a northern newspaper.

My attention was attracted by the appearance of a young man who entered the cabin supported by his servant, a strapping negro. The man was bundled up in a capacious overcoat; his face was bandaged with a white handkerchief, and its expression entirely hid by a pair of enormous spectacles. He appeared anxious to avoid notice, and before the steamer had fairly left the wharf, requested, in a low, womanly voice, to be shown his berth as he was an invalid, and must retire early —his name he gave as Mr. Johnson. His servant was called, and he was put quietly to bed.

In the morning, Mr. Johnson made his appearance, arrayed as the night before, and took his seat quietly. From the better opportunity afforded by daylight, I found that he was a slight built, apparently handsome young man with black hair and eyes and of a darkness of complexion that betokened Spanish extraction. To satisfy my curiosity,

I questioned his servant, and gained the following information.

His master was an invalid. He was now suffering principally from the "rheumatism" and he was scarcely able to walk. He was on his way to Philadelphia, at which place resided his uncle, a celebrated physician, and through whose means he hoped to be restored to perfect health. This information enlisted my sympathies for the sufferer, although it occurred to me that he walked rather too gingerly for a person afflicted with so many ailments.

Traveling first class on steamship and train, Ellen and William Craft* reached Philadelphia on Christmas morning 1848. Welcomed in abolitionist circles, they went to England after the passage of the Fugitive Slave Law.

Unlike the Crafts, Mr. and Mrs. John Little (their interviewer never learned Mrs. Little's first name) were field hands in rural Tennessee. They had been sold so often that they had picked up some knowledge of geography. When John Little was threatened with 300 blows with a paddle, the couple headed for the Ohio River. Crossing the river at Cairo, they spent three arduous months traveling to Chicago; from there, they were helped to Canada. Interviewed in 1855, Mrs. Little described the psychological as well as physical hazards of their trip. She was seventeen years old when she left Tennessee.

My shoes gave out before many days—then I wore my husband's old shoes till they were used up. Then we came on barefooted all the way to Chicago. My feet were blistered and sore and my ankles swollen but I had to keep on. There was something behind me driving me. At the first water we came to I was frightened. It was a swift but shallow stream. I felt afraid at getting into a boat to cross the Ohio River. I had never been in any boat whatever. "John" said I, "Don't you think we'll drown?" "I don't care if we do" said he.

We never slept at the same time: while one slept, the other kept watch, day or night. At Cairo, the gallinippers [mosquitoes] were so bad, we made a smoke to keep them off. Soon after I heard a steamboat bell tolling. Presently there she was, a great boat full of white men. We were right on the river's bank, and our fire sent the smoke straight up. Presently they saw our fire, and hailed, "Boat ashore! boat ashore! runaway niggers!" We put out our fire and went further back from the

---

*Light-skinned Ellen Craft became the inspiration for "tragic mulatto" characters in novels of the 1850s and later. The heroine of *Clotel; or, The President's Daughter*, by William Wells Brown, escaped from slavery in the same way Ellen did.

river, but the musquitoes were so bad, we made another fire. But a man with a gun then came along, looking up into the trees. I scattered the fire to put it out, but it smoked so much the worse. We at last hid in a thicket of briers, where we were almost devoured by musquitoes for want of a little smoke.

One morning, being on a prairie where we could see no house, we ventured to travel by day. We encountered an animal, which we at first supposed to be a dog; but when he came near, we concluded it to be a wolf. We went on, and then we saw three large wood wolves, sneaking around as if waiting for darkness. As we kept on, the three wolves kept in sight, now on one hand now on the other. I felt afraid, expecting they would attack us, but they left us. Afterward we made a fire with elder stalks, and I undertook to make some corn bread. I got it mixed, and put it on the fire,—when I saw a party of men and boys on horseback, apparently approaching us. I put out the fire; they turned a little away and did not appear to perceive us. I rekindled the fire and baked our bread. John managed to keep us well supplied with pies and bread. We used to laugh to think how people would puzzle over who drank the milk and left the pitchers and who hooked the dough.

Lear Green escaped from slavery by having herself shipped to Philadelphia in a sailor's chest. This illustration, in William Still's *The Underground Railroad*, 1872, was made from a photograph taken shortly after she won freedom.

Most runaways came from the border states, traveling on foot, in stolen carriages, and as stowaways on coastwise vessels. Lear Green, a young house servant, had herself packed into a sailor's chest and shipped as freight from Baltimore to Philadelphia, while her fiancé's mother traveled north on the same steamer. Jane Johnson, whose

Jane Johnson took her children and walked away from her master when he brought her to a free state. (*From Still's* The Underground Railroad)

picture appears here, was brought to Philadelphia by her master, John H. Wheeler, the U.S. minister to Nicaragua. When members of Philadelphia's Vigilance Committee informed her that she was entitled to her freedom, she quietly took her children's hands and walked away with them.

Harriet Tubman was a field hand on Maryland's Eastern Shore. Whipped frequently as a child, she "prayed to God to make me strong and able to fight." In 1849, five years after her marriage to John Tubman, a free man, her master died, and she learned that she and her brothers were to be sold to the Deep South. Unable to persuade her husband or brothers to accompany her, she set out alone for the North. Walking at night, hiding by day, she at last reached Pennsylvania. As she crossed the state line, she recalled, "I looked at my hands to see if I was the same person. Dere was such a glory ober eberything, de sun came like gold trou de trees, and ober de fields, and I felt like I was in heaven." Then loneliness assailed her.

Maria Weems disguised herself as a boy when she ran away from her master. (*From Still's* The Underground Railroad)

I knew of a man who was sent to the State Prison for twenty-five years. All these years he was always thinking of his home, and counting the time till he should be free. The years roll on, the time of imprisonment is over, the man is free. He leaves the prison gates, he makes his way to the old home, but his old home is not there. The house in which he had dwelt in his childhood had been torn down, and a new one had been put in its place; his family were gone, their very name was forgotten, there was no one to take him by the hand to welcome him back to life.

So it was wid me.* I had crossed de line of which I had so long been dreaming. I was free; but dere was no one to welcome me to de land of freedom, I was a stranger in a strange land, and my home after all was down in de old cabin quarter, wid de ole folks and my brudders and sisters. But to dis solemn resolution I came; I was free, and dey should be free also; I would make a home for dem in de North, and de Lord helping me, I would bring dem all dere.

In Philadelphia and in Cape May, New Jersey, Harriet Tubman worked as cook, laundress, and scrubwoman, saving her money in order to return to the South. In 1850 she went to Baltimore to rescue a sister and her children who were about to be sold. A few months later, she brought away a brother and two other men. In 1851 she returned for

*Sarah H. Bradford, a white friend who wrote down Tubman's story as she dictated it, switched back and forth between plantation dialect and standard English.

Harriet Tubman was probably in her forties when this photograph was taken. *(Library of Congress)*

John Tubman, only to find that he had taken another wife and refused to see her. Reluctant to discuss this painful episode, Harriet mentioned it only briefly during an interview in 1865.

At first her grief and anger were excessive. She said "she did not care what massa did to her, she thought she would go right in and make all the trouble she could, she was determined to see her old man once more," but finally she thought "how foolish it was just for temper to make mischief," and that, "if he could do without her, she could do without him," and so "he dropped out of her heart," and she determined to give her life to brave deeds. Thus all personal aims died out of her heart and she began the work which has made her Moses, the deliverer of her people.

Although Tubman wrote off her marriage and the hope of having children of her own, she maintained close ties with her family. In the course of nineteen trips into slave territory, she led out six of her brothers, their wives and fiancés, nieces, nephews, and, in 1857, her elderly parents. Delivering her parents took some doing, as Thomas Garrett, the Underground Railroad station operator in Wilmington, Delaware, recalled.

She brought away her aged parents in a singular manner. They started with an old horse, fitted out in primitive style with a straw collar, a pair of old chaise wheels, with a board on the axle to sit on, another board swung with ropes, fastened to the axle, to rest their feet on. She got her parents on this rude vehicle to the railroad, put them in the cars, turned Jehu herself, and drove to town in a style that no human being ever did before or since. Next day, I furnished her with money to take them all to Canada. I afterward sold their horse, and sent them the balance of the proceeds.

SEVEN

Resettlement

Homeless, jobless, fearful of pursuit, *most runaways felt lost during their first weeks in the North. Bethany Veney, a slave for forty-three years, described her feelings when she arrived in New England.*

A new life had come to me. I was in a land where I had the same right to myself that any other woman had. No jailer could take me to prison, and sell me at auction to the highest bidder. My boy was my own, and no one could take him from me. But I had left behind everyone I had ever known and it was no wonder, perhaps, that a dreadful loneliness and homesickness came over me.

Fugitives who reached the free states by way of Philadelphia made their first friends in the persons of William and Letitia Still. As secretary of the local Vigilance Committee, William Still interviewed the runaways when they arrived, often boarding them in his home until he could send them farther north. He also acted as a mail drop, forwarding messages to their families and, when possible, arranging for reunions. Still's journal and the almost 100 letters that he kept give the runaways' reactions to freedom.

Mary Epps, who changed her name to Emma Brown when she arrived in Philadelphia, had had fifteen children; all but one of them were sold or dead. "At the sale of one of her children," Still wrote in his journal, "she was thrown into such a state of grief that she lost her speech for a month in consequence there of Convulsions was brought on. Her husband, Frances Epps, a Slave also, paid $100 for her passage here, hoping that by sending her on ahead the chance for himself could the more easily be obtained." As soon as she reached Canada, she asked Still to write to Petersburg, Virginia, where her husband was waiting to hear from her:

Dear Mr. Still: Toronto, [Canada,] March 14, 1855
    I take this opportunity to inform you that I arrived here to day. I had no difficulty in getting along. The two young men that was with me left me at Suspension Bridge. They went another way.
    I cannot say much about the place as I have ben here but a short time but so far as I have seen I like very well. If you have not written to Petersburg you will please to write as soon as can. I have nothing More to Write at present but yours Respectfully
        Emma Brown (old name Mary Epps)

Rebecca Jones's husband escaped from slavery six years before she did. He kept in touch with her at first, but then ceased to write. When she escaped with their three daughters, she would have nothing to do with him. Still described her as "about 28 years of age, molato, good looking, naturally very intelligent and gives evidence of marked mind & purpose." Her letter to Still, written after seven months of freedom,

*indicates that she was working in Boston's noted hotel, probably as a
chambermaid.*

My Dear Sir: Parker House, Boston, October 18, 1856
I can hardly express the pleasure I feel at the receipt of your kind
letter; but allow me to thank you for the same.
And now I will tell you my reasons for going to California. Mrs.
Tarrol, a cousin of my husband, has sent for me. She says I can do
much better than in Boston. And as I have my children's welfare to
look to, I have concluded to go.
I should like to hear from my brothers and sisters once more, and
let me hear every particular. You never can know how anxious I am
to hear from them; do please impress this upon their minds.
I suppose you think I am going to live with my husband again.
Let me assure you 'tis no such thing. My mind is as firm as ever.
And believe me, in going away from Boston, I am going away
from him, for I have heard he is living somewhere near. I hope that
yourself, wife and family are all quite well. Please remember me to
them all. I should be most happy to have any letters of introduction
you may think me worthy of, and I trust I shall ever remain Yours
faithfully,
Rebecca Jones.
P.S.—I do not know if I shall go this Fall, or in the Spring. It will
depend upon the letter I receive from California, but whichever it may
be, I shall be happy to hear from you very soon.

*In an urgent note to Letitia Still, Roseann Johnson, who now called
herself Catherine Brice, inquired about two slaves.*

Mrs. William Still: Albany, [New York,] January 30, 1858
I sit don to rite you a fue lines in saying have you herd of John
Smith or Bengernin Pina? I have cent letters to them but i have know
word from them. John Smith was oned by Doker abe Street, Benger-
min oned by Mary hawkings. I wish to kno if you kno, and if you will
let me know as swon as you get this. My lov to Mis Still. I am much
oblige for those articales. My love to mrs george and verry thankful to
her.
Rosean Johnson oned by docter Street
When you cend the letter rite it 63 Grand St in the car of
andrue Conningham rite swon. Dela it not. Write my name Cathrin
Brice.

Louisa F. Jones, a lady's maid, traveled from Norfolk, Virginia, by steamer disguised as a man. She was light of skin "with a passable education, and very refined in her deportment," Still reported. She was welcomed in abolitionist circles in Boston and became a fashionable dressmaker.

Dear Friend: Boston, [Massachusetts,] May 15, 1858
I arrived hear on Thursday last, and had a lettor of intoduction giving to me by one of the gentlemen at the Antoslavery office in New York, to Mr. Garrison in Boston. I found him and his lady both to bee very clever. I stopped with them the first day of my arrivel hear. Since that Time I have met with so menny of my acquaintances that I all most immagion my self to be in the old country. I have not been to Canaday yet, as you expected. I suffored much on the road with head ake but since that time I have no reason to complain. Please do not for git to send the degarritips. Tell Julia Kelly, that through mistake, I took one of her pocket handkerchift, that was laying on the table, but I shall keep it in remembranc of the onner. I must bring my lettor to a close. Believe me to be your faithfull friend.
                                        Louisa F. Jones.

Most of the runaways quickly disappeared from public view. They made friends in the black communities of the North, joined local churches, and found jobs, usually as domestic workers. A small number became involved in antislavery work. Propelled into the limelight for a season, Ellen Craft and her husband appeared at abolitionist meetings in New England. Elizabeth Blakesley, a stowaway from North Carolina who had traveled to Boston in the hold of a vessel, was welcomed at a Massachusetts Anti-Slavery Society convention by Lucy Stone, then an antislavery and woman's rights lecturer. Miss Paulyon (first name unknown) lectured in New York seven years after her escape from slavery. The Weekly Anglo-African *described her talk.*

She commenced a narrative of her early slave life, part of which was very affecting, calling forth many tears, especially from the female portion of the audience. She afterwards spoke at length upon our condition in this country. In speaking of caste the lady frequently alluded to the manner in which most of the white people taught their children prejudice against colored people. She was frequently interrupted with shouts of applause. And we should think it had a wholesome effect on the audience, many of whom were white. The lady did not think it a good policy to narrate her escape from slavery, as it might involve certain parties who aided her. Suffice it to say she was 16 years old when she made her escape, suffering hunger, thirst, and cold on her journey. Since she has been in the North she had learned needle-work, geography, arithmetic, grammar, painting, together with one or two other of the fine arts, all through her own exertions. She also writes poetry, several anti-slavery pieces of which she sung, which created some mirth, excepting one entitled the "Slave's Farewell" at which many eyes filled with tears.

Although charismatic male runaways were the authors of best-selling autobiographies in the years before the Civil War only one woman fugitive wrote a narrative of her life as a southern slave. Harriet Brent Jacobs escaped to the North around 1842 and found employment as nurse and housekeeper in the family of Nathaniel P. Willis, a popular journalist.* After Mrs. Willis's death, Jacobs had full responsibility for the Willises' baby daughter, bringing her to England where the baby's maternal grandmother lived and to Boston to stay with an aunt. By the time Willis remarried in 1846, Jacobs was an indispensable member of his household. She remained in his employ until 1861, except for an interval in 1849–50 when she helped her brother John establish an antislavery reading room in Rochester, New York. John S. Jacobs had escaped from slavery in 1841 and had become an antislavery speaker, sharing platforms with Frederick Douglass and other notables. In Rochester, where Douglass was then publishing the North Star, *Harriet Jacobs became friendly with members of the Western New York Anti-Slavery Society and particularly with Amy Post† who was also a founder of the new woman's rights movement. After Jacobs's return to New York, she corresponded with Post. More than thirty of her letters have survived, recording her struggle to make her way in the North and to bring her family together. They also depict a woman who longed to strike a blow against slavery. In the Willis household, Harriet Jacobs was a faithful servitor—"our intelligent housekeeper," Willis described her in a* Home Journal *column. Only in her letters to Amy Post could she speak of the issues that were close to her heart, and of*

---

*Editor of the weekly *Home Journal* and author of some two dozen books, Willis was a member of New York's literary establishment. Visitors to his home included Washington Irving, Charles A. Dana, and Bayard Taylor. His sister Sarah, writing under the pen name of Fanny Fern, was also a successful author of novels, essays, and short stories.
†Amy Kirby Post (1802–89) left the Society of Friends in 1845 after she identified herself with the antislavery movement. A participant in the first Woman's Rights Convention at Seneca Falls in 1848, she was an organizer of the convention that met in Rochester two weeks later.

*her first faltering attempts to write about them. Selections from the
letters, spanning the years 1849 to 1861 follow.*

My Dear Friend: New York, February 12, [1851–52]
     This is the third letter that I have written to you, the two previous
ones were filled with trouble and care. I burned them. I determined
not to write again untill I felt some encouragement. I am still with Mrs.
Willis. Louisa* is with me at the present but expect to return to Mr.
Brackett this spring. I shall go with her and if I can possibly stretch
my visit as far as Rochester I will.
     I had three letters from my Brother† during the last month. He
was well and doing well. I had a letter from him last July and he had
just completed his arrangements to commence his work in the bed of
the river and seemed so full of hope. Said that he would write the next
month and send me some gold. I did not get another line until December and it was a sad letter. My Brother said that he had been so
burdened with care that he could not write. He said before he commenced working he was offered five hundred for his share which he
refused and worked until October and came out poorer than he went
in. The Claim below him at the same time paid each man two thousand dollars. He then left and went to the dry diggings where they have
done very well. There is five in the party and they have gone so far
under the hill that they work by candle light. My Joseph has gone to
his Uncle. Brother is very anxious to have me go. He thinks that I could
do well out there but he wants Louisa to remain at Mr. Bracketts until
I go and see for myself and if I like after a years time come for her.
She is much opposed to being left behind. I intend to go if possible.
You must write me what you think of it. I could do anything for the
sake of a little shanty to call home and have my children to come
around me.
     Dear Amy I have tried to do the best that I could. Last year I paid
eighty five dollars of my own earnings for Louisa so I have left no debt
there and brother sent me a hundred dollars. With that I intend to
pay balance on Louisa schooling which is sixty two dollars. Then once
more I shall be happy.
     I wish I could just run in and spend a little [time] with you and
your dear good Husband, to whom I know that you will allow me to
give my kindest love. I have not heard from the South in a great while.

*Born in 1836, Louisa Jacobs had worked as a housemaid until her mother and uncle
were able to send her to boarding school in upstate New York.
†John Jacobs had followed the gold rush to California. He was joined by Harriet's son
Joseph, then about twenty years old.

I never go out in the day light accept I ride inside. Dear Amy, May God bless you and crown you with his choicest blessings is the prayer of Harriet.

When Jacobs spoke of riding only in closed carriages, it was because her owner, "Dr. Flint," and his son-in-law made repeated attempts to capture her. After she had been forced to hide from them on many occasions, the Willises purchased her freedom. Secure in her own person at last, she told Amy Post that "I cannot be happy without trying to be useful in some way." "Being useful" meant furthering the antislavery cause. Both Amy Post and Cornelia Willis urged her to tell the story of her life to Harriet Beecher Stowe, whose Uncle Tom's Cabin *had just become a spectacular success. Jacobs was hesitant, fearful that the truth about her affair with "Mr. Sands" would ruin her reputation and brand her children as illegitimate. At last she yielded and asked Amy Post to get in touch with Stowe.*

My Dear Friend: Cornwall, [New York,] [1852–53]
 Yours of the 24th was received and my pen will fail to describe my greatful feelings on reading it. It is a blessing that we can say a word in this way to each other. Many far more deserving than myself has been debared from this privilege.
 Your proposal has been thought over and over again but not without some most painful remembrances. Dear Amy, if it was the life of a Heroine with no degradation associated with it. Far better to have been one of the starving poor of Ireland whose bones had to bleach on the highways than to have been a slave with the curse of slavery stamped upon yourself and Children. Your purity of heart and kindly sympathies won me to speak of my children. It is the only words that has passed my lips since I left my [grand]mothers door. I had determined to let others think as they pleased but my lips should be sealed and no one had a right to question me. For this reason, when I first came North I avoided the antislavery people because I felt I could not be honest and tell the whole truth. Often have I gone to my poor Brother with my grieved and mortified spirits. He would mingle his tears with mine while he would advise me to do what was right. My conscience approved it but my stubborn pride would not yield, I have tried for the last two years to conquer it and I feel that God has helped me on. I never would consent to give my past life to any one without giving the whole truth. If it could help save another from my fate it would be selfish and unchristian in me to keep it back.
 Mrs. Willis thinks it would do much good in Mrs. Stowe hand but

I could not ask her to take any step. Mr. W is too proslavery. He would tell me that it was very wrong and that I was trying to do harm or perhaps he was sorry for me to undertake it while I was in his family. Mrs. Willis thinks if its not done in my day it will [be] a good legacy for my children to do after my death. But now is the time when their is so much excitement everywhere.

My dear friend would you be willing to make this proposal? I would rather have you do it than any one else. If Mrs. Stowe would undertake it I should like to be with her a Month. I should want the History of my childhood and the first years in one volume and the next and my home in the northern states in the second. Besides I could give her some fine sketches for her pen on slavery.

Give my love to your dear Husband and kiss Willie* for me.

Yours
Harriet

After Amy Post wrote to Harriet Beecher Stowe, Jacobs had another idea. Stowe was going to England. Why not ask her to take Louisa with her as a "representative of a Southern Slave"? The suggestion was not as presumptuous as it might seem. British abolitionists welcomed ex-slaves and would have been particularly receptive to a young educated woman. This time Cornelia Willis wrote to Stowe, and was rebuffed.

My Dear friend: [New York] April 7, [1853]

I should have written you before but I have been waiting with the hope of having something to tell you from our friend Mrs. Stowe. I hardly know where to begin for my thoughts come rushing down with such a spirit of rivalry, each wishing to be told you first. Mrs. Stowe recieved your letter and Mrs. Willis. She said it would be much care to her to take Louisa. She was afraid that if her situation as a slave should be known it would subject her to much petting and patronizing which would be more pleasing to a young Girl than useful and the English was very apt to do it and she was very much opposed to it with this class of people. Remember that I were to pay Louisa expenses.

Your letter she sent to Mrs. Willis asking if this most extraordinary event was true and if she might use it in her key.† I had never opened my lips to Mrs. Willis concerning my Children. In the Charitableness of her own heart she sympathised with me and never asked their origin.

*Willet E. Post, Amy Post's youngest son.
†Stowe's *Key to Uncle Tom's Cabin*, containing factual reports of slave life, was published on April 16, 1853.

She knew it embarrassed me at first but I told her the truth but we both thought it was wrong in Mrs. Stowe to have sent your letter. She might have written to enquire.

Mrs. Willis wrote her a very kind letter begging that she would not use any of the facts in her key, saying that I wished it to be a history of my life entirely by itself which would do more good and it needed no romance. But if she wanted some facts for her book that I would be most happy to give her some. She never answered the letter. [Mrs. W.] wrote again and I wrote twice with no better success. It was not Ladylike to treat Mrs. Willis so. I think she did not like my objection. I can't help it.

[Letter breaks off]

Harriet Brent Jacobs did not readily forgive Harriet Beecher Stowe's slurring remark about "this class of people." She later wrote, "Think dear Amy that a visit to Stafford House* would spoil me as Mrs. Stowe thinks petting is more than my race can bear? Well, what a pity we poor blacks can't have the firmness and stability of character that you white people have." Her brush with "the Great Lady," as she called her, seemed to increase her own self-confidence. After reading a newspaper article in which Julia Tyler, wife of the ex-President, said that slaves were not sold away from their families except under "peculiar circumstances," she wrote her first words for publication. Her reply to Julia Tyler was written at a time when Jacobs was preoccupied with moving the Willis household from New York City to a country estate in Cornwall, N.Y., as she explained in a breathless note to Amy Post.

My Dearest Amy: Cornwall, [New York,] June 25, [1853]
I stop in the midst of all kind of care and perplexities to scratch you a line. When I was in New York last week I picked up a paper with a piece alluding to the buying and selling of Slaves, mixed up with some of Mrs. Tylers views. I felt so indignant I determined to reply to it. [We] were to leave next day. I had no time for thought but as soon as every body was safe in bed I began to look back that I might tell the truth and every word was true accept my Mother and sisters. It was one whom I dearly loved. It was my first attempt and when morning found me I had not time to correct it and copy it. I must send it or leave to some future time. The spelling I believe was every word correct. Punctuation I did not attempt for I never studied Grammar. Therefore I know nothing about it, but I have taken the hint and will

*Stafford House was the London residence of the Duchess of Sutherland. British women met there in 1853 to draft a protest against American slavery.

commence that one study with all my soul. This letter I wrote I sent
to the Tribune. I left the same morning. The second day it was in the
paper. It came here while Mr. W was at dinner. I glanced at it. After
dinner he took the paper with him. It is headed Slaves Sold under
Peculiar Circumstances. It was Tuesday 21st. I thought perhaps it
might be copied in the North Star. If so will you get two and cut the
articles out and enclose them to me? I have another but I can not offer
it before I can read over the first to see more of its imperfections. Please
answer this dear Amy as soon as possible. I want to write you a long
letter but I am working very hard preparing the new house. Mrs. W
cant give me any assistance. She is so feeble.*

Give a great deal of love to all my much loved friends. God bless
is my prayer.

Harriet

*Jacobs's "Letter from a Fugitive Slave," ran for almost a column
in the* New York Tribune *of June 21, 1853. In it she described the
seduction of a fourteen-year-old girl by her master and her subsequent
sale. To give it verisimilitude, she called the girl her sister; in reality,
as she had explained to Amy Post, the victim was a close friend. An
excerpt illustrates Jacobs's purple prose, modeled on the popular fiction
of her day.*

At fifteen, my sister held to her bosom an innocent offspring of her
guilt and misery. In this way she dragged a miserable existence of two
years, between the fires of her mistress's jealousy and her master's
brutal passion. At seventeen she gave birth to another helpless infant,
heir to all the evils of slavery. Thus life and its sufferings was meted
out to her until her twenty-first year. Sorrow and suffering had made
its ravages upon her—she was less the object to be desired by the fiend
who had crushed her to the earth . . . . In the dead hour of the night
this young deserted mother lay with her little ones clinging around her.
When the sun rose that brokenhearted mother was far on her way to
the capital of Virginia. And where she now is God only knows.

Oh ye Christians while your arms are extended to receive the
oppressed of all nations, while you exert every power of your soul to
assist them to raise funds, put weapons in their hands, while Americans
do all this, they forget the millions of slaves they have at home, bought
and sold under very peculiar circumstances.

*Two more letters to the editor (the first about a fugitive who was
caught and beheaded, the second opposing African colonization) were*

*Cornelia Willis was in the last months of a pregnancy.

published in the Tribune *that summer while their author took charge of the three Willis children, the baby born in September, and innumerable house guests.* "We have eighteen rooms and we have been crowded out of our dens by company," *she wrote Amy Post.* "It made Mrs. W. ill so they have promised to live retired for a while. I am glad for I do not have time to think, only for other folks." *By fall Jacobs was fully committed to writing her autobiography:*

My Dear Friend: [Cornwall, New York,] October 9, [1853]
I was more than glad to receive your welcome letter. I should have written before this but we have had a little member added to the family and I have had little time for anything. It makes me sad to tell you that I have not heard from my Brother and Joseph and dear Amy, I have lost that Dear old Grandmother that I so dearly loved. Her Death was beautiful. May my last end be like hers. Louisa is with me. I dont know how long she will remain. I shall try and keep her all winter as I want to try and make arrangements to have some of my time.

Mrs. Stowe never answered any of my letters after I refused to have my history in her key. Perhaps it is for the best. Have you seen any more of my scribbling? They were marked "fugitive." William Nell* told Louisa about the piece and sent her a Copy. I was careful to keep it from her and no one here never suspected me. I would not have Mr. W to know it before I had undertaken my history for I must write just what I have lived and witnessed myself. Dont expect much of me dear Amy. You shall have truth but not talent. God did not give me that gift but he gave me a soul that burned for freedom and a heart nerved with determination to suffer even unto death in pursuit of that liberty which without makes life an intolerable burden.

And now my dear friend, dont flatter me. I am aware of my many mistakes and willing to be told of them. Only let me come before the world as I have been, an uneducated oppressed slave. But I must stop. Love to all. God bless you. Excuse the hasty scrawl, 1 o'clock.
Yours Harriet

Like other creative black women, from Phillis Wheatley, an eighteenth-century poet, to Zora Neale Hurston, a leading writer of the Harlem Renaissance in the 1920s, Harriet Jacobs labored in the nursery and kitchen by day and wrote at night. A number of important literary figures were guests in Cornwall during the years she worked on her narrative but she never overstepped the bounds of class, race, and

*Jacobs met William C. Nell in Rochester when he was publisher of the *North Star.* He later returned to his native Boston where he wrote *The Colored Patriots of the American Revolution* and led a fight against the city's segregated schools.

sex to ask for advice. Only Amy Post knew of her struggles and self-doubts.

My dear Friend: Cornwall, [New York,] January 11, [1854]
If I was not so tied down to the baby house I would make one bold effort to see you. Patience. Perhaps it will not be always thus. I have kept Louisa here this winter so that I might have my evenings to write, but poor Hatty name is so much in demand that I cannot accomplish much. If I could steal away and have two quiet months to myself I would work night and day. To get this time I should have to explain myself, and no one here accept Louisa knows that I have even written anything to be put in print. I have not the courage to meet the criticism and ridicule of educated people. The old proverb where there is much given much is required. With myself nothing given and their must be but little expected.

William wrote me that you was in New York while he was there. I was in New York the week before, Louisa and myself. I stayed ten days to do the Winter shoping for Mrs. Willis. Having a young baby she could not go herself. I had the little girl portrait painted while there. I had a long distance to go to the Artist and they refused one day to take me in the cars.* It made Mr. Richard Willis very angry and he wrote a long article and inserted it in his own paper.† He is Brother to Mr. N. P. Willis and he is the couloured Man's friend. Dear Amy, will you let me know if you have heard any thing of Brother? I have not had a letter and I think it so strange. I dont know where to write. Will you please try and get my Brother Daguerotype from Miss Charlotte Murray and keep it for me. If this said Book should ever come in existance I want to have an illustrated Edition and the whole family in.

Yours truly
Harriet

My Dear Friend: Cornwall, [New York,] March [1854]
Let me thank you for your generous offer of the hospitality of your pleasant home but I cannot decide. As yet I have not written a single page by daylight. Mrs. W wont know from my lips that I am writing for a Book and has never seen a line of what I have written. I told her in the autumn that I would give her Louisa services if she would allow

---

*Seven months after Harriet Jacobs was refused a ride on a New York horsecar, Elizabeth Jennings, another black woman, sued the Third Avenue Railroad Company and won the right to ride.
†Richard Willis was editor of *Musical World.*

me my winter evenings to myself but with the care of the little baby and the big Babies I have but a little time to think or write but I have tried in my poor way to do my best and that is not much.

Just now the poor Book is in its Chrysalis state and though I can never make it a butterfly I am satisfied to have it creep meekly among some of the humbler bugs. I must stop this rambling letter. Lou sends much love to you. I am sorry you dont know her better. You would love her. God bless you. Yours

H. Jacobs

Once the narrative was completed, Harriet Jacobs set about the practical business of getting it published. When she asked Amy Post to write a preface, Post questioned her about the book's purpose. She replied:

My Dear Friend: [Cornwall, New York,] June 21, [1857]

I would dearly love to talk with you but as I cannot I will try to explain myself on paper. I have Striven faithfully to give a true and just account of my own life in slavery. There are some things that I might have made plainer—woman can whisper her cruel wrongs into the ear of a dear friend much easier than she could record them for the world to read. I have placed myself before you to be judged as a woman, to come to you just as I am, a poor slave Mother—not to tell you what I have heard but what I have seen—and what I have suffered—and if their is any sympathy to give—let it be given to the thousands of slave Mothers that are still in bondage. Let it plead for their helpless Children that they may enjoy the same liberties that my Children now enjoy.

Say anything of me that you think best—ask me any question you like—in regard to the father of my Children I think I have stated all. Perhaps I did not tell you that he was a member of Congress at that time. All of this I have written.

I think it would be best for you to begin with our acquaintance, you[r] advice about giving the history of my life in Slavery. Mention that I lived at service all the while that I was striving to get the Book out but do not say with whom I lived as I would not use the Willis name neither would I like to have people think that I was living an Idle life—and had got this book out merely to make money. My kind friend, I do not restrict you for you know far better than I do what to say.

I hope you will be able to read my uncorrected scraal. I have been called away so often that I hardly know what I have written. Baby is just 4 weeks old this morning—housekeeping and looking after the Children occupy every moment of my time. We have in all five children—three Girls and two boys.

I would so like to go away and sell my Book—I could secure a copywright to sell it both here and in England and by identifying myself with it I might do something for the Antislavery cause. To do this I would have to get letters of introduction from leading Abolitionist of this country to those of the Old. When you write tell me what you think of it. Much love to all my friends—and believe ever yours

Harriet

Taking a leave of absence from the Willises, Harriet Jacobs traveled to England where she visited abolitionists and saw her brother who was then a seaman sailing out of London. She found a friendly audience for her manuscript, but no publisher. At last in 1860, a Boston firm agreed to bring it out.

My Dear Friend: [Cornwall, New York,] October 8, [1860]

When I returned home from Europe I said that I would not mention my MS. again until I had done something with it—little dreaming of the time that might elapse. This Autumn I sent it to Thayer and Eldredge of Boston. They were willing to publish it if I could obtain a preface from Mrs. Child.* They had no objection to the one I had—but that it must be by some one known to the public to effect the sale of the book. I had never seen Mrs. Child. Past experience made me tremble at the thought of approaching another sattellite of so great magnitude, but I resolved to make my last effort. Through W. C. Nells ready kindness I met Mrs. Child at the A. S. Office. Mrs. C is like yourself a whole souled Woman. We soon found the way to each others heart. I will send you some of her letters.

Mr. Wendel Phillips has agreed to take one thousand copies.† I take four hundred at the wholesale price to dispose of myself—the book will be out 1st November. I have ten per cent. I hope my Dear Friend that you will like my arrangement. I long to see you. I shall try

*Lydia Maria Child (1802–80) was one of America's first professional women writers. An editor of the *National Anti-Slavery Standard* and author of antislavery books and pamphlets, she also wrote historical novels and such how-to books as *The Frugal House-wife* and *The Mothers Book.*

†Thayer and Eldredge failed before selling a single copy, but Jacobs managed to scrape together the money to buy the plates and keep the book in print. Even with the help of Wendell Phillips and Lydia Maria Child, *Incidents* probably made little money for its author.

very hard to get to Rochester this winter. Remember me most kindly to my dear old friend Mr. Post and believe me the same always
HJ

In one of the letters that Jacobs forwarded to Post, Lydia Maria Child explained the changes that she was making in the manuscript:

I have very little occasion to alter the language, which is wonderfully good, for one whose opportunities for education have been so limited. The events are interesting, and well told; the remarks are also good, and to the purpose. But I am copying a great deal of it, for the purpose of transposing sentences and pages, so as to bring the story into continuous *order,* and the remarks into *appropriate* places. I think you will see that this renders the story much more clear and entertaining.

She also suggested the use of fictitious names, to protect Jacobs's friends in North Carolina and "out of delicacy to Mrs. Willis." Thus Harriet Brent Jacobs became Linda Brent and the identities of her master and her lover were obscured. Jacobs had planned a trip to Boston to go over the edited manuscript, but the Willis household once again kept her tied down:

Dear Mrs. Post: [Cornwall, New York,] November 8, [1860]
When your letter came Mrs W had been ill in bed four weeks and the next day gave birth to an infant, a fine little girl. It died from the effects of its Mothers illness. Not expecting it so soon I had to be both accoucher and nurse. When the doctor came he pronounced all right for which I was very thankful.

For this reason my dear friend I could not attend to my own business as I should have done. I know that Mrs. Child will strive to do the best she can, more than I can ever repay but I ought to have been there that we could have consulted together, and compared our views. Although I know that hers are superior to mine yet we could have worked her great Ideas and my small ones together. The book will not be out until the first of December. I had hoped to have it out in October.

God bless you. Think of me as one who loves you dearly
Harriet

Incidents in the Life of a Slave Girl with an introduction by Lydia Maria Child and an afterword by Amy Post was published early in 1861; an English edition appeared the following year. In a prefatory note, Harriet Jacobs wrote, "I do earnestly desire to arouse the women of the North to a sense of the condition of two million of women at the South, still in bondage, suffering what I suffered, and most of the time far worse." Whenever the Willises could spare her, she traveled to antislavery meetings to publicize her book. By that time, however, the Civil War had begun, and there was a new life in store for Harriet Jacobs and her sisters.

Part II

Free Women, 1800–1861

EIGHT

First Freedom, 1800–1831

IN 1800, 47,000 FREE BLACKS *lived in the North. For some, freedom dated back to Colonial times; most were emancipated after the American Revolution when the states north of the Mason-Dixon line gradually freed their slaves.* By every demographic measurement, these free blacks were at the bottom rung of the ladder. Disfranchised, denied employment, excluded from schools, they had the lowest incomes and the highest mortality rates in the region. Yet, somehow, they survived. Their numbers doubled, then tripled and quadrupled until, by the time of the Civil War, they had built a multilayered society organized around their own churches, schools, and other institutions.*

With rare exceptions, black women worked. "The Women generally, both married and single wash clothes for a livelihood," a study done in Philadelphia in 1795 reported. In the first decades of the nineteenth century the majority were "in service" or did day's work for white families. Sometimes, particularly in country places, they were permitted to keep their children with them. "She has a child, but it is no detriment to her" an employer wrote in an 1809 letter of recommendation. More often, the children were bound out as indentured servants.

In Philadelphia, which had the largest black population in the North, the Pennsylvania Abolition Society† supervised indenture agreements to make sure that both child and employer were treated fairly. Boys were sometimes apprenticed to tradesmen; the girls were taught only "the Art, Trade, and Mystery of Housewifery." In the examples of indentures that follow, the first was handwritten; the

---

*Emancipation was gradual indeed. Slavery lingered on in New York State until 1827, in New Jersey until 1846. The census of 1850 reported 236 slaves in the North.

†The society, incorporated as the Pennsylvania Society for Promoting the Abolition of Slavery, for the Relief of Free Negroes Unlawfully held in Bondage, and for Improving the Condition of the African Race, was founded in 1775. Its first president was Benjamin Franklin, its secretary Thomas Harrison. Still in existence, the society celebrated its bicentennial in 1975 by microfilming its extensive records.

second was drawn up on a printed form, indicating that the rules laid down were characteristic of the place and time. Outside of the Abolition Society's orbit, girls did not always receive schooling or "Freedom Dues."

Know all men by these Presents—that I Negress Violete Hendricks, Wife of Tho^S Hendricks having a Female Child Before I was married to him Name Metilda Waker now age of 7 ^{seven} years Eight months and 8 days—and being desirous she should be properly placed out until she should be eighteen years old with sutch schooling & freedom dues as may be Proper—
I hearby authorise Tho^S Harrison & Isaac J. Hopper to take Full Charge of her & Bind her out agreeably to the above having full confidence that they will have Justice done to her in the Process. Witness my hand and Seal this Thirteenth day of September One Thousand Eight hundred and three—
Witness Present
William Price Douglass   Negress   her
                                              X   Violete
                                              mark

THIS INDENTURE

Witnesseth That Mary Kerr a mullattress now Illegitimate aged eight years and three months and with the advice of her next friend Tho^S Harrison one of the members of the Abolition Society of Philad^e Hath put herself, and by these Presents,
                DOTH voluntarily, and of her own free Will and Accord, put herself Apprentice to Mary Lewis a Black who has bro^t up and supported the said Mary Kerr from her Infancy—at her own expense—to learn the Art, Trade, and Mystery of Housewifery, and after the Manner of an Apprentice to serve her the said Mary Lewis —from the Day of the Date hereof, for and during, and to the full End of Term of Nine years & nine months next ensuing. During all which Term, the said Apprentice her said Mistress faithfully shall serve, her Secrets keep, her lawful Commands every where readily obey. She shall do no Damage to her said Mistress nor see it to be done by others, without letting or giving Notice thereof to her said Mistress. She shall not waste her said Mistresses' Goods, nor lend them unlawfully to any. She shall not commit Fornication nor contract Matrimony within the said Term. She shall not play at Cards, Dice or any other unlawful Game, whereby her said Mistress may have Damage. With her own Goods, nor the Goods of others, without Licence from her said Mis-

tress she shall neither buy nor sell. She shall not absent herself Day nor Night from her said Mistress Service, without her Leave: Nor haunt Ale-houses, Taverns, or Play-houses; but in all Things behave herself as a faithful Apprentice ought to do, during the said Term. And the said Mistress shall use the utmost of her Endeavor to teach or cause to be taught or instructed the said Apprentice, in the Trade or Mystery of Housewifery and procure and provide for her sufficient Meat, Drink, apparrel Lodging and Washing, fitting for an Apprentice, during the said term of nine years & nine months & shall cause her to be taught to Read, Write & Cypher & when free shall give her two suits of Cloathes one of which to be new—AND for the true Performance of all and singular the Covenants and Agreements, aforesaid, the said Parties bind themselves each unto the other, firmly by these Presents. IN WITNESS whereof, the said Parties have interchangedly set their Hands and Seals hereunto. Dated the fourteenth Day of June Annoque Domini, One Thousand Eight Hundred and Three—

Sealed and delivered
in the Presence of   Mary Lewis
Peter Browne
One of the Justices of the   her
peace in & for the County   Mary   X   Kerr
of Philad^e   mark

Although most black domestic workers toiled anonymously, the life stories of a few, usually the most energetic and resourceful, were recorded. Elleanor Eldridge (1785–1865), born in Warwick, Rhode Island, of African and Indian ancestry, was ten years old when her mother died, leaving nine children for her father to care for. Young Eldridge bound herself to a local family, agreeing to work for a year for twenty-five cents a week. For the next seventeen years, she remained in service, mastering a variety of household skills. After that she struck out on her own, shrewdly managing to advance despite a lack of schooling. Frances Whipple McDougall,* an admiring white friend, detailed Eldridge's work experiences.

She learned all the varieties of house-work and every kind of spinning; and plain, double and ornamental weaving. This double weaving i.e. carpets, old fashioned coverlets, damask, and bed-ticking, is said to

---

*Frances Whipple Greene McDougall (1805–68) was active in both the antislavery and labor movements. In 1842–43 she edited the *Wampanoag and Operatives Journal,* a periodical published on behalf of women mill workers.

be a very difficult and complicated process; and I presume there
are few girls of fourteen, capable of mastering such an intricate business. Yet she was pronounced a competent and fully accomplished
weaver.

In the commencement of her sixteenth year, Elleanor took leave
of her kind patrons and went to live next at Capt. Benjamin Green's
at Warwick Neck, to do their spinning for one year. At the expiration
of the year she was engaged as dairy woman. Elleanor continued in this
situation eight years. She took charge of the milk of from twenty-five
to thirty cows; and made from four to five thousand weight of cheese

Elleanor Eldridge's portrait, whitewash brush in hand, was the frontispiece to
Memoirs of Elleanor Eldridge. Published in 1838, it was one of the earliest
pictures of an Afro-American woman. *(Brown University Library)*

annually. Every year our heroine's cheese was distinguished by a premium.

Elleanor remained at Capt. Green's until 1812, being then twenty-seven years old. At this time the death of Capt. G. occasioned alterations in the family; so our heroine returned home to live with her oldest sister Lettise. Elleanor now, with her sister, entered into a miscellaneous business, of weaving, spinning, going out as nurse, washer, &c. She also, with her sister, entered considerably into the soap boiling business. Of this article they every year made large quantities, which they brought to the Providence market, together with such other articles as they wished to dispose of. By this time the earnings of Elleanor had amounted to a sum sufficient to purchase a lot and build a small house, which she rented for forty dollars a year.

She remained with her sister three years,—and was then induced by another sister to come to Providence; where she soon arrived and commenced a new course of business, viz—white-washing, papering, and painting; which she has followed for more than twenty years.

The above occupations she generally followed nine or ten months in the year; but commonly, during the most severe cold of winter, she engaged herself for high wages, in some private family, hotel, or boarding house.

About sixteen years ago, Elleanor, having six hundred dollars on hand, bought a lot, for which she paid one hundred dollars, "all in silver money," as she has herself assured me. She then commenced building a house which cost seventeen hundred dollars. This house was all paid for, with no incumbrance whatever. After it had been built three or four years; she built an addition on the east side, to live in herself; and subsequently one on the west side, to accommodate an additional tennant. This house rented for one hundred and fifty dollars per anum.

Eldridge was in her fifties when an avaricious neighbor and a dishonest sheriff conspired to swindle her out of her property. "No man would have been treated so" wrote McDougall, "and if a white woman had been the subject of such wrongs, the whole town—nay, the whole country, would have been indignant." After a group of Providence women published McDougall's Memoirs of Elleanor Eldridge *and Elleanor's* Second Book, *Eldridge traveled through New England and as far away as Philadelphia, selling copies.*

Eventually, Elleanor Eldridge was able to buy back her house. When McDougall asked her why she had never married, she explained that "she has determined to profit by the advice of her aunt, who told

*her never to marry, because it involved such a WASTE OF TIME!
for, said she, 'while my young mistress was courting and marrying, I
knit five pairs of stockings!' " There were sound economic reasons for
Eldridge's unromantic attitude. Although white women usually retired
from the labor market after marriage, most blacks were obliged to keep
on working to augment their husbands' earnings. Black men worked
in unskilled jobs, as laborers, porters, window washers, or they went to
sea, a profitable but hazardous occupation. More often than not, their
wives and widows took responsibility for the planning and scrimping
that gave them some security.*

*Chloe Spear (1750–1815) was born in Africa and sold in Boston's
slave market as a child. Married to Cesar Spear, she bore several
children before they were set free. A "Lady of Boston" who wrote a
Memoir of Mrs.* Chloe Spear *described her as tall and cheerful, speaking "extremely broken" English. Chloe, she reported:*

felt an increasing desire, to possess, some time or other, a little
habitation that she could call her own. Stimulated by this desire, she
worked early and late. She not only assisted her husband in the care
of a family of boarders, who were seamen, or labourers, but she also
took in washing, and went into various families as a washerwoman, &c.
And whatever she could save of her earnings, she carefully laid up.

The families for whom she worked, frequently gave her their cold
meat and vegetables and as her husband was more particular to have
enough to eat, than to inquire from whence it came, and was in the
habit of submitting the chief management of domestic affairs, to his
"cleber wife," she had opportunities in this way, of adding to her little
stock.

After returning from a hard day's work, she many a time, went to
washing for her customers in the night, while her husband was taking
his rest, —extended lines across her room, and hung up her clothes to
dry, while she retired to bed for a few hours; then arose, prepared
breakfast and went out to work again, leaving her ironing to be done
on her return at night. Cesar, having been accustomed to cooking, &c
could, on these occasions, wait upon himself and boarders, during her
absence; but was quite willing that she should make ready a good
supper, after she came home.

Her husband was fond of finery and show, and would sometimes
say to her, "Chloe, why you don't wear silk gown, dress up smart, like
udder colour women?" "Well," she would reply, "you give me money,
I can buy silk gown, well as any body." The money, he would give to

her; but instead of an extravagant dress, something cheap, and comfortable satisfied good Chloe, and the surplus augmented her treasury. One day hearing of an unfinished house for sale, she made inquiries respecting it, and critically examined her capital. Having satisfied herself, and being aware that the purchase must be made in her husband's name, " 'cause he de *head,* "* she said to him, "Cesar, house to sell; I wish we buy it." He laughed at her, for thinking of such a thing, but asked her, "how much e price ob it?" "Seben hundred dollar," she answered. *"Seben hundred dollar!!"* exclaimed Cesar, "I no got de money, how I buy a house?" "I got money," said Chloe. He then was pleased, and very readily agreed to the purchase which, with the advice of her friends, was soon effected. But the house was unfinished. She therefore proposed that themselves should occupy the most inferior part of it, and let out the remainder, until, from the income, they could finish one room after another, and thus increase the rent, which, with the blessing of Providence, might serve to support them, should they live to grow old. That also was effected. But during the lapse of time, her husband, after a long and painful illness was removed by the hand of death.

At Chloe Spear's death in 1815, she left a house on Hanover Street in Boston, $500 to a grandson, and smaller bequests to friends.

Born in Newburyport, Massachusetts, in 1799, Nancy Gardner Prince was of African and Indian ancestry. She was thirteen years old when her mother, widowed for the third time and left with seven children to raise, broke down under the strain. "Her grief, poverty and responsibilities were too much for her. She never again was the mother that she had been," Prince later wrote. In her autobiography, published in 1850, Prince described her early life and that of her sister, Silvia, who was "deluded away" to a house of prostitution. The following excerpt from the Narrative of the Life and Travels of Mrs. Nancy Prince *begins with her stepfather's death.*

I was at this time, in Captain E. W. Sargent's family. I thought I would go home a little while, and try and comfort my mother. My brother and myself stayed at home that summer. We gathered berries and sold them in Gloucester; strawberries, raspberries, blackberries and whortleberries. With the sale of these fruits, my brother and myself nearly supported my mother and her children. We stayed with our

---

*Under common law, married women had no right to own property and no legal existence apart from their husbands. In 1848 the first, and limited, Married Women's Property Act was passed in New York State.

mother until every resource was exhausted; we then heard of a place eight miles out of town, where a boy and girl were wanted. We both went and were engaged. We often went home with our wages, and all the comforts we could get; but we could not approach our mother as we wished.

My eldest sister, Silvia, was seventy miles in the country, so we were scattered all about. Soon as the War [of 1812] was over, I determined to get more for my labor. I went to Salem in the month of April, and thought myself fortunate to be with religious people. There were seven in the family, one sick with a fever, and another in a consumption. Sabbath evening I had to prepare for the wash, soap the clothes and put them into the steamer, set the kettle of water to boiling and then close in the steam, and let the pipe from the boiler into the steam box that held the clothes. At two o'clock, on the morning of Monday, the bell was rung for me to get up; but, that was not all, they said I was too slow, and the washing was not done well; I had to leave the tub to tend the door and wait on the family, and was not spoken kind to, at that. Hard labor and unkindness was too much for me; in three months, my health and strength were gone. In the year 1814, they sent me to Gloucester in their chaise.

In the spring of 1815, I returned to Salem, accompanied by my eldest sister, and we obtained good places. She took it into her head to go to Boston, as a nursery girl, where she lived a few months and was then deluded away. February 7th, 1816, a friend came to Salem and informed me of it. To have heard of her death, would not have been so painful to me, as we loved each other very much.

It was very cold, but I was so distressed about my sister that I started the next morning for Boston, on foot. I was young and inexperienced, but God knew that my object was good. Mr. Brown, when he learned my errand, kindly offered to assist me. He found where my sister resided, and taking with him a large cane, he accompanied me to the house, on Sabbath evening. My sister I found seated with a number of others around a fire, the mother of the harlots at the head. My sister did not see me until I clasped her round the neck. The old woman flew at me, and bid me take my hands off her; she opened a door that led down into a cellar kitchen, and told me to come down; she attempted to take my hands off my sister. Mr. Brown defended me with his cane; there were many men and girls there, and all was confusion. When my sister came to herself, she looked upon me and said, "Nancy, O Nancy, I am ruined!" I said, "Silvia, my dear sister, what are you here for? Will you not go with me?" She seemed thankful to get away; the enraged old woman cried out, "She owes me, she cannot go." Silvia replied, "I will go." The old woman seized her to drag her down into the kitchen; I held on to her, while Mr. Brown at my side, used his great cane; he threatened her so that she was obliged to let my sister go, who, after collecting her things, accompanied Mr. Brown and myself.

When Nancy was twenty-five years old, she escaped from the rut of service jobs by marrying Nero Prince, a widower many years her senior. Prince was a man of standing in black New England, a grand master of the Prince Hall Masonic Lodge and a sailor who had spent a dozen years as a footman at the court of the Russian czar. Returning to St. Petersburg with him, the new Mrs. Prince was received at court (where "there was no prejudice against color") and was given an opportunity to educate herself. For the next nine years she ran a profitable business in St. Petersburg:

I learned the language in six months, so as to be able to attend to my business, and also made some proficiency in French. My time was taken up in domestic affairs; I took two children to board, the third week after commencing housekeeping, and increased their numbers. The baby linen making and childrens' garments were in great demand. I started a business in these articles and took a journeywoman and apprentices. The Empress gave me much encouragement by purchasing of me garments for herself and children, handsomely-wrought in French and English styles, and many of the nobility also followed her example.

But the long Russian winters affected her lungs and she was forced to return to the United States. Her husband expected to follow her but died before he could make the trip. For the rest of her life, Nancy Prince was active in American reform movements, traveling, lecturing, teaching, and writing.

A small amount of capital enabled some women to go into business. Elizabeth Hewlett Marshall (1780–1861), who had roots in New York's white as well as black communities, worked as a domestic during periods of widowhood. When her last husband left her some property, she opened a bakery to support herself and her four children. Her granddaughter, Maritcha R. Lyons, recalled:

She and her sister Mary, in common with girls of their station, were apprenticed; grandmother lived with the Quaker family of Mott until an early marriage. Before she was twenty she had become wife and

widow. She shortly wed again to a John Bray. After a few years, Mr.
Bray also died. Her final matrimonial venture was the union of her
fortunes with those of my grandfather, Joseph Marshall. He worked so
diligently as a house painter that he became able to purchase four lots
of the ground now included in the domain of Central Park. He also
built on Centre Street, a house for his family. After his decease,
grandmother erected a rear house and converted the basement of the
front dwelling into a store in which she opened a bakery. When, in
her declining years, she became a member of our household, the
avails accruing from the sale of this property sufficed for her personal
needs.

Going uptown meant for her going about as far as Bond Street, the
journey consuming half a day, for a team was required and the horses
had to be fed and rested before the return trip was undertaken. Up the
Hudson to Albany in a sailing vessel was one of her annual recreations.
Though she worked hard she always indulged in a vacation once a year.
The length of a water trip was always uncertain and preparations had
to be made in consequence. This included various wraps, extra garments, bedding, and a full hamper of food of all kinds.

The first day young Lord and Taylor opened a dry goods store on
Catherine Street, she hurried over to make an early purchase of a yard
of white ribbon, to give the "boys" good luck, for she knew them both
very well. When the DeForrests, former employers, found coal in
Pottsville, Pa., she was always sure of a full bin in winter, something
to be thankful for as winters then were long and continuously severe.

*Nancy Lenox Remond (1788–1867) who was born free in Newton,
Massachusetts, was a fancy cake maker when she married John Remond of Salem. Although he became a successful merchant and ca-
terer, their daughters were taught trades. While Sarah Parker Remond
became an antislavery lecturer, her sisters, Cecilia Remond Babcock
(d. 1912), Maritcha Remond (1816–95), and Caroline Remond Putnam (1826–1908) operated the fashionable Ladies Hair Work Salon
in Salem. Their wig factory was the largest in the state, and Mrs.
Putnam's Medicated Hair Tonic sold widely as an antidote for hair
loss. Maritcha Lyons, who visited Salem often as a child, described
Susan Remond (b. 1814), who had followed her mother's calling:*

She worked at home, her bread, cakes, pastry, jellies and confec-
tions and more substantial desserts were in constant demand and
brought excellent prices. She also served, in a small dining room, where
none were eligible to entrance save the most exclusive of the townsmen
and their specially invited guests. Messengers were continually going

to and from Susan's kitchen for she controlled the trade of Salem in culinary productions. This famous kitchen was below street level in the basement of a large, straggling building, but it was well lighted and spotlessly kept, and the utensils were white as snow and as shining as gold. My earliest recollections are connected with this room where children were welcome and "treated" with goodies. Her turbaned head, her large white apron, her basket of keys at her side, these made a distinctive uniform. Her kitchen was a Mecca where gathered radicals, free thinkers, abolitionists, female suffragists, fugitives. Susan ministered freely and assisted each weary one to renewed strength and hope.

Other women became boarding-house keepers, milliners, and dressmakers. Some ventured to advertise their services in Freedom's Journal, *the first black newspaper:*

BOARDING & LODGING
The subscriber respectfully informs her friends and the public generally, that she has opened a house for the accommodation of genteel persons of colour with Boarding and Lodging at No. 88 South-Fourth St. above Lombard-st. Philadelphia. Citizens and strangers in want of Boarding and Lodging may depend upon having every attention paid to them on the most reasonable terms.
                    GRACY JONES
Philadelphia, April 23, 1828.

BOARDING & LODGING
The subscriber respectfully informs her Friends, and the public in general that her House No. 28 Elizabeth street, is still open for the accommodation of genteel persons of colour, with Boarding & Lodging.
P.S. In addition to the above establishment, the subscriber keeps on hand a quantity of best Refreshments, Oysters, &c. served up at the shortest notice. Her house is in a healthy and pleasant situation, and she hopes by the unremitted attention that will be paid to all those who may favour her with their patronage, to be entitled to public favour.
                    ELIZA JOHNSON
Philadelphia, June 2, 1828

LEGHORN BONNETS
MRS. SARAH JOHNSON

No. 551 Pearl-Street, respectfully informs her Friends and the Public, that she has commenced Bleaching Pressing and Refitting Leghorn and Straw Hats, in the best manner. Ladies Dresses made, and Plain Sewing done on the most reasonable terms.

Mrs. J. begs leave to assure her friends and the public that those who patronize her may depend upon having their work done faithfully, and with punctuality and despatch.

New-York, April 29, 1828.

Perhaps it was one of these entrepreneurs who contributed to Freedom's Journal a letter that came close to being a feminist statement. Some of the phrasing of "Matilda"'s letter indicates that she had read Hannah Mather Crocker's* pamphlet, "Observations on the Real Rights of Women." While accepting women's place as the home, Crocker rejected female inferiority and called for equal educational opportunities.

Messrs. Editors: [August, 1827]

Will you allow a female to offer a few remarks upon a subject that you must allow to be all-important? I don't know that in any of your papers, you have said sufficient upon the education of females. I hope you are not to be classed with those, who think that our mathematical knowledge should be limited to "fathoming the dish-kettle," and that we have acquired enough of history, if we know that our grandfather's father lived and died. 'Tis true the time has been, when to darn a stocking, and cook a pudding well, was considered the end and aim of a woman's being. But those were days when ignorance blinded men's eyes. The diffusion of knowledge has destroyed those degrading opinions, and men of the present age, allow, that we have minds that are capable and deserving of culture. There are difficulties, and great difficulties in the way of our advancement; but that should only stir us to greater efforts. We possess not the advantages with those of our sex, whose skins are not colored like our own; but we can improve what little we have, and make our one talent produce two-fold. The influence that we have over the male sex demands, that our minds should

*Hannah Mather Crocker (1752–1829), granddaughter of Cotton Mather, published her tract in 1818.

be instructed and improved with the principles of education and religion, in order that this influence should be properly directed. Ignorant ourselves, how can we be expected to form the minds of our youth, and conduct them in the paths of knowledge? How can we "teach the young idea to shoot" if we have [no knowledge] ourselves? I would address myself to all mothers, and say to them, that while it is necessary to possess a knowledge of cookery, and the various mysteries of pudding-making, something more is requisite. It is their bounden duty to store their daughters' minds with useful learning. They should be made to devote their leisure time to reading books, whence they would derive valuable information, which could never be taken from them. I will no longer trespass on your time and patience. I merely throw out these hints, in order that some more able pen will take up the subject.

Matilda

A handful of other early letters have survived. Written by women of diverse backgrounds, they offer a glimpse, however incomplete, of black society in the post-Revolutionary period. Margaret Harrison (1743–1811) of Providence, Rhode Island, was thirty years old when her owner, Moses Brown*, converted to Quakerism and freed his slaves. Before emancipation, they had been taught to read and write; afterwards, Brown urged them to turn to him not as master but as friend. To encourage thrift, he invested their savings for them and paid them interest. Although Harrison moved to Boston where she did days' work, she continued to write to Brown. Her letter and her daughter's illustrate the poverty that average blacks faced, as well as the dependent relationships that bound some of them to their former masters.

My friend: Boston, November 1, [1809]
    I rit you these fue lines to let you know that i stand in need of your kind asistence to Me. If you plese to Send me 20 Dollars. The disstressing times is So hard opon me that obligeged me to send to you for you are the only frind on earth that i have to send to. I hop that you wont think that its idleness or any such a thing. My husban he is old but provident and fathefl. [It is] as much as he can do to pay his reant. I pray that you wood Sent it in the letter as quick as posble for i am in

---

*Moses Brown, Rhode Island's leading antislavery advocate, was a wealthy merchant and philanthropist. When he encouraged his ex-slaves to save, there were no banks in all of Rhode Island. He helped to start the Providence Bank in 1791, at the same time that he, with Samuel Slater, established the first water-powered cotton mill in the United States.

a great State. Plese to Direct your letter to john tucker clerk of the court for safte. Plese to send it by the mail stage, I remin your friend Peggy harrison

Our dear friend: Boston, April 25, 1811
    We have met with the greatest loss in the world that is we have lost our dear mother. She died on the 15 of April and she was very willing to die and go to the lord above and she desird me when diing to let you know of our disstresses & she told me not give up the note to any body but you. There is A society of coloured people to wich my father belogs. They buried my mother. They wanted security before she was put in the ground. My father found the note and give it up to those people that buried her and they wount give it up to us. If you will please to let us have some mony to pay the expences of the burieng and dets she ode. My brother returned the same night on wich his mother Peggy Harrison died and he has been cast away and lost everything that he was worth wich was one 100 dollars. If you will please to send us some mony you will relieve the distressed. If you will please to inclose it in a letter and direct it to Ann Armstrong in Belknap street & we shal get it your friend and servent
                    Ann Harrison

A decade before the American Revolution, African-born Cuffe Slocum and his wife, Ruth Moses, a member of the Wampanoag tribe, bought a farm in Westport, Massachusetts, a coastal village near New Bedford. Their ten children formed the nucleus of a close-knit family group, part black, part Indian, whose traces can still be found in the Westport area. The family was headed by Paul Cuffe, who built a fleet of merchant ships that sailed to Europe, the West Indies, and Africa; by 1810, Cuffe was the wealthiest and most respected black man in the United States. Preserved with his logbooks and papers are several letters from female family members. Cuffe's younger sister, Freelove Slocum* (1765–1834) left the family compound for New York where she supported herself by keeping a school, investing in brother Paul's voyages, and selling goods that he brought from abroad. Although several letters from Paul and John Cuffe to sister Freelove have survived, the following is the only letter in her hand. It shows her as a woman of business acumen. The "60 Dollars in silver" was partial

---

*Freelove Slocum was the only family member to retain her father's name, the name of his master. The others dropped the cognomen Slocum and replaced it with their father's given name about 1778.

repayment of her investment in Cuffe's last African voyage; she also
wanted her brother to invest young Anthony Pease's savings so that
they could be "gaining something."

Dear brother: New York, December 9, 1816
    I received your kind and welcom letter the 3 of this month by the
hand of Abner Davis with 60 Dollars in silver money. Abner told me
you desired him to pay me thirty more but I told him no I should right
to you my self. I want to speak to you a bout taking some money in
your hands for Anthony Peas. I have got same in care for him but I
think it is best to [be] gaining sumthing. He ses he wishes Capten
Cuffe to have it in his hand till he is of age, then he thinks of taking
a voige in Africa if life and health permits. When I get it all together
there will be twenty or thirty pounds. He is twenty next April. I wish
you to right me soon if you can
    I remain your loveing sister
                        Freelove Slocum

*Mary Wainer Mastens was Paul Cuffe's niece, the daughter of his
sister Mary and of Michael Wainer who captained many Cuffe vessels.
When her mariner husband, John Mastens, deserted her, she moved
to upstate New York where her brother, Gardner Wainer, lived. The
following letter was written to Paul Cuffe, executor of her father's
estate. Michael Wainer had died a year earlier, leaving a house and
land to his daughter, but dividing his household goods between her and
his third wife.*

                        Scipio, Cayuga [County, New York,]
Dear Uncle: December 7, 1816
    I recivd your letter the last of September. I never have had an
opportunity to answer before. I was glad to hear of your Healths. You
wrote about the division. You must not Be uneasy about it but let it
stand as it [is]. She shall not have none of my house and lot. She has
got enuf Already. I dont see no other way but if you see any better way
for me I want you should do it. As for Michael I cant hear a word from
him. We have looked for him but he dont come. I am coming to dig
Clambs again if I live so dont Destroy them all if you can help it. My
love to aunt else and aunt Lidia* and all enquiring friends. I want to
see you all once more. It wont be a joy to me. Westport looks very
lonesome and desolate to me. [I spend] many hours in lonesomeness.

*Michael was Michael Wainer, Jr.; Aunt Else was Paul Cuffe's wife, Alice; Aunt Lidia
his sister, Lydia Cuffe.

I did not get away from it by coming away. I must conclude, from thy affectionate and loving Cousin

Mary Mastens

Usually it was a woman's task to inform relatives and friends of a death in the family. Twenty-two-year-old Rhoda Cuffe wrote to James Forten of Philadelphia three days after Paul Cuffe died. Her letter followed what was almost a prescribed pattern: an account of the deceased's last days; the deathbed scene; and the comforting thought that "our loss is his eternal gain." For a young woman educated only in the village school that her father had started, it was a creditable letter.

Dear Sir: Westport, [Massachusetts,] September 10, 1817

It has pleased Almighty God to remove from this transitorial world my affectionate and venerable father after a long and severe sickness. Three weeks before his departure, he was able to walk from one room to the other which gave us hopes of a speedy recovery, but how soon was our joy turned into Mourning—his indisposition again made rapid progress. We then called in an eminent physician from Rhode Island who gave great encouragement. He wished the physician not to encourage, but said the Lord's will, not mine, be done. He refused his medicine, saying it was not in the power of medicine to remove the disorder. But should it please the Almighty to raise him up once more to His own honor and glory, He would do it. He bore his indisposition with great fortitude and resignation in full confidence of being rewarded in an after state.

He has not been well one day since last February. Of his illness at that time, perhaps he apprised you. Since then has constantly complained of his stomach and great weakness. In the morning of the 27th of 8th mo he appeared to be perfectly resigned and took a solemn leave of his wife and family and near connections and bid us a long and eternal farewell.

Being asked if he would not take a little Nourishment, answered, by no means, but let me pass quietly away. About six o'clock in the evening he said, I can no longer strive against nature. All is well; and said to his sister-in-law Jane who was attending on him, feed my sheep and my lambs. Then, calling for some water that came from the boiling spring, he drank it through a quill. After drinking two glasses he was strong enough to hold the tumbler and drink freely of seven glasses.

He had much to say to his family and friends, but his strength would not permit it. There is no doubt it is well with him and that our loss is his eternal gain. It is very gloomy since his departure. The plains that knew him shall know him no more.

I presume you will excuse the liberty I have taken in writing to you. My education has been a limited one, and I am not accustomed to writing to strangers. My Mother sends her love to you, your wife and children, and respects to all our friends. Hoping at some future day to visit your region should health and strength permit of it.

Paper will not permit of further additions. Must therefore stop the course of my pen after bidding you adieu.

Affectionately
Rhoda Cuffe

Like the Cuffe women, Grace Bustill Douglass (1782–1842) came from a large and supportive family. * *Her father, Cyrus Bustill, the son of a slave, baked bread for George Washington's army during the Revolution and later operated a bread, cake, and biscuit business in Philadelphia. Her mother, Elizabeth Morey, was part English, part Delaware Indian. Growing up in a metropolis where a school for black children opened in 1770, Douglass had a good education for her day. Despite her father's comfortable income, she learned a trade and operated a millinery store from her Arch Street home. Although her husband, the Reverend Robert Douglass, was a founder of the First African Presbyterian Church, Grace Douglass attended meetings of the Society of Friends. The following letter was written to the Reverend John Gloucester, a colleague of her husband's.*

Dear Friend: Philadelphia, February 28, 1819

It has been said by our enemies among the whites, that it is doing us harm to set us free. We cannot, say they, maintain ourselves decently and respectably. Some of them must manage for us. To prove which, they bid us look around and see the many poor distressed objects of our color with which this city abounds, where we have every encouragement to do well for ourselves, overlooking the manner in which most of us have been brought up. Very many, in great families where they live on the best, dress in the finest and most fashionable clothing. Of course they carry these customs into their own families. They work hard, therefore they have money to spend, and must enjoy it in the way they have seen others do. And they are apt, too, to think they have a right to do so, as they have *worked* for it.

When I was first married I found myself precisely in this way. We

---

*The Bustill family can trace its history from 1732. Its most illustrious member was the actor, singer, and political activist Paul Bustill Robeson (1898–1976). He was a great grandnephew of Grace Douglass.

had our parties and tea-drinkings; we must have the best wine and the best cake; our friends had it and we must give them the same they gave us, or be considered mean. But when it pleased the Lord to open my eyes, these things became a burden to me. I thought I would assist the poor if I had the means some people had, but I have no more than I want myself; how can *I* help the poor? Then it occurred to me that Christ lived a self-denying life, and I began to think how I might deny myself, take up the cross and follow him, when dress presented itself to my view. Now a pair of morocco shoes cost one dollar and 50 cts.: a pair of leather will do just as well, and I shall have 50 cts. for the poor. A fine muslin dress costs five dollars: I can buy a very good calico one for three, and have two dollars to spare. I reasoned in this manner till my dress was reduced to the standard which you see. I wore a plain straw bonnet with a white ribbon. The ribbon often soiled and required to be changed. I thought if I wore a plain silk one the strings will last as long as the bonnet, and here will be something saved.

These things were very trifling in themselves, but oh! the peace of mind and the liberty I gained by it more than doubly compensated me for the mortification I at first endured in seeing others who could not afford it so well, better dressed than myself. I could now go to meeting let the weather be as it would, I was not afraid of spoiling my shoes or any part of my dress. I no longer felt disturbed as to whether my appearance was better than my neighbor or not, and I always had something for the poor.

Now, dear friend, if you please, read this in one of your meetings and beg them to try my plan for one year, and I think they cannot fail to be much benefited by it.

I remain your friend with much regard,

Grace Douglass

NINE

Daughters of Africa
Daughters of America

A RELIGIOUS REVIVAL swept through New England and New York State in the early nineteenth century. During that period, white women organized hundreds of church-related societies, including char-

itable organizations, missionary groups, temperance societies, literary clubs, and maternal associations. Their objective was to "do good": to assist the poor, convert the heathen, and lift up the fallen. Above all, they were concerned with improving themselves in order to be better equipped for their most important role—motherhood. The maternal associations that sprung up in almost every village and town between 1815 and 1835 were founded by women "aware of our highly responsible situation as Mothers" who met to discuss how best "to train up our children."

Black women had notably different priorities. They formed missionary and temperance societies around their churches, rather later than the white women, but in their first years of freedom being do-gooders was a luxury few of them could afford. They only had to cross their own door sills to confront poverty and all of its attendant ills.

As far back as the 1790s, they organized societies for mutual relief —primitive insurance companies whose members pooled their dues to pay sick and death benefits and to assist widows and fatherless children. An 1830 study of Philadelphia's mutual benefit societies found sixteen male societies that paid $2,202.71 in benefits that year, and twenty-seven female societies that disbursed $3,616.58. The oldest society in the study was the Female Benevolent Society of St. Thomas, which was formed in 1793, two years before its male counterpart, the African Friendly Society of St. Thomas. Although records of the earliest female societies have not been found, there are reports from two 1821 organizations. One is represented only by a note in Grace Douglass's neat handwriting:

Visited Mrs. Jones with the Committee and gave her 50 cts worth of groceries. She had been confined 10 days.
Grace Douglass

The second is an "Order Book" belonging to the Daughters of Africa. Covering the years 1821–29, the record book meticulously details the society's expenditures: payments to the sick, loans for funerals, and expenses for furnishing a meeting room. Also included are members' names, dues payments, and a list of their deceased (members, husbands, and children). None of the middle-class women whose names would become familiar in the antislavery struggles a decade or two later appear in the Order Book. The Daughters of Africa were nearly 200 working-class women who banded together to help them-

selves.* *Their crudely written, misspelled records tell much of their life and times. Some typical entries follow.*

Philadelphia September 12 1821
Hannah Morris Treaser of the Society Dauther of Africa will pay to Eliza Douse the Sum of 18/3 cents to pay for one pound of Candenls [candles]
By a majority of the committe

Mary   her   Vanable   Elissabeth Mathews sucruetary
     mark
Vice present

Mrs. Hannah Morris please to pay to Mrs. Elissabeth Moon Three Dollars for four benches for the Daughter of Africa Society
Phoeby Lewis Prisident
Elissabeth Mathews Sucr

December 28, 1821
Mrs. Hannah Morris please to pay to Mrs. Elissabeth Emery Five Dollars for the President [s] Chaire of the Daughter of Africa
Phoeby Lewis Prisident
Elissabeth Matthew Sucr

March the 1, 1822
Mrs. Morris Treasure Please to Pay to Sidney Buck and Elissabeth Griffith for Ann Hacket a sick member of the Daughter of Africa Society her weekly allowance $1 50 cent

Hannah Morris Treasure Plese to Pay E. Griffith for Leah Gibson a sick member $1 50 from the Daughers Africa Society
Pheb Lewis President
Elizab Mathews Sucry

April the 25 1822
Hannah Morris plesse to Pay Sidney Buck $1 for Book paper ink for the Daughter Africa Society
P. Lewis Pres.
Elizabeth Mathews Sucretary

*In 1830, the Daughters of Africa paid $149.97 in benefits. Eight other female societies paid more; the largest amount, $428.50, came from the African Female Band Benevolent Society of Bethel.

May the 5 1822

Committee of the Daughters Africa Lent Ann Hacket a member a lone acordian [according] to 10 article of the Constution the sume of four dollars for the burial child.

E. Mathew Sucrtary

July 5 1822

Mrs. Morris Treasuer of the Daughter Africa Society Please to pay Sidney Buck one of the Committee the Sume eighteen dollar for the funurall expence of Rachel Conks one of the members of the D

Phoebe Lewis Pres E. Mathews Sucr

November the 15 1822

Mary Brown borrowed of Commitee the sume of 4 wich she is to pay in 3 month to the Society for the Burial of her child

Sarah Pratte ten dollars for the lost of hir housband

The African Female Benevolent Society of Newport, Rhode Island was another early black women's organization. Once the leading slave port of New England, Newport had a large black population. Its men organized a Free African Union Society in 1780 and in 1808 started an African Benevolent Society to raise money for a school. The Benevolent Society was open to "any person of colour whether male or female," but only male members were permitted to vote or hold office. Perhaps because they wished for autonomy, Newport's women formed their own society in 1809. Welcomed by the men with "great satisfaction" and much good advice, the officers of the Female Society, both African-born ex-slaves, politely replied.

Gentlemen: [Newport, Rhode Island, October 1809]

We received your address dated April 14 by our President which address was very gratifying indeed. We thank you for the approbation you seem to express of our Society and we hope that by our forming this Society like that of yours in Substance will give you not only our approbation of yours but encouragement to persevere. Surely nothing could induce us to form this Society but the good of our posterity which we trust you have in view and we receive into our Society all good and moral Characters.

We cannot forbear to inform you the encouragement we have in seeing so many of our sects [sex] coming forward and joining us to the

Support of this institution beyound all our expectation. We also received your three Committee [men] namely Newport Gardner John Mowatt Tunbridge Hammond whom you sent to enquire of us what prospect we have of affording the school assistance with regard to the expences. We have voted that ten dollars be taken out of our treasury at this time and to be carried by three of our Directors Viz—Patience Mowatt Catherine Sheffield & Sarah Malbone To your treasury and we hope it may be acceptable as the Widows mite. Finally—may the Lord enable both Societys to persevere in Supporting this Institution is the Sincere wish of your Humble Servants—

By order and in the behalf of the Society

Orbour Collins President
Sarah D Lyna Secrettary pro tem

A year later their report was less high spirited. The school, supported by white as well as black contributions, limped along until 1842 when the city of Newport finally opened a public school for black children.

Usually the constitutions of the mutual aid societies were formal documents that followed white models. When forty Massachusetts women met in 1818 to start the Colored Female Religious and Moral Society of Salem, they wrote their own regulations. Straightforward in style, some of the articles sound as if they were intended as a guide to "consciousness-raising." Although the officers were better educated than the Daughters of Africa or their Newport sisters, the dues of a penny a week that they assessed themselves give a notion of their disposable income.

CONSTITUTION
of the
Colored Female Religious and Moral
Society of Salem

Article I.—At the weekly meeting of the Society, when the appointed hour arrives, and a number are convened, the exercises shall begin by reading in some profitable book, till all have come in who are expected.

Art. II—A prayer shall then be made by one of the members, and after that, a chapter in the Bible shall be read, and religious conversation be attended to, as time will allow.

Art. III—Four quarterly days in the year, in January, April, July and October, beginning on the first day of every January, to be observed as day of solemn fasting and prayer.

Art. IV—We promise not to ridicule or divulge the supposed or apparent infirmities of any fellow member; but to keep secret all things relating to the Society, the discovery of which might tend to do hurt to the Society or any individual.

Art. V—We resolve to be charitably watchful over each other; to advise, caution and admonish where we may judge there is occasion, and that it may be useful; and we promise not to resent, but kindly and thankfully receive such friendly advice or reproof from any one of our members.

Art. VI—Any female can become a member of this Society by conforming to the Constitution, and paying in fifty two cents per year.

Art. VII—This Society is formed for the benefit of the sick and destitute of those members belonging to the Society.

Art. VIII—If any member commit any scandalous sin, or walk unruly, and after proper reproof continue manifestly impenitent, she shall be excluded from us, until she give evidence of her repentance.

Art. IX—When any person shall manifest to any one of us a desire to join the Society, it shall be mentioned in one of our meetings that all may have opportunity, who desire it, to satisfy themselves respecting the character and conversation of the person offering to join; and if at the meeting on the next week, there be no objection to her being admitted, she may apply to the head of the Society, who will read our Articles to her, and if she is willing and does sign them, she shall be considered as a member of the Society, regularly admitted.

Art. X—As to any other matters which we shall hereafter find conducive to the benefit and good regulation of our Society, we engage to leave to the discretion and decision of a major part of us, to whose determination we promise quietly to agree and submit.

President—Mrs. Clarissa C. Lawrence*
Vice-President—Mrs. Eleanor Jones
Treasurer—Miss Betsey Blanchard
Secretary—Mrs. Sally Colemen
Visiting Committee—Mrs. Mercy Morris
                              Mrs. Nancy Randolph

Black women's societies, some patterned after white do-good groups, continued to multiply. Free black women in the slave city of Washington, D.C., formed the Coloured Female Roman Catholic

*Clarissa Lawrence later became an officer of Salem's integrated Female Anti-Slavery Society and a delegate to the 1839 Anti-Slavery Convention of American Women.

Beneficial Society in 1828.* A Colored Female Charitable Society, for which the objective was "the visiting of widows and orphans in their afflictions and, as far as possible, to mitigate their sufferings," was founded in Boston in 1832; Female Benevolent Societies were started in Troy, New York, in 1833 and in Portland, Maine, in 1840. In New York City, which had the second largest black community in the North, the earliest known female society was the African Dorcas Association, founded in 1827 to supply clothing to children in the African Free Schools. Unlike other women's organizations, the Dorcas Association had considerable male supervision. An Advising Committee of the city's black ministers arranged its first meetings and kept its records; its constitution was "prepared expressly" by the white principal of the school. It was the women, however, who held weekly sewing meetings to make jackets, trousers, and dresses for the students.

As a second generation of free women matured, their "African" societies became "colored," and "mutual relief" was broadened to include "mutual improvement." By the 1830s members of a small middle class organized literary associations and held what were called "mental feasts," hoping not only to educate themselves but also to combat white racism. A Female Literary Association of Philadelphia held its first meeting on September 20, 1831. "As daughters of a despised race," its constitution said, "it becomes a duty . . . to cultivate the talents entrusted to our keeping, that by so doing, we may break down the strong barrier of prejudice." Three months later the Afric-American Female Intelligence Society of Boston was founded "for the diffusion of knowledge, the suppression of vice and immorality, and for cherishing such virtues as will render us happy and useful to society."

Within the next year, women in Providence, Rhode Island, had associated "for mutual improvement in literature and morals"; by 1834 New York had a Colored Ladies' Literary Society and Philadelphia a Minerva Literary Association. While male societies sponsored public lectures and debates, the women usually met in members' homes to read essays and poems that they had written. After attending a mental feast in Philadelphia in 1832, one white woman described the program.

Soon after all were quietly seated, a short address, prepared for the occasion, was read by the authoress, (Sarah Douglass) a copy of which is herewith sent. The fifty-fourth beautiful and encouraging chapter of

---

*Its formal printed constitution may have been drawn up by a sympathetic priest, Father Vanlomen, who helped start a school for colored girls in 1827. The school was headed by Maria Becraft (1805–33), a free black.

Isaiah was then read. After sitting a short time under a solemn and impressive silence that ensured the reading of the chapter, one of the company vocally petitioned our Heavenly Father for a continuation of his favor, &c. The remainder of the evening was occupied principally by their severally reading and relating affecting slave tales, calculated to bring forcibly into view the deplorable situation of our fellow creatures at the south—both the oppressor and the oppressed. This interesting interview was closed with singing an appropriate hymn.

Sarah Mapps Douglass (1806–82), the daughter of Grace Douglass, was secretary of the Female Literary Association. A talented young schoolteacher, she also wrote and drew. When the Liberator *initiated*

This depiction of a chained slave was engraved in 1835 by Patrick Reason, a black artist. Widely reproduced, it was usually accompanied by the motto, "Am I Not a Woman and a Sister?" *(Dorothy B. Porter)*

a ladies department, its columns headed by the cut of a kneeling female slave, Douglass and other members of the literary association found their first forum. A selection from her essay on "Family Worship," one of several signed Sophonisba, is typical of her earnest didacticism.

Come, gentle lady, let us screen ourselves with this luxuriant honeysuckle, and look through the open window into the cottage of Albert Lindsey. Step lightly, for the family are assembled to offer their morning sacrifice; and now the voice of the mother falls like sweet music on the ear, as she reads a portion from the book of books and the meek and loving expression on the countenances of her children bears witness, that it is happiness to be thus employed. O, lady, would that we might see all the families of our people so engaged! how would the sunshine of such an example disperse the mists of prejudice which surround us! Yes, religion and education would raise us to an equality with the fairest in our land.

The Ladies' Literary Society of New York, like its Philadelphia counterpart, was made up of the elite of the black community, the wives and daughters of ministers, teachers, and small businessmen. In celebration of their third anniversary in 1837, they held a public exhibition to demonstrate the range of their accomplishments. The Order of Exercises included poetry readings, music, and an "Address on the Improvement of the Mind." Miss Jennings, the orator of the occasion, was probably Elizabeth Jennings, a schoolteacher who was later involved in a civil rights suit. Her father was a tailor, her sister Matilda a dressmaker, her brother a dentist. "On Improvement of the Mind," with its call to the "daughters of America," reiterated the arguments for self-improvement. An excerpt:

It is now a momentous time, a time that calls us to exert all our powers, and among the many of them, *the mind is the greatest,* and great care should be taken to improve it with diligence. Neglect will plunge us into deep degradation, and keep us grovelling in the dust, while our enemies will rejoice and say, we do not believe they (colored people) have any minds; if they have, they are unsusceptible of improvement.

My sisters, shall we bring this reproach on ourselves? Awake and slumber no more—arise, put on your armor; ye daughters of America and stand forth in the field of improvement. You can all do some good.

It was indeed a "momentous time." Only three months earlier, in May 1837, members of the Ladies' Literary Society had participated with almost 200 women in the First Anti-Slavery Convention of American Women. The convention was the culmination of five years of city-by-city organization of women's antislavery societies. The abolitionist movement in the 1830s, which was sparked by the publication of the Liberator,* differed from its all-white predecessors in two important ways. It called for the immediate, rather than the gradual, abolition of slavery and invited blacks and women to join in the good work.

The first Female Anti-Slavery Society was organized by a group of black women in Salem, Massachusetts, on February 22, 1832. Their constitution, excerpted below, combined mutual improvement and a commitment to antislavery.

CONSTITUTION OF THE FEMALE ANTI-SLAVERY SOCIETY OF SALEM

We, the undersigned, females of color, of the commonwealth of Massachusetts being duly convinced of the importance of union and morality, have associated ourselves together for our mutual improvement, and to promote the welfare of our color, as far as consistent with the means of this Society, therefore we adopt the following resolutions.

Resolved, That this Society be supported by voluntary contributions, a part to be appropriated for the purchasing of books, &c.: the other to be reserved until a sufficient sum be accumulated, which shall then be deposited in a bank for the relief of the needy.

Resolved, That the meetings of this Society shall commence and conclude with prayer and singing. Any member who wishes to speak, is allowed the privilege: when any member speaks, there shall be no interruption.

Resolved, That the Society shall be governed by a President, Vice President, Corresponding Secretary. Recording Secretary, Treasurer, And Librarian, who are hereafter to be instructed in the duties of their offices.

MARY A. BATTYS, *President*
E. A. DREW, *Vice President*
CHARLOTTE BELL, *Corresponding Sec'y*
ELEANOR C. HARVEY, *Treasurer*
DOROTHY C. BATTYS, *Librarian*

Conventions of American Women were also held in 1838 and 1839. Separate conventions were abandoned, however, after women

---

*The Liberator was started by William Lloyd Garrison on January 1, 1831, but blacks had been politicized earlier by *David Walker's Appeal* (1829) and by the Conventions of Colored Men held in 1829 and 1830.

were admitted on an equal basis to the American Anti-Slavery Society. The female societies continued with their work, and women circulated tens of thousands of petitions, flooding Congress and state legislatures with their appeals. They held annual fairs, which started as local sales of "useful and fancy articles" sewn by members but became, by the 1850s, elaborate and fashionable gatherings with lectures, concerts, and tables of goods from abroad.* These fairs called for managerial skills of a high order and provided substantial amounts of money for antislavery publications. Early meetings of the female societies were addressed by men; tentatively at first, then with increasing confidence, women began to speak in public. The story of the female antislavery societies as a training ground for the woman's rights movement has been told, but a study of black women abolitionists is overdue. They were present from the first days of the struggle, working alongside whites wherever they were welcomed.† Of the eighteen women who signed the constitution of the Philadelphia Female Anti-Slavery Society in December 1833 at least seven were black; one, Margaretta Forten, was elected recording secretary. At the Convention of American Women held in New York in 1837, perhaps one out of ten of the members was black. Grace Douglass was elected a vice-president and Sarah L. Forten contributed a poem that the convention printed:

> We are thy sisters. God has truly said,
> That of one blood the nations he has made.
> O, Christian woman! in a Christian land,
> Canst thou unblushing read this great command?
> Suffer the wrongs which wring our inmost heart,
> To draw one throb of pity on thy part!
> Our skins may differ, but from thee we claim
> A sister's privilege and a sister's name.

At the convention in Philadelphia in 1838, two black delegates from Boston were chosen as officers. Susan Paul served as a vice-president and Martha V. Ball‡ as secretary, while Sarah Douglass was elected convention treasurer. At the third and last convention the

---

*The Boston women held their first fair in 1834; a year later Philadelphia followed with a fair that raised $300.

†In Philadelphia and Boston as well as in Rochester, New York, and Salem and Lynn, Massachusetts, female antislavery societies were integrated. In New York City, after the two leading societies turned them away, black women formed their own organization.

‡Susan Paul was a counselor of the Boston Female Anti-Slavery Society, Martha V. Ball its recording secretary and her sister, Lucy M. Ball, served for a time as treasurer. In 1839 when the abolitionist movement was divided by factional disputes, the Balls were among the leaders of a conservative faction which broke away to form the Massachusetts Female Emancipation Society.

following year, Grace Douglass was again a vice-president, Martha Ball a secretary, and Sarah Douglass, treasurer.

Names and numbers, however, cannot convey the quality of the relationships that developed across the color line, relationships that ranged from grudging acceptance to intimate friendship. In the decades before the Civil War, it took strength and sensitivity on the part of both sets of "sisters" to meet and socialize. Black women steeled themselves to endure snubs and condescension and whites faced social ostracism; both found that the battle against racism sometimes called for physical as well as moral courage. Their most trying moments came at the 1838 convention when a mob, tacitly backed by the legal authorities, overran Philadelphia. Stones were thrown through the windows of Pennsylvania Hall where they were meeting; crowds blocked the doors, threatening the delegates as they walked to their lodgings. That night the hall was burned down because, said a spokesman for the mob, it had housed "an audience promiscuously mixed up of blacks and whites, sitting together in amalgamated ease." The women responded to the rioters by meeting again the next morning to reiterate their stand on "amalgamation."

Resolved,

That prejudice against color is the very spirit of slavery, sinful in those who indulge it, and is the fire which is consuming the happiness and energies of the free people of color.

That it is, therefore, the duty of abolitionists to identify themselves with these oppressed Americans, by sitting with them in places of worship, by appearing with them in our streets, by giving them our countenance in steam-boats and stages, by visiting them at their homes and encouraging them to visit us, receiving them as we do our white fellow citizens.

Some cautious abolitionists, including Dr. Joseph Parrish, president of the Pennsylvania Abolition Society, opposed the women's resolution, fearing that it would further antagonize white Philadelphians. In a letter to her son-in-law, Lucretia Mott* described Parrish's efforts to have the resolution rescinded.

Our proceedings tho' not yet published have greatly aroused our pseudo-abolitionists, as well as alarmed such timid ones as our good Dr. Parrish who has left no means untried to induce us to expunge from

---

*Lucretia Mott (1793–1880) was a pioneer of the antislavery and woman's rights movement. Ignoring social barriers, she invited black friends to tea and dinner as early as 1833. During the 1838 and 1839 conventions, black delegates from Boston stayed with the Motts.

our minutes a resolution relating to social intercourse with our colored brethren—in vain we urged the great departure from order & propriety in such a procedure after the Convention had separated—he and Charles Townsend were willing to take the responsibility if the publishing committee would consent to have it withdrawn—and when he failed in this effort, he called some of the respectable part of the colored people together at Robert Douglass' and advised them not to accept such intercourse as was proffered them & to issue a disclaimer of any such wish. This they have not yet done—but it has caused not a little excitement among us.

Before the convention assembled the following year, Philadelphia's mayor called on Mott to ask that the women "avoid unnecessary walking with colored people." Her reply, as reported in the "Proceedings," was that "we had never made a parade of walking with colored people and should do as we have done before—walk with them as occasion offered:—that she was expecting delegates from Boston of that complexion, and should, probably accompany them to the place of meeting." During the convention, delegates wrote a special four-page "Appeal to American Women on Prejudice Against Color," which reminded readers of "the indignities and the outrages" to which blacks were subjected. "Would it be believed that our museums, our literary and scientific lectures, our public exhibitions, which contribute so much to the intelligence of a people, are generally closed against this portion of our population?" The "Appeal" asked, "on behalf of our colored sisters, for an equal participation with yourselves, in every social advantage, moral, literary and religious."

Black women did not often take the floor, but on the final day Clarissa C. Lawrence, vice-president of the Salem Female Anti-Slavery Society, responded to the resolutions against racism. She was attending her first Convention of American Women, and she spoke with obvious feeling.

We meet the monster prejudice *everywhere*. We have not power to contend with it, we are so down-trodden. We cannot elevate ourselves. You must aid us. We have been brought up in ignorance; our parents were ignorant, they could not teach us. We want light; we ask it, and it is denied us. Why are we thus treated? Prejudice is the cause. It kills its thousands every day; it follows us everywhere, even to the grave; but, blessed be God! it stops there. You must pray it down. Faith and prayer will do wonders in the anti-slavery cause. Place yourselves, dear friends, in our stead. We are blamed for not filling useful places in society; but give us light, give us learning, and see then what places we can occupy. Go on, I entreat you. A brighter day is dawning. I bless God that the young are interested in this cause. It is worth coming all the way from Massachusetts, to see what I have seen here.

The methods of fund raising and political organizing that evolved in the female antislavery societies soon came into widespread use. The handbill below is an example.

The Ladies (of color) of the town of Frankfort propose giving a **FAIR**, at the house of **Mrs. RILLA HARRIS,** (*alias*, Simpson,) on Thursday evening next, for benevolent purposes, under the superintendence of **Mrs. Rilla Harris.**

All the delicacies of the season will be served up in the most palatable style----such as *Ice Creams, Cakes, Lemonades, Jellies, Fruits, Nuts, &c. &c.*

It is hoped, as the proceeds are to be applied to benevolent purposes, that the citizens generally will turn out and aid in the enterprise.

JULY 6, 1847.

(Clements Library, University of Michigan)

Black women who had helped to raise money for the Liberator *also organized the Woman's Association of Philadelphia to support Frederick Douglass's weekly, the* North Star. *The preamble to their constitution follows:*

Whereas, the necessity of an efficient organization for the support of our cause has long been apparent and its absence deplored; and

Whereas, believing Self-Elevation to be the only true issue upon which to base our efforts as an oppressed portion of the American people; and believing that the success of our cause depends mainly upon Self-Exertion and that the Press and Public Lecturer are the most powerful means by which an end so desirable can be attained: Therefore, we do agree to form ourselves into an Association to be known as the Woman's Association of Philadelphia, the object of which shall be, to hold Fairs or Bazaars for the support of the Press and Public Lecturers, devoted to the Elevation of the Colored People in the United States.

Black New Yorkers followed with a North Star Association, which held fairs in 1850 and 1851. Several of the women who signed their solicitation were former members of the Ladies' Literary Society. New York women also led the way in raising money for charitable purposes. Their most successful fund-raising event in the antebellum years was a fair in 1860 for the benefit of New York's Colored Orphan Asylum. * *The managers of the fair (all but one clergymen's wives) listed themselves as Mrs. J. N. Gloucester, Mrs. C. B. Ray, Mrs. A. N. Freeman, and Mrs. W. J. Wilson. Their use of their husbands' rather than their own first names suggests that they were more conventional† than the black women in other cities. Their fair, described at great length in the* Weekly Anglo-African, *was not only a successful financial undertaking but an impressive social event.*

The long-contemplated Colored Orphan Asylum Fair was one of the gayest and most elegant assemblages, perhaps, ever witnessed in the vicinity of New York. In speaking of the assemblage, a [white] gentleman remarked that it was really the finest he had ever seen. "I wish," said another "that the entire white population could, by some means, this night see this people. They would go from hence divested of most, if not all of their foolish prejudices." "What a splendid company!" said a lady, "Are these the colored people we are in the daily habit of seeing?"

Such are but a few of the many like expressions which fell from the lips of the Anglo-Americans‡ while the fair was in progress. The room is spacious, and was elegantly lighted. The Brooklyn branch of the managers were all decked in pretty calico gowns, all, or nearly all, of the same stripe, giving thereby a most picturesque effect. The various stands bore inscriptions which informed the visitors from whence they hailed. On one side we noticed the ladies of New York City, while

*Founded by white women, the orphanage housed more than 1,200 children when it was burned down during the 1863 Draft Riot.

†*Conventional* is a relative word. First Directress Emma Gloucester, for instance, was also a friend and supporter of John Brown. A letter from her enclosing a check and her "most ardent wishes" for his success was found in Brown's carpetbag when he was captured at Harpers Ferry.

‡Anglo-African and Anglo-American were the newspaper's designations for blacks and whites.

opposite were the ladies of Brooklyn. We also noticed a table of very beautiful articles bearing the inscription of Troy, and another of Oberlin, Ohio. Perhaps no one fair ever held by our people ever realized so fine a profit to the beneficiaries. From all we have been able to gather, the figures stand somewhat as follows:

Total proceeds of fair and exhibition $1,400
Total expenses 300
Net proceeds $1,100

We congratulate ourselves and the public upon the results of the fair and the fact that we have women among us able to accomplish so much. These women deserve the highest praise that can be awarded them for this noble work and the faithful manner in which they have accomplished it.

TEN

The Antislavery Ladies

WHEN REFORMERS FROM *England or New England visited Philadelphia they were first taken to Independence Hall and Fairmont Park, and then to 92 Lombard Street, the home of James and Charlotte Forten. A revolutionary war veteran, Forten was a sailmaker who was worth $100,000 by the 1830s. There were richer men in Philadelphia, but none whose great-grandfather had been an African slave. For two generations, the Fortens's three-story brick residence was a symbol of black achievement and a home-away-from-home for abolitionists. Overshadowed by her husband, Charlotte Forten (1784–1884) was described by one reformer as an "excellent motherly wife." She was also a competent manager who presided over a large household with ease and grace, brought up five children, and still found time to participate in the work of the Philadelphia Female Anti-Slavery Society.*

Along with her daughters and her intended daughter-in-law (Mary Wood, who married Robert B. Forten in 1836), Charlotte Forten was a founder of the society and a consistent supporter of its activities. Her daughters, Margaretta, Harriet, and Sarah Louise, were tutored at home, learning perhaps as much at the long family dinner table in the company of Harriet Martineau, William Lloyd Garrison, and John

Charlotte Forten, Sr., matriarch of the Forten family, lived to be 100 years old. *(Moorland-Spingarn Research Center, Howard University)*

Greenleaf Whittier, as they did from their schoolbooks. Whittier who visited the Fortens often when he was editing the Pennsylvania Free-man wrote a poem "To the Daughters of James Forten," which was published in the Liberator.

Margaretta Forten (1808–75), who for at least thirty years taught a small private school in Philadelphia, was an officer, usually recording secretary or treasurer, of the Female Anti-Slavery Society from the society's inception until its dissolution after the Civil War. She was also a supporter of the woman's rights movement. Harriet Forten (1810–75) married Robert Purvis, who was in the forefront of antislavery and Underground Railroad activities. Purvis who inherited his father-in-law's mantle as a model of black achievement, became president of the Pennsylvania Anti-Slavery Society and of the Pennsylvania branch of the Underground Railroad. *Their home in Byberry, some fifteen miles from Philadelphia, had comfortable parlors for their friends and a special room, reached only by trap door, for runaway slaves. Sallie Holley, an abolitionist lecturer, visited the Purvises in 1852, and wrote:*

> I am now staying at the elegant country home of Robert Purvis. It may be called "Saints' Rest" for here all the abolitionists find that "the wicked cease from troubling and the weary are at rest." The house and extensive grounds are in tasteful English style. Mr. Purvis is a coloured man, but so light that no stranger would suspect it. His wife is very lady-like in manners and conversation; something of the ease and blandness of a southern lady. The style of living here is quite uncommonly rich and elegant.

At Byberry, Harriet Purvis was hostess on a grand scale, tendering hospitality to reformers as her mother had done and ministering to the needs of thousands of fugitives. In addition to her own children, she was a surrogate mother to her brother Robert's small daughter, Charlotte, after Mary Wood Forten died. A delegate to the 1838 and 1839 Anti-Slavery Conventions of American Woman, Harriet Purvis was active in abolitionist and woman's rights affairs until her death in 1875.

Sarah Louise Forten (b. 1814) was the most literary of the three sisters. Signing herself "Magawisca" and "Ada," she contributed more than a dozen creditable poems and essays to the Liberator *and the* Abolitionist *between 1831 and 1837. At least one, "The Grave of the Slave," was set to music by Frank Johnson, a black band leader, and was often heard at antislavery functions. A founder of the Female Anti-Slavery Society and a member of its Board of Managers, she helped organize antislavery sewing circles and worked on the annual fairs. In 1837–38, she married Joseph Purvis, Robert Purvis's brother, and moved to a country home near Byberry. Her letters to Elizabeth Whittier, sister of the poet, give the flavor of antislavery Philadelphia as seen from 92 Lombard Street.*

My Dear Friend: Philadelphia, March 23, 1835
   I am now hastily penning a few lines to inform you of the visit of our noble friend and advocate George Thompson.*. He has paid us two visits, and four admirable lectures from him have quite captivated our

---

*A British abolitionist who frequently lectured in the United States. His scheduled appearance at a meeting of the Boston Female Anti-Slavery Society seven months later precipitated a riot.

good citizens; never before have we listened to such surprising powers of oratory—never has there been such an awakening of conscience—his eloquence surpasses any thing ever before heard. On Saturday last he addressed the Female Anti-Slavery Society, and spoke to the hearts most feelingly. After the address fifty six ladies signed their names to our constitution; so you see this was doing a great deal among our pleghmatic people. I have had many opportunities of being in Mr. Thompsons Society—and find him a most delightful and companionable person. He is witty—full of anecdote;—and very lively. He staid at my Sisters—Mrs. Purvis—and we really loved him—not only for his greatness—but for his goodness. He has had large audiences each night of his lectures—and so crowded was the church the evening on which he commenced his admirable address on St. Domingo that the gallery —from the tremendous pressure had nearly given way—the alarm was excessive—and the meeting adjourned in great confusion. This was truly unfortunate, as the accident occured in the middle part of this most admirable subject. Tomorrow evening he intends to finish his lecture. I anticipate great pleasure and information from it.

You will scarcely be able to read this hasty scrawl. I am now writing with four or five gentlemen (all abolitionists) talking about Thompson. Of course I cant help giving my ears to them, while my eyes *only* rest upon the paper. I've stoped just now to join in a hearty burst of laughter, elicited by the repetition of one of Mr. T's delightful anecdotes. Mr. Garrison is also in the City—and his brother-in-law Mr. Benson—the latter gentleman is staying at Mr. Purvis'—so you perceive that we are indeed highly favoured in having three such highly valued friends with us. I send this letter by Mr. Garrison to put in the Post office at Boston. Will you have us kindly remembered to your family. My Fathers regards to your Brother—and believe me always your friend

Sarah L. Forten

PS,

I have been looking over this badly written letter and am almost ashamed to send it—if I had time I would really write another yet you will forgive it and attribute its defects to the haste in which it was "thrown off"—rather than to any other cause. I recall with feelings of shame, Hannah More's* advice to young Ladies—wherein she recom-

---

*Hannah More's *Strictures on the Modern System of Female Education*, published in 1799, was read by women for many decades afterward. More was the first person to enunciate "the cult of true womanhood"—that being a wife and mother was a woman's "profession."

mends them, "never to write a letter in a careless or slovenly manner —it is a sign of ill breeding or indifference" &c.&c. *My* excuse is haste —and one which I hope will for this time, at least, be accepted.

Yours SLF

My Dear Elizabeth: Philadelphia, December 25, 1836

I have delayed replying to your kind letter until now because I wished to give you an account of our Anti Slavery *Fair*—and I knew you would be gratified by a description of it—and of the good success we had. Our Society have been making Preparations for the last four months to get up this Sale—and many very beautiful fancy productions did they manufacture for the occasion. We hired the Fire Mens Hall in North St—below Arch—and decorated it with evergreens—and flowers—and had it brilliantly lighted. There was six tables—including a refreshment Table—on which most of the eatables were presented —three large Pound Cakes—Oranges—and Grapes were given to us —so our expenses were not great—and the proceeds amounted to more than three hundred Dollars. We only had the Hall for a day and two evenings—so you may see we done well for so short a time. There was twelve Ladies Superintending the Tables. We had a Post Office opened—for letters to be distributed at 12½ cts a piece. A young lady and myself were superintending *Post Mistresses*—and we delivered upwards of one hundred letters—nearly one half of which we were obliged to pen ourselves. We were as busy as we could be all the time —and much amusement was afforded by the dispatch with which the mails arrived. I wish you could have been here—to contribute and receive a share of the general satisfaction. Our excellent friend and advocate Gerrit Smith has been here—and we are more than gratified by an acquaintance with him. He has brought his Wife and Daughter* a girl of fourteen years—to spend the Winter in our City—and we are delighted with them both. Miss Smith's health has not been good and her Parents think a change of air will be of service to her. Mrs. S is one of the Plainest woman in her dress I ever saw—I learn that she devotes nearly *all* her income to benevolent purposes. This is so praiseworthy that I could not forbear to mention it to you. She is also one of these lovely goodnatured looking women who takes ones heart on the instant.

As this is Christmas and two or three of my Relatives have come

*Gerrit Smith's daughter, Elizabeth Smith Miller, was the originator of the bloomer costume. She first wore her short dress and Turkish trousers when she visited her cousin Elizabeth Cady Stanton in 1851.

in to pass the day with us—I am unable to arrange my letter in better order—for a half dozen voices are holding forth on different subjects —making it rather impossible to write in a collected manner. You will therefore receive my excuses for whatever errors you should find. Please accept from myself and family the usual congratulations of the Season with the hope that you may be spared to see many returns of it. I send you one of my Brother Robert Purvis's addresses.

I will no longer intrude upon your time My Dear Friend—but ask you to write me *only* when you are at leisure

Your Friend

Sarah L Forten

Shortly before the first Anti-Slavery Convention of American Women, Angelina Grimké* asked Sarah Forten to tell her of the effect prejudice had had on her life. Sarah Forten replied:

Esteemed Friend: Philadelphia, April 15, 1837

In making a reply to the questions proposed by you, I might truly advance the excuse of inability; but you well know how to compassionate the weakness of one who has written but little on the subject, and who has untill very lately lived and acted more for herself than for the good of others. I confess that I am wholly indebted to the Abolition cause for arousing me from apathy and indifference, shedding light into a Mind which has been too long wrapt in selfish darkness.

In reply to your question—of the "effect of Predjudice" on myself, I must acknowledge that it has often embittered my feelings, particularly when I recollect that we are the innocent victims of it for you are well aware that it originates from dislike to the color of the skin, as much as from the degradation of Slavery. I am peculiarly sensitive on this point, and consequently seek to avoid as much as possible mingling with those who exist under its influence. I must also own that *it* has often engendered feelings of discontent and mortification in my breast when I saw that many were preferred before me, who by education— birth—or worldly circumstances were no better than myself—thier sole claim to notice depending on the superior advantage of being *White*—but I am striving to live above such heart burnings and will learn to "bear and forbear" believing that a spirit of forbearance under such evils is all that we as a people can well exert.

*Angelina Grimké (1805–79) and her sister Sarah (1792–1873) were the daughters of South Carolina slave owners. Rejecting slavery, they became leaders in the abolitionist and woman's rights movements. In 1838 Angelina Grimké married abolitionist Theodore Weld.

No doubt but there has always existed the same amount of predjudice in the minds of Americans towards the descendants of Africa. Even our professed friends have not yet rid themselves of it. To some of them it clings like a dark mantle obscuring their many virtues and choking up the avenues to higher and nobler sentiments. I recollect the words of one of the best and least predjudiced men in the Abolition ranks. Ah said he, "I can recall the time when in walking with a Colored brother, the darker the night, the better Abolitionist was I". He does not say so now, but my friend, how much of this leaven still lingers in the hearts of our white brethren and sisters is oftentimes made manifest to us—but when we recollect what great sacrifices to public sentiment they are called upon to make, we cannot wholly blame them.

For our own family—we have to thank a kind Providence for placing us in a situation that has hitherto prevented us from falling under the weight of this evil. We feel it but in a slight degree compared with many others. We are not much dependant upon the tender mercies of our enemies—always having resources within ourselves to which we can apply. We are not disturbed in our social relations—we never travel far from home and seldom go to public places unless quite sure that admission is free to all—therefore, we meet with none of these mortifications which might otherwise ensue. I would recommend to my Colored friends to follow our example and they would be spared some very painful realities.

My Father bids me tell you that White and Colored men have worked with him from his first commencement in business. One man (a white) has been with him nearly thirty seven years—very few of his hired men have been foreigners—nearly all are natives of this country—the greatest harmony and good feeling exists between them. He has usually 16 or twenty journeymen, one half of whom are White—but I am not aware of any white Sailmaker who employs colored men. I think it should be reciprocal—do not you?

Do you know wether the Ladies have fixed on the day for holding their Convention? There will probably be a large delegation from our society. My sisters purpose going but not as Delegates. I presume there will be a sale of fancy articles there, as we were requested to send some of our work.

Shall I apologize for taking up such a large share of your valuable time as will be requisite to peruse this long letter? But in writing to you I forget that I address you for the first time. We *all* feel deeply sensible of your labors of love for our people, and we trust that you may continue to receive strength from above to sustain you in your trials. My Parents and Sisters unite with me in affection to you and your excellent sister.

Yours affectionately

Sarah L. Forten

I have seen by your letter to S[arah] Douglass that you were kind enough to make application for us to stay at Mr. Greens house. We thank you for this attention to our wants. We expect to be able to avail ourselves of the hospitality of Rev. P. Williams* while in New York.

The Douglasses, like the Fortens, were sought by white travelers who wanted to meet blacks of culture and breeding. "In company with Lucretia Mott I visited several families of negroes," wrote Fredrika Bremer of Sweden, author of Homes of the New World. *"I was most interested by a young mulatto woman, Sarah Douglass, a charming girl,† with a remarkably intelligent countenance. She was the teacher of a school of about sixty children, negroes and mulattoes. She herself was one of the most beautiful examples of true cultivation among the colored people."*

Brought up in the middle class, Sarah Douglass might have accepted domesticity as her vocation had it not been for the steady erosion of the civil rights of black Pennsylvanians. As the state's black population increased, legislators considered a ban on black immigration and a forced exodus to Liberia. In 1832 when a bill was introduced that would have required all blacks to carry passes, Sarah Douglass was propelled into public affairs. At a mental feast she proposed that "reading and conversation should be altogether directed to the subject of slavery," explaining:

One short year ago, how different were my feelings on the subject of slavery! It is true, the wail of the captive sometimes came to my ear in the midst of my happiness, and caused my heart to bleed for his wrongs; but, alas! the impression was as evanescent as the early cloud and morning dew. I had formed a little world of my own, and cared not to move beyond its precincts. But how was the scene changed

*Friendship, business, and family ties linked leading black families. The Reverend Peter Williams, an Episcopalian clergyman, had been an associate of Paul Cuffe and James Forten. His daughter, Amy Matilda, married Charles Lenox Remond and was active in Salem antislavery circles.

†Sarah Douglass who was sometimes uncomfortable in her role of token black might have lifted an eyebrow at being called "girl." She was forty-four years old when Bremer visited her.

when I beheld the oppressor lurking on the border of my own peaceful home! I saw his iron hand stretched forth to seize me as his prey, and the cause of the slave became my own. I started up, and with one mighty effort threw from me the lethargy which had covered me as a mantle for years; and determined, by the help of the Almighty, to use every exertion in my power to elevate the character of my wronged and neglected race.

A leader in black women's organizations, from the Female Literary Association of 1831 to the Woman's Association of 1849 and the Sarah M. Douglass Literary Circle ten years later, Douglass was also the most active black member of the Philadelphia Female Anti-Slavery Society. At various times she served on its Board of Managers and Fair Committee and was librarian and recording secretary. Her minutes of a typical meeting follow.

At a Stated meeting of the Phil^a Female Anti-Slavery Society held November 8th 1838—finding our usual place of meeting closed against us, we adjourned to the school room of Sarah Douglass who informed that there had been some dispute among the members of the Phoenix Hose company about letting us have the use of their room, which induced the committee who had charge of renting the Hall to resign.

The minutes of the last meeting and of the Board of Managers were read and adopted. Teresa Himber reported that a large number of the Delegates attended the meeting of the State Society at Coatesville.

The Committee appointed to procure lecturers to address a public meeting reported that there was a large meeting which was addressed by Charles Burleigh and William Chase.

A letter was read from the Secretary of the County Society informing that a meeting of the Society would be held on Tuesday evening the 20th inst at 6½ o clock and requesting this Society to send a large delegation.

Mg adj.

Above all, Sarah M. Douglass was a teacher, the first in a long line of outstanding black educators. Philadelphia's segregated public schools were overcrowded, dirty—and taught by whites. Those families who could afford the tuition sent their children to private schools. After teaching for a time in New York, Douglass returned to Philadel-

phia to open a female academy, the only school in the city, and for a time in the country, that offered a high school education to black girls. When the Reverend Samuel Cornish, editor of the Colored American, visited the city in *1837*, he reported:

We cannot, in justice to our own feelings and the merits of the institution, close this article without some special notice of Miss Sarah Douglass' school. Wednesday last, we passed two of the most gratifying, satisfactory hours of our life with Miss Douglass and her *interesting, improving scholars.* The school numbers over 40, selected from our best families, where their morals and manners are equally subjects of care, and of deep interest. All the branches of a good and solid female education are taught in Miss Douglass' school, together with many of the more ornamental sciences, calculated to expand the youthful mind, refine the taste, and assist in purifying the heart.

Miss Douglass has a well-selected and valuable cabinet of shells and minerals, well-arranged and labelled. She has, also, a mind richly furnished with a knowledge of these sciences, and she does not fail *through them* to lead up the minds of her pupils, through Nature, to Nature's God.

Keeping the school going was always a financial struggle. When she told members of the Female Anti-Slavery Society, in 1838, that the school "did not yield sufficient income to continue," they voted to take it over, paying her a salary of $300 a year and spending an additional $200 on rent, new desks, and other school expenses. The arrangement continued until 1840 when Douglass, probably wanting to be independent, asked the society to relinquish its management of the school. The minutes recorded:

A letter from Sarah Douglass was read, announcing her intention to withdraw her school from our charge and expressing her gratitude for the assistance which we have afforded her—Lucretia Mott and Sarah Pugh were appointed a committee to confer with her on the subject.

When the committee failed to convince her to change her mind, the members resolved:

That this Society deeply regret the withdrawal of the school taught by Sarah Douglass from their charge, the supervision & maintenance of which has been a source of pleasure to them, & that they wish for it a continuance of prosperity and usefulness under her care.

Since the society used her schoolroom for its meetings, it continued to subsidize her to some extent, paying from $90 to $120 a year rent until 1849. In 1853, after the Philadelphia Institute for Colored Youth was started under Quaker auspices, Douglass took over the girls' preparatory department. She taught at the Institute until her retirement in 1877. In addition to giving her pupils a "good English education," Douglass pioneered in science teaching, at first with her "cabinet of shells and minerals," and later with illustrated lectures on anatomy and physiology. Anatomy was a dark secret to most women until the 1840s when Paulina Wright lectured in the East and Midwest, using a female manikin which caused some members of her audience to faint when she unveiled it. Sarah Douglass trained herself in this new field by attending classes at the Female Medical College of Pennsylvania in 1852–53 and at Penn Medical University from 1855–58. In 1858 she gave a course of lectures to black women at her home; these were so successful that the following year she lectured by request in New York. While the Weekly Anglo-African *defended the lectures against those "who argue that such knowledge is inconsistent with the delicacy of woman's character" members of her audience resolved:*

That our most hearty thanks are due Mrs. Douglass for imparting to us a knowledge of ourselves and enabling us to perceive the great importance of womanly health.

That women owe it not only to themselves, but to their posterity to study intimately their structures and those natural laws pertaining to their bodily and mental well-being.

That we specially appreciate the lecture "Origin of Life," to which we have just listened, with the profoundest feelings of veneration—not only for the elegant and chaste language in which her thoughts were expressed, but also for the modest and dignified manner in which it has been given.

Living out her long life in the Quaker city of Philadelphia and associating both professionally and socially with Friends, Sarah Douglass struggled constantly to conceal the anger and pain that their color prejudice evoked. There were exceptions, of course—Lucretia Mott, who early offered a hand in friendship, Abby Kelley, and Sarah and Angelina Grimké. After the tumultuous convention of antislavery women in 1838 when Kelley addressed a "promiscuous audience"* for the first time, Douglass wrote her:

---

*A promiscuous audience in the 1830s meant an audience made up of both men and women.

My Dear Abby: Philadelphia, May 18, 1838

Will you accept this little volume in token of my ardent love; in token of my respect and gratitude to you, for having stood forth so nobly in defence of woman and the slave.

May the Lord Jesus Christ bless you and the noble band of New England women who came up with firm hearts and true to our convention. Our hearts have been cheered and animated and strengthened by your presence. Altho our enemies call us ungrateful, believe me dear friend, it is *vile slander,* we fully appreciate your kindness. Do write to me sometimes, it rejoices my very soul to meet with an Abolitionist who has turned her back on prejudice.

Affectionately yours,
Sarah M. Douglass

Sarah Grimké who was her senior by fourteen years broke through Sarah Douglass's armor and got her to talk of humiliating encounters with whites. In several letters, excerpted below, she explained why her mother, who had adopted the dress and language of Friends, had never joined the Society:

While her children were in their infancy she had a great concern to become a member of Friends Society not only because she was fully convinced of the excellence of the principles professed by that society, but because she earnestly desired that her children should receive the guarded education Friends give to theirs. She mentioned her concern to a Friend who said do not apply, you will only have your feelings wounded. Friends will not receive you. Thus admonished, and feeling that prejudice had closed the doors against her, she did not make her concern known to the Society. There was nothing but my Mother's complexion in the way to prevent her being a member, she was highly intelligent & pious; her whole life blameless.

As you request to know particularly about Arch Street Meeting, I may say that there is a bench set apart at that meeting for our people, that my mother and myself were told to sit there, and that a friend sat at either end of the bench to prevent white persons from sitting there. And even when a child my soul was made sad with hearing five or six times during the course of one meeting this language of remonstrance addressed to those who were willing to sit by us. "This bench is for the black people." "This bench is for the people of color." I have not been in Arch Street meeting for four years, but my mother goes once a week and frequently she has a whole long bench to herself. Mother does not recollect distinctly the circumstances that occurred at the New York Mtg. but thinks this is the substance. After she had been in Mtg. sometime a Friend came in & sat by her, & asked her who she lived with. Mother said she did not live with any one. The Fd. then said that the colored people sat up stairs "as Fds. do not like to sit by thy color" & added she had no objection herself to sit by her, but that when she came again she had better sit up stairs. She did not go to the Mtg. again; she was attending the Women's Convention in N. Y. 1837 & was a stranger there, it was the first time she attempted to go to Fds. Mtg there.

When Sarah Douglass was teaching in New York she too was ostracized.

I had been attending meeting one month when a friend accosted me thus, "Does thee go out ahouse cleaning." I looked at her with astonishment, my eyes filled with tears & I answered no. "What does thee do then". "I teach school," "Oh then thee's better off". Judge what were my feelings, a stranger in a strange land, think of the time, the place & this the first salutation I received in a house consecrated to Him. I wept during the whole of that mtg. & for many succeeding sabbaths & I believe they were not the tears of wounded pride alone.

The two Sarahs corresponded for almost forty years, confiding their most intimate problems to each other. Along with other professional black women, Sarah Douglass did not marry until late in life. She was close to fifty years old when the Reverend William Douglass, rector of St. Thomas Episcopal Church and a widower with nine children, began courting her. Five years older than she, he was described as attractive and diffident, with a musical voice and a tendency to pun. When she sent some of his letters to Sarah Grimké, the latter replied:

Dearest Sarah—   [1854–55]
So far as I can judge from the letters I think Mr. D must be a good man, a pleasant companion, an affectionate friend. I greatly admire too the sprightly mirthful tone of some of his letters, such as that about your age, and sadly was I surprised to find that you were displeased at his innocent raillery. Dear you need a guard here, you have lived so long without the animating influences of cheerful companionship, that you are morbidly sensitive to an innocent & right degree of sportiveness, it seems to you unbecoming; but try to overcome this prejudice, wear yourself the bridal robes of cheerfulness, yea of pleasant mirthfulness, & you will find it diffuses a charm over your own life & over all around

you. Can you bring me acquainted with Mr. Douglass, I should greatly love to see him & with your permission to converse with him relative to your union.

Yours most affy S.M.G.

Still unsure about marrying, Sarah Douglass again consulted her friend. Her letter to Sarah Grimké has not survived, but Grimké's response makes its contents evident.

Dear Sarah: Newark, [New Jersey,] June 19 [1855]

I am glad you can reciprocate Mr. Ds affection, and that you have told him so. Oh Sarah how earnestly I hope you may find in him a husband in spirit & in truth. I do not wonder you shrink from sexual intercourse, yet, I suppose in married life, it is as much the natural expression of affection as the warm embrace & ardent kiss. Time will familiarize you with the idea, and the more intimate your union with Mr. D. the less you will turn from it. I am sorry you feel as if you could not marry until a certain time has elapsed, there is a right time to do right things, seek for that dear Sarah, be governed by the still small voice within.

Yours in haste affy S.M.G.

Sarah and William Douglass were married on July 23, 1855, but they did not live happily ever after. Perhaps he was more orthodox in religion and had less abolitionist fervor than she; perhaps she was too humorless and unbending. Whatever the reasons, several of Sarah Grimké's letters spoke of Douglass's "grievous trials" and "the painful results" of her marriage; Douglass herself later said of her friend, "How she comforted me during the years I was in that School of bitter discipline, the old Parsonage of St. Thomas." Nevertheless, when William Douglass died in 1861, his widow wrote in a letter recounting his last days:

In sound judgment, in power of mind, in a richly cultivated intellect, my husband was greatly my superior. I gloried in his superiority! He had his weak points, it is true, yet where he was *weak* I was *strong,* and so we held each other's hands during life's journey.

When Sarah Grimké died in 1873, Sarah Douglass continued to correspond with Angelina Grimké, her husband, Theodore Weld, and their son Charles whom she had known since his infancy. She was almost seventy and still teaching when she wrote the following letter to Charles Weld.

Philadelphia, June 1, 1876

Oh, dear Charley, what a comfort your letters would be to me if I could only read them! I have to study over your letter in order to find out all about Mr. Garrison and the memoirs. I thank you for the sweet pieces of poetry you were so kind as to send me. Surely, Charley, you are gifted with a *great* gift.

I suffer greatly from rheumatism, cannot do any house work not even sweep a room. Yet I go to school every day because my bread depends on it. I ride part of the way because it is so difficult for me to walk. I enjoy being in school. I love my work, God wills me to do it. It is sweet work.

Alas, Charley you cannot go with me to Quaker meeting. My health is so poor I do not get to meeting often. You would not know me, since my 60th year I look old. Silver lines are shining in my once dark hair.

My two brothers* and myself make up the family. A woman comes on Saturdays and cleans up. My brothers help me a great deal. I do not know what I should do without them. I should be desolate indeed.

Thanks for telling me all about yourself. I always want to know how dear Aunt Sar's boy Charley is. Dear Father and Mother! I think I can see them in their loving beautiful old age. I am suffering severely today from pain in my hips but my heart is full of love to you, dear Charley. Fare thee well.

S. M. Douglass

By the 1840s black men had begun to lecture for the antislavery societies. As they toured the North and traveled to Canada and Great Britain, they were away for months, sometimes years, leaving their wives in charge of their households. Frederick Douglass, the most famous of the absentee husbands, had met Anna Murray (1813–82), a free woman, in Baltimore while he was still a slave. Two weeks after his escape, she came north and married him. Their daughter Rosetta (1839–1906), described her parents' first months together in My Mother As I Recall Her.

She had brought with her sufficient goods and chattels to fit up comfortably two rooms in her New Bedford home—a feather bed with pillows, bed linens, dishes, knives, forks and spoons, besides a well filled

---

*After Grace Douglass's death, Sarah kept house for her brothers, Robert Douglass, Jr., and James Douglass. Robert, Jr., was a portrait painter and daguerrotypist who studied in Philadelphia and in England. Despite his ability, his sister was usually the household's chief breadwinner.

trunk of wearing apparel for herself. She had previously sold one of her feather beds to assist in defraying the expenses of the flight from bondage. The early days in New Bedford were spent in daily toil, the wife at the wash board, the husband with saw, buck and axe. After the day of toil they would seek their little home of two rooms and the meal of the day that was most enjoyable was the supper nicely prepared by mother. Father frequently spoke of the neatly set table with its snowy white cloth—coarse tho' it was.

After three years of freedom, Douglass became a lecturing agent for the Massachusetts and American Anti-Slavery Societies. Naturally eloquent, he was a popular speaker and, by 1844, had written the best-selling Narrative of the Life of Frederick Douglass. *After its publication he spent twenty-one months lecturing in the British Isles. Although Anna Douglass received some income from sales of the* Narrative, *she supplemented it by working as a shoe binder. The industrial system that permitted women to labor in their homes at piece-work rates was ordinarily denied to blacks. Anna Douglass probably was able to obtain the work through her antislavery connections. Rosetta Douglass reported:*

Father built a nice little cottage in Lynn, Mass., and moved his family there, previously to making his first trip to Europe. It was then that mother with four children* struggled to maintain the family amid much that would dampen the courage of many a young woman of to-day. I had been taken to Albany by my father as a means of lightening the burden for mother. Abigail and Lydia Mott, cousins of Lucretia Mott, desired to have the care of me.

During the absence of my father, mother sustained her little family by binding shoes. Mother was a recognized co-worker in the A.S. Societies of Lynn and Boston. There was a weekly gathering of the women to prepare articles for the Annual A.S. Fair held in Faneuil Hall, Boston. At that time mother would spend the week in attendance having charge, in company of a committee of ladies, over the refreshments. It became the custom of the ladies of the Lynn society for each to take their turn in assisting mother in her household duties on the morning of the day that the sewing circle met so as to be sure of her meeting with them. It was mother's custom to put aside the earnings from a certain number of shoes she had bound as her donation to the A.S. cause. Being frugal and economic she was able to put by a

*Rosetta was born in June 1839, Lewis in 1840, Frederick, Jr., in 1842, and Charles in 1844. A fifth child, Annie, born in 1849, died ten years later.

portion of her earnings for a rainy day.

During [my father's] absence abroad, he sent, as he could, support for his family, and on his coming home he supposed there would be some bills to settle. One day while talking over their affairs, mother arose and quietly going to the bureau drawer produced a Bank book containing deposits of her own earnings—and not a debt had been contracted during his absence.

The greatest trial, perhaps, that mother was called upon to endure was the leaving her Massachusetts home for Rochester where father established the "North Star." The atmosphere in which she was placed lacked the genial cordiality that greeted her in Massachusetts. There were only the few that learned to know her, for she drew around herself a certain reserve, after meeting her new acquaintances that forbade any very near approach to her.

Rosetta was not being fully candid when she wrote this. The antislavery women of Rochester, a group that included Susan B. Anthony and Amy Post, Harriet Jacobs's friend, were no less cordial than the women of Lynn. Anna Douglass's reserve grew out of an ambiguous situation in her household. Her husband had returned from England in triumph, a leader of the antislavery movement and a public figure who was most attractive to women. Soon after the North Star *started, a cultivated Englishwoman, Julia Griffiths, arrived in Rochester to help edit the paper and to raise money for its support. For three years she lived with the Douglasses, reading aloud to Frederick when he was tired or depressed, worrying about his health, traveling with him when he lectured outside the city. Her letters often spoke of his "home trials." "Poor fellow!" she wrote on one occasion, "the quiet & repose he so much needs are very difficult for him to attain in his domestic circle."*

Anna Douglass wrote few letters because she never learned to write. During their first summer in Rochester, her husband hired a tutor for her and the children, but she gave up quickly, protesting that she was too old to learn. The following note, dictated to eleven-year-old Rosetta, was in sharp contrast to Frederick Douglass's eloquent and polished writings. It was addressed to Ruth Cox Adams, a former slave, who had lived with the Douglasses in Lynn.

My Dear Sister: Rochester, [New York], March 11, 1851

I was very glad to recive your letter. Frederick got home Saturday evening. We are all well I hope you are two. You said that you had heard that Frederick had moved to Albany. He has not and has not

Anna Murray Douglass in her middle years. *(Library of Congress)*

any thought of moveing. I showed the letter to Frederick that you wrote to me. He says he would be very happy to see you and hopes you will come and Perry and the babe.* I wish you would come two very much for I want see you about as bad as you want to see me. It is very cold this month. We think it is going to fix for a rain. George Thompson is hear and will lecture all this week. Lewis Frederick and Charles Rosetta and Annie are all well. Annie she is fast asleep upstairs all alone. I understand that your little Daughter is name is Ann so if you [come] and bring your babe their will be Ann and Annie. Frederick has gone to the office a little while ago. I said Annie was asleep but she has got up now. Frederick and Charlotte† sends thier love to you. From your sister

Anna Douglass

N.B. Please to write as soon as you get this and tell me when you start.

Griffiths left the Douglass household in 1852, but her friendship with Douglass and her activities on behalf of the paper continued—and so did the gossip surrounding their relationship. When William Lloyd Garrison, who was then estranged from Douglass, wrote that

---

*Ruth Cox's husband, Perry Adams, and her daughter, Matilda Ann.
†Charlotte was probably Anna Murray Douglass's sister.

Douglass's printing office contained "one whose influence has caused much unhappiness in his own household," he received an answer purporting to come from Anna Douglass, but which Rochester abolitionists were sure had been "concocted by Fred and Julia." It was published in the Liberator under the heading, "LETTER FROM MRS. DOUGLASS."

William Lloyd Garrison: Rochester, November 21, 1853
    Sir,—It is not true, that the presence of a certain person in the office of Frederick Douglass causes unhappiness in his family. Please insert this in your next paper.
Anna Douglass.

Anna Douglass, who was described by one visitor as "dark, stout and plain," made no attempt to compete with polished Julia Griffiths on her terms. Instead, she retreated, keeping her marriage and her dignity intact by becoming her husband's efficient housekeeper. Rosetta wrote:

She watched with a great deal of interest and no little pride the growth in public life of my father, and in every possible way that she was capable aided him by relieving him of all the management of the home as it increased in size and in its appointments. It was her pleasure to know that when he stood up before an audience that his linen was immaculate and that she had made it so, for, no matter how well the laundry was done for the family, she must with her own hands smooth the tucks in father's linen and when he was on a long journey she would forward at a given point a fresh supply.

Father was mother's honored guest. He was from home so often that his home comings were events that she thought worthy of extra notice. Every thing was done to add to his comfort.

Perhaps no other home received under its roof a more varied class of people than did our home. From the highest dignitaries to the lowliest person, bond or free, white or black, were welcomed, and mother was equally gracious to all. During her wedded life of forty-four years, she was the same faithful ally, guarding as best she could every interest connected with my father, his lifework and the home.

Despite her loyal support of her mother in public, Rosetta Douglass's sympathies were with her father, as her letters* to him make

*Rosetta Douglass wrote her first letter to her father when she was seven years old, and she continued to correspond with him throughout his life. Because of her mother's illiteracy, she was for many years the family secretary, apprising her father during his travels of events back home.

clear. Even more than other middle-class blacks, she grew up in a white culture. Much of her childhood was spent with Lydia and Abigail Mott, kindly Quaker sisters who, although devoted to the abolitionist cause, were not likely to give their ward pride in her black heritage. In Rochester with her family, Rosetta attended the fashionable Seward Seminary* until her father discovered that she was being taught in a room apart from the other girls. Then came a white governess followed by a year in the preparatory department of Oberlin College. Her formal education completed, she returned home to practice the piano and answer her father's mail when he was away.

Rosetta Douglass's letters indicate that it was not easy to be the daughter of the best-known black man in the world. Sheltered, less mature than other black girls her age, she nevertheless struggled to live up to her father's expectations. In 1862, she went to Philadelphia to look for a teaching position. Staying with the Dorseys, well-known caterers who were members of Philadelphia's black elite, she was expected to be a model of propriety.

My dear father: Philadelphia, April 4, 1862

To night your letter has reached me. You cannot imagine how grateful I was to receive it for I need something to cheer me. I did not know I could be so unhappy and friends so false or at least unkind but six weeks have shown me. Tonight for the first time in my life have I ever heard anything detrimental to my character. Mrs. Dorsey told me to night that I was a *street woman* and used some pretty harsh language. She said that my father had told her that she was to keep me from the boys, and said it to me before a room full of folks and it sounded quite badly that you should send me here but that I must be kept from the boys as if that was my particular failing and she was to watch me. Now the reason for her passion. Twice I went out walking by myself so as to feel at home in the city and feel a little independent. Yesterday afternoon I called on a Miss Gordon a young lady who had previously made me a call. She asked to accompany in a walk and show me a part of the city. I accepted and she came around by Mrs. Dorsey's and left me at the door before tea time. About noon to day I went out to mail a letter. I found my way to Mrs. William Dorsey's. She was glad to see me and prevailed upon me to stay to dinner. I did so and got back before tea and now Mrs. Dorsey called me a *street woman.* I asked what she meant by that term and she said I knew devilish well or something to that amount—for words of that kind escape her lips

*Rochester's public schools were closed to blacks until 1857.

often. I never had any one speak to me in that manner before.

Miss Ada Minton's coming tomorrow to ask me to go walking with her. I do not know how Mrs. Dorsey will receive her but I am fearful of her explosion. But two gentlemen have called, Mr. Minton and Mr. Cato a teacher in the school,* and they are respectable too. I anticipated so much pleasure in an innocent way and nothing but unhappiness has followed.

All the time I am here I feel in bondage. Mrs. Dorsey does not wish me to go out unless I tell her when I am going and where I am going. I am willing to tell her *when* but I wish people to think me capable of going just *where* is right. That is more than Mother and yourself have required of me to Always tell *where* I am going.

I would like to come home but feel ashamed because I did so very much wish to get a school and pay my board and I then could feel independent but a school here I cannot get.

Please give my love to my mother and the boys. Much love to yourself

Yours affectionately
Rosetta Douglass

When she failed to find work in Philadelphia, Rosetta went to Salem, Massachusetts, one of the few cities that employed blacks in its public schools. Securing a teaching job, she boarded with her mother's brother, Perry, and his wife, Elizabeth, who had come from Maryland after the outbreak of the war. Here too she found people curious, and gossips who waited for her first misstep.

Salem, [Massachusetts,]
September 24, 1862

My Dear Father and Mother:

Father, your conjectures were right when you supposed my home with Uncle was growing unpleasant. My reason for not saying much of them lately was because I did not wish to utter any more complaints, 1st because I told you much of my disappointment in Philadelphia that I thought if I began to utter more from here you would begin to think me a great fault finder and 2d I thought if I was not successful after haveing asked you to give me a little start you would not feel like risking again so that I was determined to make one desperate effort, even if I did undergo a few hardships, though when I begin to enumerate these trials they will appear trifling to those you have undergone.

I am now with a family of the name of Gibbs friends of Mrs.

---

*The Mintons were members of a leading black family. Octavius Catto, son of the Reverend William Catto, taught at the Institute for Colored Youth.

Reckless.* During my stay in Uncle's family they never exacted board from me [but] when I had money the most of it went in the family. If I had not done so I should many times have gone supperless to bed as Uncle is busy paying for his house and his family were obliged to just live on as little as possible. When I went there I found they had but one towel and every body used it. I could not get use to that. I bought three towels. I found that while I was going to bed the rest remained in the dark and as I usually take my time when I am in my room I was often hurried so that I bought myself candles which the family used also and so I went on getting little things when I had money only saving enough for myself to buy my paper and ink and postage stamps and thread.

But my reasons for becoming disconsolate are these. Uncle's wife was repeatedly asking me questions. She had heard I was driven from my home on account of my growing intimacy with men and again on account of my quarrelsome disposition towards my mother. Lucy Oliver from New Bedford had said I was in New Bedford living at one Martha Fletchers but my father had come and removed me, he had taken much pains with my education having taken me to England for that purpose. This part of the story I knew who was meant. Wm Brown's daughter.† I was questioned had I been in New Bedford, did I know the Fletchers. I told them yes New Bedford was my birthplace but I left when but little more than a baby. I knew of Mrs. Fletcher that she was a lady of respectability living there but I was too small to have any recollection of her. That was enough. I had been in New Bedford knew of Mrs. Fletcher. The fact is not believed that I left a mere child. I wanted the school and I became a little frightened about these stories but did not heed them until some of the Quakers came and questioned me. Where was thee born, was thy father married to Perry's sister before he left slavery? and many more inquisitive questions. One day a lady and daughter called and talked about many things questioning mostly about my school in Claysville.‡ The daughter said I wonder at thee going there to teach them. I told her I did not feel the least ashamed of the task admitting that they were of course much neglected and were quite low and degraded. She curled her lip she said I would not care to go to school with such children and would not be engaged in teaching them. I was quite indignant then and I tried to

*Mrs. Reckless was probably related to Hester Reckless, an early member of the Philadelphia Female Anti-Slavery Society.
†William Wells Brown's daughters lived in New Bedford with Mrs. Fletcher.
‡A country school where she taught for a short time while waiting for the Salem position.

show as well as I could that much of degradation was owing to the whites. Much was said on both sides. A week or so afterwards Uncle who having heard the conversation repeated by someone else came home and told me he had not liked it. He did not think it was proper to say such things to persons who were our friends and a number of things he said not worth while to mention for I knew he did not understand me or the Quakers. I told him I should certainly say what I thought when people speak so carelessly of Slavery. Well he says you cannot speak here. I saw he was cross and said many things concerning these stories about me, but I certainly did not wish to hear them and as soon as I could conveniently proceeded to go to my room, when his wife jumped up and dodged me first one way and then another to prevent my going up stairs. I started up when she followed accusing me of closing the door in her face and shook her fist in my face saying what she should do if I did it again. I laughed and said you seem determined to have a little row with me Aunt Lizzy for I left you to escape and you have followed me here. I remained until now which is three weeks since the above happened. During this time she was more exacting and overbearing than ever. Monday she shook me as if I were a child and threatened to pitch me out doors and my washing after me.

[letter breaks off]

In reply to a despondent letter from her father, Rosetta commented on their family life.

My Dear Father,   Salem, [Massachusetts,] October 9, 1862
    Yours of the 4th inst arrived night before last and found me more than usual wearied with my days work. Lewis use to think I would make a pretty severe school mistress but I do not think I can be as all my scholars appear to love me and the school is very orderly and the scholars more or less are attentive. I *am careful* of my change and I make a few cents at spare times by knitting edging and doing embroidery. I am doing a piece now for the lady with whom I board who is doing my washing and ironing for pay. I have done it since I have been in my school but I find it rather difficult and go to school too. My walk is a mile and a half, from my boarding place I walk it in twenty five minutes. With my night school and knitting and embroidery, I can make sufficient pin money and save my salary which is my object. My evening school will commence next Tuesday evening if nothing prevents. My evenings are Tuesday, Wednesday, Thursday and Friday, as Monday and Saturday my pupils being mostly those in service could

not come on those evenings. Oh! I trust I shall succeed.

I was greatly surprised to find the little sum of money you so generously sent me. I thank you *very* much for it. I often think of your loneliness for I well perceive the necessity of congenial companions. I flatter myself if I were at home I might in a measure contribute to your happiness as well as to mother's. I think my position in the family rather a singular one for I wish to be all you would have me be and I wish also to do something to make mother happy and if both were interested in the same pursuits it would be much easier for me to be just what I wish to be, a comfort to both parents. Most of my ideas of morality and uprightness of character I have learned from you father for though I never said much when our table talks were going on I made resolutions to follow your lessons. Although you may think you were talking in vain here is one that remembers. My reading has done much and for smaller things also mother has given some counsel.

Father you are mistaken in supposing that I spread family differences or in suspecting that to be the cause of Sarah's [Dorsey] pettiness. I never speak of my home except with pleasure and contrasted with the Dorsey's I could but speak of it in that light. And you also mistake when I wrote that Uncle's family was a happy one but poor. I had just left Philadelphia and was so unhappy there that when I came here and found this family so pleasant with itself I could but make the contrast. I had no thought of home at that time for I have seen no home since I left Rochester any happier than our own for I find every family has a something. Father I trust I have too great a family pride, pride for yourself to say any thing to make people acquainted with such things with which they have no business. I have not been asked any impertinent questions about my home, except what Aunt Elizabeth told me she had heard I was sent from home on account of my ill conduct that you and mother could not live with me, but as I knew that was so untrue I did not allow it to disturb me. Our home I should like to help keep. I have begun work and I will strive to make another year more profitable to me as well as others.

When I go to Philadelphia I will go to Mrs. Hunn's for I wish you to see how large I have grown. My dresses that I had made last winter are too tight for me. I am fearful now I am to be large like Aunt Charlotte, I hope not for I am not as tall. No I have no need to parade destitution for I have everything to carry me through for sometime yet —as regards clothing Mrs. Reckless said she *wished* to make me some present and could think of nothing but shoes and as she persisted I accepted. I wish much to see your monthly for October. Mrs. Reckless has a friend who takes the Tribune and she has kindly got her friend

Rosetta Douglass as a young woman. *(Anacostia Neighborhood Museum, Smithsonian Institution)*

to save me up the dailies and I go every Saturday and get them. Miss Adams sent me this week a couple of the Rochester Express one of which contained your letter to Senator Blair on the Central American scheme.* I suppose I shall see it in the Monthly. I should think it costs something to go to Syracuse so often unless Lewis† has a *free pass.* I

*When President Lincoln issued his preliminary emancipation proclamation in September 1862, he coupled the promise of freedom with a plan for a black homeland in Central America. In the October issue of *Douglass' Monthly,* Douglass replied to Postmaster General Montgomery Blair (not Senator Blair), who was one of the proponents of the colonization scheme.

†Lewis Douglass traveled to Syracuse to see his fiancée, Amelia Loguen. Four months after Rosetta's letter, he and Charles Douglass were in the U.S. Army.

am glad to know he is growing fine looking. I did not use to think he was but I noticed within the last year or two a change, a little of the sharp edge taken off and he will do. I think I see him give me a queer look at this criticism on his manners. My love to Mother and Lewis Frederick and Charles, to Aunt Charlotte and all friends
Much to Yourself
I remain Your affectionate Daughter
Rosetta Douglass
Please don't grow despondent and write soon.

Rosetta Douglass continued to teach in Salem until 1863 when she married Nathan Sprague, an ex-slave and Union soldier.

"Wm Brown's daughter" in Douglass's letter of September 24, 1862, referred to William Wells Brown and his daughter Josephine. Given the stereotyped notions of blacks that most whites held, it is not surprising that people confused the Browns and Douglasses. Brown was also a talented fugitive slave who became an antislavery lecturer, wrote the best-selling Narrative of William W. Brown, *and was involved in a scandal that was reported in the* Liberator. *But there the resemblances ceased. Brown, who was to become America's first black man of letters, escaped from slavery in 1834 and married Elizabeth Schooner, a free woman, the same year. The couple set up housekeeping in Buffalo where they had two daughters, Clara, born in 1836, and Josephine, in 1839. After a decade as a steward on Great Lakes steamers, Brown went to work for the Western New York Anti-Slavery Society. Left alone with the children for long periods of time while her husband lectured, Elizabeth Brown became involved with another man. When Brown discovered the affair, he moved his family to a village 100 miles away. But life in a small town with her husband absent only exacerbated Mrs. Brown's restlessness. In the spring of 1847 she wrote Brown, telling him to take the girls because she was leaving.*

He brought the children east to New Bedford and put them in school. A year later Elizabeth Brown turned up in Boston with a baby. Denouncing Brown to officers of the Massachusetts Anti-Slavery Society, she demanded that they dismiss him as their agent unless he supported her. "Anxious that nothing should be done to injure the cause of the slave," the Society appointed a committee to investigate the matter. After interviewing both parties, the committee exonerated Brown, finding that he had shown his wife "great forbearance" and "was entitled to the sympathy of his friends." Elizabeth Brown spent her next years, until her death in 1851, in a fruitless effort to regain custody of her daughters. She wrote to Isaiah C. Ray, a New England abolitionist.

Dear Sir: Cleveland, [Ohio,] August 5, 1849
    It is now nearly a year since I left Boston and until yesterday I had never heard from my two Children which were in New Bedford as C. L. Remond called to see me, and informed that Wm has gone to England yet he could not inform where he had those two daughters of mine. I feel great anxiety to know as by some Hypocritical means I can never receive one word from their hand. It is very likely they never receive mine as I have writen number of times since I saw them. Is not this hard for a mother who has toiled as I have, and now not permitted to even hear that they yet live. Must so much injustice sleep for ever. After I left Boston last fall Wm sent me twenty five dollars to Buffalo, the last of which I received in Jan. Since I have never heard from him only through the press. Mr. Ray you know not how those Hypocritical friends of the opressed has worked against me and my desert child. Wm did agree last fall to send me 25 dol per quarter for her support but has not done so. I suppose his reason is that I will not hold my tongue and be quiet under all his vile slander.
    I have Had a certificate drawn up in Buffalo which I did intend to Publish and probably may yet. I will send you a copy of it, and shall [ask] you to do me the kindness to write me how is best for me to act and also give some information on how and where my two daughters are. I will now mention my Book which I have written about my Garrison friends treatment to me through out this unfair investigation of Wms notorious falsehoods. If you will give me a little advice about my book and also what papers I had better send my Certificates to be published in, that I may have justice done me. You will excuse my mistake in this letter. With respect
                           Elizabeth Brown

Her certificate, signed by Buffalo residents attested to her "un-spoted" reputation and commended her "unsurpassed" example as a mother. When she sent it to the New York Tribune *with a statement of her marital difficulties, the editor dismissed her with a paragraph.*

She says she is penniless and her child destitute, while the husband and father is living in clover, and adds, "Mr. Brown has become so popular among the Abolition ladies that he did not wish his sable wife any longer," &c.&c. We know none of the parties, but we suspect Elizabeth is slightly malicious.

While their parents battled at long distance, Clara and Josephine Brown lived in New Bedford, at first with Nathan Johnson* and then with Martha Fletcher. A devoted father, Brown visited them as often as he could. When he went to England in 1849, he intended to remain abroad for only a year but the Fugitive Slave Law, enacted in 1850, made his friends fear for his safety if he returned home. Determined to see his daughters, he arranged for them to travel to London. After attending a boarding school in France, they passed a rigorous competitive examination for the Home and Colonial School, a highly rated Preceptor's College in London. Less than three years after their arrival in Great Britain, both were school mistresses. Josephine Brown wrote to her father's friend, Samuel May, Jr., general agent of the American Anti-Slavery Society.

My Dear Mr. May: Woolwich, [England,] April 27, 1854
    I read very attentively the anti-slavery papers which come to my father, and often think I should like to be in my native land again. Yet the treatment I receive from the people here is so different from what I experienced in the United States, that I have great admiration for the English. While we resided in Buffalo, I did not go to school, owing to the fact that colored children were not permitted to be educated with the whites, and my father would not send me to the colored school, because it would have been giving sanction to the proscriptive prejudice. And even after coming into Massachusetts, where we were allowed to receive instruction in the same school with white children, we had to occupy a seat set apart for us, and therefore often suffered much annoyance from the other children, owing to prejudice. But here we have found it totally different.
    On our arrival in this country, we spent the first year in France, in a boarding-school, where there were some forty other young ladies, and never once heard our color alluded to in disrespectful terms. We afterwards returned to London, and entered a school where more than two hundred young ladies were being educated; and here, too, we were always treated with the greatest kindness and respect. As we were trained in the last mentioned school for teachers, we were somewhat afraid that our color would be a barrier against our getting employment, but in this were happily disappointed. My sister is mistress of

*Johnson, a leader in New Bedford's black community, was the first person to befriend the Douglasses when they arrived in his city.

a school at Berden, in Essex, about forty miles from London. I have a school here with more than one hundred pupils, and an assistant two years older than myself. My pupils are some of them sixteen years of age, while I am not yet fifteen. I need not say to you, that both my assistant and pupils are all white. Should I return to America, it is scarcely probable that I could get a school of white pupils, and this makes me wish to remain here, for I am fond of teaching.

Believe me to remain,
Yours, very respectfully,
Josephine Brown

After British friends purchased his freedom, Brown returned to the United States. Josephine joined him there for a brief period. She spoke at antislavery meetings and wrote Biography of an American Bondsman, by his Daughter, *an account of her father's life. Soon after its publication in 1856, she returned to England to join her sister. As far as is known, they remained abroad for the rest of their lives.* In 1860 Brown married Annie Elizabeth Gray; their daughter, Clotelle,† was born two years later.*

A handful of writings from other abolitionist families have been found. John and Mary R. Jones (1819–1910) were the prosperous leaders of Chicago's small black community. Operators of an Underground Railroad station, they also offered hospitality to Frederick Douglass and John Brown. Mary Jones's tart recollections of John Brown give a picture of a conventional housewife who often performed unconventional work:

The first time I ever met John Brown he came to our house one afternoon with Fred Douglass. Mr. Douglass said he was a nice man, and Mr. Jones wanted to know if I could make some provision for him to stay all night. I told Mr. Jones I thought he was a little off on the slavery question, and that I did not believe he could ever do what he wanted to do. The next morning I asked him if he had any family. He said: "Yes, madam, I have quite a large family, besides over a million other people I am looking out for, and some of these days I am going to free them." I thought to myself, How are you going to free them?

---

*After the Civil War, black expatriates in Europe also included William Craft, Jr., Edmonia Lewis, Sarah Remond, and her sisters, Maritcha Remond and Caroline Remond Putnam.

†She was named after the heroine of Brown's book, *Clotel; or, The President's Daughter,* the first novel by an Afro-American.

Well then, after that, he dropped into our house most any time. He would talk about the slavery question and say what might be done in the hills and mountains of Pennsylvania; and Mr. Jones would say: "Why, Mr. Brown, that is all wind, and besides, you would lose your life if you undertook to carry out your plans." And I remember how Mr. Brown looked when he snapped his finger and said: "What do I care for my life–if I can free those Negroes?"

After being in Kansas awhile, he came on here with thirteen slaves. One morning some one rang the bell, and Mr. Jones went down and answered about daylight, and I heard several men talking. I had been reading about how many men he had around him and I said to my husband: "I do not want John Brown's fighters. I am willing to take care of him, but not his fighters," but he said: "They are here, and I am going to let them in." Four or five of the roughest looking men I ever saw [came in]. They had boots up to their knees, and their pants down in their boots, and they looked like they were ready to fight, but they behaved very nicely. Mr. Brown said: "Now, Mr. Jones, if you will

Mary R. Jones, from a portrait painted in 1865. *(Chicago Historical Society)*

give my men a little bite as they have had nothing to eat, we will go away and won't be heard of any more today." So we all had breakfast. Sure enough, these men went away and nobody was at the house but John Brown and I. By and by I answered the door, and there was Mr. Pinkerton* whom I had met before. It made me feel a little nervous, as I did not know whether he was on the right side or not. But he said "Is John Brown stopping with you?" I thought the truth was best and asked him to come in. As soon as he saw John Brown I knew they were friends. Mr. Pinkerton said he had been to see the slaves Mr. Brown had brought in. "I am going to get money enough to send these negroes out of the city," he said; "Mrs. Jones will take good care of you today," and of course I said "Yes." And then their anti-slavery friends came up to see John Brown and Dr. Dyer† suggested giving him a suit of clothes and said that would be a good disguise for him. One man was about the same size as John Brown, and he went down in town and fitted the clothes on himself. He brought them to John Brown, and I guess John Brown was hung in these same clothes.

After John Brown's capture, Frederick Douglass fled to England to avoid arrest as a coconspirator. He returned home as soon as he learned of his daughter Annie's death. Mary Jones wrote to offer condolences.

Dear Mr. Douglass: Chicago, May 29, 1860
    We are glad that you are home with your dear family. The head in one of our daily papers only a short time before your return [said] that you were making preparations to visit France. We are sorry that things of so sad a nature has forbid your making the trip. We deeply sympathize with your self and family in your late affliction. We felt that the blow would fall heavily upon you in a foreign land. Since Mr Jones received your letter his buisness has been of such a pressing nature that he excuses himself for not writing to you. He told me this morning that I must write to Douglass for he had not the time to write such a letter as he would like too. Friend H. O. Wagoner‡ is trying to sell out his Hominy Machine to go to Pikes Peak. Brother Richardson is in Pikes Peak since last February he expects to return home in

*Allan Pinkerton was an Underground Railroad worker and a member of the Chicago police force. During the Civil War, he headed Lincoln's secret service; afterwards, his Pinkerton National Detective Agency became notorious as a paramilitary strikebreaking organization.

†Dr. Charles V. Dyer was also an Underground Railroad worker and supporter of John Brown.

‡Henry O. Wagoner worked with Jones, Pinkerton, and Dyer in Chicago's Underground Railroad. He later became a pioneer black settler in Colorado.

the fall and send his sons out. He has opened his business there and is doing well. The Doctor looks as if he lays himself over to the left as much as ever. Perhaps he will become more erect, now some relative of his died down east last winter and left him some money which he is investing in a farm. Money has a good influence and then again it hurts. Remember us kindly to your dear family. Daughter is well and wishes not to be forgotten. Since I wrote the above Mr. Jones has come in to dinner and says to put in this slip of paper cut from the Chicago Daily Democrat and it will save him the trouble of describing his building to you that he has lately erected and is now doing business in the same.

Yours as ever
Mary Jones

ELEVEN

Women with a Special Mission

THE MOST REMARKABLE *black woman of the antebellum period was a former slave named Isabella Baumfree (c. 1797–1883), who spoke English with a heavy Dutch accent and never learned to read or write. Emancipated by New York State law in 1827, she worked as a domestic in New York City until June 1, 1843, when, with a bundle of clothing in one hand and a basket of food in the other, she traveled wherever "the Spirit" called her. Meeting her twenty years later when she was a well-known figure at antislavery gatherings, Harriet Beecher Stowe reported:*

I do not recollect ever to have been conversant with any one who had more of that silent and subtle power which we call personal presence than this woman. Her tall form is still vivid to my mind. She was dressed in some stout, grayish stuff, neat and clean, though dusty from travel. On her head she wore a bright Madras handkerchief, arranged as a turban. She seemed perfectly self-possessed and at her ease; in fact there was almost an unconscious superiority, not unmixed with a solemn twinkle of humor, in the odd composed manner in which she looked down on me.

"So this is *you*," she said.

"Yes," I answered.

"Well, honey, de Lord bless ye! I jes' thought I'd like to come an' have a look at ye. You's heerd o' me, I reckon?" she added.

"Yes, I think I have. You go about lecturing, do you not?"

"Yes, honey, that's what I do. The Lord has made me a sign unto this nation, an' I go round a'testifyin', an' showin' their sins agin my people. My name was Isabella; but when I left the house of bondage, I left everything behind. I wa'n't goin' to keep nothin' of Egypt on me, an' so I went to the Lord an' asked him to give me a new name. And the Lord gave me Sojourner, because I was to travel up an' down the land, showin' the people their sins, an' bein' a sign unto them. Afterward I told the Lord I wanted another name, 'cause everybody else had two names; and the Lord gave me Truth, because I was to declare the truth to the people.

"Ye see some ladies have given me a white satin banner," she said, pulling out of her pocket and unfolding a white banner, printed with many texts, such as, "Proclaim liberty throughout all the land unto all the inhabitants thereof." "Well," she said, "I journeys round to camp-meetin's, an' wherever folks is, an' I sets up my banner, an' then I sings, an' then folks always comes up round me, an' then I preaches to 'em. I tells 'em about Jesus, an' I tells 'em about the sins of this people."

Sojourner Truth's speeches and witty sayings have been so widely reprinted that this section includes only a report of a meeting in rural Indiana at which proslavery auditors challenged her to strip to the waist to prove that she was a woman. In 1858, when the meeting was held, women did not even dare to bare their ankles. Sojourner, however, proved equal to the challenge:

At the close of the meeting, Dr. T. W. Strain, the mouthpiece of the slave Democracy, requested the large congregation to 'hold on,' and stated that a doubt existed in the minds of many persons present respecting the sex of the speaker, and that it was his impression that a majority of them believed the speaker to be a man. The doctor demanded that Sojourner submit her breast to the inspection of some of the ladies present, that the doubt might be removed by their testimony. There were a large number of ladies present, who appeared to be ashamed and indignant at such a proposition.

Confusion and uproar ensued, which was soon suppressed by Sojourner, who, immediately rising, asked them why they suspected her to be a man. The Democracy answered, "Your voice is not the voice of a woman, it is the voice of a man, and we believe you are a man."

Sojourner Truth, from a photograph made during the Civil War. *(Sophia Smith Collection, Smith College)*

Dr. Strain called for a vote, and a boisterous "Aye," was the result. A negative vote was not called for. Sojourner told them that her breasts had suckled many a white babe, to the exclusion of her own offspring and she quietly asked them, as she disrobed her bosom, if they, too, wished to suck! She told them that she would show her breast to the whole congregation; that it was not to her shame that she uncovered her breast before them, but to their shame.

Maria W. Stewart also felt a special call to speak, to write, to teach for the benefit of her race. Born Maria Miller (1803–79), she started life as a servant girl. Her laconic autobiographical statement:

I was born in Hartford, Connecticut, in 1803; was left an orphan at five years of age; was bound out in a clergyman's family; had the seeds of piety and virtue early sown in my mind; but was deprived of the advantages of education, though my soul thirsted for knowledge. Left them at fifteen years of age; attended Sabbath schools until I was twenty; in 1826 was married to James W. Stewart; was left a widow in 1829.

Her husband, a veteran of the War of 1812, was a shipping master on Boston's waterfront, outfitting whaling and fishing vessels. Relieved of the need to support herself, Maria Stewart read widely, absorbed not only in the Bible ("the book that I mostly studied") but also in David Walker's Appeal to the Colored Citizens of the World, a pamphlet that called for armed rebellion in the South. Cheated out of her husband's estate after his death, and once more thrown on her own resources, she became a born-again Christian. Her conversion transformed her into "a strong advocate for the cause of God and for the cause of freedom. I felt that I had a great work to perform." In 1831 Maria Stewart found her way to the newly opened office of the Liberator. A half-century later, William Lloyd Garrison wrote to her:

You were in the flush and promise of a ripening womanhood, with a graceful form and a pleasant countenance. You made yourself known to me by coming into my office and putting into my hands, for criticism and friendly advice, a manuscript embodying your devotional thoughts and aspirations, and also various essays pertaining to the condition of that class with which you were complexionally identified. You will recollect, if not the surprise, at least the satisfaction I expressed on examining what you had written—far more remarkable in those early days than it would be now, when there are so many educated persons of color who are able to write with ability. I not only gave you words of encouragement, but in my printing office put your manuscript into type, an edition of which was struck off, in tract form, subject to your order. I was impressed by your intelligence and excellence of character.

Encouraged when Garrison published two of her essays, Stewart went on to speak in public, initially to the women of the Afric-American Female Intelligence Society and then to "promiscuous audiences." Her speech in Boston's Franklin Hall on September 21, 1832, was the first public lecture by an American woman,* anticipating the Grimkés by five years. Although she said, "I borrowed much of my language from the Bible," her message was secular: "Daughters of Africa, awake! arise! distinguish yourselves":

O do not say, you cannot make anything of your children; but say, with the help and assistance of God, we will try. Perhaps you will say, that you cannot send them to high schools and academies. You can have them taught in the first rudiments of useful knowledge, and then you can have private teachers, who will instruct them in the higher branches.

It is of no use for us to sit with our hands folded, hanging our heads like bulrushes, lamenting our wretched condition; but let us make a mighty effort, and arise. Let every female heart become united, and let us raise a fund ourselves; and at the end of one year and a half, we might be able to lay the corner-stone for the building of a High School, that the higher branches of knowledge might be enjoyed by us.

Do you ask, what can we do? Unite and build a store of your own. Fill one side with dry-goods and the other with groceries. Do you ask, where is the money? We have spent more than enough for nonsense to do what building we should want. We have never had an opportunity of displaying our talents; therefore the world thinks we know nothing.

A domestic worker speaking to audiences of domestic workers and day laborers, her consuming question was, "How long shall the fair daughters of Africa be compelled to bury their minds and talents beneath a load of iron pots and kettles?"

Few white persons of either sex, are willing to spend their lives and bury their talents in performing mean, servile labor. And such is the horrible idea that I entertain respecting a life of servitude, that if I

---

*British-born Frances Wright shocked American sensibilities when she made her first public speech in 1828.

conceived of there being no possibility of my rising above the condition of servant, I would gladly hail death as a welcome messenger. O, horrible idea, indeed, to possess noble souls, aspiring after high and honorable acquirements, yet confined by the chains of ignorance and poverty to lives of continual drudgery and toil. Neither do I know of any who have enriched themselves by spending their lives as house-domestics, washing windows, shaking carpets, brushing boots, or tending upon gentlemen's tables. I have learned, by bitter experience, that continued hard labor deadens the energies of the soul, and benumbs the faculties of the mind; the ideas become confined, the mind barren. Continual hard labor irritates our tempers and sours our dispositions; the whole system becomes worn out with toil and fatigue and we care but little whether we live or die.

I do not consider it derogatory, my friends, for persons to live out to service. There are many whose inclination leads them to aspire no higher: and I would highly commend the performance of almost anything for an honest livelihood; but where constitutional strength is wanting, labor of this kind, in its mildest form is painful: and, doubtless, many are the prayers that have ascended to heaven from Afric's daughters for strength to perform their work. Most of our color have dragged out a miserable existence of servitude from the cradle to the grave. And what literary acquirements can be made, or useful knowledge derived, from either maps, books or charts, by those who continually drudge from Monday morning until Sunday noon?

An occasional apostrophe to white women was tinged with bitterness.

O, ye fairer sisters, whose hands are never soiled, whose nerves and muscles are never strained, go learn by experience! Had we had the opportunity that you have had to improve our moral and mental faculties, what would have hindered our intellects from being as bright, and our manners from being as dignified as yours? Had it been our lot to have been nursed in the lap of affluence and ease, and to have basked beneath the smiles and sunshine of fortune, should we not have naturally supposed that we were never made to toil? And why are not our forms as delicate and our constitutions as slender as yours? Is not the workmanship as curious and complete?

In a vivid sketch of Boston's black community, Stewart was sympathetic to the males but also critical.

Look at our young men—smart, active, and energetic, with souls filled with ambitious fire; if they look forward, alas! What are their prospects? They can be nothing but the humblest laborer, on account of their dark complexion; hence many of them lose their ambition and become worthless. Look at our middle-aged men, clad in their rusty plaids and coats. In winter, every cent they earn goes to buy their wood and pay their rent; their poor wives also toil beyond their strength, to help support their families. Look at our aged sires, whose heads are whitened with the frosts of seventy winters, with their old wood-saws on their backs. Alas, what keeps us so? Prejudice, ignorance and poverty. But ah! Did the pilgrims, when they first landed on these shores, quietly compose themselves, and say: "The Britons have all the money and all the power, and we must continue their servants forever?" Did they sluggishly sigh and say: "Our lot is hard; the Indians own the soil, and we cannot cultivate it?" No, they first made powerful efforts to raise themselves. And, my brethren have you made a powerful effort? Have you prayed the Legislature for mercy's sake to grant you all the rights and privileges of free citizens, that your daughters may rise to that degree of respectability which true merit deserves, and your sons above the servile situations which most of them fill?

When she lectured at the African Masonic Hall in 1833, her criticism had grown sharper.

Is it blindness of mind or stupidity of soul or want of education that has caused our men never to let their voices be heard nor their hands be raised in behalf of their color? Or has it been for fear of offending the whites? If it has, O ye fearful ones, throw off your fearfulness and come forth. If you are men, convince them that you possess the spirit of men. Have the sons of Africa no souls? Feel they no ambitious desires? Where are our lecturers on natural history and our critics in useful knowledge? There may be a few such men among us, but they are rare. It is true, our fathers bled and died in the revolutionary war, and others fought bravely under the command of Jackson, in defense of liberty. But where is the man that has distinguished himself in these modern days by acting wholly in the defense of African rights and liberty? You are abundantly capable, gentlemen, of making yourself men of distinction: and this gross neglect on your part causes my blood to boil within me. Here is the grand cause which hinders the rise and progress of the people of color. It is the want of laudable ambition and requisite courage. Most of our color have been taught to stand in fear of the white man from their earliest infancy, to work as soon as they could walk, and to call "master" before they scarce could lisp the name of *mother.* Continual fear and laborious servitude have in some degree lessened in us that natural force and energy which belong to man. But give the man of color an equal opportunity with the white from the cradle to manhood, and from manhood to the grave, and you would discover the dignified statesman, the man of conscience, and the philosopher. O ye sons of Africa, when will your voices be heard in our legislative halls, in defiance of your enemies, contending for equal rights and liberty?

I would implore our men, and especially our rising youth, to flee from the gambling board and the dance-hall; for we are poor, and have no money to throw away. I do not consider dancing as criminal in itself, but it is astonishing to me that our young men are so blind to their own interest and the future welfare of their children as to spend their hard earnings for this frivolous amusement; for it has been carried on among us to such an unbecoming extent that it has become absolutely disgusting. Had those men among us, who have had an opportunity, turned their attention as assiduously to mental and moral improvement as they have to gambling and dancing, I might have remained quietly at home and they stood contending in my place. O ye sons of Africa, turn your mind from these perishable objects. Form yourselves into temperance societies. Let our money, instead of being thrown away as heretofore, be appropriated for schools and seminaries of learning for our children and youth.

Although Stewart's exhortations did not differ greatly from the sermons of black ministers, the fact that she was a woman made her message unacceptable. She encountered such hostility that she decided to leave Boston. In a farewell address on September 21, 1833, she defended, with a surprising amount of learning, the right of a woman to speak.

What if I am a woman; is not the God of ancient times the God of these modern days? Did he not raise up Deborah to be a mother and a judge in Israel? Did not Queen Esther save the lives of the Jews? And Mary Magdalene first declare the resurrection of Christ from the dead? Among the Greeks, women delivered the oracles. The respect the Romans paid to the Sybils is well known. The Jews had their prophetesses. And in most barbarous nations all things that have the appearance of being supernatural, the mysteries of religion, the secrets of physic, and the rights of magic were in the possession of women.

In the thirteenth century, a young lady of Bologne devoted herself to the study of the Latin language and of the laws. At the age of thirty, she taught the law to a prodigious concourse of scholars from all nations. She joined the charms and accomplishments of a woman to all the knowledge of a man. And such was the power of her eloquence, that her beauty was only admired when her tongue was silent.

What if such women as are here described should rise among our sable race? And it is not impossible; for it is not the color of the skin that makes the man or the woman, but the principle formed in the soul.

I am about to leave you, for I find it is no use for me, as an individual, to try to make myself useful among my color in this city. It was contempt for my moral and religious opinions in private that drove me before a public. Thus far has my life been almost a life of complete disappointment. God has tried me as by fire. Well was I aware that if I contended boldly for his cause I must suffer. I can now forgive my enemies, bless those who have hated me, and cheerfully pray for those who have despitefully used and persecuted me.

Fare you well! farewell!

Maria Stewart's Boston experience left deep scars. When she moved to New York, where there was a larger black community, she kept a low profile. She joined the Ladies' Literary Society, attended the Anti-Slavery Convention of American Women, and worked for the North Star Association, but she never spoke from a public platform again. The Reverend Alexander Crummell, sixteen years her junior and a college student when Stewart arrived in the city, later wrote:

I remember very distinctly the great surprise of both my friends and myself at finding in New York a young woman of my own people full of literary aspiration and ambitious of authorship. In those days, that is at the commencement of the anti-slavery enterprise, the desire for learning was almost exclusively confined to colored young *men.* There were a few young women in New York who thought of these higher things and it was a surprise to find another added to their number.

Mrs. Stewart came to New York with less of the advantages of education than this small literary circle but full of the greed for litera-ture and letters. Her eagerness for instruction was gladly met by the school teachers of New York, and in the circle of my own acquaintance young women willingly aided her in the study of arithmetic, geography, grammar and other branches. Ere long she became a member of a "Female Literary Society," and I remember listening, on more than a few occasions, to some of her compositions and declamations.

From the beginning she advanced to sufficient fitness to become a public school teacher, and served as such in New York and Brooklyn. In 1853 she came South and has since been engaged in teaching in Baltimore and Washington.

After the war, Mrs. Stewart joined Washington's public school system and later became matron of Freedmen's Hospital. In 1879, the last year of her life, she proudly reprinted the speeches and writings of the 1830s under the title Meditations from the Pen of Mrs. Maria W. Stewart.

Born free in the slave city of Baltimore, Frances Ellen Watkins (1825–1911) was also orphaned when young but was brought up by an aunt and uncle. Her uncle, William J. Watkins, a shoemaker by trade, was an abolitionist and the teacher at a small private school. Frances Ellen attended his school until she was thirteen years old and then went to work as a servant in the household of a Baltimore bookseller. She took care of the children, learned sewing, and in her free time was permitted to read in her employer's extensive library. Talented and ambitious, she published Forest Leaves, *a collection of poems and essays, about 1845, and* Poems on Miscellaneous Subjects, *with a preface by William Lloyd Garrison, nine years later. By this time she had left Baltimore and given up domestic work for teaching, a vocation which she came to dislike. Writing to a friend* around 1852, she asked for advice:*

What would you do if you were in my place? Would you give up and go back and work at your trade (dress-making)? There are no people that need all the benefits resulting from a well-directed education more than we do. The condition of our people, the wants of our children, and the welfare of our race demand the aid of every helping hand. It is a work of time, a labor of patience, to become an effective school teacher; and it should be a work of love in which they who engage should not abate heart or hope until it is done.

When a class of fifty-three active children proved too much, she pledged herself to the antislavery struggle. "It may be that God himself has written upon both my heart and brain a commission to use time, talent and energy in the cause of freedom," she wrote. In the summer

---

*The friend was William Still who corresponded with her throughout his life and published excerpts from many of her letters in his postwar book, *The Underground Railroad.*

of 1854 she was in New England lecturing on "Education and the Elevation of the Colored Race" and reciting some of her poems. She supported herself by selling copies of her book until the Maine Anti-Slavery Society hired her as a lecturer. Selections from letters written during her first months on the antislavery circuit:

Well, I am out lecturing. I have lectured every night this week; besides addressed a Sunday-school, and I shall speak, if nothing prevent, to-night. My lectures have met with success. Last night I lectured in a white church in Providence. Mr. Gardener was present, and made the estimate of about six hundred persons, Never, perhaps was a speaker, old or young, favored with a more attentive audience. My voice is not wanting in strength as I am aware of, to reach pretty well over the house. My maiden lecture was Monday night in New Bedford on the Elevation and Education of our People.

The agent of the State Anti-Slavery Society of Maine travels with me, and she is a pleasant, dear sweet lady. I do like her so. We travel together, eat together and sleep together. (She is a white woman.) In fact I have not been in one colored person's house since I left Massachusetts; but I have a pleasant time. I have met with some of the kindest treatment up here that I have ever received.

I spoke on Free Produce,* and now by the way I believe in that kind of Abolition. Oh, how can we pamper our appetites upon luxuries drawn from reluctant fingers. Oh, could slavery exist long if it did not sit on a commercial throne? I have reason to be thankful that I am able to give a little more for a Free labor dress, if it is coarser. I can thank God that upon its warp and woof I see no stain of blood and tears; that to procure a little finer muslin for my limbs no crushed and broken heart went out in sighs. If the liberation of the slave demanded it, I could consent to part with a portion of the blood from my own veins if that would do him any good.

Eloquent and expressive, with a voice that could be heard in the back rows yet was never harsh or grating, she was an instant success on the platform. "She has a noble head, this bronze muse," wrote Grace Greenwood, a popular journalist. "She stands quietly beside her desk, and speaks without notes, with gestures few and fitting. She is never assuming, never theatrical." A Maine abolitionist described her in the Portland Advertiser:

*Supporters of the Free Produce movement boycotted cotton, sugar, and other products of the slave South, patronizing Free Produce stores that sold goods produced by free labor.

Miss W. is slightly tinged with African blood, but the color only serves to add a charm to the occasion which nothing else could give, while at the same time it disarms the fastidious of that so common prejudice which denies to white ladies the right to give public lectures.

Frances Ellen Watkins (Harper).

One cannot but feel, while listening to the recital of the wrongs inflicted upon her race, and to her fervent and eloquent appeals in their behalf that hers is a heavenly appointed mission. Although Miss W. is slender and graceful both in personal appearance and manners, and her voice soft and musical, yet the deep fervor of feeling and pathos that she manifests, together with the choice selection of language which she uses arm her elocution with almost superhuman force and power over her spellbound audience.

A selection from an 1857 speech illustrates her rhetoric.

Ask Maryland with her tens of thousands of slaves, if she is not prepared for freedom and hear her answer "I help supply the coffle* gangs of the South." Ask Virginia with her hundreds of thousands of slaves if she is not weary with her merchandise of blood and anxious to shake the gory traffic from her hands and hear her reply: "Though fertility has covered my soil, though I hold in my hand a wealth of water-power enough to turn the spindles to clothe the world, yet one

*Coffles were groups of slaves who were being taken from one part of the country to another. Usually they were tied to each other with ropes or chains.

of my chief staples has been the sons and daughters I send to the human market." Ask the farther South, and all the cotton-growing States chime in, "We have need of fresh supplies to fill the ranks of those whose lives have gone out in unrequited toil on our distant plantations."

A hundred thousand new-born babies are annually added to the victims of slavery; twenty thousand lives are annually sacrificed on the plantations of the South. Such a sight should send a thrill of horror through the nerves of civilization and impel the heart of humanity to lofty deeds. So it might, if men had not found out a fearful alchemy by which this blood can be transformed into gold. Instead of listening to the cry of agony, they listen to the ring of dollars and stoop down to pick up the coin.

In a letter written in 1858, Watkins described one of the hazards that black travelers faced.

Now let me tell you about Pennsylvania. I have been in every New England state, in New York, Canada and Ohio, but of all these places, this is about the meanest of all, as far as the treatment of colored people is concerned. The other day I, in attempting to ride in one of the city cars, after I had entered, the conductor came to me and wanted me to go out on the platform. Now, was not that brave and noble? As a matter of course, I did not. Someone asked that I be permitted to sit in a corner. I did not move but kept the same seat. When I was about to leave, he refused my money and I threw it down on the car floor and got out, after I had ridden as far as I wished. Such impudence!

On the Carlisle road I was interrupted and insulted several times. Two men came after me in one day. I have met, of course, with kindness among individuals and families; all is not dark in Pennsylvania, but the shadow of slavery, oh, how drearily it hangs.

When her book of poems sold well her extra income went to William Still to support Underground Railroad work. In one letter she said:

How fared the girl who came robed in male attire? Do write me how many come to your house; and, my dear friend, if you have that much in hand from my books, will you please pay the Vigilance Committee two or three dollars to help carry on this glorious enterprise. Now, please do not write back that you are not going to do any such thing. Let me explain a few matters to you. In the first place, I am able to give something. In the second place, I am willing to do so.

Like Sojourner Truth, Watkins thought of money only as a means of helping others. In this she disagreed with some of her male colleagues who believed that wealth in black hands would put an end to prejudice. She attacked this notion in "Our Greatest Want," an essay in the Anglo-African Magazine:

The idea if I understand it aright, is that the greatest need of our people at present is money, and that as money is a symbol of power, the possession of it will gain for us the rights which power and prejudice now deny us. It does not seem to me that money is our greatest want. We want more soul, a higher cultivation of all our spiritual faculties. We need more unselfishness, earnestness and integrity. Our greatest need is not gold or silver, but true men and true women. We need men and women whose hearts are the homes of a high and lofty enthusiasm, and a noble devotion to the cause of emancipation.

I am not aiming to enlist a fanatical crusade against the desire for riches, but I do protest against chaining down the soul to the one idea of getting money. The respect that is only bought by gold is not worth much. The important lesson we should learn and be able to teach, is how to make every gift, whether gold or talent, subserve the cause of crushed humanity and carry out the greatest idea of the present age, the glorious idea of human brotherhood.

While John Brown was in prison awaiting execution, Frances Watkins wrote to Brown and his wife. Her letter to Mary Brown follows:

Farmer Centre, Ohio

My Dear Madam: November 14, [1859]

In an hour like this the common words of sympathy may seem like idle words, and yet I want to say something to you, the noble wife of the hero of the nineteenth century. Belonging to the race your dear husband reached forth his hand to assist, I thank you for the brave words you have spoken. A republic that produces such a wife and mother may hope for better days. Not in vain has your dear husband periled all. From the prison comes forth a shout of triumph over that power whose ethics are robbery of the feeble and oppression of the weak, the trophies of whose chivalry are a plundered cradle and a scourged and bleeding woman. Enclosed I send you a few dollars as a token of my gratitude, reverence and love.

Yours respectfully,

Frances Ellen Watkins

After Brown's execution, she asked Still to send a box of gifts to the other condemned men explaining:

You see Brown towered up so bravely that these doomed and fated men may have been almost overlooked, and just think that I am able to send one ray through the night around them. Please send me the bill of expenses. Along with this letter I send you one for Mr. Stevens and would ask you to send him a box of nice things every week until he dies or is acquitted. I understand the balls have not been extracted from him. Spare no expense to make the last hours of his life as bright as possible with sympathy. Now, my friend, fulfil this to the letter. Oh, is it not a privilege, if you are sisterless and lonely to be a sister to the human race?

Her letter to Aaron D. Stevens enclosed her poem, "Bury Me in a Free Land," which began:

> Make me a grave where'er you will,
> In a lowly plain, or a lofty hill,
> Make it among earth's humblest graves,
> But not in a land where men are slaves.

Replying, Stevens thanked her "for those beautiful verses which go to the inmost parts of my soul." Before his execution he copied the poem; it was found in his trunk among his most precious possessions afterwards.

In several of her letters, Frances Watkins spoke of her own loneliness. At the age of thirty-five she married Fenton Harper, a widower, and invested her small savings in a farm near Columbus, Ohio. The birth of their daughter, Mary, gave her a new role, but, after three and a half years of marriage, Fenton Harper died. Frances Watkins Harper then headed east with small Mary to resume her lecturing. (Her postwar career is described in Part V.)

Compared to Frances E. Watkins and Maria W. Stewart, Mary Ann Shadd (1823–93) had privileged beginnings. Born in Wilmington, Delaware, the oldest of Harriet and Abraham Shadd's thirteen children, she was part of a close-knit family of political activists. Her father was a delegate to the annual Conventions of Free People of Color and served as convention president in 1833. By then the family had moved to West Chester, Pennsylvania, where their home, attached to Abraham Shadd's prospering boot and shoe store, was an Underground Railroad station. Having received her primary education in Wilmington, Mary Ann Shadd spent six years at a Quaker school in West Chester; her teacher, Phoebe Darlington, was a delegate to the 1838 Anti-Slavery Convention of American Women. Shadd started teaching when she was sixteen years old, at first in Wilmington, later in Pennsylvania, New Jersey, and New York. A journalist who met her when she was teaching in New York's Colored Grammar School No. 4 in the 1840s later described her:

Miss Shadd is rather tall, but of a fine physical organization—wholly feminine in appearance and demeanor—has a well moulded head set upon a rather slender neck, which gives her, when erect or speaking animatedly, what white folks would say, a very saucy look. An anecdote of her will best illustrate this. In New York, and coming down Broadway at a time when colored women scarcely dared to think of riding in the stages, Miss Shadd threw up her head, gave one look, and a wave of her hand. There was such an air of impressive command in it that the huge, coarse, ruffianly driver, who had been known to refuse colored ladies as though suddenly seized with paralysis, reined up to the curb, and she entered, and, without hinderance, rode to the end of her journey.

Only known photograph of Mary Ann Shadd (Cary). *(Public Archives Canada)*

She was in New York when the Fugitive Slave Law of 1850* was passed and thousands of former slaves and their families who had been living free for years left homes and jobs to flee to Canada. Canada

*The law, which threatened the liberty of every black person in the North, gave unprecedented powers to slave owners. Any white man could swear that any black man was his runaway slave. Without allowing the black to testify in his own defense, a U.S. commissioner was required to send him into slavery.

promised more than a haven for runaways. It was also a land of opportunity where black men could buy land, vote in provincial elections, and send their children to school and college. Over the next decade, more than fifteen thousand U.S.-born blacks, including such solid businessmen as Abraham Shadd, settled there. Looking for wider fields for her talents, Mary Ann Shadd led the exodus of her family. During her first fortnight in Canada West (now Ontario) she sent a letter of advice to her younger brother, Isaac.

Dear Brother: Toronto, [Canada,] September 16, 1851
 I heard you were in Buffalo—I have not time to say much to you for I leave here for Sandwich Canada West to-day. I have been here more than a week, and like Canada. [I] do not feel prejudice and repeat if you were to come here or go west of this where shoemaking pays well and work at it and buy land as fast as you made any money, you would do well. If you come be particular about company—be polite to every body—go to church, every body does to be respected. Start keeping a first rate business. You could attend to the business and Take lessons and discard swearing company. If boarding go where white & cold board. [Every] man is respected and patronized [according] to his ability and respectable stand he takes. I would [give] much to see you. All were well at home when I left. If you see Rev. Mr. Campbell* in Buffalo tell him to write to me at Sandwich about the school.
 Yours dear brother, M. A. Shadd

 She settled in Windsor, a village across the river from Detroit, which was the first stopping place for fugitives from Ohio and the West. Within weeks she was teaching school. In New York she had taught in a well-equipped building with books and salaries paid by a philanthropic society. In Windsor she found a bare room in an abandoned army barracks where some refugees were housed. No desks, no books, no teacher's salary. At the suggestion of a local minister, she applied to the Reverend George Whipple, secretary of the American Missionary Association† for help. She estimated that "$250 per annum would be the smallest sum reasonable" to enable her to maintain the school. When the AMA countered with an offer of half-support at $125, she promptly accepted. At the end of the year, she reported to the AMA Executive Committee:

*The Reverend Jabez P. Campbell, a Buffalo minister.
†Founded in 1846 by a group of Christian radical abolitionists, the American Missionary Association believed in spreading the gospel through good works. For more than a century, the AMA has played a significant role in the education of Afro-Americans.

Gentlemen: Windsor, [Canada West,] October 24, 1852

Since the commencement, 56 persons (children and adults) have attended the day school; 12 adults attended the evening school held last winter and 15 attend the school at present. The difference between those in attendance at any one term can be accounted for by considering the character of the population. The nearness of this point to the U.S. make it a desirable crossing point for fugitives and other settlers; here they locate for periods varying from a few weeks to several months, or until prepared to move into the interior, the children they send to school while they remain.

The ages of those at school, have varied from four to forty-five. When the school was opened, no one could read well,—two had previously been studying Grammar and Geography; at present there are 2 classes in Geography, History, 1 Arithmetic, 2 Grammar, 1 3d Reader, 1 2d Reader, 1 Written Arithmetic, 1 Botany. The friends of education in the vicinity are astir and from their voluntary contributions the frame-work of a Schoolhouse is now erected, and the building it is hoped will be completed before the very severe weather sets in.

There have been two desks made, each sufficiently large to accommodate five, a table, black-board and other *et-ceteras*. The fuel is no longer provided by the parents, their contributions in that particular having been meager in quantity and bad in quality (*wet gum* & but one cord last winter.) The receipts to Nov. 1, 1852 excepting your society $50.31¼. Two dolls. were recd from a Mr. Allen of Ohio to buy books with, and they were expended in purchasing six 2d Readers and six small arithmetics. The receipts from all sources fall short of the sum thought necessary for a teacher's support. I mean to be understood, that a teacher cannot subsist at this point contiguous to a large city at so small a rate as he could in the interior.

In conclusion, you will please permit me to state the conviction: for religious and educational purposes, the field is very important, but the work is incessant and arduous.

Yours respectfully,

Mary A. Shadd

Despite the "incessant and arduous" work, Mary Ann Shadd was busy outside of her schoolroom. Many black leaders agreed with Frederick Douglass that they must remain in the United States to fight to overthrow slavery; others urged a mass migration to Canada, the West Indies, or to Africa. Shadd had been in Canada only six months when she joined the migrationists with a forty-four-page pamphlet titled "A

Plea for Emigration or, Notes of Canada West, in its Moral, Social and Political Aspect." Crammed full of facts about Canada's climate, geography, job opportunities, and so forth, it was a handbook for would-be emigrants that, at 12½ cents a copy, remained in print for years. While the pamphlet painted a rosy picture of Canadian life, Shadd had become aware of a darker side too. The flood of fugitives had encouraged groups and individuals to come forward, some to aid the refugees, others to exploit them. Among the latter, she classed Henry and Mary Bibb and the Refugee Home Society. Handsome, glib, and nimblewitted, Bibb had escaped from slavery in 1837 and had been a successful antislavery lecturer until the Fugitive Slave Law drove him into exile. His weekly paper, The Voice of the Fugitive, made him a spokesman for the blacks of Canada. His wife had taught in the East and Midwest before opening a school in Sandwich. Shadd, who disapproved of her initially as "a profane swearer and drug taking woman" who ruled her husband, soon uncovered a scandal that went beyond personalities.

In letters to Whipple she charged that donations to the Refugee Home Society, founded to buy land for the fugitives, went to line the Bibbs's pockets instead. At the request of many fugitives she exposed Bibb in the Liberator, the Pennsylvania Freeman, and the Western Evangelist. Bibb responded with attacks on her in the Voice, while his white associates went to the AMA offices in New York to complain of her "outrageous slanders." "What a vast amount of mischief a man like H. Bibb can do with an organ of his own to 'fling' away the reputation of others," she replied. "I have not a paper of my own and must leave the result with God."

In this instance, God was on the side of the heaviest battalions. In January 1853 Mary Ann Shadd received a letter from George Whipple. Her AMA support had been discontinued because her "evangelical sentiments" were not in accord with those of the association. This dismissal did not, however, teach her prudence. If there was a lesson to be learned from her first crusade, she had already voiced it: I have not a paper of my own.

Two months later, she had one. Although volume 1, number 1, of the Provincial Freeman listed Samuel R. Ward, a prominent black minister, as editor, along with an all-male Committee of Publications, the actual editor, business manager, and factotum was Mary Ann Shadd. It took her another year to collect money and subscriptions for a second issue, but from March 1854 until 1859,* the Provincial

---

*Although the last extant issue is dated September 15, 1857, the paper was published irregularly through 1859.

Freeman *raised its sometimes eloquent, sometimes strident, voice on behalf of the black people of Canada. At first she signed herself "M. A. Shadd, Publishing Agent" and responded to letters addressed to "Brother Shadd," but by the end of a year, it was generally known that the* Freeman *had an "editress." William Still wrote, "She is justly entitled to the credit of being the* first *colored woman on the American Continent, to Establish and Edit a weekly newspaper." Assisted by her twenty-three-year-old sister, Amelia, and her brother Isaac, she wrote, edited, and canvassed for subscriptions. In weekly editorials and letters from the field, she supported friends, both white and black, and took pot shots at her enemies. (Henry Bibb died in 1854, but there was no lack of wrongdoers to berate.) One editorial replied to a prejudiced white editor.*

INTEMPERANCE—A colored man passed under the windows of this office on Saturday, "full of strange oaths," and very indiscreet expressions, the promptings of the god to whom he had been pouring in his libations. There is a law against furnishing drink to Indians, and we cannot but think that a similar restriction applied to the "sons of Ham" would be a wholesome protection both to themselves and others —*Planet.*

The *Planet* gets worse, and worse! Whenever it can put a word in edge-wise which will bear unjustly upon colored men it does so. The colored people are not *wild* Indians, neither do they drink more whiskey than their white friends hereabouts. Every colored man must be prohibited from drinking because one drank freely. Who patronize the saloons, taverns &c in this place? Indians and colored men only? No! We believe in passing a strict prohibitory law that will not only prevent Indians and colored men from getting drunk, but will stop white men as well and not only the "inferior" classes but a drunken Editor occasionally.

Another editorial chided subscribers who did not pay for their papers.

For weeks past we have been calling upon those indebted to pay up, as we have pressing liabilities to meet. A few of our local subscribers have acted promptly, but numbers of others have put us off—some with abuse—some with "I'll pay on" that worst of all pay days "Saturday," but when Saturday comes, not a head makes his appearance. Some "I want the Freeman—it must live—. If I could get some money I'd *give* you my subscription." The hypocrites! For no sooner is a new fashion, than out come the family in fine style—the paper is not paid for, but the merchant is paid for the finery. You see the merchant is *white*, and that sometimes makes a great difference in the payment of a debt.

Much of her time was spent traveling in Canada and the Midwest where she lectured on the "practicability of an en masse Emigration of Colored Americans to the Canadas" and sold subscriptions to the Freeman. *It was a strenuous life, particularly in winter as William Still reported.*

In order to maintain the *Freeman,* she has not only had to forego the ordinary recreation and rest so essential to health, but not unfrequently has been obliged to make long journeys on Rail Roads and Steam Boats (some times on the burthern trains or upper decks to save expenses) in the most inclement weather, even when in delicate health. Sometimes without a dollar, though having regularly to meet the weekly expenses of the office. Last winter, while on a Lecturing and Canvasing tour in Indiana and Ohio, she was quite severely frosted about her face, to say nothing of the insults and injuries which she was regularly subjected to on Rail Roads &c by insolent Conductors and others, on the score of prejudice.

In the fall of 1855 she went to Philadelphia, hoping to address the eleventh Colored National Convention, something no woman had ever been permitted to do. Frederick Douglass' Paper *reported the discussion that preceded her recognition.*

There was much opposition manifested to her admission, on the part of some of the members, among them a rough, uncouth, semi-barbarous fellow who wished to know "if we would admit Abby Kelley also?" He was soon silenced. F. Douglass and others endeavored to show the utter inconsistency of the rejection of Miss Shadd by the convention. Mr. Wears and others opposed her admission. She was, finally, admitted,* and addressed the convention on the subject of Emigration to Canada. Her views which were ably expressed, did not, however, receive much sympathy from the majority.

Another correspondent was more enthusiastic:

Miss Shadd's eyes are small and penetrating and fairly flash when she is speaking. Her ideas seem to flow so fast that she, at times

*Yeas, 38; nays, 23.

hesitates for words; yet she overcomes any apparent imperfections in her speaking by the earnestness of her manner and the quality of her thoughts. She is a superior woman; and it is useless to deny it; however much we may differ with her on the subject of emigration. She obtained the floor and succeeded in making one of the most convincing and telling speeches in favor of Canadian emigration I ever heard. It was one of the speeches of the Convention. She at first had ten minutes granted her as had the other members. At their expiration, ten more were granted, and by this time came the hour of adjournment; but so interested was the House, that it granted additional time to her to finish, at the commencement of the afternoon session; and the House was crowded and breathless in its attention to her masterly exposition of our present condition, and the advantages open to colored men of enterprise.

While in Philadelphia, she lectured, attended a benefit given in her honor and took part in a formal debate on the question "Shall the Free Colored People of the United States Emigrate to Canada?" Her opponent, a noted debater, pompously announced that he would treat her "precisely as he would a gentleman—no special favor or courtesy." To his surprise, the judges voted Shadd the winner. Despite her triumphs, the trip netted only seventy-five dollars, and the Freeman's *finances were as precarious as ever. Frustrated at the lack of support she received, she sometimes lashed out at the male establishment:*

The self-called "prominent" colored men, who are everlastingly growling at, hating, or toasting one another, except, when peacock-like, they call public attention to their individual merits, and high importance. The constant whirr and din about *status,* "position," gentlemanship, and influence, have so addled the brains of our young people in both countries—and hoary headed men also—so many brilliant moths and "wandering stars" infest us, that the weightier matters of life are despised by the majority. Better far to have a class of sensible industrious wood-sawyers, than of conceited poverty-starved lawyers, superficial professors, or conceited quacks.

Her ability and her assertiveness antagonized potential supporters. Black men, no less than white, did not want a member of "the unfortunate sex," to use her phrase, as their spokesman. Admitting that "many persons do not like the Freeman," *Shadd attempted to find a "gentleman editor." When a local minister agreed to take over, she wrote her "Adieu."*

With this number of the paper we consign to other hands the literary department, and in the course of a few weeks, shall pass over the keys of the business department also, and content ourself with active efforts to get subscribers. We want the *Freeman* to prosper and shall labour to that end. We have worked for it through difficulties such as few females have had to contend against, except the sister who shared our labors for awhile. We present it afresh to the patronage of friends to truth and justice and its editor, the Rev. Wm. P. Newman to their kind consideration. To its enemies, we would say, be less captious to him than to us; be more considerate, if you will; it is fit that you should deport your ugliest to a woman. To colored women, we have a word—we have "broken the Editorial ice" for your class in America; so go to Editing, as many of you as are willing, and able; and to those who will not, we say, help us when we visit you, by subscribing to the paper, paying for it, and getting your neighbors to do the same.

Newman responded with a "Salutatory," which hailed Shadd as "one of the best editors our Province ever had" even if she "did wear the petticoats instead of the breeches." She would still occupy the editorial chair were it not for "a wrongly developed public sentiment that would crush a woman whenever she attempts to do what has hitherto been assigned to men." Less than a year later, Newman resigned and the Freeman *masthead listed Isaac D. Shadd, H. Ford Douglass, and Mary A. Shadd as joint editors. Douglass, a talented young man from New Orleans, worked with the Shadds until 1858.*

Meanwhile, Mary Ann Shadd had married Thomas F. Cary, the operator of a barber shop and bathhouse in Toronto. Although a man of limited education, he was an active supporter of the paper and of Mary Ann. The marriage was clearly an unconventional one. Cary, a dozen years her senior with three children from a former union, remained in Toronto, while she traveled for the paper or edited it in Chatham, some 180 miles away.* Five days after their marriage on January 3, 1856, she was on her way to Chicago for a midwestern tour that lasted almost six months. Selections from her letters to the Freeman *follow.*

Returned to Chicago and next day started for Rockford. The advocates of Women's Rights should go there, as the citizens are so conservative on the question as not to tolerate lectures from women.

---

*In the 1850s Chatham was known as "the colored man's Paris." Blacks from the United States, who made up a third of the town's population, found work there as tradesmen, surveyors, gunsmiths, shoemakers, innkeepers, farmers, printers—and editors.

I was permitted, however, to present the claims of the paper to the young ladies of the Seminary, by which I was enabled to get subscribers. I proceeded to Aurora and two days after started for this more Northern country, [Wisconsin] after having made a bitter cold journey by sleigh, of many miles, and having "roosted" for one night on a very narrow platform at the Geneva station, in company with several belated snow-delayed mortals of both sexes. Held a very lean meeting at St. Charles indeed, the Congregationalists do not let their church for anti-slavery lectures—one at least, of the hotels is afraid to take colored female travellers, and altogether the moral pulse throbs but feebly.

Came by cars and stage to Sycamore [Illinois] in time for an appointment on Tuesday night. After the meeting a list of names which I herewith send was added to your subscribers. Though rather indisposed from such incessant "going," I hope to proceed on my journey today.

　　Back in Chatham, Mary Ann Cary edited the paper and took care of her husband's children, Ann, Thomas, Jr., and John. Cary visited from time to time and wrote to her frequently. Although in the first letter, below, he seems to be laying down the law, the bulk of their correspondence indicates mutual respect and affection.

Dear Wife:　　　　　　　　　　[Toronto, Canada, Fall, 1856]
　　I write you a few lines in answer to yours of the 14 instant. It afforded me great satisfaction to here that you and the children was well altho I am in deep distress of mind in Regard to my affairs. You spoke of packing the things in the front Room, up stares and letting it out. Such an a Rangement does not meet my approbation and never would for I am altogether *opposed* to any sutch arrangement and if you do you have it all to your *self.*
　　　　　　　　　[Signature lost]

Dear Wife:　　　　　　　　Toronto [Canada,] May 21, 1857
　　I Received your very long and gratifying letter and was glad to heare that you and children togeather with Miss F.* was enjoying good health as this leves me and Ike [Isaac D. Shadd], whom is eating Enough Every day to *kill* a pigg. I was yesterday at the legislative Council to see their doings and here their sayings for a few minuets. Today I was to have had an interview with Mr. J. C. Tarbutt at the

*Amelia Freeman of Pittsburgh who opened a school in Chatham and soon afterwards married I. D. Shadd.

Crowndland [Crown Land] Dept, But in Consequence of to day being a holy day with the church of *Roam* business is susspended. Therefour I shall have it to morrow if I am spared. I here with forward to you $2. and hope that I will be able to send you some more next weak.

I want you to Rite me a long letter So that I will get it on Sunday morning and it will be food for me on that day as I keep in my Shell all of that day boath Ike and my Self. He pore devil has but one Shirt and I have a half Doz new ones from you. See I am Rich in that direction. We are all well. Nothing more.

your affectionate husband
Thos. F. Cary

The Carys' daughter, Sarah Elizabeth, was born in August 1857, their son, Linton, in 1860. Even during their infancy, Mary Ann Cary continued to manage the Freeman, *assisted at home by her nineteen-year-old sister, Sarah. The following letter to her husband, its first page missing, was written from Michigan when their daughter was thirteen months old. By then, illness and a business depression had brought Cary to Chatham where he worked in the* Freeman *office.*

[Michigan, September 1858]

Miss [Frances] Watkins & Mr. [William] Nell come back to Detroit and she is to go West a ways. Why the whites & colored people here are just crazy with excitement about her. She is the greatest* female speaker ever was here, so wisdom obliges me to keep out of the way as with her prepared lectures there would just be no chance of a favorable comparison. I puff her as strongly as any body in fact it is the very best policy for me to do so as otherwise it would be set down to jealousy.

I have just seen Mr. Campbell again. He will assist me in getting up meetings at Saginaw and other places in that region. I saw old Mrs. Young yesterday. She told me to tell you you must get religion & meet her in Heaven. She preached to me for a long time.

Now a word to you. You smoke an old clay pipe. Some one has said that a Meershaum absorbes the oil in the tobacco and so prevents it from doing smokers so much injury. Do not you think you had better get a Meershaum as you will smoke? Please tell me in your letter if Dr. Watson said anything about Ann Arbor. Miss Watkins has been there so that I suspect they will have enough to digest for one while. Tell Isaac to put in as much reading matter as he can crowd into the

---

*Frances Watkins was a more eloquent speaker than Mary A. Cary, but observers who criticized Cary's platform manner were impressed by her original ideas and sound logic.

Freeman as that is the only way to get up an interest in it. Douglass & those men put in more than we do. Arouse you up and drive out. It will exercise you and help restore your health. My love to Sarah & the children

Your affectionate wife

M. A. S. Cary

The last years before the war were difficult ones. After a long illness, Thomas Cary died in November 1860, leaving Mary and the children without funds. With the Freeman appearing more and more irregularly, she turned her energies to the Chatham school that Amelia Shadd had started. After traveling to New York and Boston to raise money, she pocketed her pride and appealed to the American Missionary Association. Help from the AMA and the Refugee Home Society enabled the school to stay open until 1864. While she made a bare living as a teacher, Cary continued to write. After Osborne Anderson, the Freeman's printer and the sole black survivor of John Brown's* raid returned to Chatham, she compiled his reminiscences in a slim volume, A Voice From Harper's Ferry. *She was also a regular contributor to the* Weekly Anglo-African, *lashing out at the leaders of a Haitian emigration movement as vehemently as she had supported the exodus to Canada a decade earlier. Her activities during the war and afterwards are covered in succeeding sections.*

Sarah Parker Remond (1824–94), one of the younger daughters of Nancy and John Remond of Salem, Massachusetts, grew up in the antislavery movement. Her father was a life member of the Massachusetts Anti-Slavery Society; her brother, Charles, fourteen years her senior, was the society's first black lecturer, and her mother and sisters were members of the Salem Female Anti-Slavery Society and hosts to such antislavery dignitaries as William Lloyd Garrison, Wendell Phillips, and William Wells Brown. Although her sisters followed their parents' trades by becoming caterers, bakers, and hairdressers, Sarah, according to a family friend, "was dedicated from birth to the cause of freedom. The parents and other women of the family looked after her training, supplying all her personal needs, only requiring of her that when ready [she was] to war against the traffic in human flesh." Despite her family's solicitude, she later wrote "Our home discipline did not —could not, fit us for the scorn and contempt which met us on every

---

*In 1858 John Brown came to Chatham looking for recruits. Thomas F. Cary, I. D. Shadd, and Osborne Anderson were among the men who met with him in the office of the *Provincial Freeman* and in the colored schoolhouse. No women were invited to the formal business meetings, but Mary Cary knew and admired Brown.

hand when face to face with the world, a world which hated all who were identified with the enslaved race." The sensitive girl's first hostile encounter came in 1835 when she passed the examination for Salem's high school, but was refused admission. Her parents reacted to the exclusion by moving to Newport, Rhode Island, where their daughters attended a private school for blacks. After their return to Salem in 1841, Sarah Remond continued her education by reading widely and attending concerts and lectures. Active in the Female Anti-Slavery Society and the Massachusetts and Essex County Anti-Slavery societies, she came to public notice in 1853 when a policeman ejected her from a Boston theater, handling her so roughly that she fell down the stairs. Her suit for damages forced theater owners to admit black spectators on a basis of equality.

In 1856 she went to work for the American Anti-Slavery Society. Accompanied by her brother, Charles, and a team of lecturers, which included Garrison, Wendell Phillips, Abby Kelley and her husband, Stephen Foster, she toured New York State. Despite her inexperience, Garrison praised her "calm dignified manner, her winning personal appearance and her earnest appeals to the conscience and heart." The success of her first speaking engagements led to others, including an appearance at the National Woman's Rights Convention in 1858. In a warm note to Abby Kelly Foster, she explained why she had hesitated so long before taking up antislavery work.

Salem, [Massachusetts,]

My Dear Friend Mrs. Foster December 21, 1858

    I find myself thinking of you very often. First of all, let me ask after your hearts treasure, your daughter.* I have made frequent inquiries of your friends, and have not received such answers, as I wished. How much I should like to see you, and relate to you some of the anti slavery incidents, which have occurred since we parted. We have attended some interesting meetings in this state, and my only regret is that I did not sooner begin to do what little I might, in this particular field of labour. I feel almost sure I never should have made the attempt but for the words of encouragement I received from you. Although my heart was in the work, I felt that I was in need of a good English education. Every hour since I met you I have endeavoured as far as possible to make up this loss. And when I consider that the only reason why I did not obtain what I so much desired was because I was the possessor of an unpopular complexion, it adds to my discomfort. I sail

*The Foster's eleven-year-old daughter, Pauline, had developed a curvature of the spine.

for England on the 29th of this month. I go alone but do not think it will make much difference. With love for your daughter, husband, and yourself, I am very truly Yours,

Sarah P. Remond

The Supreme Court's Dred Scott decision, which declared that black people had no rights that whites were bound to respect, drove many blacks from the United States. When Sarah Remond was invited to lecture in England, she welcomed the opportunity. Although it was unusual for a woman to cross the Atlantic without a male protector, the "dread" mentioned in the following letter to a British abolitionist, referred not to her lack of a chaperon but to the likelihood that she would be forced to travel in steerage during the voyage.

Dear Friend: Salem, [Massachusetts,] September 18, 1858

Your letter dated August 18th was received. It reached my home while I was absent attending an anti-slavery convention at Cape Cod, in the town of Harwich, in company with Parker Pillsbury,* Mr. Foss and my brother. Our meetings, eight in number, were well attended. On Sunday, although we had a large hall, many were obliged to go away unable to obtain entrance. I never looked upon a more closely packed audience. We endeavored to speak the word of truth to them, and I am sure the meeting was a very successful one.

There is a very strong effort being made on the part of the slave-holders and their allies to legalize the slave trade. Only think of it, in the nineteenth century, a nation which years ago declared the slave trade piracy, endeavoring to legalize traffic in bodies and souls of men and women. Is it not enough to make one's heart sick? It is true the traffic in slaves has always been carried on, but now there will be an attempt made to throw around this infamous crime the sanction of law. "And why not?" I may ask, "When the Supreme Court of the United States has declared that men and women with a dark complexion 'have no rights which white men are bound to respect.' "

I hope to reach London before winter, but I dread starting for many reasons. I do not fear the wind nor the waves, but I know that no matter how I go, the spirit of prejudice will meet me. I shall take passage from Boston in an English steamer. Parker Pillsbury will write to a friend of his to meet me at Liverpool and I shall hope to get along very well.

I am very truly yours,

Sarah Parker Remond

*A New Hampshire minister who was a founder of the antislavery movement.

As the first black woman of culture—"a lady every inch"—that the British had seen, Sarah Remond was warmly welcomed. She toured England, Scotland, and Ireland under the sponsorship of Ladies and Young Men's Anti-Slavery societies, speaking to as many as two thousand people at a time. For her, the high point of the tour was a ladies meeting at which she received a watch "Presented to S. P. Remond by Englishwomen, her sisters." Deeply moved because, "I have been received here as a sister by white women," she was encouraged to pursue a cherished dream—to go to college. The letter below was written to Maria W. Chapman of the Boston Female Anti-Slavery Society. Both women were angry because George Thompson had prevented Sarah Remond and Ellen Craft from speaking at a London antislavery meeting, presumably because of their sex.

Warrington, [England,]

My dear Mrs Chapman: October 6, 1859

    It was my intention to send you a long letter by our friend Mr. [Samuel] May who sails for home this month but as usual I can only

Sarah Parker Remond. *(Essex Institute, Salem, Massachusetts)*

write a hurried note. On the 12th of this month I go to London, to attend the lectures at the Ladies College. I shall on every occasion that I can still continue to lecture and do all I can for our cause. I have lectured very frequently, in fact had more invitations recently than I could fill. Lectured on three successive evenings last week, which was rather too much for me and I am now with my friends Mr. & Mrs. Robson,* for a little rest, then go to York, to lecture there. In reference to Mr. Thompson, I must say that I made one mistake in the beginning. I placed him in a wrong position. I thought he belonged to a class of men like Garrison, Phillips, Jackson, &c. Men of the most reliable stamp. But alas! I am satisfied he is not of them. Please remember me most kindly to all my anti slavery friends and with warmest regard for yourself, I am most truly yours,

Sarah P. Remond

Can you give me Mrs H. B. Stow's address, as I should like to see her when she is in London.

Remond remained in Great Britain, studying at Bedford College for Ladies (now a part of the University of London) and lecturing. She had a role to play during the Civil War when the Union needed British acquiescence to its blockade of the Confederacy. As a member of the London Emancipation Society and the Freedmen's Aid Association, she did much to influence public opinion. Her letter to Garrison was printed in the Liberator.

Dear Mr. Garrison: London, October 22, 1864
    Please accept the accompanying donation of five dollars, as my "mite" for the *Liberator*. The *Liberator* is associated with my earliest recollections, and I have always looked there, and never failed to find words of hope and sympathy for my most oppressed race.
    You probably know that I am residing with a dear friend, Mrs. P. A. Taylor, the honorary secretary of the "Ladies' London Emancipation Society." Mrs. Taylor is the wife of P. A. Taylor, Esq., M. P., whose voice in and out of Parliament, has been heard in behalf of the American slave, and whose testimony is recorded against a Southern Confederacy based upon chattel slavery.
    We are now waiting with some anxiety and intense interest, the result of the Presidential election. Abolitionists generally desire the re-election of Mr. Lincoln, as any influence which defeats the "Copperheads" must, to some extent, promote our cause. It is quite certain that the election of McClellan would be received by the Confederates

*Remond had met William Robson, a British abolitionist, in 1858 when he visited the United States.

with enthusiasm, and also give fresh courage to their allies in Great Britain and France.

But I only intended to write you a line. I am sincerely and most gratefully yours,

Sarah P. Remond

After a brief trip to the United States in 1866 to lecture on behalf of the Equal Rights Association, Sarah Remond returned to Europe and its unsegregated society. At the age of forty-two she entered medical school in Florence, Italy. Marrying an Italian, she practiced medicine in Florence. In 1885 she was joined in her self-imposed exile by her sisters, Maritcha Remond and Caroline Remond Putnam.

TWELVE
Teachers and Pupils

ALTHOUGH BLACK PEOPLE BELIEVED *that education was the way to achieve equality if not fraternity, their opportunities for study were limited. In 1827* Freedom's Journal *surveyed the African Free Schools in the Northeast and found:*

Portland, Me. *With a colored population of 900 provides one school under the care of a mistress.*

Boston, Mass. *With a colored population of 2000 provides three schools, two primary under the care of African female teachers, and a Grammar School under a master.*

Salem, Mass. *With a colored population of 400, put a school into operation last year, but it closed after six months.*

New Haven, Conn. *With a colored population of 800 two schools three months during the year.*

Providence, R.I. *With a colored population of 1500, and Hartford, Conn., with 500 provide* none.

Philadelphia *With a colored population of 15,000 provides three schools.*

New York *With a colored population of 15,000 provides two schools.*

These early schools were sustained by white philanthropy. By the 1830s the larger cities began to support public schools for blacks. In

small communities, however, the children went to private schools or none at all. *This was the situation in Canterbury, Connecticut, in 1832 when Sarah Harris asked Prudence Crandall, a white teacher, if she might attend her select Female Boarding School as a day student. Crandall recalled their first meeting.*

A colored girl of respectability—a professor of religion and daughter of respectable parents, called on me some time during the month of September last, and said in a very earnest manner, "Miss Crandall, I want to get a little more learning, enough if possible to teach colored children, and if you will admit me to your school, I shall forever be under the greatest obligation to you. If you think it will be the means of injuring you, I will not insist on the favor."

I did not answer her immediately, as I thought perhaps, if I gave her permission some of my scholars might be disturbed. In further conversation with her, however, I found she had a great anxiety to improve in learning. Her repeated solicitations were more than my feelings could resist, and I told her if I was injured on her account I would bear it—she might enter as one of my pupils.

The girl had not long been under my instruction, before I was informed by several persons, that she must be removed, or my school would be greatly injured. That was unpleasant news for me to hear, but I still continued her in school.

When her white pupils withdrew, Crandall announced the opening of a school for "Young Ladies and little Misses of Color." Despite the fact that the school cost twenty-five dollars a quarter, twenty young women from New York, Boston, Providence, and nearby Connecticut towns assembled in Canterbury on April 1, 1833. Like the youngsters of Little Rock and New Orleans 125 years later, Miss Crandall's pupils were harassed in school and out. Storekeepers would not sell them food, and ministers barred them from church. Rotten eggs were thrown through the windows, manure dumped in the well, and the local doctor refused to treat them. Part of a letter from one student was published in the Hartford Intelligencer:

Sir: Canterbury, [Connecticut,] May 24, 1833
Agreeable to your request, I write you, knowing your anxiety for the school here. There are 13 scholars now in the school. The Canterburians are *savage*—they will not sell Miss Crandall an article at their shops. My ride from Hartford to Brooklyn [Connecticut] was very unpleasant, being made up of blackguards. I came on foot here from

Brooklyn. But the happiness I enjoy here pays me for all. The place is delightful; all that is wanting to complete the scene is civilized men. Last evening the news reached us that the new law had passed. The bell rang, and a cannon was fired for half an hour. Where is justice? In the midst of all this Miss Crandall is unmoved. When we walk out, horns are blown and pistols fired.

The "new law" passed by the legislature forbade the teaching of blacks from out of state, without permission of local authorities. When Miss Crandall was arrested for defying the law her pupils, who were called as witnesses, refused to testify. Crandall won the case on appeal but was forced to close the school after townspeople set the building on fire and smashed walls and windows with heavy iron bars.

Although the Prudence Crandall case won recruits for the antislavery movement, Sarah Harris and her contemporaries still had no school to attend. In 1837, more than a decade after Emma Willard and Catherine Beecher had started their seminaries, a black minister told an antislavery convention, "When we hear you talk of female seminaries and of sending your daughters to them, we weep to think our daughters are deprived of such advantages. Not a single high school or female seminary in the land is open to our daughters." Two years later the Colored American *found few attempts to educate "colored females":*

We as much need good seminaries for girls as for boys; the culture of their minds requires more care and attention and it should not be neglected. We expect our females to be educated and refined; to possess all the attributes which constitute the lady, yet we fail to provide the means whereby they can acquire an education which shall fit them to become the wives of an enlightened mechanic, a storekeeper or clerk.

More practically, higher education was needed to prepare young women to teach. The first schools for black children were taught by whites, but as more schools were established, parents began to demand black teachers. Some of the early teachers were barely literate, as the following letters to the administrators of Philadelphia's Clarkson Schools demonstrate.

To the board of education
Gentelman: [Philadelphia] March 11, 1847
    I have wrote these few lines to Ascertain from the board of education If they would be wiling to alow me one dollar And fifty cents more

added to my months saleray. Friends my reason for asking this favour
of the is Where i now reside they have raised my rent One dollar higher
on account of getting the hydrant water in.

As it respects the Schol friends i am not yet Tierd and feel a
willingnes to do the best That lays in my power towards the children.

Jane Stekley assistant teacher
At the infant school*

To the Board of Education of the Pennsylvania Society
for Promoting the Abolition of Slavery &c
Sirs: Philadelphia, February 18, 1849

Haveing heard their will be a vacancy shortly in the school, and also
your intention to employ Coloured Teacher's and haveing received a
good plain English Education; I take this method of makeing application for the situation. The branches which I teach are reading, writing,
Arithmetic and English Grammar, including sewing and Marking.

Yours with Respect
Martha B. Gordon

*Boston's segregated Smith School, run by the city's School Com-
mittee, set higher standards. When Chloe A. Lee, teacher of the
primary grades, was dismissed she appealed the firing in a series of
dignified, well-reasoned letters. The following was written after the
committee had given her an enthusiastic recommendation.*

To the Sub Committee of the Smith School
Gentleman   [Boston, April 1847]

I have been a Teacher in the Smith School now for more than six
years, and no hint has ever been given to me that there was any wish
for my removal till Monday the 29th of March last, when Mr. Welling-
ton† the Principal of the school came into my room and said that he
thought that it would be well for me to resign, as he wished to have
a better Teacher in my place, and stating he had consulted the Committee and that they had authorised him to select such Teacher as he
should wish, and that one would be procured who would take my place
on the 1st of April. I was so surprised and grieved that I hardly knew
what I said to him. He wished me to send in a communication to you
resigning my situation which I declined but told him he could tell the
committee what was proper, and I heard nothing further; till you came

*The Infant School accepted children as young as two years of age.
†Parents protesting the "caste school" charged that Ambrose Wellington, its white
principal, was prejudiced against blacks.

and introduced the new Teacher; and then I was so embarrassed that I could not speak as I would have wished.

Had Mr. Wellington, or the Committee, previous to that, ever expressed any dissatisfaction, and pointed out wherein I was deficient I should have tried to remedy the faults, and if I were *not* able to remedy them, I should have been ready and desirous to give place to some person who would render better satisfaction. But on reading your certificate and finding that you certify to my having "conducted myself with remarkable propriety; performed my duties with conscientious fidelity," and that you "take pleasure in recommending me to others," I am satisfied that I did wrong in my confusion, in so hastily suffering Mr. Wellington to say I would resign and I beg leave to recal any such *implied* resignation. I hope therefore, that you will allow me to continue to discharge the duties of an office, which I have hitherto fulfilled in such a manner as to merit the approbation of the School Committee.

Your obedient servant
Chloe A. Lee

In 1849, after a parent boycott of the Smith School, the School Committee hired a black principal, Thomas Paul, and rehired Chloe Lee as assistant instructress. During her years of unemployment, she had attended a normal school in nearby Newton to qualify herself to teach higher grades. The black community succeeded in closing the segregated school in 1855.

Teaching conferred a higher status than domestic work, but its financial rewards were limited. Susan Paul (1809–41) was the most respected black woman in Boston. She ran her own school, directed the Garrison Junior Choir, which gave benefit concerts for the abolitionist movement, and was active in the Female Anti-Slavery Society. "She was educated and intelligent and abolitionists associated with her and invited her to their homes as a friend," a white woman wrote. Yet no white realized that she lived on the ragged edge of solvency until she turned in desperation to Lydia Maria Child. Child appealed to Jonathan Phillips, Wendell Phillips's wealthy cousin:

To Jonathan Phillips Esq
Dear Sir: [Northampton, Massachusetts,] January 23, 1838
Miss Susan Paul is the daughter of the Revd Mr. Paul, late colored clergyman in this city. For several years she has taught a primary school, the proceeds of which have supported her, and assisted in the maintenance of a widowed mother. About a year ago, they were

---

JUVENILE CONCERT,

UNDER THE DIRECTION OF

MISS SUSAN PAUL.

☞ A JUVENILE CONCERT of the Colored Children, constituting the Primary School, No. 6, under the direction of Miss Susan Paul, will be given shortly. Notice of the time and place next week.

ORDER OF EXERCISES.

Overture.—Marseilles Hymn.

PART I.

1. *Duet & Chorus.*—If ever I see.
2. *Chorus.*—In school we learn.
3. *Duet & Chorus.*—The Lark.
4. *Duet & Chorus.*—Italian Hymn.
5. *Duet & Chorus.*—Pleasures of Innocence.
6. *Chorus.*—Sweet Home.
7. *Solo & Chorus.*—Strike the Cymbal.

—

Grand Symphony.

PART II.

1. *Chorus.*—O speed thee, speed thee.
2. *Recitative & Chorus.*—Suffer little children to come unto me.
3. *Chorus.*—Little Wanderer's Song.
4. *Chorus.*—The Little Weaver.
5. *Solo & Chorus.*—Prayer for the Commonwealth.
6. *Duet & Chorus.*—Good Night.

☞ Tickets 25 cents each; to be had at the Bookstore of Dea. James Loring, Washington-street; at the store of Mr. James G. Barbadoes, No. 26, Brattle-street; at the office of the Liberator; and at the door of the Hall.   Jan. 4.

Children's Concert in Boston directed by Susan Paul was announced in the *Liberator,* January 11, 1834.

obliged to leave the house they had a long time occupied, because its ruinous condition rendered it uninhabitable in storms. The few streets where colored people are allowed to live were so much crowded, that she could obtain no tenement at the humble price suited to her finances. At last, she hired a small building in a street occupied by white people, but the neighbors assured her that the family would not be allowed to remain there in comfort and safety. She could hear of no other house, except one in Grove St. in the midst of a colored neighborhood. The rent ($200) [a year] was more than she could pay; but the family of a respectable and worthy colored man offered to take half the house. It appears probable that they honestly meant to pay their proportion of the rent, but sickness, and the loss of money due to him reduced them to such distressing poverty, that the whole burden came upon Miss Paul.

In addition to this, her sister died about a year since, leaving four helpless children, that may be termed orphans; for their worthless father is leading a profligate life at N. Orleans. The few hours when she is not in school are diligently employed in sewing for their support. Her mother is aged, and can do little more than the family work. Her only brother* (almost white) formerly earned something as a printer in the Liberator Office; but he is now a charity student at Dartmouth. He cannot assist his family at the present time.

Day before yesterday, she sent for me, and told me her distress, and how she had struggled with it, rather than make it known. She said she abhorred the idea of depending upon others, she had never before incurred debt—nor should she have done so in this instance, could she have foreseen that the whole responsibility of paying the rent would come upon her. Her mind appeared to be in a state of pitiable anxiety and perplexity. If she could but obtain a hundred dollars, she could pay personal debts, and not exceed her income in future. She was desirous to borrow this sum, and pay it slowly, by small instalments; but her ability to do this, with four orphans to support, appears to me very precarious.

I have spoken to a few abolitionists, who have contributed five dollars a piece; and I shall ask others. But I prefer that you should understand all the bearings of the case, and do as seemeth to you good.

With sentiments of the highest respect & esteem,
L. M. Child

When Jonathan Phillips sent thirty dollars, "Miss Paul was affected even to tears all the more deeply, because the measure of kindness extended to our colored population is but scanty," Lydia Maria Child wrote him. "The few individuals among them, who have any considerable degree of intelligence or refinement, are, like Tantalus, continually tormented with the sight of fruit they may not eat,

*Thomas Paul, Jr., who later became principal of the Smith School.

and fountains at which their thirsty souls are not allowed to drink." This was literally as well as figuratively true of Susan Paul who, despite her light skin, had many brushes with Jim Crow. When she traveled to New York by steamboat, she was driven from the ladies' cabin and forced to spend the night on deck during a northeast storm. The cold she caught then settled in her lungs and she died of tuberculosis when she was thirty-two years old.

In the generation after Susan Paul's, small numbers of blacks began to go to school with whites. Harriet (Hattie) Purvis (1839–post 1903), daughter of Harriet (Forten) and Robert Purvis, was tutored at home until she went to Eagleswood, a boarding school in New Jersey run by the Welds and Sarah Grimké. Most of her friends were the children and grandchildren of white abolitionists, yet even this privileged young woman could not escape discrimination. The chatty letter that follows was written to a former Eagleswood classmate, Ellen Wright, who was then attending Sharon Boarding School in Pennsylvania. Wright, later the wife of William Lloyd Garrison, Jr., was a niece of Lucretia Mott. Several of the young people including George and Lucretia Hopper and Anna C. Davis were Mott grandchildren; others mentioned in Purvis's letter came from well-known Quaker families.

My Lovely Ellen: Byberry, [Pennsylvania,] January 16, 1856
I think of you and lots of others often but of you the most, I know you will say you dont much believe it, just what you said when I said your letters did me good. You like Jos. Pierce, do you? Well thats more than I do. He comes to see me sometimes, takes me out sleighing. Ellie dont you miss your music? I practice two hours every day. Yesterday was my birth-day, I was seventeen. I am getting old. Did you get any Christmas presents? I did, my brother Bob gave me a very pretty ring, George Barker gave me a beautiful bottle.

Does Miss Anna C. Davis, come to Sharon often, you like to have her come to see you, dont you dear? Ellie, in one of your letters a long time ago, you charged me with being afraid of Anna, what made you think so? I dont *think* I am, not much any-how, she is hard on a fellow sometimes, but I love her for it.

Ellie, only think of poor little Georgie Hopper;* isn't it sad? poor Lue! I feel very sorry. I have been teaching my little brothers and sister, this winter, for there is no school here for them to go except a *Public School,* and there they are made sit by their selves, because their faces

*George Hopper died in 1856, his sister Lucretia in 1862.

are not as white as the rest of the scholars. Oh! Ellie how it makes my blood boil when I think of it; Dame Fortune has not been *very good* to us.

So John Plumly presented you with a quire of note paper. I feel *very very* jealous! Tell me just what you are doing—who do you room with? *somebody nice.* Are your teachers kind and good. How is Eliza Schofield? Give my love to her, tell her to write to me (that is if she wants to.)

Now—good-by dear, as ever
Your friend Hattie Purvis

A member of the Philadelphia Female Anti-Slavery Society, Hattie Purvis continued to be active in reform movements after the war. As late as 1900 she was on the executive committee of the Pennsylvania Woman Suffrage Association and a delegate to the National American Woman Suffrage Association. She never married.

Charlotte Forten (1837–1914), Hattie Purvis's cousin, was the daughter of Mary Wood and Robert B. Forten. Because her mother died when she was small, she spent her childhood with grandmother Charlotte Forten and with the Purvises. When she was sixteen years old she went to Salem to live with the Remonds and attend one of the city's newly integrated schools. Intelligent and attractive, with a decided literary bent, she enjoyed the mentorship of such abolitionist luminaries as Garrison and John Greenleaf Whittier who had known her grandfather. Their warmth, however, did not compensate for the coolness with which most of her schoolmates greeted her. Her response to their snubs was a determination to excel in order to prove that blacks were as capable as whites. Hers was a reaction that others shared. Maritcha Lyons* (1848–1929) was sixteen when her family moved from New York to Providence, Rhode Island. After her mother appealed to the governor, she was the first black student admitted to the local high school. In her memoirs she recalled:

Having passed the required examination, I entered the high school "the observed of all observers." During the first year I occupied one sitting at a double desk, the other having been left vacant, though pupils sat in window seats and on corners of the platform, for there was an overflow attendance. The second year the only desk with a single seat was assigned to me. This I held for a month only, for the

---

*After the Civil War, Maritcha Lyons joined New York's school system, becoming assistant principal of a public school in Brooklyn.

Maritcha Lyons as a schoolgirl. *(Schomburg Center, New York Public Library)*

teacher, a gentlewoman and a Quaker, cleverly arranged my removal. A student, sitting directly behind me invited me to share her bench. Upon reaching the senior year, I pre-empted a sunny window seat and my quarters were the admiration and envy of many of my associates. A proficient pianist, on special occasions I would "condescend" to play the accompaniments for our chorus club. By this time I had become one of the foremost of the leaders [but] the iron had entered my soul. I never forgot that I had to sue for a privilege which any but a colored girl could have without asking. Most of the classmates were more or less friendly. If any girl tried to put "on airs" I simply found a way to inform her of my class record. As I never had less than the highest marks, to flaunt my superiority in scholarship was never hard.

Although more than ten thousand free blacks lived in Washington, D.C., there were no public schools and few private ones for blacks until

Myrtilla Miner, a white woman from upstate New York, opened a School for Colored Girls in 1851. In spite of white hostility, she kept the school going for a decade and in the process trained a corps of teachers for the public schools of the District and the surrounding area after emancipation. An energetic woman with high standards for her pupils, Miner provided an enriched curriculum, including scientific studies as well as the usual "female accomplishments." Pupils were taken to museums and other places of interest; well-known people, encouraged to visit the school, were pressed into service as lecturers. Two decades later, a former student wrote:

Miss Miner gave special attention to the proper writing of letters and induced a varied correspondence between many prominent persons and her pupils. At one time Mrs. Horace Mann delivered lectures on some important subject, and her niece gave us drawing lessons. Rev. Moncure D. Conway gave a course of lectures on the "Origin of Words". Mr. Walter W. Johnson gave us very elaborate lessons in astronomy. She obtained from Northern friends, a large number of newspapers and periodicals which were great helps to increase our knowledge of general matters. She also gathered quite a library, which afforded great benefit and pleasure to her pupils.

A flawed heroine, Miner let her pupils know that she looked down on them but was determined to bring them up to her level. A white associate recalled:

She was often severe in her kindness as no doubt many of her old pupils will remember. Perfectly intolerant of bad odors because the result of generations of unwashed bodies—perfectly indifferent to the luxurious meals often prepared for her, because of the untidiness of the homes where these tables were spread. She was, certainly, also very impatient in spirit—she could not wait for results. She wanted her scholars to attain at once & be very beautiful in body and mind. I remember two little girls who travelled with her extensively through the North. How scrupulously neat she obliged them to be.*

Some pupils dropped out but others, spurred on by her criticisms, worked to win her approval. Matilda Jones, an excellent student, wrote to the daughter of a backer of the school:

*George Downing, a black spokesman, accused Miner of admitting only light skinned pupils to her school. While it was true that most of her students were light skinned, they were representative of Washington's "better class of colored," she said.

Miss Dewey*
Dear friend: Washington, [D.C.,] June 25, 1855

Two years ago your mother asked our school, "if we would be *more happy*, with these educational advantages?" & I was among the number, who replied to the question. Two years have passed since then, giving us a great experience, & some can truly say, I am much happier with the knowledge obtained during that time. My feelings are entirely different, from what they were when I first came to Miss Miner's school. I not only needed intellectual cultivation, but partially a moral development of character, as did many others.

We need [education] more than your people do, & ought to strive harder, because the greater part of our people, are yet in bondage. We that are free, are expected to be the means of bringing them out of Slavery, & how can we do it, unless we have proper educational advantages? We must get the knowledge, & use it well.

Alexander Dumas is famous for what? For writing novels. If he is gifted by nature to write, would it not be better for him to write on scientific subjects—books that will be useful, & do good in the world? If there were more Douglasses, & less Dumases in the land, "The world would be better for it." Frederick Douglass is a man, whom all can appreciate for aiding his people.

Emily Brent one of our number, has gone to Wilmington Del to teach, & has so far succeeded. This does us all good, & shows that Miss Miner has not calculated wrongly, respecting our capabilities.

Accept our thanks, & believe me,

Ever yours,
Matilda A. Jones

On behalf of the school

Emma V. Brown† (c. 1843–1902) another of Miss Miner's star pupils, was the daughter of Emmeline Brown, a widow who supported her family as a mantua maker (dressmaker) and owned a substantial brick home in Georgetown. When Miner, verging on a breakdown, went North to recuperate, Emma assisted Emily Howland, a white woman who had come from New York to take Miner's place. Even when she was away, Miner prodded young Emma to continue her education, encouraging her to dream of

---

*Miss Dewey was the daughter of the Reverend Orville Dewey, a Congregational minister from Boston.

†Although she always signed herself Emma V. Brown, her full name was probably Emmeline Victoria Brown. Many black girls of the midcentury were named after the British queen.

*Oberlin College. Following are selections from Emma Brown's replies
to Miss Miner.*

Dear Miss Miner: Georgetown, D.C., August 23 [1858]
      I received your last and of course was very much pleased. You gave
the same advice with regard to my going to school that my mother has
already given. Do you imagine that I could possibly be all that you
recommended me to become? What a glorious life you pictured! It is
too noble a destiny for me to ever hope to win.
      I know that you could have taught cultivated schools elsewhere and
have been surrounded by congenial friends, but you turned to us
ignorant and uncultivated as we were. And how have you been repaid?
For having taught us contumely and reproach were heaped upon you
by your enemies and ours—enemies that you would never have made
but for us. Yet still you falter not, but continue your labors for us,
regardless of failing health, regardless of ingratitude and bitter enemies. Why is it that with all this you still toil nobly on?
      Hurriedly yours,

                              E. V. Brown

My dear friend: Georgetown, D.C., November 5, 1858
      Miss Howland has returned accompanied by Miss Anna Searing (a
Quaker) as assistant teacher. When I found that my services were no
longer needed I had some idea of opening in Georgetown, but Miss
Howland persuaded me to study and delay teaching until spring. I am
studying with all diligence *now,* but know not how long I shall be able
to stay as my mother's circumstances have altered since you were here.
      Miss Searing teaches the first class Botany which class I have
joined. I am reviewing Mental Algebra with the same class, and practical Arithmetic and Algebra alone. The first class will take up Astronomy next week, that I will also study. Miss Howland thinks that
without apparatus I can do nothing with Chemistry. I would be glad
if you would tell me what studies would benefit me most, for you know
best what I need.
      You know not how I rejoice that you are raising funds for the
school. Your perseverance is a marvel to me. I did not dream when you
left us last winter that by this time so much would be collected.
                        I am, truly, yours
                        Emma Brown

My dear friend: Georgetown, [D.C.,] February 20, 1859
      I am much grieved to hear of your ilness and trust that you are
much better now. Do take care of your health, and let your mind &

body be thoroughly rested. You have already sacrifice much—your *life* is entirely too valuable to be given for us—none of us are worth the sacrifice of *that.*

I am glad that you approve of my plan to open a school in Georgetown. If the school that Miss Howland has is large enough I will be employed there in the spring if not I will open on my own account. I spent the afternoon and night there a few days ago. Miss Searing read the "Merchant of Venice" aloud. I know that you would like Miss S. I attended several lectures with Miss Howland at the Smithsonian, they were uninteresting however. The subject was Rome.

You spoke of the necessity of bathing all over every day. I do it regularly & have done so for some time. I have become so accustomed to it, and find it very delightful that there is not the slightest danger of my discontinuing it. I am not really well though. For some years I have had a humor in my blood. Once it fell in my eyes occasioning blindness, then it went to my head and I suffered oh! intensely. My father was then living and he employed four physicians, they poured medicine by the wholesale down my throat and I suppose only made the humor worse. Now it has gone to my head, and I suffer very much at times. I tremble lest it is scrofula.

You asked if the leisure moments were all employed. I answer no they have not been all well employed. Many have been squandered away uselessly, but I will now endeavor to do better. Instead of being at work, I have been accustomed to dream away the moments of life. Instead of engaging in some healthful employment, I have scribbled trash on paper, but I will not do it any more. The moments *shall* be well employed. I know not why it is, but I tremble, for fear that I will not go to Oberlin next fall. If I do not it will be the greatest disappointment of my life. Oh! you dont know how happy I felt when I received your first letter that spoke of it. It was truly the happiest moment of my life. Allow me to thank you ten thousand times for your kindness.

Hoping that you are much better, believe me, truly yours,
Emma Brown

The flattering, self-deprecating tone that Emma Brown adopted when she wrote to Myrtilla Miner was not in her letters to Emily Howland.* Warm and sympathetic, Howland did not share Miner's contempt for blacks. She and Emma lived together in the teachers' quarters at the school and, despite a difference in age, became good

*Miss Miner's school introduced Emily Howland (1827–1929) to the world of abolition and reform. A Quaker from a prosperous Cayuga County, N.Y., family, she was a major supporter of black education in the South after the war. She was also active in the woman's rights, peace, and temperance movements.

friends. Emma Brown's letters to Emily Howland, written over a period of forty years, offer a rare opportunity to follow the development of an educated black woman. The following was written when Howland was at home with her sick mother and Brown was in charge of the School for Colored Girls.

My dear friend: Georgetown, [D.C.,] October 7, 1858
    My school is prospering. There are twelve scholars, all interested in their studies and endeavoring to excel. I tried to get up a class for the students you mentioned but all say that they have their living to work for and though they would like to learn, have no time to spare. I earnestly entreated them to form the class at the cost of some personal sacrifice—but they did not manifest any interest concerning it. I spoke of the advantages to be derived from a knowledge of Astronomy and of the delight of wandering in thought [through] the sky, among myriads of stars, but all to no purpose. They replied that it would be of no use to them, at least of practical use. I spoke of Algebra, but they said it was useless for *women* to study Algebra. I spoke of the pleasure of studying Botany, but they had no time for plants and flowers. I told them how much they needed a more thorough knowledge of literature, but their time was too precious. There is no hope of educating the girls that are grown. The only hope is in the younger portion whose minds are free.
    They are trying to pass a bill here, the object of which is to make all free colored persons pay five dollars for the privilege of living in the capital of this *free and glorious republic.* It is to [be] hoped that such an unjust and odious bill will be cast aside. The girls that I asked to organize a class are indignant because of this detestable bill, yet will not endeavor to elevate themselves by education, and thus overthrow such vile laws, which must be annihilated by the *mightiest* of weapons —knowledge.
                        Ever yours
                        Emma V. Brown

In the summer of 1859 Emma Brown was teaching her own school in Georgetown while preparing to go to Oberlin. Founded by abolitionists, Oberlin was the first coeducational, interracial college in the country. By the 1850s small numbers of black girls were traveling to Ohio to attend its preparatory school or to take the Ladies' Course, leading to a literary degree. Many of Oberlin's black students came from the South, the children of slave mothers whose white fathers wanted to educate them; others like Rosetta Douglass were the daugh-

Oberlin's Young Lady Graduates, Class of 1855, including one black, Ann Maria Hazle. *(Oberlin College Archives)*

ters of influential black men. For sixteen-year-old Emma Brown, backed only by Miner and Howland, enrollment there was a major undertaking, emotionally as well as financially.

Dear Miss Howland: Georgetown, D.C., July 14, 1859
    I am not superstitious but I had a dream that has left a powerful impression on my mind. I had been thinking a great deal about Oberlin and at length fell asleep. I dreamed that a friend set out on a journey with me. After a time we came to two paths one was smooth and beautiful and down in a valley. The other was rugged and very high.
    My friend asked me to go in the smooth path. I answered, "no, I will not travel in such a low path. If I cannot go higher I will not go at all. I scorn that road." He left me and continued his journey. My path tho' high was filled with rocks, they hindered my progress considerably but I managed to climb over them. At last I came to a river which looked peaceful and I tried to pass over, but felt myself sinking. A voice then cried "Why did you not choose the lowly path. Behold your danger and retrace your steps, it is not yet too late." I answered "I *will* see the end of it." I passed that river and climbed over rocks until I came to another river. As before I commenced to sink and looking ahead I saw my friend continuing his journey on the opposite bank. I called to him to save me, but he was too far ahead to hear.
    So I struggled for awhile but in vain. I felt that I was lost *forever.*

Just at that moment I awoke. Oh, the remembrance of that anguish caused me to shudder. Tis said that angels warn us in dreams. Perhaps I saw my future life path. Perhaps I am rejecting the smooth path, and choosing the rugged one, but I cannot believe that it will end in misery. I still desire ardently to go to Oberlin in spite of the dream. I shall look anxiously for a letter. Mother sends love.

Truly and gratefully
Emma

Traveling under the protection of a Washington businessman, Emma Brown and Matilda Jones arrived at Oberlin in February 1860, in time for the spring term. In Ladies' Hall, the girls' dormitory, Emma obeyed the rules—rising at 5 A.M. and retiring at 10 P.M.—and plunged into her studies. Almost immediately she was attacked by blinding headaches. At first she ascribed them to the need for acclimating herself to Oberlin's colder climate. As they continued, she searched for a cure. Conventional medicine leaned heavily on pills and purges; many reformers preferred homeopathic doctors who prescribed drugs in infinitesimal doses and recommended exercise and fresh air. At Oberlin, however, exercise was limited by the regulations for lady students. Mrs. Dascomb, mentioned in the letter below to Howland, was Marianne Dascomb, Oberlin's lady principal.

My dear friend: Oberlin, [Ohio,] April 30, 1860

It seems hardly possible that nearly a month has elapsed since I received your letter. I am sorry you felt solicitous concerning my health. All the home-sick feelings have vanished. I grew so sick that the people here persuaded me to see a physician—much against my inclination I consented. He gave me some of the bitterest medicine I ever tasted. It took away what little appetite I had and made me sicker than I was before I took it. Just at that awful period a friend of mine —a young physician who graduated from another college in this state, came to Oberlin. He advised me to throw my books and medicine into the fire. I thought it would be rather expensive to do so. He went with me to visit pleasant people and brought me Homeopathic medicine. Thanks to him I am now well. You advised me to ride. They will not allow the Lady students to ride on horse-back.

Last Sunday, Prof. Monroe made an eloquent appeal to the students in behalf of a colored woman* who is trying to purchase her mother. He introduced the woman to the congregation. All stood up to welcome her. I felt so happy to see so much respect paid to a

---

*The woman was probably Louisa Picquet who collected enough to buy her mother's freedom by October 1860. See pages 50–51.

representative of the "despised race." I think they collected quite a sum for her. I gave a portion of the money you enclosed to her. The balance shall be used for similar purposes. Excuse me but I think as I am stronger it is much better to appropriate it in this way than in riding.

Mrs. Antoinette B. Blackwell lectured here last week. Her subject was "Men and Women". It was an excellent lecture. Carl Schurz also delivered a lecture a few evenings ago.

Today we had Monthly Rhetorical exercises.* A number of young men declined. One young Lady read an essay. All did well. I have come to the conclusion that I will take Mrs. Dascomb's advice and instead of working entirely for my board, after my funds are exhausted permit my board to be paid from the Avery fund† and after I finish teach and refund the money. Mrs. D. told me that sufficient time would be given me to pay it. When you write please tell me what you think of it. I would willingly pay my board by work, but I am not so strong as I thought. I can go through a course quicker in this way. I must thank you again for the [*National Anti-Slavery*] Standard. A number of the students read my papers. When Wendell Phillips' speeches are published the papers are passed around the table at a wonderful rate.

We are obliged to be in bed at 10. It now lacks only a few minutes. I must bring this hastily written letter to a close.

Ever yours,

Emma

Matilda sends love. Oh! the bell is ringing in the passage and I am not in bed—tomorrow I will have to report‡ a failure. Well I can't help it.

E.

As the headaches continued she agreed to a drastic remedy, as she reported to Emily Howland.

My dear friend: Oberlin, [Ohio,] May 22, 1860

I have been thinking for a number of days whether it is best to tell you about my troubles or not—and have come to the conclusion that I will. The terrible acclimating ordeal is not entirely through. My head

---

*When Lucy Stone and Antoinette Blackwell were students at Oberlin, the rhetorical essays were confined to men. Women were not permitted to read their own essays until 1858.

†When philanthropist Charles Avery died in 1858, he left a trust fund for "the education and elevation of the colored people of the United States."

‡At General Exercises every Tuesday, students were required to report their own "failures," infringements of rules.

aches from morning until night. The physician gave orders that my
hair must all be shaved off. I hesitated for some time. Now I have come
to the conclusion to have it done. My hair is very thick now, and ere
this reaches you I shall be minus hair. I think then I shall gain relief.
It is not very pleasant to think of, but I suppose it must be done—this
afternoon I will have a bald pate. I cannot help *laughing* at the idea
—there is something so ludicrous about it. I am determined that I will
not go to the table nor to church with a cap on. I have a large Shaker
bonnet and therefore I can attend recitations very conveniently.
The lady of the house will allow me to take my meals alone. Well, I
do not think it is so terrible after all, yet I doubt much whether my
hair will ever grow long again. The folks at home know nothing
about it.

I went to my Algebra recitation this morning. This term closes
tomorrow. This week nearly all the classes are examined and each
student is marked. Without feeling much elated (it is impossible for
me not to feel a little pleased) I inform you that I received six* marks.
This is the very highest number. Philosophy & Elocution examinations
will take place this afternoon & tomorrow morning. The directress
advised me not to attend but rest until the beginning of the next term
but I think I must go. While I am in the class my head does not ache
but as soon as the excitement is over it throbs terribly. I am not at all
alarmed—it is only the natural result of change of climate.

Yesterday we had Monthly Rhetoricals—they were very interesting. One mean young man who is I must confess a brilliant orator
under took to define the position of the colored people in America. He
advocated the Colonization doctrine warmly. He was frequently ap-
plauded—a number of colored persons hissed—I felt ready to cry
Shame! shame! A colored young man spoke as well as any other—much
better than many. I felt proud that he did so nobly. His subject was,
"Let the people rule". Many said that he was the very best speaker.
His voice is clear and powerful.

There was a grand torchlight procession here last Saturday night.
The names of Lincoln and Hamlin were heard all over the village.
There were bonfires, music and much cheering. Many regret that Mr.
Seward is not the Republican candidate for the presidency. I care not
whether they elect a Democrat or Republican—I do not believe one
will do one particle of good more than the other.

The students are getting up parties, exhibitions and picnics for the
coming holiday—they anticipate a joyous time. I attended a picnic two

*Marks ran from 1 to 6, with 6 the highest grade.

weeks ago given by the boarders of the Ladies Hall. A young gentleman called for Matilda and me with a large buggy. There is considerable prejudice here which I did not at first perceive therefore I was surprised that the gentleman came for us. We enjoyed ourselves very much. Charades were played as well as other interesting games. We returned home at 8 o'clock in the evening.

Do write soon and speak a word of consolation. I need it. I cannot forget my poor bald head that is to be. Matilda says that I keep up wonderful spirits—I am not homesick at all. I feel more satisfied each day, and bless the stars that I am here. Do write me.

Ever yours,
Emma

For seventeen-year-old Emma to give up her crowning glory was a measure not only of her desperation but also of her will to succeed. Lucy Stone too had suffered intense headaches at Oberlin, but Emma Brown had more stress to contend with. Although Oberlin prided itself on being antislavery, some students and teachers were thoughtlessly racist, a few deliberately so. And there was no escape either in dormitory or lecture hall.

My dear friend: Oberlin, [Ohio,] May 27, 1860
I am very sorry that I told you of my sickness. I should have kept the knowledge of it from you as well as from my mother. You are sorry you advised me to come and I am so glad I came here. Please do not reproach yourself any more. I am willing and able to endure this sickness. I am now much better.

It is true my hair is shaved off but I get along nicely without it. I deemed myself brave enough to bear having it taken off with scarcely a pang, but when I saw it fall around me on the floor and when I glanced at the reflection of my head in a mirror, I found that I was only a weak silly girl. I will confess that I burst into tears. The barber left a little hair in front and I wear a net lined with black silk. I get along pretty well and go to the table and to church—as usual. My head has been better since my hair was taken off and I know that I can study much better during the ensuing term.

Mr. Giddings* was escorted through the streets of Oberlin last week. He delivered an address at the church—the ladies of the Institution were not allowed to attend. A number went without being allowed. I was strongly tempted but resisted the temptation.

*Joshua Giddings, Ohio's antislavery congressman and a founder of the Republican party.

You wish to know how many students there are. During the spring term there were 870. Some are now engaged in teaching—others have gone home to spend the summer. There are 300 lady students. Quite a number. The number increases constantly during the fall and spring terms and decreases in the summer. There are very few colored students—that is comparatively speaking. I believe there is only one in the Theological Department. There is one colored girl taking a Classical Course. I have been told that she is a pretty good scholar. Two young ladies (col'd) who are taking the 'ladies course' will graduate in Aug. One seems to be very intelligent—the other is a miserable affair. A colored man will graduate at the same time. I believe there are about twelve other colored students in the college and I suppose 20 in the preparatory. I wish there were more.

Our studies will be resumed next Wednesday—I am already tired of vacation. I made a dress last week for myself, the first one I ever made. I am really proud of it. My sister sent me word that she knows they would like to get it for the Patent Office, but it is not a curiosity —a very nice respectable-looking dress. Besides the dress I have learned to wash clothes since I have been in Oberlin. Oberlin is a grand teacher of many branches.

I must prepare for church. As I am not entirely well they allow me to go when I choose. Did I tell you that we are not allowed to walk out on Sunday? Miserable!

Ever yours—
Emma

The letter below to Emily Howland is another indication of Emma Brown's courage. The Reverend Charles Grandison Finney was not only president of Oberlin College, he was also the most prominent evangelist of his time, a preacher who had converted thousands. Some of his converts became leaders of the antislavery movement, but Finney was a moderate abolitionist who opposed the Garrisonians. Perhaps Emma's spirited encounter with President Finney emboldened her to express her true feelings about Miner.

My dear friend: Oberlin College, [Ohio] November 29, 1860
This is Thanksgiving day—Everyone in the Hall myself alone excepted has gone to church. I concluded to employ the day in a pleasanter and more profitable way than by hearing Mr. Finney. I must tell you something that amused but annoyed me. They have prayer meetings every afternoon. We are not compelled to attend, but they wish us to. Well yesterday I happened to be visiting at Mrs. Finneys. The

President was busily engaged in writing but he called me into his study and we talked about religion of course. Then we discoursed upon politics and reform. It seemed to me that he denounced everything that is noble and good. He said Theodore Parker* was a liar and infidel, John Brown an enthusiast and fool, Wendell Phillips and Garrison fanatics. I wish I could tell you all the absurd arguments he used to convince me that this was true. I dared to argue with him. I never would have commenced such a conversation with the President of the Institution, but as he forced it upon me I would defend those noble men. While we were talking the bell commenced to ring. He invited me to go to church with him. Of course I dared not refuse. He told me to stand up and ask the people to pray for me (as is the custom here). I told him I would not do it. After a number of prayers had been offered, he requested the folks to pray for a young lady with whom he had conversed that afternoon who was in an awful state. Then he told what I said. Imagine my unpleasant feelings and yet there seemed something so ludicrous in it that I could not restrain my laughter. I shall not visit over there again very soon.

I have thought of your suggestion about my applying to the trustees for Miss Miner's school. I do not like or respect Miss M. I know this is wrong, but I cannot help feeling so, or explain my feelings. Yet I owe her an eternal debt of gratitude. I should not have been here, & might have remained in ignorance forever if it had not been for her instrumentality. I shall write to Mr. Rhoads† and ask if Miss Miner has given it up entirely. If she has I shall apply for it. When I left home, she said she wished to remain Principal and wished me to be asst teacher. I shall never teach there while she has anything to do with it. I suppose there will be openings elsewhere. The colored people seem so little interested about education. I wish they could be stirred up more.

With many thanks for your last suggestion and all other kindness I have received at your hands believe me truly & gratefully yours,

Emma V. Brown

Anna Searing, referred to in the letter below, was Howland's friend, who enrolled at Oberlin in the spring of 1861.

Dear friend: Oberlin, Ohio, April 9, 1861

Your last letter accompanied by the sleeves came some weeks ago, for both I thank you, also for the package you sent by Miss Searing.

*Noted Unitarian minister and abolitionist.
†Samuel Rhoads was a trustee of the School for Colored Girls.

I wanted to write some time ago, but have not been very well. This must be my apology.

Mother thinks I can stay in Oberlin until next fall. I am glad of this. I shall return your kind loan pretty soon. I did hope to return it with this letter but was disappointed.

I have been reading Carlisle's "Sator Resartus." Have you read it? What a strange thing it is. I have all the books I want from the library. The members of the Ladies Society get them for me. There are two of these Societies; in August they have an exhibition, at which time several ladies read essays. I was invited to join and read next summer, but refused. I guess I have enough of reading essays at exhibitions.

I am compelled to stop. I am ashamed of this letter, but I despair of being able to write a better one. I am too nervous to write.

Yours sincerely

Emma

The next month Emily Howland learned that Emma Brown's headaches had given way to insomnia. "She cannot sleep during the night," Anna Searing wrote. "Her nervous system is sadly deranged and she has in common with many young people a weariness at times of life. She spent the afternoon here on Friday. We had a good talk. She has more originality than ever so many of these students put together. If she could go on with her studies I predict that the Institution would not turn out many who are her equals." Forced to give in at last to the demands of her "nervous system," Emma Brown left Oberlin in June 1861. At home, against a background of stirring events, she recovered quickly. By the time the slaves of the District of Columbia were emancipated the following spring, she had her own school in Georgetown. (Her correspondence with Emily Howland during the war years and afterwards appears in Part III.)

Emma Brown's contemporaries at Oberlin included Mary Jane Patterson and Fanny Jackson (Coppin), noted educators, and Edmonia Lewis, the sculptor. Little is known about Mary Jane Patterson (1840– 94) beyond the bare facts of her life. Born in Raleigh, North Carolina, she moved to Oberlin with her family when she was a child. After a year in the preparatory school, she enrolled in the so-called gentlemen's course* and earned a Bachelor of Arts degree in 1862. Recommending

---

*Most women took the two-year Ladies' Course. The "gentlemen's course," a four-year classical course, led to a Bachelor of Arts degree. Although Mary Jane Patterson is usually referred to as the first black woman to receive a B.A., Grace A. Mapps of Philadelphia was graduated from the short-lived New York Central College at McGrawville in the 1850s. A cousin of Sarah M. Douglass, Mapps also taught at the Institute for Colored Youth.

Mary Jane Patterson, who was awarded a Bachelor of Arts degree from Oberlin in 1862. *(Oberlin College Archives)*

her for a job, a professor described her as "a light quadroon, a superior scholar, a good singer, a faithful christian, and a genteel lady." She taught at the Institute for Colored Youth in Philadelphia and then went to Washington where she became principal of the new Preparatory High School (later the prestigious Dunbar High School). Serving as principal for twelve years, until a male principal was hired, she continued to teach there until her death. Neither she nor her two sisters, also Oberlin-educated teachers, ever married.

Unlike Emma Brown who learned to sew and wash at college, Fanny Marion Jackson (1837–1913) was a domestic worker until she went to Oberlin. Born a slave in Washington, the daughter of her master, Jackson was purchased by an aunt and sent to live with another aunt in Massachusetts. In her autobiography, written in the last years of her life, she recalled her struggle for an education:

[My aunt] put me out to work, at a place where I was allowed to go to school when I was not at work. But I could not go on wash day, nor ironing day, nor cleaning day, and this interfered with my progress. Finally I found a chance to go to Newport. I was now fourteen years old and felt that I ought to take care of myself. So I found a permanent place in the family of Mr. George H. Calvert, a great grandson of Lord Baltimore, who settled Maryland. Here I had one hour every other afternoon to take some private lessons. After that, I attended for a few months, the public colored school. Mrs. Calvert taught me to sew beautifully and to darn and to take care of laces. My life there was most happy, and I never would have left her, but it was in me to get an education and to teach my people. This idea was deep in my soul.

After graduating from Rhode Island State Normal School, Fanny Jackson went to Oberlin in 1860. More mature than most of her classmates, she had her own order of priorities. "About clothes do you not think there are some girls who actually cannot take care of their apparel?" her Oberlin landlady wrote. "Fanny Jackson was a great trial to all her friends in this respect—and she never had anything fit to wear." Although she may have neglected her appearance, Jackson was well aware of her position in the classroom, where she too took the gentlemen's course. "I never rose to recite in my classes at Oberlin but I felt that I had the honor of the whole African race upon my shoulders. I felt that, should I fail, it would be ascribed to the fact that I was colored," she later recalled.

Fanny M. Jackson (Coppin) in 1865. *(Oberlin College Archives)*

Graduating in 1865 with a Bachelor of Arts degree, Jackson went to work at the Institute for Colored Youth in Philadelphia, at a salary of $500 a year. She was principal of the school from 1869 until 1902, training two generations of girls and boys. Many of her students became leaders of their struggling people. In the letter below, written after a decade of teaching, she explained her driving force.

Dear Mr. Frederick Douglass: Philadelphia, March 30, 1876
     I cannot tell you how proud and glad I was to get your letter. Many and many a time when you have been to Philadelphia have I wished that I could see and speak with you a little while. I used to wish so much to tell you what I was trying to do here and what purpose has animated me all my life. I feel sometimes like a person to whom in childhood was entrusted some sacred flame: it has burned more dimly sometimes than at others, but it always has and always will, burn steadily and persistently for it will never go out but with my life. I need not tell you, Mr. Douglass, that this is the desire to see my race lifted out of the mire of ignorance, weakness and degradation: no longer to sit in obscure corners and devour the scraps of knowledge which his superiors fling him. I want to see him crowned with strength and dignity; adorned with the enduring grace of intellectual attainments, and a lover of manly deeds and downright honesty.
     I wish you could hear how I speak to the School sometimes. I pour out upon them what my heart is so full of, sometimes I think that it falls upon deaf ears, and then again, I think that it does not. At one time, feeling very much discouraged, I asked them all if there was any one among them who ever thought about what I said to them: that is, my desires for them aside from their merely making fine scholars: several hands went up, and I—well—I took courage and took up the burden again. I fear, Mr. Douglass, that I have not got over my childhood entirely. If I planted beans and they did not put in, or rather put out, an appearance as soon as I thought they ought to I used to take them up and see if they were all right. Experience has deepened my trust in the laws of nature, but I am ashamed to say that I sometimes feel very much like going among the children, pulling up my intellectual corn and beans and noting progress. Ah well, I have to teach myself patience. A most worthy man said to me, "Remember, Fanny that it is seed time now and not harvest." The golden harvest may be reaped in time—who knows? But I must not trespass longer upon your time.
     And now, Mr. Douglass, I beg to sign myself—always with gratitude and high esteem

F. M. Jackson

Edmonia Lewis (1845–c. 1911), another of Oberlin's black students, was the daughter of a Chippewa Indian and a black man. Interviewed in 1866, she gave the following account of her childhood.

My mother was a wild Indian, and was born in Albany, of copper color and with straight black hair. There she made and sold moccasins. My father who was a Negro, and a gentleman's servant, saw her and married her. I was born at Greenhigh, in Ohio. Mother often left her home, and wandered with her people, whose habits she could not forget, and thus we, her children, were brought up in the same wild manner. Until I was twelve years old I led this wandering life, fishing and swimming and making moccassins. I was then sent to school for three years at McGraw,* but was declared to be wild—they could do nothing with me. From this school I was sent to another at Oberlin, in Ohio, where I remained four years.

With financial help from her brother who became a California gold miner, she studied at Oberlin from 1859 to 1862. Boarding at the home of John Keep, a founder of the college, she seems to have been accepted by her classmates, despite brusque manners and a distaste for conventional standards of respectability. In January 1862, during a college recess, she became the pivotal figure in a bizarre mystery. Two of her fellow boarders fell seriously ill while on a sleigh ride with male students. They immediately charged that Edmonia Lewis had poisoned them with mulled wine she had served before their departure. The drug she was accused of administering was cantharides, or Spanish fly, which was used as a blistering agent, diuretic, and aphrodisiac. While straight-laced Oberlin buzzed with the scandal, unknown persons seized Lewis and gave her a severe beating. She was still on crutches when she appeared in court to answer the charges.

Lewis's lawyer, John Mercer Langston,† disclosed that the contents of the young women's stomachs had never been analyzed. There was neither proof of poisoning nor evidence pointing to a poisoner. The case against Edmonia Lewis was dismissed, but the questions surrounding it remain unanswered. Did this "wild" seventeen-year-old spike her friends' wine with cantharides or an herb decoction of her own? Or did the male students procure the aphrodisiac? A sleigh ride, with the passengers bundled together under blankets, offered a rare opportunity for sex play. It is not difficult to imagine that the couples tried the drug and finding that they had overdosed put the blame on their black classmate. In support of this theory is the fact that none of the whites involved returned to Oberlin while Edmonia Lewis who

*The school she attended at McGraw, New York, may have been connected with New York Central College at McGrawville.
†The son of a black mother and white father, Langston, an 1849 Oberlin graduate, had a distinguished career as lawyer, college administrator, and U.S. congressman.

Edmonia Lewis. *(Dorothy B. Porter)*

had the support of her landlady and other boarders remained at college
for some time.

Although she never spoke publicly about the case, the accusation
and the beating must have taken their toll. "I thought of returning to
wild life again," she said in an interview, but a consuming interest in
art brought her to Boston. Assisted by abolitionists, she studied with
a local sculptor and, in 1865, went to Rome where she modeled busts
and heroic figures, many of them based on black and Indian themes.
Her best-known early work was a group originally titled "The Freedwoman on first hearing of her liberty."* Later works included portraits
of John Brown, Wendell Phillips, and a memorial monument for the
grave of Harriot Hunt, one of the earliest women doctors. Employing
twenty workers in her studio, she was a popular success by the 1870s.

*Later called "Forever Free," it is now at Howard University.

Although she visited the United States to exhibit and sell her work, she lived in Rome for the rest of her life.

In every class at Oberlin were women who came for a semester or two and then dropped out. Mary Sampson Patterson (1835–1914), part black and part Cherokee Indian, attended the preparatory department in 1857–58 and returned to the classroom in 1864–65 and 1867–68. She would have remained unnoticed had it not been for her marriage to Lewis Sheridan Leary who fought and died with John Brown at Harpers Ferry. In her first years of widowhood, she received financial assistance from both black and white abolitionists. The following letter was addressed to James Redpath, an associate of John Brown, who helped her to buy a house in Oberlin and to educate her daughter.

Mr Redpath
Dear Sir: Cleveland, Ohio, February 22 [1861]

Some weeks past I dropped you a line Concerning a hous that I thought of trying to purchase. I have now closed the trade. It first went at $500, but afterwards the man said he would not take less than $600 but since then he came to the conclusion that I could have it at $550. I am to pay the 1 of April next $183.33 next October $183 33/100 April 1862 $183.33. If I can pay for the hous I can find work to support my

Mary Leary (Langston) about 1910. *(Yale University Library)*

self and child. I am a Milener by trade and in Oberlin I can find work stady and I know that it will be best for my child. I am sorry to trouble you so much but if I can get a home of my own I will ask for no more. I said I would ask for no more but I must say that you will also send me your Likeness if it is not asking too much and then I will cease to trouble you. With much respect

Mary S. Leary

Mary Leary later married Charles Langston, brother of John Mercer Langston; their daughter Carrie was author Langston Hughes's mother.

Not everyone could be a hero. Susan Bruce (1850–66) was a bright eight-year-old when Emily Howland first taught at Myrtilla Miner's school. She became Howland's protégé, dividing her time between her parents in Washington and the Howland family in Sherwood, New York. In September 1865 Emily Howland sent her to Oberlin. Although Howland was well able to pay for Bruce's education, it was part of her creed—and Oberlin's—that students pay their way. She was supported in this by the abolitionist Sallie Holley, an Oberlin graduate who helped Bruce get settled. "I don't want her to spend her thought and time in dress—walking out with the young men—and generally idling away her precious opportunity here," Holley wrote Howland. "She can by diligence and alertness and alacrity, earn most of her board." Susan Bruce tried to live up to their expectations, but it was clear from her first letters to Howland that she lacked the physical stamina or the sense of urgency that drove Emma Brown and Fanny Jackson.

During Bruce's first weeks at Oberlin, Howland paid her board directly to her landlady, Mrs. Rayl, and Bruce's work in the boarding hall was credited against it. Her "side ache" was chronic, masking a real illness. She was shrewd enough to use it to play her mother off against Howland; neither woman liked the other.

My dear friend: Oberlin, Ohio, September 13, 1865

    I have just this evening received your two letters and of course am in high glee to hear from you. I do not have but two studies Grammar and Arithmetic as I could not possibly get along with my Physiology and work. Tis true I do work but two hours a day, one at cleaning knives & forks for which I receive 5 cts. & the other I set tables & wash tumblers receiving four cts. which I think very small wages only nine cts. a day. I will however work the four if you wish by working one more in the A.M. and depriving myself of my walk after tea. I can not learn my lessons at night for I have such a short memory I could not tell a word when my recitations came, so I must work three in the A.M. & one in the P.M. I will omit the practising [music] until next Summer as you see that four hours a day at the rate of four cts. an hour will not allow me to spend a cent of your money in practising. I think you might let me keep my own money instead of Mrs. Rayl. I will not spend it and it looks so mean kind of to me. Of course I do not mean it looks mean of you but it seems so funny to think I cannot keep my own money. I will nevertheless be content with any way you think proper.

Father did supply me with paper, envelopes & soap enough to last me some time. I am learning to be very economical. I cannot possibly wash any. It makes my side ache so dreadfully and I know you do not believe in the kind of smartness for which we sacrifice health & strength, and will not wish me to work beyond my ability. Mother does not even wish me to do my own washing. She thinks she knows my strength even better than yourself & wished me to find out how much it will cost and either she or my brothers would pay for my washing this winter. I find I can have it done at the rate of 5 or 6 shillings a doz. which number I shall not always have and besides can wash all my collars, handkerchiefs & cuffs & stockings. The woman will also find soap & starch, for that price.

I do go to Presbyterian Church where Pres. Finney preaches and like him very much, I also go to prayer meetings, Young People's religious meetings and everything of the sort always being in my room at study hours in the evening which begin at half past seven. I am very happy to inform you I have broken none of the rules and have had but one failure which was in Grammar lesson to-day when I had worked so hard I could not have time to study before class.

I have three pairs drawers & three chemises & one night gown. My old underclothes are entirely worn out, I would like one more night gown and one more chemise. The drawers are sufficient. Can I not have some kind of spencers.* I will have to remodel that red one it is such a horrid shape. If I can save enough may I not get some kind of pretty dark calico?

I do not like the boarding hall keepers as indeed no one hardly does. We have the same all the time. Breakfast boiled potatoes, beef hashed, bread and butter and warm drink under the assumed name of coffee which last of course I do not want. Dinner Boiled beef boiled potatoes good bread and most always strong butter with some kind of pudding

*A spencer was a short close-fitting jacket.

smeared up with bread crumbs rice and all sorts of stuff, always the same kind. Once in a while and always on Sunday we have pies. Supper bread, butter, some kind of nasty cakes generally taste as if made of water, flower, a sprinkling or else a great dash of sugar, tho' to-night we had real nice cake I don't know what kind, sometimes molasses syrup and either peaches or apples whole sour and raw sometimes not half ripe. Sunday we have the same with the exception of warm dinner. We have a slice of pie some cake and bread & butter. We have splendid eating at Oberlin Boarding Hall!

With love to all,
Susie

When the following letters to Howland were written Bruce was boarding with E. A. Peck whose husband, Professor Henry E. Peck, was in Haiti, serving as U.S. minister.

My dearest friend: Oberlin, Ohio, December 13, 1865
Yours of the 4th was rec'd this P.M. with much joy altho'it did make me put on rather a long face when I found it contained a curtain lecture for me. Well I suppose I need it. I intend to do as much as possible & take a course. I will try to work for all my board & will surely not be afraid of the work. I am sorry you still continue to have such a poor opinion of me, but I feel confident you will change when you hear my report.

I can tell you what I did yesterday & hope you will give me a little credit. I got breakfast, washed the dishes & was done my work in kitchen at eight. I then went to washing a few things for Mrs. P. & myself. At nine I had to go to class & at ten also. I got home here at half past eleven & the children coming in from school I got dinner. Having fixed the children (4) off to school I went to washing again. Cleared off the table piled up the things & then boiled two boilers of clothes. I then rinsed them and hung them out. I emptied the water, washed the dishes, cleaned the sitting room & bedroom, mopped the kitchen and at four had the clothes all in & folded as the wind blew so hard they dried in a very short time. Well every day I spend an hour in studying my Latin with another girl. The Prof & Mrs. D [Dascomb] made me take Latin. Said one term of Latin would be worth three of English grammar to me so I had no choice & now can do very well, but as I was saying just then at four the girl came. We studied our hour & after she went I commenced my ironing having heated the irons, made starch & so on while studying. I ironed until 15 min. past five & then got the children's suppers, while they were eating I ironed and kept on till seven. Then I put them to bed and at eight had done every bit of the ironing, washed the supper dishes & got the sitting room fire all built & ready to light in the morning. I then studied my Latin until half past eight. Now was I not smart? Today I have worked a great deal & having read a half hour this eve to the children & Mrs. P. I mended eight pairs of stockings & have now written a long letter to mother besides this one.

I do not have to find wood or lights here and Mrs. P. says she is not sure she shall charge me $4 a week, I eat so little. Well, I guess this letter will weaken your eyes some, so I will stop. I shall have a little over a dollar for my shoes. I find I can get a real thick nice pair for 3 or 3½ or a thicker still for four. I shall save all to that end. I am very near barefoot as far as concerns shoes but guess I shall do with my rubbers until I can get some. Love to your father & mother.

Yours,
Susie

My dear friend: Oberlin, [Ohio,] February 7, 1866
Can you possibly let me have two or three dollars? I will try to pay it back as soon as possible. I have expected some money from mother. She sent $4 about Christmas time but I gave it to Mrs. P. as I had to borrow money from her with which to buy books. I owe her a few cts. on them yet. I also need money to pay for the hire of the arithmetic for two terms which will be about .50.

I went to hear Miss Anna E. Dickinson* last night, on Flood-tide. Isn't she splendid. I think she puts Emerson in the shade entirely. She was dressed in a black dress (empress cloth I guess) with gold chain, diamond ring, emerald ring (it looked like) bracelet, (with a flashing little gem in it) and point lace. Quite superb but not equal to the words!

I have studied so well in my latin that Tutor Shurtleff declares I will soon be able to talk latin. Goodnight, I know this letter will not please you, but I cannot help it, I try to do the best I can. O! I would like the purple lawn waist I forgot to tell you.

Yours ever aff.
Susie.

While Susan Bruce continued to emphasize her achievements, Peck reported that she was not studying or working in a disciplined way. When she fell ill, Emily Howland decided to bring her home.

*Anna Dickinson (1842–1932) was a well-known orator. After the Civil War she became a star on the lyceum lecture circuit.

Dear, dear Miss Howland: Oberlin, [Ohio,] May 8, 1866
   Mrs. Peck rec'd a letter from you last might wh.' she read to me
and I was very much surprised to hear your proposal that I should come
home. Now if I co'd come right to you and go to teaching I would
almost willingly come home but if I have got to stay in that old
Washington I should feel miserably to leave Oberlin. If I can stay till
my year is up I will be so glad, but actually I am not able to work out
here and study too. If I were just to work awhile and not study I have
no doubt I should do very well but I cannot do both. Mrs. Peck said
one very strange thing which I can't get out of my head, it was this:
When Dr. came the first time, she told him that I had got all used up
with studying, working &c. that I was not strong enough for it. Well
he had hardly left the house before the Madam came to me and
astounded me by saying I had worked scarcely any and she thought if
you knew of it, would be very much displeased. Well that puzzled me
for she told the Dr. & me directly opposite stories. I am sorry I have
such a large Dr's. bill but I have felt this coming on all the spring and
don't think it could have been helped. Please write to tell me if I may
stay or come be with you. Good bye, God bless my darling "Mamma
Howland." Your loving,

                                 Susie

   *Poor Susie Bruce! Depressed by her failure at Oberlin, she was also
seriously ill by the time she reached Washington. Four months later
she died of a "disease in her bowels." "So all is over, hopes, fears, and
plans, the grave ends all," Emily Howland wrote afterward. "I think
she would not have disappointed me could she have lived."*

THIRTEEN

Black Women and the
Impending Crisis

   *By 1860 MORE THAN 225,000 free blacks lived in the North,
the majority in urban ghettoes known by such names as Little Africa,
Nigger Hill, and New Guinea. Although blacks had their own
churches, schools, and social organizations, their cultural models were*

largely white. The "corn-field ditties," which ex-slaves had brought from the South (those songs that would later be known as Negro spirituals), were rejected in favor of Stephen Foster melodies and Methodist hymns. Folktales handed down from African grandmothers were deemed old fashioned; those who could read preferred Gothic novels from the circulating library. Two thoughtful commentators lamented the community belief that "White is beautiful." William J. Wilson, writing for Frederick Douglass' Paper *in 1853, said:*

We despise, we almost hate ourselves, and all that favors us. Well may we scoff at black skins and woolly heads, since every model set before us for admiration, has a pallid face and flaxen head. Every one of your readers knows that a black girl would as soon fondle an imp as a black doll—such is the force of this species of education upon her. I remember once to have suddenly introduced one among a company of twenty colored girls, and if it had been a spirit the effect could not have been more wonderful. Such scampering and screaming can better be imagined than told. No, no; we must begin to tell our own story, write our own lecture, paint our own picture, chisel our own bust, acknowledge and love our own peculiarities.

Martin H. Freeman wrote in the Anglo-African Magazine *in 1859:*

The child is taught directly or indirectly that he or she is pretty, just in proportion as the features approximate the Anglo-Saxon standard. Hence flat noses must be pinched up. Kinky hair must be subjected to a straightening process—oiled, and pulled, twisted up, tied down, sleeked over and pressed under, or cut off so short that it can't curl, sometimes the natural hair is shaved off and its place supplied by a straight wig. Thick lips are puckered up and drawn in. Beautiful black and brown faces by the application of rouge and lily white are made to assume unnatural tints, like the livid hue of painted corpses. Now all this is very foolish, perhaps wicked, but under the circumstances it is very natural.

Most recreation was centered in church and home, but small upper-class groups, particularly in New York, copied the ways of white society. The Weekly Anglo-African *reported on a ball given by the thirteen members of the Victoria Club.*

The Victoria Club gave a grand holiday entertainment to their numerous friends on the evening of Friday, Jan. 3, 1862, at the Hall.

Having received a *billet doux,* we repaired thither at the hour of ten and after putting aside our overcoat and chapeau, we entered the reception hall which was beautifully decorated with bunting and the emblems of the season. We found two hundred guests already assembled, and they continued to arrive up to the hour of twelve, at which time they numbered about two hundred and fifty. The sexes were about equal in numbers, and made a splendid appearance; the gentlemen being uniformly dressed in fashionable suits of black, and the ladies, God bless them! were the most beautiful collection of forms and faces that eyes ever beheld.

Dancing was going on merrily. At 1 o'clock, while the band performed a grand march, we entered the banquet room where we found a most magnificent supper. The table was beautifully decorated. In the centre was one of Prof. H. Maillard's superb pyramids, composed of various fruits and *nugua* in imitation of an Oriental *Jet de Eau,* surmounted by a sea nymph surrounded by a shower of silver spray. During the repast our ears were continually assailed by the discharge of green seal artillery and Sherry and Madeira musketry.

At the close of the banquet the guests repaired to the reception hall, where dancing went merrily until the clock told the hour of 5 A.M. when all departed in peace and harmony, pleased with themselves and all the world.

In limited ways the status of blacks had improved since 1800. Black men could vote in five New England states. They could sit on juries and ride first class on railroads in Massachusetts and send their children to public schools in New York. But spotty gains in education and civil rights could not compensate for actual losses in the economic sphere. While the factory system was expanding across the nation, the word was "No Blacks Need Apply." Denied access to skilled trades as well as factory jobs, they also faced increasing competition from Irish immigrants for the unskilled work that had traditionally been theirs. In 1847 a census of free blacks in Philadelphia found that 5 percent of the men were stevedores or hod carriers. By the time of the U.S. census of 1850, the proportion was down to 1 percent. In three years the number of black hod carriers had decreased from 98 to 28, of stevedores from 58 to 27.

As male employment opportunities narrowed, women's wages became increasingly important to their families' survival. In urban areas as many as eight out of ten women were day workers, most of them laundresses. James McCune Smith, New York's leading black doctor,

contributed a sketch of "The Washerwoman" to Frederick Douglass'
Paper.

Saturday night! *Dunk!* goes the smoothing-iron, then a swift glid-
ing sound as it passes smoothly over starched bosom and collar, and
wristbands, of one of the many dozen shirts that hang around the room
on horses, chairs, lines and every other thing capable of being hanged
on. *Dunk! dunk!* goes the iron, sadly, wearily, but steadily, as if the very
heart of toil were throbbing its penultimate beats! *Dunk! Dunk!* and
that small and delicately formed hand and wrist swells up with knotted
muscles and bursting veins!

The apartment is small, hot as an oven, the air in it thick and misty
with the steam rising from the ironing table; in the corners, under the
tables, and in all out-of-the way places, are stowed tubs of various sizes,
some empty, some full of clothes soaking for next-week's labor. On the
walls hang pictures of Brother Paul, or Sammy Cornish:* in one corner
of the room a newly varnished mahogany table is partly filled with
books—Bunyan's Pilgrim's Progress, Watts' Hymns, the Life of
Christ, and a nice "greasy novel" just in from the circulating library;
between the windows stand an old bureau, the big drawer of which is
the larder, containing sundry slices of cold meat, second handed toast,
"with butter on it," and the carcase of a turkey, the return cargo of
a basket of clothes sent down town that morning. But even this food
is untasted: for, the Sabbath approaches, and old Zion, and the vivid
doses of hell fire ready to be showered from the pulpit, on all who do
labor on the Day of Rest. Dunk! dunk!! dunk!!! the iron flies as a
weaver's shuttle, shirts appear and disappear with rapidity from the
heated blanket and at a quarter to twelve, the groaning table is cleared,
and the poor washerwoman sinks upon her knees in prayer.

Sunday evening! Can it be the same apartment? No sign of toil is
there, everything tidy, neat and clean; all the signs of the hard week's
work stowed away in drawers or in the cellar. The washerwoman
dressed up in neat, even expensive, garments; and her boy with his
Sunday go-to-meetin's on, one of the pockets stuffed with sixpence
worth of "pieces," [candy] which he had made Stuart the Confectioner
sell him, as he came back from carrying home clothes, that morning.

*Perhaps 15 percent of the female work force were dressmakers and
hairdressers; another 5 percent operated lodging houses or small shops.
Some advertisements from black newspapers in 1860–62 follow.*

*Nathaniel Paul and Samuel Cornish were ministers; Cornish was also an editor of
Freedom's Journal and the *Colored American.*

Fashionable
DRESS MAKING,
SHIRT MAKING, EMBROIDERING, AND
QUILTING
Mesdames F. A. Hamilton, D. A. Newton,
and Miss A. M. Hamilton
187 Navy Street, Brooklyn

Ladies' and Children's dresses cut and made in the most fashionable style and warranted to fit.

SHIRTS of all paterns made, and plain sewing executed with neatness; and durability of work guaranteed. Orders for EMBROIDERING promptly attended to, and QUILTING executed with dispatch.

Public patronage is respectfully solicited

WANTED—COLORED YOUNG LADIES
to learn to operate on Sewing Machines. Work dispatched at shortest notice. Shirts made to order. Apply at 718 Russel st.—Philadelphia.
S. R. Given

MRS. SARAH A. TILMAN
FANCY HAIR BRAIDER
In all its branches—such as
BRACELETS, EAR-RINGS, WATCH
GUARDS, FINGER RINGS, CHARMS, ETC.
Residence-120 St., between 3d and 4th Avenues,
Harlem

BOARDING AND LODGING
By Mrs. Mary Johnson, 120 West 20 Street, New York. This house is very pleasantly situated in very healthy and convenient part of the city.

Boarding for Ladies	$2.50
" " Gentleman	3.00
Lodging per week	75

A cooperative grocery store in New York with 100 female members was a unique enterprise. "We believe this is the first successful organized effort of this kind among the colored people of this city and we cannot in too decided terms express our admiration," wrote an editor of the Colored American *as he called attention to the store's advertisement:*

THE FEMALE TRADING ASSOCIATION

Continue their establishment, consisting of *Dry Groceries* of every description, at 157 Orange st., (near Grand st.) where they dispose of articles, cheap for cash. They solicit the patronage of their friends and the public. No pains will be spared to accommodate the public. Families will do well to call and examine for themselves.

Flour, Indian meal, grits, hominy, rice, beans, peas, coffee, cocoa, teas, chocolate, hams, pork, beef, fish, shoulders, butter, lard, soap, starch, candles, cheese, oil, raisins, citron, spices of all descriptions, sugars, white and brown, brooms and brushes.

The Female Trading Association was short lived, but large numbers of black women were learning the ways of business. Elizabeth Gloucester made enough money buying and selling real estate in Brooklyn to contribute to John Brown's cause. Nancy Ruffin (1816–74), another entrepreneur, had moved from Richmond, Virginia, to

Nancy Ruffin. *(Amistad Research Center)*

Boston in 1854 in order to educate her eight children, while her husband, a barber, remained in the South. From time to time, he shipped barrels of fish or crates of fruit that she and her sons marketed. Although he sent money for their support, the responsibility of managing their property and bringing up the children was hers. Two of her letters follow.

My Dear Husband: Boston, November 12, 1858
   I received your letter dated the 5th of November and was very much disappointed at not receiving the money. It is very disagrable to me to have to go to first one person then to another to borrow money to pay when it is due. I would rather take my children and go to the poor-house. I did not like to ask Mr Lockley for the sixty $. I asked Mr. Smith* for it. He had to take it out off the bank. They charge sixty two cents intrust to get it with out giving notice. Mr. Lockley spoke for 4 tons of coal which will be due the first of January is 22$ that will not last me all the winter. I would like to get two tons more and one cord of wood. The people give you notice here in plenty time when it is time for you to pay your bills and when it is due you must have the money. They will not wate for nothing and soon the water rent will be due. This house has so manny dets hanging on it makes me so low spirited that I dont know what to do. I reckon we had better try and get rid of the place and trye and get a cheaper place. If you cant spare the money sell the bed for I would rather pay my dets than to keep the bed. I received the barrel of fish. Let me here from you as soon as you can and send this money on for the people will not wate.
                         Your Wife
                         Nancy Ruffin
                         No 18 Grove St

My Dear Husband: Boston, December 16, 1859
   I write you on this day for it is the 16th and George† is twenty-five years old to day and I think it hard that we have been living to gether so long as to have a child so old and to be separated from each other and the winter is cold and I sleep cold.
   I think I shall haft to take a few boarders. I don't like to take a

*Probably John J. Smith who had moved from Richmond to Boston in 1840 and was also a barber.
†George Ruffin became a lawyer and judge in Massachusetts. He married Josephine St. Pierre Ruffin (1842–1924), who was editor of *Woman's Era* and the founder of the National Federation of Afro-American Women.

nother family in the house do not like to have strangers about. I want to get some carpeting. I would like for you to help me to fix up a little. Sis send her love to you and says please to send her a Christmas present.

And for the Lord's sake do try and sell that property. It is of no use to wate for a grate price and come away from there. I am not very well I have a right bad cold. The rest of the children are well.

I remain your wife
Nancy Ruffin

Ignoring the part that black women played in supporting their families, the early black newspapers published innumerable articles on what was called woman's sphere, some reprinted from the white press. One wonders what a washerwoman or seamstress thought when she read "Counsel for Ladies," "Duties of Wives," or "Ladies Beware." Excerpts from articles in Freedom's Journal *and the* Colored American:

Women are not formed for great cares themselves, but to soften ours. Their tenderness is the proper reward for the dangers we undergo for their preservation. They are confined within the narrow limits of domestic assiduity, and when they stray beyond them, they move out of their proper sphere and consequently without grace.

Employ yourself in household affairs. Wait till your husband confides to you, and do not give your advice till he asks it. Always appear flattered by the little he does for you. Never wound his vanity, not even in the most trifling instance. A wife may have more sense than her husband but she should never seem to know it.

In the 1840s, as the woman's rights movement got under way and progressive black spokespersons emerged, these sexist articles virtually disappeared. The change in masculine attitudes, at least among leading men, was formally noted at a Convention of Colored Freemen in 1848 when, after some discussion, the delegates voted:

Whereas, we fully believe in the equality of the sexes, therefore, Resolved, That we invite females hereafter to take part in our deliberations.

Although organizations in the black community continued to be male dominated, women played an important part in the Underground Railroad. Because Mary Lyons's husband operated a Colored Sailors' Home, runaways frequently found their way to her door. Her daughter, Maritcha, recalled those days.

Mary Marshall Lyons came from an old New York family. *(Schomburg Center, New York Public Library)*

Father's connection with the underground railroad brought many strange faces to our house, for it was semi-public and persons could go in and out without attracting special attention. Under mother's vigilant eye, refugees were kept long enough to be fed and to have disguises changed and be met by those prepared to speed them on in the journey toward the North Star. Father use to say humorously this part of his business was "keeping a cake and apple stand". He estimated he had been of help to a thousand persons, thanks to mother's devotion and discretion.

Sometimes women's roles were more militant. In 1836 when two fugitive slave women were rescued from a Boston courtroom and carried away to freedom, "the rush was made, and the liberated prisoners were born out by the colored females *in attendance, and not by the* colored men," *the* Liberator *reported. The "Abolition Riot," as Boston newspapers called it, was followed by a similar attempt in New York, which the* Colored American *deplored: "Everlasting shame and re-morse seize upon those females that so degraded themselves yesterday. We beg their husbands to keep them at home and find some better occupation for them." The rescues set a standard for direct action that was widely copied in later years. Thomas B. Hilton, the son of Lavinia Hilton, who as a member of the Boston Female Anti-Slavery Society may have taken part in the "Abolition Riot," recalled another occasion when women routed a slave catcher. The time was 1847, the place Smith Court where many ex-slaves lived.*

One day between eleven and twelve o'clock, A.M., there was a ripple of excitement in the rear of Smith's Court. Some children had reported that a slave holder was in Mrs. Dorsey's. It being working hours scarcely a colored man was seen in the vicinity; but there were those around that showed themselves equal to the occasion. Among these was Mrs. Nancy Prince, a colored woman of prominence in Boston who, with several others, hurried to the scene. Mrs. Prince had seen the kidnapper before. Only for an instance did [her] fiery eyes rest upon the form of the villain, as if to be fully assured that it was he, for the next moment she had grappled with him, and before he could fully realize his position she, with the assistance of the colored women that had accompanied her, had dragged him to the door and thrust him out of the house. By this time quite a number, mostly women and children had gathered near by, whom Mrs. Prince commanded to come to the rescue, telling them to "pelt him with stones and any thing you can get a hold of," which order they proceeded to obey with alacrity. The slaveholder started to retreat, and with his assailants close upon him ran out of the court. Only once did the man turn in his head-long flight when, seeing them streaming after him terribly in earnest, their numbers constantly increasing and hearing in his ears their exultant cries and shouts of derision he redoubled his speed and, turning the corner was soon lost to view.

After the passage of the Fugitive Slave Law, men and women, black and white, worked together in every city of the North to save runaways from going back to slavery. A dramatic rescue took place in 1859 in Troy, New York, with Harriet Tubman as mastermind of the event. Sarah H. Bradford, her friend and biographer, told the story.

The instant Harriet heard the news [of the fugitive's arrest], she started for the office of the United States Commissioner, scattering the tidings as she went. An excited crowd was gathered about the office, through which Harriet forced her way, and rushed up stairs to the door of the room where the fugitive was detained. A wagon was waiting to carry off the man, but the crowd was so great that the officers did not dare to bring the man down. Harriet, seeing the necessity for a tremendous effort for his rescue, sent out some little boys to cry *fire*. The bells rang, the crowd increased, till the whole street was a dense mass of people.

At length the man was brought out—with his wrists manacled together, walking between the U.S. Marshal and another officer. The moment they appeared, Harriet threw up a window, and cried to her friends; "Here he comes—take him!" and then darted down the stairs like a wild-cat. She seized one officer and pulled him down, then another, and tore him away from the man; and keeping her arms about the slave, she cried to her friends, "Drag us out! Drag him to the river!" They were knocked down together, and while down, she tore off her sun-bonnet and tied it on the head of the fugitive. When he rose, only his head could be seen, and amid the surging mass of people, the slave was no longer recognized. Harriet's outer clothes were torn from her, and even her stout shoes were pulled from her feet, yet she never relinquished her hold of the man, till she had dragged him to the river, where he was tumbled into a boat, Harriet following in a ferry-boat to the other side.

Across the river, after another scuffle with the law, Tubman and a group of women succeeded in putting the fugitive in a wagon heading west. The Troy Whig *reported his safe arrival in Canada a day later.*

Although the first battles against segregated accommodations were initiated by men, women like Frances E. Watkins, Mary Ann Shadd, and Sojourner Truth were soon raising their voices to demand equal rights. During the 1850s protests focused on the horse cars that had become the chief form of urban transportation. In New York Elizabeth Jennings sued the Third Avenue Railroad Company after she had been put off a horse car. She won $225 for damages for herself and the right to ride for all "colored persons, if sober, well-behaved and free from disease." Her account of the incident that precipitated the lawsuit was read at a mass meeting of black New Yorkers:

Sarah E. Adams and myself walked down to the corner of Pearl and Chatham Sts. to take the Third-Av. cars. We got on the platform when the conductor told us to wait for the next car. I told him I could not wait, as I was in a hurry to go to church.

He then told me that the other car had my people in it, that it was appropriated for "my people." I told him I had no people. I wished to go to church and I did not wish to be detained. He still kept driving me off the car. I told him I was a respectable person, born and raised in New York, did not know where he was born.* He took hold of me and I took hold of the window sash. He pulled me until he broke my grasp. I took hold of his coat and held on to that. He then ordered the driver to fasten his horses and come and help him put me out of the cars. Both seized hold of me by the arms and pulled and dragged me down on the bottom of the platform, so that my feet hung one way and my head the other, nearly on the ground.

I screamed, "Murder," with all my voice and my companion screamed out, "You'll kill her. Don't kill her." The driver then let go of me and went to his horses. I went again in the car and the conductor said, "You shall sweat for this." Then told the driver to drive until he saw an officer or a Station House. The officer, without listening to anything I had to say, thrust me out and then tauntingly told me to get redress if I could.

For every woman who fought for civil rights, hundreds were too preoccupied with personal problems to protest. Two women who were "in trouble" appealed to Wendell Phillips for help. Their letters make it clear that having a child out of wedlock was not looked on with favor in the black community.

To Wendell Phillips
Dear Sir: Hartford, [Connecticut,] December 15, 1858
My unfortunate condition compels me to acquaint some one of my imprudence. I am in great trouble by Carl Formes that is at present singing at the Boston Theater. I have acquainted him of it and receiving no reply and being destitute of funds I borrow 7 dollars and visited New York two weeks ago. I wrote him two letters and the last one on the day of my leaving New York for this city. I inform him that as he was soon to visit Boston that I should try what the laws of that State would do in my behalf.

I would like you to go and see him & plead for me. I do not wish to make it a Public affair on the account of my Mother who is a respectable Woman in Florence, Mass. where I became acquainted with him. Pleas to do all that you can for me as privately as possible unless Mr. Formes is determin to doubt my word and then I will come

*The conductor was born in Ireland. Jennings's anti-Irish bias was typical of blacks who saw the newly arrived Irish moving into jobs that were denied to them.

on and prove it for I am now nearly six months in advance. Do pleas to use all the influence that you can for me for I must not go home to my Mother. I cannot give you directions where to find him only at the Boston Theater in company with Madll. Picclomini & others. Pleas to pardon the liberty I have taken to write you of my serious troubles & let them apollogiz for so unfortunate person as Susan P. Randall No. 52 Village Street

After investigating Randall's claim, Phillips convinced the man who had "wronged" her to contribute to her support.

Mr. Phillips
Sir: Hartford, [Connecticut,] April 26, 1859
    I am still at No 52 Village St and through your kindness am doing as well as can be expected. My little Boy was five weeks old last Saturday and is quite well. I do not intend to remain here any longer than it is necessary for me to do so.
    It is a pleasure to me to inform you what a relief your timely assistance gave me. I shall soon be able to earn my living again I can never forget your kindness to me as a stranger. I wish it was in my power to give you something for your trouble or in any way to express my thanks as I could wish. Believe me truly greatful and accept the humble thanks of
                                            Susan P. Randall

The fate of Mary E. Daniels, author of the letter which follows, is not known.

Mr. Phillips
Sir: Hartford, Conn[ecticut,] March 26, 1859
    I trust you are acquainted with a Colored young man by the name of Charles L. Mitchell a Printer in Boston which came to the aforesaid City 5 years ago. At that time my sad story commences. He left me in trouble. We both resided under the same roof and had kept company for a year or more previous to his leaving Hartford. He promised to mary me but has since treated me with neglect and indifference and was at that time the cause of my being treated with the greatest severiety by my Mother who died last August and from the time of my misfortune up to the time of my Mothers Death we lived very unhappily as she said I had disgraced her. At that time I was under age. Oh Sir I have been cruelly Deceived. He has broken his promises and all the assistance he has ever rendered me was 10 dollars. I have not been well since my misfortune. His Mother wrote to him of my

sickness and has entreated him to do what was right by me but he has not as yet answered her letter. I am Sir greatly in need of assistance and protection as I have neither Father or Mother and my health is delicate.

Very respectfully

Mary E. Daniels

Deserted by her husband, Paul Cuffe, Jr., Mary Cuffe wrote to William Rotch, the Quaker businessman who was executor of her father-in-law's estate. In his will, Cuffe, Sr., had provided that "five hundred dollars be retained and put to interest, the income of which I order to be used annually for the support of my son Paul Cuffe's family, forever."

Nantucket, [Massachusetts,]
Respected Friend William Rotch Jr.:   November 2, 1836
I have a copy of Paul Cuffe's will before me, in which it appears, that the income of 500 dollars is ordered to be used annually for the support of my husband's family. I believe, that on *reflection* you will deem it very unconscionable for the income to be used up by a man who lives in a state of idleness & inaction, and makes no provision for the support of himself or family, and while his family are destitute of the comforts & necessaries of life.

The fact is, my husband is a hale, stout, strong, hardy man, and ought to be made to know that he *shall,* at least support *himself.* We have a Law of this Commonwealth enacted for the very purpose of punishing Common Drunkards—Idlers &c. Were my husband sick, lame or otherwise providentially disqualified for labor, I would cheerfully be his nurse & do all I could to render his situation comfortable —But this is not the case. He is well & hearty and has abandoned me. He has thrown me upon the mercy of an unfeeling world.

I am told that my husband is a first rate whaleman—And is abundantly qualified for a Boat Leader, and might obtain an excellent Lay.* Shall he under those circumstances remain idle & inactive and use up the annual pittance which ought to be appropriated for the support of his Wife & children. Here I am, exposed to the inclemency of an approaching winter. I submit my case in full confidence that you will do right.

your friend

Mary Cuffe

*A lay was an individual seaman's share in a whaling voyage.

Mary Cuffe's persuasive letter convinced Rotch to send her money, but a later note from Paul Cuffe, Jr., told the executor to "pay no more of that interest to no one til I give orders." He also confided, "I have stop drinking any thing but Cider."

Despite unfeeling lovers and delinquent husbands, black women's most serious problems were caused by whites. Reputed to be women of easy virtue, they always had to be on guard against rape. This taboo subject was never mentioned in the black or abolitionist press. Only in Chatham, Canada, a town with a large black population, did a woman bring charges against her attacker—and only in Chatham did a woman editor dare to print her story. Mary Ann Shadd Cary published the following account of attempted rape, noting that the victim was "a very respectable colored lady" who taught in the public school and that her assailant, J. F. Grady, was "an Irishman, A Dentist."

On Saturday last, the 21st Feb'y, about 4 o'clock P.M., I went in the Dentist room of the accused, for the purpose of getting a tooth extracted. I proposed having another set in place. Defendant said he would charge ten dollars, which I declined giving. Defendant then asked me if I was married to the gentleman with me. I said I was not. I told him I was a married woman, but that my husband was absent, he then said he would charge four dollars, fixed the day for me to call, which was Tuesday. As I turned to go out at the door he clasped me, so that I had no use of my hands and then locked the door. I desired him to let me alone and threatened to scream out murder; he still held me and tried to push me to a lounge in the lower part of the room. I asked him what he wanted? He said that I knew how it was with a young unmarried man. I again threatened to scream murder, and after tusseling around the room some ten minutes, I told him I would take the law of him; he found he could not accomplish his design when he let me go. He offered an apology which I refused to take; but said I would expose him. He then said if I would not expose him he would unlock the door, I still said I would expose him, and if he did not unlock the door, I would break a pane of glass and scream for help. He then unlocked the door and I left.

Signed,
Sarah Armstrong

Grady found it expedient to leave town. Tried in absentia, he was convicted of assault and fined £4 2s 6d and court costs.

The crime of kidnapping was far more commonly reported. No black woman, man, or child could feel safe from the blackbirders who cruised in poor neighborhoods looking for victims to sell into slavery. Reports of lost children were common. The affidavit below and the letters that follow are from the files of the Pennsylvania Abolition Society. The society's officers prosecuted kidnappers and reunited families who had been separated.

Personally appeared before me the Mayor of the City of Philadelphia Rebecca Thompson a free Coloured Woman who being duly sworn doth depose and say that she is well acquainted with a coloured boy Named Henry Johnson the son of her husbands Sister whose name was Hester Johnson; that the said Henry was born in the house of this deponent in the City of Philadelphia and that his mother who is deceased left the lad to the care of this deponent and that he continued to live with her till about Two months past when this deponent sent him as usual to Sweep the Philadelphia Library and make the fires which he did but never returned. This deponent does not recollect at this time any particular marks about him but that his 2nd toe is as long as his large toe and is somewhat raised over it he is about 14 years of age and is rather Short of his age but stout and of a very dark complexion and large good teeth.

Respected Sir: Milford, [Delaware,] December 4, 1822
I would wish you to enquire into the fate of my son and let me know the consequence. I am very unhappy on the occasion. I wish you and lawyer Norris to pry into this business and I shall be very much obliged to you. If you get him keep him and I will come after him. My child was free by law. I wish to know how it is for I am very uneasy. Remain your most duitufl and humble St
                    Amyntia Conner

Levina Johnson's letter, probably written by someone else, was addressed to her husband. Philip Lee, her uncle, could testify that she was freeborn.

Mr. Isaac Johnson   Augusta, [Georgia,] July 7, 1824
Dear Sir: I write you a few lines that you may know where I am and how I came here. I was kidnapped by Jacob Purnal Joseph Johnson & Ebenezer Johnson at the Cross Roads the division of Maryland and Delaware. I am now in Augusta Georgia owned by John Filpot. I was brought to Georgia by the above named Johnson's & Sold to Mr. Filpot, myself & two Children. Mr. Philip Lee I wish also to know where I am & my two Brothers, Littleton Stevens & his Brother James

please inform them I am in Augusta Georgia, and how I came here. I once was Free but now am a slave. I wish to inform you all that I am still striving to get to Heaven & if I should not see you all in this world I hope to meet you all in Heaven there to part no more. I hope you are well and I remain the Same yours
Levina Johnson

Rachel and Mary Elizabeth Parker, sisters who worked as domestics in Chester County, Pennsylvania, were both kidnapped in 1851. When Rachel Parker's white employer, Joseph Miller, attempted to rescue her, he was lynched by a Maryland mob. Public outrage was so great that the governor of Pennsylvania intervened and, after a year in captivity, the young women were returned to their homes. Rachel Parker described her kidnapping.

I was taken from Joseph C. Miller's about twelve o'clock on Tuesday, by two men who came up to the house by the back door. One came in and seized me by the arm and pulled me out of the house. Mrs. Miller called to her husband, and he ran out and seized the man by the collar. The other, with an oath, then told him to take his hands off, and if he touched me he would kill me. He then told Miller that I belonged to Mr. Schoolfield, in Baltimore. They hurried me to a waggon, where there was another large man, put me in, and drove off. We stopped at a tavern near the railroad, and I told the landlord that I was free. I also told several persons at the car-office. I was taken to Baltimore to jail. The next morning a man with large light-colored whiskers took me away by myself, and asked me if I was not Mr. Schoolfield's slave. I told him I was not; he said that I was, and that if I did not say I was he would 'cow-hide me and salt me, and put me in a dungeon.' I told him I was free and that I would say nothing but the truth.

In September 1852 Anne Northup, the cook at Carpenter's Hotel in Glen Falls, New York, received a letter from her husband who had been kidnapped eleven years earlier. She appealed to the governor.

To His Excellency, the Governor of the State of New York:
The memorial of Anne Northup, of the village of Glens Falls; respectfully sets forth—
That your memorialist, whose maiden name was Anne Hampton, was forty-four years old on the 14th day of March last, and was married to Solomon Northup, on the 25th day of December, A.D., 1828. That the said Solomon, after such marriage, lived with your memorialist in

said town until 1830, when he removed with his family to the town
of Kingsbury, and remained there about three years, and then removed
to Saratoga Springs, and continued to reside in Saratoga Springs until
about the year 1841, when Solomon started to go to the city of
Washington, in the District of Columbia, since which time your
memorialist has never seen her husband.

And your memorialist further states, that in the year 1841 she
received information that said Solomon had been kidnapped in Washington, put on board of a vessel, and was then in such vessel in New
Orleans, but could not tell how he came in that situation, nor what
his destination was.

That your memorialist ever since the last mentioned period has
been wholly unable to obtain any information of where Solomon was,
until the month of September last, when another letter was received
from Solomon, post-marked at Marksville, in the parish of Avoyelles,
in the State of Louisiana, stating that he was held there as a slave.

That your memorialist and her family are poor and wholly unable
to pay or sustain any portion of the expenses of restoring said Solomon
to his freedom. Your excellency is entreated to employ such agent or
agents as shall be deemed necessary to effect the restoration and return
of Solomon Northup, in pursuance of an act of the Legislature of the
State of New-York, passed May 14, 1840, entitled "An act more
effectually to protect the free citizens of this State from being kidnapped or reduced to slavery." And your memorialist will ever pray.
November 19, 1852

                              Anne Northup

*Solomon Northup was returned to his wife and children two
months later. His story of his years in the South,* Twelve Years a Slave,
*became a best-selling narrative and an authoritative account of slave
life.*

*The kidnappings continued during the war. In Washington, where
the warden of the District jail was notorious for selling free people into
slavery, a domestic worker barely escaped.*

My name is Julia Blackwell. About half past nine o'clock on Tuesday night I was going on an errand to a grocery store. I had got but
a short distance from Dr. McConnell's door, when two men came up
to me, one of whom caught hold of me and shook me, threatening if
I made a noise to choke me. He said that he was going to take me to
jail; that I was a runaway slave. I began to cry, and told him that I was
a free woman, begging him all the while to let me go. He cursed and

swore at me, and again threatened to strangle me if I made a noise.

I was then taken to a magistrate's office. They put me in a back room and Keese asked me where I was born, where my parents lived, and if I was a free woman. I told him that I was free. He then said that it was a lie, that he knew my master and that he had sold my brother Daniel. I again began to cry and begged him for God's sake to let me go. He then gave me a Bible and told me that if I would swear I was a slave he would set me free, and would give me my free papers. I refused to swear, when he told me that I would have to go to jail. Several gentlemen then came into the office. They asked me if I was free and where I lived. I told them I was free and lived with Dr. McConnell. One of the men said "I believe she tells the truth and is a free girl." The man who arrested me then told me that I could go. I was very much frightened. It was near 12 o'clock when I returned home.

Even middle-class women felt insecure. Elizabeth Shadd William-son had been planning to leave her home in Delaware to join the Shadd family in Canada when she learned that her nephew, I. D. Shadd, had been arrested in Chatham after he had rescued a fugitive. She poured out her fears in a letter to Mary Ann Shadd Cary, her niece.

Wilmington, [Delaware,]
My dear Mary Ann: November 2, 1858

I was struck panic on looking over the Standard of last Saturday to see it announsed that I D Shadd had bin sent to Prison. It made me so sick and so bewildered that I could scaircly attend to my duty. I am much afraid that Canada is not going to prove what it was crackd up to be. I was afraid that the Resaprosity Bill would let Yankee influence in their and so it will be in time and what they could not do by the sworde they will by money. Canada will eventually bicome hunting ground for the American Bloodhound and when the friends of the fugative attemps to rescue them the Riott Act will [be] brought against you and Cram you into Prison—the yankees is like the Porke-pine. They had their nose in already and that Bill let their Boddy in. Now all they want is to get their tail in and they will soon molde the Government to their likin and, if Queen Victorya begins to feel the pointe of their quills and complains they will inform her Laydeship that the place suites them and if she dont like she can walk out.

I want if you have time that you will inform me by letter how long him and his Companions will have to stay. This case of Isaac turning out as it has makes me begin to think I had better stay where I am than to go from bad to worse. My best love to Mr. Cary and the Children and believe me now as ever your Affectionate Aunt E. J. Williamson

The ultimate in assaults against persons took the form of mobs invading black neighborhoods, looting, burning, and killing. Starting in 1829 there were periodic race riots in Cincinnati, Philadelphia, New York, and Detroit. The most disastrous took place in New York in July 1863 when men who resented being drafted in "a war for the niggers" turned in fury on black citizens. Dozens of blacks were hung from lampposts or beaten to death; thousands were left homeless. The Colored Orphan Asylum was burned to the ground. Maritcha Lyons, then fifteen years old, described the attack on her parents' home in Brooklyn.

On the afternoon of July [13th] a rabble attacked our house, breaking windowpanes, smashing shutters and partially demolishing the front door. Before dusk arrangements had been effected to secure the safety of the children. As the evening drew on, a resolute man and a courageous woman quietly seated themselves in the hall, determined to sell their lives as dearly as may be. Just after midnight a second mob was gathering. As one of the rioters attempted to ascend the front steps, father advanced into the doorway and fired point blank into the crowd. The mob retreated and no further demonstration was made that night. The next day a third and successful attempt at entrance was effected. This sent father over the back fence while mother took refuge on the premises of a neighbor.

In one short hour, the police cleared the premises. What a home! Its interior was dismantled, furniture was missing or broken. From basement to attic evidences of vandalism prevailed. A fire, kindled in one of the upper rooms, was discovered in time to prevent a conflagration. Under cover of darkness the police conveyed our parents to the Williamsburg ferry. Mother with her children undertook the hazardous journey to New England. We reached Salem tired, travel-stained, with only the garments we had on.

The family escaped with their lives, but her father's business was destroyed, and he was never able to rebuild it. Once prosperous, he spent his last years as the sexton of a church.

Other eyewitness reports were far worse.

Mrs. Nancy Robinson says that her husband in order to escape dressed himself up in some of her clothes and in company with herself and one other woman left their residence and went towards one of the Brooklyn Ferries. Robinson wore a hood which failed to hide his beard. Some boys seeing his beard, lifted up the skirts of his dress, which exposed his heavy boots. Immediately the mob set upon him and the atrocities they perpetrated upon him are so indecent, they are unfit for publication. They finally killed him and threw his body into the river. His wife and her companion escaped across the Grand street Ferry to Brooklyn.

Mrs. Statts told this story:

At 3 o'clock the mob arrived and immediately commenced an attack with terrific yells, and a shower of stones and bricks. In the next room to where I was sitting was a poor woman, who had been confined with a child on Sunday, three days previous. Some of the rioters broke through the front door with pick axes, and came rushing into the room where this poor woman lay, and commenced to pull the clothes off from her. Knowing that their rage was chiefly directed against men, I hid my son behind me and ran with him through the back door, down into the basement. In a little while I saw the innocent babe, of three days old, come crashing down into the yard; some of the rioters had dashed it out of the back window, killing it instantly. In a few minutes streams of water came pouring down into the basement, the mob had cut the waterpipes with their axes. Fearing we should be drowned (there were ten of us, mostly women and children, there) I took my boy and flew past the dead body of the babe, out to the rear of the yard, hoping to escape with him through an open lot; but here, to our horror and dismay, we met the mob again; I, with my son had climbed the fence, but the sight of those maddened demons so affected me that I fell back, fainting into the yard; my son jumped down from the fence to pick me up, and a dozen of the rioters came leaping over the fence after him. Two ruffians seized him, each taking hold of an arm, while a third, armed with a crow-bar, deliberately struck him a heavy blow over the head, felling him to the ground. (He died in the N.Y. hospital two days after). I believe if I were to live a hundred years I would never forget that scene, or cease to hear the horrid voices of that demoniacal mob resounding in my ears.

New York's Draft Riot marked the end of an era. The city's leaders —none of them abolitionists—raised money for the homeless and helpless victims of the mob. Afterwards, despite Copperhead opposition, they secured authorization from the War Department to raise a black regiment. *Eight months after the riot, the Twentieth Regiment U.S. Colored Troops marched down Broadway to Union Square, and whites as well as blacks lined the streets to wave handkerchiefs and cheer. "There has been no more striking manifestation of the marvelous times that are upon us than the scene at the departure of the first of our colored regiments," said a* New York Times *editorial. "It is only on such occasions that we can realize the prodigious revolution which the public mind everywhere is experiencing."*

Part III

The War
Years

FOURTEEN

Slavery Chain Done Broke at Last

"GOD BE PRAISED!" *Frederick Douglass wrote when Confederate forces captured Fort Sumter. "The slaveholders have saved our cause. They have exposed the throat of slavery to the keen knife of liberty."*

Liberty for the slaves was a long time coming. In the White House Abraham Lincoln listened with equal patience to abolitionists and to spokesmen from the border states who had remained loyal to the Union and loyal to slavery. He heard the soldiers singing as they marched across the bridge into Virginia:

> To the flag we are pledged, all its foes we abhor.
> And we ain't for the nigger, but we are for the war.

"My policy is to have no policy," Lincoln said. *"What I want is to get done what the people desire to have done, and the question for me is how to find that out exactly."*

The war was only a month old when the slaves began to shape a policy for the president. Wherever Union forces set up camps in the South, men and women stole away from the plantations to join them. At first Lincoln's generals returned the fugitives to their masters. But when slaves who had been building Confederate fortifications presented themselves at Fortress Monroe, General Benjamin Butler declared them "contraband of war" and put them to work on a bakehouse for his men. By the end of the first year of war thousands of contrabands were in camps outside of Washington, in tidewater Virginia and South Carolina, and in Union-held territory along the Mississippi. Mary Barbour was a small child when her parents took her to join the Yankees:

One of de fust things dat I 'members wuz my pappy wakin' me up in de middle o'de night, dressin' me in de dark, all de time tellin' me ter keep quiet. One o'de twins hollered some an' pappy put his hand ober its mouth ter keep it quiet. Atter we wuz dressed he went outside an' peeped roun' fer a minute den he comed back an' got us. We snook out o' de house an' long de woods path, pappy totin' one of de twins an' holdin' me by de han' an' mammy carryin' de odder two.

I reckons dat I will always 'member dat walk, wid de bushes slappin' my laigs, de win' sighin in de trees, an' de hoot owls an' whippoorwills hollerin' at each other from de big trees. I wuz half asleep an' skeered stiff, but in a little while we pass de plum thicket an' dar am de mules an' wagin.

Dar am er quilt in de bottom o' de wagin, an' on dis day lays we youngins. An' pappy an' mammy gits on de board cross de front an' drives off down de road. We trabels all night an' hid in de woods all day. When we gits ter New Bern de Yankees takes de mules an wagin. My pappy wuz a shoemaker, so he makes Yankee boots, an' we gits 'long pretty good.

Mill and Jule who had been slaves on a plantation on the Mississippi River told a white abolitionist* of their final encounter with their mistress.

One day she say, "Mill, I reckon that's a gunboat comin'. Now, if the Yankees do stop you all run and hide, won't you?" I didn't answer till I see the big rope flung on the bank. An' mistress got wild-like. "Yes, they are stoppin'. Mill an' Jule run, tell all the niggers in the quarters to run to the woods an' hide; quick, for they kills niggers. Mill, why don't you go?"

I said, "I ain't feared the Yankees," "Jule, you run and tell all the niggers to run to the woods, quick. Yes, here they are coming, right up to the house. Now, Mill, you won't go with them, will you?" I felt safe, and said, "I'll go if I have a chance." "Jule, you won't go, will you?" "I shall go if Mill goes." She began to wring her hands and cry. "Now, 'member I brought you up. You won't take your children away from me, will you, Mill?" "Mistress I shall take what children I've got lef'." "If they fine that trunk o' money or silver plate you'll say it's your'n, won't you?" "Mistess, I can't lie over that; you bo't that silver plate when you sole my three children." "Now, Jule you'll say it's your'n, won't you?" "I can't lie over that either." An' she was cryin' an' wringin' her han's. "Yes, here they come, an' they'll rob me of every thing. Now 'member I brought you up." Here come in four sojers with swords hangin' to their sides, an' never looked at mistess, but said to

*Laura Haviland (1808–98) was a leader in the antislavery movement in Michigan. A teacher, Underground Railroad operator, and abolitionist lecturer, she worked closely with the freedpeople during and after the Civil War.

me, "Auntie, you want to go with us?" "Yes, sir," I said, an' they
looked to Julie an' say, "You want to go?" "Yes, sir," "Well, you can
all go; an' hurry, for we shall stay but a little while." An' Jule jus' flew
to the quarters an' they all tied up beds an' every thing, an' tote 'em
down to the gunboats. An' we all got on the boat in a hurry; an' when
we's fairly out in the middle of the river, we all give three times three
cheers for the gunboat boys, and three times three cheers for big
Yankee sojers, an' three times three cheers for gov'ment; an' I tell you
every one of us, big and little, cheered loud and long and strong, an'
made the old river just ring ag'in.

*Sometimes slave owners visited the camps in an effort to retrieve
their property. "I jus' trimble" a woman said.*

My ole missus come las' week and she tried mighty hard to get us
to go back wid her. Den she went to General Grant, an' he say, "If
your people want to go back they may." Den she try us again; but not
one would go, 'cause we knows her too well—she's mighty hard on us.
Den she went back to the general, an' begged an' cried, and hel' out
her han's and say, "General, dese han's never was in dough—I never
made a cake o' bread in my life; please let me have my cook." An' she
took on so I's feared he'd tell me to go wid her. But all her cryin' didn't
help her. General say, "I can't help you, madam; if your cook wants
to go wid you she can; but she is free, an' can do as she likes about
it." An she went off cryin'; and we could jus' kiss de groun' General
Grant walks on ever since.

*Few Union officers were as compassionate as General Grant.
When the commander of Camp Nelson, Kentucky, was confronted by
what he called the "Nigger Woman Question," he drove away hundreds of women and children, whipping some and returning others to
their former owners. From camps across the South, there were complaints of rape. An indignant white man reported an episode at Fortress Monroe.*

About a week since, four soldiers went to the house of two colored
men, (father and son-in-law.) Two of them seized a colored woman in
the front yard, each in turn gratifying his brutal lusts, while the other
stood guard with sword and pistol. The other two went to the house,
one stopping at the door to stand guard. The other, after a desperate
struggle, succeeded in ravishing a young woman in the house in the
presence of her father and grandfather. The father gave vent to his
bitter anguish by an irrepressible groan, when the guard at the door

rushed upon him and struck him. The grandfather and girl came to us and told us the sad story of their wrongs but there were then some fifteen thousand soldiers at Newport News and the villains were not found.

In the Union camps family groups were separated as the women worked as laundresses and cooks while the men dug ditches, built roads and bridges, and, after 1863, joined the army. More than 186,000 black men fought for the Union; a third were dead or missing by the end of the war. On the Confederate side, a "Negro soldier law" was not passed until February 1865, too late for enlistments, but numerous slaves went to the front with their masters as body servants or were drafted as laborers. Several letters from women whose husbands were at the front have been found. The following was addressed to Norfleet Perry, a slave who accompanied his master's son, a member of the Texas Cavalry. It was probably written for Fannie by her young mistress.

My Dear Husband: Spring Hill, [Texas,] December 28, 1862.
     I would be mighty glad to see you and I wish you would write back here and let me know how you are getting on. I am doing tolerable well and have enjoyed very good health since you left. I haven't forgot you nor I never will forget you as long as the world stands, even if you forget me. My love is just as great as it was the first night I married you, and I hope it will be so with you. If I never see you again, I hope to meet you in Heaven. There is no time night or day but what I am studying about you. I heard once that you were sick but I heard afterwards that you had got well. I hope your health will be good hereafter. Master gave us three days Christmas. I wish you could have been here to enjoy it with me for I did not enjoy myself much because you were not here. Mother, Father, Grandmama, Brothers & Sisters say Howdy and they hope you will do well. Be sure to answer this soon for I am always glad to hear from you. I hope it will not be long before you can come home.
                            Your Loving Wife
                                Fannie

The poignant letter which follows was sent to Solomon Steward, a member of the First South Carolina Volunteers, the first regiment of ex-slaves to be mustered into the U.S. service. Although the recruits had been promised allotments for their families, pay and rations were often in arrears.

My Dear Husband:　　　　Fernandina, Florida, February 8, [1864]
This Hour I Sit Me Down To write you In a Little world of sweet sounds. The Choir In the Chapel near Here are Chanting at The Organ and Thair Morning Hymn are sounding and The Dear Little birds are joining Thair voices In Tones sweet and pure as angels whispers. But My Dear a sweeter song Than That I now Hear and That Is The song of a administering angel Has Come and borne My Dear Little babe To Join with Them. My babe only Live one day. It was a Little Girl. Her name Is alice Gurtrude steward. I am now sick in bed and have Got nothing To Live on. The Rashion That They Give for six days I Can Make It Last but 2 days. They dont send Me any wood. I dont Get any Light at all. You Must see To That as soon as possible for I am In want of some Thing To Eat.

All the family send thair love to you. No more at pressant
Emma Steward

Until the final days of the war the vast majority of slaves remained on the plantations. Some owners "refugeed" them, sending wagon trains of livestock and people to Texas, Arkansas, and even California. "Us travel all day and half de night and sleep on de ground," Ella Washington said. Other masters tried to hold them by warning that the Yankees were devils with horns and tails who would sell them all to Cuba. "He said that you all had for legs like a hors and had one eye before and one behind and a horn on each side," Emma Bolt wrote after her escape. The women listened to these stories but kept their own counsel. When the Yankee soldiers appeared, no horns could be seen. However, haloes were also conspicuously absent. Cheney Cross of Alabama recalled:

I 'members de Yankee raid like it was just yesterday. I'se settin' dere in de loom room, and Mr. Thad Watts' little gal, Louise, she's standin' at the window. She says: "O-o-Oh! Dem's de Yankees comin'!" Before I can catch my breath, de place is covered. Feets sounded like mutterin' thunder. Dem bayonets stick up like dey just settin-on de mouth of dey guns. Dey swords hanging on de sides singin' a tune while dey walk. A chicken better not pass by. If he do, off comes his head!

When dey pass on by me, dey pretty nigh shuck me outa my skin. "Where's de men's?" dey say and shake me up. "Where's de arms?" Dey shake me till my eyeballs loosen up. "Where's de silver?" Lord! Was my teeth droppin' out? Dey didn't give me time to catch my breath. Look like dem soldiers had to sharpen dey swords on everything in sight. De big crepe mullein bush by de parlor winder was bloomin' so pink and pretty, and dey just stand dere and whack off dem blooms like folks' heads droppin' on de ground. De sergeant run his bayonet clean through Miss Mary's best featherbed and rip it slam open! With dat, a wind blowed up and took dem feathers every which way for Sunday. You couldn't see where you's at. When dey left de next day, de whole place was strewed with mutilation.

Sarah Debro of North Carolina said:

I 'members de first time de Yankees come. Dey come gallipen' down de road, jumpin' over de palin's, tromplin' down de bushes an' messin' up de flower beds. Dey stomped all over de house, in de kitchen, pantries, smoke house, an' everything. I was settin' on de steps when a big Yankee come up.

"Whare did dey hide de gol' an silver, Nigger?" he asked me.

I was skeered, but I tole him I didn't know nothin' bout nothin.' I just set. Den he pushed me off de step an say if I didn dance he gwine shoot my toes off. Skeered as I was I sho done some shufflin'. Den he give me five dollars an tole me to go buy jim cracks, but dat piece of paper won't no good.

Occasionally a soldier with abolitionist sympathies came along. Eliza Sparks of Virginia never forgot the first time she was addressed as "Mrs."

I was nursin' my baby when I heard a gallopin', an' fo' I could move here come de Yankees ridin' up. An', chile, I wasn't scared of 'em. Not a bit. Never in my life, fo' or since, has I seen setch people. The officer mought of been a general—he snap off his hat an' bow low to me an' ast me ef dis was de way to Gloucester Ferry. Den he lean't over an' patted de baby on de haid an' ast what was its name. I tole him it was Charlie, like his father.

Den he ast, "Charlie what?" an' I told him Charlie Sparks. Den he reach in his pocket an' pull out a copper an' say, "Well, you sure have a purty baby. Buy him something with this; an' thankee fo' de direction. Goodbye, Mrs. Sparks." Now, what you think of dat? Dey all call me "Mrs. Sparks!"

Rumors about the Emancipation Proclamation traveled by grapevine. On one Virginia plantation, all of the slaves decamped when they heard them.

We done heared dat Lincum gonna turn de niggers free. Ole missus say dey warn't nothin' to it. Den a Yankee soldier tole someone in Williamsburg dat Marse Lincum done signed de mancipation. Was winter time an' moughty cold dat night, but ev'ybody commence gittin' ready to leave. Didn't care nothin' 'bout Missus—was goin' to Union lines. An' all dat night de niggers danced an' sang right out in de cold. Nex' mornin' at day-break we all started out wid blankets an' clothes an' pots an' pans an' chickens piled on our backs, 'cause Missus said we couldn't take no horses or carts.

For most slaves formal emancipation followed "de surrender," the April day in 1865 when Generals Lee and Grant met at Appomattox.* Matilda Dunbar, mother of the poet, Paul Dunbar, described how she felt when she heard the news.

I was in the kitchen getting breakfast. The word came—"All darkies are free". I never finished that breakfast! I ran 'round and 'round the kitchen, hitting my head against the wall, clapping my hands and crying, "Freedom! freedom! freedom! Rejoice, freedom has come!" Oh, how we sang and shouted that day!

Other ex-slaves recalled the day of jubilee.

Oh, baby! Dem Freedom Days! Never was no time like 'em befo' or since. Niggers shoutin' an' clappin' hands an' singin'! Chillun runnin' all over de place beatin' tins an' yellin'. Ev'ybody happy. Sho' did some celebratin'. Run to de kitchen an' shout in de winder:

> Mammy don't you cook no mo'
> You's free! You's free!

Run to de henhouse an shout:

> Rooster don't you crow no mo'
> You's free! You's free!

Go to de pigpen an' tell de pig:

> Ol' pig, don't you grunt no mo'
> You's free! You's free!

An' some smart alec boys sneaked up under Miss Sara Ann's window an shouted:

> Ain't got to slave no mo'
> We's free! We's free!

---

*Emancipation was not acknowledged in Texas until June 19, 1865; in some remote places, masters were able to conceal the news for years.

Was the glorious news true? One way to make sure was to confront Mistress. Maggie Lawson recounted a story that her grandmother had told:

Caddie had been sold to a man in Goodman, Mississippi. It was terrible to be sold in Mississippi. In fact, it was terrible to be sold anywhere. She had been put to work in the fields for running away again. She was hoeing a crop when she heard that General Lee had surrendered. When General Lee surrendered that meant that all the colored people were free! Caddy threw down that hoe, she marched herself up to the big house, then, she looked around and found the mistress. She went over to the mistress, she flipped up her dress and told the white woman to do something. She said it mean and ugly. This is what she said: "Kiss my ass!"

But when the day of jubilee was over, exultation often gave way to bewilderment. What was freedom anyway? A Mississippi woman puzzled over its dimensions.

I used to think if I could be free I should be the happiest of anybody in the world. But when my master come to me, and says— Lizzie, you is free! it seems like I was in a kind of daze. And when I would wake up in the morning I would think to myself, is I free? Hasn't I got to get up before daylight and go into the field to work?

In South Carolina ex-slaves sang of "No more driver's lash for me/ No more mistress call for me." In Virginia, freedom was defined as "No mo' selling."

Member de fust Sunday of freedom. We was all sittin' roun' restin' an' tryin' to think what freedom meant an' ev'ybody was quiet an' peaceful. All at once ole Sister Carrie who was near 'bout a hundred started in to talkin':

> Tain't no mo' sellin' today,
> Tain't no mo' hirin' today,
> Tain't no pullin' off shirts today,
> Its stomp down freedom today.
> Stomp it down!

An' when she says "Stomp it down," all de slaves commence to shoutin' wid her:

> Stomp down Freedom today—
> Stomp it down!
> Stomp down Freedom today.

FIFTEEN

View from the North

IN THE OPENING MONTHS OF THE WAR, *as northern white women rolled bandages, knitted socks, and packed boxes of delicacies for the soldiers, black women remained on the sidelines. They had little choice, for the War Department rejected their men's offers to fight while at the same time the President tried to persuade them to emigrate to Central America. As soon as contrabands began to make their way to the Union lines, however, there was work to be done. Harriet Jacobs and Elizabeth Keckley, a former slave from Virginia, were among the first to come forward to aid the refugees.*

Harriet Jacobs was speaking to antislavery groups in Pennsylvania about her newly published Incidents in the Life of a Slave Girl *when Philadelphia Friends asked her to go to Washington to report on the contrabands. When she arrived in the capital in the spring of 1862, she found some 400 homeless, penniless people. A year later, ten thousand had gathered in Washington, with an additional three thousand across the river in Alexandria, Virginia. By war's end, black newcomers in the District of Columbia were estimated at forty thousand. Nominally under army jurisdiction, they needed substantial aid from northern philanthropists. Jacobs's long letter to the* Liberator, *excerpted below, was one of the earliest accounts of the freedpeople.*

Dear Mr. Garrison: [Washington, D.C., August 1862]

I went to Duff Green's Row,* Government headquarters for the contrabands here. I found men, women and children all huddled together without any distinction or regard to age or sex. Some of them were in the most pitiable condition. Many were sick with measles, diptheria, scarlet and typhoid fever. Some had a few filthy rags to lie on, others had nothing but the bare floor for a couch. They were coming in at all times, often through the night and the Superintendent had enough to occupy his time in taking the names of those who came in and those who were sent out. His office was thronged through the day by persons who came to hire the poor creatures. Single women hire at four dollars a month, a woman with one child two and a half or three dollars a month. Men's wages are ten dollars per month. Many of

*Duff Green's Row was on East Capitol Street where the Folger Shakespeare Library now stands.

them, accustomed as they have been to field labor, and to living almost entirely out of doors, suffer much from the confinement in this crowded building. The little children pine like prison birds for their native element. It is almost impossible to keep the building in a healthy condition. Each day brings the fresh additions of the hungry, naked and sick.

Hoping to help a little in the good work I wrote to a lady in New York, a true and tried friend of the slave, to ask for such articles as would make comfortable the sick and dying in the hospital. On the Saturday following an immense box was received from New York. Before the sun went down, I had the satisfaction of seeing every man, woman and child with clean garments, lying in a clean bed. What a contrast! They seemed different beings.

Alexandria is strongly Secesh; the inhabitants are kept quiet only at the point of Northern bayonets. In this place, the contrabands are distributed more over the city. The old schoolhouse is the Government headquarters for the women. This I thought the most wretched of all. In this house are scores of women and children with nothing to do, and nothing to do with. Their husbands are at work for the Government. Here they have food and shelter, but they cannot get work.

Let me tell you of another place—Arlington Heights, General Lee's beautiful residence,* which has been so faithfully guarded by our Northern army. The men are employed and most of the women. Here they have plenty of exercise in the open air and seem very happy. Many of the regiments are stationed here. It is a delightful place for both the soldiers and the contraband.

My first visit for Alexandria was on a Saturday. To the very old people I gave some clothing. Begging me to come back, they promised to do all they could to help themselves. One old woman said, "Honey, tink when all get still I can go and fine de old place. Tink de Union 'stroy it? You can't get nothing on dis place. Down on de ole place you can raise ebery ting. I ain't seen bacca since i bin here. Neber git a livin here, where de peoples eben buy pasley." This poor old woman thought it was nice to live where tobacco grew, but it was dreadful to be compelled to buy a bunch of parsley.

Some of them have been so degraded by slavery that they do not know the usages of civilized life; they know little else than the handle

*Originally owned by George Washington Parke Custis, grandson of Martha Washington, the Arlington estate became the home of Robert E. Lee after his marriage to Custis's daughter. Occupied by Union forces during the war, it was later purchased by the government as the site of Arlington Cemetery and Fort Myer.

of the hoe, the plough, the cotton-pod and the overseer's lash. Have patience with them. You have helped to make them what they are; teach them civilization. You owe it to them and you will find them as apt to learn as any other people that come to you stupid from oppression.

Linda*

Jacobs remained in Washington to assist the refugees. "My health is better than it has been for years," she wrote to Amy Post. "The good God has spared me for this work. The last six months has been the happiest of all my life."

In Freedmen's Village† in Alexandria where more than a thousand ex-slaves were raising food for the army and living in cabins paid for out of their first earnings, she distributed clothing to the needy, nursed the sick, and helped the able bodied find jobs. After her daughter Louisa joined her, they organized sewing circles and schools. Not all of the lessons were taught in classrooms. When whites insisted on taking charge of a school that the freedmen had built, Jacobs intervened and secured the school for Louisa and a teacher who had accompanied her from Massachusetts. She reported the incident in a letter to Hannah Stevenson, then in charge of the Teachers Committee of the New England Freedmen's Aid Society.

Dear Miss Stevenson: Alexandria, [Virginia,] March 1 [1864]
   I found the school house not finished for the want of funds. I also found many missionary‡ applicants waiting to take charge of the school. I thought it best to wait and see what was the disposition of the Freedmen to whom the Building belonged. The week before the school room was finished I called on one of the colored Trustees, stated the object of bringing the young ladies to Alexandria. He said he would be proud to have the ladies teach in their school, but the white people had made all the arrangements without consulting them. The next morning I was invited to meet with the Trustees at their evening meeting. I extended the invitation to the parties that were contending for the school. I wanted the colored men to learn the time had come when it was their privilege to have something to say. A very few words

*Because Jacobs had used the pseudonym, Linda Brent, when her book was published, abolitionists referred to her as Linda or Linda Jacobs.
†Freedmen's Village was built on seventeen acres of land that George Washington Custis had deeded to Marie Syphax, his daughter by a slave woman.
‡Teachers who went to the South to work with the freedmen were often called missionaries, in the sense that they were people with a mission. Many, of course, were evangelical Protestants who hoped to bring the ex-slaves to salvation.

decided the matter. Miss Jacobs was to have charge of the school with Miss Lawton her assistant. One gentleman arose to lay his prior claim before the people. A black man arose and said —the gentleman is out of order. This meeting was called in honor of Miss Jacobs and the ladies. After this discussion the poor people were tormented. First one then another would offer to take the school telling them they could not claim the Building unless a white man controlled the school. I went with the trustees to the proper authorities, had their lease for the ground on which the building was erected secured to them for five years. I do not object to white teachers but I think it has a good effect upon these people to convince them their own race can do something for their elevation. It inspires them with confidence to help each other.

After the school room was finished there was a debt of one hundred and eighty dollars to be paid. I wrote to some of my friends in Mass. to beg for some of the articles that might be left over at their fairs. Louisa wrote to a friend in New York. Through their kindness we opened a fair with a handsome fancy table, cleared one hundred and fifty dollars, paid on the school house one hundred and thirty dollars, leaving a surplus in my hands. All day we have three classes at the same time reciting in this room. It makes such confusion. I am anxious to add a small room for recitations. It will cost two hundred dollars. If [you are] willing for the money [you sent] to be used for this purpose, I can raise one hundred and we shall be at work in a few days.

Believe me Grateful
H. Jacobs

The Jacobses worked in Arlington until 1865 when the New York Society of Friends sent them to Savannah, Georgia, to a newly built freedmen's hospital. While Louisa taught school, her mother distributed shipments of clothing from the North and assisted the community with their first efforts at subsistence gardening.

After Elizabeth Keckley (1818–1907), a Virginia-born slave, bought her freedom she moved to Washington to open a dressmaking shop. A stately woman with great poise and charm, she soon employed twenty girls in her establishment and was modiste for the wives of cabinet ministers and senators, including Mrs. Jefferson Davis. Introduced to Mary Todd Lincoln the day after Lincoln's inauguration, Keckley became the First Lady's dressmaker and close confidante. Many years later she told an interviewer:

I dressed Mrs. Lincoln for every levee. I made every stitch of clothing that she wore. I dressed her hair. I put on her skirts and

Elizabeth Keckley, in a photograph taken many years after the Civil War. *(Anacostia Neighborhood Museum, Smithsonian Institution)*

dresses. I fixed her bouquets, saw that her gloves were all right, and remained with her each evening until Mr. Lincoln came for her. My hands were the last to touch her before she took the arm of Mr. Lincoln and went forth to meet the ladies and gentlemen on those great occasions.

Early in the war Keckley's son, who had been light skinned enough to join a white regiment, was killed in action. In her grief Keckley was particularly sensitive to the problems of the contrabands in Washington and proposed that well-to-do blacks assist the freedpeople. In Behind the Scenes, *her autobiographical account of White House life, she discussed her effort.*

[In August 1862] I made a suggestion in the colored church, that a society of colored people be formed to labor for the benefit of the unfortunate freedmen. The idea proved popular, and in two weeks "the Contraband Relief Association" was organized with forty working members.

In September of 1862, Mrs. Lincoln left Washington for New York, and requested me to follow her. I was glad of the opportunity to do so, for I thought that in New York I would be able to do something in the interests of our society. Armed with credentials, I took the train for New York, and went to the Metropolitan [Hotel] where Mrs. Lincoln had secured accommodations for me. The next morning I told Mrs. Lincoln of my project; and she immediately headed my list with a subscription of $200. I circulated among the colored people, and got them thoroughly interested in the subject, when I was called to Boston by Mrs. Lincoln, who wished to visit her son Robert, attending college in that city. I met Mr. Wendell Phillips, and other Boston philanthropists, who gave me all the assistance in their power. We held a mass meeting at the Colored Baptist Church, Rev. Mr. Grimes, in Boston, raised a sum of money, and organized there a branch society. The society was organized by Mrs. Grimes, wife of the pastor, assisted by Mrs. Martin, wife of Rev. Sella Martin. This branch was able to send us over eighty large boxes of goods, contributed exclusively by the colored people of Boston. Returning to New York, we held a successful meeting at the Shiloh Church. The Metropolitan Hotel, at that time as now, employed colored help. I suggested the object of my mission to Robert Thompson, Steward of the Hotel, who immediately raised quite a sum of money among the dining-room waiters. Mr. Frederick Douglass contributed $200, besides lecturing for us. Other prominent colored men sent in liberal contributions. From England a large quantity of stores was received. In 1863 I was re-elected President of the Association, which office I continue.

The Contraband Relief Association, which became the Freedmen and Soldiers' Relief Association of Washington after black men were enrolled in the army, continued its activities throughout the war, aided by contributions from many cities. In New York black women gave a ball for the benefit of the contrabands; in Boston funds were raised through dramatic readings; in Philadelphia, members of Mother Bethel Church organized a Contraband Committee. Contributing as best they could from their slender resources, black women also supported the numerous Freedmen's Aid Societies organized by whites.

After President Lincoln's assassination, Elizabeth Keckley was the first person Mary Todd Lincoln turned to. The two remained intimate

*friends until 1868 when Keckley's autobiography was published. Writ-
ten with the help of James Redpath,* Behind the Scenes *presented
details of the Lincolns' private lives that Mrs. Lincoln found offensive.
Except to speak of her derisively as "the colored historian," Mrs.
Lincoln refused to have anything more to do with the woman she had
once called "my best living friend." Although Lincoln scholars consider Keckley's book a valuable source, it conferred neither prestige nor
money on its author. She continued to support herself as a dressmaker
and, in her later years, as a domestic science teacher at Wilberforce
University.*

*Sojourner Truth was living in Battle Creek, Michigan, when Jose-
phine Griffing (1814–72) of the National Woman's Loyal League†
persuaded her to hold rallies in Indiana where Copperheads controlled
the legislature. Defying a new law that forbade blacks from entering
the state, Sojourner was arrested several times during her tour. When
Rebel sympathizers threatened to burn down the hall in which she was
to speak, she said, "Then I will speak upon the ashes." She described
her meeting in Angola, Indiana.*

The ladies thought I should be dressed in uniform so they put upon
me a red, white, and blue shawl, a sash and apron to match, a cap on
my head with a star in front, and a star on each shoulder. When I was
dressed I looked in the glass and was fairly frightened. Said I, "It seems
I am going to battle." My friends advised me to take a sword or pistol.
I replied, "I carry no weapon; the Lord will [preserve] me without
weapons."

When we were ready to go, they put me into a large, beautiful
carriage with the captain and other gentlemen, all of whom were
armed. The soldiers walked by our side and a long procession followed.
As we neared the court-house, I saw that the building was surrounded
by a great crowd. I felt as I was going against the Philistines and I
prayed the Lord to [deliver] me out of their hands. But when the rebels
saw such a mighty army coming, they fled, and by the time we arrived
they were scattered over the fields, looking like a flock of frightened
crows, and not one was left but a small boy, who sat upon the fence,
crying "Nigger, nigger!"

We now marched into the court-house, escorted by double files of

---

*Redpath later collaborated with Jefferson and Varina Davis when they wrote their
recollections of the war.

†The National Woman's Loyal League, organized by Elizabeth Cady Stanton, Susan
B. Anthony, Lucy Stone, and others in May 1863, pledged its support to the government
as long as it waged a war for freedom.

soldiers with presented arms. The band struck up the "Star Spangled Banner," in which I joined and sang with all my might, while amid flashing bayonets and waving banners our party made its way to the platform upon which I advocated free speech with more zeal than ever before, and without interruption.

Accompanied by her fourteen-year-old grandson, Sammy Banks, Sojourner Truth went to Washington in the fall of 1864. With the help of Elizabeth Keckley, she and a white companion, Lucy N. Colman, had an interview with President Lincoln. She wrote to a friend:

He was seated at his desk. Mrs. C. said to him, "This is Sojourner Truth who has come all the way from Michigan to see you." He then arose, gave me his hand and said "I am glad to see you." I said to him, "Mr. President, when you first took your seat, I feared you would be torn to pieces, for I likened you unto Daniel, who was thrown into the lions' den." I then said, "I appreciate you, for you are the best President who has ever taken the seat." He replied—"I expect you have reference to my having emancipated the slaves but," said he, mentioning the names of several of his predecessors and particularly Washington "They were just as good and would have done just as I have, if the time had come. And if the people over the river," pointing across the Potomac, "had behaved themselves I could not have done what I have."

I replied, "I thank God you were the instrument selected by Him and the people to do these things." I presented him with one of my shadows* and songs, for which he thanked me. He then showed me the splendid Bible presented to him by the colored people.

Although Sojourner said "I never was treated with more kindness and cordiality than I was by Abraham Lincoln," Lucy Colman disagreed.

Mr. Lincoln was not himself with this colored woman; he had no funny story for her, he called her aunty, as he would his washerwoman, and when she complimented him as the first Antislavery President, he said "I am not an Abolitionist; I wouldn't free the slaves if I could save the Union any other way."

Appointed a counselor to the freedpeople by the National Freedmen's Relief Association, Sojourner Truth settled in Freedmen's Vil-

---

*Sojourner Truth sold her "shadows" (photographic portraits mounted on cards) as a way of supporting herself.

lage to instruct "the people in the habits of industry and economy. Many of them are entirely ignorant of housekeeping," she wrote, but "they all want to learn the way we live in the North." In addition to teaching the women how to take care of their homes and persons, she too taught them to assert themselves. The following was one of several letters to Amy Post who had been her friend for many years. Although she addressed Post as "my dear daughter," she also sent messages to her real daughters, Sophia and Elizabeth, who were working in Rochester at that time.

Mason's Island,* Virginia,

My Dear Daughter: November 3, 1864

And here I am in the midst of the Freedmen, Women, and Children—and I am in a comfortable place here at the house of Rev. D. B. Nichols,† superintendent of Freedmen and am treated *very* kindly indeed. I do not know but what I shall stay here on the Island all winter and go around among the Freedmens camps. They are all *delighted* to hear me talk. I think I am doing good. I am *needed* here. The people here (white) are only here for the *loaves* and *fishes* while the freedmen get the scales and crusts.

In the Colored Home they *never* knew that Maryland was free‡ until I told them. One old woman clung around my neck and most choked me she was so *glad*. I had good chance to tell the colored people things that they had never heard.

I am agoing around among the colored folks and find out who it is sells the clothing to them that is sent to them from the North. They will tell me for they think a good deal of me.

How are my daughters Elizabeth and Sophia. Sammie§ and I are *perfectly* well and he is *delighted* with the place. He thinks he can be useful. I don't calculate to ask the Government for anything only what I have to eat for the colored people must be raised out of bondage. Say to my daughter Sophia to go and see her son Charlie and if his place aint good to take him home again. I calculate to go and see President Lincoln again. I hope *all* will do *all* they can in putting him in President again. I have a very comfortable room here with

---

*Mason's Island, an island in the Potomac near Freedmen's Village, is now known as Roosevelt Island, after President Theodore Roosevelt.

†The Reverend Danforth B. Nichols of Oberlin was superintendent of the contrabands in the District of Columbia.

‡The slaves of Maryland, a loyal border state, were formally emancipated on November 1, 1864.

§As different people wrote Sojourner Truth's letters at her dictation, the spelling of her grandson's name varied. Usually it was written "Sammy."

Sammie. Direct to me at Washington D.C. Care of Rev. D. B. Nichols,

Sojourner Truth

After the war Sojourner Truth was asked to work in Freedmen's Hospital. Despite the recognition that she received from Freedmen's Bureau officers, she still encountered "the old slaveholding spirit," she told Amy Post.

My dear friend: Washington, [D.C.,] October 1, 1865
    A few weeks ago I was in company with my friend Josephine S. Griffing,* when the Conductor of a street car refused to stop his car for me, although [I was] closely following Josephine and holding on to the iron rail. They dragged me a number of yards before she succeeded in stoping them. She reported the conductor to the president of the City Railway, who dismissed him at once, and told me to take the number of the car whenever I was mistreated by a conductor or driver. On the 13th inst I had occasion to go for blackberry wine, and other necessities for the patients in the Freedmen's Hospital where I have been *doing* and advising for a number of months. I thought now I would get a ride without trouble as I was in company with another Friend Laura S. Haviland of Michigan. As I assended the platform of the car, the conductor pushed me, saying "go back—get off here." I told him I was not going off, then "I'll put you off" said he furiously, clenching my right arm with both hands, using such violence that he seemed about to succeed, when Mrs. Haviland told him, he was not going to put me off. "Does she belong to you?" said he in a hurried angry tone. She replied "She does not belong to me, but she belongs to Humanity." The number of the car was noted, and conductor dismissed at once upon the report to the president who advised his arrest for assault and battery as my shoulder was sprained by his effort to put me off. Accordingly I had him arrested and the case tried before Justice Thompson. My shoulder was very lame and swolen, but is better. It is hard for the old slaveholding spirit to die. But *die* it *must.* Write immediately. Tell me where my children are and *how* they are.
    Mrs. Haviland is here on business, and will remain a week or ten days longer. She does the reading and writing for me while here. As ever I am your friend

Sojourner Truth by L. S. H.

*Josephine Griffing, then general agent of the National Freedmen's Relief Association of the District of Columbia, had been in large part responsible for the creation of the Freedmen's Bureau, officially the Bureau of Refugees, Freedmen and Abandoned Lands.

Before the trial was over, "the inside of those cars looked like pepper and salt" and conductors were inviting black women to "walk in, ladies," Sojourner reported. While she made her daily rounds at the hospital, preaching "order, cleanliness and virtue" she was still concerned about the inhabitants of Freedmen's Village. Throughout the war, members of benevolent societies had endeavored to find jobs for the freedwomen. Apparently it did not occur to anyone that women with children should remain at home to take care of them. Sojourner Truth, Harriet Jacobs, and Josephine Griffing all agreed that the freedwomen must support themselves and not depend on charity. Because employment opportunities in Washington were limited, organizations like the Pennsylvania Abolition Society shipped hundreds of women to employers in the North. White housewives blended philanthropy and self-interest as they wrote to the society to indicate their preferences:

I should like a woman who understood cooking, washing and ironing and would be obliging and willing, age between 25 and 35 without a child with her.

I would like to have a coulored Girl from 12 to 14 years of age of rather dark coulor of sprightly appearance, one that would be well calculated for general housework in the country.

I want a Black boy, say 12 to 14 years old one who can milk. I don't want a yellow boy, but as black as he can be.

At war's end, after black soldiers were demobilized and black laborers dismissed from the army, the numbers of unemployed freedpeople in Washington soared. While Griffing, acting for the Freedmen's Bureau, opened employment offices in several northern cities, Sojourner Truth conducted her own job placements. Selections from two letters to Amy Post:

Dear Friend: Washington, [D.C.,] July 3, 1866

I would like to know if you can find some good places for women that have children. There has been a great many gone on to the west but there are yet some good women here that want homes. These have all been slaves. There are some that have no children. Also, I shall most likely leave here this month & would take them along if you or some of the friends of the Cause would find homes for them.

There has been about 140 sent west and we have heard that the men get 36 dollars a month & the women 1.25 a week. These were from the Hospital & there are some here now full as smart as those that have gone. I wish you would let me [know] what can be done for them in Rochester for I want to see them provided for before I leave here. Please be kind enough to write as soon as you get this. Remember me to my children and accept my love & best respects for yourself.

Sojourner Truth

Dear Friend: Washington, [D.C.,] April 25, 1867

I shall I think reach Rochester Wednesday or Thursday night next week with ten or twelve Freedpeople men & women & few children. In May I shall get a large company. I think by the 16th of May they will be there sure. I am coming with them & shall come back for the rest. I will have some *first* rate folks next *time*. We are working with all our might—Mrs. Griffing & I.

Tell Elizabeth to have things *all in order* when I come. Be at the Depot Wednesday night. If I dont come be there Thursday night. I shall be there if transportation is ready. Bureau helps me with all their might.

Yours with love,
Sojourner Truth

P.S. Have good people who are coming this time. Now do be ready for us when we come.

The effort to resettle freedpeople in the North soon came to an end. Many women preferred to return to their old homes. The small number who could be placed by benevolent societies scarcely diminished the population of Freedmen's Village and other refugee camps. Returning to Battle Creek, Sojourner Truth continued to write to Amy Post to learn how "her" women were getting along, but she realized that a broader solution to the problem of these displaced people was needed. Her campaign to obtain public lands in the West is discussed in Part V.

After the War Department authorized regiments of free blacks, the last lingering doubts about the goals of the war disappeared. Black women quickly undertook the traditional work of women in wartime —preparing food and clothing for their soldiers, sewing regimental flags, and writing letters to the front. With the passage of a stiff new Conscription Act requiring each state to draft men if there were not enough volunteers to fill quotas, black recruits were in demand. Prominent men, including Frederick Douglass, William Wells Brown, and Charles L. Remond became recruiting agents. Paid by the states, they traveled as far as Canada and to Union-held territory in the South to obtain black volunteers. They were aided by women like Josephine Ruffin, then a young bride in Boston, and by Harriet Jacobs, who wrote from Alexandria, "I hope to obtain some recruits for the Mass. Cavalry, not for money, but because I want to do all I can to strengthen the hands of those who are battling for Freedom." Mary Ann Shadd Cary who had been supporting her two children by teaching school became the only woman officially commissioned as a recruiting agent. She was brought to the work by her friend Martin R. Delany* who wrote:

Mrs. Cary
Madame: Chicago, December 7, 1863
    I have just returned from the East where I have completed a contract with the State authorities of Connecticut, with the sole right of raising Black Troops in the west and South-west. She wants 5,000 men to make up her quota, and as many of them as can be obtained may be Black. The first black regiment to be raised is the "29th Regt. Conn. Volunteers."
    To all "slaves" obtained, a state-bounty of $120, cash will be paid *immediately* on being sworn in, with the same pay per month, clothing and political status as white men. Free colored men get $200 Bounty cash. This difference in the Bounty has to be made, in consequence of all the contingencies attending the obtaining of our "slave" brethren.
    I will pay you $15 (fifteen dollars) cash for all slave men (or freedmen as the case may be) on delivery and examination by me here in Chicago, I bearing the expense of *transportation.* This is one of the best measures yet entered into, and presents a good opportunity to do good to the oppressed, and justice to those who help them.
    I should have said that I will pay $5 (five dollars) on delivery for every free born man, but do not desire to get many from so great a distance as the cost is hardly justifiable.
    Please write me by return mail as I am anxious to hear from you, and to get all the men I possibly can in the shortest possible time. I am still an agent for Rhode Island and if any prefer Heavy-Artillery, you may take them for that, always designating the service intended for, whether Infantry or Artillery.
                        Very respectfully, dear sir,
                        M. R. Delany

*A doctor, black nationalist, and African explorer, Delany became the first black man to be commissioned as a major in the U.S. Army.

After helping to fill the ranks of the Connecticut Volunteers, Cary was employed by the state of Indiana as a recruiting officer. According to a brief biography of her that appeared in William Wells Brown's book The Rising Son *she also secured soldiers for Massachusetts regiments.*

Mrs. Carey raised recruits in the West, and brought them on to Boston, with as much skill, tact and order as any of the recruiting officers under the government. Her men were always considered the best lot brought to head-quarters. Indeed, the examining surgeon never failed to speak of Mrs. Carey's recruits as faultless. This proves the truth of the old adage, that "It takes a woman to pick out a good man."*

Even before the first northern black regiments were authorized, Harriet Tubman saw action in the South. She arrived in Beaufort, South Carolina, in May 1862, six months after the Sea Islands had been captured by a Union fleet. The ten thousand slaves who had been left behind when their masters fled interested both the government and northern philanthropists—the government because it wanted to ensure a continuing supply of the long-staple cotton for which the region was noted; the philanthropists because they hoped to prove that free black people would work without the incentive of the lash.

Tubman who traveled south on a government vessel in the company of a group of missionary-teachers, found the black Sea Islanders wary of her at first. They had never heard of "Moses," the Underground Railroad leader and friend of John Brown. They saw a woman with skin as dark as their own but whose customs and language were different. The freedpeople spoke Gullah, a dialect containing hundreds of African words, and Tubman addressed them in the accents of her native Maryland. "Dey laughed when dey heard me talk, an' I could not understand dem, no how," she said. When she found that they were suspicious of her because she received army rations as the white teachers did, she relinquished the privilege and paid her way by selling pies, gingerbread, and root beer that she prepared at night. To help the freedwomen become self-supporting she taught them how to do the soldiers' washing and built a washhouse, which she paid for out of her earnings. She was also in demand at the army hospital where she nursed both soldiers and contrabands. She described the hospital routine.

*The sketch of Cary that Brown published was written by William Still. Who was responsible for "the old adage" is not known.

I'd go to de hospital early eb'ry mornin'. I'd get a big chunk of ice, I would, and put it in a basin, and fill it with water; den I'd take a sponge and begin. Fust man I'd come to, I'd thrash away de flies, and dey'd rise, like bees roun' a hive. Den I'd begin to bathe der wounds, an' by de time I'd bathed off three or four, de fire and heat would have melted de ice and made de water warm, an' it would be as red as clar blood. Den I'd go an' get more ice an' by de time I got to de nex' ones, de flies would be roun' de fust ones black an' thick as eber.

Noted for herb remedies, she was asked by an army officer to go to Fernandina, Florida, to nurse soldiers who were "dying off like sheep" from dysentery. She cured many with a medicine she prepared from roots dug out of the marshes, but she also utilized a more traditional drug, as the following note to a commissary officer indicates.

Beaufort, [South Carolina,] August 28, 1862
Will Cap. Warfield please let "Moses" have a little Bourbon whiskey for medicinal purposes.
Henry L. Durant, Act. Ass. Surgeon

Her most valuable service to the Union was as a spy and scout. Under the command of Colonel James Montgomery of the Second South Carolina Volunteers, Tubman headed a corps of local black men, most of them river pilots. Dressed as a freedwoman, with a bandanna on her head, this short plain woman could travel anywhere in Rebel territory without arousing suspicion. When she and her scouts returned from their forays, she was able to pinpoint the location of cotton warehouses, ammunition depots, and slaves who were waiting to be liberated. Noted as a guerrilla fighter, Montgomery made numerous expeditions in the coastal areas of South Carolina, Georgia, and Florida based on information from Harriet Tubman and her squad. On his most celebrated raid up the Combahee River in June 1863, Tubman led the way. An account of the raid appeared on the front page of the Boston Commonwealth *a month later.*

Col. Montgomery and his gallant band of 800 black soldiers, under the guidance of a black woman, dashed into the enemies' country, struck a bold and effective blow, destroying millions of dollars worth of commissary stores, cotton and lordly dwellings, and striking terror to the heart of rebeldom, brought off near 800 slaves and thousands of dollars worth of property, without losing a man or receiving a scratch!

A letter dictated by Tubman was excerpted in the Commonwealth'*s next issue. It told of some of the special hazards that a woman in the military encountered.*

Beaufort, South Carolina, June 30, 1863

Last fall, when the people here became very much alarmed for fear
of an invasion from the rebels, all my clothes were packed and sent to
Hilton Head and lost; and I have never been able to get any trace of
them since. I want, among the rest, a *bloomer* dress, made of some
coarse, strong material, to wear on *expeditions.* In our late expedition
up the river, in coming on board the boat, I was carrying *two pigs* for
a poor sick woman, who had a child to carry, and the order "double
quick" was given, and I started to run, stepped on my dress, it being
rather long, and fell and tore it almost off, so that when I got on board
the boat there was hardly anything left of it but shreds. I made up my
mind then that I would never wear a long dress on another expedition
of the kind, but would have a *bloomer* as soon as I could get it. So
please make this known to the ladies, for I expect to have use for it
very soon.

You have without doubt seen a full account of the Combahee
expedition. We weakened the rebels by bringing away seven hundred
fifty-six heads of their most valuable livestock. Of these seven hundred
and fifty-six contrabands, nearly or quite all the able-bodied men have
joined the colored regiments here.

I have now been absent two years almost, and have just got letters
from my friends in Auburn, urging me to come home. My father and
mother* are old and in feeble health, and need my care and attention.
I do not see how I am to leave at present. Among other duties which
I have, is that of looking after the hospital here for contrabands.
Most of those coming from the mainland are very destitute, almost
naked. I am trying to find places for those able to work, so as to
lighten the burden on the Government as much as possible, while at
the same time they learn to respect themselves by earning their own
living.

Faithfully and sincerely your friend,

Harriet Tubman

*Harriet wore her bloomers in a number of guerrilla forays before
leaving South Carolina in May 1864. "She was proud of the fact that
she had worn 'pants' and carried a musket, canteen and haversack,
accoutrements which she retained after the war," an Auburn resident*

*Harriet Tubman had built a home for her parents in Auburn, New York, providing for
them as best she could before going South.

reported. Ill after her return, she was heading back to South Carolina in March 1865 when she was persuaded to go instead to the contraband hospitals on the James River in Virginia. At the end of the war she was employed as matron of the Colored Hospital at Fortress Monroe.

SIXTEEN

The Schoolmarms

DURING THE CIVIL WAR, and for decades afterwards, northern women went to the South to teach the freedpeople. Under the auspices of philanthropic societies,* they opened schools in church basements, slave pens, and army barracks. Teaching children by day and adults at night, organizing Sabbath schools and visiting the homes of their pupils, these women sought to "uplift" the former slaves and to indoctrinate them with the moral values of the North. Although scholars have written about these "saintly souls," as W. E. B. Du Bois called them, who brought "the gift of New England" to the ex-slaves, few have mentioned that scores of the calico-clad crusaders were black.

The schoolmarms followed the Union armies, bringing primers and Bibles to liberated areas, and, at war's end, to districts throughout the South. The first teacher to be supported by a northern society was Mary S. Peake, a black Virginian who started a school in Hampton, Virginia, in September 1861, a month after the town had been evacuated by Confederate forces. Born free and educated in a private school in the District of Columbia, Peake had taught slaves and free blacks before the war. When Lewis Lockwood was sent to Hampton by the American Missionary Association, he found her already at work. He reported:

I have just visited the school of Mrs. Peake (the colored teacher). The school numbers forty-five children and others are expected. She offers to teach a school for adults in the afternoon. She has several classes that spell well in the book and out of it. She is also teaching

*The American Missionary Association, which supported more than five thousand teachers in the South between 1861 and 1876, was the largest of the freedmen's aid societies. Others included the Friends Associations of Philadelphia and New York, the Pennsylvania Freedmen's Relief Association, New England Freedmen's Aid Society, National Freedman's Relief Association, Freedmen's Aid Society of the Methodist Episcopal Church, and the American Freedman's Union Commission.

Mary S. Peake, from a pamphlet published in 1862. *(Amistad Research Center)*

writing and the elements of arithmetic with encouraging success. She intersperses the Lord's Prayer, the Ten Commandments, catechismical exercises, singing, etc. She surely deserves compensation, though she began without any such expectation feeling that she should be fully rewarded in having the privilege of doing good.

Soon afterwards Peake wrote to the Association.

Fortress Monroe,
Dear Brethren and Friends: Virginia, November 1861
    With many thanks I acknowledge the donation received from you. After our church was burned, we had no place of worship, and we were in a most deplorable condition in respect to our spiritual welfare. But the efforts of brother Lockwood have brought us together again. Although we have lost many of our earthly comforts, we are better off than many of the poor soldiers, who are suffering from wounds and exposure to weather. Some of them take part in the Sunday school and assist us to teach the children, who improve very fast.
    I have been teaching about fifty small children. Some are beginning to read very well, and are very anxious to learn, also quite a

number of adults. In regard to the church and school, we feel thankful; our condition is quite prosperous. We have had many interesting marriages performed, since brother Lockwood has been with us.

Most respectfully,

M. S. Peake

She wrote again in January 1862 to thank the AMA for donations of clothing and bedding and to report that her school was "still improving," with fifty-three scholars in the day school and twenty at night. Ill with tuberculosis, she continued to teach from her bedside until her death a month later. "She was indeed a queen among her kind," wrote Lockwood. "We never shall see her like again."

Mary S. Peake, who died at the age of thirty-nine, leaving a husband and child, was not typical of the black schoolmarms. An examination of the backgrounds of some thirty women who taught the freedpeople in the 1860s shows that all were northern born, middle class, single, and childless. Almost all were in their twenties, with an above-average education acquired at Oberlin, the Institute for Colored Youth, or at normal schools near their homes; almost all had taught locally before going South. A few familiar faces were in the group: Charlotte Forten was at work in South Carolina in 1862, and Emma V. Brown became the first teacher in Washington's new public school system for black children. For the most part, however, these crusaders were youthful idealists who were leaving home for the first time to take part in the most significant movement of their day. "I am myself a colored woman, bound to that ignorant, degraded long enslaved race," one teacher explained. "They are socially and politically 'my people', and I have an earnest and abiding conviction that the All-Father requires me to devote every power with which he has endowed me to the work of ameliorating their condition." In earnest letters to officers* of the American Missionary Association, these young teachers elaborated on their reasons for wishing to go South.

Rev. S. S. Jocelyn   Newport, [Rhode Island,] June 13, 1863

Sir:

I have a great desire to go and labor among the Freedmen of the South. I think it is our duty as a people to spend our lives in trying to elevate our own race. Who can feel for us if we do not feel for ourselves? And

*Officials with whom the schoolmarms corresponded included the Reverends George Whipple, M. E. Strieby, and Simeon S. Jocelyn, secretaries; the Reverend E. P. Smith, general field agent; the Reverend Samuel Hunt, superintendent for education; and William E. Whiting, assistant treasurer.

who can feel the sympathy that we can who are identified with them? I would have gone upon my own responsibility but I am not able. I thought it would be safer for me to be employed by some Society. Then, I shall not be troubled about my livelihood, for it cramps ones energies to have to think about the means of living.

I suppose I must tell you something of myself. I teach the common English branches, viz. Reading, Writing, Arithmetic, Geography and Grammer. Should there be an opportunity for me to be employed will you please to inform me what the Salary will be and all the particulars. I shall be ready to leave Newport as soon as I can settle my present business. I have a Select School but I believe I can do more good among the Freedmen.

Please write me if there is any prospect and you will much oblidge me.

Yours most respectfully,

E. Garrison Jackson

P.S. I was born in Concord, Mass, and am a member of the Baptist Church in Joy St. Boston. E. G. J.

In this 1863 photograph of northern teachers in Virginia, the black women were relegated to the back row. Although the names of some of the white women are known, the blacks remain unidentified. *(Quaker Collection, Haverford College)*

Rev. George Whipple
Dear Sir: Cleveland, Ohio, January 19, 1864
    I am a colored woman, having a slight admixture of negro blood
in my veins; and have been for several years a teacher in the public
schools of Ohio. Since the providence of God has opened in the South,
so vast a field for earnest and self-abnegating missionary labor, I have
felt a strong conviction of duty, an irresistible desire to engage in
teaching the freed people; to aid, to the extent of what ability God has
given me, in bringing the poor outcast from the pale of humanity, into
the family of man.
    Possessing no wealth and having nothing to give but my life to the
work, I therefore make this application to you. Can I become a teacher
under the auspices of the American Missionary Association? I should
be very glad and happy if it might be so.
    No thought of suffering, and privation, nor even death, should
deter me from making every effort possible, for the moral and intellectual elevation of these ignorant and degraded people. I know that the
efforts of a single individual seem small and insignificant but to me this
is of the most vital importance.
                              Very respectfully Yours
                              Sara G. Stanley

    *The AMA replied to each applicant with a cautionary circular.
Teachers must not only have a "missionary spirit," but they must also
have good health, energy, culture, and common sense. "This is not a
hygienic association, to help invalids try a change of air, or travel at
others' expense," its officers warned. "None should go who are influenced by either romantic or mercenary motives." Few were likely
to go for mercenary motives. The initial salary offered to women* was
ten dollars a month, plus board and travel expenses; fifteen dollars was
the highest anyone could aspire to. Many of the white teachers they
worked with had independent means; the black teachers needed their
pay not only to support themselves but also to contribute to their
families. Two women apologetically asked for more money.*

    Your circular informs me that ten dollars with board is the salary
allowed by the A.M. Asso. for female teachers. This, I would consider

---

*Black and white women received the same pay, but men were paid more. A male
teacher's starting salary was $25 a month; superintendents and ministers might receive
$1,000 a year. Although salaries rose after the war, the male-female differential re-
mained. In November 1865 an AMA superintendent in South Carolina wrote of three
of his black teachers: "Miss Weston and Miss Rollin are much above the average and
deserve I think $30.00 and Mr. Weston, being a Male, will get, I suppose $60.00 at
least."

a liberal remuneration if it were not that I have a mother, towards whose support I am obliged to contribute to some extent. As this is the case, I am compelled to ask an increase of 2 dollars. Please inform at the earliest convenience if the committee will agree to give me twelve dollars.

I spoke to Mr. Strieby when here, regarding my salary. If it would be quite convenient to give me fifteen dollars per month instead of ten, as hitherto, I would be very glad. I regret extremely the necessity of asking for it. It has always seemed to me that our work in this field should be entirely a gratuity, and it is painful to feel that indigence forces me to ask for money, when I would, if the ordering of circumstances were mine, make the labor a labor of love.

Although the printed application failed to say so, women with children were not accepted by the AMA. Lucie Stanton Day had impeccable references. Born in Cleveland, Ohio, she completed the Ladies' Course at Oberlin in 1850 to become the first black woman college graduate. An experienced teacher, properly religious, she had two significant drawbacks—a seven-year-old daughter and a delinquent husband. William Howard Day, then a prominent spokesman for black nationalism, had gone to England for five years of lecturing without providing for his family. "He desires a divorce or rather desires me to obtain one—which I have not made up my mind to do," she wrote in one letter to the AMA. She believed that the hardships she had endured in his absence had prepared her for the work in the South.

Rev. George Whipple
Respected Sir: Cleveland, [Ohio,] April 26, 1864
    I thank you for the circular given me by Rev. J. A. Thome through whom I learned that my child would be an objection. This was the reason for not writing you sooner: for although I knew that under ordinary circumstances Florence—who is over seven years old—who can sew, knit, sweep and do thoroughly many little services that children are not expected to perform, at her age, would not interfere with my duties—yet I could readily perceive that others might not think with me.
    I will try to answer the questions put in the circular. I Lucie Stanton Day am over thirty years of age. Have for the last two or three years supported myself by dress-making. My health has been uniformly good. I am married though myself and child are entirely dependant upon my exertions for support. I hold a diploma as a graduate from the

Ladies Department of Oberlin College. Have taught District School in Columbus Ohio some years since, also Select School. Have been a member of the Presbyterian Church for years. I wish to engage in this work because I desire the elevation of my race.

With respect—

Lucie Stanton Day

Perhaps unwilling to offend William H. Day, who was well known in reform circles, perhaps fearful of the stigma attached to divorce, the AMA rejected Lucie Stanton Day. In 1871 she went South on her own to teach in Mississippi's public school system. She taught there and in other southern states until 1903.*

Most of the young women who went South were starry-eyed when they arrived at their posts. "I am prepared to give up everything even life for the good of the cause," an Oberlin student wrote from Virginia. In frequent enthusiastic letters, the teachers reported on the progress of the freedpeople.

When I first opened my school I found the children exceeding ignorant. Not having had the advantage of any teaching at all, there were only two out of thirty that *knew the first letters of the Alphabet.* But they are exceedingly anxious to learn. During the short time I have been teaching them they have all learned the alphabet and many of them are reading small pieces in the Freedmens Primer. They attend punctually and never absent themselves except in case of sickness.

During the time I have been here, I have visited several families, mostly the parents of my scholars. Their moral and religious character as far as perceptible is generally good. The Colored Ladies here have organized a sewing circle. The object of which is to provide clothing for the poor.

The interest in the evening school is quite as great, if not greater than that which characterized it last year. I have a class of adults some of whom, three weeks ago, did not know a letter of the alphabet, but are now spelling. As much of my time as I could well afford has been spent in the hospital at Portsmouth, writing letters for the sick and wounded. Many of these men have acquired some knowledge of reading and writing while others who have hitherto been deprived of this privilege are striving to master the minor elements of education.

---

*After divorcing Day, Lucie Stanton married Levi N. Sessions of Mississippi. An active clubwoman and temperance worker, she died in Los Angeles in 1910.

The days were seldom long enough for all that needed to be done.

My labors have not been confined to the school-room alone. I have appointed meetings at the Church and addressed them at different times. The house is usually crowded, and my audience listen with great earnestness, a small fee is charged for admission and that assists in supporting the school. I have received numerous invitations to deliver addresses in the neighboring villages which I have complied with. I have formed an Educational Society for the moral, and intellectual promotion of the members and as an auxiliary in supporting the school. It meets monthly. A subject is selected a certain number appointed at each meeting to make remarks, until every member has participated, then another is selected &c. Each member pays an admission fee, and a monthly contribution.

To enrich the lives of their pupils, the teachers celebrated holidays and marked the end of the school year with elaborate exhibitions. Martha L. Hoy described a program at her school in Prince Frederick, Maryland.

The rear and sides of the building were festooned with Cedar. The windows decked with Holly, and between each window hung paintings of "Grant building his Log House," "Colored Volunteers," "Battle of 54th Mass. Regt," and the "African Prince". In the centre of the house hung a large "Union Flag" with a portrait of our "Martyred President Lincoln" hung on it. The word Progress was formed and covered with Cedar on the wall above the Flag. On each side were the words PERSEVERE AND ADVANCE. A stage was erected for the occasion and the number of pupils present was 75. Our exercises commenced with Prayer by the Pastor, then followed Chants, Addresses, Recitations, Dialogues, Spelling and Definitions by 1st Class &c. We had 59 selections and the performances continued two and one half hours. The children did remarkably well.

At the close of the Exhibition a table was laid, extending the length of the room laden with Fowls, viands, oysters & etc., together with Fruits and other delicacies of the season. We had also a table with Lemonade and Raspberry Syrup. We continued two nights. Our efforts were crowned with success. The proceeds amounting to seventy dollars and six cts. which will be used for school and church purposes.

The schoolmarms made the best of barely tolerable working conditions. After traveling over "one of the worst roads that were ever made," Ellen Garrison Jackson found that her school in Port Deposit, Maryland, had "nothing convenient about it, no desks on which the scholars can write & no desk for me to keep my books in and but one seat with a back. The want of seats and desks is a serious obstacle." Sara G. Stanley drew a bleak picture of her school in St. Louis.

The school to which I had been assigned was in the basement of one of the colored churches. When I first beheld it, I recoiled with a shiver that could not be repressed. On opening the door nothing was immediately perceptible, but as the eye gradually became accustomed to the darkness I was enabled to discern a long low room, furnished with ungainly movable seats, and containing perhaps one hundred and fifty children. It was bare and dreary, the smoked and blackened walls unrelieved by a single map, tablet or blackboard. Through the dusty window the dim light struggled for admission and the chill March wind found entrance through numberless broken panes. I looked about me with a feeling akin to despair. How can I ever counteract the influence of this room, which must rest like an incubus upon the minds & hearts of the children.

I am glad to be able to report that the aspect of our room has somewhat improved. I have succeeded in procuring a blackboard which I have ornamented with bits of landscape, figures of animals, diagrams of the planets, etc. By marvellous good fortune, I have obtained a number of discarded, obsolete outline maps, upon which I have sketched, with crayon, the present geographic boundaries. Having no school apparatus and no facilities whatever for teaching, I find my inventive faculties called into frequent requisition, for example, I illustrated the rotation of the earth on its axis with a ball borrowed of one of my pupils, poised between thumb and forefinger and whirled from left to right.

The schoolmarms were not superwomen. The stress of teaching in an unfamiliar and often hostile environment and the heavy emotional investment in their pupils brought on headaches, neurasthenia, and mental breakdowns. Yet few dropped out of the work for long. Even when recuperating at home, they were eager for reassignment. The letter below is typical.

Rev. Geo. Whipple
Dear Friend: Philadelphia, August 12, 1865
I cannot say that I am enjoying my vacation as much as might be expected for my heart and wishes are constantly straying toward my

brethren and sisters in the South. It seems to me to be wrong to be away from those dear ones so long & to be wasting time that might be used in working for them. I feel that I cannot do too much or work too constantly for the elevation of my race and for the banishment of those prejudices which have so long formed a barrier to our rise and progress in the world.

Hoping that my appointment to my future field may be an early one, I am truly yours,

S. L. Daffin

After the war, the freedpeople were expected to help pay for their schools. Trustees chosen by the black community worked with the Freedmen's Bureau and the philanthropic societies to raise money for schoolhouses, books, and teachers' salaries. Sometimes the all-male school boards were ambivalent about the teachers who came from the North with so much knowledge and advice. Although they were grateful for the instruction given to their children, the men nevertheless resented the schoolmarms' assumption of superiority. For their part, some schoolmarms tended to exhibit more energy than sensitivity in their zeal for reform. Martha Hoy of Brooklyn, New York, was one of several schoolmarms who antagonized local trustees. She had been teaching in Prince Frederick, Maryland, for more than a year when she told AMA officials:

Much good has been accomplished in our neighborhood during the past few weeks. On Saturdays I have travelled 20 and 25 miles, *yea* on one occasion I went 35 miles to address the people concerning Education & Temperance. Showing them the necessity of and fruits of an Education and *many* of the evils of Intemperance. Of course the use of Tobacco was not excluded.

I have prepared an article upon Liberty, Education and Temperance which numbers about 50 pages and occupies one hour and twenty minutes to read it. It is beneficial to the people in two ways. 1st Advice. 2nd The money which is rec'd from said reading, after expenses in traveling are deducted, is given to assist in supporting their school.

Six months later she reported "a dissatisfaction among the people, particularly the trustees," which climaxed when three of them locked her in the schoolhouse and attempted to have her arrested. Although she taught in another Maryland small town for the balance of the summer of 1870, Hoy decided that her talents were better suited to an urban area. By 1873 she was in Washington working as a clerk in the office of the New National Era, a weekly published by Frederick Douglass and his sons and lecturing on "woman's work."*

In rural communities the schoolmarms "boarded 'round" with the families of their pupils, encountering varying degrees of discomfort. In letters from James City, Virginia, a teacher wrote:

I am in the most convenient and comfortable dwelling there is in the neighborhood but that is not saying much, for the wind has free access to my room in spite of all my efforts to the contrary. I have 4 panes of glass in my sash which affords me sufficient light to write by in the daytime. I had to be very persevering or I should have had none. My room was the most forlorn looking place I ever saw for respectable people to live in, it was minus everything but dirt and something they nicknamed a bed. My first night was spent with my Cashmere Shawl snugly wrapped about me, not to sleep but to wait as patiently as I could until day.

After some little delay I obtained some fuel and began to feel a little more comfortable. The style of living is unlike any that I have ever seen. They do not use lamps or candles, but light wood† instead. I found the few articles of comfort and convenience which I usually carry with me of real service. I would advise everyone who comes out into the country to teach to carry a few things with them, such as a Knife and fork, spoon, cup & saucer etc. They will be needed.

In towns teachers employed by the same association usually lived together. Wherever possible the AMA provided mission homes patterned after traditional households. A minister-superintendent served as "father", his wife as "mother" and housekeeper, and the teachers were the loving (and sometimes rebellious) "daughters." Although the "families" offered guidance and support to young women away from home, they also contained sources of friction. The philanthropic societies were officially colorblind, but some white "family" members objected to sharing quarters with blacks. In the letters below Sara G. Stanley, who lived in a mission home in Norfolk, Virginia, complained of the "malign prejudices" of William L. Coan, a missionary, and of Fannie Gleason, a matron. The first letter (to which Edmonia High-

---

*The New National Era reported that her lecture advocated "that justice which would concede to woman the right to labor in such fields as she may see fit to select, for the furtherance of her own temporal welfare."
†Resinous pine knots supplied light as well as heat.

gate, another black teacher, added a postscript) was addressed to William L. Woodbury, superintendent for the Norfolk area who was on leave in the North.

Prof. W. H. Woodbury
Dear Friend: Norfolk, Virginia, July 24, 1864
    When great principles are involved, I deem silence criminal. If your presence here had never effected any good beside serving to keep Mr. W. S. Coan's peculiar secession, pro-slavery, anti-Christian, negro hating principles, and malign prejudices, in abeyance, or preventing the expression of them, I think your services to the cause will have been sufficiently great. Since your departure he seems to have set aside whatever restraint he may have thought proper, and does not hesitate, or rather I should say, takes an especial pleasure in advocating the inferiority of "negroes" and the necessity of social distinctions, with special application to colored missionary teachers. You have been informed of his conversation with one of our teachers, when it was her deliberate choice to occupy a room with Miss Highgate (whom she esteemed not only for her talents but as a personal friend) and so expressed to him. He said furthermore to the young lady who committed the heinous offense refered to, that had she been in his house he would never have permitted it, but would have slept on the floor himself, and caused his wife to sleep on a sofa, and given their bed for her occupancy, if no seperate room could have been provided for her.
    You will please understand, Professor, that I am not advocating a social unity of the races in New York or New England. I fully apprehend the distinctions of Society, and at the North Mr. Coan would have an incontrovertible right to select his own circle of acquaintance but here, in the missionary field, it is different. For the success of our efforts there should be a christian unity and sociality among the laborers. Hitherto there has been in a large degree, but if Mr. C. is to administer affairs, the kindness, forbearance and love which you have so carefully cultivated among us will soon be dissipated. We will be no more as one family, but resolved into discordant and irreconcilable elements.
                                    Very Truly Yours
                                    Sara G. Stanley

    Prof. Woodbury. I fully and heartily concur with my gifted friend. Do not think either of us aroused to a spirit of merciless denunciation by mere galling manifestations of the spirit of caste. No sir! It is the deep underlying principle.

Edmonia G. Highgate.

Rev. Geo Whipple

Dear Friend: Norfolk, Virginia, October 6, 1864

I spoke to you in a former note regarding Miss Gleason, who has emphatically affirmed to the wife of one of the military officers at this post, that "if all colored teachers are not removed from Mission House No 80 Main Street she will not return to it." I am what is called a colored teacher, am an inmate of the Mission House referred to and consider the remarks as having direct application to myself.

These exhibitions of prejudice on the part of Missionary teachers supposed to be in this work because the love of Christ constrained them, is to me very sad to contemplate. As for Miss Gleason, we might, in consideration of the fact that her intellect and training* has not perhaps been as thorough and extended as some others of us, pass by this expression of her feelings with indifference. But as the character of individuals, communities, societies, depends upon the character of individuals composing them, there can be Truth, Honesty, Equity in the whole, only as these qualities inhere in individuals.

Oh! Mr. Whipple if we could have in this work only earnest, humble, true-hearted Christians—regarding all mankind as brothers; feeling not that the great desire of all hearts should be to wear a Saxon complexion, how blessed it would be.

Truly yours,

· Sara G. Stanley

Life in the South offered other unpleasant surprises for black northerners. "In the evening it is considered unsafe to go out, that is for colored people for they are stoned and driven about at the pleasure of the rowdies. This seems somewhat strange to me," Ellen Garrison Jackson of Concord, Massachusetts, reported. In a second letter she narrated "a little incident which befell me:"

I was walking with a friend on my way to a lecture to be delivered at Bethel Hall. We were walking very leisurely along when some one came up behind me and trod on my dress at the same time angrily

---

*The black schoolmarms were often better educated than their white companions. Sara G. Stanley had attended Oberlin for three years and held a first-class teaching certificate from the Ohio public schools.

exclaiming I wish you would not take up all of the sidewalk. Somebody else wants to walk as well as you. Accordingly I stopped one side and politely told him he could pass by if he wished. He then called me a nigger and told me he would not have any of my sass and told me he would slap me in the mouth. At this point I thought it best to interfere having a particular regard for my mouth. I told him in a very decided manner he would not do it. He then passed on. I have found out one thing about these people if they attack you be careful to stand your ground and they will leave you but if you run they will follow.

Ellen Jackson, one of the older teachers, could doubtless remember when the railroads of her native state were segregated. But she had never encountered a Jim Crow waiting room until she and another teacher were waiting for a train to go back to school after a weekend in Baltimore.

Rev. S. Hunt
Dear Friend: Port Deposit, [Maryland,] May 9, 1866
An outrage has just occurred which demands attention. It was nothing less than the forcible ejection of myself and Miss Anderson from the ladies' sitting room at the depot of the Philadelphia Baltimore & Washington Rail Roads in the city of Baltimore.

We arrived at the depot a few minutes before 6 o'clock took our seats in the ladies room from which we were *thrown out.* We were injured in our persons as well as our feelings, for it was with no gentle hand that we [were] assisted from that room and I feel the effects of it still.

I made up my mind to make a complaint to the Supt. of the Freedmen's Bureau General Stannard whose headquarters are at Baltimore. I did so in person. The General told me that he would do all in his power to ascertain whether respectable people have rights which are to be respected.* Thus you see it will be a question of much importance. It will not benefit us merely as individuals also but it will be a standpoint for others. I feel anxious to have your opinion and I hope you will write as soon as you receive this. General Stannard wrote me yesterday requesting me to come to Baltimore as soon as possible but I cannot go until Friday evening after school. It is different from the past. We can now give evidence.
                                   Yours truly,
                                   E. Garrison Jackson

*Ellen Jackson was paraphrasing the Supreme Court's Dred Scott decision.

Backed by the Freedmen's Bureau and the black people of Baltimore, Jackson brought the railroad and conductor to court. This action took "a great deal of moral courage," she wrote. "Our soldiers went forth with sword and bayonet to contend for right and justice. We could not do that. But we contend against outrage and oppression wherever we find it."

Sara Iredell, a graduate of the Institute for Colored Youth and a former Oberlin student, encountered another form of segregation in Maryland. Her comments are excerpted from a twenty-six page letter to Christian Fleetwood whom she married a year later.

My Kind Friend: Frederick, [Maryland,] February 21, 1868
Frederick, yes it is a pretty little city (if you please) but the people, ah, a long drawn sigh will express it all better than any words of mine. Last Sabbath in company with an old lady I visited the Episcopal church. Judge of my disgust when I found that our seats were benches ranged against the wall and separated from the body of the pews by an isle through which the congregation passed to their seats, brushing the colored christians with their saintlike robes. O! a curse on such Godliness. I think I shall not go again and yet when I so decide the thought comes;—do you worship God, or man or self? have you a right to withdraw from the house of God and refuse to do him public homage, forsooth, because your fleshly pride must suffer?

Have you read Jane Eyre? I've just finished but I cant say that the book exactly suits me—I like the bold free style of the writer—the language at times elegant—the individuality of her characters and the true, vivid pictures of them—yet for all that there's a moral that the work bears that is not pleasing to me—what do you think of it?

Good night—I believe I should say good morning,
Your friend
Sara

In the Deep South after the war the egalitarian principles of the freedmen's aid societies were severely tested. When hostile whites charged them with advocating "social equality," some prudent officials bowed to southern custom. "For a time at least we must not think of carrying out the same habits here that we did North. We had better pursue that course which would excite the least prejudice and opposition to our whole work," the Reverend Selig Wright told Blanche V. Harris, an Oberlin graduate, when she went to Mississippi in 1866. Harris accepted segregated housing in silence until protests from the

black community reached George Whipple's attention. Mr. Litts,
mentioned in Harris's letter, was the Reverend Palmer Litts, "father"
of the AMA teachers in Natchez.

Rev. George Whipple
Esteemed Friend: Natchez, Mississippi, March 10, 1866

You wish me to give you facts. We were placed to board with a
very nice colored lady; this we preferred, as we knew our influence
would be greater, if we were to board with our own people. We
remained at this place one month. Mr. Wright called on me one day
and stated, that my board was too expensive, more than the society
were willing to pay. That arrangements were being made for me to
come to the Mission house, that I would be obliged to room with two
of the domestics. And that I must not expect to eat at the first table.
And might come in the sitting room sometimes. My room was to be
my home.

I consulted with some of the old citizens (colored) they did not
think it would be right. I then rented a room, one quite small, open,
poorly ventilated but the best I could do, and commenced teaching,
hoping they would pay my rent and board. After the holiday I rented

Blanche V. Harris when she graduated from Oberlin. *(Oberlin College*
Archives)

two rooms larger, but not large enough, but we are doing as well as could be expected. Mr. Litts and Mr. Wright seemed determined to have us go in the country or any place but Natchez. And the colored people seemed equally determined to have us remain. Mr. Litts has lost the confidence of the greater, and richer portion of the colored people here, by giving them to understand when he was building the new school house that the colored teachers were not to go in there. The colored people were anxious that the colored teachers should have one of the churches to teach in. Mr. Wright remarked although he had brought us down we could not compare with the white ladies. One of the Ministers baptist, wished to know if we had lost our knowledge coming down here. Sometimes we get discouraged and think we had better resign, then we know that we must suffer many things. We wish to do right. Money is not the object nor change of place, but we know and feel that there is plenty of work to be done and feel willing to sacrifice much to see our race elevated.

Respectfully
Blanche V. Harris

Litts defended himself to Whipple by saying that the Harrises had been placed "in respectable colored families," because his mission house was too small to accommodate everyone. Wright added, "I never proposed to those teachers to live with our servants. I said 'We abhor the idea of treating you in that way but if we take [you] into the house with us and should not put you to eat at the second table we should be liable to be mobbed.' " Blanche Harris reluctantly returned to Natchez for a second year and then went to North Carolina to teach under the auspices of the Society of Friends. Married twice and the mother of a daughter who also graduated from Oberlin, she taught for more than a half-century in Tennessee, Ohio, and North Carolina.

Ostracized by the white society around them, members of the mission "family" depended on one another and a small group of transplanted northerners for companionship. Not surprisingly, romances developed between young lonely teachers and the men with whom they were thrown in contact each day. Although the black teachers had the black community to reach out to, the cultural gap between educated woman and ex-slave was not easily bridged. The small number of black teachers who are known to have married while in the South chose their mates from the corps of missionary teachers or other northerners. Carrie Highgate, a New Yorker who taught in Mississippi, and Sara G. Stanley, then in Alabama, married white *men.** *Stanley married Charles A. Woodward, a former Union soldier who was cashier of the Freedmen's Bank in Mobile. Her request to be married in the mission home where she had lived for a year was addressed to Jacob R. Shipherd, secretary of the American Missionary Association's Chicago office.*

Rev. J.R. Shipherd
Dear Friend: Mobile, [Alabama,] April 6, 1868

Mr. Putnam† has informed you of my engagement with Mr. Woodward and of our intention of being married in Mobile. He has stated to me that we "cannot be married at this house" (as I very innocently supposed it to be the only proper place here, where a teacher should be married) and "that if such marriage is allowed to take place he will immediately resign." Surprised, indignant and grieved by this manifestation of a spirit of caste and prejudice, my dignity and self-respect forbid my ever holding any farther communication with Mr. P. on the subject. If I had anticipated any objection to my marriage being solemnized at the Home I would have addressed you in the first instance. As an officer of an Association established upon the principle of human Brotherhood, you see the matter in the light of simply right and justice, rather than that of unchristian prejudice. I do deny that our quiet and unostentatious marriage here, will "create a talk", as is asserted or do injury to anyone. The injury Mr. P. purposes doing me would be far greater than any injury caused to others by a contrary course. Something is due me in the matter as a woman simply. Your delicacy of perception will at once show you how my character would be compromised by a refusal to be allowed to be married in the house where I have lived, and to be required to skulk away as if I were committing a crime. It is well perhaps to say, that I do not wish to remain here one moment after the marriage is solemnized.

My marriage at this house I consider as an act of common justice, and willingly leave the matter now to your sense of honor and right, not doubting that your decision as a christian gentlemen will be such as I feel myself justified in expecting.

I remain, Very Truly yours,
Sara G. Stanley

AMA officials were usually sympathetic to the personal problems of the schoolmarms but in this instance Shipherd, with the backing of George Whipple in New York, took refuge in a technicality to reject

---

*Propinquity worked in both directions. At least two black men employed by the AMA married white teachers.
†George L. Putnam was in charge of AMA work in Mobile.

Stanley's request. To Putnam, he explained, "I acknowledge the perfect lawfulness of the relations upon which she proposes to enter. Upon its expedience I do not choose to pass. I simply apply to her case the law that no teacher has a right to contract an important relation without obtaining the full and explicit assent of the Association."

Sara G. Stanley and Charles A. Woodward were married, but not in the mission home. Sara Woodward taught for a time and then worked as assistant cashier in the Freedmen's Bank. A year after their marriage her husband wrote "Savings Banks: Their Origin, Progress and Utility, with a History of the National Savings Bank for Colored People," an enthusiastic account of the bank. The Woodwards left Mobile in 1874 after he was accused of misappropriating $3,375. Little is known of their later life. In 1885, after her husband's death, Sara Stanley Woodward applied for a pension as the widow of a Civil War veteran. She was then an accountant and engraver, living in New Jersey. Later pension records show that she went South again to teach in Lucy Laney's Normal and Industrial Institute in Augusta, Georgia, in 1894. She died in 1916.

Three remarkable women, perhaps the most talented of the schoolmarms, have left letters that shed further light on their crusade and on their own personalities. Charlotte Forten, the darling of the abolitionists, was the first of these to go South. Her employment secured by friends of the family, she arrived in South Carolina in October 1862, under the auspices of the Philadelphia Port Royal Relief Association (later the Pennsylvania Freedmen's Relief Association). In

Charlotte L. Forten. *(Schomburg Center, New York Public Library)*

a letter to William Lloyd Garrison, she gave her first impressions of Sea Island life.

St. Helena's Island, South Carolina,
My Dear Friend: November 20, 1862
    St. Helena's Island, on which I am is about six miles from the mainland of Beaufort. I must tell you that we were rowed hither from Beaufort by a crew of negro boatmen, and that they sang for us several of their own beautiful songs. There is a peculiar wildness and solemnity about them which cannot be described, and the people accompany the singing with a singular swaying motion of the body which seems to make it more effective.

    As far as I have been able to observe, the negroes here rejoice in their new-found freedom. It does me good to see how *jubilant* they are over the downfall of their "secesh" masters. I do not believe that there is a man, woman, or even a child that would submit to be made a slave again. They are a truly religious people. They speak to God with a loving familiarity. Another trait that I have noticed is their natural courtesy of manner. There is nothing cringing about it, but it seems inborn, and one might almost say elegant. It marks their behavior towards each other as well as to the white people.

    My school is about a mile from here, in the little Baptist church, which is in a grove of white oaks. These trees are beautiful—evergreen—and every branch heavily draped with long, bearded moss, which gives them a strange, mournful look. There are two ladies in the school besides myself—Miss T[owne] and Miss M[urray]* both of whom are most enthusiastic teachers. At present, our school is small—many of the children being ill with whooping cough—but in general it averages eighty or ninety. It is a great happiness to teach them. I wish some of those persons at the North who say the race is hopelessly and naturally inferior, could see the readiness with which these children, so long oppressed and deprived of every privilege, learn and understand.

    I have some grown pupils—people on our own plantation—who take lessons in the evenings. It will amuse you to know that one of them,—our man-of-all-work—is named *Cupid*. (Venuses and Cupids are very common here.) He told me he was "feared" he was almost too old to learn, but I assured him that that was not the case, and now he

---

*Laura Towne (1825–1901) left Philadelphia for St. Helena in April 1862. Founder of the Penn School, she served the black community of the Sea Islands as teacher, physician, and friend for almost forty years. Ellen Murray, a New Englander, worked alongside her. The Penn School still exists on St. Helena as a community center.

is working diligently at the alphabet. One of my people—Harry—is a scholar to be proud of. He makes most wonderful improvement. I never saw anyone so determined to learn.

I wish someone would write a little Christmas hymn for our children to sing. I want to have a kind of festival for them on Christmas, if we can. The children have just learned the John Brown song and next week they are going to learn the song of the "Negro Boatmen." The little creatures love to sing. They sing with the greatest enthusiasm. I wish you could hear them.

C. F.

A sensitive listener, Forten was quick to appreciate the cadences of the Negro spirituals and work songs, which northerners were hearing for the first time.* In a second letter to the Liberator, *she wrote:*

These people have really a great deal of musical talent. It is impossible to give you any idea of their songs and hymns. They are so wild, so strange, and yet so invariably harmonious and sweet. There is one of their hymns—"Roll Jordan Roll"—that I never listen to without seeming to hear, almost to feel, the rolling of waters. There is a great rolling wave of sound through it all.

Despite her appreciation of the islanders' songs, she concentrated on teaching her pupils new music: the John Brown song and two hymns by John Greenleaf Whittier, the "Song of the Negro Boatmen," written in a synthetic dialect, and a Christmas hymn composed at her request. The irony of teaching a New England version of the boatmen's song to Sea Island children who heard the genuine music every day was not apparent to Forten or to her white associates. Although she was an ardent champion of the cause of the freedpeople, she did not feel comfortable with their culture. They were too black, too crude, too African. In her journal and in articles for the Atlantic Monthly, *from which the following is excerpted, she remained the ethnocentric observer, sympathetic but patronizing.*

After the lessons, we talk freely to the children, often giving them slight sketches of some of the great and good men. Before teaching them the "John Brown" song, which they learned to sing with great spirit, Miss T. told them the story of the brave old man who had died for them. I told them about Toussaint, thinking it well they should

*In 1867 Lucy McKim Garrison, William T. Allen, and Charles P. Ware published a collection of songs from the Sea Islands. Their *Slave Songs of the United States* introduced Negro spirituals to a wide audience.

know what one of their own color had done. They listened attentively
and seemed to understand. We found it rather hard to keep their
attention in school. It is not strange, as they have been so entirely
unused to intellectual concentration. It is necessary to interest them
every moment, in order to keep their thoughts from wandering. Teaching here is consequently far more fatiguing than at the North.

In the evenings, the children frequently sing and shout for us.
These "shouts" are very strange,—in truth, almost indescribable. The
children form a ring and move around in a kind of shuffling dance,
singing all the time. Four or five stand apart, clapping their hands,
stamping their feet, and rocking their bodies to and fro. These are the
musicians, to whose performance the shouters keep perfect time. The
shouts of the grown people are always in connection with their religious
meetings. It is probable that they are the barbarous expression of
religion, handed down to them from their African ancestors, and
destined to pass away under the influence of Christian teachings.

After the [church] service, there were six couples married. Some
of the dresses were unique. One was particularly fine,—doubtless a
cast-off dress of the bride's former mistress. The silk and lace, ribbons,
feathers and flowers, were in a rather faded and decayed condition.
But, comical as the costumes were, we were not disposed to laugh at
them. We were too glad to see the poor creatures trying to lead right
and virtuous lives. The legal ceremony, which was formerly scarcely
known among them, is now everywhere consecrated. Nearly every
Sunday there are several couples married in church. Some of them are
people who have grown old together.

*For their part the freedpeople were not sure how to react to
Charlotte Forten who, during most of her stay on St. Helena, was the
only black teacher. "The people on our place are inclined to question
a good deal about 'dat brown gal,' as they call Miss Forten. Aunt Becky
required some coaxing to wait upon her and do her room. Aunt Phyllis
is especially severe in the tone of her questions. I hope they will respect
her," Laura Towne wrote in her diary the day after Forten arrived.
"When they heard her play on the piano it quite put them down, and
soon all grew fond of her," Thomas Wentworth Higginson* wrote a
year later. "Miss Towne says she is the pet and belle of the island."
Forten was the pet not only of the black people but also of the army*

---

*A Unitarian clergyman from Worcester, Massachusetts, Higginson had been an active
abolitionist and friend of John Brown's before his appointment to head the First South
Carolina Volunteers.

officers and plantation superintendents stationed there, many of them abolitionists who had known her or her family in the North. *Colonel Robert Shaw, commanding officer of the Fifty-Fourth Massachusetts Volunteers, took tea with Charlotte Forten a fortnight before the assault on Fort Wagner in which he lost his life. Colonel Higginson, and his regimental surgeon, Dr. Seth Rogers, appointed her the Daughter of the Regiment, an honor that might more appropriately have gone to the wife or daughter of an enlisted man. Much of her leisure time was spent with David Thorpe, a plantation superintendent from Rhode Island with whom she explored St. Helena and the neighboring islands. She knew, however, that the rules of caste had not been repealed even for James Forten's granddaughter. An entry in her journal:*

> After school rode to Mr. T[horpe]'s. Returning Mr. T came with us. T'was intensely dark. I rode Mr. T's horse, a splendid, swift, high spirited creature. C'ld hardly hold him. But enjoyed the ride exceedingly. I like Mr. T. Report says that he more than likes me. But I *know* it is not so. Although he is very good and liberal he is still an *American*, and w'ld of course never be so insane as to love one of the proscribed race. The rumor,—like many others, is entirely absurd and without the shadow of a foundation.

After eighteen months in the South, Charlotte Forten returned home. Her health, always delicate, had given way under the strain of teaching and, perhaps, her anamolous position in Sea Island society. In a later letter to Lucy Chase, a white teacher, she described the blinding headaches that led her to fear insanity.

Dear Miss Chase: Boston, [Massachusetts,] June 7, 1867

Indeed I did think you sincere in your inquiries after my health. I have been better, thank you, since warmer weather has come. All the spring I suffered dreadfully with my head. I dread unspeakably spending another winter here, & if I am well enough to teach, I think I shall try to go to Florida, next year. I long to enter into the work again. I feel that I ought to go South, if I am able to teach. But the last year of my experience there taught me that it would be folly for me to attempt teaching again, anywhere, until my head should be better. Often, I was haunted by the fear of insanity, & indeed, I think I should have become insane had I continued to teach. Oh, if one could only be well! I am disgusted with myself. I feel as if my life were a failure. Not one of its long cherished aspirations has yet been fulfilled.

I need not tell you how deeply I sympathize with you in your self-sacrificing labors, & in the discouragements, too, with which you have to contend. But, dear friend, you have the noblest of compensations—the knowledge that you are giving your life to the regeneration of a down-trodden & long suffering people. I envy you; I who find it so hard to believe, "They also serve who only stand & wait." But do not wear yourself out.

Very truly your friend
Charlotte L. Forten

When she wrote to Chase, Forten was working for the Teachers Committee of the New England Freedmen's Union Commission. With the title of clerk and a salary of ten dollars a week, she corresponded with teachers in the field and their northern supporters and kept a daily journal of committee activities. Excerpts from this journal for February 1869 and a typical letter illustrate the scope of her work.

From Mrs. Hawkes—has reopened her school—has several large girls from over the river some of whom work for their board others sleep at her house & board themselves.

Mrs. John Ware came in—the Lancaster Society ask if they can use the $70 which they owe us on their old account, for Miss Knight's benefit—she expects to have a school-house built on Edisto & that after this year the colored people will support the school themselves.

Wrote to Gen Howard asking Transportation for Mrs. Cheney* & Miss Crocker.—

From Mr. Shaw, New York Society—would like to dispose of their property in Richmond, consisting of School-House, Teachers' Home, & outbuildings—would sell them for the amount of indebtedness for which they are pledged, & wish to have a voice in the further disposal of the property.—*Referred to Com.*

Wrote Miss Lucy Chase that she could deduct the $6.58 expressage on books—from her receipts for books.

From Miss Fowles—Gordonsville—is much in need of salary as she is in debt for her board—the average attendance of their school is very good—have begun a Sabbath School—would like more Temperance tracts,—Sent her one month's salary.

From Miss Jenkins—Columbus—school is very flourishing—

---

*Ednah Cheney (1824–1904) was secretary of the Teachers Committee of the New England Freedmen's Union Commission from 1867 to 1875. She was in charge of all the teachers that the society sent to the South.

wishes that those who are really unable to pay might be exempted from the tax—some of her brightest scholars are too poor to pay it—*Referred to Com.*

From Mrs. Vaughan—St. Helena I.S.C.—the Supt. of the Bureau in Beaufort will allow her a salary from the first of Jan., so she will no longer need our help—wishes her name omitted from our list as she must now report her school as supported by the Bureau in Beaufort—

From Paulina A. Vanderhoop, has a very pleasant school. The scholars are making good progress. She speaks with special pleasure of their entire freedom from profanity.

Forten also wrote to Reuben Tomlinson, superintendent of education in South Carolina under the Freedmen's Bureau.

Boston, Massachusetts,
Dear Mr. Tomlinson: December 24, 1866
I am trying to get at the whole number of scholars in our schools for this year in order to print a list in the Record as soon as possible. There is quite a number of native teachers in S.C. from whom we have had no report, & as this w'ld make, probably, a material difference in our numbers (of course we wish to appear as "extensive" as possible) will you notify these delinquents that we w'ld like to have them report to us *immediately.* Will you also have the kindness to tell us where Miss Jane Knight now is,—whether she is still on Edisto I. & will you ask her please to report to us, as she is still in the employ of this Society.

We have every prospect of a rainy Christmas—dismal, isn't it? We've had every variety of weather within the last ten days—rainy, cold, *bitter* cold, snow, rain, culminating in slush (expressive words) indescribable, & to be found in Boston only, in perfection.

A happy Christmas to you in barbarous S.C.!
Very truly
C. L. Forten

Charlotte Forten worked for the New England Freedmen's Union Commission from October 1865 to October 1871, and then returned to South Carolina to teach in Charleston at the Shaw Memorial School (named in honor of Colonel Robert Shaw). After a year in the South she went to Washington, teaching in the Preparatory High School until her appointment as a clerk in the Treasury Department in July 1873. "It is a compliment to the race that Miss Forten should be one of fifteen appointed out of five hundred applicants," the New National Era reported. In December 1878 she married the Reverend Francis J.

Grimké,* pastor of the Fifteenth Street Presbyterian Church. The bride was forty-one years old, the groom twenty-eight. A daughter born the following year died in infancy. Marriage put an end to Charlotte Forten's work outside of the home; she continued to write articles and poetry for publication. Despite recurrent bouts of illness, she lived until she was almost seventy-seven.

Washington was an exciting place both educationally and politically during the 1860s and '70s. With reformers as plentiful as office seekers, the capital was the first southern city to have a free, tax-supported school system for blacks. On March 1, 1864, the Board of Trustees of Public Schools of the District of Columbia opened a school in Ebenezer Church on Capitol Hill. Its teacher was Emma V. Brown. Paid a salary of $400 per year she was assisted by Frances W. Perkins, a white woman supported by the New England Freedmen's Aid Society. With an initial enrollment of forty, the school tripled in size in a short time, as Emma Brown wrote Emily Howland. Dr. Daniel Breed, mentioned in her letter, was a school trustee whom she had known since her days at Myrtilla Miner's.

Dear friend: Georgetown, [D.C.,] July 18, 1864
    I have not seen you since I have been teaching in Washington. Dr. Breed offered me the Corporation school and I felt that I should like to help establish the first district i.e. colored school. We have had an average attendance of one hundred and thirty pupils. There is only one room for this multitude. Miss Perkins prefers to have the primary department. She teaches from the charts you gave. Her scholars recite in concert and I must have my classes at the same time. We have a regular Bedlam.
    This is hard work—it has been too hard for me and Dr. Breed closed the school a week earlier than he intended because I was too sick to teach longer. I gave completely out.
    Would you believe that I hate teaching now? I grow sick at the very thought of going back to teaching. I can scarcely realize that I who loved teaching so dearly should feel so. Dr. B. is kind and considerate, Miss P. I am devoted to, she is a faithful friend and an excellent teacher, the children have been good, yet the mere thought of going back to that school makes me sick.
    I must work—there is no alternative, yet it is not right to teach

*Francis J. Grimké (1850–1937) was the son of Nancy Weston, a slave, and Henry Grimké, brother of Sarah and Angelina Grimké. Sent north to be educated during the war, he was a graduate of Lincoln University and Princeton Theological Seminary. He became a leading spokesman for black people.

with this feeling. What shall I do? How can I overcome this loathing, this hatred of teaching?

I have boarded in Washington but am at home now. The enemy made a daring attempt recently.* Many of our citizens were alarmed. I did not believe they could get in. Is it not a shame that W. is so poorly defended? The rebels are far more solicitous about Richmond. The rebels are so daring, so courageous that were it not for the remembrance of Fort Pillow† I fear I should be a sympathizer.

Yours ever,
E. V. Brown

Emma Brown continued to teach in Washington public schools until 1869, when she worked briefly as a clerk in the Pension Office and then spent a term in the South. Although her letters to Howland were not as frequent as they had been, they were always frank and often acerbic. Sometimes she was critical of blacks, as in the following description of an 1866 church service.

Last Sunday night I went to Watch meeting. The folks howled, yelled & did everything. A few minutes before twelve the minister said "Let us kneel and sing the Covenant hymn". It really was solemn. They knelt, filling every aisle. The singing was of peculiar minor sort that makes one feel rather sad. Just before twelve the minister said, "The old year is almost dead—let us kneel in silent prayer". They all began to scream, groan and cry right out. I can give you no idea of it. They looked like so many lost souls struggling in purgatory. It was terrible to hear the noise and see the arms thrown wildly about. Suddenly the preacher said—This is the New Year. The people sprang up and sang, "What a happy New Year." They were all as happy then as could be. I said to myself, Truly we are a peculiar people.

Emma Brown resented platitudes even when delivered by General Oliver Otis Howard, head of the Freedmen's Bureau, or the Reverend John W. Kimball, the Bureau's superintendent of education for the District. In the following letter to Howland she described a monthly meeting of the association of teachers in Washington's colored schools.

*Five days before Brown's letter was written, General Jubal A. Early and his men threw Washington into a panic by crossing the Potomac and attacking the fortifications that guarded the city. President Lincoln watched the battle in which Union forces drove them away.

†On April 12, 1864, Confederate forces led by Nathan Bedford Forrest captured Fort Pillow in Tennessee and murdered more than 100 soldiers, mostly black, after they had surrendered. "Remember Fort Pillow!" became a rallying cry for black troops.

She referred to them as "the N.T.'s" (Nigger Teachers) using the pejorative that southerners applied to all the schoolteachers whether their skins were white or black.

My dear friend: Georgetown, [D.C.,] February 3, 1867
    I need not tell you that I was very very glad to get your good letters. Our work goes on—we still have the teachers' meetings. Last Friday Gen. Howard addressed the N.T's at the Soldiers' Library. His address was as tame as he looks. He said several original things such as these, "Teachers you are doing a noble work—you are glorious laborers in the cause—You will have high places assigned you in heaven." Just as he said this I looked at Miss Smith and mentally resolved to ask the Lord please to let me have a low seat as I did not care to sit with the N.T's. Well the General's discourse came to an end—then Rev. Kimball rose and said "Teachers, how many of you think these children can learn as well as white children?" The teachers voted on that. Then he said How many think that these children are as honest as white children of the same class? One damsel said she thought they were not as honest as their favored brethren and sisters. One other teacher who looked to be of the "poor white trash" species, said in a very injured tone that she had "never associated with or come into contact with the low class of whites". I looked at her and perceived that her bump of benevolence had not begun to sprout. The colored teachers as though they had known of this ridiculous performance beforehand and had together resolved on their course, declined taking any part in the debate. None of us voted. All looked just what they thought. At the close I wished I had remained in school teaching my children to be as honest as white folks. Poor Kimball! I could have been angry only the man is so insignificant—is such a consummate fool.
    Why do you say that I toil on heroically? You cannot know how often I falter—how near I am to being shipwrecked. The battle rages fiercely within. There is no more peace nor quiet within than there was months ago. I cannot accept my destiny—I cannot be resigned. I scarcely care for anything—yet it is necessary that I should work—that I should keep up. I am impatient, cross and hateful. My brother can get no work of any kind.* He is moody and disagreeable because of this. My mother cannot collect any money. The whole burden falls on me. Of course I am glad to help them but it seems as if everything goes wrong. I cannot make them economical. We get in debt. I tried to effect a reform, but what could I do with folks who have so long been

*A sharp business decline in Washington after the war meant a high rate of unemployment for black males.

accustomed to have all they want. My brother would perhaps get well if he could be employed. I have tried to get work for him but everything fails. My brother-in-law too is unable to get work. Sometimes it seems to me I shall go mad listening to their complaints. There are many people here white and colored who find it impossible to procure employment of any kind.

My mother and aunt send love.

Yours very sincerely,

E

Nineteen months before the Fourteenth Amendment was ratified, Congress voted to permit unrestricted manhood suffrage in the District. In the spring of 1867 black men registered to vote in Washington's municipal election, and Sayles J. Bowen (see Brown's letter, below) was elected mayor. The Bowens and Danas, also mentioned in the letter, were old friends of Emily Howland's.

My dear friend: Georgetown, [D.C.,] March 23, 1867

I believe I wrote you a dreadfully forlorn letter. I was very tired and had very nearly lost the small stock of sense I usually possess. I have seen Mrs. Dana once since you left. She was as sweet and gushing as ever. Miss Mann* is trotting around with the "Life of Horace Mann" written by Mrs. H. Mann. Maria is indignant because "Mr Wormley, Mr. Slade and such men will not buy it for their sons. It does not matter so much about the girls, but, really, I think every colored person should have it." I wish I could send her hateful tone. She cannot understand why it is that colored folks do not worship "Uncle Horace".

A number of colored teachers, i.e. three, have recently been appointed by Mr. Bowen. Poor Rebecca Perry was the only one examined —she could not answer the questions asked her by the Rev. John Kimball. How I hate the wretch. I know he would gladly have all white teachers if he had the power to turn out colored ones. I forgot to state that Mr. Bowen's sudden preference for colored teachers is easily accounted for. Colored men can vote now. Mr. B. hopes to be Mayor so say folks. Colored men are now annoyed with bows, scrapes and hearty grasps of the hand from white men who did not know them a few weeks ago. Truly this is a strange world.

Are you really coming next month? Mother sends love.

Very truly your friend

Emma

*Maria W. Mann, niece of the noted educator Horace Mann, taught in the colored schools. Her patronizing manner antagonized many black people including, no doubt, James T. Wormley and William Slade, who were community leaders.

Fortunately, Howland disobeyed Brown's injunction to burn the letter that follows.

My dear friend: Georgetown, D.C., March 29, 1868
    I have wanted to write you before but have been too ill to do anything after school hours. I have come home each day completely exhausted. Now my head is aching severely—it has ached for three days. I sent for a physician to-day. He told me what I knew before, that I am worn out—that my liver is disordered.
    We have been seriously disturbed. A bold, bad girl got into trouble. She discovered that she would become a mother and accused my brother of being her seducer. The girl's father has told Richard* to marry her, he refused and the man threatened to shoot him. The girl is that Kate Barker who once accompanied me on a visit to you. I have tried to save her from ruin but in vain. This girl got herself into trouble with some white man—she could not force him to marry her—then she tempted my brother. This he confessed to me with his face buried out of sight. I felt for him—I blamed him—but I could not condemn him as I did that wicked girl. We could have had the father put under bail to keep the peace, but dreaded the publicity of the affair. My mother was sick and almost worn out. She would start in her sleep and scream out. I thought the best thing I could do would be to send my brother off which I did. He is now in the West. He is looking for employment but has not yet obtained work. I know it must be hard to be in a strange place without work—but he has sinned and must expect to suffer. He has been petted and spoiled I fear. I have felt almost hopeless over this.
    I hope to be a better correspondent when my health is better.
                        Very sincerely yours,
                        E. V. Brown
Please burn this letter.

Working in South Carolina and Mississippi in 1870 when black men were in positions of power, Emma Brown suddenly found herself a belle. Although she had known James Lynch in the past, the others mentioned in the following letter—Francis L. Cardozo, Jonathan Wright, and the "bright particular stars of South Carolina"—were new acquaintances. Since Mississippi's House of Representatives had thirty black members in 1870, it is hard to guess who the annoying suitor was.

*Richard H. Brown was twenty-five years old when this incident took place. Many years later Brown told Howland that "he is a very clear-headed business man and a man of strict honor and integrity. He is becoming as good a man as my mother was a woman."

My dear friend: Jackson, Mississippi, May 27, 1870
Your letter was handed me a day or two ago. It was sent from Charleston. I liked C. very much so far as company and gayety were concerned but I did not like the school. It was such a miserable affair —composed of ugly, impertinent, stupid scholars. In a fit of disgust I resigned and came to Jackson. I saw Mr. Cardozo, Sec't'y of State of S.C. He is refined and polished—in fact, he is altogether splendid. Judge Wright is one of my best friends. I was introduced to all the bright, particular stars of S.C. (colored ones I mean). I enjoyed life in Charleston and grew strong and healthy—but this climate does not seem to agree with me. I am not teaching but copying the Acts of the Legislature. I have visited the Capitol. Both the Senate and House presented a very orderly appearance, but they do have some fighting and shooting. Jeff Davis was in town yesterday. He had not the courage to visit the Capitol and see colored men sitting there.

You know, I presume, that my friend, Rev. James Lynch is Sec't'y of State of Miss. I am at his house. His wife was very anxious for me to come here.

I have had about six love affairs on hand since I left home. Only this morning a letter containing an offer of marriage came from the most prominent member of the Lower House. Singular, is it not? He confessed that he is engaged to the most beautiful girl in Jackson (I have seen her). He calls himself a villain but says he will do anything —leave Miss., sacrifice the girl and everything else. Of course I shall decline the honor—but it does seem strange. I arrived here two weeks ago to-day. I wish I had remained in Charleston for the Negro men have annoyed me almost beyond endurance.

This is a mean, dirty, dusty little city and I intend to go back to Charleston early in the fall. Direct to care of Hon. James Lynch.
Very sincerely your friend,
E. V. Brown

Instead of returning to Charleston, Brown went back to Washington to become principal of the John F. Cook School on Capitol Hill. Two years later she received the most prestigious appointment in the District school system, the principalship of the new Sumner School with a salary of $900 a year. "One of the most magnificent public edifices in the city" and one of the finest schools in the country, according to the New National Era, *it contained ten classrooms, playrooms, offices, and an auditorium, all heated by steam and equipped with the "most improved" desks, chairs, clocks, and electric bells. Named after Senator Charles Sumner, the building was a showplace* *to which visitors to the city came. Until 1877 it also housed the Preparatory High School, which was presided over by Mary Jane Patterson, Brown's contemporary at Oberlin.*

With responsibilities commensurate with her talents, Brown had little time for correspondence. When Caroline F. Putnam, who had known her as a pupil of Myrtilla Miner's,* visited Sumner School, however, she had to tell Emily Howland about it. Putnam, one of Howland's oldest friends, was then teaching black children in Lottsburgh, Virginia.

My dear friend: Washington, [D.C.,] January 25, 1875
    During the last two weeks I have been examining, promoting and grading. On Friday we finished and I went home ill. The severe labor brought on a nervous headache which has not entirely left me.
    On Thursday Miss Putnam in company with a lady friend passed near our building. Attracted by the name Sumner School, they entered. Miss Putnam while in one of the primary rooms, asked the teacher if she knew anything of Emma Brown. "Oh yes, said the teacher she presides over this bd'g. Imagine Miss P's surprise—she came up stairs to see me. I escorted the ladies over the building. Miss Putnam was in raptures. She praised the order and discipline. I know that her judgement is worth considerable. She said "Emily Howland ought to feel that this is her work."
    You will pardon my egotism if I inform you that this school is a success. I glory in it. It is just the field I like—wide enough for my ambition. It is *your* school for you incited or rather inspired me with zeal. With no talent—with nothing but energy I have I feel accomplished a little.
    My German friend† and Oberlin became mutually disgusted. I suppose Michaelis smoked, played chess on Sunday and did various other dreadful things. He has gone to another Theological school. He wishes me to unite my destiny with his at once. Alas! Michaelis is the most impractical being in existence. I am too cowardly—too selfish if you will to face poverty so I cannot consent to such an arrangement.
    When are you coming to Washington? Do write soon—pardon egotism and everything else that is obnoxious in this letter.
                        Yours in love—
                        Emma V. Brown

*A columnist for the *New National Era* was the first to point out that the Sumner School was only a square or two away from the original location of Miner's school where Emma V. Brown had received her early education.
†Michaelis, Brown's German friend, had been a suitor for a decade.

In another letter the same year, Brown reported on two black Mississippians, U.S. Senator Blanche K. Bruce, who had just arrived in Washington, and Representative John R. Lynch, who had served in the House since 1873. Her woman's-eye view of portly Blanche Bruce, the first black man to serve a full term in the Senate, is in amusing contrast to the standard historian's portrait. Bruce, who was thirty-four years old at the time he was squiring Emma married Josephine Wilson, an Ohio teacher, in 1878.

My dear Miss Howland: Washington, [D.C.,] March 31, 1875

I have waited for a letter from you but vainly. I have been worked almost to death this year; our teachers have been ill—one gave out and so much additional labor has been thrown on me. I get home exhausted.

I was escorted to a concert last night by Senator Bruce of Miss. The single ladies here rave over his good looks—he *is* goodlooking or rather very fine looking but I do not especially admire him. He is a great big good natured lump of fat. He wears the finest broadcloth, a lovely beaver the finest linen, diamond studs and his wellshaped hands are encased in the loveliest kids. He is gentlemanly and very jolly. Just the fellow to go around with. It is customary for Senator Bruce, Representative Lynch and myself to attend evening church, concerts &c in company. The beautiful ladies are quite disgusted and say in the hearing of the gentlemen "There goes that heartless Emma Brown, with no style and no beauty. What Bruce sees in her, or Lynch either it is difficult to imagine." The gentlemen are exceedingly amused at these comments and appear more devoted. These people do not know that a year ago Mr. Bruce stood above the grave of his betrothed. They do not know how his heart aches to-day. I know the story and as I do know it he knows that his friendly feeling toward me will not be mistaken. I knew both gentlemen in Miss.

My school is still flourishing. I am enjoying it. Do write soon.

Yours in love,

Emma

Because married women were forbidden to teach in the District schools—and in most urban school systems—Emma V. Brown's teaching career came to an end after her marriage, at age thirty-six, to Henry P. Montgomery. Montgomery, nine years younger than his wife, had been a Mississippi slave until he ran away to the Union army during the war. Educated in Vermont by the surgeon of the regiment that protected him, he came to Washington as a teacher in 1876. He was

*principal of the John F. Cook School when they married in 1879, and
supervising principal* of a group of schools, including Sumner School,
from 1882 until his death in 1899. Although Emma V. Montgomery
was no longer gainfully employed, she continued to interest herself in
black education. For many years she served as corresponding secretary
for the Manassas Industrial School, a Virginia school that was patterned after Hampton and Tuskegee. Lonely and ill as she grew older,
she died in October 1902 at the age of fifty-eight. The following may
have been her last letter to her friend Emily Howland.*

My dear friend: Washington, [D.C.,] April 15, 1902
    Your card sent from Va. was most welcome, but I have not been
able to answer earlier. I was unable to call on you for some days after
that blissful day you spent with me and when I did go you had left the
city. It is cool and damp here—when the weather grows warm, I shall
try to reach the sea shore. It is rather forlorn going alone but I have
no one to go with me. My friends are poor and it is as much as I can
do to make myself comfortable. I feel that my life is very narrow but
what can I do when I am only a poor nervous invalid?
    My best regards to the inmates of your home.
                                Sincerely yours,
                                E. V. Montgomery

*Intense, hard working and self-assured, Edmonia G. Highgate
was the daughter of ex-slaves who struggled to educate their children.
Born in Syracuse, New York, in 1844, she graduated with honors
from the local high school and was principal of a public school in
Binghamton, New York, when she asked the AMA to send her to
the South.*

Rev. George Whipple   Binghamton, [New York,]
Dear Sir: January 18, 1864
    I write to make an application to go South or Southwest as mission-
ary. I have been engaged as teacher for two years and a half among my
own people. I am about twenty years of age and strong and healthy.
I know just what selfdenial, selfdiscipline and domestic qualifications
are needed for the work and modestly trust that with God's help I
could labor advantageously in the field for my newly freed brethren—
I am engaged at present as teacher here but will resign as soon as an

---

*His younger brother, Winfield S. Montgomery, served as principal of the Preparatory
High School and as assistant superintendent of schools. His *Historical Sketch of Education for the Colored Race in the District of Columbia, 1807–1905* is a primary source
of information about early schools in the District.

opportunity to go south presents itself. Please answer at your earliest convenience and oblige,

Yours for Christ's poor—

Edmonia G. Highgate

Arriving in Norfolk, Virginia, in March 1864, she was deeply moved by her first encounters with the freedpeople. "I never felt so intensely as when listening to their expressions of joy at being free," she wrote. Throwing herself into the work, she taught day and night, feeling herself "blessed in the effort."

Reverend Geo Whipple
Dear Sir: Norfolk, [Virginia,] June 1, 1864

The most earnest months of my existence were the two last which have just passed. I have been able to get so near to so many of my people who have spent most of manhood's and womanhood's freshness in slavery. There are peculiar crushing emotions which, at first, check even my utterance but go away and leave me with such deep compelling motive power to "do with my might whatsoever my hands find to do."

A case came under my notice of a woman and her three little girls who lived in the hollow of a tree several months to elude the vigilance of her rebel pursuers who aimed to send them to Richmond. She related many little incidents of her life in the tree amid audible smiles. It is predominating mirthfulness and appreciation of the ridiculous that enable these people to be so light hearted in spite of weighty sorrow. One old woman said she had not been to church for six months, because she had to leave her clothes all behind her, and flee for her life from her bachelor master. "I used to have plenty of clothes but now I have got only a few old rags and the folks that used to be jealous of me now jeer at me and I can't stand that nohow," she said. But through the benevolence of some home friends I have been enabled to fit her out so comfortably as to see her at class meeting the following Sabbath.

It would be useless to attempt to report in one letter the various thrilling cases with which I am daily permitted to meet. I have lately taken the school of fifty second-grade pupils taught by Miss Hill. I have just commenced teaching from four till six at the Rope walk* and feel blessed in the effort. My evening class of men who are studying geogra-

---

*Newly arrived freedpeople, as many as 500 at a time, congregated at the Rope Walk in Norfolk. Because they had just escaped from their owners, they were the neediest of the refugees.

phy arithmetic &c afford me decided recreation. Oh how inspiring the thought that these dear souls are "forever free."

Truly yours,

E. G. Highgate

Overwork and the intensity of the experience proved too much. By the end of the summer, Highgate had a mental breakdown and was sent home. The teacher who escorted her to Syracuse reported her "deranged . . . perfectly wild." Once home, however, she recuperated rapidly. Three days after her return, she addressed the National Convention of Colored Men then meeting in Syracuse. Nine years had passed since Mary Ann Cary had spoken at a Colored Convention. Delegates and officers were still only male, and Highgate and Frances Ellen Watkins Harper,* were the sole female speakers. Introduced by Frederick Douglass who compared her to Anna Dickinson, then at the height of her fame as an orator, twenty-year-old Edmonia Highgate addressed the nation's leading black men. Although her speech, as summarized in a black newspaper, contained nothing original, it demonstrated her burgeoning interest in politics.

Miss Highgate was unwell, and labored under a little difficulty in speaking, but her remarks were most attentively listened to by all, except as they were interspersed with applause. Miss Highgate said she would not be quite in her place, perhaps, if a girl as she is, she should tell the Convention what they ought to do; but she had, with others *thought* about what had been proposed and those thoughts she would tell them. Miss Highgate was evidently a strong *Lincoln* MAN; so much so, that she felt that Gen. Fremont ought not to be a candidate. He was now removed and she believed that Mr. Lincoln would be re-elected for the four years to come. Miss Highgate urged the Convention to press on, to not abate hope until the glorious time spoken of to-night, shall come.

A month after her breakdown the AMA authorized her to solicit money and clothing for freedmen's relief. As antislavery workers had done, she traveled from town to town in upstate New York, lecturing nightly in order to raise funds. In March 1865 she returned to teaching. Sent to Darlington, a rural town in northern Maryland, she made no secret of the fact that she found the assignment beneath her and that she wanted to be sent further south. An excerpt from a letter to the men "in the rooms," that is, the AMA office in New York:

*Widowed five months earlier, Harper had just resumed her speaking career.

[April 13, 1865] I am about to do as I proposed to do when I left "the rooms" for this place. That is to resign after I started the school. I do not conceive it to be my duty to stay here in the woods and teach thirty four pupils when I have an opportunity of reaching hundreds. I hope to have a good teacher in my place. Have just received word that my brother is at City Point Hospital. He was wounded five times at the taking of Petersburg.

When her brother died, Highgate placed her mother as teacher in Darlington, and she accepted a more rewarding position in New Orleans. That the "men in the rooms" acquiesced to her arrangement and continued to take an interest in her welfare is an indication of the esteem in which she was held. As she explained in her letter to the Reverend Strieby who had been her pastor in Syracuse before becoming an AMA official, New Orleans' schools were supported by the Freedmen's Bureau until a cutback in February 1866.

Reverend M.E. Strieby   New Orleans, [Louisiana,]
Dear Friend: February 8, 1866
The schools of New Orleans have been sustained without aid from northern Associations. But commencing with this month, the government has withdrawn its pecuniary assistance. While the Freedmen's Bureau still retains its supervision i.e. regulation of tuition fees, provision of school houses and school property, yet the colored people must compensate the teachers by making an advance installment of $1.50 per mo. for each child they send. This plan was proposed by Maj. Gen. Howard because the Bureau owes an arrearage on teachers salaries of four months standing. Consequently the number of teachers in the city which up to Feb'y 1st was 150 has been reduced to twenty-eight. I need scarcely inform you that something like 3000 children have been shut out of our schools because their widowed mothers are "too poor to pay." Their fathers being among the numbers "who made way for Liberty and died."

There is a class mostly Creoles, who have for years, paid an educational tax to support the schools of the whites, themselves deriving no benefit there from. They cannot afford to pay that tax and teachers also. I refer now to the poorer class of Creoles. Of course some of them are wealthy but do not feel in the least identified with the freed men or their interest. Nor need we wonder when we remember that many of them were formerly slaveholders. You know the peculiar institution cared little for the ethnology of its supporters.

The question is this dear sir, can the American Missionary Association pay several teachers under the F. Bureau's supervision? The people's fees will not warrant the salary of even the twenty eight teachers retained. The Fred. Douglass school of which I am principal, numbered 800 pupils, now it has but 127. Board and other expenses are exorbitant here. We still draw rations from the Government yet those who have to wait for so long for their salary are reduced to sad straits. It may perhaps amuse you to know that the building in which I teach was formerly a slave pen but now conveniently fitted up as a graded school.

Very truly yours,

Edmonia G. Highgate.

On July 30, 1866, white rioters attacked white and black Unionists who were holding a constitutional convention in New Orleans. Forty-eight men were killed and 166 wounded. After the riot, Highgate left the city to teach in a country parish some 200 miles away. Her letter is one of the few reports on the black Creoles of rural Louisiana.

Rev. M. E. Strieby   Lafayette Parish, Louisiana,
Dear Friend: December 17th 1866

After the horrible riot in New Orleans in July I found my health getting impaired, from hospital visiting and excitement so I came here to do what I could and to get stronger corporally. I have a very interesting and constantly growing day school, a night school, and a glorious Sabbath School of near one hundred scholars. The school is under the auspices of the Freedmen's Bureau, yet it is wholly self supporting. The majority of my pupils come from plantations, three, four, and even eight miles distant. So anxious are they to learn that they walk these distances so early in the morning as never to be tardy. Every scholar buys his own book and slate &c. They, with but few exceptions are french Creoles. My little knowledge of French is put in constant use in order to instruct them in our language. They do learn rapidly. A class who did not understand any English came to school last Monday morning and at the close of the week they were reading "easy lessons." The only church of any kind here is Catholic and any of the people that incline to any belief are of that denomination.

There is but little actual want among these freed people. The corn, cotton and sugar crops have been abundant. Most of the men women and larger children are hired by the year "on contract" upon the plantations of their former so called masters. One of the articles of agreements is that the planter shall pay "a five per cent tax" for the education of the children of his laborers. They get on amicably. The adjustment of relation between employer and former slaves would surprise our northern politicians.

Most all of them are trying to buy a home of their own. Many of them own a little land on which they work nights and Sabbaths for themselves. They own cows and horses, besides raising poultry. The great sin of Sabbath breaking I am trying to make them see in its proper light. But they urge so strongly its absolute necessity in order to keep from suffering that I am almost discouraged of convincing them. They are given greatly to the sin of adultry. Out of three hundred I found but three couple legally married. This fault was largely the masters and it has grown upon the people till they cease to see the wickedness of it. There has never been a missionary here to open their eyes. I am doing what I can but my three schools take most of my time and strength. I am trying to carry on an Industrial School* on Saturdays, for that I greatly need material. There are some aged ones here to whom I read the bible. But the distances are so great I must always hire conveyances and although I ride horseback I can seldom get a horse. There is more than work for two teachers yet I am all alone.

There has been much opposition to the School. Twice I have been shot at in my room. My night scholars have been shot but none killed. The rebels here threatened to burn down the school and house in which I board before the first month was passed yet they have not materially harmed us. The nearest military protection is two hundred miles distant at New Orleans. Even the F. M. B^au agt [Freedmen's Bureau agent] has been absent for near a month. But I trust fearlessly in God and am safe. Will you not send me a package of "The Freedmen" for my Sunday School? No matter how old they are for there has never been a Sunday School paper here.

Yours for Christ's poor

Edmonia Highgate

Returning to New Orleans, Highgate became a leader (the only woman officer) of the Louisiana Education Relief Association. Founded after the Freedmen's Bureau withdrew its support of black schools, the association backed the concept of integrated education as a way to eradicate race prejudice. When the New Orleans school board announced plans for a segregated public school system, the association met to debate the issue. Speaking against separate schools, Highgate said she "would rather starve than to stoop one inch on that question. If it should be regarded as proper to transfer the school under my

---

*An industrial school probably meant a sewing class for women and girls.

*charge to the control of the old school board, all I have to say is that
Edmonia G. Highgate will then resign as its teacher." By refusing to
teach in a segregated school system, Highgate gave up a substantial
salary* as well as her chance to influence young people. She was not
as far ahead of her time as it might seem, for in January 1871 New
Orleans desegregated its schools, the only southern city to do so. Until
the end of Reconstruction, up to a thousand black pupils studied with
whites each year. Highgate, however, had left Louisiana for Mississippi. In a letter published in the* American Freedman *she described
the life of a Yankee schoolmarm in a small town in the eastern part
of the state.*

Our Kind Friend: Enterprise, Mississippi, October 31, 1868
    A well-situated family with whom I boarded last winter, yielded to
the strong force of circumstances; its head avowed himself a Democrat,
and voted accordingly. The white Democrats, not satisfied with that,
demanded that he should turn the Yankee teacher out of doors, which
he did. I am now in a very open, cold house, and any aid I can get in
making it somewhat homelike would be well bestowed. My school
numbers sixty-eight. I collect monthly from the people, never more
than fifteen dollars, and sometimes less than eight.
    I have some twenty-five bright pupils, some of whom are studying
to be teachers. I wish in my instruction properly to represent Northern
normal school training; but how can I without charts, maps, or a globe?
The school-books which each child has bought, were paid for by real
hard labor. Industry, self-help, my scholars are taught to consider
cardinal virtues. Teachers among these people need a fund from which
they can draw for medicines for very needy cases. Some children are
yet "held to service" and brutally used, and, when really very ill, are
wantonly neglected and left to die. I am constantly appealing to the
Freedmen's Bureau for redress, sometimes not vainly.
    I must establish a sewing school here. The girls and women greatly
need this training. I have no material; can you aid in supplying me?
I want those who learn to make garments to have them for their own.
                    Edmonia G. Highgate

*By the spring of 1869 Edmonia's mother and two sisters, Carrie
and Willella, were teaching in Mississippi under the auspices of the
American Freedmen's Union Commission. Worn out after four strenuous years in the South, Edmonia returned to New York that fall.*

*During Reconstruction teachers in some southern cities were paid $1,000 a year.

While regaining her strength, she raised money to repair "a miserable little church building" in which her sister was teaching and to furnish an industrial school in Jackson for her mother. For more than a year she remained in the North, speaking in New York, New England, and Canada on behalf of the freedpeople. In February 1870 she gave a prophetic speech at the last convention of the Massachusetts Anti-Slavery Society, warning the abolitionists that their work was "not yet half done; and if not now thoroughly done, it will have to be done over again." Critical of the other schoolteachers, she also urged a radical solution to the land problem.

Even in the instruction given to the ignorant there lacks some of the main essentials of right instruction. The teachers sent out by the evangelical organizations do very little to remove caste-prejudice, the twin sister of slavery. We need *Anti-Slavery* teachers who will show that it is safe to do right.

As to lands for the freedmen, and other help proposed for them, all we can do is only a part of what the nation owes to the colored people. It is no gratuity. These men and women have earned more than all we can do for them; and not only is their state necessitous, but in the interior rural districts considerable numbers are yet held in positive slavery.

Her occasional letters to the AMA and to her old friend Gerrit Smith indicate that she was at a crossroads in her life. On the one hand, she felt committed to return to the South; on the other, her lectures had begun to attract the attention of men like Theodore Tilton, the editor of the Independent, *who was a successful lyceum speaker. While she was in New York City, she wrote to Gerrit and Ann Smith.*

Dear and highly esteemed friends: New York, June 10, 1870
The good and gifted Theodore Tilton said to me not long since, "You must write a lecture to interest the general public, deliver it as other lecturers do and you will then be on your way to secure the funds necessary to aid the cause to which you are so devoted." He promised me ever so much aid in way of influence next fall.

How I need exalted surroundings and access to books in order to prepare my lecture Light in Dark Places. I am just hesitating about accepting Mr. Smith's most hospitable invitation "to come and see us" in order to do something towards utilizing Mr. Tilton's advice. Do you think I could advance the cause of Temperance by delivering an

address on that subject whenever opportunity offered. No one feels
more deeply on that subject than I do.

You will accept my highest regards and believe me,

Yours most truly,

Edmonia G. Highgate

*Yet a month later she asked the AMA for an appointment to
Tougaloo, the new college to be located outside of Jackson.*

Rev. E. P. Smith

Dear Sir: Cortland, New York, July 25, 1870

I sincerely trust you still intend to send me to Tougalo Miss. to take
a position in the Normal School. I have no other expectation and much
prefer to devote the remainder of my years to that branch of the work.
Perhaps you may know that my normal school training has been such
that I hold a certificate from the Syracuse Board of Edc. which entitles
me to a position in its excellent public schools—only caste prevents me
from occupying it. Please write to this place when you wish me to start
&c.

Very truly yours,

E. G. Highgate

*"I have no other expectation . . . the remainder of my years." These
were strangely gloomy phrases from a capable and ambitious woman
of twenty-six. During her year of lecturing, Edmonia Highgate had
fallen in love with a white man, John Henry Vosburg. Writing to
Gerrit Smith on behalf of Vosburg's sister, a sculptor, she described
Vosburg as "the assist.-editor of The National Quarterly Review* who
is also a poet some-what similar in style to Keats and Shelley. He is one
of the purest, most exalted gentlemen some what delicate in health."
She failed to mention, however, that Vosburg was married, with two
children and a wife in a mental institution.*

*At the same time that Edmonia Highgate became friendly with the
Vosburgs, her sister Carrie was also involved with a white man, Albert
T. Morgan, a Union army officer who had settled in Mississippi after
the war. Active in Reconstruction politics, Morgan was sheriff of
Yazoo County and a state senator. After meeting Carrie, he shep-
herded a bill through the legislature to repeal the antimiscegenation
law that prevented their marriage. Soon after the bill's passage, they
married and took a honeymoon trip to the North. Edmonia wrote Ann
Smith about them.*

*A learned quarterly published from 1860 to 1880.

[McGrawville, New York,]
My highly esteemed friend: September 2, 1870
    In July Mr. Smith very kindly invited me to visit you in this month.
I write to ask permission to transfer the pleasure I would have in
accepting the invitation to my sister—now Mrs. Col. A. T. Morgan.
She has been married a month to one of the noblest gentlemen in the
world. Most of that time they have spent boarding at a hotel in
Cleveland O. They have their share of disagreeable things to contend
with owing to the prejudice against the two races inter marrying. They
are however so admirably suited to each other that they are happy. Col.
Morgan is a noble type of abolitionist and is very desirous to meet Mr.
Smith before his duties compel his return to Mississippi which will be
in November. They have reason to apprehend considerable danger in
Miss. but Col. Morgan is state senator and must brave what comes.
They barely escaped being mobbed the night of their marriage.
                          Most respectfully yours,
                          Edmonia G. Highgate

    The Morgans visited the Smiths in September before spending a
month with sister Edmonia in McGrawville, New York. On October
8, 1870, she wrote to Gerrit Smith to thank him for his kindness to
"my noble brother." It was her last letter to him. Nine days later, the
Syracuse Daily Courier *published a story headed "Melancholy and*
Sudden Death."

    Last Friday morning Undertakers Ryan were notified that a woman
died suddenly at the house of a woman named Mrs. Paine. They
immediately notified the Coroner, who held a post mortem examination which showed that the woman was enceinte and died from the
effects of treatment for abortion. The body of the unfortunate victim
who thus lost her life while endeavoring to hide her shame, was identified as that of Miss Edmonia Highgate, a mulatto, and a school
teacher by profession. She was dressed in a brown suit, with a black
silk overskirt. She also wore a gray balmoral skirt with a plaid border.
She had with her a satchel, filled with underclothing. In the satchel
were found her wallet, containing something over $5 in money and a
pawn ticket she having pawned her trunk and contents for $16.55.
Miss Highgate was wellknown in this city, as she was born and educated here, and at one time taught school in the Eighth Ward. But
she has now fallen a victim to her own shame and guilt and is a sad
warning to others to beware how they trifle with their lives, as God
often visits the death penalty upon those who would act contrary to

both the laws of nature and of nature's God. We hope that the guilty miscreant who administered the antidote that caused the death of the unfortunate woman will be discovered and get what he justly merits.

Edmonia Highgate, the young woman of shining promise, had died penniless and alone, in an abortionist's shabby boarding house. A lengthy inquest established that she had burned "an apronful of letters" during the last days of her life. In her trunk the coroner found Virginia and Other Poems *by John Henry Vosburg.* "She was so good and pure, we can't believe it," Albert Morgan wrote Gerrit Smith. "My darling wife is nearly crazy." In a later letter he offered an explanation.*

Honored Friend: McGrawville, New York, October 21, 1870

From what we have since learned we are satisfied she was some time ago married secretly to a John Henry Vosburg, of whom she had frequently spoken to her family and who had frequently visited her. He is known to have proposed such a marriage—giving as a reason that because of his infirmities being a cripple—he was to some extent dependent upon his family for support and they would have withdrawn all support had he married a colored woman. Edmonia loved him—his sister was a bosom friend & confidant. I have now no doubt they were married. The sequel is a terribly sad commentary on that condition of society that made such a marriage desireable to such as Edmonia. How long will this prejudice continue to work destruction and ruin? How great in *his crime.* God, I feel sure, will forgive her. The *world* will not very greatly condemn him. The world will condemn *me* for an honorable choice and an honorable courtship and marriage [more] than it will Vosburg for this cowardly murder with the world as accessory of a true, noble, Christian woman.

Sincerely & Respectfully

A. T. Morgan

Edmonia Highgate who was murdered "with the world as accessory" was buried in Oakwood Cemetery in Syracuse, alongside her father and brother. Still grieving for "our Eddie," Carrie Highgate Morgan returned to Mississippi with her husband. Driven from the state when the Reconstruction government fell, they lived in Washington for a decade, with Morgan clerking in the Pension Office until

---

*Published in 1864, the book included a poem about the end of a love affair: "I am content;—'tis best we so should part; / Our love was like a summer flower, / Too bright, too frail to last when cold winds start."

southern Democrats forced his dismissal. From Washington they went to a racially mixed community in Kansas. After repeated business failures, Morgan traveled to Colorado to mine silver, leaving Carrie and their six children. Passing as white, she and her daughters went on the stage with a musical act. Despite moderate success, tragedy stalked their lives. A son died in an accidental shooting; one daughter committed suicide and another went insane when their racial background was revealed. Finding comfort in Christian Science, Carrie Highgate Morgan lived with her daughter Angela, a poet, until her death in the 1920s.

Part IV

Freedwomen

SEVENTEEN

New Beginnings

"WHEN FREEDOM COME, folks left home, out in the streets, crying, praying, singing, shouting, yelling and knocking down every-thing. Then come the calm. So many folks done dead, things tore up, and nowheres to go," a woman said. "We just sort of huddle round together like scared rabbits. Didn't many of us go, 'cause we didn't know where to of went," another added. Freedom imposed on its beneficiaries the need to make decisions, the most urgent being where to live and with whom. For some, this was a frightening experience. Anne Evans was twenty-two years old when freedom came.

I asked my old owner to please let me stay in with dem; I didn't have nowhere to go nohow. So he just up and said "Anne, you can stay here if you want to, but I ain't goin to give you nothing but your victuals and clothes enough to cover your hide, not a penny in money do no nigger get from me." So I up and said, "Why boss, they tells me dat since freedom we get a little change," and he cursed me to all de low names he could think of and drove me out like a dog. I didn't know where to go so I sauntered off to a nearby plantation where a colored slave kept home for her bachelor slave owner and she let me stay with her, and her boss drove me off after two days. I was bare-footed, so I asked Moses Evans to please buy me some shoes. My feet was so sore and I didn't have no money nor no home neither. So he said for me to wait till Saturday night and he'd buy me some shoes. Sure 'nough, when Saturday night come, he buyed me some shoes and handkerchiefs and a pretty string of beads and got an old man neighbor to let me stay at his house. Den in a few weeks me and him got married, and I was might glad to marry him to get a place to stay.

Mary Lindsay was nineteen.

Mistress say we all free and the War over. She say "They say I got to pay you if you work for me, but I ain't go no money to pay you. If you stay on I will feed you and home you and I can weave you some good dresses if you card and spin the cotton and wool." I stayed on, 'cause I didn't have no place to go, and I carded and spinned the cotton and wool, and she make me just one dress. Mistress go off about a week, and when she come back I see she got some money, but she didn't give me any. Den I starts to feeling like I ain't treated right. So one night I just put that new dress in a bundle and set foot right down the big road a-walking west!

Other women reacted with decisiveness. When Delia was asked to remain on the plantation she replied, "No, Master. If I'm really free I must go and find my husband." Lucy Skipwith, on the other hand, used her freedom to leave her husband of many years. In her last known letter to John Hartwell Cocke,* she also rejected Cocke's offer to send her to Liberia.

My dear Master: Hopewell, [Alabama,] December 7, 1865
I Received your letter a few days ago. I was truly glad to see that you were still alive & not yet gone the way of all the Earth. I was sorry that I had to part from Armistead but I have lived a life of trouble with him, & a white man has ever had to Judge between us, & now to be turned loose from under a master, I know that I could not live with him in no peace, therefore I left him. If you have any hard feelings against me on the subject, I hope that you will forgive me for Jesus sake.

I Have a great desire to come to Va to see you & my relations there & I hope that I maybe able some day to do so. I have looked over my mind in regard to going to Liberia but I cannot get my consent to go there, but I thank you for your advice. None of our people are willing to go. I am still carrying on my School on the plantation & the Children are learning very fast. I have been thinking of putting up a large School next year as I can do more at that than I can at any thing elce, & I can get more children than I can teach.

I am glad that one of your Grandsons is comeing out this winter. We are looking for him every day. Our Turnip patch failed this year. Our Crop of Potatoes were very small also. Some of every bodys black people in this Neighbourhood have left their homes but us. We are all here so far but I cannot tell how it will be another year.

I will now bring my letter to a Close hopeing soon to hear from you again. I am as ever your Servant
Lucy Skipwith

*When Cocke died in 1866, he left Skipwith an annuity of twenty-five dollars.

All during that first summer of freedom, women struck out across the fields or followed the railroad tracks. "They had a passion, not so much for wandering, as for getting together," wrote a Freedmen's Bureau officer. "Every mother's son seemed to be in search of his mother; every mother in search of her children." Years later ex-slaves described reunions with their mothers.

After de war my ma come to de place an' tol' de marster she want her chillun. At firs' I was scared of her, 'cause I didn't know who she was. She put me in her lap an' she mos' nigh cried when she seen de back o' my head. Dey was awful sores where de lice had been an' I had scratched 'em. Us lef' dat day an' went right on to Tuscaloose. My ma had married again an' she an' him took turns carrying me when I got tired.

My mother came and demanded that her children be given up to her. This, mistress refused to do, and threatened to set the dogs on my mother if she did not at once leave the place. My mother remained with some of the neighbors until supper time. Then she got a boy to tell Caroline to come down to the fence. When she came, my mother told her to go get Henry and myself as quick as she could. Then my mother took Henry in her arms, and my sister carried me on her back. We climbed fences and crossed fields, and after several hours came to a little hut which my mother had secured on a plantation.

One day my mammy came to de big house after me. I didn' want to go. I wanted to stay wid Mis' Polly. I grabbed Mis' Polly an' held so tight dat I tore her skirt.
"Let her stay wid me," Mis' Polly said to Mammy.
But Mammy shook her head. "You took her away from me an' didn' pay no mind to my cryin', so now I'se takin' her back home. We'se free now, Mis' Polly, we ain't gwine be slaves no more to nobody."

Even women who had their children with them longed to return to the home place. Isabella Soustan asked her former master to send for her.

Master Manual: Liberty, Virginia, July 10, 1865
    Master, I am cramped hear nearly to death and no one ceares for me heare, and I want you if you pleas Sir, to Send for me. I dont care if I am free. I had rather live with you. I was as free while with you as I wanted to be. John is still hired out and doing Well only greaveing

about home. He want to go home as bad as I do, if you ever send for me I will send for him immediately and take him home to his kind Master. Hoping to bee at your Service Soon—yes befor yonders Sun Shal rise and Set any more.

May I Subscribe myself your most affectionate humble friend and Servt—

Isabella T. Soustan

Freedwomen who had been living in the North shared this impulse to go home, if only for a visit. Bethany Veney traveled from Massachusetts to Virginia soon after the war.

I had saved some money; and, as soon as it was deemed safe by my friends, I undertook the journey. I purchased my tickets taking me to Culpepper Court House via railroad. I did not wait for the stage to take me on my journey, for I was too eager to reach the end. I engaged a colored boy to take my satchel, to whom I was proud to pay one dollar in advance; and we started on foot for the top of the mountain, over which my course lay. Remaining there over night, I pursued my way on the next day, reaching Luray before night. I found my daughter Charlotte grown to womanhood, married, and had one child. My old masters expressed pleasure at seeing me, and had many questions to ask of people and things at the North. My dear, kind old mistress, Miss Lucy, had been paralyzed; and her face was drawn on one side, which greatly changed her. She was delighted with a pair of cloth shoes that I carried to her.

After visiting about for six or seven weeks, I turned my face again to the North, my daughter, her husband and child, coming with me. Three times since I have made the same journey, bringing back with me, from time to time, in all sixteen of my relatives.

For those who had been sold to the Deep South or refugeed to Texas, the search for family members went on for a long time. Just as survivors of the Nazi Holocaust still travel to Europe or Israel in the hope of hearing of a long-lost relative, these victims of an earlier dispersion persevered in similar efforts. In the 1870s crowded excursion steamers ran from Savannah and Charleston to ports in Virginia. "Aged women and grayhaired men journeyed from far-off Georgia hoping to hear some word or perchance to meet sons and daughters whom they bade farewell at the auction block," the New National Era *reported. "Many had the fortune to find those they sought and their greetings were pathetic beyond description." Until the end of the century, black newspapers published advertisements like the following:*

INFORMATION WANTED—Mrs. Thos. L. Johnson, of Richmond, Va. who was sold away from Georgetown, D.C. when quite a child, is very desirous of finding her father, Joseph Thompson, who for many years was a gardner in and about Washington. Her grandmother Rachel Marlin, lived at Rev. Mr. Gillis's and was a member of Asbury M.E. Church, Washington. Her sisters, Cecilia and Priscilla, lived with a Mrs. Mincaster, of Georgetown, and her brother, Henson Thompson, lived in Montgomery Co. Md., before the breaking out of the war. Any information in regard to these persons will be thankfully received by Thos. L. Johnson, Richmond, Va.

Charlotte Brock wishes to hear from her son Alonzo; was taken from her about 1859, to Memphis, Tenn; lived there with a family named Morrison. Think he was in the army during the rebellion. Any information concerning him will be thankfully received by his aged mother. Address John W. Brock, Green street Baptist Church, Lexington, Kentucky.

Martha Ward wishes information concerning her sister, Rosetta McQuillin, who was sold from Norfolk, Va., about thirty years ago to a Frenchman in Mobile, Ala. She is about forty-nine years of age, light complexion, and much freckled. Her former master was Mr. McQuillin, who resided on Brigg's Point. Any information concerning her whereabouts will be kindly received by addressing to P.O. Box 216, Norfolk, Va.

Children could not always be taken from a master's home. When emancipation was imminent, slave owners drew up apprenticeship agreements binding young slaves to long terms of service. The practice began in Maryland after slaves were freed on November 1, 1864. A day later, wagonloads of black children were brought to orphans' courts throughout the state to be apprenticed to their former owners. So many children were bound out without their parents' consent that General Lew Wallace, ranking Union officer in the state, offered to intervene in their behalf. He and his aides were besieged with appeals from mothers, fathers, and grandmothers.*

Baltimore, [Maryland,]
Major Gen. Wallace   November 21, 1864
Dear Sir: I, the undersigned your humble servant, beg of you to aid me in the recovery of my two children now in the possession of Thomas R. Brown, my late master. My oldest daughter Susan, about

*In Kent County alone, 130 slave children were apprenticed by late November; the parents of 102 of the children protested the court action.

fourteen years of age, he has now on his farm near Chestertown, and the youngest, eight years of age, in service with his family in Baltimore.

He has refused to let me have my children, saying that the courts have bound them to him. May it please your honor that I am able to provide for and with the aid of my husband the father of them to protect them. Hoping that your honor will aid me to recover them,

I am your most ob't servant,

Mary Ann   her X mark   Ran

Baltimore, [Maryland,] November 22, 1864

Mrs. Mills and her Son, holds my child in slavery, I went there and they ordered me out of the house to-day, and they locked the door and took the key out of the door, and they tell her not to live with me. I want her to come home and go to school. I feel myself perfectly able to support her, she never was in a church in her life and don't know the Lord's prayer.

By her Mother,
Rebecca Sales

Sir: Baltimore, [Maryland,] January 10th, 1865

I wrote you a letter some time ago, and having received no answer, I thought I would write again. It is hard that I should be deprived of my daughter's aid now in my old days, and that she should be kept a prisoner here in a free land. We were delighted when we heard that the Constitution set us all free, but God help us, our condition is bettered but little; free ourselves, but deprived of our children. It was on their account we desired to be free, for the few years we have to live, what need we care. Give us our children, and don't let them be raised in the ignorance we have; help us, and God will help you at the last day. Very respectfully,   her

Lucy   X mark   Lee

Even after the Supreme Court declared these apprenticeships unconstitutional, the practice continued all over the South. "Not a day passes but my office is visited by some poor woman who has walked perhaps ten or twenty miles to try to procure the release of her chil-

dren," wrote a Freedmen's Bureau officer. Some typical complaints to
the Bureau follow.

Grenada, Mississippi, July 20, 1866

Mary Smith (colored) complains her daughter 8 years old is held
by Hardin Smith, he claiming to have her apprenticed to him—Mary
says she never gave her consent.

Sally Saunders makes the same complaint in regard to her son
about 17 years of age. Boys name is Lewis Washington.

Starkville, Mississippi, September 14, 1867

Harriet Saunders, a colored woman states on oath that she is the
mother of Lucius & Gracy Ann two minor children, that these children
were bound out to Green W. Walker with her consent but that her
consent was obtained by fraud & misrepresentation and that she did
not know what "bind out" children meant, that he promised to give
up the children whenever she became dissatisfied & left, but she has
some time since left & he refuses to give them up—that her son
Richard Oliver is over fourteen years of age & was bound out to Dr.
Josephus Walker. That she is able to take care of & provide for said
children & prays for an order setting aside said letters of apprenticeship.

Harriet   her **X** mark   Saunders

[Athens, Georgia, June 22, 1868]

Elizabeth Pollard (Col'd) states that she has been to get her Grandchild Georgiana of Mr. Mobley Forsythe Geo., that Mobley refused
to give her & says that she is properly bound to him until she is 18 years
old. Elizabeth now wishes that the indenture be cancelled on the
ground that Georgiana is treated badly & is beaten by Mr. Mobley &
she wishes to get the child to educate her & bring her up properly.

*Wives and husbands who lived on neighboring plantations moved
in with each other easily, but those who had been sold to other parts
of the country had difficult adjustments to make. Many who had been
forced to take new mates found themselves with two families after
emancipation. Willie Ann Grey and her daughter, Maria, had been
sold from her husband in the 1850s. Remarrying, she had three more
children; her second husband was killed in the war. When Philip Grey
tracked her down afterwards, she agreed to join him if he would care
for all of her children.*

Dear Husband: Salvisa, Kentucky, April 7, 1866
    I received your letter the 5 of this month and was very glad to hear
from you. You wish me to come to Virginia. I had much rather you
would come after me but if you cannot make it convenient you will
have to make some arrangement for me and family. I have 3 little
fatherless girls. My husband went off under Burbridge's command and
was killed at Richmond Virginia. If you can pay my passage I will come
the first of May. I have nothing much to sell as I have had my things
all burnt. You must not think my family to large and get out of heart
for if you love me you will love my children and you will have to
promise me that you will provide for them as well as if they were your
own. I heard that you spoke of coming for Maria but were not coming
for me. I know that I have lived with you and loved you then and I
love you still. I was very low spirited when I heard you was not coming
for me. My heart sank within me in an instant. You will have to write
and give me directions how to come.
    Maria sends her love to you but seems to be low spirited for fear
that you will come for her and not for me. No more at present but
remain your true wife. (I hope to be with you soon.)
                        Willie Ann Grey

*Fanny Smart had mixed emotions when she heard from her hus-
band who had gone off with the Union army. Reproaching him for his
failure to remember his family, she was also careful to tell him that she
had recently had a baby "a little brighter than you would like." The
tone of her letter was doubtless influenced by the fact that their former
master was writing it for her.*

To Adam Smart
Dear Husband: Woodville, Mississippi, February 13, 1866
    I received your letter yesterday. I heard that you was dead. I was
glad to hear from you. I now think very strange, that you never wrote
to me before. You could not think much of your children, as for *me*,
I dont expect you to think much of as I have been confined, just got
up, have a fine *daughter* four weeks old, and a little *brighter*, than you
would like to see. You wish to know what arrangements I have made.
I expect to stay here this year. I have made a contract to that effect.
I am doing very well. My children I have all with me, they are all well,
and well taken care off, the same as ever, if one get sick, they are well
nursed. I now have eight children, all dependent on me for a support,
ondly one, large enough to work for herself, the rest I could not hire
for their victuals & *cloths*. I think you might have sent the children

something, or some money. *Joe* can walk and talk. *Mat* is a great big boy, *bad as ever.* My baby I call her *Cassinda.* The children all send howda to you they all want to see you.

From your wife Fanny Smart

For others with multiple spouses, "things is powerfully mixed up," an ex-slave said. When Jane Ferguson learned that her first husband had survived the war, she made plans to join him, despite the existence of a second husband. She explained her situation to Elizabeth Botume, a northern schoolmarm.

Martin Barnwell is my husband, ma'am. W'en de secesh sell him off we nebber 'spect to see each odder more. He said, "Jane take good care of our boy, an' w'en we git to hebben we will lib togedder to nebber part no more." You see, ma'am, w'en I come here I had no one to help me. So Ferguson come an' axed me to be his wife. I told him I never 'spects Martin *could* come back, but if he did he would be my husband above all others. An' Ferguson said, "That's right, Jane;" so he cannot say nothing, ma'am. And now, please, ma'am, write a letter for me to Ferguson—he was with the Thirty Fourth Regiment.

Many couples agonized over the choices they made. "It will not do for you and I to meet," Laura Spicer's husband wrote when he learned her whereabouts. "I am married and my wife have two children, and if you and I meets it would make a very dissatisfied family." They began to correspond, although he wrote "every time I gits a letter from you it tears me all to pieces." Below is an excerpt from one of his letters.

Send me some of the children's hair in a separate paper with their names on the paper. Will you please git married, as long as I am married. My dear, you know it never was our wishes to be separated from each other and it was never our fault. Oh, I can see you so plain, at any-time. The woman is not born that feels as near to me as you do. I think of you and my children every day of my life. My love to you never have failed. Laura, truly, I have got another wife, and I am very sorry, that I am. You feels and seems to me as much like my dear loving wife as you ever did.

A Virginia freedwoman wept when she encountered her first husband.

'Twas like a stroke of death to me. We threw ourselves into each others arms and cried. His wife looked and was jealous, but she needn't have been. My husband is so kind, I shouldn't leave him, but I ain't happy. White folks got a heap to answer for the way they've done to colored folks!

Under the influence of northern missionaries who followed the Union forces, slave couples legalized their marriages. Hundreds were married in mass ceremonies; thousands more registered their names with justices of peace or Freedmen's Bureau officers. In part this was in response to the missionary warning that God would no longer tolerate "adultery and fornication"; in part it was a recognition of the rules governing a free society and an eagerness to conform to them. For a woman, a legal marriage offered security, qualifying her for child support in case of desertion and for a veteran's pension in case of death. Thus, marriage "by de book" made her right with both God and man.

In the first postwar years, freedmen acquired a new image of themselves. A slave who had been called boy all his life became a man when he joined the army. After the war, friend and foe alike told him that he was the head of his household and must support his family. It was the men who were called on to sign work contracts, to serve on church and school boards, and to attend political rallies. With their first vote, freedmen were formally initiated into the patriarchal society. Observing the changes on St. Helena, Laura Towne noted in her journal:

Today in church Mr. Hunn* announced another [political] meeting next Saturday. "The females must stay at home?" asked Demas.† "The *females* can come or not as they choose," said Mr. Hunn, "but the meeting is for men voters." Demas immediately announced that "the womens will stay at home and cut grass," that is, hoe the corn and cotton fields—clear them of grass! It is too funny to see how much more jealous the men are of one kind of liberty they have achieved than of the other! Political freedom they are rather shy of, and ignorant of but domestic freedom—the right, just found, to have their own way in their families and rule their wives—that is an inestimable privilege! Several speakers have been here who have advised the people to get the women into their proper place—never to tell them anything of their concerns, etc. etc.; and the notion of being bigger than woman generally, is just now inflating the conceit of the males to an amazing degree.

---

*John A. Hunn, a New Jersey Quaker, came to St. Helena in 1862 to open a store for the freedpeople. Charlotte Forten lived with him and his daughter while she was on the island.
†Demas, an ex-slave, was a church elder.

Missionaries, schoolteachers, and Freedmen's Bureau officials were all eager to tell the freedpeople how to live. General Clinton B. Fisk, the popular head of the Freedmen's Bureau in Tennessee, gave a series of lectures titled "Plain Counsels for the Freedmen." "Be a Man," Fisk said:

Husbands must provide for their families. Your wives will not love you if you do not provide bread and clothes for them. They cannot be

"A Happy Family," as depicted in Clinton B. Fisk's *Plain Counsel for the Freedmen,* 1866. *(Library of Congress)*

happy and greet you with a kiss, when you come home, if they are hungry, ragged, and cold. By industry and economy you can soon provide a real good home, and plenty of food and clothing for your family; and you should not rest until this is done.

To the female members of his audience he said:

Do not think of getting married until you know how to knit and sew, to mend clothes and bake good bread, to keep a nice clean house and cultivate a garden, and to read and write.

A wife should take good care of her person, be clean, neat, tidy, and look as pretty as possible. I do not see how a man can love a slovenly woman, who goes about with her heels out of her stockings, her dress unpinned, her hair uncombed with dirt under her finger nails and snuff or tobacco in her mouth. A wife must do her very best to help her husband make a living. Much of the beauty and happiness of home depends on the good sense, economy, and industry of the wife.

When Fisk's lectures were published as a pamphlet, they were illustrated with a picture captioned "A Happy Family" (see previous page), which showed three generations of black people living in middle-class comfort. Accepting a feminine role would have seemed a small price to pay for pictures on the wall, a stove in the kitchen, and leisure to rock by the fire. Unfortunately, the real situation was very different. Austa French, a white teacher, described a typical South Carolina cabin.

The only furniture inside the hut is a washtub, in which water is carried on the head often from long distances; hominy-pots, ever stewing in the ashes, boards propped up so as to form a kind of table, some few dishes on a shelf against the wall, or on the table or floor, some children eating beans from small wooden buckets, a bench, and sort of berth, where a heap of rags shows it is used as a bed.

To the occupants of these windowless, dirt-floored huts who did their cooking over an open fire and who lacked even a chamber pot, the home of the "Happy Family" represented an ideal which, their well wishers assured them, could be achieved if they adopted the standards of New England. Curtains and carpets, candles and calicoes, were all part of a "civilizing" process. A yearning for consumer goods was conducive to hard work, and honest labor was, of course, good for*

*Freedpeoples' homes had neither wells nor outhouses. The first sanitary privies were built on the Sea Islands in the 1890s.

A Beaufort, South Carolina, family photographed after being freed by Union forces in 1862. *(Library of Congress)*

the souls of black folk.* All over the South, freedwomen flocked to sewing classes, learned to bake bread with yeast and wheat flour, and dreamed of bringing up a generation of black Yankees. And all over the South, planters complained that freedwomen were "putting on airs," desiring "to play the lady and be supported by their husbands like the white folks."

Few women however, were permitted to "play the lady." Angered by behavior that seemed to place blacks on an equal footing with

---

*And the harder they worked, the more money they would spend on northern manufactured goods. With the hindsight of over a century, it is easy to recognize the economic motivation that went hand-in-hand with abolitionist zeal. While northern schoolmarms taught the freedwomen to sew with northern-milled cloth and to bake with northern-milled flour, northern merchants were the first to introduce these goods in plantation stores.

whites, planters insisted that women and children work alongside the men. Henry Adams, a freedman who traveled through the Southwest in the first postwar years, reported:

I seen on some plantations on Red River where the white men would drive colored women out in the fields to work, when the husbands would be absent from their home, and would tell colored men that their wives and children could not live on their places unless they work in the fields. The colored men would tell them they wanted their children to attend school; and whenever they wanted their wives to work they would tell them themselves; and if he could not rule his own domestic affairs on that place he would leave it and go somewhere else. So the white people would tell them if he expected for his wife and children to live on their places without working in the field they would have to pay house rent or leave it; and if the colored people would go to leave, they would take everything they had, chickens, hogs, horses, cows, mules, crops, and everything and tell them it was for what his damn family had to eat, doing nothing but sitting up and acting the grand lady and their daughters acting the same way, for I will be damn if niggers ain't got to work on my place or leave it.

Even without planter disapproval, "the evil of female loaferism" was not likely to become widespread because the pay freedmen received made two incomes necessary. "My husband never did like for me to work; he used to ask me how come I work when he was doing all he could to give me what I wanted," a Tennessee freedwoman recalled. "But I'd say 'I just help you 'cause I don't want you to break down. If you put a load on one horse it will pull him down, but two horses can pull it jest as easy.'" A South Carolinian described her family's struggle to get ahead.

I picked out Jery Walker from a baker's dozen of boys, hot footin' it 'bout mammy's door step, and us never had a cross word all our lives. Us had nine chillun. Us moved 'round from Pillar to post, always needy but always happy. Seem lak us never could save anything on his $7.06 a month and a peck of meal and three pounds of meat a week.

When de chillun come on, us try rentin' a farm and got our supplies on a crop lien, twenty-five percent on de cash price of de supplies and paid in cotton in de fall. After de last bale was sold, every year, him come home wid de same sick smile and de same sad tale: "Well, Mandy, as usual, I settled up and it was—'Naught is naught and figger is a figger, all for de white man and none for de nigger.' "

"I nebber was no rockin' chair setter," said Dolly Haynes:

I ain't nebber had no time to set down and do nuthin'. After freedom I mar'd Paul Haynes. Paul wanted to preach but nedder of us had no learnin' an' I say to Paul, "Does you think you got nough learnin' to lead a flock of people? I don' wan' you to git up an' mek me shame." I tell him to go to de Benedicts* an' see what book he needs to study, come by town bring a pair of broggans for me, 'cause I wuz a-gwine to wuk and he wuz a-gwine to school. For t'ree long years I plowed de farm an' sent Paul to de Benedicts 'til he wuz edicated. De briars cut my legs an' de breshes tore my skirt, but I tuck up de skirt an' plow right on 'til I bought my little farm. Paul preached right up to de day he died.

Mattie Curtis was also ambitious.

I got married before de war to Joshua Curtis. I always had craved a home an' a plenty to eat, but freedom ain't give us notin' but pickled hoss meat an' dirty crackers an' not half enough of dat. Josh ain't really care 'bout no home but through dis land corporation I buyed dese fifteen acres on time. I cut down de big trees dat wus all over dese fields an' I hauled out de wood an sold hit, den I plowed up de fields an' planted dem. Josh did help to build de house an' he worked out some. All of dis time I had nineteen chilluns an' Josh died, but I kep' on.

I'll never fergit my first bale of cotton an' how I got hit sold. I was some proud of dat bale of cotton, an' atter I had hit ginned I set out wid hit on my steercart for Raleigh. De white folks hated de nigger den, 'specially de nigger what was makin' something so I dasen't ax nobody whar de market wus. I rid all day an' had to take my cotton home wid me dat night 'case I can't find no place to sell hit at. But dat night I think hit over an' de next day I axes a policeman 'bout de market.

I done a heap of work at night too, all of my sewin' and such and de piece of lan' near de house over dar ain't never got no work cept at night. I finally paid for de land.

Some northern observers though that the freedwomen worked harder than their husbands. Elizabeth Botume wrote:

---

*Benedict Institute, in Columbia, South Carolina, was founded in 1870 to educate men of the Baptist faith for the ministry and to train teachers. Little more than an elementary school at first, it became Benedict College in 1894.

Most of the field-work was done by the women and girls; their lords and masters were much interrupted by their political and religious duties. When the days of "conwentions" came, the men were rarely at home; but the women kept steadily at work in the fields. As we drove around, we saw them patiently "cleaning up their ground," "chopping

Freedwoman carrying more than forty pounds of rice stalks on her head. From Edward King's *The Great South*, 1875.

down the old cotton stalks and hoeing them under," gathering "sedge" and "trash" from the river-side, which they carried in baskets on their heads, and spread over the land. And later, hoeing the crops and gathering them in.

We could not help wishing that since so much of the work was done by the colored women,—raising the provision for their families, besides making and selling their own cotton, they might also hold some of the offices held by the men. I am confident they would despatch business if allowed to go to the polls; instead of hanging around all day, they would exclaim,—"Let me vote and go; I've got work to do."

In "Inside Southern Cabins," a series of articles in Harper's Weekly *in 1880, the anonymous author found that in Georgia:*

The women accept it as a settled fact that they are to support their husbands, and many of them work almost day and night in order to send him to school, because, perhaps, he imagines himself a born preacher. This sacrifice is always accepted as a lawful tribute to his

A South Carolina field worker, late nineteenth century.

superiority, and he generally has an extempore sermon on hand from some of Paul's dicta about women.

In South Carolina:

Generally, the woman is the provider for the whole family and even when the man works, the wife takes in washing or sewing, or goes out to day's work, it being an understood thing that she is to provide clothing, while he undertakes for the rent and food. In most cases, however, the woman takes care of the whole family.

In Alabama:

I met a woman who lived a few miles from Talladega, and she showed me $98, the receipts from her own little cotton patch, and, said she, "I plowed, and I sowed, and I hoed every lick of it myself, and I picked it, and got it baled and sold it too."

This is no extraordinary case. I met everywhere in the neighborhood of Talledega women not only able but willing to do more than a man's work, if by it they could send their children to school. I noticed also, as a result of this predominating female energy, that here the *girls* as well as the boys are sent to school.

Although these observations may have been tainted by prejudice against black men, there is little doubt that freedwomen as a group were hard working. A significant number* of them were the widows or deserted wives of Civil War soldiers and laborers who had to support themselves and their children. The tasks they performed and the rewards they received for their labor are spelled out in the files of the Freedmen's Bureau. The Bureau's chief assignment was to set the economy of the South in motion again. To ensure a stable labor supply, employers and workers were required to sign annual contracts that listed the obligations of both groups. The employer usually furnished lodgings and rations, as he had done during slavery, plus a small cash payment or a share of the crop that was raised. The worker agreed to work diligently and to be humble and obedient.

Georgia Brooks County
Contract Between James Alvis and Dianna Freedwoman.

Said Dianna agrees to work for said Alvis for the year 1866 till the day of December at any kind of labor Said Alvis direct and to serve him faithfully and constantly.

*More than sixty thousand black Union soldiers were dead or missing at war's end; black Confederate casualties were also sizable.

Should such labors be faithfully performed Said Alvis on his part agrees to furnish quarters and food for said Dianna and her two youngest children, he further agrees to furnish her with Cards Spinning wheel and Cotton to Spin for herself as much as she shall Spin at night after having performed her said Service for said Alvis, and further said Alvis agrees to pay Said Dianna twenty five Dollars in cash at the expiration of said Service.

Said Dianna is to be respectful to said Alvis & family allways submissive to their orders and Should she be impudent or idle or neglectful of her duties she is subject to be discharged and forfeit, as shall be just and right between parties

Signed in presence of

William Alvis James Alvis
A. Buckner

her
Dianna X
mark

Unlike Dianna, Emmie Gray worked in the fields as well as the house. In the contract which follows, her employer, probably her former master, spelled out in detail the restrictions on her private life. During slavery, medical care was paid for by the slave owner; after emancipation, it was the responsibility of the freedpeople.

State of South Carolina
Anderson District

This agreement entered into between I. A. Gray of the one part and Emmie (a freedwoman) of the other part.

Witnesseth that the said Emmie does hereby agree to work for the said Gray for the time of twelve months from the first day of January 1867. She agrees to do the cooking washing and all other necessary work about the house. She is to obey all lawful & reasonable commands issued to her by said Gray or his agent, and to be kind & respectful to the same. She is not to leave the premises of said Gray without permission. She is to receive no company or visits of any kind without the permission of said Gray or his agent. For all time lossed by her from sickness or otherwise twenty-five cents per day shall be deducted from her wages. For every day lossed without permission she is to forfeit one dollar and if more than two days be lossed without permission she can be dismissed from the plantation by said Gray with a forfeit of her entire interest in the crop.

In consideration of the foregoing service duly performed I. A. Gray agrees to turn over to the said Emmie one half of the corn & cotton cultivated by herself during the term above mentioned. Said Gray agrees to furnish & feed the necessary horses and farming implements for cultivating said crop. The above mentioned Emmie agrees to board & clothe herself. If she is sick during the year she is to procure if necessary a physician & medacine at her own expense. It is further agreed by & between the party above mentioned that for all supplys of provision clothing or monies advanced & supplyed by said Gray to said Emmie he the said Gray shall have and hold a lien upon her entire portion of the crop until they have been paid for. It i⋅ further agreed that should the said Gray fail to perform his part of this agreement the said Emmie shall have & hold [a] lien upon the entire crop cultivated by herself during the term above mentioned to the full value of what may be due her and until the same is paid over to her.

Witness our hands the 22nd day of February 1867

Signed in presence of   I. A. Gray
W. J. Simpson
D. Sadler   Emmie   her
                                          X   Gray
                                         mark

Freedwomen were always paid less than the men. On one Georgia plantation male hands received $140 a year, women from $60 to $85. In Adams County, Mississippi, Sarah Nelson was promised $10 a month; John, a man working alongside her received $15:

Contract entered into this first day of March A.D. 1866, between Jonathan Rucker, of Adams County, Mississippi of the one part, and John, freedman, and Sarah Nelson, freedwoman, both of said County and State, of the second part.

Witnesseth: that the said Jonathan Rucker, employs the services of the said freedpeople as laborers on his plantation, to assist in preparing, planting and harvesting crops of cotton, corn, &c, &c, and to do all manner of usual plantation labor, each agreeing to work honestly and faithfully and continuously until the first day of January, A.D. 1867, and at all times to be respectful and obedient towards their employer, and towards his agent or manager on said plantation. The said employer is to furnish each with good and comfortable quarters, and good and wholesome rations, that is to say four pounds of Miss pork, and a peck of meal each week, and is to allow each a small garden patch for vegetables, &c, but not cotton, and is to furnish each with material to make a suit of summer and winter clothes, viz: for a Shirt and pair of pants in Summer for John, and in winter for a Shirt pants and coat.

For Sarah, in summer, material for an out dress and one under ditto, and, for winter, one out and two under dresses, and to each a pair of shoes.

They are each to receive wages. John at the rate of Fifteen dollars per month, and Sarah at the rate of ten dollars per month, the one half of the wages respectively to be paid them every three months, dating from their time of service, the residue to be paid them at the close of the year. In case of continued disobedience of orders, idleness, or bad conduct, the employer shall have the right to discharge either or both of said laborers from his employ, and he or she shall not be permitted to remain on the plantation. The employer is to give kind care and attention in case of sickness, but if a Physician has to be Sent for the laborers will have to pay the same.

his
Jonathan   X   Rucker
mark

her
Sarah   X   Nelson
mark

The real worth of a contract became clear only on settling-up day at the end of the planting season. Then the employer added up the "deducts," that is, the pay forfeited for illness or disobedience and the charges for purchases at the plantation store, and paid the balance due. To the freedpeople's dismay, they found that they had worked all year for a few dollars or less. When the Baldwin family contracted with J. R. Thomas in 1867, David Baldwin was promised $140 for the year, Matty Baldwin $85, and Mariah Baldwin $60. On "countin' day" David Baldwin received $12.40, Matty Baldwin $48.53, and Mariah Baldwin $3.15. Thomas's account book showed that Mariah who worked a seven-day week had forfeited $34.20 for days lost because of sickness, rain or "against orders," and had spent $22.65 at his store. Thomas's account for her for the first three months of the year was:

1867 Mariah Baldwin Dr
     To James P. Thomas

January 19th	Lost time & rations 1 Day by sickness		50
" 22	" " " 1 Day " "		50
" 25	Half Plug of Tobacco		25
" 27	Lost time & ration by sickness ½ day		25
" 31	" " " " 1 day		50
" "	3 Yds of Osnaburg*	1	30

*A coarse cloth known before emancipation as slave cloth.

Feb.	2	Lost time & rations 1 Day by sickness	25
"	4	" " " by sickness	50
"	5	" " 1 Day	50
"	6	" " & rat by sickness	50
"	7	" " " "	50
"	8	Lost time & rat by sknss	1 00
"	9	" " " 1 Day	50
"	16	" " " ⅓ day	25
"	23	" " " 1 Day	50
"	27	" " " 1 day by sick	50
Mch	2	Lost time & rations 1 day do	50
	8	" " " 1 Day Do	50
	9	" " " 1 Day Do	50
	15	" " " 1 Day Do	50
	18	" 1 Plug of tobacco	25
	21	Lost time & rations 1 Day	50
	27	Lost time & rations 1 Day	50
	28	½ Gal of syrup	60
	30	Lost time & rations 1 Day	50
			$11.65
			−9.25
			2.40

In the course of her year's labor, Ellen Latimer lived somewhat more lavishly than Mariah Baldwin, judging from the debits logged against her. A year's work left her owing $9.43 to her employers.

1867 Ellen Latimer—
        To Helsman & Ely Dr-

May 8.	1 blank book 12½—8 yds calico $2	2.12½
Sept 15	1 pr shoes—1.75 Nov 9 1 pr do 3.00	4.75
Mch 30	order W.W. Kendrick	5.00
June 1st	1 pr shoes 3.00 5 yds homespun 1.25	4.25
"	1 umbrella	1.50
	Coleman & Doughtys Act	21.50
	39½ day sick & lost & rations a 40ᶜ	15.80
Nov 30	cups saucers & plates	2.75
Dec 28	Cash paid	1.76

The large number of days lost from work stemmed in part from a refusal to work on Saturdays and Sundays despite contractual require-

ments. Women who needed time for household chores or for their vegetable gardens simply took the days off and the penalty that went with it. Arriving late in the field was another form of resistance. As slaves, they had to rise before dawn in order to prepare breakfast for their families. To celebrate their new status, they rose with the men, cooked breakfast, and then went to work. Recognizing their tardiness as an assertion of independence—impudence many called it—planters sometimes exploded with rage. Linda Pearson had been working for H. J. Pearson for more than five months but she "couldn't do to please him," she told a Freedmen's Bureau agent.

My contract was to work the crop of corn, cotton & potatoes. I was to get one fourth of everything. Mr. Pearson's treatment is such that I cant stay with him. I can do nothing to please him. He was always quarreling at me. I cant get breakfast soon enough can't get out soon enough. I hurry all I can. The sun was up when I go to work, I had to wait for the children to get them breakfast. Mr. Pearson frequently told me that it wouldnt do to stay at the home so late, that I must git up and git my breakfast & git to work or we could never gather the crop. Mr. Pearson hit me on the head with the grubbing hoe handle, with both hands. He said to me "You yaller bitch you, you aint a cutting grass" & struck me. I was cutting all I could then.

EIGHTEEN

Slavery Made Us Tough[*]

MOST FREEDWOMEN WORKED as sharecroppers, tenant farmers, or wage laborers. Only a small number were able to buy land. They were scarcely better off economically than they had been as slaves, but they had some control over their own lives. To a limited extent, they could define their working hours. If dissatisfied with the boss's settlement of accounts—and they usually were—they could change employers at the end of a contract year. Most important, they could marry and bear children without fear of having their families broken up.

[*]From a verse by Frances E. W. Harper: "We soon got used to freedom, / Though the way at first was rough; / But we weathered through the tempest / For slavery made us tough."

Any changes that spelled freedom for the ex-slaves were reminders of defeat for their former owners. By 1866 the South had a stable and, in general, docile labor force, but most planters were angered by the slightest sign of independence on the part of blacks. Did a woman ask for planking for the dirt floor of her cabin? Or take time off to care for a sick child? She was impertinent, ungrateful, and in need of instant punishment. "I acknowledge her freedom," said one employer, "but I do not acknowledge her right to do as she wishes."

There was a tacit recognition, however, that ex-slaveholder and ex-slave were economically dependent on each other. Accordingly, they struggled to work out a new etiquette of race relations with the Freedmen's Bureau acting as referee. Bureau agents were required to hold regular office hours to listen to complaints and to attempt to rectify them. Their registers of complaints, which contain the only substantial body of black testimony from this period, make grim reading, but their very existence signified a break with the past. For the first time, freedpeople had the right to appeal to authority when unjustly treated, with some hope of relief.

An examination of more than 100 registers of complaints from six southern states* provides a firsthand report on freedwomen's lives. It was common practice, many testified, for employers to dismiss them without pay as they neared the end of their contract year.

Monks Corner, South Carolina, September 8, 1867
Elizabeth Bash, Col^d complains that she worked last year on the plantation of Brantley Pettigrew, white, about 10 miles from Florence, that she left there last January, and did not get anything but her Share of Potatoes. She says she is entitled to a Share of Cotton, Corn, Peas, Rye and Blades. Laborers were to get one-third of the crop.

Baton Rouge, Louisiana, March 25, 1868
Rachel Caruth, freedwoman Presents an agreement between Mrs. E. J. Penny and herself that Rachel agrees to wash, iron, and milk for Mrs. Penny for one year, and Mrs. Penny agrees to give Rachel ($6 00/100) Six dollars a month payable at the end of the year. In the month of December about one week before Christmas, Mr. and Mrs. Penny turned her off without any kind of settlement, and also ordered her (Rachel) to move from the place immediately. Rachel asked for the wages due her and both Mr. and Mrs. Penny told her (Rachel) to go off that they have not got any money. Rachel states that while in

*Alabama, Georgia, Louisiana, Mississippi, South Carolina, and Virginia.

the employ of Mrs. Penny, she received *one* dress and *two* under-skirts.

Athens, Georgia, April 15, 1868
Manervia Anderson States that Harvey Wood (White) of Athens Ga. owes her $1 for washing done by her for him and that he (Wood) Says he dont intend to pay me. I asked him this morning for it and he said I acted damned smart. I said Well I want my money. My child is sick. I asked him why he would not pay me. He said I was too damned saucy for him.

Slave owners used to tell themselves that the whippings they administered were necessary to improve performance and to maintain discipline on the plantation. But the spurting anger and the brutal beatings of the first postwar years could not be explained by a this-hurts-me-more-than-it-does-you paternalism. With the old relationships gone, former slave owners used violence to express their frustrations. Any attempt on the part of an ex-slave to test "de feel of bein' free" was likely to bring on a storm.

Murray County, Georgia, February 8, 1868
The Freedwoman had made a verbal contract to work for Thomas by the day in the absence of her husband who was at work on the R.R. On the last of January 1868 Thomas ordered her to the field very early in the morning before she had had time to properly take care of her child. She refused to go at that time and he cursed and abused her when she told him she was as free as he. On this he kicked her in the head and knocked her down seriously injuring her.

Women were beaten for attempting to protect their children.

Baton Rouge, Louisiana, June 26, 1866
Rhody Ann Hope Col; Samuel Davison, Beat her with fist and with the trase of an artillery harness. Alledged cause: Daughter of freedwoman was not there at dinner time to keep the flies off the table.

Aberdeen, Mississippi, August 30, 1867
Angiline Hollins Col'd gst James Lea. Complaints are made that you abused her very severely because she would not let her child go to the field to work before breakfast.

They were beaten when they asserted themselves in the mildest way.

Baton Rouge, Louisiana, May 12, 1867
Hetty Richardson complained that Mr. Lee on Fish Pond Plantation
shot her goose and that she went to him and said Mr. Lee you shot
my hog and would not pay for it. Now you have shot my goose and,
because I spoke in defence of my rights and property he struck me with
a gun and snapped it at me and used threats against me.

Athens, Georgia, May 13, 1867
Helen Palmer (colored) States that she went to Mr. Hoover's store,
for the purpose of dealing; while there Helen asked a little boy to
please move when Charles Hill steped up to her and violently
remarked to me to shut my mouth a dam whoreing bitch as he
would knock my god-damned brains out with a 10 lb. weight which he
held in his hand. He remarked that if they wished to report it to the
damd "Yankees" they could do so. He did not care a god-damn for
them.

*They were beaten when they were late to work or failed to perform
to their employer's satisfaction.*

Anderson District, South Carolina, June 29, 1866
Amanda a freedwoman, employed by Samuel Newell, farmer says: I
was sitting in my Room putting on my shoes to go milk the cows when
said Newell came to the house and entering he took hold of my hair
and pulled me across the floor. He then pushed me out of doors causing
my head to strike the door. He then pushed me down on the ground,
hurting me very much. I saw him pick up a stick. He threatened to
kill me if I did not go to the cow pen.

Coffeeville, Missippi, April 20, 1867
Mary Connor (Col^d) complains that Mr. Isaac Tanksley with whom
she was living whipped her with a stick in the field, and afterwards
beat her with a chair at the house, because she "did not know how to
plow."

Oglethorpe County, Georgia, April 16, 1868
Margaret Martin (Col'd) States that she went to Macon on last Saturday and returned home to Jake Edwards (white) where she was employed and when I got home Mr. Edwards beat & choked me because
I diden come home on Sunday evening and not returning until Monday morning. I told Mr. Edwards the reason why was because my
Sister Emily Child was lying very low and likely to dye. Margrt further
states Mr. Edwards says if I come back on his place again he will
kill me.

They were abused whether they cohabited with the boss or rejected his advances.

Aberdeen, Mississippi, August 1867
Emma Cox complains tht she has been at work for Barry at $3 per week
—Commenced work in July last. She done house work. Barry (white) cohabited with her, but on the morning of Aug 9 Emma caught Barry hugging a white woman stopping at his house named Carrie Naben. This caused a jealousy & Barry ordered her away & said he would keep Carrie. Emma would not leave & thereupon Barry beat her & struck her with his fist, she left but soon returned to get her clothes. Words ensued between him & her & he took a horse whip & beat her violently causing bruises & taking skin off her back and shoulders and her thighs and legs. Has paid her nothing but a pair of Shoes & a dress.

Franklin County, Georgia, November 27, 1867
Bowers, Lucinda col'd States that she worked for Solomon Tomison a white citizen of the above county. After I was driven off Mr. Tomison's two daughters sent me word to come and get my articles away or they would burn them. I went and before I got them all the two girls Mrs. Frick and Florence Tomison followed me to the creek and Mrs. Frick called for a gun to shoot me and Miss Florence said she would give me just one week to get out of Franklin County. Mrs. Frick then asked me what lies I had been telling. I said I had not lied and what I had said I would say again. The question was then asked me if I did not say that Mr. Tomison wanted to take improper liberties with me. I said yes, and I would not consent to it. Then Mr. Frick who is Mr. Tomison son-in-law jumped at me, caught me by the throat, and choked me to the ground. Then Mrs. Tomison said take your damd young one and leave here and I did leave that night.

They felt the wrath of white women as well as white men.

Baton Rouge, Louisiana, October 4, 1867
Elisabeth Stingles freedwoman States that on the 24th day of July last, Mrs. Henderson hired her to work about the house for $8.00 per month. This morning Mrs. Henderson had a falling-out with Elisabeth and struck her with a dusting pan three times over the head, telling her to leave the house. Elisabeth asked her for her wages, and Mrs. Henderson answered she would not give her one cent.

Franklin County, Georgia, July 7, 1868
Ann Edins Col'd States that she has lived with Mr. Edins three years and has never received anything for her work except 1 pair shoes &

1 Bunch of thread. On Tuesday the 6th day of July 1868 while Ann was cleaning off the table Mr. Edins daughter a little girl about eleven years of age, asked Ann to pass her the dish cloth. Ann told her that she was in a hurry & that she must wait upon herself, whereupon the little girl struck Ann in the face with a glass tumbler, which caused a tea-cup to fall & break. The little girl told her Mother that Ann broke the cup and her mother struck Ann & told her to leave there a stinking black bitch. You dont eat no more of my meat & bread unless you steal it as you have already done. Ann said she never had stole from her. Ann started out with some dishes. Mr. Edins threw the scrubbing broom at her & struck her on the back part of the head & Mr. Edins said now leave here.

Sometimes freedwomen were punished for complaining to the Freedmen's Bureau.

Calhoun, Georgia, 1867
Matilda Frix Freedwoman States that on Tuesday Night on or about the 20th of August 1867 Late in the Night 3 men came into the house where myself and Cheany Ransom Colored are living, in the town of Calhoun about 50 yards West of the Rail Road depot. We had the door fastened by putting a Shovel under it. These 3 men forced the door open, came in cursed & swore tore around generally. Came and pulled the cover from me. Said they would get into bed. I complained of being Sick. One of the party fired off his pistol.

On the Evening of the 24th we got some men to come and put a fastening on our door so that no person could come in, went to bed. Some time in the Night was awakened by some party throwing large rocks in thro the window. The reason for their doing so was because Cheany Ransom had complained to the Bureau agent about Mrs. Hunt oweing her for services and could not get anything from her. They had a trial over it before Mr. Blacker the Agt and he ordered Mrs. Hunt to pay Cheany $20⁰⁰/100. Mrs. Hunt said if she had to pay her that Cheany should not live here to enjoy it.

Oglethorpe County, Georgia, January 1868
Rhoda Robinson (col'd) says that on the first day in Christmas I went on a visit to Joe Glenns plantation in Oglethorpe Cty, that Aleck Glenn came to the house on Friday night & said you are the very damned lady I am looking for, asked me what business I had there. I said I had come down to see my folks, he said did I not tell you not to come where I was again. He then took hold of me & took the

knitting out of my hand & jerked the watch out of my belt saying he wanted me to take a walk with him. Henry Glenn my uncle tried to prevent Aleck Glenn taking me out whereupon Mann Tiller came in told my uncle that if he chafed he would blow his damned brains out & Bill Turner came in & with Aleck Glenn took me out about 200 yds from the big dwelling house stripped me to the waist & beat me with hickory rods & a walking stick & said that they were paid by the Bureau to sleep days and thrash niggers at nights & were paid $10 for every nigger they whipped & that they had particular instruction to whip me for reporting Glenn to the Bureau last fall.

Among the hundreds of assaults reported, no one complained of anything as casual as a slap on the face. With monotonous regularity, the women were set upon with clubs, hoes, guns, ropes, and knives.

Calhoun, Georgia, July 30, 1866
Viney & Julia col'd state that they are under contract with one Oliver Perry and that a son of Perrys named John struck Viney with a bone and cut her head and then drew his knife threatened to kill her and that they have left the crop for which they were working on shares and are afraid of their lives.

Dallas County, Alabama, August 15, 1867
Adaline Smith FW Complains that on Thursday the 13th, Mr. Howard whipped her with a stirrup strap from his saddle. He sat on her head and lashed her with her clothes draw up exposing her person telling her if she hollowed he would take his knife and cut her throat. His wife Tilla Howard whipped at the same time another girl "Emma" who was staying at Mr. Howards. She tied her to the Bed-post & made her take her clothes off & then whipped her with sticks & a strap.

For sheer meanness, the following complaints are hard to surpass.

Clarke County, Georgia, July 6, 1868
Martha Martin (Col'd) States that is living with one Kenny (white) of Clarke Co, Ga, and that on Saturday her child was bit by a rattlesnake and died, and that Kenney charges her one dollar for ground to bury the child on and five dollars for a coffin and that the child has been dead two days out of the ground and that she is out of money and cant raise that amount. She further states that she offered to pay Kenney for the Ground to bury the child and Kenney Said he would not do it unless I would give him all my crop, I told him I could not do that.

Habersham County, Georgia July 10, 1868
Amanda Redmond, col'd States as follows. I went to live with Sterling
Yerwood during the war, did not want to go. My mother did not want
me to go, and Sterling Yerwood tied my mother up to a tree, whipped
her & drove her away. Mr. Yerwood then whipped me for crying
because he whipped my mother. I never got enough to eat or wear
while at Yerwood's house. He was going to whip me in Christmas 1867
because I said I did not want to live with him and his wife prevented
it. I was whipped several times for reasons unknown to me. He would
whip me at times when he would come home drunk. When his children would whip me Mrs. Yerwood would whip them. Then when Mr.
Yerwood would find it out, he would whip me. I do not want to go
back to live with Mr. Yerwood. I want to remain with my Mother &
Grand Mother. I am not able to perform the duties required of me by
Yerwood. I am only nine years old.*

*Conscientious bureau officers tried to settle disputes over wages
and to reprimand abusive employers. But unless they were near enough
to a military post to call for a squad of soldiers, they could not enforce
their decisions. When serious assault cases were turned over to the
local authorities the results were predictable. After Rhody Ann Hope
complained that her employer, Samuel Davison, had beaten her, the
bureau agent referred her to Justice of Peace James Halton.*

After Plaintiff had made her complaint [Halton] said he knew said
Davison well and that he did not believe he beat her but that if he did
she deserved it. Told her that she had better not have it investigated.
Also said if she failed to sustain the charges against Davison she could
be sent to the penitentiary. Warrant was issued. At the trial defendant
acknowledged that he beat her but claimed that she used impertinent
language to the wife of Dr. Thornton. Case dismissed. The woman
made to pay cost.

*Freedmen's Bureau agents might fail to prosecute cases against
whites, but they were quick to tackle domestic quarrels. One amused
officer wrote that he regularly delivered lectures on "connubial bliss";
others gave the warring couples in their districts "a full explanation of
their duties as husband and wife" or "advised [them] to get along
peacably." During slavery, master or overseer had arbitrated domestic
disputes. Afterwards, as freedmen assumed their new roles as heads of*

---

*The bureau agent who took Amanda's deposition added, "I certify that the above
statements are the exact words that the child Amanda Redmond stated to me."

*families, they sometimes resorted to fists or clubs to assert their domi-
nance. Registers of complaints included numerous entries similar to
the following:*

Chatham County, Georgia, July 24, 1866
Personally appeared before me one Rose Freeman "Freedwoman" who
upon oath states that her husband (David Freeman "Freedman" to
whom she has been married about nine months) has beaten her repeatedly and refuses to support her. We lived at Fernandina Fla about four
months—during that time he beat and abused me. I reported it to the
Officer in charge of the Freedmans Bureau; he had him arrested & he
got out of the *Guard House* & left the place, remaining away until a
new officer took charge—he (my husband) then came back & beat me
again—I had him arrested—he knocked the officer down & ran away
& came here to Savannah. This in May 1866. Since that time he has
abused me & refuses to pay for the rent of my room & has not
furnished me with any money, food or clothing. I told him that I would
go to the Freedmans Bureau. He replied—damn the Freedmans Bureau—I'll cuss you before them. On Saturday night he came to my
room, took all his things, some four linen sheets & some underclothes
belonging to me & tore up two nice dresses of mine—he told me he
would rather keep a woman than be married—because she could not
carry him to law & I could.

Anderson District, South Carolina, August 23, 1866
Esther, a freedwoman being duly sworn deposes: I am the wife of a
freedman named Joseph and have been living with him this year at Dr.
Crumley's. He has frequently whipped me and otherwise maltreated
me and has threatened to poison me. I fear bodily harm from him by
reason of his menaces. I further swear that I do not make this complaint out of malice or for mere vexation.

Vicksburg, Mississippi, April 25, 1868
Julia Gibson (col) states that on Tuesday last her husband beat her over
the head, and bit her hand. She has been laid up since till today. When
she appr'd to make complaint, she showed a severe cut on her head
and a very sore hand where he bit her. Her husband goes by the name
of Willis Berkly and lives on Carters place.

Randolph County, Georgia, August 17, 1868
Julia Ray Complains that Alec who is her husband has beaten her badly
& her appearance is such as to indicate a gross assault. Appeared and
the assault acknowledged by dfdt, but as his wife had made up the

quarrel she declined to prosecute. Ray said he did not before know that he could not whip his wife.

In the absence of a quantitative study it is hard to know how widespread wife beating was, but women in the Sea Islands sang as they picked cotton:

> Black men beat me
> White men cheat me
> Won' get my hundud all day

In one Louisiana parish, women's complaints elicited the following notice:

I have had a great deal of Trouble with Freedmen whipping Women. I will have every Man punished in future who maltreats (or beats) Woman. The Colored people are now free and are governed by the same law as the White Man. If a Man strikes a Woman the Law says he shall be fined and imprisoned.

      J. H. Camp, A.S.A. Com. BR.F.&A.L., Trinity, La.

When Frances E. W. Harper traveled through the South to meet with freedwomen she found herself "preaching against men ill-treating their wives." During a lecture in Alabama, the Mobile Register *reported:*

She urged the cultivation of the home life, the sanctity of the marriage state, and the duties of mothers to their daughters. "Why," said she, in a voice of suprise, "I have actually heard since I have been South that sometimes colored husbands positively beat their wives! I do not mean to insinuate for a moment that such things can possibly happen in Mobile but I did hear of one terrible husband defending himself for the unmanly practice with, "Well, I've got to whip her, or leave her." We heard a darkey near us say, "If she will just stay here a few days, she will find plenty of them sort of husbands."

Freedwomen also complained of infidelity and desertion.

Columbia, South Carolina, April 16, 1866
Brown, Charlotte Vs Brown George States that she was Lawfully married to George Brown 14 Years ago and for several years he has been having illicit intercourse with a worthless white woman named Amelia Tines. Last Saturday night her husband left home and she mistrusted he had gone to this woman (although he had promised to abandon his bad conduct with her) and she went to this woman's house

and found her husband there with the woman and she gave the woman two licks when her husband jumped upon her and held her off the woman and put her out of the yard and picked up a stick & struck her with it and put a large hole in her head. She has four children to support, is in ill health and her husband contributes very little.

Dalton, Georgia March 15, 1868
Complainant Betty Ann Ellington Freedwoman; Defendant Harry Ellington Freedman, Betty found her husband in bed with a strange woman in her own house. On Speaking to her husband about the affair he Seized her by the throat and choked & beat her. He then took his things & the strange woman & left the house & has not returned to his family since. She has three children & has no way of making a living but by washing.

Corinth, Mississippi, 1867–68
Harriet Buchanan (Colored) complained that her husband Alfred Buchanan (Colored) was keeping another woman living with her in Adultery and had driven her off with two (2) of his children to support and had beaten her because she had said he was living with the other woman.

When lectures on "connubial bliss" were ineffective, delinquent husbands were fined, jailed, and required to support their children. In Louisiana, a bureau officer ordered a father to pay four dollars a month for his daughter's support until she was ten years old. In Georgia, a new bastardy law* required payments of fifty dollars a year until the child was fifteen. As bastardy laws were passed, freedwoman also filed claims against white fathers. Harriett Ogleby's claim went back to slavery days.

Clarke County, Georgia, August 25, 1868
Before me came in person Harriett Ogleby, (Col'd) who after being duly Sworn disposes and Says that She was delivered of a male bastard child on the 23 day of Dec'r 1862. The child name is Beauregard, and that one Drew Oglebly (white) is the father of said bastard child and that she is unable to support the child by reason of her poverty and that the said child must become an expense to the State of Georgia. She prays that Drew Oglebly (white) may be dealt with and compelled

---

*Laws passed during Reconstruction not only held white men responsible for their mulatto children, but also permitted these children to inherit property from their fathers. Some observers felt that these laws acted as a check on rape and casual liaisons. They were repealed or ignored after Reconstruction.

to support the Said bastard child as the laws of Georgia provides in Such cases.

Ellen Nesbit was one of four freedwomen from Athens, Georgia, who received lump sum payments of fifty to sixty dollars from the white fathers of their children. Her complaint stated:

Clarke County, Georgia, May 12, 1868
Before me came in person Ellen Nesbit (Col'd) who after being duly sworn disposes and says that on the 10th day of November 1867 She was delivered of a Male bastard Child by the name of Frank and that one Frank Lumpkin (white) of the County of Clarke and Town of Athens is the father of said bastard Child and that the child is likely to become an expense to the Government of the United States.

Putative fathers often denied the freedwomen's charges or accused them of being "notorious strumpets." Some whites threatened to murder the freedwomen if they were named.

Anderson District, South Carolina, August 11, 1866
Personally appeared Patsy a freedwoman who being duly sworn deposes and says:—About two months ago, I was delivered of a female child which was begotten by William Harper, he being a white man. Before the child was born he told me that if I had one and it became known that he was the father of it he would kill me. Columbus Harper, a nephew of William Harper told me one day this week that he heard I was going to swear the child to him (William Harper) and that if I did I would certainly be killed.

When called to account by bureau agents, whites blamed their behavior on their victims. Harriet Brown's boss beat her because her "irritable and abusive language exasperated him to extremes." John Bass pistol-whipped Ann May until she bled profusely; she "provoked [me] to strike her" he said. Will Tyson beat Isabella Colman "in a most brutal manner almost breaking her jaw." He was "sorry for striking her," he told a bureau officer, "but was provoked to it." Freedwomen responded in different ways to assaults on their persons. Some walked off their jobs when employers struck them and refused to live with battering husbands. Others, submissive by temperament or training, tried to divert violence through flattery and feigned mirth. Still others became chronically bad tempered, directing their rage at blacks as well as whites. Freedmen's Bureau records do not include many women like Emeline Ellaby, but she was a recognizable personality.

Louisiana, November 21, 1867

Mr. L. P. Conner called at this office to answer to the complaint made against him by Emeline Ellaby (Col) charging him with having discharged her without [paying] her the wages due. Mr. Conner stated that the complainant and several other Freedwomen were continually quarrelling. After warning all parties that he could not allow such things any longer and notifying their husbands the complainant again commenced to quarrel using language unfit to be repeated and raised a thorough disturbance among the hands thereby delaying the work. Harriet White (col.) States: that on or about Oct. 20 1867 as she and Martha were going along talking, Emmeline Ellaby jumped out of the cotton and called them damned bitches and said that everyone of them damned bitches there was shitting and pissing through one quill, and she would put her foot into we dam-d bitches ass so deep that we would have to saw her foot off: Said she would kick me until she brought blood &c etc. I would not say anything to her but went to Mr. Conner about it.

As Agent of the Bureau I consider it my duty to stop such things and as this woman made use of language disgraceful to anything human, and a disgrace to the race that all eyes are watching, I consider it my duty to make an example of this case by allowing Mr. Conner to discharge her with forfeiture of all back pay.

The bureau's files also include reports of parents beating their children. Freed children were not battered in the modern sense of the word. Rather, they were whipped frequently "for their own good." Women who had been brought up by the lash were firm believers in corporal punishment, to the dismay of their northern friends. When Ellen Craft returned to Georgia after living in England and New England for more than two decades she forbade whippings in her school and "made the plan that when the parents wanted to whip their children, they should take them into the grave yard, and when they got there to kneel down and pray." While this succeeded on the Crafts' plantation, other schoolmarms could not change the old ways. The following is from a letter from Virginia.

We have our sympathies called out, almost every day, for the innocent children who are harshly beaten by their harsh mamas. Close by us lives a black woman who lashes her little boy with a raw-hide. We have remonstrated repeatedly, but she "Reckons I shall beat my boy just as much as I please." "A few licks now and then, does 'em good," a sweet woman said to us once in extenuation of her practice of beating. Many a father and mother have begged me to beat their children at school. "Spare the rod and spoil the child," is on every mother's tongue. "Now you whip her and make a good girl out of her," the kindest mother says when she trusts her sweetest child to us.

NINETEEN

White Folks Still on Top

AFTER THE PASSAGE OF the Reconstruction Acts, relations between blacks and whites took a new turn. Black men could vote and hold office. In five southern states they made up a majority of the electorate. Faced with the spectre of black political power, whites put aside random acts of violence in favor of organized terror. One month after Congress passed the first Reconstruction Act over President Andrew Johnson's veto, leading southerners met in a Nashville hotel to draw up a constitution for "an institution of Chivalry, Humanity, Mercy, and Patriotism"—the Ku Klux Klan.* "Our main and fundamental objective," its founders stated "is the MAINTENANCE OF THE SUPREMACY OF THE WHITE RACE." Operating outside the law, bands of armed men, including doctors, lawyers, storekeepers, and poor whites, roamed the countryside at night. Their officers had names like Grand Giant, Grand Titan, Grand Wizard; their uniforms consisted of grotesque caps and masks and long black, red, or white gowns. This hocus-pocus had a double purpose: to strike terror in the hearts of superstititous freedpeople and to disguise the wearers so that they could commit murder, arson, and rape with impunity.

Declaring war on the Radical Republicans, Klansmen shot political leaders, both black and white, whipped voters, and intimidated working people to keep them from the polls. Their activities and those of similar vigilante groups† peaked between 1868 and 1870 when thousands were killed and tens of thousands driven from their homes. The mass murders at last moved Congress to pass the Ku Klux Act of 1871,

*Although a small group of ex-Confederate soldiers founded the Ku Klux Klan in Pulaski, Tennessee, in December 1865, it did not become a widespread organization until April 1867.
†Similar groups included the Knights of the White Camelia, the White Brotherhood, the Society of the Pale Faces, and the White League.

which proposed fines and imprisonment for "those who go in disguise" to deprive others "of the equal protection of the laws." While federal prosecutors brought some Klansmen to trial, a joint Congressional committee traveled south for an on-the-spot investigation. Their twelve-volume report, Testimony Taken by the Joint Select Committee to Inquire into the Condition of Affairs in the Late Insurrectionary States, includes numerous eyewitness accounts of the Klan terror.

The Klan's chief targets were politicians and members of state militias. Betsey Westbrook, one of a procession of widows who traveled to the county courthouses to talk to the Congressmen, said that her husband was killed because "He just would hold up his head and say he was a strong radical."

They first came and shot about seven barrels through the window, at the end of the house. They said "You had better open it, it will be better for you." They went to the fence and got a rail and broke down the outside door. We shut ourselves up in another room at the back of the house and they got another rail and busted open the back door, and one of them said "Raise a light." I was sitting on a little basket on the hearth. They picked it up and pitched it into the fire and it had grease on it, and it blazed up and made a light. Then one of them began to strike him over the head, and says "You are that damned son of bitch, Westbrook?" He says, "Yes, I am." The man struck him with his gun. Then my husband took the dog-iron up and he struck three or four of them. They got him jammed up in a corner, and one man went around behind him and put two loads out of a double-barreled gun in his shoulders. Another man says, "Kill him, God damn him," and he shot him right down. He didn't live more than a half hour after they shot him.

Although he was badly wounded, Martha Hendricks's husband survived a Klan attack.

They came on Sunday night. We were in bed. I was awake, for my baby was fretting. I said, "Mr. Hendricks, somebody is calling you. And he said "Who is that?" They said "A friend; get up and come out." I said, "Mr. Hendricks, you make up a light before you go to the door to anybody; make up a good light." As soon as he made a light Sam Edmunds bursted the door down and came right in. I had got out of bed, with my baby in my arms. Mr. Edmunds held me, and told my husband if he moved, he would shoot his damned head off.

Q. What has any of them against your husband?

A. I do not know. My husband was appointed by Governor Bullock as one of the managers of election; my father told me that he heard several of them say that no negro should be a manager of election; that they would kill him first.

Joe Johnson's wife described her husband's execution.

They made me and my children wrap our heads up in bed-quilts and come out of the house, and they then set it on fire, burning it up, and my husband in it, and all we had. They then took all my husband's papers from me. There were about fifty or sixty of them. They killed him because he refused to resign his office as constable, to which he was elected on the Republican ticket. They sent him several notices, warning him to leave his place and resign his office, but he said he would not, so they burnt him near to death; at least they thought he was dead, but he was not quite dead; he got out and fell into a hole of water and lay there: but all the skin was burnt off of him. So the white men saw him and shot him and he died and leaves me, a poor widow with a housefull of children, and no one to help me.

Although the Klan was boldest in the country districts, politicians all over the South felt threatened. The daughter of a black Congressman, Ann J. Edwards* recalled an attempt on the life of the Reverend Richard J. Cain. Cain who lived in Charleston at that time, served two terms as U.S. congressman from South Carolina.

From the moment [father] became delegate to the Constitutional Convention [1868] a guard was necessary night and day to watch our home. We, his family, lived in constant fear. The climax of the resentment against him took place when he was Republican candidate to the House of Representatives. A day or two before election a mob gathered suddenly in front of the house, and we thought the end had come. Father sent us all upstairs, and said he would, if necessary, give himself up to the mob and let them satisfy their vengeance on him, to save the rest of us.

While he was talking, mother noticed another body of men in the alley. Father told us to prepare for the worst, saying, "What they plan to do is for those in front to engage the attention of ourselves and the guard, then those in the rear will fire the place and force us out." He was calm, but mother was greatly agitated and I was crying.

*Born a slave in 1856, Ann J. Edwards was adopted by the Reverend Richard Cain in 1861. While Cain was in Congress, she attended Howard University and married one of its graduates.

The mob leader demanded that father come out for a talk. Then the sheriff and deputies appeared and told them if harm came to us the city would be placed under martial law. The men then dispersed.

State Senator George Ashburn, a white Georgian who had joined the Radical Republicans, was marked for assassination by the Klan. When he came to Columbus, Georgia, in the spring of 1868, the only person who would shelter him was Hannah Flournoy, a twenty-eight-year-old black woman. Testifying three years later in Atlanta where she had been living "since they run me from Columbus," she told the Congressional Committee about Ashburn's murder.

They went around to all the boarding-houses and got them to promise not to take him. He walked all day, and come to my house about 3 or 4 o'clock. He said "Hannah, can you feed me?" He said he had been to every boarding-house in the place, and could get no chance to stay.

I said "You are a republican, and I am willing to die for you. I am a republican, tooth and toe-nail." I took Mr. Ashburn through the house, which contained five rooms. Colored people rented three of them, and a white girl had one. I then said "Amanda and I will sleep here in this room and you can have her room." I furnished the sheets and pillow-slips for Mr. Ashburn, and she furnished the other bedding. After he came there, I had the gate locked every night, and made the boy bring me the key. The white people next to my house had a very severe dog, and nobody could go up and down the alley after night, but what the dog would bark. Generally, I would go to bed after supper, and then when all the rest had gone to bed, I would get up and sit up all night, and take a nap during the day.

The white girl who boarded at Flournoy's tried to bribe her to betray the senator.

She said she had money enough to buy me. I said, "Not now, I used to be for sale, but I am not now; if you have so much money you had better pay your board."

On the night of March 29, 1868, Flournoy's neighbor's dog was strangely silent when a crowd of masked men broke in.

I saw them lighting candles and fingering their pistols. I went into Mr. Ashburn's room and said "Lord, Mr. Ashburn, the room is full of men; they are disguised and showing their pistols." He put on his coat and walked up and down with his pistol in his hand. He said, "Go out, and take care of yourself; the Lord will take care of me." I turned and just as I was coming out a Mr. George Betts and Mr. Sergeant Marshall bolted right in and commenced shooting. I looked at the men. They were disguised but I knew a great many of them.

I went down to the courthouse, and if Captain Mills had put out his men when I first went down there, he would have caught every one of them. An officer there said, "I am liable to be shot down." For eight weeks I was afraid to stay in the house at night. I staid with a double-barrel shot-gun in my lap.

Threatened because she could identify Ashburn's murderers, she fled Columbus, leaving her household goods behind. "What business were you engaged in?" a Congressman asked. She replied.

Washing and cooking for anybody that wanted me to do it. I was working honorably for my living. I took Mr. Ashburn in for I thought it right to take him in. He was owing me thirty dollars before he went to the convention. He said to me "I suppose you want some money." I said "You go on. If you come back you can pay me; if you don't I can collect money for my washing and pay my house-rent. You had better keep your money, for if you go there without money, you may get into trouble."

After politicians, teachers came next on the most-wanted list. "Your wife, the damned bitch, is teaching a colored school," Columbus Jeter's employer complained. "I work for her and maintain her; why should she not teach?" replied Jeter. "The laws of the country permit her to do so." But wherever the Klan was the law, colored schoolhouses were burned and teachers, black and white, were driven away. Whole communities began "lying out" at night, sleeping in the woods and fields in order to avoid Klan visits. If the man of the house was lying out, the night riders "took the[ir] spite out on the women," Harriet Hernandez said.

They came in; I was lying in bed. They took me out of bed; they took me up in their arms and toted me out—me and my daughter Lucy. He struck me on the forehead with a pistol. Says he, "Damn you, fall!" I fell. Says he, "Damn you, get up!" I got up. Says he "Damn you, get over this fence!" and he kicked me over; and then he went on to a brush pile and they laid us right down there, both together. They had dragged and beat us along. They struck me right on the top of my head, and I thought they had killed me; and I said, "Lord o'mercy, don't kill my child!" He threw my arm over my head so I could not do anything with it for three weeks.

Q. How do colored people feel in your neighborhood?

A. They have no satisfaction to live like humans, no how. It appears to me like all summer I have been working and it is impossible for me to enjoy it.

Q. What do the colored people do for their safety?

A. They lie out all night. Some families say they don't think they can get tamed to the house in five years.

Q. Does this fear extend to women and children?

A. Yes, sir; they just whipped them all—they did them scandalous.

Sixty-four-year-old Abraham Brumfield was lying out until his rheumatism became too painful. His wife, Emeline, described her confrontation with the Klan.

They came to my house some time in March. Mr. Brumfield had been lying out for four weeks; he came in all swelled up, and told me to make poultices and poultice his arms and shoulders, and I did, and he laid down, and I laid on two chairs before the fire until midnight, and then his poultice got cold, and he told me to warm it, and when I did, he says, "Now, you go and lay down." I went to bed and was woke up by the alarm of the dog. I seed persons coming up through the woods, running and I says "Ku-Klux! Ku-Klux!" and he just throwed the house 'twixt him and them and run back for the fence. They called for Brumfield, and I says, "Brumfield ain't here," and a man that had come up says, "You're a God-damned liar." I throwed open the door and says, "If I am a God-damned liar, you may come in and get him." He said "Now, you have got to tell me where he is; if you don't I will blow your God-damned brains out." I says, "Then you will have me to shoot tonight."

Emeline Brumfield's courage was not unusual. Mary Brown panicked when the Klan came, but "I got over my scare, for I said to myself 'I have not done anything; I have not stolen anything or murdered anybody; so I will not be scared.'" Harriet Postle was frightened too, but had enough presence of mind to seat herself over the loose plank in the floor that concealed her husband's hiding place.

I was asleep when they came; they made a great noise and waked me up, and called out for Postle; my husband heard them and jumped up; when I got up I found he was gone; they kept on hallooing for Postle and knocking at the door; I was trying to get on my clothes, but I was so frightened I did not get on my clothes at all. My oldest child ran under the bed; one of them saw him and said "There he is; I see him;" and with that three of them pointed their pistols under the bed; I then cried out, "It is my child;" I begged them not to hurt my child; I then took a chair and sat it back upon a loose plank,* and sat down upon it; one of the men stepped up; he just jerked the chair and threw me over while my babe was in my arms, and I fell with my babe to the floor, when one of them clapped his foot upon the child, and another had his foot on me.

They asked me if Postle was there; I said no; they told me to make up a light, but I was so frightened I could not do it well. Then they asked me where my husband was; I told them he was gone for some meal. One of them comes to me and says: "You are a damned lying bitch;" and he had a line, and commenced putting it over my neck; when he had the rope around my head he said "I want you to tell where your husband is." I commenced hallooing, and the one who had his foot on my body mashed me badly, but not so badly as he might have done, for I was seven or eight months gone in travail; then I got outside of the house and I called the little ones to me, for they were all dreadfully frightened. My child was scared well nigh unto death, and now when the dog barks it looks like it would go into fits.

Although the avowed goal of the Klan was to destroy the political power of the Radical Republicans, the night riders kept a sharp eye out for "smart-assed niggers." Caroline Smith of Walton County, Georgia, and Lucy McMillan who lived near Spartanburgh, South Carolina, told of their efforts to be submissive.

The colored people dare not dress themselves and fix up, like they thought anything of themselves, for fear they would whip us. I have been humble and obedient to them—a heap more so than I was to my master, who raised me.

They never had anything against me. I was mighty good to the white folks. When they called on me to work, I worked as good as I could. If they were a mind to pay me, I took it. If they wouldn't, I had to do without it. I took whatever they gave me.

Despite their attempts to be conciliatory, McMillan's house was burned after she said she wanted to own land, and Smith was given forty licks with a hickory to remind her not to "sass any white ladies."

*Details in the women's testimony indicated that blacks' homes were larger and more comfortable than they had been in the first postemancipation years. One woman spoke of curtains at her windows, another of wooden floors.

*A brush with a white woman also brought the Klan to Diana Wil-
liams's house. The widow of a Union soldier, she gave the following
affidavit.*

The early part of May I was sent by the man for whom I am
working to the spring to get water; after I left the spring a Mrs. Susan
Perry come, and accused me of stealing some soap she had left at the
spring, which I denied doing; I told her I did not take it—you can
search me; and then she said that she would not let any nigger bitch
sass her, and if I did not shut up she would shoot me. I continued my
work, and she said she would have me whipped. On Saturday night,
the 12th, about midnight, five men came into the house. One of them
put his gun to my breast, saying that if I did not go he would kill me.
Putting me down they commenced to beat me over the head and back
with sticks until I fell to the ground; then they said "You go back
home, and if you ever say anything about the Ku-Klux being here we
will kill you."

*Wallace Fowler, who was over seventy-five years old, caught a
white boy stealing his watermelons. The boy's father called in the Klan
to settle their private grievance, with a fatal result. Charlotte Fowler
gave this tender account of her husband's last days.*

I was taken sick on Wednesday morning and laid on my bed
Wednesday and Thursday. He went out working on his farm. We had
a little grandchild living with me—my daughter's child. He kept coming backward and forward to the house to see how I got and what he
could do for me. I never ate nothing until Thursday night. When he
came home he cooked something for me to eat and said "Old woman,
if you don't eat something you will die." Says I: "I can't eat." Says he,
"Then I will eat, and feed the little baby." That is the grandchild he
meant. I says, "You take that little child and sleep in the bed; I think
I have the fever and I don't want you to get it. He called to the
grandchild, Tody—she is Sophia—and he says: "Tody, when you are
ready to come to bed, come, and grandmother will open your frock,
and you can go to bed." I reckon I did not lay in bed a half an hour
before I heard somebody by the door; it was not one person, but two
—ram! ram! ram! He heard it as quick as lightning, and he said to
them, "Gentlemen, do not break the door down; I will open the door";
and just as he said that they said "God damn you, I have got you now."
The little child followed its grandfather to the door—you know in the
night it is hard to direct a child. Just then I heard the report of a pistol,

and this little child ran back to me and says, "Oh, grandma, they have killed my poor grandpappy." He was such an old gentleman that I thought they just shot over him to scare him; but sure enough, as quick as I got to the door, I said, "Gentlemen, you have killed a poor innocent man." My poor old man!

"Uppity blacks," that is, those who were successful, also felt the wrath of the Klan. Mary Elder and her husband were driven from their farm because "we were two quiet hard-working people, doing well." Eliza Lyon's husband had built "an elegant blacksmith shop" in Choctaw County, Alabama, and was saving money "to buy him a piece of land and build him a house," she said, when the Klansmen came. Despite her attempt to protect him, he was killed almost instantly.

Hannah Tutson, forty-two years old, and her husband Samuel, fifty-three, had worked and saved to acquire 160 acres of land in Clay County, Florida. Her years as a slave had accustomed her to beatings. When whites threatened to dispossess her, she told one, "In the red times, how many times have they took me and turned my clothes over my head and whipped me? I don't care what they do to me now if only I can save my land." But when her neighbors came in their Klan robes the punishment they meted out was worse than "in the red times." The Tutsons fled to Jacksonville where she told her story.

Just as I got into bed five men bulged right against the door, and it fell right in the middle of the floor. George McCrea ran right to me and gathered me by the arm. As I saw him coming, I took up the child —the baby—and held to him. Cabell Winn catched hold of my foot, and then there were so many hold of me I cannot tell who they were. George McCrea catched the little child by the foot and slinged it out of my arms. I screamed and they got me out of doors. They tore down the fence and jerked me over, just as if you were jerking a dumb beast. The old man was ahead of me and I saw Dave Donley stamp on him. They carried me about a quarter of a mile from the house to a pine, just as large as I could get my arms around, and then they tied my hands there. They whipped me for a while. George McCrea would act scandalously and treat me shamefully. He would make me squat down by the pine, and say, "What are you trembling for?" He would get his knees between my legs and say, "God damn you, open your legs. Old lady, if you don't let me have to do with you, I will kill you." They whipped me and got liquor of some kind and poured it on my head, and I smelled it for three weeks, so that it made me sick. I had been working and washing for them. I had not been two weeks from [Cabell

Winn's] mother's house, where I washed every week. There were four men whipping me at once, with saddlegirths, with surcingles off the saddles. They whipped me from the crown of my head to the soles of my feet. I was just raw. After I got away from them I ran to my house. My house was torn down.

Q. Did you find your children?

A. I did next day. When they got away they went out into the field, and my little daughter said that as the baby cried she would reach out and pick some gooseberries and put them in its little mouth. When she could hear none of them any more she went up to a log heap and staid there with her brother and the baby. At daylight the old man came by.

Q. Did the baby get hurt?

A. Yes, sir, in one of its hips. When it began to walk one of its hips was very bad, and every time you would stand it up it would scream. But I rubbed it and rubbed it, and it looks like it was outgrowing it now.

Q. You spoke about some of them "wanting to do with you". Did you give way?

A. No sir; George McCrea acted so bad, and I was stark naked. I tell you, men, he pulled my womb down so that sometimes I can hardly walk.

Q. What does he follow for a living?

A. He was a deputy sheriff when he came and whipped me.

"Splitting a nigger woman," the coarse phrase of an Alabama doctor, was not only considered a white man's prerogative, but was also a way to express his anger and contempt. Sexual assaults on black women ranged from whispered words on the street and attempted seductions to mutilations and gang rapes. In almost every recorded case, beatings accompanied the assaults.

Mary Jane Forrest of Baton Rouge, Louisiana, complained to the Freedmen's Bureau about Joseph McKitrick.

McK stopped her on the sidewalk and asked her to s--k his privates. She refused and he thrust her against the fence and beat her. They watched for and beat her a 2d time as she was going home from this office. Pete McKitrick & Frank Young were with him.

Lydia Anderson and her daughter rejected their employer's advances. She talked about this to visiting congressmen in Macon, Mississippi.

Mrs. Richards wanted to go up to Choctaw to see her children. She said "If you will stay here and take care of my things I will give you a good present when I get back." The old creature started Monday morning, and then Monday night and Tuesday morning her husband commenced some of his talk. He says, "The witches rode me last night." I didn't know what he meant. He says, "You ought to come in and keep me company. The old lady told you to take good care of me." I says, "I am going to cook your victuals and make your bed and take care of you." He kept talking that way, and finally I found out what he was talking about, and I said, "No, sir; my old master raised me like his own child; that's not my disposition." In that week my daughter came there. When she came he dropped off with me and flies to this young girl, young woman grown. I never let on; I said if he became too free she will tell me after a while. On Friday morning, they thought I was gone out milking, but I stopped behind the chimney, and I heard him say, "What do you want me to fetch you from Macon?" She said, "Nothing; I don't want nothing you have got." She says, "If I did such a thing as that you want, she would beat me nearly to death." Says he, "Oh, your mother won't know it." She says, "Yes, she will; my mother don't allow no such bother and I am right to mind my mother."

After the Andersons left his employ, Richards's sons, wearing Klan costumes, took Lydia from her bed and whipped her. She was luckier than Rhoda Ann Childs of Griffin, Georgia:

Myself and husband were under contract with Mrs. Amelia Childs and worked until the crops were laid by. Then we were called upon one night and my husband was demanded. I said he was gone to the watermelon patch. They then seized me and took me some distance from the house, where they "bucked" me down across a log, shipped my clothes over my head, one of the men standing astride my neck and beat me across my posterior. In this manner I was beaten until they were tired. Then they turned me parallel with the log, laying my neck on a limb which projected from the log, and one man placing his foot upon my neck beat me again on my hip and thigh. Then I was thrown upon the ground on my back, one of the men stood upon my breast, while two others took hold of my feet and stretched my limbs as far apart as they could, while the man standing upon my breast applied the strap to my private parts until fatigued into stopping and I was more dead than alive. Then a man supposed to be an ex-Confederate soldier, as he was on crutches, fell upon me and ravished me. During the whipping one of the men ran his pistol into me, and said he had a hell of a mind to pull the trigger, and swore they ought to shoot me, as my husband had been in the "God damned Yankee Army." There were concerned in this affair eight men.

In North Carolina a U.S. commissioner testified that "The most outrageous cutting that I saw was the cutting of a woman who was cut in her private parts."

Frances Gilmore came to my office and complained that disguised persons had visited her house in the night-time, taken her out, and whipped her with a board, turned her over and whipped her again; then with matches burned the hair from her private parts and cut her with a knife; and that she had been lying there about three weeks, unable to get to me before. I asked her if she could identify any of the parties. She said she could not.

Q. What political objects were to be obtained by such proceedings?

A. The driving of the whole negro race out of the country, I should suppose.

TWENTY

Washerwomen, Maumas, Exodusters, Jubileers

ALTHOUGH THE KLAN DID NOT SUCCEED *in driving black people out of the country, it ended Reconstruction in Georgia and North Carolina and contributed to Conservative victories in Virginia, Tennessee, and the border states. Tired of lying out at night, numbers of field hands migrated from Georgia to Alabama and Mississippi, or sought refuge in urban areas. In Atlanta and Columbia, Jackson and Mobile, women from the plantations found that they had marketable skills. "I have done a mountain of washing and ironing in my life," one freedwoman sighed. Washerwomen were so indispensable to city life that they ventured to get together to ask for higher wages. In June 1866, the* Daily Clarion *of Jackson, Mississippi, published a politely worded ultimatum.*

Mayor Barrows
Dear Sir: Jackson, Mississippi, June 20, 1866
At a meeting of the colored Washerwomen of this city, on the evening of the 18th of June, the subject of raising the wages was considered, and the following preamble and resolution were unanimously adopted:

Whereas, under the influence of the present high prices of all the necessaries of life, and the attendant high rates of rent, we, the washerwomen of the city of Jackson, State of Mississippi, thinking it impossible to live uprightly and honestly in laboring for the present daily and monthly recompense, and hoping to meet with the support of all good citizens, join in adopting unanimously the following resolution:

Be it resolved by the washerwomen of this city and county, That on and after the foregoing date, we join in charging a uniform rate for our labor, and any one belonging to the class of washerwomen, violating this, shall be liable to a fine regulated by the class. We do not wish in the least to charge exorbitant prices, but desire to be able to live comfortably if possible from the fruits of our labor. We present the matter to your Honor, and hope you will not reject it. The prices charged are:

$1.50 per day for washing
$15.00 per month for family washing
$10.00 per month for single individuals

We ask you to consider the matter in our behalf, and should you deem it just and right, your sanction of the movement will be gratefully received.

Yours, very truly,

THE WASHERWOMEN OF JACKSON

The Clarion *failed to print further news of the women's struggle, nor is anything known about the outcome of a more militant effort in Texas a decade later. When the washerwomen of Galveston went on strike in 1877, their cottage industry faced competition from steam laundries and Chinese laundrymen. The* Galveston News *reported:*

Monday night colored women, emboldened by the liberties allowed their fathers, husbands and brothers decided to have a public hurrah of their own, and as the men had demanded two dollars for a day's labor they would ask $1.50 or $9 per week. As women are generally considered cleansers of dirty linen, their first move was against the steam laundry, corner of Avenue A and Tenth Street, owned by J. N. Harding.

About 6.30 A.M. colored women began collecting around his house, until they numbered about twenty-five. The laundry women were soon seen coming to work. When met and told that they should not work for less than $1.50 per day, four turned back; but, one, a Miss Murphy went into the house and began working. Seeing this, the women rushed in, caught her and carried her into the street, and by threats forced her to leave.

This success emboldened the women to further demonstrations. The cry was raised, "Let's lock them out for good; here's nails I brought especially." An axe lying in the wood pile was grabbed, and the laundry house doors and windows secured. Then off they started for the heathen Chinese, who "washes Mellican man clothes so cheapee". Down Market street they went, led by a portly colored lady, whose avoirdupois is not less than 250.

Each California laundry was visited in turn, beginning at Slam Sing's and ending at Wau Loong's corner of Bath Avenue and Postoffice Street. At these laundries all the women talked at once, telling Slam Sing, Wau Loong and the rest that "they must close up and leave this city within fifteen days or they would be driven away," each Chinaman responding "Yees, yees," "Me go, yees," and closed their shops. The women scattered after avowing they would meet again at 4 o'clock and visit each place where women are hired, and if they receive less than $1.50 per day or $9 per week they would force them to quit.

There were probably organizing efforts in other cities, but it is unlikely that any surpassed the scope of the one in Atlanta in 1881 when three thousand washerwomen struck and were joined in their demand for pay increases by cooks, nurses, and other servants. A police captain told a reporter for the Atlanta Constitution *that the organization had started a year earlier but had failed.*

This year however, they have been successful and to-day nearly 3,000 negro women are asking their white friends who supported them during the cold, hard winter to pay them a dollar a dozen for washing. Three weeks ago twenty negro women and a few negro men met in Summer Hill Church and discussed the matter. The next night the negro preachers in all the churches announced a mass meeting of the washerwomen. The meeting was a big one and the result was an organization. Officers were elected, committees appointed and time and places for meetings read out. Since then there has been meetings every night or two, and now there is a society or club in every ward in the city.

"What do they do at these meetings?" the reporter asked.

Make speeches and pray. They swear they never will wash another piece for less than one dollar a dozen, but they will never get it and will soon give in.

"They are trying to prevent those who are not members from washing, are they not?"

Yes. The committee first goes to those who have no connection with the organization and try to persuade them to join. Failing in this they then threaten them with cowhides, fire and death if they disobey. The men are as bad as the women. When a woman refuses to join the society, their men threaten to 'whip 'em' and the result is that the ranks are daily swelling. Why, last night there was a big meeting at New Hope church and fifty additions were made to the list. They passed resolutions informing all women not members of the society to quit work or stand the consequences. I tell you, this strike is a big thing.

White Atlanta fought back. The police arrested strike leaders for disorderly conduct and threatened to fill up the chain gang. Landlords raised rents, and the city council proposed an annual license fee of twenty-five dollars for each washerwoman, the same fee that downtown merchants paid. Although the license fee caused some strikers to withdraw, others sent a defiant letter to the mayor.

Mr. Jim English, Mayor of Atlanta   Washing Society,
Dear Sir: Atlanta, Georgia, August 1, [1881]

We, the members of our society, are determined to stand to our pledge and make extra charges for washing, and we have agreed, and are willing to pay $25 or $50 for licenses as a protection, so we can control the washing for the city. We can afford to pay these licenses, and will do it before we will be defeated, and then we will have full control of the city's washing at our own prices, as the city has control of our husbands' work at their prices. Don't forget this. We hope to hear from your council Tuesday morning. We mean business this week or no washing. Yours respectfully,

From 5 Societies, 486 Members

The "Washing Amazons," as the Atlanta Constitution called them, lacked the economic power to hold out indefinitely. When their strike fund and savings were exhausted, the women were forced to return to their tubs at the old rate of pay.

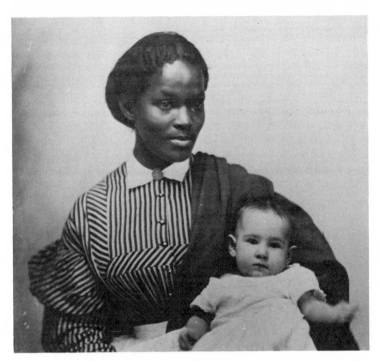

A nursemaid and her charge, from a daguerrotype circa 1865. *(Valentine Museum, Richmond, Virginia)*

As independent contractors working in their own homes, washerwomen had somewhat more control over working conditions than domestic workers did. Servants worked seven days a week, from breakfast until the last dinner dish was washed and put away. Most insisted on living at home so that they could have a modicum of family life when their day's work was done. They lacked the power to bargain for better wages and hours but asserted their independence in small ways. In what might be called sit-out strikes, a woman who had worked all weekend could be "too ailing" to arrive on time on Monday; by Thursday she might develop "a mis'ry" in her back, which kept her at home. If too many tasks were assigned, she could do them poorly or not at all. Since tardiness and sloppy work were part of the whites' stereotype of blacks, these derelictions from duty were met with little more than "What-can-you-expect-from-them?" To compensate to some extent for their low wages, domestic workers were given their employers' cast-off clothes and the food left from the whites' dinner.

The "service pan," which black women brought home each day, was often the major source of food for their families. Creola Wilson's mother, a New Orleans cook, brought her up on food pans.

I can 'member that my ma went to work early every mornin'. She was a short brownskin lady. She says my pa was brownskin too. I used to ask her why I'm so chocolate and she used to laugh and say, "We plucked you out of a dark cloud that was hangin' low one day." Fo' the longest I believed that.

She took me to church every Sunday. She didn't do no runnin' around neither. I ain't never seen my ma wid no man. She was a hard-working woman, and she brought the pans right home. Then we'd sit down and eat out of the pan and she'd tell me all about how them white folks like her cookin' and what they said.

Then mamma commenced gettin' old. I was hittin' around sixteen years old and gettin' kind of lively. Well, mamma got sick and she put me in her place. Miss Graves says to me, "Honey child, does you think you can do my cooking?" I says yes'm. She give me five dollars a week fo' cookin' and cleanin' up the house. It was some house, a two-story house. We had some scuffle. I took care of my mamma off of five dollars a week. Talkin' about making a dollar stretch!

In Congo Square in New Orleans market women did a thriving business in spruce beer, popcorn, and peanuts. Marchandes des calas *sold rice croquettes; the purveyors of sweet potato cakes cried their wares in "gombo" French.*

> Bel pam patat, Bel pam patat.
> Madam, ou-lay-ou le bel pam patat

The blackberry women came to town in May, announcing:

> Blackberries, fresh an' fine,
> I got blackberries, lady,
> Fresh from de vine,
> I got blackberries, lady,
> Three glass fo'a dime,
> I got blackberries, I got blackberries

Charleston's broad-chested, big-hipped "vegetable maumas" balanced fifty-pound baskets of vegetables on their heads while chanting:

> Red rose To-may-toes
> Green peas! Sugar peas!

Carrying baskets of strawberries on their heads, women in Norfolk,
Virginia, sang:

> I live fore miles out of town,
>   I am gwine to glory.
> My strawberries are sweet an' sound,
>   I am gwine to glory.
> I fotch 'em fore miles on my head,
>   I am gwine to glory.
> My chile is sick, an' husban' dead,
>   I am gwine to glory.
> Now's de time to get 'em cheap,
>   I am gwine to glory.
> Eat em wid yer bread an' meat,
>   I am gwine to glory.
> Eat dees strawberries when you please,
>   I am gwine to glory.

Other female enterpreneurs ran boarding houses, opened restau-
rants, and grocery stores. Hagar Ann Baker, a waitress during slavery,
became a businesswoman afterward. Her daughter who taught school
in Savannah wrote:

In 1867, soon after the death of my father, who had served on a
gunboat during the war, my mother opened a grocery store, where she
kept general merchandise always on hand. These she traded for cash
or would exchange for crops of cotton, corn, or rice, which she would
ship once a month, to F. Lloyd & Co., or Johnson & Jackson, in
Savannah. These were colored merchants, doing business on Bay Street
in that city. Mother bought her first property, which contained
ten acres. She next purchased fifty acres of land. Then she had a
chance to get a place with seven hundred acres of land, and she
bought this.

Annie L. Burton, also a Georgia freedwoman, was a domestic
worker in the North when her sister died, leaving an eleven-year-old
son. Taking the boy and another sister with her, Burton went to
Florida.

My idea was to get a place as chambermaid at Green Cove Springs,
Florida, through the influence of the head waiter at a hotel there,
whom I knew. After I got into Jacksonville, the idea of keeping a
restaurant came to me. I found a little house of two rooms where we

could live, and the next day I found a place to start my restaurant. Caroline's cookstove had been left in Macon. After hiring the room for the restaurant, I sent for this stove. Then I went to a dealer in second-hand furniture and got such things as were actually needed, on the condition that he would take them back at a discount when I got through with them.

Trade at the restaurant was very good, and we got along nicely. One day the cook from a shipwrecked vessel came to my restaurant, and in return for his board and a bed in the place, agreed to do my cooking. After trade became good, I changed my residence to a house of four rooms, and put three cheap cots in each of two of the rooms, and let the cots at a dollar a week apiece to colored men who worked nearby in hotels. Lawrence and I did the chamber work at night, after the day's work in the restaurant. Lawrence, who was about eleven years old, was a great help to me. He took out dinners to the cigarmakers in a factory nearby.

At the end of the season, about four months, it had grown so hot that we could stay in Jacksonville no longer. From my restaurant and my lodgers I cleared one hundred and seventy-five dollars, which I put into the Jacksonville bank. Then I took the furniture back to the dealer, who fulfilled his agreement.

After the Florida venture, Burton returned to the North where, at various times, she ran a restaurant, worked in a hotel and "rented a lodging house, and lost money on it." Married in 1888, she and her husband were able to send Lawrence to Hampton Institute for schooling.

Little is known about the southern black women, most of them free-born, who had received some education before the war. Occasional glimpses of them can be found in black newspapers. In Louisiana, a woman who signed herself "Mattie" was an occasional correspondent for the New Orleans Louisianian. *Writing from a rural parish, she was particularly interested in seeing freedmen buy land.*

Thibodaux, Lafourche Parish, [Lousiana,]
Editor Louisianian: September 23, 1871

The weather has been very rainy during the past month, but it has not seriously impeded the gathering of the rice crop. Complaints are made by some of the larger planters that they are unable to haul their wood, but the last few days of dry weather has somewhat dried up the mud, and hopes are entertained that the roads will be in a passable condition before the time for "cutting."

It seems as if something might be done to show a large majority of our race, the necessity of owning houses, and especially their own small farm. In the present system of large plantations, the laborer gets $20 per month and a ration of meat and meal. Of course a portion of these wages must go for food and clothes, so that when the end of the year comes round they have not much more than they had when they began. The great trouble with them (and I have talked with many of the most intelligent of the laborers about this) is the ignorance of where to buy, and how to buy land for their homes.

For example, there are at least a hundred colored men in this town who have bought and paid for their lots; built neat and substantial dwelling places on them, while their *"work"* is perhaps six, or seven miles distant from their homes. Now if they could have purchased, say twenty arpents of land to cultivate with this same money, they would have a certain source of revenue their entire lives.

If the columns of the *Louisianian* were to take up the matter, our race would have confidence to buy a farm and pay for it gradually. Perhaps I have made my letter too long, but I wish to hasten the time when my race will own their own plantations, and work for themselves. Then we shall see the death, and burial of the senseless caste and prejudice now so common in the South.

Truly your,
Mattie

*Sarah H. Thompson, a Memphis teacher, wrote to Senator Charles Sumner who was sponsoring a Civil Rights Act.**

Hon. Charles Sumner
Dear Sir: Memphis, Tennessee, February 5, 1872
Last winter, while coming from Cincinnati to this city, myself and four small children, the oldest of whom was not eleven years old we were not allowed to enter the ladies' sitting room in Louisville, Kentucky. Therefore, to keep ourselves warm, we were obliged to walk to and fro in front of the depot in the sleet while my dear children were suffering and crying from the severity of the cold. In faltering accents one of them inquired of me, "Why is this, ma? What have we done? Why can't we go in there and warm just like others?" When the time arrived for the train to leave we were conducted into the smoking car. Here we were obliged to sit and inhale the fumes of tobacco rising from the cigars and pipes of all who wished to come into that car; also, to

*His Civil Rights Act became law in 1875 but was declared unconstitutional by the Supreme Court in 1883, a decision that was not reversed until 1964.

hear all manner of obscene and profane language. Such as my children had never heard before.

A friend of mine came from the North for the purpose of going into Mississippi to teach. On her way from this city to Jackson, she was ejected from the ladies' car. And because she dared to "talk back" as they call it down here to the baggage master, he slapped her in the face. It is futile for me to try and enumerate the many instances of this kind; they are occuring almost every day, and we have no means of redress.

I sincerely hope your bill may pass, and believe the colored people owe you a debt of gratitude which they can never repay. Long may the name of Charles Sumner live in the hearts of the colored people of America.

Yours gratefully,
Sarah H. Thompson

A second letter from Sarah Thompson appeared in the New National Era and Citizen *the following year.*

To the Editor: Hernando, Mississippi, November, 1873

Nearly two months ago I thought of writing you from Memphis in regard to our new school-house which has been built for the colored children. While I was preparing to write, the yellow-fever broke out and caused me to forget for a time everything except the suffering of the sick and the dying.

At present, myself and family are sojourning in Hernando, Mississippi. This is a small town, situated a little over twenty miles from Memphis. There are about seven hundred inhabitants. About three hundred are colored. Since I have been here I have heard little besides politics. As far as I can learn, the colored people here and in the surrounding country will vote for Ames. This is as it should be. If I could have my way, every colored man throughout the length and breadth of Mississippi would march to the polls in one solid phalanx and vote for Ames. If a colored man could be found so lost to the cause of justice and humanity as to vote for Alcorn,* after his voting against the Civil Rights Bill in Congress, such a man should be treated to a coat of tar and feathers and ducked in the nearest creek.

It is a fact greatly to be deplored, that the colored people here manifest but little interest in the public schools. Two white men have been appointed trustees over the school. These men showed the inter-

*Adelbert Ames, Republican governor of Mississippi, was driven from office in 1875. Senator James L. Alcorn, a former slave owner, worked with the Republicans for a brief period.

est they felt in the progress of the colored people by giving the school a white man instead of a colored lady. I am not opposed to white teachers; but I think where colored teachers can be found equally competent they should have a preference in the colored schools. Let a colored person be ever so competent he can never hope to gain a position in a white school. I am aware that in an educational way, we have received a great deal from the whites. But are we always to be led by them? Are we never to "go it alone"?

Respectfully
Sarah H. Thompson

A small number of women, those whose husbands were ministers, officeholders or skilled workers, were able to stop work and keep house for their families. Cora Gillem had been a field hand until her marriage.

Gillem was a blacksmith and had a good business but he got into politics in Little Rock. I don't know how many times he was elected to the city council. He was the only colored coroner Pulaski county ever had. He was in the legislature, too. I used to dress up and go to hear him make speeches. Even after the colored folks got put out of public office, they still kept my husband for a policeman. It was during those days he bought this home. All my nine children was born right in this house. I never have worked since I came here. My husband always made a good living. I had all I could do caring for those nine children. When the Democrats came to power, then my husband went back to his blacksmith trade.

Wives and daughters of black politicians, particularly those who had some education, were part of a select social group in the capital cities of the South during Reconstruction. Emma V. Brown's letter of May 27, 1870 (p.291) gives some impression of the social whirl in Jackson, Mississippi, during a legislative session. In Columbia, South Carolina, the Rollin sisters, Charlotte, Katherine, Louisa, and Frances, reportedly presided over a salon, wielding influence in Radical Republican circles. Born free in Charleston, educated in Boston and Philadelphia, the sisters were described as light skinned, beautiful, and talented. A southern woman said that their drawing room was called Republican Headquarters.

Thick carpets covered floors; handsome cabinets held costly bric-a-brac; a $1,000 piano stood in a corner; legislative documents bound in morocco reposed with big albums on expensive tables. In their salon, mingling white and dusky statesmen wove the destinies of the old Commonwealth.

Reports of these elegant, intriguing women appealed to racist audiences. In the research about the Rollin sisters it is difficult to separate fact from fiction. Charlotte and Katherine Rollin were living in Columbia in the summer of 1868 when the first Reconstruction legislature met; Louisa Rollin joined them there at least by the following spring because in March 1869 she spoke for woman suffrage on the floor of the House.* The sister about whom the most is known is Frances Anne Rollin (1847–1901). After attending the Institute for Colored Youth in Philadelphia, she taught school in Charleston at the end of the war and then went to Boston to write a biography of Major Martin R. Delany.† After the book's publication, she returned to South Carolina to clerk for William J. Whipper, a northern-born lawyer and legislator. Whipper, a widower, soon convinced the attractive twenty-one-year-old woman to marry him. During their brief courtship and the first month of their marriage, Frances Rollin kept a diary. Although she was recording her private life, it was characteristic of the time and place that her first and last entries told of violence.

Aug. 2 [1868] Reached Columbia about six o'clock. Mr. Whipper met me at the depot with his buggie and took me to my boarding place where an elegant and spacious room awaited me. Charlotte came to see me in the morning but Kate did not. Went to Church in the morning. The Gov. and all the members [of the legislature] were there. Quite an excitement created on account of the disappearance of Joe Howard after the riot of the Ku Klux‡ last night.

Aug. 3 Went to the Committee Room this morning, copied a few

---

*The New York Times wrote of Louisa Rollin, "Her argument (so-called) was to the effect that inasmuch as the Constitution did not define the voter as male, the intent and scope of that paper were that sex was unknown to the Constitution, and that, accordingly, women have as much right to vote as men have." Her sisters were also suffragists. Katherine Rollin was secretary of the Southern Carolina Woman's Rights Association; Charlotte Rollin represented the group at the 1872 Convention of the American Woman Suffrage Association in New York.

†Excerpts from her Boston diary can be found on pp. 455–61.

‡"The riot of the Ku Klux" was a tragicomedy that ended with the death of Dallas P. Smith, a white postal agent. After a night of heavy drinking, Smith and some friends entered a boarding house where black legislators lived. The white men thought they were going to a brothel. The blacks who lived in fear of a Klan attack drew their guns to repel the invaders. In the ensuing scuffle, Smith was killed and eight residents of the boarding house, including Joseph Howard, were accused of his murder. In the end no one was brought to trial because the coroner could not get his jury of seven whites and five blacks to agree on a verdict.

bills and left early. Joe Howard heard from at Kingsville. The young man Dallas Smith who was shot and Joe's disappearance made capital of by the rebels. This afternoon on his arrival he was arrested but Mr. Whipper got out a writ of Habeas Corpus and got him out. Joe seemed terribly frightened about it. Kate came to see me this morning.

Aug. 4 At the Committee Room. Joe Howard came in and spoke. Appeared much frightened. I advised him to get Mr. Whipper to go with him to the examination before the coroner. In the afternoon went back, wrote several letters for Mr. Whipper. He accompanied me home.

Aug. 5 At the Committee Room. Mr. William Johnson* called there to see me on business, walked home with me. When there he raved about Mr. Whipper sending for me to clerk for him. He told me he felt like cutting his throat when he learned I was to come home under Mr. Whipper's auspices.

Aug. 8 Went to Committee Room in afternoon. Went out to dine with Mr. Whipper, to the races but did not go in for the reason no ladies were there.

Aug. 13 This morning at the Committee Room. Quite a time about the Civil Rights Bill.

Aug. 14 I wrote an answer to Mr. Whipper's letter asking a delay of the *decision* (matrimonial). Mr. W. was at the office when I got there also one of the Committee. I waited my chances and placed it between the leaves of a book which he was reading. I saw him take it out.

Aug. 18 To be, or not to be. Wrote all day and the Justice of the Peace Bill in the afternoon. In evening W. came and spoke over the affair. I felt he did not want a *No.* I said *yes.* He kissed me good night.

Aug. 19 Feeling the most curious this morning. Wondering how W. felt. Received a letter from him. I wonder how he will meet me this evening. Went shopping. W. came while at supper. He froze me up completely. Spent a most curious time which baffles all of my philosophy. What was it? Was the [ghost] of his departed wife present, unseen, unwilling to give up her claim or what? Both of us were unlike our real selves.

Aug. 20 Woke early wondering whether to throw up the sponge or accept a loveless life. Felt as though W. could not love anyone. A letter came from him today which restored and invigorated me. A real love letter.

Aug. 29 Left this morning for Charleston. Things home disheartened me. Ma looked much the same. Carried my book home for Pa. Told

*Probably the Reverend William E. Johnston, a state representative from Sumter.

Loady [Louisa] about my intended marriage.

Aug. 31 Sent letter to W. today. Went shopping for myself and the children. Loady took the nightgown, chemises and promises to make the dress. Miss Sophia will make the drawers and the reception dress.

Sept. 2 Started for Columbia for my darling.

Sept. 14 Left Columbia for Charleston. Met Pa on returning home. From dusk till nearly midnight the contest lasted between Pa and I. Pa consented at last not to interfere and allow the marriage to come off on Thursday morning. He thought it was too soon, etc.

Sept. 16 Busy as a bee. Could not stop to think how I felt. I was at Miss Sophia Morris to try on the dress. I have not felt yet as though I am to be married tomorrow. W. came in the afternoon to bring the ring to try.

Sept. 17 Up by times this morning getting ready. *Married* by Mr. Adams. *Very nervous.* Left for Columbia. Elliott and Lee at the depot. A. O. Jones, Lottie & Katie Ella Tolland at the house. Quite an ovation. In the evening a grand reception. All the State officers nearly ditto for the members of both Houses, a few outsiders.

Sept. 18 Today I am beginning to realize the affairs of the past few days but am happy to have them behind me. W. seems very happy too. May God enable us to continue it. Visitors. In the afternoon Mrs. Cardozo and Mrs. Henry Cardozo, Mr. and Mrs. Ransier, Bob De-large. Bob and W. not speaking. W. E. Johnson come up and congratulated Willie.

Sept. 20 Did not go to Church. Read Enoch Arden for W. and Smalls. In afternoon lots of company. Also John Langston, Purvis and Randolph took tea with us. Mr. Cardozo came to invite W. and I to dinner with him on Monday.

Sept. 21 Clear and bright. Felt put out just a little because W. did not come home in time to dress to go to the dinner. Had a pleasant time at Mr. Cardozo's—Randolph, Haynes, Mr. and Mrs. Adams. John Langston spoke that evening and paid quite a tribute to Willie. Took the girls home.*

*Almost all of the names in the September 17–21 entries are those of black lawmakers. Robert Brown Elliott, Alonzo J. Ransier, Robert De Large, and Robert Smalls served in the state legislature and later became U.S. congressmen. Samuel J. Lee was Speaker of the South Carolina House; A. O. Jones, its clerk. Francis L. Cardozo had been principal of the school where Frances Rollin taught; in 1868 he was South Carolina's secretary of state. Other legislators included Henry Cardozo who served in the state senate from 1870–74, Henry E. Hayne, and Henry W. Purvis, the son of Hattie and Robert Purvis of Philadelphia. In 1868 John Mercer Langston visited Columbia as inspector of schools for the Freedmen's Bureau.

Oct. 18 At church today heard of the brutal murder of poor Randolph*
at Cokesbury on Friday last.
Oct. 19 Randolph buried this afternoon at Columbia.

*Although the Rollin sisters and Emma Brown took tea and dinner
with lawmakers, they were seldom present when political business was
transacted. Receptions for black congressmen in Washington, ban-
quets to honor such old stalwarts as Frederick Douglass, and suppers
to greet up-and-comers like P. B. S. Pinchback were elaborate all male
affairs. Someone was sure to toast "The Ladies—God Bless 'em!"; no
one requested their presence. Women were not members of Union
League clubs or local Republican organizations; they did not attend
conventions or sit in smoke-filled rooms when candidates for office
were chosen. But when men were intimidated by violence or tempted
by bribes, it was sometimes their wives who kept them in line. In*
Sketches of Southern Life *published in 1872, Frances E. W. Harper
had Aunt Chloe say:*

> You'd laughed to see Lucinda Grange
> Upon her husband's track
> When he sold his vote for rations
> She made him take 'em back.
>
> Day after day did Milly Green
> Just follow after Joe,
> And told him if he voted wrong
> To take his rags and go.
>
> I think that Curnel Johnson said
> His side had won the day,
> Had not we women radicals
> Just got right in the way.

*During the crucial election campaign of 1876 when the Red
Shirts, armed bands of Democrats, who threatened South Carolina
voters in order to elect Wade Hampton as governor, women
ripped the red shirts from the backs of their few black sympathizers. Congressman Robert Smalls, a prominent member of the
white-tie banquet circuit in Washington, appealed to the women*

*Benjamin F. Randolph, an Oberlin graduate who had been chaplain of the Twenty-
Sixth U.S. Colored Troops and a Freedmen's Bureau agent, was a state senator and
chairman of the State Executive Committee of the South Carolina Republican party.
He was gunned down by three assassins in a bold daylight attack. No one was ever
punished for his death.

of the Sea Islands in down-home language. Two Sea Islanders reported:

Robert Smalls went there before the election and said to the women that if their husbands voted the Democratic ticket to throw them out of the house. "When John went to Massa Hampton and pledged his word to vote for him and returned back home his wife told him 'she would not give him any of that thing if you vote for Hampton.' John gone back to Massa Hampton and said 'Massa Hampton, I can't vote for you, for woman is too sweet, and my wife says if I vote for you she won't give me any.' And, ladies, I think, if you all do that, we won't have a Democratic ticket polled on Parris Island." (These are the words of Robert Smalls.)

Robert Smalls give us to understand any gentleman courting the ladies to not marry them until we get through voting. If a gentleman vote the Democratic ticket, to don't marry them. Dose what is married "don't service to them in bed." He got a little wife, and if he was to talk of voting the Democratic ticket, his wife would throw hot lead in his throat when sleeping; and in going to the polls, he wants every womens to follow her husband with her club in hand, and dare him to vote any Democratic ticket.

On Election Day, a witness said, the women armed themselves.

Womens had sticks; no mens were to go to the polls unless their wives were right alongside of them; some had hickory sticks; some had nails-four nails drive in the shape of a cross—and dare their husbands to vote any other than the Republican ticket. My sister went with my brother-in-law to the polls and swear to God if he voted the Democratic ticket she "would kill him dead in his sleep."

Democratic guns controlled most polling places in 1876, however, and black voters had good reason to be intimidated. Although the Klan was disbanded, its goal of a lily-white South had been adopted by new terrorist organizations. The White League in Louisiana waged pitched battles with guns and cannon; hundreds of blacks were killed in a single skirmish. * *Mississippi whites had a Shotgun Plan whose slogan was*

---

*General Philip H. Sheridan, in command at New Orleans, wrote in January 1875, "Since the year 1866 nearly 3500 persons, a great majority of whom were colored men, have been killed and wounded in this state. In 1868 the official records shows that 1884 were killed and wounded. From 1868 to the present more than 1200 persons have been killed or wounded on account of their political sentiments. Frightful massacres have occurred in the parishes of Bossier, Caddo, Catahoula, Saint Bernard, Grant, and Orleans."

"Carry the election peacefully if we can, forcibly if we must." South Carolina's Red Shirts turned up at Republican meetings with pistols cocked. "Every Democrat must feel honor bound to control the vote of at least one Negro, by intimidation, purchase, keeping him away," their battle plan said. "Never threaten a man individually. If he deserves to be threatened, the necessities of the times require that he should die."

Hundreds died. Once again widows told their stories to visiting congressmen. In Jackson, Mississippi, eighteen-year-old Ann Hodge described her last moments with her husband.

The white people came after him. They asked where Square was and I did not tell. Then he said "If you don't tell, I will shoot your God damned brains out." They started to shoot under the house— mother put the children under the house and I told them that nobody was under but the children. Then they came into the house and turned back the bed and made him come out and called him a damned son of a bitch. They told him to put his shoes on, and I got them, and said I will put them on; and I could not tie them very well; and some one said, "Let the God damned shoes be; he don't need any shoes." I put my brother's coat on him, and they carried him before them. I never did find him for a week, until the next Saturday. The buzzards had eat the entrails; but from the body down here (indicating) it was as natural as ever. His shoes were tied just as I had tied them.

She was followed in the witness chair by Margaret Ann Caldwell whose husband, Charles Caldwell, had been a state senator and the captain of a militia company. "When did he die?" a congressman asked.

Thursday night, in the Christmas. Him and his brother was killed. I was at my room until just nearly dark and the chapel bell rang. We live right by it. I knew the minute the bell tolled what it meant. The young men that lived across the street, when the bell tolled, they rushed right out. They all ran to the chapel and got their guns. I went down town and some of them wanted to know who I was, but I hid my face as well as I could. I just said "woman" and did not tell who I was. As I got to town I went to go into Mr. Chilton's store. All the other stores were closed. As I put my foot up on the store steps they cussed me and threatened to hurt me. I knew there was two dead men there. As I stood there they said to me, "If you don't go away they would make it very damned hot for me." I didn't say anything, and walked off. I went over to the house, and went upstairs to my room and laid down a widow.

After the bodies were brought to my house the train came from Vicksburgh with the "Murdocs".* They all marched up to my house and went into where the two dead bodies laid, and they cursed them, those dead bodies, and they danced and threw open the window, and sung all their songs, and challenged the dead body to get up and meet them, and they carried on there like a parcel of wild Indians over those dead bodies, these Vicksburgh "Murdocs". Just one or two colored folks were sitting up in the room and they carried on all that in my presence, danced and sung and done anything they could.

This time the federal government did not intervene. The North was tired of "these annual autumnal outbreaks in the South", the U.S. attorney general said. Besides Democratic support was needed if Rutherford B. Hayes was to win the contested presidential election. With black congressmen systematically excluded from the bargaining sessions, a deal was worked out. On March 4, 1877, Hayes was sworn in as president of the United States; a month later the last federal troops were withdrawn from the South, and white Democrats took over the machinery of the state governments. "The whole South—every state in the South—had got into the hands of the very men that held us slaves," Henry Adams said.

While black politicians waged a last-ditch struggle to retain their positions—or fled to Washington to look for new ones—working people in the states bordering the Mississippi River turned their faces to the North and the West. In the spring of 1879 an extraordinary migration began. Hundreds of families camped out along the river banks waiting for steamboats to take them to Kansas; hundreds more traveled by team from Texas or crossed the river from Tennessee to Arkansas. In the space of a few months about six thousand freedpeople arrived in Kansas. By 1880 fifteen thousand black migrants were at work on the farms and in the towns of the Prairie State.

The suddenness of the exodus and its magnitude caused consternation in the South and in Washington. Frederick Douglass joined Blanche Bruce, U.S. Senator from Mississippi, who saw his constituents disappearing up-river, in deploring the move. Other black leaders and such old-time abolitionists as William Lloyd Garrison and Wendell Phillips agreed with Sojourner Truth who called the exodus "the greatest movement of all time" and helped organize a Freedmen's Aid

---

*Members of a vigilante group called themselves Modocs, after the Modoc Indians who had been at war with the United States in 1872–73.

Waiting for a Mississippi riverboat. *(Library of Congress)*

Association to assist needy migrants until they found jobs.

But who had started the movement? When the Exodusters first crowded the Kansas City docks, the public believed that they had been duped by the false promises of unscrupulous emigration agents. Continuing investigations as well as the inevitable congressional hearings turned up individuals who tried to take credit for the exodus, but did not identify any one leader who had actually initiated or directed it. When asked why they had left their homes, one woman explained, "Tax man make me pay three dollars for my license for washin' for people. My ole man had to hide away for his life 'case two men shot dead a few days afore we lef'." Another said "I don't have no home nohow if they shoots my ole man an' the boys and gives me no money for the washin'." A Mississippi teacher wrote to the governor of Kansas.

Governor John D. St. John
Respected sir:

Clay County, Mississippi,
June 18, 1879

I write a few lines to you for information about our emigrating to your state next fall. We are hard working people but can not reap the benefit of our labor. I went to the State of Ohio in 1877 [and] found there is better living in a grain fruits and stock growing state than in a cotton growing one. Rev. Ephraim Strong my brother served in united states army three years during the war of 1861 and was honorable discharged at its close desired me to write to you for information. We wants to know if we can get any assistance from the government or any society to emigrate to Kansas. We have seen some papers from there and feel if we could get there we could make a better support.

I have been teaching public schools in the districts ever since they began in Miss. in 1871. When the republican laws rule the state I made right good support at it but since the democratic power has got in we can scarcely board and clothes ourselves. All the people in district I taught are wanting to emigrate to Kansas this fall if they can get assistance from any quarter. If I can get information from you that I can get in any business or a support and get assistance to get there my brother father and husband and I am coming. [A] great many desired me to Write to Kansas for information. I see in the Mo. Republican that you have a freedmen aid society thinking perhaps we could get assistance from it. Please answer our letter and let us know if you can aid us. By doing so you will [aid us] and a great many more and we will be grateful in our hearts. Your humble obedient and grateful Servant

Roseline Cunningham

No black woman was called to testify before the Senate committee which investigated what it called "the Causes of the Removal of the Negroes from the Southern States," but a male witness told of the Committee of Five Hundred Women of New Orleans, headed by Mary Jane Garrett, which published an address demanding "every right and privilege that the Constitution guarantees" and calling on husbands and brothers to "take them where they could live in security and peace and get homes for themselves and educations for their children." An article about the committee in the Nashville Weekly American *shed some light on its goals and considerably more on southern white attitudes. Headlined "A Colored Exodus Threatened," the article said, in part:*

Five hundred working women of New Orleans have addressed a letter to Ben Butler* terribly denunciatory of Mr. Hayes and the southern people. These sable workwomen claim that they are exposed to robbery, murder, swindling and all other foibles and pleasantries.

*Congressman Benjamin Butler of Massachusetts, who had been military governor of New Orleans in 1862, was trusted by blacks and detested by southern whites.

They have organized an emigration society and say they propose to move.

The truth about these people is that they do not, and will not, accept their own situation. Savages a few decades ago, slaves a few years ago, they expect to step at once into the position of social leaders, rulers, cocks of the walk, every way the equals of those who belong to a race which has had a thousand years of progress in civilization. For all their schemes of emigration they will clamor and grumble and finally settle down to the facts as they are, that they are a people, ignorant, without money, under a terrible necessity to labor and to wait.

Willianna Hickman, an Exoduster from Kentucky was thirty-one years old when she traveled with her minister husband, their six children, and 140 other colonists to the all-black settlement of Nicodemus* on the Kansas plains. The railroad left them in Ellis, some thirty miles from their destination, on March 3, 1878. She recalled:

I had some trouble getting housed as my children broke out with measles on the way. We dwelled at a farm house that night. The next night members of the colony had succeeded in stretching a tent. This was our first experience of staying in a tent. We remained in the camp about two weeks. Several deaths occurred among the children while we were there.

We left there for Nicodemus, traveling overland with horses and wagons. We were two days on the way, with no roads to direct us save deer trails and buffalo wallows. We traveled by compass. At night the men built bonfires and sat around them, firing guns to keep the wild animals from coming near. We reached Nicodemus about 3 o'clock on the second day.

When we got in sight of Nicodemus the men shouted, "There is Nicodemus." Being very sick I hailed this news with gladness. I looked with all the eyes I had. I said, "Where is Nicodemus? I don't see it." My husband pointed out various smokes coming out of the ground and said, "That is Nicodemus." The families lived in dugouts. The scenery to me was not at all inviting and I began to cry.

From there we went to our homestead fourteen miles west of Nicodemus. Rev. S. M. Lee carried us to the farm in his wagon and

---

*Nicodemus was the best known of several black towns in Kansas. Flourishing in the 1880s when the Missouri Pacific was expected to reach it, it slowly declined after the railroad passed it by. By the end of World War II it was virtually a ghost town, but its population, largely black, has grown in recent decades.

as usual there was no road and we used a compass. I was asleep in the wagon bed with the children and was awakened by the blowing of horns. Our horns were answered by horns in the distance and the firing of guns, being those of my brother Austin, and a friend, Lewis Smith. They had been keeping house for us on our new homestead. Driving in the direction of the gunfiring, we reached the top of the hill where we could see the light of the fire they had built to direct our way.

Days, weeks, months, and years passed and I became reconciled to my home. We improved the farm and lived there nearly twenty years, making visits to Nicodemus to attend church, entertainments, and other celebrations. My three daughters were much loved school teachers in Nicodemus and vicinity.

In 1880 the stream of migrants became a trickle. The Exodusters built sod huts and planted wheat, cultivating their own land in colonies like Nicodemus, or working as farm laborers and domestics. Some who had arrived without resources moved on to Nebraska and Oklahoma; a small number returned to the South. When Sarah Smith found herself stranded in Indiana, she appealed to her former employer. Having lost thirty of the fifty tenant families who had worked his plantation, he gladly sent her the railroad fare to come home. Smith's letter and others like it were publicized in southern newspapers.

Mr. S. I. Wooten
Sir: Putnam Co., Indiana, January 5, 1880
    I am now in Ind. in the worst fixt I ever was in in all the days of my life. I am out of cloes, and I have not got no where to go and no house to stay in day or night and no boddy wount let me in with them and I have not got nothing to eat and nothing to dow to get not a cents worth for myself nor my children to eat. No boddy wount implore a woman that have childdran and no husband. Brother Allen would let me stay with him but the man that he lives with dont want him to take no orther famly with him and I am a sufren here. Please send me some money to get back with to your plantation and I will work with you till you say you are pad and never will leave again.
                              Mrs. Sarah Smith

In the states of the old Confederacy Sarah Smith and others worked for ten dollars a month or a share of the crop, knowing full well that at settling-up time "deducts" would gobble up their earnings. A few courageous men continued to vote until lawmakers drew up new constitutions containing an "understanding clause," a "grandfather clause," or a "good character" clause, all of which meant "Blacks, stay away from the polls." The violence continued, too, with undisguised lynch mobs taking the place of costumed night riders. A year after Mississippi rewrote its constitution to disfranchise blacks, a group of women appealed to a sympathetic northerner.

Waynesboro, Missippi,

Mr. Albion W. Tourgee:* December 17, 1891

We are women of Wayne County Miss and we thought we would write and let you know what is going on as the men was afraid to do it for fear it would not be very good for them to let it be known. The white people of this county are taking the colored men and beating them and putting them in Jail. They beat a young man nearly to death this week and put him in Jail and said they would take him out and mob him. The men have to pay a too dollar Poll Tax and them that cannot write cannot vote. A colored man cannot get any charge made against a white man here. They take the colored man and send him to the penitensiary and the law is not executed on the white man at all. We will have to have some protection or else go away from here. We cannot live here much longer. I cannot write any more now

Yours truly
Jane Evans
Minnie Evans

During those dark years, the only rays of hope for most freedpeople came from the church and the school. The church promised a better life in the hereafter. Schools offered the children of slaves a more immediate possibility—a chance to equip themselves for living in the world beyond the plantation. The public school systems that had begun in Reconstruction were cut back or dismantled; by the 1880s less than a third of the black children of the South received free schooling.† The dreams of black parents centered around the private schools and colleges, places like Fisk, Howard, and Atlanta Universities, Hampton Institute, Talladega College, and hundreds of smaller institutes and seminaries. Intended to train teachers, the early colleges began as elementary schools. When Hampton Normal and Agricul-

---

*Albion Tourgee, a liberal columnist and civil rights activist, was the lawyer for New Orleans's Citizens Committee to Test the Constitutionality of the Separate Car Law. When their test case, known as *Plessy* v. *Ferguson,* was heard by the Supreme Court in 1896, the justices ruled that "separate but equal" accommodations were constitutional, and thus legitimized Jim Crow for another half-century.

†In 1889–90, only 32.8 percent of school-age blacks in the South were enrolled in public schools. A decade later the figure had risen to 51.46 percent.

*tural Institute, which evolved from Mary Peake's wartime school,
opened its doors in 1868, it required students to be of "good character"
and to read and write at fifth-grade level; two decades later it offered
the equivalent of a high school education.*

*Della Irving Hayden (1854–1924), an 1877 graduate of Hampton,
became one of a group of distinguished educators, along with women
like Lucy Laney and Mary McCleod Bethune, whose schools were
beacons for black southerners. After a childhood in slavery, she attended public school in Franklin, Virginia, for four years. Determined
to become a teacher, she entered Hampton when she was eighteen
years old. In a short autobiography written in 1917, she described her
first days away from home.*

When we went in to supper, they had a big yellow bowl with
sassafras tea, what we called 'greasy bread', and a little molasses. There
were three or four new students and one old student. When we were
seated he began to eat. We were waiting, and he said, "Why don't you
eat?" We said we were waiting for them to put supper on the table.
He told us this was all we would get. We had sassafras tea and corn
bread and syrup for supper all those two years. That first night I slept
on the floor with seven other girls. We were all new and there was such
a rush of girls they had no other place to put us. We didn't know
anything about bells, and the next morning when we woke up, everybody had had breakfast and gone over to Academic. We got up and
dressed. I had a little piece of cheese and some crackers in my trunk
and I ate them.

Then they gave me a room in the barracks with three other girls.
They gave us ticks and we carried them to the barn and filled them
with straw. We took two pillows and filled them too. We had regular
wooden bedsteads. When it rained, it always leaked. I had an old
waterproof of my mother's and many a time I put that waterproof on
my bed, with a tin basin, too, to catch the water. I could not turn over
for fear of upsetting the basin full of water. The boys all slept outdoors
in tents. They had a little stove in each tent. There was no heat in the
room except what my lamp gave. Miss Mackie [the Lady Principal]
made me bathe every morning in cold water, and I have often broken
the ice in my pitcher.

*When her money ran out, she taught in a rural school for two
years.*

I was in the woods, twelve miles from the railroad at a place called
Indian Town, in Southampton County. The family with whom I went

to board were a man, his wife, and two daughters, and they lived, cooked, ate, and slept in one room about 20 by 24 feet—a log cabin. It had four beds, a table, pots, kettles. When I looked around and felt that I had to sleep there I was very discouraged and began to cry. The old lady came to me like a dear mother, and putting her arms around me, she said, "Don't cry, little teacher, I'm going to hang up some bedquilts across the room." So she strung a rope across the room and hung some heavy bedquilts on it, so that it separated my room from the rest of the family.

When I went to school, I had thirty bright-eyed children. I told them to ask their fathers to come to the schoolhouse to see me on business. The men came right from the fields to the schoolhouse to see what the young teacher could want. I was the first teacher they had ever had. I told them I wanted to stay but I would not feel satisfied to sleep in the room with the family. I said to the men: "Why can't you go out in the woods, take your axes, and cut down some trees and add another room to the house. I'll give the nails if the men will give the work." All the men agreed to come the next day and cut down the trees and build the room. I sent to the store and bought nails. The room was notched up in the old fashioned way and daubed with clay, after which I pasted newspapers inside to make it comfortable. They built me a log chimney where I could have a good fire. I moved into my little room and was as happy as a queen.

Returning to Hampton in 1876, she graduated with honors a year later. For more than a half-century, she taught in Franklin's public schools, in Virginia Normal and Industrial Institute, and in her own Franklin Normal and Industrial Institute. Widowed shortly after her marriage to a Hampton classmate, she brought up two adopted children, owned her own home, two cows, and a parlor organ. Her account of the founding of Franklin Institute, was typical of the beginnings of many schools that gave black youngsters the education denied them elsewhere.*

I rented a little room 15 by 20 feet, bought two dozen chairs, got a blackboard, stove, table and broom. I had twenty-one students the first month. We had five acres of land donated to us by Mrs. Marriage Allen of London, England. I taught school in the week and went on Sundays and begged money at the churches, so we were finally able to put up a building with four classrooms that cost about $1,000.

The first year I was alone, but now I have three teachers besides

*In 1900 there were only ninety-four public high schools for blacks in the seventeen southern and border states.

myself. In addition to this building we have a dormitory for the girls, with 22 rooms, costing $6,000. We borrowed the money for ten years, and we still owe $3,800 of it. Eight hundred fifty students have attended this school and 40 have graduated. Some are teaching, others are in business, and several have gone to other schools.

At Howard University in Washington, founded by the Freedmen's Bureau in 1867, students could take high school and college courses and graduate degrees in medicine, law, and theology. Sidney Ann Taliaferro, a protégé of Emily Howland's, was better prepared than most freshmen because she had spent the previous winters working and studying in Sherwood, New York, where Howland's family lived. Her letter is one of dozens written to her mentor over a period of thirty-five years.

Howard University, Washington, D.C.
January 7, 1876

Dear friend:

It has been a long time since I wrote you but we have been having a good deal to do since school opened and I could not find time so now will take a few minutes before the bell rings. I am so *very* much obliged to you for the things you sent, the dress I wore the first night I got it to a entertainment given by one of ladies in the city. We had a very pleasant time. I paid the wash woman and also had to pay my room mate one dollar for the one I had to borrow from her to have a tooth extracted. The dentist's here are all so dear in their work. Each tooth is one dollar. We had a good deal of rain during the holidays but now it is as warm and mild as spring. I went to see Miss Brown* and we had not been there long before she passed us cake and wine, and I told her that I was going to tell you that she offered me wine first thing after I entered the house, but of course I refused for I have become disgusted with the sight of wine all other drinks for every body has it where ever one may call. I hope you will not infer from what I have said that I have taken any of these drinks for I feel like breaking the glass when ever it is offered to me. I suppose you had a Merry Christmas and happy New Year. Prof. Robinson bought my books for me and says he will wait for pay because he wanted us to begin study the very day school opened. They were as follows.

Chemistry	$1.15
Physiology	1.15
Material for book keeping	.50
total	$2.80

*Emma V. Brown was then principal of Sumner School.

I am so glad we have Phys. for I think it is something that we all should know about. The room rent this term $19.00 and washing for Dec. 1.00 total 22.80. I am trying to be as saving as I can, but will some day make what I have spent while at school and return it. Please do not scold me for writing with a lead pencil. Oh I think the picture is splendid of you, Mr. H, and Grant.* I must close in haste from

Sidney

Fisk University,† which began as Nashville's Colored High School in 1866, was able to offer college courses five years later. Although it received support from the American Missionary Association, the school was poor and its students poorer still. Family members pooled their resources to pay tuition for their children. One freedwoman hired herself out as the university cook in order to educate her three sons; another scraped together the money to send her niece "in hopes of seeing her a useful ornament in society." She sent a concerned letter to Fisk's principal, John Ogden.

Mr. J. Ogden
Sir: St. Louis, Missouri, November 16, 1868
    I write to inform you that my niece will be to your city this week & also with the expectation of being one of the pupils of your school. I shall start her on Thursday the 19 of this present month. As she is not known in your city—I hope you will see that she is properly cared for as she will be amongst strangers entirely and no one to see to her. If you will do this favor for me I will be under many obligations. You can expect her either Friday or Saturday. I send her to try to learn to be of use to her self & her people who so long have been oppressed. I want a certain degree of restriction put on her. Your own judgment I have been assured will be sufficient. I do not know whether she can pass the required examination or not. I fear for her as she has not been to school for 2 years nor applied her mind during that period. She has no mother. Her father is a labouring man & tries to do for his family. He bought himself & wife and 4 children just before the emancipation & is now trying to give the oldest daughter an education as far as his scanty means will allow. I raised her from a girl of 8 years up to the present. Now I still live in hopes of seeing her a useful ornament in society. Therefore I leave her in your charge & hope you will do her justice. I am very respectivly

Mrs. E Cole

*The picture showed Emily Howland, her father, Slocum Howland, and their dog, Grant, on the verandah of their home in Sherwood.
†Named after General Clinton B. Fisk, one of its founders.

Most students studied for a term or two, then taught in a rural school until they had earned another semester's expenses. Sarah Grant's letter to George White, Fisk's treasurer, was typical of the students' struggles:

Mr. Geo White   Chattanooga, Tennessee,
Dear Friend & Teacher: September 28, 1870

I received your long looked for letter. But I being very busy could not write sooner. I have now 39 Scholars, and half of them have not paid me. Mr. White I have been making every effort to get means to enter your school Christmas, but I do not think I will be able. I will try by the help of God to come out and pay you what I owe you. Dear Friend you know my condition. If you will give a position of some kind to work for my board I would gladly except it and by so doing I will [be] in school. If I come I will bring two others. And I wish you would write me if I could get any aid from that society north. I have no asistence at all, just what I am making here and $10.00 per month for board. And if I do not get to come to school I shall be out anyway. Please write me about this arangement and how school is progressing. I must close hoping *God* may bless you and your School. Please remember me in your prayers for I feel very weak in the cause of Christ.
Your Student
Sarah L. Grant

Maggie Carnes's mother was able to help her with $12 toward her back board bill, but she still owed $39. Board was $47 a term, tuition $4.50.

Mr. White
Sir: Memphis, Tennessee, July 18, 1871

I am happy to inform you that we are all well a present. Mr. White mother send threw the bank $12.00 on account of my board. She would of send it before now but the Gentleman who owed her went to Saint Louis and when he come back he did not have any money so she will send you some more money before long and please send her word how much she will owe you then. Give my love to Miss Sheppard and Ida & Flora. Mother want to start me and my other sister by the 9 of september. I know 8 more young girls will want to enter in the school in September. This is all please let us know if you got the $12.00.
From Maggie A. Carnes

Ella Sheppard, one of Fisk's leading students, was born a slave in 1851 but was purchased by her father three years later. Living in

*Cincinnati at the end of the war, she received a rudimentary education
including music lessons, although she had to enter her teacher's home
by a back door after dark, so that no one would see the black pupil.
Her father's sudden death when she was fifteen left her penniless. She
later wrote:*

I tried every honorable opportunity to make a living. I took in
washing and ironing, worked in a family, and had a few music pupils
who paid me poorly. Finally I left Cincinnati and taught school in
Gallatin, Tennessee. In five months I realized my deficiencies and
came to Fisk School in September, 1868, with all my possessions in a
trunk so small that the boys immediately called it "Pie Box". I had six

Ella Sheppard, from Gustavus D. Pike's *The Jubilee Singers,* 1873. *(Amistad
Research Center)*

dollars and when Mr. White, the Treasurer, said that this amount
would keep me a little over three weeks, I decided to stay until my
money ran out.

Exceptional musical advantages, then very rare for colored girls in
the South, secured me three pupils, who paid me four dollars each per
month. Wednesdays and Saturdays I went to the city and taught each
pupil one hour, which made it impossible for me, running all the way

over the rough, rocky hills, to get back in time for supper; so I went without supper and waited on the table one day and washed dishes the other day. The school was very poor and food was scarce yet it filled one. The beef was so tough the boys called it "Old Ben" and declared that every time they met a cow they felt like apologizing.

There were no helpful "mission barrels" in those days; many of us shivered through that first winter with not an inch of flannel upon our bodies. In spite of our poverty and hardships we were a jolly set of girls, and when we had a chance romped and played with all the abandon of children. We were especially fond of music and gladly gave half of our noon hour and all spare time to study under Mr. George L. White.* We made rapid progress, and soon began to help our school by going Fridays and Saturdays to neighboring towns to give concerts.

Those noon-hour classes were the beginning of a remarkable success story. In September 1871 Fisk's finances were at a low ebb. "There was no money even for food," Ella Sheppard wrote.

Many a time special prayer was offered for the next meal. The American Missionary Association decided that the school must be given up. Teachers, pupils felt that this would be a calamity, but no one could see how nor where to get the money even for our necessities.

When Mr. White proposed to take a company of students to the North to sing for the money, there was consternation at Fisk. Such a plan was looked upon as "a wild goose chase." Prayers for light, guidance and patience went up daily. While we waited for guidance Mr. White called for volunteers from his singing class. He selected eleven voices.

Our teachers caught the vision and enthusiasm of Mr. White and helped to get us ready, dividing their clothing with us. Not one of us had an overcoat or wrap. Mr. White had an old gray shawl. Taking every cent he had, all the school treasury could spare, and all he could borrow, Mr. White started, October 6, 1871, with his little band of singers to sing the money out of the hearts and pockets of the people.

The Jubilee Singers—named in memory of the year of jubilee— began by singing "white man's music," Ella Sheppard explained.

The slave songs were never used by us in public. They were associated with slavery and the dark past, and represented things to be

*White was a northerner who came to the South with the Union army and served with the Freedmen's Bureau before joining Fisk's faculty. Although he had had no formal musical training, he was noted for his ability to get good singing from his pupils.

The Jubilee Singers. Ella Sheppard is seated at organ, left, Maggie L. Porter, right. *(Fisk University Library)*

forgotten. Then, too, they were sacred to our parents who used them in their religious worship and shouted over them. We finally grew willing to sing them privately, and sitting upon the floor (there were but few chairs) we practiced softly, learning from each other the songs of our fathers. We did not dream of ever using them in public. Had Mr. White suggested such a thing, we certainly had rebelled. After many months we began to appreciate the wonderful beauty and power of our songs; but continued to sing in public the usual choruses, duets, solos, etc. Occasionally two or three slave songs were sung at the close of the concert. But the demand of the public changed this order. Soon the land rang with our slave songs.

After eight months on the road, this talented troupe of ex-slaves —six women and four men—had earned more than enough to pay Fisk's debts. At the end of seven years, the Jubilee Singers had given $150,000 to the university and had brought the cause of black education to the attention of millions. By introducing their parents' unique folk music to the world, they had also profoundly influenced the course of musical history. A second tour in the United States was followed by *a year abroad in the course of which they sang for Queen Victoria and the royal family, the Russian czarina, and members of the British Parliament. Maggie Porter, born in slavery in 1853, described "the day of all days, the day we appeared before Queen Victoria."*

Poor ignorant me! I received the greatest disappointment of my life. The Queen wore no crown, no robes of state. She was like many English ladies I had seen in her widow's cap and weeds. But it was the Queen in flesh and blood. I saw her; I heard her deep, low voice saying, "Tell them we are delighted with their songs, and that we wish them to sing John Brown." I wondered why the Queen did not speak these words to us. But what could I know of English court etiquette?

On a second European trip that lasted from May 1875 to July 1878, they traveled on the Continent, singing for the king and queen of the Netherlands, Kaiser Wilhelm and Crown Prince Frederick of Germany, and the duke and duchess of Saxony. At the first concert in Berlin, Germany's leading music critics occupied front seats, which was, according to Ella Sheppard, "the worst place from which to judge us."

Maggie L. Porter in Pike's *The Jubilee Singers. (Amistad Research Center)*

We trembled. One of our basses was absent, which left only one bass to balance nine voices. We grouped as usual, leaned heads toward each other, and paused for oneness of effort. Then everything else forgotten, in a musical whisper, "Steal Away" floated out so perfectly that one could not tell when it began. The astonishment upon the fixed, upturned faces of the critics told us that we had won; we were again at ease and did our best to maintain the good impression. Our concert was received with great enthusiasm. The audience, representing the greatest and best of the city, was in evening dress. We had never seen such an array of sparkling jewels as were worn that night. After the concert many came up and congratulated us. One [newspaper] article was filled with such expressions as these: "What wealth of shading! Such a pianissimo, such a crescendo and decrescendo as those at the close of 'Steal Away' might raise envy in the soul of any choir master. Something may be learned from these Negro singers."

The singers learned too. Unsophisticated when they left Nashville, they not only acquired musicianship of a high order, but also behaved with poise and dignity. "Their heads were not turned," a Fisk official wrote. "They feel more at home on the concert platform than they did at first, but their manners have remained as natural and unaffected— as free from professional 'airs' as if they had never sung outside their school-room." None of the singers returned to Fisk to complete their schooling, but they received a priceless education abroad. No wealthy youngster on a Grand Tour could have seen more sights of literary and historic interest or have been treated with greater kindness by Europeans. Instead of having to fear insult or Klan attack they were sometimes mobbed by well-wishers. In Holland, reported America Robinson who joined the troupe in 1875, "The people are kind but they weary us with their much talking."

Last night a lady was in the waiting room to speak with us. She looked very rusty & common place & the singers being tired paid no attention to her. Finally she engaged in a conversation with me. I suppose I must have pleased her for she gave me 60 florins for the institution & some books—about $25.00. The town seemed to have some nice avenues & we thought to explore it but could not go out on account of the mob that would follow us around the streets. Hundreds met us at the station, some climbed upon the busses & carriages to get a glimpse of us. At night when we went to the concert they had assembled at the front door of the hotel to accompany us to the "Kirk"

but we slipped out the back entrance through the stable yard & beat
their time.

*Born in slavery, America Robinson entered Fisk's first college class
in 1871. Just before graduation she left to go abroad with the singers.*

America Robinson. *(Fisk University Library)*

*While in Europe she wrote regularly to her fiancé, James Burrus, a
serious-minded classmate, who went on to teach mathematics at Fisk
and pursue advanced studies at Dartmouth College (with financial
help from Robinson). During three years abroad, as the letters illustrate, she changed from a blushing girl to a poised, self-confident
woman. The letter below was written after a year away from home.*

My *Dearest* James: London, May 22, 1876
      Your two letters came within a few days of each other. I believe
I was never happier in my life than now. I am so glad to know that
you are pleased with me. I think it sweet to meet *your* approval. When
your letter came it affected me so that I lost my appetite nearly: my
heart was so full that I had no inclination to eat or think of anything
else. You spoke of being teased about me. I have the same experience.
I know I must look guilty whenever your name is mentioned because
my face burns so & when they tell me I blush I cannot help getting
still redder.
      I used to sometimes think that you were ashamed of me but I have
no right to entertain such thoughts now since you have given me to

understand otherwise. And whatever you say is gospel to me. I love you & trust you & will do everything in my power to please you. James, I wish you would confide in me more. Some how the little things you told me have drawn me so much closer to you. I used to think that you got along so smoothly. Your life seemed to be wholly unruffled. From what you have said at different times I know that you & I are perplexed alike & that trouble is common to us both.

Your first letter I thought was delightful but the second containing what I desired above all things—your photo—was most delightful. You can not imagine how glad I was to see you looking so well. The photo is *very very* good. The glasses give you a stern & scholarly appearance. You look already like a professor. I can not possibly look at it without kissing it. It is the dearest face to me there is on earth. Of course I love mother & them at home but it is so different from what I have for you.

Last week was most delightful. I went sightseeing and visited some. The first of the week I visited the biscuit manufactory. The next day I went to Oxford and attended the races. I mean the boat races. I took tea at the Jesus College. The next morning I breakfasted with a gentleman at the Christ Church College. I went to Banbury on Thursday and saw the cross where every infant has taken his knee journey. The next day we went to Bedford the home of Bunyan. Saturday I drove in Hyde Park & around the Albert Memorial.

You wrote telling me to get Stereoscopic views. I have a few. It always makes my head ache to look through stereoscopes so I thought it best to get scraps & keep a scrap book. It is done a great deal over here. If I do not complete the book I shall call on you to assist me with it when I come home.

You said something about my learning French enough to teach you. I am so rusty that I doubt if I shall advance much myself. I will try knowing that I have an object in view namely to teach such as you —a B.A.

Give my love to your mother & family. What will your mother think of me being your wife? Will she like it or not? Excuse all mistakes and believe me

Ever true & lovingly yours

America

A year later, without consulting James, she felt sure enough of herself to ask Erastus R. M. Cravath, Fisk's president, for a raise.

At first the Jubilee Singers had received only clothing and travel expenses; during their European tours they were paid from $500 to $800 a year, with old-timers like Ella Sheppard and Maggie Porter receiving the top salaries, and American Robinson and other newcomers less.

My Dearest James: Arundel, England, May, 1877
 You may blame me all you wish for waiting so long without writing. It is so seldom we get to London that we must fix up our things when we are there. I only see my large trunk once a year, so the storing away of winter apparel & getting out summer &c&c takes abundance of time.

 But this is not the sole reason that I have not written. I had expected to go home in July or August but not being certain I did not like to write you until I did know. Mr. Cravath said when we were in Holland that all who were unwilling to stay another year would go home in July. He meditates a tour through Belgium, France, Germany & some parts of Austria for another year. When he asked the question all said they would go home save Mr. Loudin, Tom, Alexander & Maggie Porter.* Of course this would be too few to think of going on another year. They would be obliged to bring in too many new members. This would be very expensive & besides they would not produce the same harmony & effect. Maggie Carnes & I gave Mr. Cravath our reasons for leaving. It is simply this. Mr. Cravath was unwilling to give us new singers the same as the old & we were determined not to stay for less than they. Mr. C. wanted that we should work our way up— that we have done & now that we have reached the consummate point, where we would get the same amount he was unwilling to abide by it fearing the old singers would demand more. But there is not one of the old singers who feels this way save Maggie Porter & she places more value on herself than any one does for her. Even she is so anxious that Maggie & I should stay that I know she would hold her tongue on that account. The reason that I felt I ought to get the same salary was because I do the same amount of work. When we were in Holland, Jennie & Maggie P. were both sick & we new ones had the work to do. We made over £2000. Well, Saturday night Mr. C. & Gen. Fisk came down here from London. After tea they sent for Maggie & me

*Other members of the troupe were Frederick J. Loudin, Thomas Rutling, Hinton Alexander, Maggie Porter, Maggie Carnes, Jennie Jackson, Georgia Gordon, and Ella Sheppard.

in the Coffee Room. Mr. C. said he was astonished that I would let such a noble work hinge for the sake of a few hundred dollars & base my decision on money &c but one thing is sure he would calculate as long as I for the same amount. He did a lot of talking showing the Christian & not the money side but was unable to convince me that I was wrong in the course I had taken. Maggie said nothing her self but said ditto to what I had said. Gen. Fisk told Mr. C. that he thought the salaries should be equitable. He talked very nice to me indeed. Mr. C. gave me no answer as to whether he wished me on my conditions until Monday. He said he was not sure the class would remain another year but if it did why he would expect me to remain.

Do you think I did right James? I did not consult you about remaining another year. In the first place there was not time & in the second I was not sure whether you intended going to Dartmouth or not. I knew if you went there would be no use of my returning. Of course I may come home after all, but the probabilities are that I shall stay. You will not think hard of me that I did not consult you, will you? Please write me what you intend to do, if you go to Dartmouth, when will you go & all about your expenses there &c. Georgia will go home in July. Ella has said that she would not be able to work another year so Mr. C told her to go home in July.

We have come here for a fortnight's rest. Arundel is a charming little place about 60 miles from London. It is the seat of the Duke of Norfolk who has a magnificent castle here. The sea is only four miles off-

[Letter breaks off]

By July 1878 when the Jubilee Singers disbanded, the relationship between Robinson and Burrus had cooled. Disturbed by the long separation, he had sent her a letter filled with "cruel accusations." Despite his subsequent apology, America Robinson determined to break their engagement and to remain in Europe for further study. The following was her final letter to James Burrus:

My *Dear* James: Valentigney, France, August 4, 1878
    You are still dear to me and ever will be. I always have loved you. I always shall but a nearer relation between us there never can be. The decision I came to in my last is final. My dear James, I can not be your wife.

    For a long time, James, I have somehow had the thought that you had ceased to love me as formerly and only held out because you felt

in honor bound, so when I received that letter it seemed as a direct confirmation of all my doubts. I think I should have resented it from *any* one, but from *you I could not* bear it. Whatever may have passed between us, you must confess that we have never offerred an insult before. I have loved you half of my life & shall go on through eternal ages loving you. I trust that in heaven there will be a reconciliation and we shall know a better and purer love for each other.

I will ask one favor of you. I do not know whether you care to keep any of my letters, if so, will you please put them together & mark them with these words. *To be burned when I am dead.* * I should be better satisfied to know that no eye save yours had seen them. But of course they are yours to do with as you choose.

I shall be here this month or perhaps longer. Then I return to my school in Strasbourg where I shall study German, French and music. I seem doomed to be a wanderer on the face of the earth, while you have no settled home. Perhaps you may soon find a peaceful home. If we ever should meet again shall we meet in friendship? And now in conclusion, my long loved darling, I shall love you where'eer you are, what'er you do.

America

The Jubilee Singers were the first of a long procession of black artists† who won recognition in Europe that they could not find in the United States. The absence of race prejudice during their years abroad transformed their lives, making it difficult for them to live in the South again. Two male members of the troupe remained in Europe; three others, including Maggie Porter, returned for concert tours from time to time. Most of the other singers settled in the Midwest. The handful who returned to the South included America Robinson Lucas who was married and teaching school in Mississippi when Fisk celebrated the Jubilee Singers' fortieth anniversary in 1911. Ella Sheppard Moore married a minister who was an official of the AMA. She brought up three children, taught at Fisk, and was an effective public speaker and community leader. As president of the Women's Missionary Society, she lectured frequently on Negro womanhood.

Fisk University was the best-known black school in the United States until two young Hampton graduates started a normal school in

---

*James Burrus never married. After teaching at Fisk and Alcorn, he became a successful businessman. When he died in 1928, leaving his estate to Fisk, America Robinson's letters were found in his trunk.

†Including in modern times Marian Anderson and Mattiwilda Dobbs.

*Alabama, with minimal backing from the state. In the summer of
1881, Olivia Davidson (1854–89), a former slave who had studied at*

Olivia Davidson (Washington). *(Tuskegee Institute)*

*Hampton and at Framingham Normal School in Massachusetts, went
to the South to become lady principal of Tuskegee Normal and Industrial Institute. Finding the school without classrooms, furniture or
books, she appealed to Ednah Cheney, who was still supporting freedpeople's education. The colleague she referred to in the letter was
Booker T. Washington.*

Mrs. Cheney   Normal School, Tuskegee, Alabama,
Dear Madam: August 28, 1881
  In its last session the state Legislature of Alabama established a
Normal School at this place for the training of colored teachers. An
appropriation for the payment of teachers was made but none for the
purchase of books, maps or other apparatus for school work. Since then
the state has agreed to aid in the purchase of a farm with a view to
having an industrial as well as normal school, hoping by this means to
provide work for the men and women who come for instruction by
which they can pay their expenses and at the same time pursue their
studies, for, at present, they can only come a short while and then must
leave to earn means to go on again.
  Whatever aid the state can give us must go towards the payments
on the land and the erection of temporary buildings (for at present we
are teaching in a church and two adjacent buildings) though it will fall
far short of being sufficient for these purposes. For books, maps and

other apparatus, of which we are entirely destitute, not even having a dictionary, we must depend upon the donations of friends. For this reason I write to you. Can you in any way, by influence or other wise, aid us in procuring a few, at least, of the things we need so much.

I graduated from the Framingham Normal School in June. The school here began in July. At present we have an attendance of about 45 young men and women, most of whom have naught. We need help in every way—even clothes would be helpful distributed among the most needy of the young women, but our greatest need is of such things as I have already mentioned.

If you can and will aid in any, even the smallest way, I assure you it will be doing for a worthy cause.

Very truly yours,
Olivia A. Davidson

In the next decades the school flourished, supported by Ednah Cheney and other former abolitionists* and by prominent politicians and businessmen. Olivia Davidson and Booker T. Washington married in 1885. Better educated than her husband, she continued to play an influential role at Tuskegee until her sudden death four years later.

*Ednah Cheney contributed regularly to Tuskegee and left the school seven thousand dollars in her will. Emily Howland was also a substantial contributor.

Part V

The Postwar North

TWENTY-ONE

Some Old Acquaintances

THE PASSAGE OF the Fifteenth Amendment to the Constitution, which promised full citizenship to black people, marked the end of the abolitionist crusade. While veterans of the antislavery struggle continued to fight for civil rights and to support the new schools and colleges of the South, many white reformers turned to such causes as temperance, labor unions, and civil service reform. Black women leaders had no doubt about their priorities. Harriet Tubman explained:

Long 'go when de Lord tole me to go free my people I said, "No, Lord! I can't go—don't ask me." But he come anoder time. I saw him jes as plain. Den I said again, "Lord, go away—get some better eddicated person—get a person wid more cultur dan I have; go way, Lord." But he came back de third time, and speaks to me jess as he did to Moses, and he says,: "Harriet, I wants *you*," and I knew den I must do what he bid me. Now do you s'pose he wanted me to do dis jess for a day, or a week? No! de Lord who tole me take care of my people meant me to do it jess so long as I live, and so I do what he told me to.

Returning to Auburn, New York, after the war, she took care of her parents and a host of other needy people as well as aiding freedmen's schools in the South. With money raised by selling copies of her biography, she converted her residence into the Home for Indigent and Aged Negroes. The home and twenty-five acres of land that she bought to use as a community farm were later deeded to the AME Zion Church so that they would be maintained after her death.*

Among her boarders in the first postwar years was Nelson Davis, an ex-slave and war veteran. Handsome, almost six feet tall, Davis was more than twenty years younger than his landlady. Despite this difference, on March 19, 1869, according to an Auburn newspaper, "Harriet Tubman took unto herself a husband." Her many friends and her

*Rebuilt after World War II, the house is now the Harriet Tubman Home and Library.

Harriet Tubman (standing, left), her husband, Nelson Davis (seated, with cane) and some of her protégés. *(Boston Public Library)*

biographer remained silent about her marriage, perhaps disapproving. One contemporary later said that Davis was ill and that Tubman had married him to take care of him. This may be so, but they had nineteen years together before he died of tuberculosis in 1888. After his death, she was granted a pension of twenty dollars a month, not for her own war services, but for his.

Financing the home was always a pressing problem. For this reason and others, Harriet Tubman continued to speak at meetings all over the East. Her most memorable public appearance was at a convention in Washington in 1896 when two generations of women* met to organize the National Association of Colored Women. To the younger delegates, few of whom had known slavery, she was the embodiment of black women's capacity for struggle. "The audience rose as one

*By 1896 Sojourner Truth and Mary Ann Shadd Cary were dead, Harriet Jacobs confined to a wheelchair, but the participants in the historic meeting included Rosetta Douglass Sprague, Fanny Jackson Coppin, Louisa Jacobs, Frances E. W. Harper, Charlotte Forten Grimké, Ella Sheppard Moore, as well as such younger women as Josephine St. Pierre Ruffin, Dr. Rebecca Cole, Mary Church Terrell, Ida Wells Barnett, Margaret Murray Washington, Alice Moore [Dunbar], and Victoria Earle Mathews.

person and greeted her with the waving of handkerchiefs and the clapping of hands," an observer reported. During another emotional session, Mother Harriet, the oldest member of the convention, was asked to introduce the Baby of the Association, the infant son of Ida B. Wells. Many who witnessed the meeting of the aging heroine of the antislavery wars and the youthful antilynching crusader, perceived it as a moment in which a torch was passed from one strong bearer to another.

Tubman remained active for another seventeen years. The children of old-time abolitionists and such new black spokesmen as Booker T. Washington made pilgrimages to see her and to listen to her songs and stories. She died in the spring of 1913; the following year the citizens of Auburn placed a bronze tablet at the entrance of the Cayuga County Courthouse in her memory.*

Harriet Tubman in 1895. *(Boston Public Library)*

As she watched the shining promises of Reconstruction fade, Sojourner Truth emerged from retirement in Michigan for a last crusade. The freedpeople needed land of their own far from their former owners. "De government hab given land to de railroads in the West. Can't it do as much for these poor creatures?" she asked. For more than two

*Visitors to Auburn can still see the tablet that commemorates her work in the Underground Railroad and the Civil War.

years she stumped the country saying, "Give 'em land and an outset, and hab teachers learn 'em to read. Den they can be somebody." In a letter to the New York Tribune, *which a friend wrote for her, she inaugurated a petition drive:*

To the Editor of the *Tribune*
Sir: Florence, Massachusetts, February 18, 1871

I am urging the people to sign petitions to Congress to have a grant of land set apart for the freed people to earn their living on, and not be dependent on the government for their bread. I have had fifty petitions printed at my own expense, and have been urging the people of the Eastern States for the past seven months. I made up my mind last winter, when I saw able men and women taking dry bread from the government to keep from starving, that I would devote myself to the cause of getting land for these people, where they can work and earn their own living.

Instead of sending these people to Liberia, why can't they have a colony in the West? Everybody says this is a good work, but nobody helps. Please help me with these petitions. Yours truly,
                              Sojourner Truth

Her goal was "to send tons of paper down to Washington for them spouters to chaw on," but the petition campaign failed. Reformers were less responsive than they had been in the past, and Congress was busy with other matters. Then illness and the tragic death of her grandson, Sammy, who had been her constant companion kept her in Battle Creek. She was almost eighty years old when she wrote William Still to say that she wanted to visit Philadelphia for the Centennial celebration:

Dear Sir: Battle Creek, Michigan, January 4, 1876

I have been very sick since I last saw you. I had a terrible sore on my leg. The doctors pronounced it a gangrene. I returned home Dec. 10th 1874 and was taken sick 2 weeks after. My grandson Samuel the one that was with me to your house is dead. He was taken sick when we came home. He was 24 years of age. I have so far recovered as to walk without the aid of a cane. The doctors gave me up but I got a woman doctor who got me so I could walk but proud flesh got in and my leg swelled and then I got a horse doctor who took the swelling out and I am fast improving. It seems I am like a horse as no other doctor could cure me.

I have got a book of my life out an addition of 200 pages on the old one, 320 pages in the whole.* My expenses in my sickness was heavy and I had to mortgage my little house. I am between 3 and 400 dollars in debt and the [book] was got up to pay my debts and to help me in my old age. I expect to come to Philadelphia to that great time. If I should live to come down I will have an opportunity to see all my old freinds. And I can dispose of my books and can raise the mortgage off my house and have it free from debt once more. I had it all paid for but sickness brought me in debt. Samuel's funeral expenses costed me a great deal and I did not want him buried by the town.

Freind Still you have helped me years ago and maybe this is the last time I shall need any help. I want you to assist me in getting 2 rooms in your house or any place about Philadelphia you think is as good place. I have no one to send down to see about it. My grand-son the one I depended on is dead. I have got another grand-son Willie who is 14 years old but he is to young to go down there to see about a place as he has never be in a large city. He does my writing and wrote this letter. If there is any mistake please excuse them as I cannot read writing. He must come with me down there to do my writing and reading and his mother to see to me. I have another daughter that may come with me that is my oldest daughter. I want the rooms furnished as I cannot carry beds chairs etc. I am very anxious to come down for I think I can sell my book fast and then I can pay my debts. I would send a book but it cost something more than my limited means can afford but I will send a circular. My love to you and Family. I hope to see you soon.

Sojourner Truth

It is not known if she visited the Centennial, but her health improved and she returned to the rostrum, often lecturing three times a week. In 1879 when the Exodusters streamed into Kansas she teamed up with her old friend Laura Haviland to distribute food and clothing to the needy and to urge the migrants to homestead on land of their own. It was her last trip. Old age† and her ulcerated legs caught up with her, and she died in her home in Battle Creek in November 1883.

After working with freedpeople in Savannah, Georgia, Harriet

*In 1850, Olive Gilbert, a New England abolitionist, edited *Narrative of Sojourner Truth*, which was part biography and part speeches and articles. It was expanded and brought up to date in 1875 by Frances W. Titus, a Battle Creek admirer. The newspaper stories, letters, and autographs in the *Book of Life* were taken from the album that Sojourner Truth carried with her wherever she traveled.

†Although Sojourner Truth and her contemporaries believed that she was over a hundred, modern scholars estimate her age as eighty-six at the time of her death.

Jacobs paid a visit to Edenton, North Carolina, her birthplace and the scene of Incidents in the Life of a Slave Girl. *She found a community in transition, the freedpeople working as tenant farmers and welcoming such innovations as schools and suffrage. From her grandmother's home which had been willed to her,* she sent a memorable letter to Ednah Cheney:*

Dear Mrs. Cheney: Edenton, North Carolina, April 25, [1867?]

I am sitting under the old roof, twelve feet from the spot where I suffered all the crushing weight of slavery. Thank God, the bitter cup is drained of its last dreg. There is no more need of hiding places to conceal slave mothers.

I had long thought I had no attachment to my old home. As I sit here and think of those I loved, of their hard struggle in life, their unfaltering love and devotion toward myself and children, I love to think of them. They have made the few sunny spots in that dark life sacred to me.

I cannot tell you how I feel in this place. The change is so great, I can hardly take it all in. I was born here, and amid all these new born blessings, the old dark cloud comes over me, and I find it hard to have faith in rebels.

The past winter was very severe for this region. It caused much suffering, and the freedmen with but few exceptions were cheated out of their crop of cotton. Their contract masters shipped it for them, and when they ask for a settlement, they are answered I am daily expecting the returns. Many of the large plantations of the once wealthy planters is worked under the control of colored men. The owners let their plantations to the freedmen in preference to the poor whites. They believe the Negro determined to make money and they will get the largest portion of it.

Negro suffrage is making a stir. The rebels are striving to make the people feel they are their true friends, and they must not be led astray by the Yankees. The freedmen ask if Abraham Lincoln led them astray, that his friends is their friends his enemies their enemies.

I have spent much of my time [on] the plantations distributing seed and trying to teach the women to make Yankee gardens. They plant everything to mature in the summer, like their corn and cotton. I have hunted up all the old people, done what I could for them. I love to

---

*Harriet Jacobs's deed to her grandmother's property was formally recorded by the register of deeds of Chowan County in 1873. She and her daughter Louisa sold the land in 1892 for $425.

work for these old people. Many of them I have known from child-hood.

There is one school in Edenton well attended. On some of the Plantations there is from 15 to 25 Children that cannot attend school. The distance is so far. Some of the freedmen are very anxious to establish plantation schools as soon as the more advanced schools can send out teachers. Many of the freedmen are willing and will sustain their teachers. At present there is a great revival in the colored churches. The whites say the niggers sung and prayed until they got their freedom, and now they are singing and praying for judgment.

My love to Miss Daisy. I send her some jasmine blossoms. Tell her they bear the fragrance of freedom. Yours truly,

H. Jacobs

In 1868 Jacobs went to England to solicit funds for a home for orphans and aged freedpeople in Savannah. Like Harriet Tubman's old people's home in Auburn, the Savannah asylum was to be situated on fifteen acres of land so that the freedpeople could raise their own vegetables, fruit, and poultry. In an appeal published in the Anti-Slavery Reporter *she thanked British friends for their contributions as "noble evidence of their joy at the downfall of American Slavery and the advancement of human rights." Little is known of her later years when she lived in Cambridge, Massachusetts, and in Washington, D.C., with her daughter Louisa. A few days after her death in March 1897, the Reverend Francis Grimké recalled hearing her "speak of the stirring times before the war when the great struggle for freedom was going on." In a perceptive eulogy, Grimké talked of her in terms that could have applied to Harriet Tubman and Sojourner Truth as well.*

She impressed me as a woman of marked individuality and strong character. She was no reed shaken by the wind. She did her own thinking; had opinions of her own, and held to them with great tenacity. . . . There was also combined in her a heart as tender as that of a little child. How wonderfully sympathetic she was; how readily did she enter into the sorrows, the heartaches of others, how natural it seemed for her to take up all who needed to be soothed and comforted.

During the 1860s and '70s, Frances Ellen Watkins Harper supported herself and her daughter by lecturing and by selling copies of her books of poems. Speaking to white audiences on race themes, with such titles as "The Nation's Great Opportunity" and "The Colored Man as a Social and Political Force," she traveled in the South as well as the North. In a letter to William Still she described life on the road:

I am in the sunny South. I read and see human nature under new lights. Traveling, conversing, addressing day and Sunday-schools, picking up scraps of information, takes up a large portion of my time. For my audiences, I have both white and colored. On the cars, some find out that I am a lecturer and I am drawn into conversation. "What are you lecturing about?" the question comes up and if I say, among other topics, politics, then I may look for an onset. There is a sensitiveness on this subject, a dread that someone will "put the devil in the nigger's head"; still I get along somewhat pleasantly. Last week I got in conversation with a former slave-dealer, and we had rather an exciting time. I was traveling alone. . . . Last Saturday I spoke in Sumter; a number of white persons were present, and I had been invited to speak there by the Mayor and editor of the paper. Next week I am to speak in a place where one of our teachers was struck and a colored man shot, who gave offence by some words spoken at a public meeting. I do not feel any particular fear.

Her wisdom, eloquence, and beauty helped to persuade whites of the humanity of blacks. An Alabama newspaperman with a reputation as a staunch Rebel attended one of her lectures "to see how the colored citizens were managing" and came away impressed. Below are excerpts from his report for the Mobile Register.

Her voice was remarkable—as sweet as any woman's voice we have ever heard, and so clear and distinct as to pass every syllable to the most distant ear in the house. We followed the speaker to the end not discerning a single grammatical inaccuracy of speech, or the slightest violation of good taste. At times the current of thoughts flowed in eloquent and poetic expression. The main theme of her discourse was the grand opportunity that emancipation had afforded the black race. "You have muscle power and brain power," she said "You must utilize them, or be content to remain forever the inferior race. Get land, every one that can, and as fast as you can. A few acres to till and a roof, however humble, over your head, are the castle of your independence, and when you have it you are fortified to act and vote independently." That part of her lecture that dwelt on domestic relations was pitched on the highest key of sound morality. She urged the sanctity of the marriage state (a happy contrast to her strong-minded, free-love, white sisters of the North), and the duties of mothers to their daughters.

There were parts of the lecturer's discourse that grated a little on a white Southern ear, but it was forgiven in the genuine earnestness and profound good sense with which the woman spoke.

While acting as an ambassador to the white South, Harper spent most of her time with the freedpeople. "I meet with a people eager to hear, ready to listen," she told Still.

Sometimes I speak twice a day. Part of my lectures are given privately to women and for them I never make any charge or take up any collection. I am now going to have a private meeting with the women of this place. I am going to talk with them about their daughters, and about things connected with the welfare of the race. Now is the time for our women to begin to plant the roots of progress under the hearthstone. Last night I spoke in a schoolhouse, where there was not a single window glass. Today I write to you in a lowly cabin, where the windows in the room are formed by two apertures in the wall. Last night my table was adorned with roses, although I did not get one cent for my lecture.

Part of the time I am preaching against men ill-treating their wives. The condition of the women is not very enviable in some cases. They have had a terribly hard time in Slavery and their subjection has not ceased in freedom. One man said of some women that a man must leave them or whip them.

Staying in crowded, dreary cabins, sharing the freedpeople's beds and humble fare, Harper barely cleared expenses. Yet, "I live through it and find life interesting," she wrote. "I belong to this race, and when it is down I belong to a down race; when it is up I belong to a risen race." When Reconstruction came to an end, she protested vigorously. At the 100th anniversary meeting of the Pennsylvania Abolition Society in 1875, she challenged its members to continue the struggle.

Two things are wanting in American civilization—a keener and deeper, broader and tenderer sense of justice; a sense of humanity, which shall crystallize into the life of the nation the sentiment that justice, simple justice, is the right, not simply of the strong and powerful, but of the weakest and feeblest of all God's children. Instead of the North relaxing its efforts to diffuse education in the South, it behooves us to throw into the South all the healthful reconstructing influences we can command. Before our young men is another battle —not a battle of flashing swords and clashing steel but a battle against ignorance, poverty and low social condition. In the great work of upbuilding there is room for woman's work and woman's heart. We need a deep earnestness and a lofty unselfishness to round out our lives.

During most of her life Frances Ellen Watkins Harper was the nation's most popular black poet. In addition to Poems on Miscellaneous Subjects, *which went through more than twenty editions, she wrote* Moses, *a long narrative poem;* Sketches of Southern Life *with Aunt Chloe, a freedwoman, as narrator; and* Iola Leroy, *a novel about the adventures of a "tragic mulatto" during and after the war. She organized Sunday schools, worked for black education, and headed temperance work among blacks under the auspices of the National Woman's Christian Temperance Union. A founder of the National Association of Colored Women, she served several terms as a vice-president. She died in Philadelphia in 1911.*

In 1869 Mary Ann Shadd Cary gave up a teaching job in Detroit and moved to Washington, D.C., in hope of obtaining a government clerkship. When the job failed to materialize, she returned to teaching. She also became the first woman to enroll in Howard University's law school. After studying for two years, she withdrew when she was refused a law degree because of her sex.* More than a decade later she returned to school, receiving a Bachelor of Law degree from Howard in May 1883. For the rest of her life she practiced law in Washington, "with notable success," her daughter wrote.

During summers while she was teaching, she traveled in the South and West, speaking on behalf of the New National Era *and candidates of the Republican party. She went back to Michigan to sell copies of her friend William Still's book,* The Underground Railroad, *and visited members of her far-flung family. In 1885 she spoke in Mayersville, Mississippi, where her sister Amelia's son was town clerk. "When it was announced that Mrs. M. A. Shadd Cary, a colored lady lawyer and lecturer on Temperance and other reforms would lecture at the court-house, the populace turned out en masse," a correspondent wrote. "The subject of the lecture was 'Race Pride and Cooperation.'"*

In Washington she wrote two influential articles entitled "Trades for Our Boys," outlining the difficulties that black youth faced in finding jobs. "I have a boy† who must and shall have a trade, and yet where may he learn it, or where exercise it when learned?" she asked

---

*Charlotte E. Ray, who graduated from Howard Law School in 1872, became the first black woman lawyer.

†Linton S. Cary, her son, held an unskilled job as messenger and cloakroom attendant in the House of Representatives until his untimely death in 1892. Sarah Cary Evans, her daughter, was a dressmaker.

in one article. Insisting that blue-collar jobs rather than token represen-tation "at the top of the house" must be given priority, she continued:

We have a few live members of Congress. We have members of State Legislatures; also attaches of the learned professions, and aspir-ants in the field of letters, all of which is enjoyably rose-tinted and gilded as compared with the past; but we, no more than others, can afford to build at the top of the house only. Ill-timed and unseemly as it may appear, the craftsman, the architect, the civil engineer, must all come through the door opened to us by the mechanic.

At the monthly meetings of the Bethel Literary and Historical Association, organized by the black elite of Washington, Mary Ann Cary read papers and took part in debates. She was remembered as "a speaker whose clear, high treble voice and epigrammatic sentences were a signal for death-like stillness and [whose] oracular sayings nearly always met popular approval." In 1887 she went to New York for the annual congress of the Association for the Advancement of Women, joining Frances Ellen Watkins Harper and her daughter, Mary, as the only black participants. Writing for the New York Age, *she proposed that black women follow the whites' example and form clubs for philanthropic and educational purposes.*

Mary Ann Shadd Cary died in 1893. It was characteristic of her that after having worked selflessly for more than a half-century her estate consisted of household furniture "of inconsiderable value" and "a library of law & miscellaneous books"—total value about $150.

Finding work for young people was as important to Fanny Jackson Coppin* as to Mary Ann Cary. As principal of the Institute for Col-ored Youth from 1869 to 1902, she was in a better position to bring about change. Prodding her pupils to excel, she saw a remarkable number† of them become doctors, lawyers, and educators. John Dur-ham, a former student, who became an engineer, journalist, and diplo-mat, told how she had motivated him.

I first made Mrs. Coppin's acquaintance while I was in disgrace, contemplating the prospect of a sound trouncing. Mrs. Coppin walked over to me and asked me my name. She talked pleasantly to me and won my confidence by ignoring the fact that I was a candidate for a

---

*In 1881, when she was forty-four years old, Fanny M. Jackson married the Reverend Levi J. Coppin, a widower eleven years younger than she. They had no children.
†In *The Philadelphia Negro,* published in 1899, W. E. B. Du Bois listed almost 200 ICY graduates who had white collar or professional jobs. However, nearly three-fourths of them had to leave Philadelphia in order to find work.

"barking." Finally she asked me what I intended to be after leaving school. I promptly answered: "A clerk!" The prospect of sitting behind a desk and writing in big books seemed to me the remotest ideal for a student. She led me to a desk and sat in the chair next to mine. In language which was perfectly clear to me at ten years of age, she pictured the great work to be done by specialists in the learned professions, great cures to be made by colored doctors, cases to be won by colored lawyers, books to be made by colored writers. Then she said, "Mr. Venning tells me that you like arithmetic. I think that I'll have to make you a civil engineer." And she did. From that time on, until the day of the conferring of my degree sixteen years later she was my constant advisor.

What Mrs. Coppin did for me in that first interview—and it fixed the trend of my entire life—she has done for hundreds of other pupils. As a teacher, her classroom work is thorough, magnetic and abreast with the most advanced science of teaching. She is the last to deal in pedagogic-philosophy talk, and the first to apply it in her work. No student is so stupid or indifferent as to exhaust her sympathy and patience. Had she been other than an American colored woman, she would have been one of the most famous of America's school reform instructors.

Since teaching was one of the few professions open to black women, Fanny Jackson Coppin determined to make her would-be teachers the best in the nation. To supplement the institute's classical curriculum she introduced a normal school program so that pupils could study new pedagogical methods and do practice teaching. Equally concerned about the students from blue-collar families who made up the majority of her school, she lobbied long and hard for industrial training. She addressed a meeting of public school directors in 1879.

I told them the only places in the city where a colored boy could learn a trade was in the House of Refuge or the Penitentiary and the sooner he became incorrigible and got into the Refuge or committed a crime and got into the Penitentiary, the more promising it would be for his industrial training.

Speaking in Philadelphia, New York, and Washington, she at last obtained backing for an Industrial Department where boys were taught bricklaying, carpentry, shoemaking, and printing, while girls learned dressmaking, millinery, typing, stenography, and cooking. Her students acquired the requisite skills. But would anybody hire them? For the rest of her life, Fanny Coppin knocked on factory doors, appealed to church groups, spoke at political meetings in an effort to break down the barriers that denied black people access to all but the most menial work. She established a Woman's Industrial Exchange, where the mechanical and artistic skills of black women were displayed, and a Home for Girls and Young Women to provide a residence for workers from out of town.

Talented, dynamic, and innovative, she demanded even more of herself than of her pupils. Her working day began at 9 A.M. and ended after 6 P.M. In addition to teaching Greek and Latin, she administered the school, managing to keep pupils, parents, teachers, and the school committee happy. She needed all the tact she could command to smooth the ruffled feelings of male teachers who resented a female principal and to effect changes despite the conservative Quakers who held the institute's purse strings. Small wonder that in her fortieth year, she experienced an emotional crisis. In a letter to Frederick Douglass written when he was appointed marshal for the District of Columbia, she spoke of her illness and also revealed some of the charm and humor that made her success possible.

Dear Mr. Douglass: Philadelphia, April 19, 1877
    I was very very glad to think that your worth has been, in some degree, recognized, and that I have lived to see the day. Our brave President* who has dared to recognize ability and high personal character, has by that action, given an inspiration to intelligence and uprightness. He has elevated the position of President of the United States, in that he has shown he does not intend to be a huckster of political positions to the highest bidder.

    I should have discharged this very agreeable duty much sooner if it had not been that for some time I have been quite sick. I can not yet say whether my life's work is done or not; but a few months will decide. I have no one to blame but myself. Although I knew I was not well, yet for three weeks past I have worked both day and night preparing a class for examinations, and this, I fear, has been the "last straw".

    Try to work prudently, dear Mr. Douglass, for I believe that there are greater honors yet in store for you. You cannot tell what an inspira-

---

*Her enthusiasm for President Rutherford B. Hayes seems questionable today. Only nine days earlier, Hayes had withdrawn all federal troops from the South, thereby signaling the end of Reconstruction. In 1877, however, most black leaders accepted the inevitability of Hayes's policy; Douglass did not criticize it for another decade.

tion your appointment has been to the School. The boys are diving into their studies more earnestly than ever. I was very much pleased with your picture in Harper's last week. How proud I am of you!

When I came to Washington to lecture, February 8th, I was astonished to see upon the hand-bills that you were to introduce me. Dear me! I thought; suppose that I do badly: how will poor Mr. Douglass feel. I worried about it, for I was very uncertain as to how I should get on. That I had a heart full to say to them, I felt sure, but as to how I should succeed in saying it, was the question.

I was both glad and sorry when I heard that you were not in the City; sorry because I should not get to see you, and glad because I wished to speak of you in the lecture and I could not have done that freely if you had been present—and also, because if I did do badly it could not in any way affect you. After all, it turned out better than I had expected.

Very respectfully yours,
F. M. Jackson

Continuing to teach for another quarter century, she retired when her husband, elected a bishop in the AME Church, was assigned to South Africa. According to Emily Howland who talked with her in 1904, "she told the committee [of the Institute] that she must be released, her husband had been very good to let her continue teaching all the years since they married. So she left the school and went with him to Africa." While he established churches in the Cape of Good Hope Colony, she talked to African women on "the subjects of righteousness, temperance and the judgment to come." Virtually bedridden after her return from Africa, she nevertheless managed to complete her autobiography, Reminiscences of School Life, *which was published after her death in 1913. Widely acclaimed before her death and afterwards,* she became the role model for two generations of black teachers.*

Racial equality was first on the agenda of these black women activists, but the struggle for woman's rights was a close second. Virtually all of them were identified with the feminist movement.† After

*The Institute for Colored Youth still exists as Cheyney State College in Cheyney, Pennsylvania; Coppin State College in Baltimore, also a teachers college, was named in honor of Fanny Jackson Coppin.

†Active black feminists included Margaretta Forten; Harriet and Hattie Purvis; Maritcha Lyons; Louisa, Katherine, and Charlotte Rollin; and such younger women as Josephine Ruffin; Anna J. Cooper; Dr. Susan McKinney Steward; Dr. Rebecca Cole; Ida B. Wells; Mary Church Terrell; and Ellen Crum; Ellen Craft's daughter.

all, as Fanny Jackson Coppin said, "During my entire life I have suffered from two disadvantages. First, that I am a woman, second that I am a Negro."* Furthermore, when the woman's rights movement split in 1869 and two separate suffragist organizations were formed, most black spokeswomen supported the National Woman Suffrage Association headed by Susan B. Anthony and Elizabeth Cady Stanton, which was the more radical (albeit sometimes racist) of the two groups. Black women continued to work with white feminists until the end of the century when suffragist leaders, courting support from the South, made them feel unwelcome.†

Living only a few miles from Seneca Falls, birthplace of the woman's movement, Harriet Tubman's was a familiar face at suffrage meetings. She spoke at a convention in Rochester, chaired by Susan B. Anthony in the 1880s, and a decade later she traveled to Boston when the New England Woman Suffrage Association gave a party in her honor. Although she steered clear of the bitter factional disputes in the movement, she told an interviewer, "I belong to Miss Susan B. Anthony's association." Two years before her death she enrolled in a Geneva, New York, suffrage club. "Do you really believe that women should vote?" a white woman asked. "I suffered enough to believe it," Tubman replied.

Sojourner Truth began her participation in the woman's movement in 1850 when she spoke at a convention in Worcester, Massachusetts. After the war, when the American Equal Rights Association was organized, she joined Elizabeth Cady Stanton in advocating universal suffrage, at a time when other reformers believed that suffrage for black men was the more urgent goal. Speaking at the Equal Rights Association in 1867, she said:

I feel that I have a right to have just as much as a man. There is a great stir about colored men getting their rights, but not a word about the colored women; and if colored men get their rights, and not colored women theirs, the colored men will be masters over the women, and it will be just as bad as it was before. So I am for keeping the thing going while things are stirring; because if we wait till it is still, it will

---

*Eighty years later, Congresswoman Shirley Chisholm would write, "Of my two 'hand-icaps,' being female put more obstacles in my path than being black."
†There is need for an in-depth study of the participation of black women in the nineteenth century woman's rights movement. Most historians as well as modern feminists have underestimated their role. A lone exception in the literature is Terborg-Penn's essay, "Discrimination Against Afro-American Women in the Woman's Movement," in *The Afro-American Woman* edited by Harley and Terborg-Penn.

take a great while to get it going again. White women are a great deal smarter, and know more than colored women, while colored women do not know scarcely anything. They go out washing, which is about as high as a colored woman gets, and their men go about idle, strutting up and down; and when the women come home, they ask for their money and take it all, and then scold because there is no food. I want you to consider on that, chil'n.

During a later session she added:

I would like to go to the polls myself. I own a little house in Battle Creek, Michigan. Well, every year I got a tax to pay. Road tax, school tax, and all these things. Well, there was women there that had a house as well as I. They taxed them to build a road, and they went on the road and worked. It took 'em a good while to get a stump up. Now, that shows that women can work. If they can dig up stumps they can vote. It is easier to vote than dig stumps.

When suffragists attempted to vote in the presidential election of 1872,* Sojourner Truth who had been campaigning for Grant's reelection, went to the polls in Battle Creek, Michigan, and demanded a ballot. She was turned away but the Battle Creek Journal *reported, "It is Sojourner's determination to continue the assertion of her right, until she gains it." As she continued to address gatherings of suffragists, she scolded her coworkers if the occasion seemed to warrant it. At a meeting in Providence, Rhode Island, in 1870, she rebuked her listeners for their elaborate attire.*

Women, you forget that you are the mothers of creation; you forget your sons were cut off like grass by the war, and the land was covered with their blood; you rig yourselves up in panniers and Grecian-bend backs and flummeries; yes, and mothers and gray-haired grandmothers wear high-heeled shoes and humps on their heads, and put them on their babies, and stuff them out so that they keel over when the wind blows. O mothers, I'm ashamed of ye! What will such lives as yours do for humanity? When I saw them women on the stage at the Woman's Suffrage Convention, the other day, I thought, What kind of reformers be you, with goose-wings on your heads, as if you were going to fly, and dressed in such ridiculous fashion, talking about reform and women's rights? Pears to me, you had better reform yourselves first.

*Susan B. Anthony was arrested at the polls in Rochester for "knowingly, wrongfully and unlawfully" voting, and was fined $100 and court costs. She never paid the fine.

After the split in the movement, Sojourner Truth affiliated with the Anthony-Stanton organization. Her last appearance at a woman's rights meeting was as a delegate to the National Woman Suffrage Association's convention in Rochester in 1878.

Shortly after her arrival in Washington, Mary Ann Cary joined the Universal Franchise Association,* the capital's first woman suffrage organization and became its spokesperson at the Colored National Labor Union convention in December 1869. An experienced participant in male-dominated gatherings, Cary won the chairmanship of a Committee on Female Suffrage and was the only woman elected to the union's executive committee. After addressing the convention "at considerable length" on woman's rights, she presented her committee's report, which was devoted to employment problems.

The avocations of women, and particularly colored women, have been lamentably circumscribed, laundresses, teachers, clerks and domestic servants, constituting almost the entire complement of pursuits. We are pleased, however, to be able to say that a manifest desire to widen the boundaries of manual and other pursuits is apparent. Miss Edmonia Lewis among sculptors, Mrs. S. M. Douglass and Miss Cole among physicians, Miss Ketchum among clerks, illustrate an ability among colored women which, if encouraged by colored men, would be the beginning of an era of thought and effort among colored women.

We would recommend to our women to learn trades, to engage in whatever pursuits women of the most highly favored classes now pursue. In addition to present avocations, we would suggest that profitable and health-inspiring employment might be found at market-gardening, small fruit and berry culture, shop and storekeeping, upholstering, telegraphing, and insurance, and to connect themselves with cooperative building societies wherever opportunity offers. No women have had a more varied experience than those who have labored in the fields of the South, and to such we would say, engage in agriculture. Bring to the pursuits of freedom the knowledge of husbandry learned when in bondage.

Both the report and a resolution inviting women to join in the formation of unions and cooperative societies were adopted by the

---

*Founded in 1867 by such women as Josephine Griffing and Belva Lockwood, the Universal Franchise Association was allied to the Anthony-Stanton faction. At the Colored National Labor Union convention, Griffing and Lockwood were members of Mary Ann Cary's committee.

convention. For the next two decades Mary Ann Cary continued to work for woman's rights and equal employment opportunities. With other members of the Universal Franchise Association (who were the most progressive white women in the capital) she addressed the House Judiciary Committee on behalf of woman suffrage. In 1871 she was one of sixty-four District women who attempted to register to vote. When the National Woman Suffrage Association held its annual conventions in Washington, she attended as a delegate and reporter for the black press. She was also a founder of a Colored Woman's Progressive Franchise Association the purpose of which was "to take an aggressive stand against the assumption that men only may conduct industrial and other things." Its goals included the establishment of newspapers, banks, cooperative stores, and a printing establishment conducted by women.

During her travels through the South, Frances Harper displeased some black leaders by her advocacy of woman's rights. The Louisianian, a weekly owned by P. B. S. Pinchback, advertised her as "a lecturer of rare talent and powerful oratory" before she spoke in New Orleans. After listening to her "spirited defence of woman's rights," an editor was "struck dumb with consternation." Reporting on a later speech, the paper said "She has dropped the woman's rights question, and that very wisely."

A frequent participant in women's meetings in the North, she was present at the tumultuous gathering of the Equal Rights Association in 1869 when Stanton and Anthony urged delegates to repudiate the Fifteenth Amendment because it opened the way for black male suffrage while ignoring women's claims. Predicting that woman's rights would be delayed for a generation* if they failed to act "while the constitutional door is open," they favored a companion amendment that would grant suffrage to all. Because of the situation in the South where black men's votes were vital for survival, most abolitionists, including Frederick Douglass, believed that suffrage for black men should take priority. During the heated debate, angry feminists spoke of "Sambo," the ignorant black man whose rights came before those of "women of wealth, education and refinement." They balanced their racist sentiments by expressing sympathy with black women who struggled against the "tyranny and despotism" of their men. Excerpts from the minutes of the meeting follow.

*The prediction was an underestimate. The Nineteenth Amendment giving suffrage to women was ratified in 1920, fifty years after the Fifteenth Amendment became law.

PHOEBE COUZINS:* While feeling entirely willing that the black man shall have all the rights to which he is justly entitled, I consider the claims of the black woman of paramount importance. Black women are, and always have been in a far worse condition than the men. As a class, they are better, and more intelligent than the men, yet they have been subjected to greater brutalities, while compelled to perform exactly the same labor as men, with the added cares of maternity and household work, with their children taken from them and sold; suffering a thousandfold more than any man could suffer.

PAULINA W. DAVIS† said she would not be altogether satisfied to have the XVth Amendment passed without the XVIth, for woman would have a race of tyrants raised above her in the South, and the black women of that country would also receive worse treatment then if the Amendment was not passed. Take any class that have been slaves, and you will find that they are the worst when free, and become the hardest masters. The black women are more intelligent than the men, because they have learned something from their mistresses. She then related incidents showing how black men whip and abuse their wives in the South. One of her sister's servants whipped his wife every Sunday regularly. [Laughter.] She thought that sort of men should not have the making of the laws for the government of the women throughout the land. [Applause.]

THE PRESIDENT, Mrs. Stanton, argued that not another man should be enfranchised until enough women are admitted to the polls to outweigh those already there. [Applause.] She did not believe in allowing ignorant negroes and foreigners to make laws for her to obey. [Applause.]

Although Frances Harper had voiced her own criticisms of black men she could not let these statements pass without comment. According to the minutes, she said:

When it was a question of race, she let the lesser question of sex go. But the white women all go for sex, letting race occupy a minor position. . . . If the nation could only handle one question, she would not have the black men put a single straw in the way, if only the men of the race could obtain what they wanted. [Great applause.]

*Phoebe Couzins (1839?–1913), one of the first woman lawyers, was a loyal supporter of Anthony and Stanton.
†Paulina Wright Davis (1813–76), an abolitionist and suffragist, helped found the New England Woman Suffrage Association in 1868.

Frances Ellen Harper was the only leading black woman who supported the American Woman Suffrage Association headed by Lucy Stone and Julia Ward Howe until the two groups merged in 1892. She also lobbied for suffrage in black circles. Her "Dialogue on Woman's Rights," below, appeared in the New York Freeman:

JACOB
I don't believe a single bit
In those new-fangled ways
Of women running to the polls
And voting nowadays.
Now there's my Betsy, just as good
As any wife need be
Who sits and tells me day by day
That women are not free;
And then I smile and say to her,
"You surely make me laff;
This talk about your rights and wrongs
Is nothing else but chaff."

JOHN
Now, Jacob, I don't think like you;
I think that Betsy Ann
Has just as good a right to vote
As you or any man

JACOB
Now, John, do you believe for true
In women running round,
And when you come to look for them
They are not to be found?
Pray, who would stay at home to nurse,
To cook, to wash and sew,
While women marched unto the polls?
That's what I want to know.

JOHN
Who stays at home when Betsy Ann
Goes out day after day
To wash and iron, cook and sew,
Because she gets her pay?
I'm sure she wouldn't take quite so long
To vote and go her way,

As when she leaves her little ones
And works out day by day.

JACOB
Well, I declare, that is the truth!
To vote, it don't take long;
But, then, I kind of think somehow
That women's voting's wrong.

JOHN
The masters thought before the war
That slavery was right;
But we who felt the heavy yoke
Didn't see it in that light.
Some thought that it would never do
For us in Southern lands,
To change the fetters on our wrists
For the ballot in our hands.
Now if you don't believe 'twas right
To crowd us from the track
How can you push your wife aside
And try to hold her back?

JACOB
Well, wrong is wrong and right is right,
For woman as for man
I almost think that I will go
And vote with Betsy Ann.

JOHN
I hope you will and show the world
You can be brave and strong
A noble man, who scorns to do
The feeblest woman wrong.

TWENTY-TWO

Representative Women and a New Generation

WHILE Mary Ann Cary and Fanny Jackson Coppin crusaded for broader employment opportunities for black youth, Rosetta Douglass Sprague learned at first hand the damage that job discrimination could do to family life. Frederick Douglass's biographers have portrayed her husband, Nathan Sprague, as a ne'er-do-well. Perhaps he was, but a series of letters from Rosetta make him seem more victim than villain. Demobilized at war's end, after serving with the Massachusetts Fifty-fourth in South Carolina, Sprague went to Rochester where his wife and baby daughter, Annie, were living in the spacious Douglass home. An ex-slave, poorly educated, and lacking a trade, he was one of thousands of black veterans looking for jobs. While his brothers-in-law, Frederick, Jr., and Lewis Douglass, went to Colorado Territory to seek their fortunes, Sprague tried to make a go of a farm outside of Rochester. None of the trio succeeded. After two years in the West, Frederick, Jr., and Lewis joined their brother Charles in Washington. With their father's help, all three found government clerical jobs. Sprague, who lacked the education for white-collar work, tried driving a hack, working as a gardener, and selling chickens. Rosetta's letter was written shortly after he gave up his farm. Harriet was her second daughter.*

My Dear Father: Rochester, [New York,] March 26, 1867

Your affectionate letter I received a week ago but it found us busy moving and therefore prevented me from replying sooner. Nathan has already informed you why we sold. It is better to live in the city until we are able to buy a farm without such a debt hanging over us and straining every nerve to get rid of it. I have now a neat little home on a nice street. On one side of us are three American families and on the other two Irish families. Those I do not like so near, still we need not have any trouble with them. Mother came down one day and helped

---

*From 1869 to '72 Lewis and Frederick Douglass, Jr., were coeditors of the *New National Era*, a paper financed in part by their father. Both men had learned printing in the office of the *North Star* but were denied membership in the Typographical Union because of their color.

me to get somewhat put to rights. We have seven rooms and two cellars in the house, a pretty good sized cistern and not very good drinking water being land having much lime.

Mother seemed in very good spirits and wished me when I wrote to send her love. I am busy making a rag carpet for my dining room and mother I expect down to help me a day this week. Harriet grows quite good looking. Mrs. Gibbs insists that she looks something like me something like mother. I fail to see it. She is a very good and lively baby and very large. She is four months old tomorrow and weighs sixteen pounds. Annie is talking to Nathan about Grandpa and says when I ask her to send her love to Grandpa "Yes me"

Affectionately your Daughter
R. D. Sprague

A fortnight later she proudly reported her husband's newest venture.

My Dear Father: Rochester, [New York,] April 11, 1867

I should have written to you at Pittsburg but I desired to tell you all I could about Nathan's hack. He took out his license Monday and has been on the stand every day. His hack is the finest that can be found and he has a handsome span of greys. The whole establishment is very grand and attracts much attention. N. has some trouble among the hackmen. They insult him and threaten his hack. A policeman came up to him on the stand by the Osburn house and told him that he had better go to the other stand in front of the Court house, that there were too many hacks already on the Osburn house stand. Nathan refused as the Mayor told him he could stand at any place where hacks were allowed. The Policeman said I shall have to move it for you there. Another policeman came, said Mr. Sprague if there is any trouble let it be known and all will be righted. The first day he made three dollars and every day besides a dollar. He bought the hack of Mr. Cunningham for $640, paying $200 down and the rest in $40 installments monthly. Father I cannot thank you too much for your kindness, and I can assure you Nathan is grateful and proud of your good opinion of him.

I ran up to the house yesterday to see mother. She was not well at all. She complained of dizziness in the head. I gave her some pills and tomorrow I am going up again. Annie and Harriet are well. Annie is full of fun and getting quite noisy. Nathan and I went to hear Anna E. Dickinson a week ago. Subject "Something to do" It was a womans' rights lecture and failed to make the same impression that some of her former efforts have done. Mother and Nathan send much love,

Affectionately Your Daughter

Rosetta D. Sprague

The hack lasted less than two weeks. Rochester's newspapers failed to report how the hackmen put Nathan Sprague out of business, but Rosetta's letter of April 24, 1867, spoke of "the outrage on Nathan's hack," adding that Gerrit Smith had told her "not to become disheartened." After fruitless attempts to find other work, Sprague left his wife and children with her parents and went to Nebraska, which had just become a state. Determined not to come back until he had made some money, he wrote Douglass, "If I do not make it it is not because you have not did all you could to help me." But it was no easier for an unskilled black man to find work in Omaha than in Rochester. When Nathan Sprague returned with empty pockets a few months later, his self-esteem had hit a new low. Depressed, irritable with his wife, and quarreling with her brothers, he took offense when Douglass accused his children of being "all mouths and no hands". Although Rosetta attempted to defend her husband, her letter depicts a deteriorating relationship; it also casts light on her parents' home life.

My Dear Father: Rochester, New York, March 10, 1869

    I am sorry you believe Nathan is offended. He was hurt supposing you alluded to him as well as the rest for he has been very sensitive all winter because he has laid idle so long and had more than once said to me he believed father thought he could get work. I told him that you know the difficulty of getting employment in the winter. Nathan has been willing to take the taunts of the rest of the family so long as he could be worthy of your approval. I do not know that Nathan has ever been seriously offended with me only as he has been conscious of the feeling of the family towards him. I do not consider his harshness towards me just but thanks to your good advice I am able to bury it as I know that our happiness mainly depends on me. You say to me Husbands first and fathers second. I know it but I cannot help my affection for you and your words whether of censure or praise affect me accordingly. I see now that Nathan feels himself in a sort of tight jacket because he knows however much you may be satisfied he is the subject for all kinds of unkind remarks from the rest.

    You say you are a lonely man. No one knows it better than myself and the causes. I have felt it for years for I have been in a measure lonely myself but would not allow myself to analyze my feelings as I was the daughter and had duties to fulfill in that relation. I knew where my sympathies were. I do not know whether you ever thought much about it but my position at home was anything but pleasant. You used to say that we were all glad when you left, something that was so far from what was true as far as I was concerned. I never dared to show much zeal about anything where you were concerned as I could very readily bring a storm about my ears if I endorsed any of your sentiments about matters pertaining to the household. I do not wish to pain you, but I must say I have no pleasant memories of my brothers. I had my faults but none so great that their feelings of dislike should follow me to this day.

[letter breaks off]

By the 1870s the history of their marriage, in which Sprague's unemployment was a dominant theme, had begun to sound like a soap opera. When Nathan's "chicken speculations" and similar ventures proved "not as much of a success as we could wish," the Spragues returned to the Douglass household— until the house was destroyed in an incendiary fire. After a stay in Washington where Douglass had decided to make his permanent home, the Spragues returned to Rochester. There Nathan, with his father-in-law's help, obtained a job in the post office. Less than a year later his family was "disgraced and scandalized" when he was caught opening letters to steal their contents. Pleading guilty to the charge, he was sentenced to a year in the Monroe County Penitentiary. Besieged by Nathan's creditors, Rosetta sold her Rochester property and joined her parents in Washington. Her unhappy letter follows.

My Dear Father: Rochester, New York, September 17, 1876

The past two weeks have been full of events and I am having a singular time and I wonder can it be me. My breaking up has caused such a flurry among Nathan's creditors and I am being sued on every side. Mrs. Rodenbeck brought a note for me to sign of $91.48. I refused to sign it as I could not promise to pay in six months.* She was very angry and left sending a Constable to attach articles to cover the amount. I gave up the black sofa, a corner stand, 49¾ yards of Brussels carpet—that large chromo of Nathan's, three smaller chromos, two marble top stands, a chest of carpenters tools, the alarm clock, my small rocking chair, three office stools, the two rugs that were in the parlor. The constable said all left over the sale came to me and

---

*Rosetta Sprague was not as destitute as this letter implies. Before leaving for Washington she sold two Rochester properties, receiving $3,700.

then went away returning with three other men took my piano out in a drenching rain.

Everybody in the neighborhood says she has taken too much for such a debt and consider that she has acted outrageously. The piano she cannot hold at any rate. *I* cannot dispose of the furniture to pay N's debts as it is considered *his* personal property, it is *mine* for *housekeeping* purposes but [I] cannot dispose of it, but my piano is my personal property and it can [not] be seized to settle debts contracted by Nathan. District Attorney Raines assures me it cannot be kept and tomorrow morning is the time set for deciding if I can be made responsible for N's debts.

I was obliged to go to see Nathan about this Rodenbeck debt—I found him wondering at my not having written to him or been to see him. I told him I was going away and had rented the house. He did not like it that I had rented. He said he should see me but that he should not come to Washington. The next evening his keeper came with a message from him not to rent the house. If I did I would simply ruin him. I cannot understand that and propose to follow out my own plans as far as I can.

I can tell you better in a couple of days how matters stand. It is a wild night—a cold rain has fallen all day and as I write it is pouring. The wind howling around the house makes me shiver. Good night dear father. I wish I could be with you and be out of this turmoil. I never knew so little what to think in my life. Love to all.

Affectionately your Daughter
Rosetta

In Washington, Rosetta Sprague who had no career ambitions became the main support of her six children. Clerking in various government offices, she worked under her father when he was marshal of the District and recorder of deeds. *The Spragues were reconciled after Nathan's release from prison, but he never became the breadwinner he aspired to be.*

After her father's death, Rosetta Douglass Sprague was frequently called on to address public gatherings. She spoke at the founding convention of the National Association of Colored Women, contributed to a symposium on the role of educated black men, and, in

---

*The Spragues had seven children, but one died in early childhood. Lewis and Frederick Douglass, Jr., also worked in the office of the recorder of deeds while their father held that position.

one of her last public appearances, read a paper entitled My Mother
As I Recall Her.* *She died in November 1906.*

*With Frederick Douglass to fall back on, Rosetta and Nathan
Sprague were spared the poverty that most blacks faced. By 1870 there
were almost ten times as many black people in the North as there had
been in 1800. Black men's right to vote was guaranteed by the Constitution, and a growing body of civil rights laws promised an end to
discrimination in public places. But black people still had the lowest
incomes and the highest mortality rates. In Philadelphia, where the
black population has been studied more consistently than in any other
city, eight out of ten black men worked at unskilled jobs in the 1870s;
the figure for Irish immigrants was five out of ten and for native whites
fewer than two. Black male mortality rates were so high that more than
one-quarter of black women with children were widowed by the time
they were in their forties.† The death rate was even higher in Washington and New York.*

*In the decade after the war, employment opportunities for white
women had broadened. Many of them were working in factories or as
clerks in stores and business offices. Black women, however, were
confined to the kitchen or the classroom. The following letter was
published in the* Philadelphia Post; *it could have appeared in any city,
North or South.*

To the Editor of the Post
Sir: [Philadelphia,] November 1, 1871
    Being a constant reader of your valuable paper, I take the liberty
of asking you to explain to me why it is that when respectable women
of color answer an advertisement for a dressmaker, either in families
or with a dressmaker, [they] are invariably refused, or offered a place
to cook or scrub, or to do house work; and when application is made
at manufactories immediately after having seen an advertisement for
operators or finishers, meet with the same reply, sometimes modified
by bidding you "call again," "just suited," "will want more hands in
the course of a few weeks," etc.
    There are many respectable women of color competent to fill any

*Presenting only positive aspects of Anna Murray Douglass's life, this paper has been
the chief source of later writings about her.
†A study of black Philadelphia in the 1870s and '80s, "The Origins of the Female-
Headed Black Family," by Furstenberg, and others found that the number of female-
headed families varied inversely with family income. Black women became family heads
"as a result of the destructive conditions of northern urban life."

of the above named positions, and who eke out a scanty livelihood sewing at home, who would gladly take permanent situations, to sew, operate or finish; and some have advertised to that effect, making their color known, and received no answers.

The "brotherly love" for which this city is proverbial should extend to all, irrespective of color, race or creed.

                                                    A COLORED WOMAN

Hundreds of interviews conducted by W. E. B. Du Bois twenty-eight years later showed scant improvement.

A—, a dressmaker and seamstress of proven ability sought work in the large department stores. They all commended her work, but could not employ her on account of her color.

B—is a typewriter, but has applied at stores and offices in vain for work; "very sorry" they all say, but they can give her no work.

C—has attended the Girls High School for two years and has been unable to find any work; she is washing and sewing for a living.

D—is a dressmaker and milliner, and does bead work. "Your work is very good," they say to her "but if we hired you all of our ladies would leave."

E—a seamstress, was given work from a store once, to do at home. It was commended as satisfactory, but they gave her no more.

Educated women often cleaned houses or washed clothes when they could not find other employment. Sidney Taliaferro, Emily Howland's protégé, became a chambermaid after she lost her teaching job. *

Dear Miss Howland: Philadelphia, May 26, 1881

I have something better in view in regards to my obtaining a livelyhood, which is this, the old lady with whom I made my home while resting wants me to come and live with her. She says she will pay me $2 a week to help her and then she would have some one to stay with her nights, she does washing for two or three young ladies and after we are through with that I can go out to sew by the day or do any other work so I be home with her nights and I am only getting half a dollar more here where I have to help with washing and ironing do chamber work and wait table with 9 in family besides the cook and myself and I think I would do much better and even make more by

*Taliaferro was teaching at Howland School in Heathsville, Virginia, until she had an affair with a married man and was summarily dismissed for her "crime." By the time she wrote the above letter, she had won Howland's forgiveness.

going to live with the old lady. Mrs. Cliff this old widow lady has taken quite a liking to me. I remind her of her daughter that is dead, she has given me two very nice white skirts and some other little notions of the daughters and I think I will go and live with her. Then I can get to go to church and Sunday school every Sunday where in I don't get to either now. Please write me what you think of it. You can send me a card to her house no. 234 Dean Street. I am there every Thursday after-noon. I would not leave here though with out giving a weeks notice and wait till the lady got some one else. I hope you will bear with me but I must tell some one my plans and seek advice too, so please let me hear from you very soon.

                    Yours in haste,
                    S. A. Taliaferro

Sidney Taliaferro was soon able to return to teaching, but most black women found no escape from service jobs and the grinding poverty that went with them. Barbara Foule, a domestic worker, told Frederick Douglass an all too familiar tale of old age and insecurity.*

Mr. Douglass
Dear Sir: [Rochester,] New York, September 5, 1877
    I do not know whether you Remember Barbara Foule or not. But she has not forgoten you, or your kindness when i ust to do the washing for your wife, when you lived in Rochester. I have been thinking of you So much latly and dreamed twice that you came to See me in my time of need. I thought i would get one of my Children to write for me and say to you that there is one poor person at least who often says God Bless Fredrick Doughlass and family.
    I am getting old and soon will Be at rest in the grave. I thought when i got old and my Children grone up to take care of me i woud not have to work in my old age But all the help i get is from my girls. Jennie the oldest has just learned Dressmaking. My oldest boy An-thony has been gone to the Army five years, he ust to help me Some the first few years, But now he Does not even write to me. That is Breaking my heart. My Daughter Annie is still outh west. She is a widow now, she never writes to me. My old man is alive yet, But not a cent do I get from him. He spents all his pension for drink. One thing i only ask and that is that i may live if only for one day longer than he So I can enjoy one day of peace with my Children.

*Married to a Maryland farmer, Sidney Taliaferro Boyer continued to teach while raising a family. Her daughter subsequently attended a Virginia boarding school that Emily Howland and Emma V. Brown helped to support.

Dear Sir, now i feel Better for writing to you. I know you will not feel angre with me, for taking the Liburty For i know that you have got a kind heart to feel for the poor. If it is not asking to much, will you write and tell me How you and your family are. Please Direct your letter

Barbara Foule in care
William Witherspoon
27 North Washington St

Although Barbara Foule's letter reflected the poverty of the overwhelming majority of black people, there was a small group who were affluent. Some were the descendants of the caterers, druggists, and realtors of an earlier generation; others had come to the fore during Reconstruction. Black legislators disappeared from the South after 1876, but such men as Frederick Douglass, John Mercer Langston, Blanche K. Bruce, and P. B. S. Pinchback retained federal jobs* and a measure of political influence. In contemporary parlance, they were known as "representative colored men." The term representative did not mean typical. Rather they were the men who, having absorbed "white" values, were accepted as representatives of their people by the white world. A tiny privileged class, they lived in comfortably appointed homes; their children were well educated, and their wives fashionably dressed. "Our society women are lively, charming and unusually wellbred," a newspaper woman wrote in the AME Church Review:

They observe the same laws of etiquette that are observed by devotees of fashion the world over. They call, receive and dress according to their means and often beyond their means, just as other women do. She requires dainty morning gowns, elaborate dinner dresses and stylish street costumes, with hats, gloves and wraps to match, just like the rest of the feminine world. The fashionable Afro-American, like her Caucasian sisters spends her time in novel reading, card playing and in whirling through the intricate mazes of the dance. Others who have consecrated their lives to God find their time taken up with various religious and intellectual organizations.

In 1880 when blacks were still invited to White House social events (a privilege they would lose in later years) a reporter thought that the appearance of Josephine Bruce, wife of Senator Blanche K.

---

*As long as the Republican party was in power, "Negro jobs" included the recorder of deeds, marshal of the District of Columbia, register of the treasury, ministers to Haiti and Liberia, and appointments in the Post Office and Customs Service.

The Cheathams, a middle-class Richmond, Virginia, family, about 1890. *(Valentine Museum, Richmond, Virginia)*

Bruce, was "one of the most notable features" of a presidential reception:

The tall, graceful figure of Mrs. Bruce was displayed in a black velvet princess dress, elaborately trimmed with gold-colored satin, richly embroidered, and drapings of pointed duchess lace, studded with butter-cups at her waist and throat. Her soft brown hair was simply and becomingly arranged, the only ornament worn being a cluster of tiny rosebuds embedded in lace. Her jewels consisted of solitaire diamonds worn in the ears and around the neck. Mrs. Bruce's toilette was considered one of the most tasteful and magnificent of the evening.

Josephine Beall Bruce. *(Moorland-Spingarn Research Center, Howard University)*

A year later, black Republicans from all over the country descended on the capital for the inauguration of James A. Garfield. The Welcome Club of Washington gave a reception and ball:

The Hall was tastefully decorated, the music the best that could be procured, while supper would have tempted an epicure. The dresses of the ladies were simply magnificent. One pleasing feature that we noticed particularly was the profusion of jewelry worn by the ladies. A few years since diamonds were a rarity among our people, but on this occasion they could be seen on every hand, while half a dozen ladies displayed from $500 to $2000 worth of the precious gems each. This shows conclusively that we are advancing not only in education but also in wealth and taste.

Critics were quick to poke fun at the snobbery and ostentatious display of some members of the black elite. In an article, "Washington's Colored Society," written in 1877, John E. Bruce burlesqued the "fust families" who boasted of their "blue veins," that is, skin so white *that veins were visible, and "good hair".* A generation later, James Weldon Johnson, himself a representative man,† satirized "the colored aristocracy" in a song written for "In Dahomey," a popular musical play:*

> To be the leader of the color'd aristocracy
> Is my ambition
> Is her ambition
> I have a longing just the same as all the quality
> For recognition, for recognition
> To have folks say as I pass by
> She moves on a social plane so very high
> She's the leader of the colored aristocracy,
> She's the leader of the colored aristocracy.
>
> Now to establish swell society for color'd folks
> I have a yearning
> She has a yearning
> And from the high-toned 'ristocratic white folks
> How to lead
> I have been learning
> She has been learning.
>
> All that I need is lots of dough
> For that regulates the social scale you know
> To make the proper show
> As the leader of the color'd aristocracy.

In actuality, most "leaders of the colored aristocracy" were preoccupied with self-improvement rather than "lots of dough." Cut off from white society, barred from theaters and concert halls, they had to construct their own cultural life. In New Orleans, members of the

---

*The search for "good hair" and light skin was not limited to the well-to-do. Advertisements in the *New National Era* promised that "our women can excell the famed beauty of the Caucasians" if they would send \$2 for a nostrum. Later advertisements in the *New York Freeman* boosted Anti-Curl, a preparation that made "Kinky, Curly & Rigid Hair Straight, Glossy and Beautiful." There was so much emphasis on these beauty preparations that Nannie H. Burroughs, a prominent educator, wrote an essay entitled "Not Color but Character." "What does this wholesale bleaching of faces and straightening of hair indicate?" she asked. "It simply means that the women who practice it wish that they had white faces and straight hair."

†In addition to collaborating with his brother, Rosamond, and Paul Laurence Dunbar on musical comedies, Johnson was U.S. consul in Venezuela and Nicaragua and field secretary for the National Association for the Advancement of Colored People. The author of *The Autobiography of an Ex-Colored Man, Fifty Years and Other Poems,* and *Along This Way,* he is best known for "Lift Every Voice and Sing," which became the Negro national anthem.

Athenaeum Club met weekly to hear papers on literature and politics. Washington's Mignonette Club put on plays and concerts. At the Monday Night Literary Club, Charlotte Forten Grimké discoursed on Dante, and Frederick Douglass gave a speech entitled "The Philosophy of Reform"; at the Saturday Evening Club, Dr. Edward Blyden, a Liberian scholar, read an article on the late Robert Browning. Sara Iredell Fleetwood whose husband, Christian Fleetwood, organized the Mignonette Club theatricals and directed the St. Luke's Church choir, told of their "evenings at home":

Sara Iredell and Christian Fleetwood photographed on their wedding day in 1869 by Mathew Brady. *(Library of Congress)*

Charlotte Forten Grimké, holding book, and her husband, the Reverend Francis J. Grimke. With them are Anna J. Cooper, seated, Ella D. Barrier and Fannie S. Smythe. *(Anacostia Neighborhood Museum, Smithsonian Institution)*

From the first month of our marriage Mr. Fleetwood and myself have reserved Thursday evening to receive our friends—we are happy to see them at any time, but obligate ourselves to be at home on Thursday.

We adopted the following program which has proved very satisfactory. 1. Music, 2. Reading followed by conversation on the same, then an Essay and conversation on the Essay, after which answers to questions propounded at a previous meeting, followed by questions to be answered at the next meeting. The chairman of the evening then announces the Essayist and Reader for the next week. This is followed by a quotation recited by each one present. The closing exercise is music. One distinctive feature of these evenings is the well understood fact that no refreshments will be furnished, a decision that does much to insure the permanency of these entertainments.

The home of Charlotte Forten Grimké and her husband was a cultural headquarters in Washington. Francis J. Grimké, a political as well as religious leader, shared his wife's concern for the amenities. Their friend, Anna J. Cooper,* told of acquiring a taste for tea "at Mrs. Grimké's hospitable board."

Mr. Grimké was the miracle man who transformed water fresh from the spigot into brilliant amber-colored nectar. He had a three-minute glass that came from Pisa, Italy. It took just so many minutes for its fine sands to flow from the upper to the lower bulb. Just so long, not a second longer must the hot water remain on the tea leaves; and when the delighted ohs and ahs from his admiring audience announced that the performance was a complete success, Mrs. Grimké would say "Oh don't inflate his vanity by too much praise. I assure you Frank is indeed proud of the fact that he tops all competitors in the fine art of brewing tea."

Although they adopted the rituals of upper-class society, "representative colored women" were seldom ladies of leisure. Josephine Bruce managed a Mississippi plantation and real estate holdings in Washington after her husband's death; she later became lady principal at Tuskegee Institute. Sara I. Fleetwood enrolled in the new nursing school at Freedmen's Hospital when she was past fifty years of age; at sixty she became superintendent of nurses at the hospital and, six years later, was the first black woman to serve on the District's Nurses' Examining Board. Preoccupied with the duties of a minister's wife and plagued by ill health, Charlotte F. Grimké nevertheless continued to contribute to black newspapers and to such periodicals as the Boston Commonwealth *and* New York Evangelist.

For the generation growing up at the end of the war, schools were available—poor, middling, never quite equal—yet offering an escape hatch for an ambitious girl or boy. Young "representative women" began to break down barriers in every field. For them "it was an

---

*Anna Julia Haywood Cooper (c. 1858–1964), a graduate of Oberlin, was for many years principal of Washington's M Street High School. The author of *A Voice from the South by a Black Woman of the South* (1892), she later wrote *Personal Recollections of the Grimké Family.*

extraordinary period of awakening," Maritcha Lyons wrote. Women "were beginning to select their own life plans instead of tacitly accepting those arranged for them."

Where Mary Ann Cary had stood alone as a journalist before the war, scores of black women wrote for newspapers and magazines afterwards. Some like Caroline F. Bragg, editor of the Virginia Lancet, and the brilliant Ida B. Wells published their own papers; others wrote columns for the black press and, occasionally, for white publications. Among the liveliest articles in the New National Era in 1871–72 were those written by Faith Lichen.* When Mary Clemmer Ames, a white journalist, disparaged blacks in her "Woman's Letter from Washington" in the Independent, Lichen wrote a devastating reply. Ames had complained that the Senate ladies' gallery was packed with blacks when Charles Sumner spoke: "White ladies of fashion and position stood; while Dinah and Phillis in gorgeous array [sat] beside their sable 'Jefferson' and 'Washington.'" Excerpts from Lichen's answer, headed "That Woman's Letter from Washington," follow.

Maritcha Lyons was assistant principal of a Brooklyn, N.Y., school when this photograph was taken. *(Schomburg Center, New York Public Library)*

*Since no mention of Faith Lichen has been found in contemporary books and magazines, the name may have been a pseudonym concealing the identity of a teacher or government clerk.

O you awful negroes! why couldn't you have been a little late in getting into your "gorgeous array," and presenting yourselves in the Senate galleries? What did it matter that this question was of vital importance to you; was it necessary for you to show your interest by being there in time to get seats, before those "white ladies of position and fashion?" Was there no cockloft into which you might have scrambled and heard Senator Sumner?

Again this precious Woman's Letter says "it was difficult to realize that a slightly colored lady, educated and refined, might go hungry on the cars and be refused food in the hotels of Georgia while the most unctuous contraband from its slums can plunge herself beside you or possess your seat in the city of Washington."* I confess I do not quite make out what M.C.A. is chattering of just here; does she mean that the seats in the city of Washington belong to white ladies of position and fashion only? The public seats of Washington belong to those who come in time to occupy them, let this be understood, and we shall have no more growling championship of lazy or indifferent "white ladies of position and fashion" or implied tolerance of slightly bronzed ladies, educated and refined, to the exclusion of "unctuous contrabands." What natural rights should a slightly colored lady have that do not belong to an entirely black lady, or even an "unctuous contraband"?

And now, M.C.A. needles are not swords, but they make painful wounds; and this sticking and pricking of colored people whenever opportunity offers, is intensely mean, unendurable, and will be futile; for meet them in public places you will, and have them take *their* seats in the *street cars* of the city of Washington, you must.

As black publications proliferated in the postwar years, more atten-tion was paid to women's activities. Along with such magazines as Our Women and Children *and* Ringwood's Journal, *which was devoted to fashions, most weeklies carried a woman's column. This consisted largely of boiler-plate articles, reprinted from the white press, which bore little relation to the lives of black women. Reflecting southern male sentiments, the* Louisianian *printed pieces about the latest fash-ions; advice, with such titles as "Who Will Make a Wife"; and poems like "A Woman As She Should Be":*

> Submission to her husband's will
> Her study is to please him still.

*A District of Columbia law forbade discrimination in public places.

Elsewhere women's columns included relevant information on homemaking, child care, and woman's rights. Gertrude Bustill Mossell (1855–1947), a cousin of Sarah Douglass's,* edited "Our Woman's Department" for the New York Freeman *and wrote for white newspapers in Philadelphia. She interspersed practical advice with sketches similar to the following, entitled, "A Boy's Estimate of His Mother's Work."*

"My mother gets me up, builds the fire, and gets my breakfast," said a bright youth. "Then she gets my father up, and gets his breakfast and sends him off. Then she gives the other children their breakfast and sends them to school; and then she and the baby have breakfast."

"How old is the baby?" asked the reporter.

"Oh, she is 'most two."

"Are you well paid?"

"I get $2 a week and father gets $2 a day."

"How much does your mother get?"

With a bewildered look the boy said, "Mother, why, she don't work for anybody."

"I thought you said she worked for all of you."

"Oh, yes, for us she does, but there aint no money in it."

When Gertrude Mossell wrote The Work of the Afro-American Woman *in 1894, she commented on the abundance of talent that characterized her generation of black women. Attributing it to emancipation, higher education, and the woman's rights movement, she also credited "the men of the race" who "have been generous, doing all in their power to allow the women to rise with them." Mossell's position was vigorously disputed by Anna J. Cooper in her* Voice From the South.

While our men seem thoroughly abreast of the times on almost every other subject, when they strike the woman question they drop back into sixteenth century logic. They actually do not seem sometimes to have outgrown that old contemporary of chivalry—the idea that women may stand on pedestals or live in doll houses, but they must not furrow their brows with thought or attempt to help men tug at the great questions of the world. I fear the majority of colored men do not yet think it worth while that women aspire to higher education. The three R's, a little music and a good deal of dancing, a first rate dress-

*She was also an aunt to Paul Robeson.

maker and a bottle of magnolia balm, are quite enough generally to render charming any woman possessed of tact and the capacity for worshipping masculinity.

Who was correct? A modern essay* points out that black leaders were ahead of their time in championing woman suffrage. Suffrage, however, did not mean equality. In the councils of the church, which were male dominated, in the press, and in their private lives, so-called representative men often echoed the sentiments of their white contemporaries. Frederick Douglass had supported woman's suffrage from the time of the Seneca Falls convention in 1848. Yet when Dr. Monroe A. Majors asked him to suggest names of women to be included in his book, Noted Negro Women, *Douglass's reply was less than generous.*

Mr. M. A. Major
Dear Sir: Cedar Hill, D.C., August 26, 1892
     We have many estimable women of our variety but not many famous ones. It is not well to claim too much for ourselves before the public. Such extravagance invites contempt rather than approval. I have thus far seen no book of importance written by a negro woman and I know of no one among us who can appropriately be called famous.
     This is in no way a disparagement of the women of our race. We stand too near a former condition to have any famous work in science, art, or literature, expected of us. It is not well to ship the paddle wheels before we have steam to move them. You will therefore pardon me if I do not find it consistent to enlarge the list of famous negro women. Many of the names you have are those of admirable persons, cultivated, refined and ladylike. But it does not follow that they are famous. Let us be true and use language truthfully.
                                   Respectfully yours
                                   Frederick Douglass

Five years later when leading black intellectuals, including Francis J. Grimké, W. E. B. Du Bois, Paul Laurence Dunbar, and Alexander Crummell, organized the prestigious American Negro Academy "for the promotion of Literature, Science, and Art," they voted to limit their membership to men.† When Theophilus W. Steward, husband

---

*"Black Male Perspectives on the Nineteenth-Century Woman" by Terborg-Penn in *The Afro-American Woman,* edited by Harley and Terborg-Penn.
†An exception was later made for Anna J. Cooper.

of a successful doctor, was polled, he wrote, "I am decidedly opposed to the admission of women to membership. Literary matters and social matters do not mix."

Despite the lukewarm support they received from men, the daughters of slaves, by the last quarter of the nineteenth century, were becoming businesswomen, elocutionists, lecturers, actresses, and singers. Maggie Lena Walker (1867–1934) was a banker and insurance executive; Sarah Breedlove Walker (1867–1919) invented the Walker Method for hair straightening and became a millionaire. A chapter in American musical history could be written about the Hyers's sisters of California; Marie Selika Williams; Flora Batson Bergen, the "colored Jenny Lind"; and Matilda Sissieretta Jones, "the black Patti." Well-trained concert singers with rich contralto or soprano voices, they took the concert stage by storm. Singing for white audiences in Boston's Music Hall, Steinway Hall in New York, and leading auditoriums in the South, they were acclaimed at home and abroad. In her later years, Sissieretta Jones was the star of the Black Patti Troubadours, a troupe that combined operatic music and musical comedy routines. With this venture into popular music, she was a bridge between the classical musicians of her generation, most of them trained in the North and West, and such folk musicians of the South as Gertrude "Ma" Rainey, who introduced the blues in the opening decade of the twentieth century.

Black women had been nurses from their first days on the American continent, but they were barred from the professional nursing schools that opened after the Civil War. The New England Hospital for Women and Children, the first institution to introduce a formal nursing course, was also the first to accept a black student, Mary Eliza Mahoney, who received her diploma in 1879. By 1900 as many as ten black women, including Minnie Hogan who graduated from the University of Pennsylvania's Training School in 1890 and Martha Franklin who studied at the Woman's Hospital in Philadelphia, had completed nursing courses in white schools. Hundreds of others had R.N. degrees from schools affiliated with black Provident Hospital in Chicago, Freedmen's Hospital in Washington, Lincoln Hospital in New York, and Meharry Medical College in Nashville, Tennessee. Although their color kept them from the staffs of white hospitals, from the Army Nurse Corps, and the Red Cross, they found employment in black communities and as private duty nurses.

After Pauline Lyons Williamson (1850–94), the younger sister of Maritcha Lyons, was widowed, she worked as a nurse in the San

Francisco area while an aunt took care of her six-year-old son, Harry.
She discussed her problems in a series of letters to her sister:

My dear May: Oakland, [California,] November 10, 1885
     Your letter was received by me this day. Now my dear don't fash
yourself. I am not coming home at present. I shall never leave the field
until I am thoroughly convinced that I can't get a living here.

     I got along nicely with my case and got $120 for the two weeks,
but I have found that the one great obstacle is I have no certificate
to prove I am a trained nurse and with [out] one I shall have a hard
time to get established. People and doctors both require some proof
of ones proficiency, so I have been trying to get into the only training
school that there is in Frisco. I cannot enter now but I have a promise
[from] the board of directors that in the spring that will admit me on
probation and if the term is pass satisfactorily that they will give me
[permission] to take the two years course. They were willing to take me
this month but the nurse of whom there are eight would not work with
a colored person. As there accommodations are small they could not
at present accommodate me under the existing unpleasantness of the
nurse, but in the spring their new building will be completed. In the
meantime the Ladies interested will try to keep me employed as best
they can until the time comes for me to be admitted. If I once succeed
in getting in I want Harry to return to Plainfield* and stay with his
grandmother untill I come out which will be at the end of two years.
Then my mind will be at rest concerning him and I shall be better able
to attend to the duties required of me.
                                   Yours
                                   Pauline

Dear May: [San Francisco, California,]January 18, 1886
     Last Friday I went with young Dr. Blake to see an operation
performed. There was present two doctors a nurse and myself. It took
two hours to do it. The patient was a lady and her womb was taken
down, pieces of flesh cut off and parts that had been injured during
child birth were sewed up. I tell you I enjoyed it. Everything was
so scientifically done and so neatly. One doctor gave the either and
the other performed the operation. The nurse and myself assisted
the doctor by holding the Vaginia open with the speculum and
washing sponges. We took turns. The either made me deathly sick

*Williamson's parents, Albro and Mary Lyons, lived in Plainfield, New Jersey, where
Albro Lyons was the sexton of a white church.

and I did not get over it for several days.

I wish you would get together all the books that Allie* had on chemistry. I think some of them are in the next to the top drawer in the bureau in my room. Take them to Brooklyn so when Mr. Freeman comes he can bring them to me as they will be of great service. I think a glorious future is before me if I can only get the training I want for without it I can do nothing.

Just think I have been away seven months. I wonder when where and under what circumstances we will meet again. I think that Harry will enjoy the St. Nicholas.† I want to buy a dictionary. Which is the best one to get? Well now I really will not write another word. Yours with love.

Paul.

When the time came to enter nursing school, Williamson lacked the fare to send Harry back East and her aunt and uncle were unwilling to help.

Dear May: San Francisco, [California,] Jan 31, 1886

I had a message from Doctor Brown saying that upon her return, March 1st, she would make room for me to enter the hospital. It is impossible to pay Harry's board and clothe us both off of ten dollars a month which is all I would get in the Hospital the first year. Now what had I better do? I will suggest several plans to you for your opinion. The lowest board I can get for the boy is $8.00 per month for 1 year. Now if I get $10.00 in the hospital it only leaves two for clothes and other expenses per month. 2nd had I better throw up the whole thing and try to get us both back to New York, if so, what shall I do there. 3rd give up going into the hospital go to service pay board for the child save what I can and in the course of a year or two try to open a little store. I could earn $20.00 or 25.00 at service.

I will leave the place where I am first of March. I would not stay here longer, as I am not willing to do so much work as they want one person to do. I take care of four rooms & bathroom get three meals a day, and take the entire care of the lady who is paralyzed. I have to do everything for her, give her the galvanic battery every day wash and dress her and fire to make and it is very hard for she is a large woman and it strains me much to lift her. From a little after six in the morning

*Albro Lyons, Jr., a younger brother.
†Founded in 1873, *St. Nicholas* magazine delighted generations of children. Contributors included Mark Twain, Louisa M. Alcott, Jack London, and such illustrators as Howard Pyle and Frederic Remington.

until nine at night I am on the gō, and they are very close on the feed. As soon as Dr. Brown returns I will see her and hear what she has to say. Now write me a good long letter so I may have your ideas to help me out. How is everybody at home, do tell me all about them. How does your school get along.

With love

Paul

When Harry became seriously ill, Pauline Williamson was forced to give up her dream of nursing school. Returning to the East, she remarried and had a second son. After her death in 1894, Maritcha Lyons helped bring up both boys.

The most impressive achievements of the postwar generation were in medicine. Only fifteen years after Elizabeth Blackwell became the first woman medical graduate, black Rebecca Lee received an M.D. from New England Medical College and went to Virginia to practice. She was followed by Rebecca J. Cole (1846–1922), who graduated from Woman's Medical College of Pennsylvania in 1867, and by Susan Maria Smith (1847–1918), who completed her studies at New York Medical College for Women in 1870. After graduation, Dr. Cole, a Philadelphian, worked with Elizabeth and Emily Blackwell at the New York Infirmary for Women and Children. One of the first "sanitary visitors",* she paid house calls in slum neighborhoods, and taught mothers the basics of hygiene and child care. Returning to Philadelphia, she was cofounder of the Woman's Directory, which gave medical and legal aid to women. In her later years she became superintendent of the Home for Destitute Colored Women and Children in Washington.

In her role as a representative woman, Cole was asked by the all-white Ladies' Centennial Committee of Philadelphia to form a Colored Ladies Committee to support the Centennial. When she and her friends learned that their work was to be limited to the black community, Cole wrote to the newspapers that they "resented being placed in a proscribed light." The separate Colored Ladies Committee dissolved and its members decided "to work in common with American women, not as 'colored Centennial women.' " After some conciliatory gestures were made, Cole and a majority of her committee acquitted the white women of "dishonorable intentions." A substantial minority of the Colored Committee, however, repudiated Cole, accusing her of being "a party to the proposed insult, which consisted in

*The Blackwells' Tenement House Service, begun in 1866, was the earliest practical program of medical social service in the United States.

discriminating against us by reason of our color."

Despite this dispute, Cole remained a spokeswoman for black Philadelphians. Two decades later when twenty-eight-year-old W. E. B. Du Bois told a women's meeting about his new research project, the study that would become The Philadelphia Negro, *she reported on his talk in the* Woman's Era, *a Boston monthly.* Du Bois had said that blacks died of consumption in disproportionate numbers, in part because of their ignorance of hygiene. Cole, with three decades of experience in social medicine, took issue with the young scholar. Pointing out the possibility of statistical errors, she also blamed slum landlords rather than slum dwellers for the high mortality figures.*

On the point of deaths from consumption, I would say this: hosts of the poor are attended by young, inexperienced white physicians. They have inherited the traditions of their elders, and let a black patient cough, they immediately have visions of tubercles, let him die, and he writes "Tuberculosis," and heaves a great sigh of relief that one more source of contagion is removed.

And who makes up the police records? To what class do most of the men in this department belong but to Irish democracy. You see it is the question of disproportion that I am answering. There can be no doubt that the number is large and hence we are glad that a man whose sympathies are with us is seeking to gain information which will answer these two important questions: 1. Are colored people largely forced to live in unsanitary districts, and are they more ignorant and careless about the laws of health, or are they suffering the fate of all exotics?

We must attack the system of overcrowding in the poor districts by urging our men to contend for laws regulating the number in one dwelling—"Cubic Air Space Laws," we can call them—that people may not be crowded together like cattle while soul-less landlords collect fifty per cent in their investments. These are the things that we can do to attack vice disease and crime in their strongholds, for they have no complexion and they always yield to such treatment.

Dr. Susan Smith was valedictorian of her class at New York Medical College and the only woman on the staff of Long Island College Hospital when she did postgraduate work there. Probably the most successful of the pioneer doctors, she had offices in Brooklyn and Manhattan and served on the staffs of the New York Hospital for Women, the Brooklyn Women's Homeopathic Hospital, and the

---

*Started in 1894 by the Woman's Era Club of Boston, the *Woman's Era* lent support to the burgeoning women's club movement. Edited by Josephine Ruffin, its contributors included "representative colored women" from all over the country.

Dr. Susan Smith McKinney Steward. *(Moorland-Spingarn Research Center, Howard University)*

Brooklyn Home for Aged Colored People. Married to the Reverend William McKinney and the mother of two children, she was also church organist and choir master and a founder of the Woman's Loyal Union, black New York's leading women's club, and of the Equal Suffrage League of Brooklyn. Described as small and peppery, she once said of women doctors:

Fortunate are the men who marry these women,* from an economic standpoint at least. They are blessed in a threefold measure, in

*Perhaps women doctors' high incomes accounted for the fact that so many of them married not once but twice. In addition to Dr. Smith McKinney Steward, the group included Dr. Caroline Still Wiley Anderson, Dr. Halle Tanner Dillon Johnson, and Dr. Verina Harris Morton Jones.

that they take unto themselves a wife, a trained nurse, and a doctor. Unfortunate, however, is the woman physician who finds herself unevenly yoked; for such a companion will prove to be a millstone hanged around her neck. But the medically educated women are general good diagnosticians in this direction also.

Widowed when she was forty-eight, McKinney married U.S. Army Chaplain Theophilus G. Steward of the Twenty-fourth Infantry. She practiced medicine at army posts in Montana and Nebraska and, after Steward's retirement, became resident physician at Wilberforce University in Ohio. One of the few women physicians remembered today, her name has been given to the Susan Smith McKinney Junior High School in Brooklyn and to the Susan Smith McKinney Steward Medical Society, founded by black women doctors in 1975.

Most of the early doctors came from "representative" families. Susan McKinney Steward's father was a prosperous Brooklyn pork merchant. Caroline Still Wiley Anderson (1848–1919) was the daughter of William and Letitia Still and a graduate of the Institute for

Dr. Caroline Still Anderson in 1868. *(Oberlin College Archives)*

Colored Youth and Oberlin before she went to the Woman's Medical College of Pennsylvania. Dr. Halle Tanner Dillon Johnson, also a graduate of Woman's Medical College, was the daughter of a bishop of the AME Church. Dr. Consuelo Clark Stewart's father was Peter Clark, a school principal and political activist in Cincinnati. Dr. Sarah Boyd Jones, a graduate of Howard University Medical School, was the daughter of George W. Boyd, the wealthiest black man in Richmond, Virginia.

Another Woman's Medical College graduate, Dr. Matilda Arabella Evans, was born in Aiken County, South Carolina, in the 1870s and studied at Schofield Normal and Industrial School* in Aiken and at Oberlin. Evans opened a practice in Columbia, South Carolina, where there was no hospital for blacks. She took the sick into her own home until she was able to rent a building with room for thirty patients.

Dr. Matilda A. Evans, Class of 1897, Woman's Medical College of Pennsylvania. *(Medical College of Pennsylvania)*

After the railroads serving the city brought their injured employees to her and white doctors referred their black patients, she was able to establish a full-scale hospital and nurses' training school. In practice for almost a decade, she asked a Philadelphia philanthropist to help another young woman to attend medical school because "I need her greatly in my work."

Mr. Alfred Jones
Philadelphia, Pa.

Dear Sir: Columbia, South Carolina, March 13, 1907

You may remember me as being the colored student to whom you gave a scholarship to The Woman's Medical College of Penn. I graduated in the class of 1897 and came South. I have done well and have a very large practice among all classes of people.

It seemed when I came to Columbia that the harvest was ready and waiting for me. The obstacles I did not consider very much and I have had unlimited success. I was the first woman physician to hang out a

---

*The Schofield Normal and Industrial School of Aiken was founded in 1868 by Martha Schofield, a Pennsylvania Quaker who taught in the Sea Islands in the first years after the war. Her pupil, Matilda Evans, wrote an appreciative biography of her, *Martha Schofield, Pioneer Negro Educator,* which was published in 1916.

shingle in this state. Since I have returned to my native state, others have gone to our beloved College to take degrees. The last case is that of a colored woman, a friend of mine, named Melissa Thompson,* in whose behalf I am about to write you.

I have known this young woman for nine years and she has been in my nurse-training department and has helped in the dispensary at the hospital. She would be of great service, if she could get a few years in medicine and surgery. She will not be able to continue her course without some aid being given. Her sisters, who are teachers, are sending her their earnings to help her pursue her studies. I would be greatly pleased, if you can do something for her. I am sure that she will be of great service to the race and to suffering humanity. I need her greatly in my work. The poor people of her race need her.

Thanking you kindly for what you did for me and hoping that you will consider her case, I remain, yours truly,

Matilda A. Evans, M.D.

Unlike other members of the pioneer group, Dr. Georgia E. L. Patton (1864–1900) and Dr. Eliza Anna Grier were ex-slaves.† After the death of her widowed mother, Georgia Patton's sisters and brother helped her to attend Fisk University and Meharry Medical College. Patton spent two years as a doctor in Liberia and then returned to Tennessee. Establishing a lucrative practice in Memphis, she married

Dr. Georgia E. L. Patton Washington. *(Meharry Medical Library)*

*Melissa Thompson graduated from Woman's Medical College of Pennsylvania in 1910.
†Although Georgia Patton has often been referred to as the first woman graduate of Meharry Medical College, Osceola Queen preceded her by three years and Annie Gregg was in her class. Nothing more is known about these women, but they, too, may have been ex-slaves.

David Washington. Grateful to the missionary teachers who had edu-
cated her she responded generously to alumni appeals, although ir-
ritated by the way she was addressed:

Dear Brother Mason: Memphis, Tennessee, May 24, 1900
    Some weeks ago I sent you a letter with a little money inclosed.
In reply you said, "Dear Brother". I am not a brother. Do you not
remember Georgia Patton? Well, it is she, with a little more attached.
I send ten dollars more, and hope to be able to keep sending until I
have given $100, asked by you of the alumni of the schools; and even
more if possible.
                    Yours, with best wishes for the Society,
                    G.E.L. Patton Washington
P.S.—Say "Sister" next time.

Eliza Anna Grier, a Georgian described by a white journalist as "a
coal-black negress," also worked her way through Fisk. In her letter she
explained why she wanted to be a doctor.

Dr. Eliza Anna Grier, Class of 1897, Woman's Medical College. *(Medical
College of Pennsylvania)*

To The Proprietor of The Woman's Med. College,
Philadelphia, Pa.   Fisk University, Nashville, Tennessee,
Dear Friend: December 6, 1890
    It is with some hesitation I attempt to write you. I am a Negro
woman—a fair representative of my race. I have been attending this
school for seven years and God willing I hope to complete the Advanced Normal Course of Study next June. I desire to be of the most
possible benefit to my race and to my fellow creatures. I think I can

accomplish more by having a Medical Education. Few of our colored girls have dared to enter the Medical Science I presume for several reasons. Viz: on account of timidity—on account of means whereby to pursue such a course. I have no money and no source from which to get it only as I work for every dollar. I desire a thorough Med. education and I desire to enter the school to which I write now or some other good school. What I want to know from you is this. How much does it take to put one through a year in your school. Is there any possible chance to do any work that would not interfere with one's studies. Do you know of any possible way that might be provided for an emancipated slave to receive any help into so lofty a profession. If you cannot do otherwise than give me a chance—a fair chance—I will begin with that.

Please let me hear from you at once or as soon as you have had time to think.

I am yours truly
Miss Eliza A. Grier

After practicing in Atlanta, Grier opened an office in Greenville, South Carolina. Falling ill and needing financial help, she turned not to southern whites or blacks, but to Susan B. Anthony, the venerable head of the woman's suffrage movement.

Dear Miss Anthony: Greenville, South Carolina, March 7, 1901

I write to you because I believe you will listen to my appeal & in some way help me. I am a young Negro woman engaged in the practice of medicine in this city. I have made a pretty good practice, but mostly among the very poor & in neglected districts. I have been quite ill for six weeks with La Grippe. I have not been able to make a single dollar. I cannot retain my place of business unless some one will help me. Rent is $12.00 per month & this place is the only one that can be had down town now. There are a great many forces operating against the success of the Negro in business. These, however, I hope someday will be overcome. The only thing that impedes my progress is that I am illy prepared in a financial way to contend when hardships & want come on.

I graduated from the Woman's Coll. of Penn. Phila. Class '97. Please help me in this my time of severe trial. I am yours sincerely,

Eliza Anna Grier M.D.

Anthony who at eighty-one years of age was living on a small annuity given her by younger suffragists, forwarded Grier's letter to the Woman's Medical College, writing, "My sympathies are very strong

*for all these women, but my purse is not equal to helping them
financially. Cannot you suggest some way out of her troubles?"*

Like the schoolmarms of a generation earlier, most of the black
doctors went to the South, often becoming the first women, black or
white, licensed to practice in their respective states. Dr. Verina Morton Jones was the first woman doctor in Mississippi; Dr. Evans in
South Carolina; Dr. Sarah Boyd Jones in Virginia; and Dr. Halle
Tanner Dillon in Alabama. Dr. Sarah McCurdy Fitzbutler hung out
her shingle in Kentucky, and Dr. Alice Woodby McKane and her
husband established a hospital and nurses' training school in Savannah,
Georgia. All had to pass stiff qualifying examinations, often administered by hostile examiners. When Dr. Halle T. Dillon, resident physician at Tuskegee Institute, went to the state capital for the ten-day
examination, Booker T. Washington accompanied her. She described
the ordeal to the dean of Woman's Medical College.

Dr. Halle Tanner Dillon Johnson and some of her classmates, Woman's
Medical College. *(Medical College of Pennsylvania)*

Clara Marshall M.D.

Dear Doctor: Tuskegee, Alabama, October 3, 1891

Yours of Sept. 23 at hand. I have been quite ill for the past ten days with sort of general break, nervous prostration,* but am improving slowly.

I left Philada as you know on the 1st Aug. arriving in Tuskegee Aug 3rd staid there until Aug 8th when I went up to Montgomery and boarded at quiet place studying for the examination until Aug 17th and on that day about half past eight o'clock in company with Mr. Washington went to the Capitol, which is a beautiful white building situated on Dexter Ave. Mr. Washington introduced me as Dr. Dillon who came to take the State Examination. The Supervisor said very politely "any information I give &c". I said that is alright I am ready to begin *immediately* in chemistry. I also showed him my diploma & letters of introduction. The diploma especially excited comment from the Supervisor & another young doctor who was taking the examination. They both said well I have [never] seen a woman doctor before or a diploma from a Woman's Medical College. They treated [me] quite cordially and gave me a very pleasant desk by the window & I began at once on Chemistry.

There were only five questions but they involved one or two different points. The applicant is not allowed to tell the questions, but is given one question at the time and must answer that before he leaves the room. Taking the examination as a whole it is rather hard because there were so many questions, or rather a few questions which were technical in character. One question in Hygiene occurs to me now & it certainly was to my mind incomprehensible, "Discuss the *hygiene* of the reproductive organs of the female."

The School work is quite congenial to me and I hope to be able to do some good. Tuskegee is comparatively a healthy place and the students so far have not been sick to any extent. It is the first time that there has been a woman physician in Tuskegee.

I can but say that I am indeed thankful I was successful for it was quite a risk to run. With many thanks for kind wishes of success, I remain very Respectfully

Halle T. Dillon

The women physicians struggled against heavy odds. Barred because of race and gender from all medical schools in the South and

---

*Dr. Dillon's "nervous prostration" may well have been caused by the examination. Although she passed easily, Tuskegee's lady principal reported that she lacked self-confidence.

many northern schools—"The College of Medicine never ma-
triculated a 'coon' and never will as long as I am Dean," a Kentucky
administrator wrote—they also had difficulty finding hospitals that
would accept them as interns and male colleagues who would consult
with them. There were psychological barriers, too. In a biography of
her friend Dr. Susan McKinney Steward, Maritcha Lyons explained
that for Steward and her contemporaries "the bugbear was the fear
that woman would unsex herself. Only level headed, self reliant, determined women ventured upon a course of action certain to elicit un-
friendly criticism." Nevertheless, they persevered, founding clinics and
hospitals, training nurses, and teaching elementary health rules to their
patients. A quarter century after the end of slavery, there were 115
black women physicians in the United States; a decade later, the
number had grown to 160.

Anna J. Cooper in 1884. *(Oberlin College Archives)*

What sustained these representative women? To be a member of
the first postemancipation generation, Anna J. Cooper wrote in 1892,
was "to have a heritage unique in the ages."

Everything is new and strange and inspiring. There is a quickening
of the pulse, and a glowing of its self-consciousness. Aha, I can rival
that! I can aspire to that! I can honor my name and vindicate my race!
Something like this is the enthusiasm which stirs the genius of young
Africa in America and the memory of past oppression and the fact of
present attempted repression only serve to gather momentum for its
irrepressible powers.

Part VI

Epilogue:
Four Women

IN MOST OF U.S. history the black woman has been portrayed as mammy or matriarch, sex object or mindless drudge. The women who have spoken in these pages offer a refutation of such stereotypes. Loving, hostile, courageous, fearful, hopeful, dispirited—they have shown themselves to be "intensely human," as a Civil War general said of his black troops. Nowhere is the richness of their humanity better exemplified than in four diaries written by young women during the two decades after emancipation.

Diary keeping was a common practice in the nineteenth century. In their journals women noted tasks done, books read, and visitors seen; they also used their daily record to express their emotions and to take stock of their accomplishments. Many diaries kept by white women at that time have been published in the last decade. Present-day readers can learn of the inner lives of pioneer women in the West, of plantation ladies of the South, and of New England's female elite.

The black women's record is sparser. Only Charlotte Forten's journal, written before and during the Civil War, has appeared in book form. The diaries excerpted in the following pages thus offer a unique introduction to the black women of the first free generation.

Two of the diarists were born in slavery, two of free parents. All were in their early twenties when they wrote of their daily activities, their hopes, and their dreams. Three of the women were bent on achievement (although only one made a lasting mark); the fourth reflected more conventional aspirations, for a home, family, and financial security. Speaking in diverse voices, they have left for us an authentic perception of what it meant, in their time, to be a woman—and black.

Frances Anne Rollin was born free in Charleston, South Carolina, where her parents found refuge after a revolution in the Dominican Republic. She spent the war years in Philadelphia studying at the Institute for Colored Youth. Returning to Charleston in 1865, she taught at an AMA-supported school. When she was refused first-class *accommodations on the steamer* Pilot Boy *during a summer trip to Beaufort, South Carolina, she lodged a complaint with the Freedmen's Bureau, becoming the victor in an early civil rights case.* During the proceedings, she met Major Martin R. Delany, the highest-ranking black man in the Bureau. When she told him of her dream of a literary career, he proposed that she write his biography and promised her financial support while she completed the book. Rollin went to Boston in the fall of 1867 with a satchel filled with Delany's speeches, writings, and reminiscences. Boarding with the Bailey family† on Blossom Street, at the edge of the black neighborhood, she set to work.*

Delany, with a wife and numerous children to support on his Bureau salary, failed to keep his promise of monetary help and Rollin had to eke out a living with sewing and clerical work. Although she was troubled by lack of money and by concern for her parents who had lost their property during the war, her diary also reflected the excitement of life in a cosmopolitan city where there was still considerable goodwill toward a personable young black woman. The antislavery movement was divided between those who, like William Lloyd Garrison, believed that the struggle had been won, and Wendell Phillips and his followers who continued to fight for the rights of the freedpeople. Both sets of reformers took Frances Rollin to their hearts, as they had done a decade earlier with Charlotte Forten.

The black community was supportive as well. The war and emancipation had opened opportunities for a limited number of blacks. William C. Nell was working in the post office, one of the first to hold a federal job. Lewis Hayden who, with his wife, Harriet, had operated a busy Underground Railroad station in their home on Phillips Street, was a state employee, messenger to the Massachusetts secretary of state; in 1873, he was elected to the legislature. Remarried and living in Cambridgeport, William Wells Brown worked as a doctor and continued to write and lecture. Richard Greener, one of Rollin's many gentlemen callers, was a Harvard sophomore who became the first black man to graduate from the university two years later. Her friends, the Howards, were also taking advantage of expanded educational opportunities. Imogene Howard was in her last year at Girls' High and Normal School, the first black to complete her studies there. Subsequently, she became principal of a New York school while her sister, Adeline, headed a school in Washington.

---

*The captain of the *Pilot Boy* was fined $250 and ordered not to discriminate.
†Emily Bailey was a hairdresser, and John Bailey a "teacher of sparring."

Frances Rollin's diary, a small leatherbound book, now belongs to her great granddaughter. Rollin was twenty years old when she made her first entry.

January 1, 1868: A rainy gloomy day. I sent a letter to mother which I wrote last night, the latest hour nearly of the old year. The year reaches its birth today with all of its hopes and sorrows. Uncertainty and doubt are in its wake. To me and mine may God enable us to murmur not, but patiently bear, and work and labor.

January 2: Clearing up today somewhat. In evening went to the [Anti-Slavery] Fair at Horticultural Hall. Imogene Howard and I met. We had been to see "John Brown" at Child's Gallery. I do not like the painter's license. He is blessing instead of kissing the Negro child. "The bold blue eyes grew tender and the stern harsh face grew mild, as he stooped around the jeering ranks to kiss the Negro child"— history notes the act.*

January 3: Writing as hard as ever. I know not with what success I shall meet, but I feel there is a strength in the endeavor which will be of service to me hereafter. Mr. Richard Greener has gone over some of it with me, but he is cynical and apt to discourage instead of acting otherwise. He lives in a grand intellectual sphere and is accustomed to only perfection.

January 7: I spent an impatient day waiting for evening. I sat and listened to Dickens. He acted as only Dickens can. "Mr. Peggoty" was grand. It was so naturally told that we all saw him.†

January 20: Writing as usual. In the afternoon went to Mr. [Wendell] Phillips. How his grand prophet face lighted up when I inadvertently said I had succeeded. And how generously he offered to hear me read my ms. though it would take up his time. He gave me an invitation for the Anti-Slavery Festival and gave me Emerson to read. How it cheers me to spend an hour with such a masterpiece of humanity, it reconciles me to Americans.

January 22: Writing in the morning. In the afternoon dressed for the Anti-Slavery Festival. Mr. Phillips gave a generous clasp of the hand. The Redpaths were there.‡ I had a miscegenetic conversation with

---

*The story that John Brown kissed a black child while on his way to the gallows was invented by a *New York Tribune* reporter. It became "history" when John Greenleaf Whittier incorporated it into his poem, "Brown of Osawatomie," which Rollin quotes almost correctly here.

†Charles Dickens toured the United States in 1867–68, reading from his books. Mr. Peggotty was a character in *David Copperfield.*

‡Rollin knew James Redpath from Charleston where Redpath had headed a Bureau of Education at the war's end.

Mr. Pierce editor of the Watchman and Reflector.* Mr. Pierce gave me a history of a colored young lady and a young white gentleman who had loved and the prejudices kept from marrying. They feared ostracism. America is not the world.

January 23: Cloudy day. I went with Mrs. Gray to the [Anti-Slavery] meeting. Col. Higginson spoke as did Mr. Frothingham. I heard Stephen C. Foster the great hearted anti-Churchman of the Society. I agree with his church views. A. B. Alcott the metaphysical scholar. How spiritual his actual presence. Later Mr. Phillips spoke with his usual effect.†

January 28: Today a letter from Major [Delany]. Immediately answered and gave him an account of my visit to the great Wendell.

January 30: Writing in the morning. In afternoon Mr. Greener invited us to go to hear Ralph Waldo Emerson. We went and I considered it a rare intellectual treat. It was at Cambridge at the College Hall. Subject: "The Immortality of the Soul." He argued with great force that there is no death and showed that as Nature renews her form so does man.

February 5: Received a note from Mr. Nell to meet Mr. Garrison at the Freedmens Rooms. Mr. Garrison's voice is as familiar to my ears as possible, and yet I can't account for it. He was speaking of Charleston and of Sam Dickerson. His manners are as genial as his looks.‡

February 12: Mr. Wm. Lloyd Garrison spent the morning with me. I think him a grand noble soul. I felt a reverence while in the presence of this great man who came to the rescue of a dazed and helpless people. But is he an humanitarian? How can his practiced pen and ready heart remain uninterested while the same wrongs exist under another form.

February 18: Two letters from home. The first crushed me to earth with its sad contents of father's failure and his pecuniary losses. How hard that the accumulations of years should be swept away! "Ruin" is written in every homestead of South Carolina.

February 22: Washington Birthday. I am no enthusiast over Patriotic Celebrations as I am counted out of the body Politic.

*Perhaps Edward L. Pierce, a vice-president of the Freedmen's Union Commission. However, Pierce was not the editor of the *Watchman and Reflector*, a Baptist weekly.
†Mrs. Gray may have been Louisa Nell Gray, William Nell's sister. Colonel Thomas Wentworth Higginson, the Reverend Octavius B. Frothingham, Stephen S. (not C.) Foster, and Amos Bronson Alcott were familiar figures at antislavery gatherings.
‡When William Lloyd Garrison went to Charleston to witness the raising of the U.S. flag at Fort Sumter, Samuel Dickerson and his daughters presented him with a wreath of flowers on behalf of the freedpeople.

February 23: I went today to Rev. Bartol's church.* The Sexton was giving me a pew in the Gallery and I declined and left. We are compelled to be sensitive and tenacious of our rights or else we will be sunken by this Americanese. I went to the [Church of the] Advent, but was too much engrossed with the Bartol incident to enjoy my religious duties.

February 24: Home all day hard at work finishing my writing. In afternoon received a letter and check for $50. I am afraid that I cannot afford to pursue the course marked out. To write one must be above want, I should think.

February 27: Wrote all morning. In the evening went with Mr. Bailey to *Dickens.* There was the genial and grand face of Longfellow, the kingly publisher Fields,† in the same line with us, brilliant authors and handsome women.

March 1: Worked in my book. In afternoon I read Macaulay. Later Ludie Mathew came and there was a setting for spiritual[ist] purposes. The table was clearly lifted and twisted about and the spirit answered to C.L. I thought it might be Grandma. I am no sceptic. "I thank God" as Goethe said that I do not doubt the possibility of anything.

March 3: Book completed. Mr. Nell came in and I read my Finish to him. It has been no easy task writing under so many difficulties and uncertain of my prospects while it is in the hands of the publishers. I am not feeling very well about my scant pay while writing! I have not been dealt with according to the letter of the contract.

March 4: This morning I took the Ms. Mr. Fields told me he could present Mr. Garrison's letter and would let me know. I tremble for my success. I suppose it is natural for a novice to feel so. Home and sewed for Miss Emily. I wrote to Major. I feel so much better now that I am through with the Ms. Yet I know that I can better it.

March 6: I went to see Rev. Henry Ware about the school. I did not meet him, saw Miss Lottie Forten at the Freedmens Rooms.‡

March 7: Mr. Fields told me the firm refused to entertain the proposition of receiving my book. I was scarcely disappointed.

March 9: Beautiful day went out to Roxbury to Mr. Garrison. His home is built on a high rocky hill a wild romantic scenery. His parlor

---

*Cyrus A. Bartol's West Church was considered one of Boston's more liberal churches.
†James T. Fields was junior partner in the publishing firm of Ticknor and Fields and editor of the *Atlantic Monthly.*
‡With the book completed and no money from Delany, Rollin applied for a teaching job in the South. Charlotte Forten was then clerk of the Teachers Committee of the New England Branch of the Freedmen's Union Commission; Henry Ware a supporter of freedmen's education.

is adorned with sculptured busts of himself and the kingly orator Phillips and portraits of [George] Thompson and Phillips and himself.*

March 10: This morning at Lee and Shepard about the book.† After dinner went to Cambridge to Wm. Wells Brown's. They always treat me so hospitably that I can't help liking them. He seems honest in his kindly interest in me.

March 11: Went to the Freedmens Rooms to see Mr. Ware.‡ Lottie Forten conversed very freely with me and show'd me a letter of Mrs. Childs [Lydia Maria Child] to her concerning her criticism of "Waiting for the Verdict". Says Mrs. Childs: "Every quadroon and mulatto bears upon his face the refutation of the intuitive shrinking of the white race from the black."

March 16: Took my book to Mr. Lee's today and was very kindly received. I pray for success.

March 17: I went to the Studio Building to meet the ladies of the Society by whom I would be employed. I found them young and rather hesitating in their manners. I liked them very much as they meant to be kind.§ Today being St. Pat's day the Irishman was in his glory and made his parade an all day nuisance.

March 25: Saw Mr. Phillips. We conversed a long while about my prospects in the literary world and he gave me a copy of his Speeches which is as precious to me as the apple of my eye.

March 29: Went to Tremont Temple and heard a splendid sermon. Dined and went to Grimes Church.**

April 3: Went to church, after to Mrs. Hayden's. Read to Mr. H. Garrison's letter against Mr. Phillips.†† I am sorry for it. In afternoon I read and evening went to the *Dancing School* and *mirabile dictu* I actually danced even waltzed with Mr. Rob Howard! He escorted me home and played the gallant to perfection. If I intended waltzing through life, I might fancy him for a partner.

*Roxbury, now the center of black Boston, was rural when the Garrisons moved there in 1864.

†William Lee and Charles Shepard were book publishers with offices on Washington Street.

‡Probably the Reverend John F. Ware, overseer of freedpeople's schools in Baltimore, who had come to Boston for the annual meeting of the Freedmen's Union Commission.

§The offices of the Freedmen's Union Commission were in the Studio Building. The ladies of the John A. Andrew Society had agreed to "adopt" Frances Rollin, that is, pay her salary as a teacher in Maryland.

**The Reverend Leonard A. Grimes, pastor of a black Baptist Church. Like many middle-class blacks, Rollin usually attended services at white churches.

††In a letter to the *National Anti-Slavery Standard,* Garrison had responded to Phillips's criticism of him by accusing Phillips of "great self inflation" and "a pitiable hallucination of mind."

April 4: I received a letter today from Miss Lyons of Providence R.I. and one for the Association. Miss Forten informed me that the Association will not send *any teacher* as I cannot go.* Went to Haydens. They are both very kindly to me. Received a very disheartening letter from home. Ma has the dropsy. God have mercy on me.

April 5: (Palm Sunday) Feeling miserable over that triflingly written letter from home. Read all day. No visitors and I am glad of it.

April 7: Snowing furiously. I finished the History of the Girondists. I am charmed with it. I hate, respect, pity, regret Robespierre. He has more of weakness than cruelty in his nature.

April 10: Snowing furiously making this the forty second snow storm this season. Mrs. Simons very kindly sent me some rice and cow peas today. I ate though it was Good Friday.

April 13: In evening went with Addie [Howard] to Cambridge to the Leap Year Party. Mr. Greener, Mr. Rob Howard, Mr. Nell and lots of my gentlemen friends. We escorted the gentlemen to tables, helped them and played several games, sang and had a good time generally. Then returned home about two oclock next morning.

April 16: Went to Mr. Redpath's. He suggested to write a story on misceg. I will finish what I have. Mr. Lee showed me Mrs. Keckley's book. I finished reading it before five o'clock. It is well written but not by Mrs. K that's clear.†

April 30: Home all morning. In afternoon to State House was introduced to Sec. of State Mr. Oliver Warner. We conversed very freely on public affairs.‡

May 6: Sewed all morning. In afternoon went to State House. Saw Mr. Warner. Went to Wiley's with Mr. Hayden had oysters and coffee. To Lee and Shepard. Got a ticket for Mrs. Frances Kemble's Reading on Tuesday night. I am resolved to take some step forward to promote my success in Literature.

May 9: At home sewing then to the State House and wrote until four oclock. Went to Addie Howard's. Addie received today two photographs of Edmonia Lewis from Rome taken in her Studio dress. Home and sewed like a trojan until 12 oclock.

---

*After Lee and Shepard accepted her manuscript, Rollin decided against the teaching job but proposed that Therese Lyons of Providence go in her place.
†Elizabeth Keckley's *Behind the Scenes* had just been published. She came to Boston (see June 25 entry) and gave a reading to publicize the book. Her collaborator, James Redpath, who ran a lecture agency probably arranged her public appearance.
‡Lewis Hayden introduced Rollin to his boss, so that she could get clerical work. When she spoke of "writing" at the State House in later entries, she meant that she was copying legislative documents and other official papers.

May 10: Mr. Lennox came for me to go to Mr. Wells Brown's lecture. Generally it was a good instruction.* Mr. Phillips introductory was graceful and grandly eloquent as usual.

May 16: At the State House Library writing until one. Got Randolph of Roanoke from there. Read the Biography of Josiah Quincy par Edmond. Sewed on Mrs. Hare's dress. Read for Mr. Hayden at his house. The vote on Andrew Johnson impeachment taken. Ross Trumbull and Fessenden of the Rep. side voted for acquittal. Shame!

May 25: Went to Lee & Shepard, saw a sample sheet. Went to the State House and read all morning in the Library. Whittier's Prose writings and a portion of de Quincy's letters etc.

May 26: At the State House today writing. In eve to Mr. Phillips who gave me a note to admit me into the Tremont Temple to the Freedmens Meeting.

May 29: This morning went to the meeting of the Free Religion Association. Heard Messrs. O. B. Frothingham, John Weiss, Rev. Olympia Brown, Robt. Collier and [James] Freeman Clark.† R. Greener spent evening.

June 4: Nothing of importance only I am kept in a fever about the book. Not a line from Major Delany. Letters from William E. J. [Whipper], Lottie.

June 24: Mr. Baker brought me some proof sheets. We had a long conversation about literati, Oliver Optic, Julia Ward Howe, Speaker Phelps who has out a life of Grant, etc.‡

June 25: At Lee & Shepard today. Mr. Baker brought me tickets for Mrs. Keckley's reading. It was poor to say the least. It is too late in the day for her to attempt it especially without a first class teacher.

June 30: Went to the State House this morning. Mr. Warner got me to blot for him while he signed. In afternoon chills and fever.

July 1: Went out to sew today. I thought when I began literature that ended, but find it otherwise.

July 3: At Mrs. Duquesnes sewing. In evening Mathew brought a letter from Major Delany. I sat down and answered it immediately, not a dollar sent to me again. I was provoked.

---

*A handbill described the lecture as Brown's "great Historical lecture on the Origin and Early History of the African Race."

†The speakers at the meeting of the Free Religious Association, founded in 1867, were ministers who had broken away from orthodox churches.

‡Oliver Optic was the pseudonym of William Taylor Adams, author of more than 100 books for children. In 1868 Julia Ward Howe was best known for her "Battle Hymn of the Republic." Charles A. Phelps had just published *Life and Public Services of General Ulysses S. Grant.*

July 7: Mr. Baker brought me the proofs. We had a time about the dedication.* I never did approve of it but Major D. insisted. I suppose we will have a fuss about it anyhow.

July 8: The So.Ca. Legislature convened today. Went to the State house. Went up in the Cupola and viewed Boston and its surroundings. In afternoon went to State House to Mr. Hayden. God Bless his kind heart for all he has done for me. Promenaded on Washington St., met W. Wells Brown. Home and continued reading The Restoration par Lamartine. Feeling very depressed, no money.

July 28: Boston *Vale.* Up very early—my last day in Boston, dear dear Boston. Went to Lee & Shepard. Mr. Lee gave me "Planchette". Also a Yankee in Canada [and] the Memoirs of Mme Recamier. Went to see Addie for the last, Mr. Hayden, and Wells Brown. I left at five for Newport.

Although the diary failed to mention it, Rollin and her publisher decided that the reading public was not yet ready to accept a book by a black woman. When Life and Public Services of Martin R. Delany *was published in the summer of 1868, its author was listed as Frank A. Rollin.† Reprinted in 1883 with some additional material, it remains a useful reference on Martin Delany's life.*

Throughout her Boston stay, Frances Rollin thought about William Whipper. In one diary entry she had written, "I do not know how it will end with us. I think sometimes he might have done more for me when my means ran out and thereby I would have been drawn immediately to him but he acted so selfishly that the memory of it would mar our happiness if we were married." When her book was finally in press, she accepted his offer of a clerkship in Columbia. Six weeks later, they married. The marriage was not a happy one. Growing tired of Whipper's drinking and gambling, she took their three children and went to Washington in 1881. Although she continued to write stories, dreams of a literary career were put aside in favor of work as a government clerk and court stenographer. She saw all her children graduate from Howard University. Winifred Whipper became a teacher, Ionia Whipper a doctor, and Leigh Whipper a distinguished actor.‡

---

*The fuss was probably over the correctness of the Latin of the dedication, —*et niger arma Memnonis.*

†Frank was her family's nickname for her.

‡The first black member of Actors Equity, Leigh Whipper played important roles in "Porgy," "In Abraham's Bosom," "Of Mice and Men," "Lysistrata," and scores of other plays and films.

Mary Virginia Montgomery (1849?–1902?), whose diary is excerpted in the following pages, was a slave for the first fourteen years
of her life. Her parents belonged to Joseph Davis, older brother of
Jefferson Davis and the proprietor of Hurricane and Brierfield plantations on Davis Bend, a fertile peninsula in the Mississippi River some
thirty miles from Vicksburg. Joseph Davis was a paternalistic master,
and Benjamin T. Montgomery a talented slave. A machinist and inven-
tor, he not only managed his owner's enterprises, but also established
a plantation store that brought him money enough to pay Davis for
his wife's labor. Thus Mary Lewis Montgomery (1822–85) was permitted to stay at home with their children. When Mary Virginia was
about five years old, her parents hired a white man to tutor her and
her older brothers, William Thornton and Isaiah. After white neighbors protested, her formal schooling ended, but she continued to read
and study. The even tenor of her life was interrupted by the war when
the family spent two years as refugees in Cincinnati. Returning to
Davis Bend after emancipation, Montgomery leased the plantations
from his former master and established a community of black tenant
farmers. In 1866 the firm of Montgomery & Sons contracted to buy
Hurricane and Brierfield over a ten-year period; they later purchased
Ursino, an adjoining plantation.

During the turbulent years of Reconstruction, Davis Bend was a
black oasis. Benjamin Montgomery was justice of peace, and William
Thornton Montgomery was constable and postmaster. Isaiah managed
the family store while assorted Montgomery and Lewis relatives and
friends farmed, shipping their produce to market by riverboat. Although the community bore some resemblance to Joseph Davis's pre-
war patriarchal estate, there was a place in it for women, as Frances
Ellen Watkins Harper noted when she visited in 1871. Marveling at
the changes that permitted her to be "a welcome guest under the roof
of the President of the Confederacy" she told William Still that "Mr.
Montgomery, the present proprietor of between five and six thousand
acres, has one of the most interesting families that I have ever seen.
Last year his wife took in her hands about 130 acres of land, and with
her force she raised about 107 bales of cotton. She has a number of
orphan children employed, and not only does she supervise their labor,
but she works herself. One daughter, an intelligent young lady, is
postmistress and assistant book-keeper and another daughter attends
at one of the stores."

Mary Lewis Montgomery was at the center of plantation activities,
hostess to visiting dignitaries, loving daughter to aged parents, and

nurse when her first grandchild was born. She was also in charge of the Home Farm, supervising hired hands as well as a crew of orphaned children whom she raised, and working in the fields. She was responsible for the prize-winning cotton that made the Montgomery name known at state and national agricultural fairs.*

The Montgomerys and their daughters lived at Brierfield, in the one-story house with broad verandahs and Doric columns that Jefferson Davis and his wife, Varina, had occupied before the war. Mary Virginia "brushed around" her room, practiced piano, and sewed like any proper southern girl, but six days of each week she also worked in the family store at Hurricane. In an office above the store, she assisted B. L. Hickman, the bookkeeper, to keep records of sales, purchases, and tenants' credit accounts. Although "Brother T" was the U.S. postmaster, it was Mary Virginia who registered letters, canceled stamps, and prepared the mail sack for the steamboat that carried it upriver. After work she visited "Zie," her brother Isaiah, and his young wife, Martha ("Mat"), who lived at Hurricane. "Brother T" lived at Ursino where a branch store was located. Sister Rebecca ("Beck") spent time sewing and preserving and also clerked in the store.

Mary Virginia Montgomery's diary depicts an earnest twenty-three year old woman with an inquiring mind. If she seems both more cheerful and more youthful than Rollin or other contemporaries, it is probably because she was sheltered by a supportive family, had few worries, financial or otherwise, and almost no contact with whites. Unlike most representative women of her day, she was dark skinned ("as black as the ten of spades," Jefferson Davis said). Intellectually, however, she adhered to the mores of the white middle class rather than the folk culture of ex-slaves. Isolated by choice from the people of the quarters, she had few women friends her age and no male friends. Her diary reflects the rhythms of the planting seasons and her own changing goals. In the quiet winter months, she planned and planted a garden, doubtless remembering Jefferson and Varina Davis's splendid antebellum flowers. As spring gave way to summer and her companions were caught up in the excitement of the cotton harvest, she decided to break away from her protected environment and see the world.

February 3, 1872: The sun shines beautifully today. Our garden has been reploughed. I am so proud of the prospect of a flower yard & the

*Montgomery & Sons won prizes for the best bale of cotton at the St. Louis Fair in 1870 and at the Philadelphia Centennial in 1876. The cotton was grown by Mary Lewis Montgomery.

orchard improvement that I feel like one just embracing the threshold of a new life. I find now the study of agriculture most necessary.

February 4: [Sunday] All here to dinner except Mat. We had quite a lively day. Some poor woman in the Quarter lost her baby today. Two children have died in the last 3 days. After the distraction of the visitors, I busied myself in my Phrenological pursuits.*

February 5: Full of animation and spirit. I sang and played [piano] at daylight. After Breakfast I found Von saddled and very tastefully arrayed in red ribbon. The weather being pleasant, I hastened to Hurricane. On returning my horse ran off with me. The saddle turned around and I fell almost senseless. Great excitement prevailed. I was brought home in the buggy. My arm was most injured. I only cried because I had to give up today.

February 6: I cannot raise my arm without aid. Brother T came to see me having just learned of my narrow escape. He advised me to sell Von and by a gentle horse instead. I have partly consented if I can find a good master for him.

February 7: I feel much better. I tried some chrystalizing experiments was much pleased with the result. All the morning I spent studying the rudiments to Mineralogy. Afternoon read Tennyson. I tried to play [piano] but my arm failed me. We sent T. a birthday cake today as a surprise. Rec'd a very aff & grateful note in reply.

February 8: Pa designated the walks of the Garden hurriedly this morning before leaving for V[icks]burg. I was appointed general supervisor in the transplanting business and settling with hands. I only make mention of it because I of course feel proud of having a cognizable judgment. All ambitious persons do. With Mas assistance succeeded in planting fifty Rose cuttings two trees and eight Cape Jasmines. I had Von brought home. I will take care of him and hope some day to have a horse more trusty.

February 12: Up early and went to Hurricane. All hands are working in the orchard. We have Co[tton] Sales yet to finish up.† We engaged Wm Kannigan to finish our Garden Walks. I have been studying Chemistry.

February 14: Ma has all hands out ploughing. We have completed the Co Sales. We brought home some Bulbs to set out. The *Gov. Allen* went up today. She brought some meal and pork from New Orleans.

---

*Popular in the North before the war, phrenology was late reaching the South. Mary Virginia not only subscribed to *Well's Phrenological Journal* but also bought charts and a model head so that she could practice the pseudoscience.

†These were records of cotton grown in 1871.

We retire early tonight with the resolve to rise early to plant bulbs.
February 16: The [Robert E.] Lee came up about noon. Mr. I. D. and
his brother Abe* came today. After getting through in the office I with
Ma visited Grandma Aunt Susan and Bennie. I read Self Education
tonight.

February 17: Beck & I went to Hurricane. A good many persons were
at the store. Sales amounted to 155$. I made the Gin list and paid a
few of the hands. Wm Kannigan finished the Garden.

February 18: [Sunday] Morning very dark and rainy. I feared my
company would not come but presently the sun shone and Mrs. Ma-
ginnis with her little ones came afterwards Mrs. Shadd & Family.
Brother & Mrs. Green† made the appearance just before dinner. We
had just twelve to dinner. After noon we played the Piano. After the
company dispersed I busied myself studying the Ten Commandments.
On the whole I have enjoyed myself very much today.

February 21: I got up very early and played the piano first thing. I made
a few mistakes in my office work yesterday & today received a severe
castigation. I did not feel very well under the penalty. However every
cloud has its sunny side. Ma gave me a new dress tonight.

March 4: Never have I felt so much anxiety and pleasure in one day.
My dear Sister Mattie has presented a darling son. All of us are proud
of Mat & the baby.

March 5: Beck & I went to Hurricane and after admiring our darling
nephew we went to our respective duties. Ma came home & attended
to farm business awhile then returned to H.

March 19: Read a while before breakfast. The trial Balance is yet
uneven. Mr. H. has been hunting the difference in the ledger page by
page. On arriving home tonight I was much pleased to find that Beck
had cut my Gabrielle. It will be so long & fashionable. I read a little
Phrenology & retired early.

March 29: This morning is to be numbered among the most pleasant.
When I reached Hurricane, I spent some time at the house & afterward leisurely perused the papers that came up by the *Lee.* Mrs. Shadd
sent for me to witness the school examination. The school exhibited

*Isaac D. Shadd, Mary Ann Shadd Cary's brother, came South in 1870 and worked as
a bookkeeper for Montgomery & Son until his election to the state legislature. His wife,
Amelia, remained at Davis Bend teaching school. A close friend of Mary Ann Cary's,
Amelia Shadd undoubtedly influenced the young Montgomery women. Abraham
Shadd, I. D.'s younger brother, practiced law in Mississippi.
†Virginia C. Green who had come from St. Louis to teach the freedmen also brought
word of the outside world to Mary Virginia. She worked in the Ursino store and served
as hostess for bachelor Brother T.

a progression that exceeded my every expectation. The Girls recited a good part of American History and did well. This eve studied Bumpology [phrenology].

April 15: We did the office work with ease. Mr. I. D. [Shadd] entertained us very pleasantly with legislation and general news. Mr. I. D. presented to me a large volume of Scotts Poetical works. It is just what suits me and I am pleased with it.

April 16: The Office work was light. I have cut a dress since and sewed it up. After supper I took up Darwin on the Origin of the Species.* It bids to be interesting & will entertain me many nights.

April 26: Having obtained a furlough from my boss I remained home today feeling like a happy fish out of water. I began an essay on the situation and requisites of the colored people everywhere.

May 1: A messenger stated that Mr. Jefferson Davis was at Ursino and would come up after Breakfast. We sent the buggy for him. In the meanwhile I brushed around the house, and donned my white dress. Smoothed my hair and pinned on a rose or two. Mr. D. arrived accompanied by Dr. Bowmar. Both gentlemen were polished in their manners and on the whole I have been pleased with their visit.†

June 5: Mr. Haney sent in a cotton blossom this morning, his first for the season. Ma reported one two or three days ago. Would not pull it in order to have the first boll. I sat up very late trying to write an Essay on Progress, it does not suit.

June 10: Ma discovered a cotton worm in her best cotton. Tis very early for cotton worms.‡ I hope the July sun may be severe enough to protect us from its ravages.

June 11: The Fever and Ague have visited me with all force. Ma's hands found more worms. She has moved some young chickens out in different places on the ridge in front.§

June 25: I wrote the Sales book journalized it, then we posted before twelve oclock. Afternoon court was in session upstairs. Mr. H's room and all our office was occupied. Zie & I went over the upper part of

---

*First published in 1859, *The Origin of Species* was hardly conventional reading in southern homes in 1872.

†This understated entry fails to convey the drama of the occasion. Jefferson Davis and Dr. J. H. D. Bowmar, coexecutors of Joseph Davis's will, hoped to oust the Montgomerys from Brierfield. Unlike his brother, Jefferson Davis was a firm believer in black inferiority. To be greeted in his former home by a well-dressed, educated black woman must have been a disturbing experience for the ex-president of the Confederacy. The care with which Mary Virginia dressed shows that she understood the significance of the meeting.

‡The army worm, a caterpillar, was the worst pest in cotton fields until the arrival of the boll weevil.

§She hoped that the chickens would eat the worms.

Hurricane Plantation. The crops above are not as fine as those in our section. I read Plutarch.

June 27: Our office cancelled forty six letters besides sending a bundle of missent letters & papers. We also sent up Dead Letters and two or three registered. I indexed the letter book, wrote & journalized the sales books.

July 4: After preparing for company, we sat in the parlor and read. Very soon Zie came with Mat & Willie. We sent the buggy up for Grandma & Pa but they were sick. Cousin Mary Jane spent the day. We rowed tables in the dining room and gave the Hands their dinner. They were highly pleased and several made short speeches. The cannons roar & the drums beating have been heard today. The stars & stripes also floated upon the breeze. Tonight the children have a Ball.

July 24: We hurried the office work in order to attend the Public meeting. The house was full. Committees were organized and the delegates appointed. Bro. W. T. and Uncle William [Lewis] were appointed with several others. Twas very near night when the voting took place. McKee rec'd all but two votes.* After taking up a collection the meeting adjourned.

August 12: Mother has succeeded in conquering the worms in her field. The smallest boys and girls are picking cotton. Beck is sewing and picking cotton. She is confident of gathering a Bale herself.

August 15: Early this morning I watered the Geraniums, marked the cotton sacks then took up sacred History. Mother's hands picked 2170 lbs. Ginning will commence next week. Tonight we have a supplement to the N.Y. Times so full of political interest. We read until time to retire.

August 20: This morning I resumed history. Stopped in a quandary about the builders of Babel. I compared two Histories but they differ. Further perusal I judge will settle the question. We finished the office work before dinner and afterward I had time to read Demorest and the Bazar.†

August 22: Went to the Lake before sunrise. All vegetation was fresh, and sparkled with dew. I had some time to read sacred History before breakfast. Afterwards was engaged in making up mail, registered five

---

*The meeting chose delegates to Republican conventions (county and state). George C. McKee, the choice of Davis Bend voters as candidate for Congress, was a white man not noted for sympathy to blacks.

†*Demorest's Monthly Magazine* contained news of fashions and stories and poetry. *Harper's Bazar* was a ladies' version of *Harper's Weekly,* with many of the same stories and illustrations, but with fashions and patterns substituted for political articles. Mary Virginia read both Harper's publications.

letters. Still the postage increases. We must have more readers as we have subscribers.* Mother had eight Bales ginned today.

August 23: Granny and Grandpa are both sick.

August 24: The cotton was hauled to Ursino and shipped on the *Lee* last night. Trade lively at Hurricane. Small change scarce. Many settlements with Ginners, Woodmen and carpenters. Ma Beck & I went to see our grandparents. I read Harpers this evening.

August 25: [Sunday] This morning before breakfast Pa brought out a short essay on Science & Theology. After breakfast we talked, read or sang as best suited our feelings. I pasted my Scrapbook, then engaged myself in the Punic wars.

September 3: I spent a short while reading sacred History, then took a lesson in Zoology. Entered the first Co[tton] Sales of the season. We received a splendid mail papers and reading matter of various descriptions. I received one letter. How welcome! One ray of hope illumined my path.

September 5: Told papa & ma of my intentions. They assent to my wishes. Another light beams upon my future. Hope beats high.

September 8: [Sunday] After I attended the house duties this morning busied myself reading Cowpers Task.† The Quarter people had a large meeting, our children attended. Before the dispersion of the company we had Ice cream & cake. After the family retired I resumed my lessons in Zoology.

September 18: Uncle Jack called and informed us of the arrival of Mr. Cardoza, Shadd and Hunt from V[icks]burg. Court was in session most of the day at Brierfield and Squire Hunt presided. This evening Messrs Cardoza and Hunt came over and we remained to hear Mr. Cardoza speak. The meeting was well attended, and highly pleased with his address.‡

October 16: Up this morning long before light and finished my Wrap. Cut and partly made a calico "Waist" before breakfast. Mr. Crosby§ from Vicksburg is here and will deliver a speech on political issues tonight. We went to the meeting. I am sorry to say that the speaker

*Mary Virginia probably meant that the increased amount of mail indicated increased literacy on the Bend.

†William Cowper's long poem, "The Task," published in 1785.

‡With a population of sixteen hundred, only thirty of whom were white, the people of Davis Bend were wooed by Republican politicians in 1872, the first year that Mississippi freedmen could vote in a presidential election. Thomas W. Cardozo, brother of Francis Cardozo, was a political leader in the state during Reconstruction; Henry Hunt was also a black politician.

§Peter Crosby was the black sheriff of Warren County, where Davis Bend was located.

was intellectually unable to do justice to the subject of his speech. Mother has finished digging all of her potatoes, & cut the sugar cane.

October 18: I wrote to Oberlin this evening.

November 1: This first day of November I greet hopefully and cheerfully. Only two or three weeks will elapse and my highest hopes must be realized or broken. I have cut and made my Alapacca skirt. Beck and I have been looking over United States history a while today.

November 5: I went to Hurricane after breakfast. The voters were on the ground early. All hands very earnest, and looked distressed until Pa came with Tickets, a messenger brought them via New Town. The Polls were opened immediately & rushing ensued for a while. All the men in our family were engaged. I did the book work alone. Tonight four hundred and forty two votes are polled for Grant & Wilson, one for H.G.*

November 11: The long looked for information has come from Oberlin. Pa has made arrangements to procure all necessary recommendations. I sent to Town for some silk to finish my dress & a pair of shoes. Mother ordered a high chair for Willie.

November 18: I went to the Office and did my last days work perhaps for a long time. I came home, found Zie here looking for me. He says we† had better go by boat to Cairo. Our things are packed pretty well up to the present.

November 20: After Breakfast I went to the Office and wrote up the Sales Book. My mind was filled with the last scenes of the Store and Office. I have given tokens of remembrance to H[urricane] people, and received many good wishes in return. How sadly I feel tonight.

November 21: After breakfast Ben Walton and Andrew took our trunks to Ursino. Pa Ma & all of our family came down. Uncle William and cousin Betsey were down also. We received a thousand instructions in regard to our correspondence. The *Lee* came at 2 P.M. The parting was sad indescribably and even tonight sighs arise like billows.

November 22: We remained on board all night, on waking this morning, my first thought was of the parting yesterday and silently the tears stole down my cheek and moistened my pillow. Bro tried to cheer us and made fun of our grief. The *Howard* came at noon and we had a

---

*Before the introduction of the Australian ballot in the 1880s, each party printed its own ticket. Voters took the ticket they wanted and put it in the ballot box. The Democrats did not bother to bring tickets to Davis Bend in 1872. Voters chose between Grant, the regular Republican candidate, and Horace Greeley who ran as a Liberal Republican.

†Rebecca was going to Oberlin with Mary Virginia.

sad farewell to Vburg. Tonight we are nearing the northern boundary of Mississippi. This is a fine boat & accommodations. This evening I amused myself by watching the majestic curling of the dark deep waves.

November 23: As soon as I awoke the first thought was of home. I know they must be well yet tears came. We have spent the day walking from guard to guard looking at the river banks. No colored passengers except us. The managers of the boat are making an effort to please but on this boat like others we sleep downstairs.*

November 24: At dusk we arrived at Memphis. B & I walked to the front of the boat and viewed all that was in sight. This is the only day that I have not cried. I have enjoyed my Phren Journal. The maids have been kind & pleasant. We conversed with them until bedtime.

November 27: At four oclock this morning we left Cairo. Tonight at nine oclock we reached the Chicago and Cleveland junction. There rechecked our baggage and waited for the Cleveland train. We were afraid to sleep at Cairo, thinking of being left.

November 28: All night we rode and without much sleep. Feeling tired and worried we arrived at Oberlin nine oclock this morning. I cannot express my mingled joys, fears, and prayers at sight of the College. We have unpacked and are partially straight. We need Pillows and a lamp. Miss Martin† loaned us some.

November 29: I cannot yet bend my mind to study. Our term commences next week.

November 30: I made a lamp Mat this morning. B made the pillows. Afternoon we took them up town to have them filled, but no feathers were to be had until Monday. We called on Miss Martin, returned her lamp and received some instructions in regard to washing and examination. After supper we had a call from Miss Hatch and her cousin. I tried to entertain them Phrenologically, and had a lively time. I do not feel homesickness so much now.

December 2: B & I went up town after breakfast. B bot a pr shoes, a mattress, Glass Pitcher a Book case and Rocker. Miss M sent her wash woman to see me. She surprised me when she told me she would wash & Iron for 62½ cents per doz.‡ I have reviewed Geography today. I would have studied more but for that irresistible yearning for home.

December 3: This day, my most fearful anxieties have been calmed.

---

*Black passengers were relegated to the lower stern decks of the riverboats.

†Helen F. Martin, assistant principal of the Women's Department.

‡Apparently washerwomen's charges had dropped since 1865 when Susan Bruce was asked five to six shillings (62½–75 cents) a dozen. Many women students, of course, did their own washing.

The examination is passed. It was not so rigid as I expected. Prof. Smith delivered a short lecture at French Hall. His remarks were fraught with kindly words of welcome and sank deeply in my poor homesick heart. We have paid Tuition. Tomorrow our classes will be formed.

December 4: All our classes are settled. All the afternoon I have spent in studying. Tonight I study my Grammar Lessons. Three young girls called and remained about two minutes. The Bell had rung and everyone must away to their rooms and be quiet.

December 7: I was able to answer my lessons readily. Two lots of girls came in to night and made things look lively. This evening I studied Latin.

December 8: [Sunday] We went to the 2nd Congregational Church. After supper we attended prayer meeting in the Assembly Room. I enjoy the prayer meetings and feel more influence through them than in any other way. I would like to be a true Christian in heart and deed.*

December 9: No recitations this morning. Afternoon went to Rhetorical exercises. B & I have each an essay to prepare in two weeks.

December 11: Afternoon went to the Principal's Office. I received permission to take drawing lessons one hour each day. I have not as much as I can do by studying diligently. I attended Becks Geography class this evening.

December 14: Today letters from home. How sweet to know that though absent I am not forgot. Beck took her first lessons on the Piano. She rented an instrument. We have bought some adornments for our room. Our money is gone. Both Brothers expressed a willingness to send us such change as we need.

December 16: I attended Bible Class and Rhetoric. We had a lively and interesting time. Tonight we contributed twenty five cents for the Christmas tree. Wrote a long composition and a letter to Brother T. discussing general and financial subjects.

December 23: Up at five this morning. Wrote my composition before breakfast. Finished some bags for the Christmas tree then studied Latin. Beck is quite under the weather and did not attend the Rhetorical Exercises. I went and managed to read my essay without fainting. I never shall forget that first essay.

December 25: The Hall rang with lively shouts of a merry Christmas. Today my heart has yearned for the dear old Home scenes more than

---

*Since Benjamin Montgomery was anticlerical, this may have been his daughters' first experience with churchgoing. At home they had attended revival meetings as spectators but not as participants.

ever. I spent some of the day studying. Beck made wax flowers. This evening we witnessed the Tableau & Pantomimes. Enjoyed it very much. Had some lively singing too. Supper at seven. Oysters plenty and nice cake. After supper Santa Claus distributed the Gifts off the Tree. Some of them were ridiculous and created much laughter. Some of the presents were beautiful.

Mary Virginia and Rebecca Montgomery returned to Mississippi in 1874 and taught school at Davis Bend. After white conservatives regained control of the state and floods, then drought, reduced cotton yields, the family's fortunes declined. Following the deaths of Benjamin and Mary L. Montgomery, the Davis Bend plantations reverted to Jefferson Davis and to Joseph Davis's grandchildren. In 1887 Isaiah Montgomery and other family members purchased land alongside the railroad to Memphis, and founded the black town of Mound Bayou. Mary Virginia and Rebecca accompanied them and for a time taught school in Isaiah's home. In 1895 Mary Virginia Montgomery was appointed postmistress of Mound Bayou, a position she held until 1902, which was probably the year of her death.

Born in Mercer County, Ohio, where freed slaves and abolitionists had lived side by side for many decades, Laura Hamilton (1864–98?) married Freeman H. M. Murray when she was nineteen years old. They went to the East in 1884 after he passed a civil service examination, winning a clerkship in the War Department. Murray, a pillar of the church and president of the literary society, worked in Washington while Laura settled down in Alexandria, Virginia, to await the birth of their first child. Lonesome for family and friends back home, she found the churches and social clubs of black Alexandria inferior to those in Ohio. Soon after she became pregnant, "Mamma"—probably her grandmother—came to live with her and help with household duties. Despite a fair education, Laura Murray was neither an intellectual nor a feminist. Rather, she was preoccupied with housekeeping, visiting, and the changes taking place in her own body. She was twenty and in her sixth month of pregnancy when the diary began.

February 26, 1885: We have been married 14 mos today.
February 27: Mamma sick. I washed and scrubbed and now of course must suffer from the effects. I have felt *Daphne* considerable today.
March 4: Inauguration day. Went to Washington on ten Oclock train, saw President going to Capitol to take oath. Went up ave. opposite War Dept. Sat on curb of fence until parade came. Never saw so many

soldiers. Colored companies looked grand. We went down by White house and grand stand and got good look at president Cleveland V. P. Hendricks and Expresident Arthur. We hurried to cars got on just in time. Had roast chicken for supper. Oh how tired I am.

March 5: Woman I engaged did not come to wash so I did it all myself Mamma not being able. At 1 Oclock Fannie Hamilton came. Showed her the little clothes for the coming responsibility. Well we are now living under a new Administration.* How it will terminate who can tell.

March 6: I was ironing steadily 3 hrs which seemed to me a long time. Everything looked nice collars cuffs and shirts daisy. Three Ladies called in eve.

March 8: Sunday. Mamma much better. F. went to S.S. [Sunday School] and Church. I am quite large and I am afraid if I go out remarks might be made.

March 9: I gave the upstairs room a thorough cleaning. I wonder so much lately about death. Sometimes it worries me but again I am reassured and I know if I live faithful that after death will come rest. I must trust. I *do* trust. Wrote letters to Aunt Sissy and Aunt Priscilla.

March 10: Mamma's birthday 75 years old. I washed and while I was washing of *course* Miss E. Welch came. Mamma finished. In evening Mamma's birthday present from us came a rattan R. chair. Mamma seemed delighted. She sent Aunt P [riscilla] one dollar and Aunt S[issy] her log cabin quilt.

March 11: Mamma and I went up to Washington on one Oclock train. F. met us at depot. We went to Museum to see "Uncle Tom's cabin" played. Mamma has always wanted to see it. It was real nice. We had reserved seats but too close to the stage.

I hardly think of my little child that is coming. I hope I shall love it. I do not love it now.

March 14: Scrubbed and cleaned feeling badly. Baked pies in evening. F. brought home chicken Ham and apples. Letter in evening from Grandpa Bentley.† F. and I carried "Easter eggs" to Mrs. Simms for distribution among S.S. Scholars. Yesterday Freeman paid the last cent on Furniture our $70 debt. I paid [sewing] machine agent $3, leaving $35 our total indebtedness. The cat had three kittens today. My time draws near.

March 19: One year ago today I landed here, a bride of eleven wks.

---

*Cleveland was the first Democratic president since the war. Blacks were concerned about how the change in administration would affect them.
†Grandpa Bentley was probably Freeman Murray's grandfather.

I was homesick and how I wished for Mamma.

March 20: I very busy making my dress. I am worried with thoughts, sometime I really think I will go wild. The subject is death and the thought that death must come. Oh Lord let me be submissive to Thy will.

March 24: Dr. Gibson called.* He is very pleasant and I like him. I told him when I expect. He wished to examine my urine to see if there was symptoms of Kidney dicease "likely to develope with first child".

March 25: Ironing today baked apple pies. I am very tired. Making a fln [flannel] skirt for baby. So far baby's apparel has cost $9.95 *not* counting thread. I do not think that is so much.

April 2: I ironed a large ironing. Mamma made a nice cake. Mrs. Fisher and Fannie Hamilton called. Women make me so angry. They seem to think of nothing but the lower things of earth. Mrs. F. said she wanted to see if I looked like a married woman. I hope now she can rest easy.

April 8: Finished baby dress. F. to Literary at night elected President.

April 13: Washed windows. Fannie Hamilton came staid all day. We had a nice time. I really believe she has "started".† I pity her if she has. I went as far as the P.O. with Fannie. A letter from Mr. Bentley. He asked F. for ten dollars to buy a suit of clothes as folks were talking. I say let them talk if after sending them ten dollars monthly they cant clothe themselves. Let them go naked. Here poor Freeman is still wearing his wedding suit week and Sunday. Underclothes almost gone. It makes me angry to see how much cheek they have. I am not willing to give a red copper over two dollars. She a strong ablebodied woman. Since we have been here they have gotten in cash money $104 and sometimes for two and three days there has not been enough money in this house to buy a postage stamp and clothes *we* have not.

April 15: Pay day. The month is half gone. How fast my time is coming. What will be the result who can tell. There is so much to be gotten out of this pay. Bought groceries $3.09 oilcloth $1.50 dry goods 2.58 bought baby brush 25^{cts} Powder box 40 cents.

April 16: Emancipation day.‡ F. and Norman went to Washington to hear F. Douglass speak. Charged admission and they wouldn't pay so did not hear.

April 19: Sunday. It is such a lovely day. How I wish I could go to Church. Got dinner. In aft. F. and I rambled out by canal. Mamma

---

*This seems to have been Laura Murray's first contact with a doctor.
†Laura's guess was correct. See entries for August 20 and October 11.
‡Slavery was abolished in the District of Columbia on April 16, 1862.

went to church again at night. I went to Susie's. I got a head ache. S. tells such Tiresome yarns makes me sick. How I wish my time would come and all would be over.

April 21: Mamma thinks I will not "run three weeks longer". My time is out in two weeks but I think I will go to the 9th or 10th of May. We can only wait and see. *I know I am ready* come what will come.

April 24: I got the blues for a while. Think perhaps our little baby would not live but I must submit to what must come but I do not want it to die even if it is a little girl.

April 25: Not very well and F. sent Dr. Gibson here. He wrote out a prescription but I wouldn't have it filled. Went to bed rather late slept much better than usual.

April 27: Was taken with pains in morning which lasted all day growing more severe but in spite of them I kept up baked pies and so forth. F. came home on leave of absence for ten days. Oh me what I have soon to endure Lord help me.

F. went for the Dr. at 10.30. Mrs. Ross was here. F. staid right by me. Baby was born at 15 min. to One on the morn of the 28th. This is the 13th of May. I am writing from memory.

April 28: First day of confinement. Feeling very comfortable. No milk for baby. He looks like he is going to die.

April 29: Still feeling very well considering. Baby better. His name is Raymond Hamilton.

April 30: Not so well. Milk came and fever. No nipples and a terrible time.

May 3: Very sick in the evening. Sent for Dr. He prescribed camphorated oil to be rubbed on my breasts.

May 9: Better but still in bed. My breast is very bad off. I am so afraid it will gather.*

June 1: It has been a long time since I wrote. On the 15th Cousin Kate Triplett from Baltimore came. She brought to Mamma a handsome black cassimere dress. The baby a zephyr sacque and myself a pretty water pitcher. On the 18th my left breast broke. The Dr. had made his last visit he thought but we had to send for him again.

June 10: Mrs. Graham is so good. She comes and combs my hair for me. She is such a nice lady. I have such a pain under my breast that I cannot lie down at night. The Dr. sent some medicine and said he would call in the morning. If he does he *shall not* strap my breast.

---

*Mastitis, which seems to be what Laura Murray was describing, was both more common and more dangerous before the discovery of antibiotics.

June 23: I feel encouraged. Baby nurses nicely through the nipple shield. My right breast still queer. I went as far as the grocery today.

June 29: Commencement over at school house. I never saw so many colored girls in my life dressed in all manner of dresses.

July 2: F. and I went down town in evening. I bought hat (white) trimmings and all costing $3.40, gloves ($.50) black lace 2½ yds. ($1.13) pins (.05) Baby can of milk. Baby now takes the nipple nicely.

July 3: F. Wrote to Grandpap. We trimmed my hat. It looks nice. Went to Concert at night. It was miserably poor. Given by Asbury Choir Washington D.C. I wish they could hear a good concert once.

July 4: Another glorious 4th and I worked harder today than I have done for over two months. F. at home making screens for windows.

July 5: My first Sunday out since baby's birth. Folks appeared glad to see me.

July 6: My birthday. I am 21 years old. F. and I went down to stores.

July 9: I finished my lawn dress. Went to Literary at night. It is as bad as usual. I was given an essay for next time. It is very discouraging. Became unwell this morning.

July 23: Finished a dress for baby. Went to Literary read essay to a very slim crowd. *Grant* died this morning.

July 28: Baby is three months old today and as smart as he can be. Made Mamma a calico basque.

August 5: Mamma washed two quilts. I helped all I could but baby was bad. Went to see ball game in evening. Quite a crowd. I enjoyed it hugely.

August 20: F. Spoke at Teachers' Institute today subject Language. In evening I went down to Fannie Hamilton's. She is very large. Bought dress for baby 85 cents glasses for jelly 20 cents.

Had privy cleaned new box put in much larger than the other.

August 27: I went to Mrs. Graham's today. She is in a D—C—I think!*

August 28: The baby is four months old today and such a little baby. Mamma went out. The baby was very troublesome and worried me greatly.

September 6: Sunday. F. to S.S. as usual. I went to First Baptist to funeral of Mrs. Lee. Quite a crowd but poor preacher.

September 7: Mamma made some more preserves which makes 2 gallons and six glasses of jelly. Played croquet in evening. Was beaten fearfully.

*Delicate Condition.

September 14: I spent the day calling. Went to the following places
Mrs. T. Triplett gave me flowers
Mrs. Browner gave grapes and pears
" Keys
" McGruders
" Thompson
" E. Young baby very pretty
" M. Dogens gave brush
" J. Bryants not home.
September 15: Pay day. F. brought home two beautiful pins for the baby. He put $10.00 in the bank which makes $30.00 in all.
September 17: Did not iron today. Paid machine agent 3.00. Became unwell again.
September 19: I wrote letters to Aunt P. and C. We gave up Nestles milk food and use condensed again.
September 21: Nothing much of importance today except Fs grandmother sent him for a Birthday present a handsome red plush mirror.
September 22: Freeman is 26 years old today. May he live so long again. I never want him to die while I live.
September 25: Just think F. received Promotion today to $12.00. Isn't that fine. How glad I am. We went to the Dr's in the evening. He told me to continue taking Cod liver oil.
September 27: Sunday. I dressed baby and F. and I went out to Church and had him Christened but "that bottle" he had to have and when I took it from him to hand him to Bro Carroll he puckered his lip but [F.] rescued him from the squall. His dress was not as fine as the others but I was not bothered.
September 29: Baby sick today poor little fellow. I wonder if we will raise him. There is something that I think that a Christian should not think. I wonder about death and try to imagine how a person feels when he has drawn his last breath in this world then about the Hereafter. Oftentimes I think so much I feel my mind wrong and then I pray and almost immediately I find comfort.
October 1: Put short clothes on Raymond. He looks nice in them.
October 10: Mamma has been here one year today. What has happened in this year. Oh the changes. I hurried through my work. Went up to Washington on 3:23 train. F. met me at the depot. We went to Dr. Muhlburg a Homeopathic Phys. I have lumps under my arms which I fear is scrofula returning. He gave me powders.
October 11: In afternoon took a great desire to go to F. Hamilton's. Millie invited us upstairs and behold what should be there but Fannie

in bed and a little boy. Well we were surprised. She has been married nine mo. on the 15th. The baby is real fat and I am glad it is a boy.

October 18: Sunday. Mamma to Church in morn, F. and I to Bible class in afternoon. We heard of a house on Duke St. belonging to brother Mitchell for rent. F.'s new suit looks nice.

October 26: I have so much headache lately and past the time for menses so Dr. Prescribe (Bellad) and menses appeared that night.

October 27: We went to see the house. Mr. Mitchell will rent it for $7 and build a kitchen in Spring.

October 28: F. home early made final bargain concerning house. Chose paper for the two down stairs rooms. Babe 6 mo old today.

October 30: My menses are very bad worse than ever before. I hope it will prove nothing serious.

October 31: Pay day. We went to Pretzfelder and bought carpet paid 10. and F. will draw $20 out of bank to finish paying.

November 3: Moved today 7 loads brought by Mr. Countee.

November 4: Carpet came. I went to see Mr. Pretzfelder. It did not look like it was sewed right but he said it was.

November 19: Sewed all day. At night went to our church to see Ella Thompson married. She was dressed in white brocade satin front veil half yard long with dress train. The "family" was quite large, all consisting of very bright* persons not one dark face in the crowd.

December 23: I have neglected writing in my diary. Today Mamma and I with baby went up to Washington and had baby's and Mamma picture taken Card size Mamma Cabinet size Raymond's.

December 25: In eve we went to First Church Christmas Festivities. Poor of course. At night to Bazaar lecture room. Was it poor. It was simply ridiculous. I ate so much cream it made me sick.

December 26: Today we have been married two years and have only one baby which is quite good.

December 27: Oh what a headache I have. It is over two months since I was unwell and I feel so badly just like I would be sick every minute. I don't see how I can be pregnant.

December 28: Raymond is 8 months old. He is not a bad looking child now. He is quite plump and very intelligent.

December 30: Still no menses. Sometimes I shed tears fearing I am pregnant.

December 31: Mamma and I went to Watch meeting. It was grand only the old clock was slow and some one was speaking when the

*Lightskinned.

Whistles and Horns blew Happy New Year to all. It was one Oclock when we got to bed.

January 5, 1886: Washed today. Who should come home with Free. but Percy Triplett. He came on a trip to Washington and the hotel where he was was so "awful" Freeman invited him down here. He will sleep with Freeman and I with Mamma.

January 8: F. and Percy went up on the half past 11 Boat came home 5 Oclock. At night Percy sang Minstrel songs. My Percy is an enormous eater.

January 11: Percy got me a leather hand satchel. Does he think that sufficient for his board I wonder.

January 14: Percy left on the 1 Oclock train and what do you think he did. Asked us to fix him lunch to take. Cheek? No! *Gall!*

January 15: I feel free like I had been let from Prison since company left. F. got paid today. Paid Pretzfelder 7.20 bought high chair Raymond 2.00.

January 24: Snowing and snow on the ground. I was afraid to go out as I do not know yet what ails me. I am afraid I am going into Consumption.

January 25: It is now three months since I was unwell and I am not growing so what is the matter.

January 27: Went to Dr. He says lumps are smaller, must be careful or I will go into consumption. He gave me another powder to take.

February 3: Sewed some on babys shirts. My flowers all froze last week. I was so sorry I cried. F. put $10 in bank.

Laura Hamilton Murray's fears were not without foundation. Her second son was born in July 1886; a third son and two daughters followed before she died at the age of thirty-four. Marrying again, Freeman Murray became active in politics, and was associated with W. E. B. Du Bois and the nascent civil rights movement. After leaving government service he and his sons founded Murray Brothers Printing Company in Washington.

Ida Bell Wells (1862–1929) was born a slave in Holly Springs, Mississippi. After emancipation her father, a skilled carpenter, earned enough money to support his wife at home and to send his children to an AMA school in Holly Springs. Ida, the oldest, had progressed from kindergarten to college-level studies, when a yellow fever epidemic swept the Mississippi Valley, killing her parents and a baby brother. Neighbors proposed parceling out the children, but sixteen-year old Ida insisted that the family remain together. Pinning up her hair and lengthening her dresses, she found a job in a country school and came home on muleback each weekend to care for the younger children. She kept up this strenuous schedule for more than two years until her brothers, Jim and George, found farm work and an aunt volunteered to take Annie and Lily, the two youngest. Aunt Fannie Butler, a widow with three children of her own, later moved to Visalia, California.

Twenty-three years old when she began the diary excerpted in the following pages, Ida B. Wells was a teacher in a Memphis public school and a budding journalist. A year earlier, she had sued the Chesapeake & Ohio Railroad after a conductor forcibly ejected her from a first-class car on a train. A sympathetic judge awarded her damages of $500. While the railroad appealed the decision, Wells reported the incident in the Living Way, a Memphis religious weekly. Her account was so favorably received that she was asked for others. Writing a column over the signature Iola, she was soon contributing to other black newspapers —there were almost 200 of them in 1885—and corresponding with their editors. Some of her columns were reviews of lectures or plays; others were forceful political essays.

Although Memphis did not rival Boston as a cultural center, it offered a surprising number of educational opportunities for the generation of blacks who were growing up free. Plays, concerts, and revival meetings were open to all (with segregated seating), and the black community had its own lyceums, lectures, and dramatic groups. Still mourning the educational opportunities she had lost when she assumed responsibility for her family, Ida B. Wells signed up for summer courses at Fisk and at Lemoyne Institute, another AMA school, took elocution lessons on Saturdays, and studied for a principal's certificate. Striving to practice all the virtues that her parents and Yankee teachers had preached, she tried to be a big sister to Jim and George and to send money regularly to Aunt Fannie. The latter was difficult because there was so much on which to spend her meagre salary: stylish clothes, her "cabinets" (that is, the photographs of herself which she exchanged with friends) in addition to board and streetcar fare.

Attractive, tempestuous, full of contradictory impulses, Wells's flirtations, the majority carried on safely by mail, invariably led to conflicts. Although she longed for friendship and love, she rejected any relationship that threatened her independence. At a time when it was widely asserted that black women were constitutionally amoral, it is interesting to note the Victorian courtship patterns to which Ida B. Wells and her friends adhered.

January 5, 1886: School reassembled yesterday. I now have 3 classes. *The Living Way* came out Saturday with my letter in it. Taught today, feeling worse than I have for some time; my chest & head have been in an uproar all day. The winter of my discontent is made more so by Mrs. P.'s* determination to hire out at the end of the week. I ought to have the money to pay her for my board & she would not have to go. I asked a loan of Mr. G.† today; don't know what his answer will be. I hated to do it but I want to pay her even if I go. I promised to pay him 10 per cent interest.

Found a letter from Mr. F. of *Little Rock Sun* offering me a scheme to have a branch of his paper published here & I get my pay by selling the papers. He wishes me to assume editorial control & complimented me as a "powfull writer". Shall not accept as I could not make it pay. It is only 8 o'clock but I go to bed early to see if it will not help me to feel better in the morning.

January 13: Thursday was city election day; I was not interested in anything but the School Board & both colored men were beaten; we now have an entirely white Board. Jim came to the school to see me and wanted money, of course. He has gotten into trouble & can't go back where he was. I have no money & told him so, but gave him a note to Mr. F.‡ who, I knew, would help him if he could. Mrs. Powell adhered to her determination to move & altho I had paid her $4 on what I owed her & gave her a bill on Menken's [department store] for $2.50, she went and I was forced to hunt another place.

Wrote to C.S.M.§ over a week ago & received an early reply. He is pleased to receive a letter from a "genuine woman" as he has hitherto been overflooded with schoolgirl notes. I think I scent a faint odor of patronage.

January 21: Received letters from Mr. Carr, Avant, Mosely, Morris & Taylor** Mr. Morris writes a very interesting letter & sends me his picture. I told him I liked the face but it is the face of a mere boy; whereas I had been led, from his writings, to suppose him a man. I sent him a picture that I request him to return—but promise him one when I have my cabinets taken. I described myself only withholding my age till I know his, as I wish to make the unpleasant discovery that I am his senior—first. If a boy, he certainly has a man's head and a man's

*Mrs. Powell, one of Wells's many landladies.
†J. J. Graham, another teacher.
‡Mr. Froman, an older man whom Wells sometimes referred to as Dad or Pop.
§Charles S. Morris, a Kentucky newspaperman.
**Marshall W. Taylor was editor of the *South Western Christian Advocate.*

thoughts in that head. I wrote and mailed 7 letters yesterday.

January 24: Went to the Literary meeting at LeMoyne Friday night to see Macbeth but they read it. It was exceedingly dull & some of the pronunciation was execrable. Took my 3rd [elocution] lesson yesterday. Came home and ironed my clothes. No visitors except George.

January 28: Letters from Messrs. Morris & Jones. Mr. M. returned my pictures & repeated the word "boy" so often I fear it nettled him. He urges me to write the book I spoke of; to make it classical, representative and standard and I shall make myself loved, honored & respected. He speaks so authoritatively and I could accept his superior criticism if he were not my junior; he is what I have long wished for as a correspondent, an interested intellectual being who could lead & direct my wavering footsteps in intellectual paths. His youth, tho, prevents my seeking information of him as I would one who was my superior in age as well as intellectuality. He denominates my nose as my weakest feature. He phrenologizes my features minutely and unerringly, as well as amusingly. The stupendous idea of writing a work of fiction causes me to smile at myself at daring to dream of such a thing—but his enthusiasm is catching.

A letter from Mr. Bowser* who is evidently disposed to favorably regard my asking for pay & asks me to state my price—which is an embarrassing thing to do. I have no idea of its worth & shall tell him so. L. M. B. [Brown] sent me a copy of *The Bee* in which there is a marked article from the pen of his very incapable editor. The article speaks of "the star eyed goddess" as not knowing what she is talking about (as everybody is accused who differs from the *Bee.*†) He is puerile in the extreme. I would not write for him for great pay & I will write some thing some day that will make him wince.

January 30: Friday was a trying day in school. I know not what method to use to get my children to become more interested in their lessons. Had a talk with G. who informed that some one had reported me as saying any young man I went with ought to feel honored because of the privilege. He did not add that they hasted to tell the rumor thus maliciously setting all the young men against me by their cock & bull stories. I will not begin at this late day by doing that which my soul

*J. D. Bowser, editor of the *Gate City Press,* Kansas City, Mo.

†Only a month earlier, the *Washington Bee* had described Wells as a "remarkable and talented young school marm . . . about four and a half feet high, tolerably well proportioned, about twenty summers, and of ready address. She is ambitious to become a full fledged journalist, a physician, or an actress. From a mere, insignificant countrybred lass she has developed into one of the foremost among female thinkers of the race. While we wish her success in her undertakings, we do not advise her to take to the stage."

abhors: sugaring men, weak, deceitful creatures, with flattery to retain them as escorts.

February 8: Went nowhere Saturday, not even to take a lesson but took a bath in the afternoon & patched the rest of the day. I had intended retiring early in order to rise soon enough to attend the Moody & Sankey meeting Sunday morning. We got a front seat in the gallery.* His style is so simple, plain and natural. He told the old, old story in an easy conversational way that charms the listener and tells the simple truth that Christ Jesus came on earth to seek & save. Mr. Sankey's singing is a sermon in itself. I intended writing Mr. Moody asking him why ministers never touched on that phase of sin—the caste distinction—practised even in church but I had no chance.

Was to school this morning by 8.30 and felt peculiarly pleasant and —good. A day's worry with these children has brought my temper to the surface. Found a letter from Mr. C. S. M. on my arrival home. He understands and sympathizes with my position of almost complete isolation from my fellow beings on account of lack of congeniality. His fine humor & sarcasm are very refreshing & I believe I have found a thoroughly congenial correspondent, and I sincerely hope it may be the foundation of a lasting friendship such as I read about, see very rarely and have experienced—never!

Went with Ella to the theatre—not that I wished so much to go, for I had seen "The Mikado" before. It is a delightful jumble of ridiculous and laughable; a comic combination of songs, speeches and actions and dress; for everything is represented as Japanese. It is very bright and sparkling, with no suggestion of the coarse or vulgar.

February 14: Mr. G. & I had a bout last week. He renewed his question of a former occasion as if I would tell him I "cared for him" without a like assertion on his part. He seems to think I ought to encourage him to speak by speaking first—but that I'll *never* do. It's conceding *too* much and I don't think I need buy any man's love. I blush to think I allowed him to caress me, that he would dare to take such liberties and yet not make a declaration. Were he to plead with me on his knees now, for no consideration would I consider his proposition.

February 18: Mr. B. has told me an incident of Judge Greer'st court that for fear I will not remember it when I write my "novel" I will jot down now. It seems that a white and colored girl had been in the habit of passing and repassing on a narrow path in the woods. One day they

---

*Dwight L. Moody and Ira D. Sankey, the celebrated evangelists, preached to segregated houses in the South.

†Judge Greer was Wells's attorney in her suit against the railroad.

passed while the white girl's brother was with her and he pushed the girl from the path and abused her. The next day they met again when each were alone and the white girl attempted to imitate the example of her brother and they fought; the colored girl getting the best of the fight. She was reported, a complaint lodged against her and in the trial the jury brought in a verdict of guilty. The judge carried it to the utmost of his power by giving her 11 months 29 days & a half in the workhouse. One half day more would have been a penitentiary offense.

February 23: Friday I finished and sent off the article I've been preparing for the *Fisk Herald*, entitled "A Story of 1900." The Board paid us for Dec. only & as a consequence mine is gone already and no money to send Aunt F yet. Paid Menken $20, Mrs. H. $23.25, Mrs. Powell $7.00; have reserved $6.75 (after deducting 85 cts to Williams, the bookstore man) for street car fare & incidentals. Still owe Menken's $61. We hope to get some more in about two weeks & then I shall send Aunt F. some.

March 11: Took the first lesson of a new month Saturday and read all day after going home, "Bricks without Straw" by Judge Tourgee.* It deals with the Reconstruction era of Negro freedom, and I like it somewhat. Received a letter from Fortune† notifying me of the end of my subscription for the *Freeman.* His picture adorned the paper last week. My curiosity is satisfied but I am disappointed. With his long hair, curling about his forehead and his spectacles he looks more like the dude of the period than the strong, sensible brainy man I have pictured him. But then, one should not judge a person by the cut or rather uncut of his hair. C.'s card reminded me that I was in his debt one letter. He wishes to know if I can stand examination in algebra, natural philosophy, etc. and I must confess my inability. I now begin to think of the golden moments wasted, the precious hours I should have used to store up knowledge. It seems so hard to get at it (study) and I've made so many resolutions I am ashamed to make any more.

Received a letter from the [Detroit] *Plaindealer* Co. who wish to know what I will charge for 2 letters per month to their paper. Answered today and stated that I would do as he wished for $2 per article. Sent the article I have been writing on for sometime to Mr. Arneaux

---

*Albion Tourgee's popular novel, *Bricks Without Straw* was sympathetic to blacks. In later years, Tourgee and Ida B. Wells became friends.

†T. Thomas Fortune, editor of the *New York Freeman* was the dean of black newspapermen. He strongly supported Wells when she was driven from Memphis.

entitled "Our Name."* Mr. A. says for me to write the plot of my novel & for us to write in partnership.

March 18: The daily papers bring notice that 13 colored men were shot down in cold blood yesterday in Miss.—Carroll co. I think.† O, God when will these massacres cease—it was because they had attempted to assassinate a white man (and for just cause I suppose). Colored men rarely attempt to wreak vengeance on a white one unless he has provoked it unduly.

Ida Bell Wells about 1893. *(Alfreda M. Duster)*

March 23: Got my pictures and like them somewhat but the more I look at them the less I like them. Sent one to Charlie. Took the second lesson of the series in elocution but still have not learned all of Lady M's [Macbeth's] role. George came in Saturday and brought me a dollar; he stayed all night and went back on the cars Sunday, I giving him 30 cts. to do so.

April 3rd: The Board paid us for Jan. today and it's very uncertain when we will get any more. Guess I'd better hold on to this, or what's left. Gave Mr. Froman $10 to pay Judge Greer for me. The case will come up in the Supreme Court this month and a friend has unfolded a conspiracy that is on foot to quash the case.

*J. A. Arneaux, a promising actor, was also editor of the *New York Enterprise.* He was campaigning for the abolition of the word *colored,* substituting Africo-American instead.
†When a white man charged with assault by two blacks was brought to trial in Carrollton, Mississippi, a mob of white men burst into the courtroom and killed thirteen blacks. The murderers were never arrested.

April 11: Made arrangements to take up the whole of my May salary at Menken's & gave them an order on the Secretary for it. I bought enough silk to finish my dress, and buttons, thread, linings, etc. amount to $15.80. My expenses are transcending my income; I must stop.

I am in as correspondingly low spirits tonight as I was cheerful this morning. I don't know what's the matter with me. I feel so dissatisfied with my life, so isolated from all my kind. I cannot or do not make friends & these fits of loneliness will come. My life seems awry, the machinery out of gear & I feel there is something wrong.

April 20: Thursday evening Mr. L. M. B. came out and we had an interesting game of checkers, in which I beat—of course surprising him greatly.

April 25: Easter Sunday! the day on which our Lord arose from the grave. I have attended service all day; at S.S. this morning, remained to church. Went to Avery Chapel this afternoon and again at church tonight. I am thoroughly tired. Wore my new dress & hat & liked the dress very much. Paid the woman $7.60 for making it and altogether it cost a great deal.

April 29: Went to the opening of the school of manual training, and was agreeably surprised by a rare treat from Rabbi Samfield. It's the first time I ever heard a Jewish intellectual discourse. Started an article on it last night.

May 6: Mr. Dardis asked me to read a piece for his concert next week. We did not decide on anything. I like Lady Mac's soliloquy and sleepwalking scene but it is almost impossible to arrange it. I will give "Le Marriage de Convenience" or "The Doom of Claudius & Cynthia". George was in Saturday & gave me $1.15 to add to his $1.70. His pile grows slowly.

Had a talk with G. and I think convinced him of my sincerity. He called that evening and asked me to kiss him, but I gently but firmly refused.

May 9: A letter from my aunt who wants me to decide what to do.* Went to the literary Friday night. I saw Mr. F. who told me of the dirty method Mr. Cummins† is attempting to quash my case.

May 18: The school board paid two months Sat. and I paid all outstanding debts except Menken's. I went to the baseball park & saw a professional game for the first time, but lost my temper & acted in an unladylike way toward those in whose company I was.

June 3: School is out & the exhibition attempted but it was a complete

---

*Aunt Fannie wanted Wells to take a teaching job in California.
†Holmes Cummins was attorney for the Chesapeake & Ohio Railroad.

farce. The house was jammed & so noisy, we could hear nothing; so half the exercises were omitted.

Tuesday Mr. G. came home with me & told me of his love for me. I told him I was not conscious of an absorbing feeling for him but I thought it would grow. I feel so lonely and isolated and the temptation of a lover is irresistible. I should not like to go thro' another winter as weary as heretofore. We went to the picnic next day and he was unvaryingly kind & attentive. I shall patiently wait to see what the future shall bring forth.

June 15: Mr. B. and I took a long walk Saturday evening and he told me things that surprised me a little—especially about his loving me. I begged him not to spoil all by any such course; whereupon he said, as many others have, that he did not believe I had any heart or could love anyone. My affairs are always at one extreme or the other. I either have an abundance of company or none at all. Just now there are three in the city who, with the least encouragement would make love to me; I have two correspondents in the same predicament. I am an anomaly to myself as well as to others. I do not wish to be married but I do wish for the society of the gentlemen.

Received a copy of the *A.M.E. Church Review* this morning and a letter from the editor asking an article from my brilliant (!) pen. I have not decided on accepting as yet.

June 28: Mr. B. persuaded me to go walking with him & asked me directly if I were pledged to anyone. I told him that I did not love him, but I was sorry that would cause a cessation of his visits. He kissed me —twice—& it seems even now as if they blistered my lips. I feel so humiliated in my own estimation that I cannot look anyone straight in the face. I feel somehow as if I were defrauded of something. I came home and lay thinking of the awkward predicament I am in and the remark made by Mr. Settle the other morning, "you are playing with edged tools" and I feel that I have degraded myself in that I had not the courage to repulse the one or the other. I don't think I want either for a husband but I would miss them sadly as friends. It seems I can establish no middle ground between me and my visitors. It is either love or nothing.

July 4th: We have definitely concluded to go on the excursion* which leaves this afternoon for the west. Am all in a turmoil as to what I shall do. Drew $85 all the money I have in the world from the bank. The

---

*Wells took advantage of cut-rate railroad tickets to the National Education Association convention in Topeka, and a Grand Army of the Republic excursion from there to California.

rest of the day was spent in packing. We start about four this afternoon.

July 13: Topeka, Kansas. After a whole week of excitement in Kansas City we left this morning for this place. Met very many pleasant acquaintances while there. Mr. Bowser took us the first ride thro' the city in a carriage, we also visited the cable line, engine house & the Coates Hotel. Next day we went shopping and had our pictures taken. Thursday evening we went to an entertainment and had a royal time. Friday evening we went to the literary meeting. Sunday morning went to church to the Episcopal service. We returned to find the house full of company. Monday we went calling and visited a dozen houses or more, and found the people all comfortably situated.

We got here about 10 o'clock P.M. Went downtown to the headquarters of the National Teachers Association, to the Capitol Building and while there called on Mr. McCabe, the present auditor of the state of Kansas.* He is a mulatto, a polished agreeable gentleman. We went to the meetings at the opera house & the Methodist church where we heard considerable spouting.

July 20: Denver, Colorado. Had a fine time in Topeka. Met many teachers from different parts. Such crowds and crowds of people! I never saw so many teachers in my life. About 30 are of our race.

July 29: San Francisco. Have been in this place two days. Circulated around looking at the shops and public buildings and going thro' Chinatown with its thousands of "Heathen Chinee". Went to the *"Elevator"*† office yesterday and had quite a talk with the editor, who gave us flattering accounts of the negro and claimed that there were several wealthy colored men here.

Went out to the Cliff House and had a magnificent view of the ocean. The rocks in front of the house were lined with seals that looked like so many brown bags as they lay basking in the sunlight.

August 2: Visalia, California. Arrived here yesterday and found all well and very glad to see me. The children have all grown tall and Annie & Ida‡ are near my height and look very much like women. I look at them in amazement and find the little sisters of whom I spoke, shooting up into my own world.

Poor Aunt F.! She wants me to stay the year with her whether I get any work to do or not & I, seeing how careworn she is with hard

---

*Edward P. McCabe settled in Kansas in 1878. He was elected to two terms as state auditor, the first black to hold high office in the state. He later became auditor of Oklahoma Territory.

†The *Elevator* was San Francisco's black weekly.

‡Aunt Fannie's daughter, Ida, had been named after Ida B. Wells.

work and solicitude for the children—know she is right & I should help her share the responsibility. The election of teachers has not taken place yet in Memphis. I know not whether I'm on the list.

August 26: Finished & at last mailed to the *A.M.E. Church Review* my article on "Our Young Men" not because I was satisfied with it but as a trial to get the opinion of others. I think sometimes I can write a readable article and then again I wonder how I could have been so mistaken. A glance at all my "brilliant" productions pall on my understanding. I find a paucity of ideas that make it a labor to write and yet what is it that keeps urging me to write notwithstanding all?

Wrote a letter to Mr. C.* asking the loan of one hundred dollars. Will take Annie back if I get the money. Am making a dress for Aunt F.

September 1: Sunday passed in the usual dull way. I wrote to Mr. F [Froman] telling him to see Mr. C. immediately & have him forward me the money. I am very eager to get back home. Have made two dresses for my aunt.

Today witnessed my first essay in story-writing. I have made a beginning. I can portray in my mind all the elements of a good story but when I attempt to put it on paper my thoughts dissolve into nothingness.

September 4: Wrote a dynamite article to the *G [ate] C [ity] Press* almost advising murder! My only plea is the pitch of indignation to which I was carried by reading an article concerning a great outrage in Jackson Tenn. A colored woman accused of poisoning a white one was taken from the county jail and stripped naked and hung up in the courthouse yard and her body riddled with bullets and left exposed to view! O my God! can such things be and no justice for it? The only evidence being that the stomach of the dead woman contained arsenic and a box of "Rough on Rats" was found in the woman's house, who was a cook for the white woman. It may be unwise to express myself so strongly but I cannot help it.

September 9: The past 24 [hours] have been very stormy ones. At breakfast Lily brought me a card & a paper both apprising me of the result of the Memphis election. After knowing for certain I was elected I telegraphed Mr. Yates to lend me $50. After sending it a card was brought to me from Mr. Murphy, [Visalia] school superintendent & the result was an offer of the school here to begin Monday. His eagerness backed with my aunt's importunities made me yield, tho' very reluctantly. He had the contract drawn up and delivered to me

*Robert R. Church of Memphis who had become the South's first black millionaire.

by three o'clock. It was all done so swiftly there was not time to think & when I realized it all I shed bitter tears; but my calmer sober judgment coming to the rescue I see it will be a better money plan than if I go home. I'll have no board to pay for the children nor myself, & I'll have over $300 clear to take home; for I am determined to go to that railroad suit.

September 14: Letters from "Pop" F. & Mr. and Mrs. Bowser upset all my resolutions and on the former's assurance that Mr. C. had lent the money, I made up my mind to throw up the school & come home. Aunt F. talked very determinedly telling me to go & then cried half the night & all the morning. I know I owe her a debt of gratitude but she makes it so burdensome for me as to make it very distasteful. Forced acts of gratitude are not very sincere.

October 2: Nearly a month since I wrote in my diary and I am back in Memphis. I taught four days in Visalia & received the remittances from both Messrs. Church & Yates. On September 16 I determined to come home.

Met Rev. Simmons, pres. of last Press Convention* and he wheedled a picture out of me & a promise to write for him. He is very lively & jolly. Have been at work all the week with 70 pupils. Fannie H. came to see me. She will be married in two weeks & invited me to the wedding.

October 12: Have received a very flattering notice in Mr. Simmons' paper. I sent him the article Mr. T. returned & he promises to print it in full. The Editor of *The Indianapolis World* wants to engage me as a pay contributor to his paper.

October 20: It rained so I could not go to Fannie's marriage but I sent her a pair of vases costing $1.50. Wrote to Aunt F. who has not written. Wrote a letter on the Knights of Labor demonstration at Richmond, Va. Wrote one to the *Scimitar*† concerning the theatre here & it is published in this afternoon's paper. Mr. G. was married very unexpectedly last week. I wish him joy. George was in to see me Sunday & seemed somewhat constrained.

November 7: Wm. J. S. published my article "Our Young Men" last week. Sent $1.50 for *The Chatauquan*. Bought $6.00 worth of lace to go on my dress & will have to pay about $4 to get it made over besides slippers, gloves, etc.—such a nuisance but it must be done, I suppose.

---

*The Reverend William J. Simmons was editor of the *American Baptist* and president of the National Colored Press Association. He paid Wells one dollar an article, the first money she earned for her writing.

†The *Memphis Scimitar* was a white newspaper.

Bought L [ily]* $1.35 worth of books also. Met Mr. Collier & he advised me to study & get a principal's certificate & he would give me a school. Am going to studying in real earnest.

November 28: The editor of the *Indianapolis World* has at last decided on the remuneration I shall receive for the article I sent & gives me 2 years subscription to his paper! Cheeky, that. Visited Miss Rosa Sheppard Thanksgiving also went to the Strangers Church & heard a good sermon & witnessed practical evidence of "white folks' Christianity", in the haste with which they passed us by when choosing a seat.

Wednesday evening was the night of Morris & Stella's marriage. The church was crowded and the presents were many & beautiful. There were three bridesmaids, of which I was the first. Everybody said we looked "sweet" and I guess we did. The bride was simply lovely.

December 4: Went to the lecture Monday evening & was highly entertained & enthused. I never was so touched for Africa before, as when he pictured the thousands bleeding & dying in ignorance & sin, & their eagerness for the gospel.

My brother Jim came to see me Wednesday & talked freely with me; he has been roaming around & has been following a passion for gaming. I told him of the depth to which he would sink & when he said the passion would never get such a mastery of him, I asked him to promise to quit. Oh God, help my wandering boy come back to the innocence of his childhood! I have thought of prevailing on him to stay here & help me with my project i.e., to start a chicken farm & for us to go housekeeping. He went out to see George & promised to return yesterday, but it turned so bitter cold, I guess he concluded to stay. I do hope he will return.

December 21: Over two weeks since I wrote! Jim returned with George & they both went to Millington. They have concluded to make a crop up there this year & by that time I hope to be able to start my project.

Have concluded negotiations with Simmons touching the ticket to Press Convention. I am to write short twice-a-month articles for him exclusively until August & the price of my ticket will be forthcoming. *The World* sends me 2 years' subscription as pay for my article. I sent them to Jim & will write no more for them. Jim says it takes time to break up a habit that has been forming for years and signs himself "your wild & reckless brother." It is a good hopeful letter. L. M. B. has a letter in this week's *World.* He doesn't write to me any more.

December 28: Christmas has come & gone & brought the good cheer incident thereto. Received a whisk broom, a photograph album, a box

*Annie had not wished to leave California, so Wells brought ten-year-old Lily instead.

of paper. Today's mail brought me a beautiful autograph album. I gave
Mrs. M. a handkerchief & Susie a pair of stockings, George a pair of
gloves. Received a letter from California with a Christmas Gift of
$3.00 for Lily.

Sunday went to church, remained to S.S., went from there to Miss
B's to dinner, then went to the Knights of Labor to hear Mrs. Lide
Meriweather speak.* It was a noble effort. Mr. Alexander† accompanied me. I like him very much. I must not be so indifferent to the
young men; they feel and resent it.

January 3, 1887: The new year is three days old. Was at Cong. Church
yesterday & took sacrament. While there I reviewed my past year &
I resolved to connect myself with the S.S. forthwith & ask for a class
of youths & see if I can not influence them in a small degree to think
on better things. God help me to be a Christian! O help me to better
control my temper!

January 18: Received an answer from Wm. J. S. Have written two
letters for him already & two for the *Watchman* here. The *Freeman*
& *K.C. Dispatch* & *Living Way* copied my letter to the *Scimitar;* the
first named & the *Detroit Plaindealer* have an extract from the *Watchman* letter relating to the K. of L.

Sunday I went to Avery Chapel S.S. & organized a class of young
men or rather youths, just merging into manhood. I got them to say
they would come every Sunday. I am more than delighted with my
success so far & pray for it to continue, But I seem to be a failure as
far as my own brother is concerned, for I speak harshly or indifferently
& repulsively to him before I think of the consequences. I can get along
well enough with other boys but am too hasty & impatient with my
own. Have heard nothing from Jim since I wrote him last.

February 1: Vickie O. was married last week. I am the only lady teacher
in the building who is unmarried.

February 8: Interest is centered in the Godwin case that has brought
forth some shocking developments concerning the morals of high life.
A silly woman forgot her marriage vows for an equally scatterbrained
boy; who boasted of his conquest, as a result he lost his life. The brother
of the woman taking this revenge on him. It seems awful to take

---

*Wells wrote a news story praising "that grand woman, Mrs. Lide Meriweather" and
also pointing out that "every woman from black to white was seated with the courtesy
usually extended the white ladies alone. It was the first assembly of the sort in this town
where color was not the criterion to recognition as ladies and gentlemen."

†Alexander's father had been a state legislator in Arkansas during Reconstruction. His
brother John (see entry for July 13) was a cadet at West Point, and would become the
second black to graduate from the military academy.

human life but hardly more so than to take a woman's reputation & make it the jest & byword of the street. One is strongly tempted to say his killing was justifiable.

February 14: Friday I went to see Booth* play "Hamlet". It was a superb rendition & as the first time I saw either the man or the play I could form no comparison between other actors & "the greatest living actor". I saw him also the next night play "Iago". I do not like that near so well.

March 1: I went up to Mr. C's [Church's] this morning before breakfast and paid him one hundred dollars. We had a holiday last week & Mrs. S. & I went calling. We paid 22 calls in all & came home tired out.

Had 10 in the class Sunday & my contribution was 75 cts. I am so proud of my success. Father help me, I pray be more thoughtful & considerate in speech and in action.

April 11: The Supreme Court reversed the decision of the lower court in my behalf last week.† Went to see Judge G. this afternoon & he tells me four of them cast their personal prejudices in the scale of justice & decided in face of all the evidence to the contrary that the smoking car was a first class coach for colored people as provided for by that statute that calls for separate coaches but first class, for the races. I felt so disappointed, because I had hoped such great things from my suit for my people generally. I have firmly believed all along that the law was on our side and would, when we appealed to it, give us justice. I feel shorn of that belief and utterly discouraged, and just now if it were possible would gather my race in my arms and fly far away with them. O God, is there no redress, no peace, no justice in this land for us? Thou hast always fought the battles of the weak & oppressed. Come to my aid at this moment & teach me what to do, for I am sorely, bitterly disappointed.

April 18: Have just returned from what I consider the best thing out. The Negro's Mutual Protective Association had a public meeting and Mr. A. escorted me. I was very much enthused as I listened to the speeches and saw the earnestness of the men present. The Negro is beginning to think for himself and find out that strength is to be found only in unity.

May 2: Nearly a score of young ladies & gentlemen met to form

*Edwin Booth, the famous Shakespearean actor.

†In the case of *Chesapeake, Ohio & Southwestern Railroad Company* v. *Wells,* the Tennessee Supreme Court ruled that "the purpose of the defendant was to harass, and that her persistence was not in good faith to obtain a comfortable seat for the short ride. Judgment reversed."

dramatic organization, & appointed a committee of which I am the chairman to draft a plan for permanent organization. Thursday evening called on & solicited the Hon. P. B. S. Pinchback to lecture for the Lyceum. He promised to be there & I published it so. The result was we had a nice crowd out while they heard nothing extra as a speech.

May 3: The concert which was a great success is over & done with. Our program was good (so they say) & they sold out nearly every thing. I recited "Le Marriage de Convenience" and everyone admired it. Mr. Froman gave me a basket of flowers costing $1.10. Taken all together it was a big success, for we made clear nearly $60.

July 13: Nearly a month has elapsed since I scratched a pen in my diary! Last Monday, July 4th, Mr. Y & myself spent the day talking over old times; that evening we went to the Asylum & had a very pleasant time. The Cadet, Mr. Alexander's brother, was out with Miss Church* and I was glad of the opportunity to meet him. I also met President Burrus† of Alcorn University. Wednesday morning we called on Miss Church and found her the most pleasant companion. Miss Mollie was down Friday evening to call and said she wished to have a talk with me. Her ambitions seem so in consonance with mine that I offered to come up the next morning. I did go and I came away after about two hours chat—very much enthused with her. She is the first woman of my age I've met who is similarly inspired with the same desires hopes & ambitions. I was greatly benefited by my visit and only wish I had known her long ago. I shall not let the acquaintance slack.

July 16: This morning I stand face to face with twenty five years of life. The experiences of a quarter of a century are my own, beginning with this, for me, new year. I go back over them in memory. The first ten are so far away as to make those at the beginning indistinct, the next 5 are remembered as a kind of butterfly existence at school, and household duties at home; within the last ten I have suffered more, learned more, lost more than I ever expect to again. In this last decade, I've only begun to live—to know life as a whole with its joys and sorrows. Today I write with a heart overflowing with thankfulness to My Heavenly Father for His bountiful goodness to me, in that He has not caused me to want, & that I have always been provided with the means to make an honest livelihood. When I sum up my own accom-

---

*Mary Eliza ("Mollie") Church, the daughter of Robert R. Church, later became Mary Church Terrell. Although Wells's and Terrell's paths crossed frequently, they became rivals rather than friends.

†President Burrus was James Burrus, America Robinson's former fiancé.

plishments I am not so well pleased. I have not used the opportunities I had to the best advantage. I find myself as deficient in comprehensive knowledge as the veriest school-girl just entering the higher course. I heartily deplore the neglect. God grant I may be given firmness of purpose sufficient to essay & *continue* its eradication! Twenty-five years old today! May another 10 years find me increased in honesty & purity of purpose & motive!

Losing her teaching job after she criticized the inadequate schools for blacks in Memphis, Ida B. Wells became a full-time journalist and coowner of Free Speech, *a Memphis weekly. Her concern about the increasing number of lynchings peaked when three friends were lynched not for "the unspeakable crime," rape of a white woman, but because they had started a successful grocery store. After she wrote a series of investigative reports proving that most "rapes" that led to lynchings were affairs between consenting adults, her newspaper office was destroyed and she was driven from the South. With black women coalescing behind her, she launched a crusade against lynching. Lecturing from coast to coast, publishing fact-filled pamphlets, she aroused white liberals at a time when black rights were almost forgotten. She married Ferdinand L. Barnett in 1895 and had four children in fairly rapid succession, while maintaining her position as a militant public figure in the tradition of Harriet Tubman and Sojourner Truth.*

Selected Bibliography

Source Notes

Index

Selected Bibliography

Books, Articles, Dissertations

Albert, Octavia V. Rogers. *The House of Bondage.* New York, 1891.
Alexander, Leslie. "Early Medical Heroes." *The Crisis.* January 1980.
Aptheker, Bettina. "Quest for Dignity: Black Women in the Professions, 1865–1900." n.p., 1978.
Aptheker, Herbert. *A Documentary History of the Negro People.* New York, 1951.
Avary, Myrta Lockett. *Dixie After the War.* New York, 1906.
"B." "Inside Southern Cabins." *Harper's Weekly.* November 13–December 4, 1880.
Bassett, John Spencer. *The Southern Plantation Overseer as Revealed in His Letters.* Northampton, 1925.
Bearden, Jim, and Butler, Linda Jean. *Shadd.* Toronto, 1977.
Blassingame, John W. *Slave Testimony.* Baton Rouge, La., 1977.
Botkin, Benjamin A. *Lay My Burden Down.* Chicago, 1945.
Botume, Elizabeth H. *First Days Amongst the Contrabands.* Boston, 1893.
Bovoso, Carole, "Discovering My Foremothers." *Ms.* September, 1977.
Bradford, Sarah H. *Harriet the Moses of Her People.* New York, 1886.
Brewer, J. M. *American Negro Folklore.* Chicago, 1968.
Brown, Hallie Q. *Homespun Heroines and Other Women of Distinction.* Xenia, 1926.
Brown, Josephine. *Biography of an American Bondsman, by his Daughter.* Boston, 1856.
Brown, William Wells. *My Southern Home.* Boston, 1880.
———. *The Rising Son.* Boston, 1873.
Burroughs, Nannie H. "Not Color but Character." *Voice of the Negro.* July 1904.
Burton, Annie. *Memories of Childhood's Slavery Days.* Boston, 1909.
Cade, John B. "Out of the Mouths of Ex-Slaves." *Journal of Negro History.* Summer 1935.
Campbell, Randolph, and Picken, Donald K. "My Dear Husband." *Journal of Negro History.* Fall 1980.
Catterall, Helen T., ed. *Judicial Cases Concerning American Slavery and the Negro.* 5 vols. Washington, D.C., 1926–37.
Chadwick, John W. *A Life for Liberty.* New York, 1899.
Child, Lydia M. "Edmonia Lewis." *The Broken Fetter,* March 3, 1865.
Christensen, A. M. H. *Afro-American Folk Lore.* Boston, 1892.
Colman, Lucy N. *Reminiscences.* Buffalo, N.Y. 1891.
Conrad, Earl. *Harriet Tubman.* Washington, D.C., 1935.
Cooley, Rossa B. *Homes of the Freed.* New York, 1926.
Cooper, Anna J. *A Voice From the South.* Xenia, Ohio, 1892.
———. *Personal Recollections of the Grimké Family.* Washington, D.C., 1951.
Coppin, Fanny Jackson. *Reminiscences of School Life.* Philadelphia, 1913.
Cromwell, John. *History of the Bethel Literary and Historical Association.* Washington, D.C., 1896.
Culp, Daniel W. *Twentieth Century Negro Literature.* Naperville, Ill., 1902.
Daniels, Sadie I. *Women Builders.* Washington, D.C., 1970.
Davis, Elizabeth L. *Lifting as They Climb.* Washington, D.C., 1933.
DeBoer, Clara M. *The Role of Afro-Americans in the Origin and Work of the American Missionary Association.* Ph.D. dissertation, Rutgers University. University Microfilms, Ann Arbor, Mich., 1973.
De Forest, John W. *A Union Officer in the Reconstruction.* New Haven, 1948.

Douglass-Sprague, Rosetta. *My Mother As I Recall Her.* n.p., 1900.

Drew, Benjamin. *The Refugee: A North-Side View of Slavery.* Boston, 1856.

Du Bois, W. E. B. *The Philadelphia Negro.* Philadelphia, 1899.

———. *The Health and Physique of the Negro American.* Atlanta, 1906.

Dunbar, Alice Moore, ed. *Masterpieces of Negro Eloquence.* New York, 1914.

Duster, Alfreda, ed. *Crusade for Justice. The Autobiography of Ida B. Wells.* Chicago, 1970.

Eliot, William G. *The Story of Archer Alexander.* Boston, 1885.

Epstein, Dena J. *Sinful Tunes and Spirituals.* Chicago, 1977.

Farrison, William E. *William Wells Brown.* Chicago, 1969.

Fisk, Clinton. *Plain Counsels for Freedmen.* Boston, 1866.

Fisk University. *Unwritten History of Slavery.* Nashville, 1945.

Fisk University News. "The Jubilee Singers." October 1911.

Fletcher, Juanita. *Against the Consensus: Oberlin College and the Education of American Negroes, 1835–65.* Ph.D. dissertation, American University. University Microfilms, Ann Arbor, Mich.: 1974.

Fletcher, Robert. *A History of Oberlin College.* Oberlin, Ohio, 1943.

Flexner, Eleanor. *Century of Struggle.* Cambridge, Mass., 1959.

Foner, Philip. *The Life and Writings of Frederick Douglass.* New York: 4 vol. 1950.

———, and Ronald Lewis. *The Black Worker.* Vols. 1 and 2. Philadelphia, 1978.

Forten, Charlotte. *The Journal of Charlotte L. Forten.* New York, 1953.

———. "Life on the Sea Islands." *Atlantic Monthly,* May 1864.

Frazier, E. Franklin. *The Negro Family in the United States.* New York, 1948.

French, Austa. *Slavery in South Carolina.* New York, 1862.

Fry, Smith D. "Lincoln Liked Her." *Minneapolis Register.* July 6, 1901.

Furstenberg, Frank, Theodore Hershberg, and John Modell. "The Origins of the Female-Headed Black Family." *The Journal of Interdisciplinary History.* Autumn 1975.

Genovese, Eugene. *Roll, Jordan, Roll.* New York, 1974.

Gilbert, Olive, and Titus, Frances W. *Narrative of Sojourner Truth and Book of Life.* Battle Creek, Mich., 1878.

Grandy, Moses. *Narrative of the Life of Moses Grandy.* London, 1843.

Gutman, Herbert. *The Black Family in Slavery and Freedom.* New York, 1978.

Harley, Sharon, and Terborg-Penn, Rosalyn, eds. *The Afro-American Woman.* Port Washington, N.Y., 1978.

Harper, Frances E. W. *Sketches of Southern Life.* Philadelphia, 1872.

Haviland, Laura. *A Woman's Life-Work.* Chicago, 1887.

Hayden, Della. "A Graduate's Reminiscences." *Southern Workman.* January 1917.

Heard, William. *From Slavery to the Bishropic.* Philadelphia, 1905.

Hermann, Janet. *The Pursuit of a Dream.* New York, 1981.

Higginson, Thomas W. *Part of a Man's Life.* Boston, 1905.

Holt, Rosa Belle. "A Heroine in Ebony." *The Chautauquan.* July 1896.

Hutchinson, Louise. *Anna J. Cooper.* Washington, D.C., 1981.

Jacobs, Harriet. *Incidents in the Life of a Slave Girl.* Boston, 1861.

James, Edward, and Janet, eds. *Notable American Women.* Cambridge, Mass., 1971.

Jerrido, Margaret J. "Early Black Women Physicians." *Woman and Health.* Fall 1980.

———. "Black Women Physicians." Medical College of Pennsylvania, *Alumnae News.* Summer 1979.

Johnston, James H. *Race Relations in Virginia and Miscegenation in the South.* Amherst, Mass., 1970.

Keckley, Elizabeth. *Behind the Scenes.* New York, 1868.

Kemble, Frances Anne. *Journal of a Residence on a Georgia Plantation.* New York, 1863.

Killion, Ronald, and Waller, Charles, eds. *Slavery Time When I Was Chillun Down on Marster's Plantation.* Savannah, Ga., 1973.

"Lady of Boston." *Memoir of Mrs. Chloe Spear.* Boston, 1832.

Langston, John Mercer. *From the Virginia Plantation to the National Capitol.* Hartford, Conn., 1894.

Larison, C. Wilson. *Silvia Dubois.* Ringoes, N.J., 1883.

Lawson, Ellen, and Merrill, Marlene. "On the Cutting Edge: Antebellum Educated Black Women Missionaries and Teachers." n.p., 1980.

Levine, Lawrence. *Black Culture and Black Consciousness.* New York, 1977.
Litwack, Leon. *Been in the Storm So Long.* New York, 1979.
_____. *North of Slavery.* Chicago, 1961.
Loewenberg, Bert J., and Bogin, Ruth. *Black Women in Nineteenth-Century American Life.* University Park, Pa., 1976.
Logan, Rayford, and Winston, Michael. *Dictionary of American Negro Biography.* New York, 1982.
Lyons, Maritcha R. *Memories of Yesterdays All of Which I Saw and Part of Which I Was.* n.p.
McDougall, Frances Whipple Greene. *Memories of Elleanor Eldridge.* Providence, R.I., 1838.
Majors, Monroe A. *Noted Negro Women.* Chicago, 1893.
Marsh, J. B. T. *The Story of the Jubilee Singers.* Boston, 1880.
Mattison, H. *Louisa Picquet, the Octoroon.* New York, 1861.
Meltzer, Milton, and Holland, Patricia G. *Lydia Maria Child Selected Letters, 1817–1880.* Amherst, Mass., 1982.
Miller, Randall, M. *"Dear Master" Letters of a Slave Family.* Ithaca, N.Y., 1978.
Montgomery, Winfield S. *Historical Sketch of Education for the Colored Race In the District of Columbia, 1807–1905.* Washington, D.C., 1907.
Moore, Ella Sheppard. "Historical Sketch of the Jubilee Singers." *Fisk University News.* October 1911.
Morgan, Kathryn L. *Children of Strangers.* Philadelphia, 1980.
Mossell, Gertrude. *The Work of the Afro-American Woman.* Philadelphia, 1894.
Nell, William C. *The Colored Patriots of the American Revolution.* Boston, 1855.
Northup, Solomon. *Twelve Years A Slave.* Auburn, N.Y., 1853.
O'Connor, Ellen M. *Myrtilla Miner: A Memoir.* Boston, 1885.
Odom v. Odom, v. 36 (Georgia, 1867).
Olsen, Otto. "Albion W. Tourgee and Negro Militants of the 1890s." *Science and Society.* Spring 1964.
Osthaus, Carl. *Freedmen, Philanthropy, and Fraud. A History of the Freedman's Savings Bank.* Urbana, Ill., 1976.
Painter, Nell Irvin. *Exodusters.* New York, 1977.
Perdue, Charles L., Barden, Thomas E., and Phillips, Robert K., eds. *Weevils in the Wheat.* Charlottesville, 1976.
Plummer, Nellie. *Out of the Depths.* Washington, D.C., 1972.
Porter, Dorothy B. "Sarah Remond, Abolitionist and Physician." *Journal of Negro History,* July 1935.
_____. *The Remonds of Salem: A Forgotten Nineteenth-Century Family.* n.p., 1973.
Prince, Nancy. *Narrative of the Life and Travels of Mrs. Nancy Prince.* Boston, 1850.
Puckett, Newbell. *Folk Beliefs of the Southern Negro.* Chapel Hill, N.C., 1926.
Proceedings of the Anti-Slavery Convention of American Women. New York, 1837, Philadelphia, 1838 and 1839.
Proceedings of the Colored National Labor Convention. Washington, D.C., 1870.
Quarles, Benjamin. *Allies for Freedom.* New York, 1974.
Rawick, George P., ed. *The American Slave: A Composite Autobiography.* Vols. 2–17. Westport, Conn., 1972.
Report of the Committee of Merchants for the Relief of Colored People Suffering from the Late Riots in the City of New York. New York, 1863.
Richardson, Joe. *History of Fisk University.* University, Ala., 1980.
Rose, Willie Lee. *Rehearsal for Reconstruction.* Indianapolis, Ind., 1964.
Saxon, Lyle, Dreyer, Edward, and Tallant, Robert. *Gumbo Ya-Ya: A Collection of Louisiana Folk Tales.* New York, 1945.
Smedes, Susan Dabney. *Memorials of a Southern Planter.* New York, 1965.
Stanton, Elizabeth C., Anthony, Susan B., and Gage, Matilda J. *The History of Woman Suffrage.* Vols. 1–3. New York, 1881–86.
Staupers, Mabel K. *No Time for Prejudice.* New York, 1961.
Sterling, Dorothy. *Black Foremothers.* Old Westbury, N.Y., 1979.
Steward, Susan M. *Woman in Medicine.* Wilberforce, Ohio, 1914.
Steward, Maria W. *Meditations from the Pen of Mrs. Maria W. Steward.* Washington, D.C., 1879.

Still, William. *The Underground Railroad.* Philadelphia, 1872.

Stowe, Harriet Beecher. *Key to Uncle Tom's Cabin.* Boston, 1853.

Swint, Henry L. *Dear Ones at Home.* Nashville, Tenn., 1966.

Taylor, Orville W. " 'Jumping the Broomstick.' " *Arkansas Historical Quarterly,* Autumn 1958.

Taylor, Susie King. *Reminiscences of My Life in Camp.* Boston, 1902.

Thomas, Adah. *Pathfinders: A History of the Progress of Colored Graduate Nurses.* New York, 1929.

Tillman, Katherine D. "Afro-American Women and Their Work." *AME Church Review.* April 1893.

Towne, Laura M. *Letters and Diary of Laura M. Towne.* Cambridge, Mass., 1912.

U.S. Congress. *Condition of Affairs in the Late Insurrectionary States,* 42 Cong., 2d Sess. 13 vols., Washington, D.C., 1872.

———. *Report of the Select Committee to Inquire into the Mississippi Election of 1875,* 44th Cong., 1st Sess. S. Rept. 527. Washington, D.C., 1876.

———. *Report and Testimony of the Select Committee of the U.S. Senate to Investigate the Causes of the Removal of the Negroes from the Southern States.* 46th Cong., 2d Sess., S. Rept. 693. Washington, D.C., 1880.

———. *Smalls v. Tillman.* 45th Cong. 1st Sess. House Misc. Document No. 11. Washington, D.C., 1877.

Veney, Bethany. *The Narrative of Bethany Veney.* Worcester, Mass., 1889.

[Virginia] *Calendar of Virginia State Papers,* Vol. 11, Richmond, Va., 1875–93.

Vosburg, John H. *Virginia and Other Poems.* Philadelphia, 1864.

[Wallace, Lew]. *Communication from Major Gen'l Lew. Wallace in Relation to the Freedman's Bureau, to the General Assembly of Maryland.* Annapolis, Md., 1865.

Williams, George W. *History of the Negro Race.* New York, 1883.

Winegarten, Ruthe, and Hunt, Annie May. "I Am Annie May." *Chrysalis,* No. 10, 1980.

Woodson, Carter. *The Mind of the Negro.* Washington, D.C., 1926.

Works Progress Administration [WPA]. *The Negro in Virginia.* New York, 1940.

———. Georgia Writers' Project. *Drums and Shadows.* Athens, Ga., 1940.

Yetman, Norman. *Voices From Slavery:* New York, 1970.

Manuscript Sources

(Abbreviations in parentheses)

African Union Society Papers, Newport Historical Society (African Union Papers)

American Missionary Association Papers, Amistad Research Center (AMA Papers)

Archives and Special Collection on Women in Medicine, Medical College of Pennsylvania (Med. College, Pa)

Blagden Papers, Houghton Library, Harvard University (Blagden Papers)

Moses Brown Papers, Rhode Island Historical Society (Brown Papers, RIHS)

Bureau of Refugees, Freedmen and Abandoned Lands, Record Group 105, National Archives (BRFAL)

Mary Ann Shadd Cary Papers, Moorland-Spingarn Research Center and Archives, Ontario, Canada (Cary Papers, M-S and Archives, Canada)

John Hartwell Cocke Papers, Manuscript Department, University of Virginia Library (Cocke Papers)

Paul Cuffe Papers, Free Public Library, New Bedford (Cuffe Papers)

Daughters of Africa Society Order Book, Historical Society of Pennsylvania (Daughters of Africa Papers)

Department of Rare Books and Manuscripts, Boston Public Library (BPL)

Frederick Douglass Papers, Library of Congress (Douglass Papers)

Christian Fleetwood Papers, Library of Congress (Fleetwood Papers)

Garrison Family Papers, Sophia Smith Collection (Women's History Archive) Smith College (Garrison Papers, Smith)

Abigail Kelley-Foster Papers, American Antiquarian Society (Kelley-Foster Papers)

Duke Marion Godbey Papers, Special Collections, King Library North, University of Kentucky (Godbey Papers)

Francis Grimké Papers, Moorland-Spingarn Research Center (Grimké Papers)

Emily Howland Papers, Cornell University Libraries (Howland Papers)

Charles Colcock Jones Collection, Special Collections Division, Tulane University Library (Jones Collection)

Lyons-Williamson Papers, Schomburg Center for Research in Black Culture (Lyons-Williamson Papers)

Myrtilla Miner Papers, Library of Congress (Miner Papers)

Montgomery Family Papers, Library of Congress (Montgomery Papers)

Moorland-Spingarn Research Center (Moorland-Spingarn)

Freeman Murray Papers, Moorland-Spingarn Research Center (Murray Papers)

New England Freedmen's Aid Society Papers, Massachusetts Historical Society (N.E. Freedmen's Aid Papers)

Oberlin College Archives (Oberlin Archives)

Papers of the Pennsylvania Abolition Society, Historical Society of Pennsylvania (P.A.S. Papers)

William Phillips Jr. Collection, Salisbury, Conn. (Phillips Papers)

Post Family Papers, Department of Rare Books and Special Collections, University of Rochester Library (Post Papers)

America Robinson Papers, Fisk University Library (Robinson Papers)

Frances Rollin diary, in possession of Carole Bovoso (Rollin diary)

Ruffin Papers, Amistad Research Center (Ruffin Papers)

Governor John St. John Papers, Kansas State Historical Society (St. John Papers)

Schomburg Center for Research in Black Culture (Schomburg Center)

Singleton Family Papers(#1626) Manuscripts Department, University of Virginia Library (Singleton Family Papers)

Slavery in the United States Collection, American Antiquarian Society (Slavery in U.S. Coll. AAS)

Gerrit Smith Collection, George Arents Research Library, Syracuse University (Gerrit Smith Collection)

Sophia Smith Collection, (Women's History Archives) Smith College, (Sophia Smith Collection)

Superintendent of Education Papers, South Carolina Archives (Supt. of Ed. Papers)

Boyd B. Stutler Papers (microfilm), Ohio Historical Society (Stutler Papers)

Weld-Grimké Papers, William Clements Library, University of Michigan (Weld-Grimké Papers)

Ida B. Wells Diary, Regenstein Library, University of Chicago (Wells Papers)

William N. Whitehurst Papers, Department of Archives and History, State of Mississippi (Whitehurst Papers)

Elizabeth Whittier Papers, Clarke Historical Library, Central Michigan University (Whittier Papers)

Periodicals

American Freedman

Anglo-African Magazine

Atlanta Constitution, July–August 1881

Colored American

Commonwealth, Boston, July 1863

Daily Phoenix, Columbia, S.C., August 1868

Frederick Douglass' Paper

Freedmen's Record

Freedom's Journal

Liberator

Louisianian

National Anti-Slavery Standard

National Freedman

New National Era and *New National Era and Citizen*

New Orleans Tribune

New York Age and *New York Freeman*

North Star

Philadelphia Press, April–May 1873

Provincial Freeman

Rochester Union and Advertiser, August–October 1876

Syracuse Daily Courier and *Journal,* October–November 1870

Weekly Anglo-African

Woman's Era

Source Notes

Each document, except for letters and biographical writings, is identified by its initial words in italics. Initial words from my text are not italicized. Sources are given in full in the Bibliography. In the case of George P. Rawick's multivolumed *The American Slave*, volume numbers and states are included here.

Introduction

Part I ◆ SLAVERY TIME

19 *My ma say:* Rawick, vol. 2, S.C.; *They didn't:* Fisk University; *When that:* Fisk University.
20 *Us didn't* and *We was:* Yetman; *I now entered:* Jacobs.
21 *I was:* Mattison.
22 *Now I come:* Jacobs.
24 *Mr. Williams:* Mattison.
25 *Ma mama said:* Perdue and others; *Aunt Jane:* Rawick, vol. 8, Ark.; *Grandma say:* Winegarten; *My sister was:* Killion; *I don't like:* Perdue and others.
26 *LOUISA:* Odom v. Odom; *Your petitioner:* Johnston.; *She used:* Perdue and others.
28 *Mr. Mordicia:* Rawick, vol. 14, N.C.; *Once Massa:* Botkin; *Lots o'white:* Perdue and others.
29 *My mother:* Rawick, vol. 14, N.C.; *I, Walter Robertson* and *I, Thomas Wright:* Johnston.
30 *I, Philip:* Record of Wills, vol. 40, pp. 203–204, Charleston County Library, Charleston, S.C.; *The testator* and *The deceased:* Catterall, vol. II.
31 When an overseer: Bassett; Her child was worth: O. Taylor; *I was worth:* Yetman; *Dr. Ware:* Rawick, vol. 8, Ark.; *[Master] would never:* Albert.
32 *On the Blackshear:* Rawick, vol. 9, Ark.; planters utilized: Gutman, Catterall, vol. I; *Missus told:* Rawick, vol. 5, Tex.; *I heard:* WPA Georgia Writers' Project (the Gullah dialect of the speaker has been modified); "The unmarried woman": Gutman.
33 *I walk:* Yetman; *I married:* Rawick, vol. 16, Va.; *I was:* Rawick, vol. 2, S.C.
34 *My mammy:* Rawick, vol. 2, S.C.; *My first husband:* Stowe.
35 *We just:* Stowe; "Dey just puts": Rawick, vol. 5, Tex.; *We didn't:* Rawick, vol. 13, Ga.; *My mother:* Perdue and others.
36 *Your pa:* Smedes; *[Aunt Mary Jane]:* Fisk University; *Uncle Edmond Kirby:* Yetman.
37 *I was glad:* Yetman.
38 *Dere was:* Christensen; *When slaves:* Rawick, vol. 13, Ga.; *Mammy and pappy:* Rawick, vol. 5, Tex; *When the women:* Killion.
39 *When women was:* Rawick, vol. 4, Tex.; *Dere was uh:* Perdue and others.; *When my little:* Rawick, vol. 11, Mo.; *One poor woman:* Kemble.
40 *How many children":* French; *The functions:* Morgan, John H. "An Essay on the Causes of the Production of Abortion." *Nashville Journal of Medicine and Surgery,* August 1860.
41 *My master:* Albert; *Mother tole me:* Rawick, vol. 15, N.C.; *"Have you":* French; *My mammy grieve:* Yetman.
42 *Bye baby:* Puckett; *Kink head:* Yetman; *On de cold:* Rawick, vol. 4, Tex.; *My father:* Fisk University; "Saturday night": Mallard, Robert Q. *Plantation Slavery Before Emancipation,* quoted in Gutman; *My pa:* Rawick, vol. 13, Ga.; *My Pa b'longin':* Rawick, vol. 2, S.C.
43 *Farewell, fellow servants:* Epstein; *O, dat was:* Yetman.
44 Watching a white: Stowe; S. Brown letter: *National Anti-Slavery Standard,* September 16, 1841, reprinted in Blassingame; Alexander letter: Eliot.
45 Newby letters: [Virginia] *Calendar.*
46–47 Plummer letters: Plummer; S. M. Plummer letter: Woodson.
48 Russell letter: Stowe.
49 Tucker letter: Cocke Papers.
50 Ramsey letters: Mattison.
51 Gooley letter: Godbey Papers.
52 Phoebe letter: Jones Papers.
53–56 Skipwith letters: Cocke Papers, reprinted in Miller.
56 "Fight": Fisk University; *[My mother's] boss:*-Botkin.

57 *The white folks:* Rawick, vol. 16, Ky.; *[Mistress] set:* Larison (Originally
    written in phonetic spelling, this excerpt has been changed to standard
    spelling.); *I knew:* Heard; *He owned:* Botkin.
58 *She married:* Stowe; *My mother:* Grandy.
59 *A Georgia man:* American Freedmen's Inquiry Commission, reprinted in
    Blassingame; *[My mother] worked:* Botkin.
60 *My mammy was:* Rawick, vol. 7, Okla.; *I had:* Albert.
61 *My sister:* Grandy; *One of the:* Killion.
62 *"Now William":* Josephine Brown.
63 *My attention: Newark Advertiser,* reprinted in *Liberator,* February 19,
    1849.
64 *My shoes:* Drew.
67 *I knew:* Bradford.
69 *At first: Freedmen's Record,* March 1865; *She brought:* Bradford.
70–72 *A new life:* Veney; Still's journal: P.A.S. Papers; letters to Still: Still.
72 *She commenced: Weekly Anglo-African,* September 7, 1861.
74–83 Jacobs letters: Post Papers.
83 Child letter: Meltzer and Holland.

Part II ♦ FREE WOMEN, 1800–1861

87 "The Women, generally": Litwack, 1961; "She has": letter, Schomburg
    Center.
88–89 Indentures: P.A.S. Papers.
89–91 Elleanor Eldridge: McDougall; f.: "Biographical Memoir of Frances H.
    McDougall," Rhode Island Historical Tracts, no. 1, Providence, R.I.,
    1880.
92–93 Chloe Spear: "Lady of Boston."
93–95 Nancy Prince: Prince.
95 Elizabeth H. Marshall: Lyons.
96 Remond women: identified in letter from Dorothy B. Porter, 1982; Susan
    Remond: Lyons.
97–98 Advertisements: *Freedom's Journal,* May 2, June 13, May 9, 1828.
98 Matilda letter: *Freedom's Journal,* August 10, 1827.
99–100 Harrison letters: Brown Papers.
101–3 Slocum, Mastens, Cuffe letters: Cuffe Papers.
103–4 Grace Douglass letter: William Catto, *A Semi-Centenary Discourse.* Phila-
    delphia, 1857.
105 maternal associations: Nancy F. Cott, *The Bonds of Womanhood,* New
    Haven, 1977; An 1830 study: Aptheker; G. Douglass letter: Schomburg.
106 "Order Book": Daughters of Africa Papers.
107 Collins and Lyna letter: African Union Papers.
108–9 *Constitution of the Colored Female: Liberator,* February 16, 1833.
109–11 Black women's societies: *Rules and Regulations of the Coloured Female
    Roman Catholic Beneficial Society of Washington City,* n.p., *Liberator,*
    December 29, 1839, *Colored American,* April 1, 1837, *Freedom's Jour-
    nal,* February 1, 1827, *Liberator,* December 3, 1831, January 7, 1832,
    September 22, 1832, *Colored American,* September 23, 1837; *Soon after:
    Liberator,* July 21, 1832.
112 *Come, gentle lady: Liberator,* September 8, 1832; Ladies Literary Society and
    It is now: Colored American, September 23, 1837.
113 *Constitution of the Female: Liberator,* November 17, 1832.
114 Philadelphia Female Anti-Slavery Society: P.A.S. Papers; *We are thy: Pro-
    ceedings of the Anti-Slavery Convention,* 1837.

115 *Resolved, That prejudice:* ibid, 1838; L. Mott letter, June 18, 1838: Houghton Library, Harvard.

116 Before the convention and *We meet: Proceedings of the Anti-Slavery Convention,* 1839.

117 *Whereas, the: North Star,* March 9, 1849.

118 North Star Association: *North Star,* April 12, 1850; *The long-contemplated: Weekly Anglo-African,* April 7, 1860.

120 "To the Daughters": *Liberator,* September 3, 1836.

121 *I am now:* Chadwick.

121–23 S. Forten letters: Whittier Papers.

124–25 S. Forten letter: Weld-Grimké Papers.

126 Fredrika Bremer, *The Homes of the New World,* New York, 1853; *One short year: Liberator,* July 21, 1832.

127 *At a Stated meeting:* P.A.S. Papers.

128 *We cannot: Colored American,* December 2, 1837; *A letter* and *That this Society:* P.A.S. Papers.

129 Sarah Douglass trained: Med. College, Pa.; *That our most: Weekly Anglo-African,* July 23, 1859.

130–31 S. Douglass letters: Kelley-Foster Papers; Weld-Grimké Papers.

131–32 S. Grimké letters: Library of Congress.

132 *In sound judgment: Repository of Religion and Literature,* September 1862, courtesy of Dorothy B. Porter.

133 S. Douglass letter: Weld-Grimké Papers; *She had brought:* Douglass-Sprague.

134 *Father built:* Douglass-Sprague.

135 Griffiths letters: Gerrit Smith Collection; A. Douglass letter: Douglass Papers.

137 "LETTER FROM MRS. DOUGLASS": *Liberator,* December 2, 1853; "Dark, stout, and plain": F. Bremer, *op. cit; She watched:* Douglass-Sprague.

138–43 R. Douglass letters: Douglass Papers.

144 William W. Brown marriage: *Liberator,* July 12, 1850.

145 E. Brown letter: Slavery in U.S. Coll. AAS.; *She says: New York Tribune,* March 12, 1850.

146 J. Brown letter: *Liberator,* May 23, 1854.

147 *The first time:* Rufus Blanchard, *Discovery and Conquest of the Northwest.* Chicago, 1898.

149 M. Jones letter: Douglass Papers.

150–51 *I do not recollect* and *At the close:* Gilbert and Titus.

153–58 *I was born, You were in,* and other Stewart writings: Stewart; *I remember:* Stewart.

159–60 F. Watkins (Harper) letters and Greenwood: Still.

161 *Miss W.: Provincial Freeman,* March 15, 1856; *Ask Maryland: National Anti-Slavery Standard,* May 23, 1857.

162 *Now let me: Liberator,* April 23, 1858; *How fared:* Still.

163–64 *The idea: Anglo-African Magazine,* May 1859; F. Watkins (Harper) letters: Still; Stevens: *National Anti-Slavery Standard,* January 21, 1860.

165 *Miss Shadd: Frederick Douglass' Paper,* November 9, 1855.

166 M. A. Shadd (Cary) letter: Bearden and Butler.

167–68 M. A. Shadd (Cary) letters: AMA Papers.

169–70 "She is justly," *INTEMPERANCE, For weeks past,* and *In order: Provincial Freeman,* December 1, 1855, July 26, 1856, February 28, 1857, December 1, 1855.

170 *There was much* and *Miss Shadd's eyes: Frederick Douglass' Paper,* October 26, 1855, November 9, 1855.

171 *The self-called: Provincial Freeman,* May 5, 1855; "unfortunate sex" and "many persons": *Provincial Freeman,* June 9, 1855.

172 *With this number: Provincial Freeman,* June 30, 1855; "Salutatory": *Provincial Freeman,* August 22, 1855; *Returned to: Provincial Freeman,* March 8, April 26, 1856.

173 T. Cary letters: Cary Papers, Archives, Canada.

174 M. A. S. Cary letter: Cary Papers, M-S.

175 "dedicated from birth": Lyons; "Our home discipline": Porter, 1973.

176–77 S. Remond letters: Kelley-Foster Papers, *Anti-Slavery Advocate,* November 1859, reprinted in Porter, 1935.

178–79 S. Remond letters: BPL, *Liberator,* November 11, 1864.

180 *Portland, Me.: Freedom's Journal,* June 1, 1827.

181 *A colored girl* and *Sir: Liberator,* May 25, June 22, 1833.

182 "When we hear": Theodore Wright in *Colored American,* November 11, 1837; *We as much: Colored American,* November 23, 1839.

182–83 J. Stekley and M. Gordon letters: P.A.S. Papers; C. Lee letter: BPL.

184–86 L. M. Child letters: Phillips Papers.

187 H. Purvis letter: Garrison Papers, Smith.

188 *Having passed:* Lyons.

190 *Miss Miner:* O'Connor; *She was often:* S. R. Howland, March 3, 1882, Howland Papers; f.: *Frederick Douglass' Paper,* December 22, 1855–January 19, 1856.

191 M. Jones letter: Miner Papers.

192–93 E. V. Brown letters: Miner Papers.

194–202 E. V. Brown letters and Searing letter: Howland Papers.

203 "a light quadroon": E. M. Fairchild, AMA Papers. [*My aunt*] *put:* Coppin.

204 "About clothes": E. N. Peck, Howland Papers; "I never rose": Coppin.

205 F. Jackson (Coppin) letter: Douglass Papers.

206 *My mother:* London *Athenaeum* reprinted in *Lorain County News,* April 4, 1866; bizarre mystery: Langston.

207 "I thought of": Child.

208 M. Leary letter: Stutler Papers.

209–13 S. Holley and S. Bruce letters: Howland Papers; she died: Emily Howland, September 20 and 30, 1866, Howland Papers.

214 *We despise: Frederick Douglass' Paper,* March 11, 1853; *The child: Anglo-African Magazine,* April, 1859; *The Victoria Club: Weekly Anglo-African,* January 4, 1862.

216 *Saturday night: Frederick Douglass' Paper,* June 17, 1852.

217 Advertisements: *Weekly Anglo-African,* October 19, 1861, April 21, 1860, February 8, 1862, January 1, 1862.

218 *The Female Trading Association: Colored American,* June 7, 1841.

219 N. Ruffin letters: Ruffin Papers.

220 *Women are not: Freedom's Journal,* February 14, 1829; *Employ yourself: Colored American,* September 8, 1838; *Whereas, we: North Star,* September 29, 1848.

221 *Father's connection:* Lyons; "the rush": *Liberator* August 6, 1836.

222 "Everlasting shame": *Colored American,* April 13, 1837; *One day: Woman's Era,* August 1894; *The instant Harriet:* Bradford.

223 *Sarah E.Adams: Frederick Douglass' Paper,* July 28, 1854.

224–25 S. Randall and M. Daniels letters: Blagden Papers.

226 M. Cuffe letter: Cuffe Papers.

227 M.A.S. Cary and *On Saturday last: Provincial Freeman,* March 7, 1857.

228 Affidavit and letters: P.A.S. Papers.

229 *I was taken:* Stowe; A. Northup letter: Northup.

230   *My name is:* Weekly Anglo-African, March 8, 1862.
231   E. Williamson letter: Bearden and Butler.
232   *On the afternoon:* Lyons.
232–33   eyewitness reports: *Report of the Committee of Merchants.*
234   "There has been no": *New York Times,* March 7, 1864.

Part III ♦ THE WAR YEARS

237   "God be praised": *Douglass' Monthly,* May 1861; "My policy": Carl Sandburg, *Abraham Lincoln: The War Years,* New York, 1939; *One of de:* Rawick, vol. 14, N.C.
238–39   *One day she* and *My ole missus:* Haviland; *About a week: Liberator,* August 22, 1862.
240   F. Perry letter: Campbell and Picken.
241   E. Steward letter: Higginson; "Us travel": Rawick, vol. 5, Tex.; "He said that": Swint; *I 'members:* Yetman.
242   *I 'members:* Rawick, vol. 14, N.C.; *I was nursin':* WPA, *Negro in Virginia.*
243   *We done heared:* WPA, *Negro in Virginia; I was:* Hallie Q. Brown; *Oh, baby:* WPA, *Negro in Virginia.*
244   *Caddie had been:* Morgan; *I used to think: American Freedman,* July 1869; *Member de fust:* WPA, *Negro in Virginia.*
245–46   H. Jacobs letter: *Liberator,* September 3, 1862.
247   H. Jacobs letter: BPL.
248   *I dressed Mrs. Lincoln: Minneapolis Register,* July 6, 1901.
249–50   [*In August 1862*]: Keckley.
251   *The ladies thought:* Gilbert and Titus.
252   *He was seated: Liberator,* December 23, 1864; *Mr. Lincoln was:* Colman.
253–56   S. Truth letters: Post Papers.
255   *I should like:* P.A.S. Papers.
257   M. Delany letter: Cary Papers, M-S.
258   *Mrs. Carey:* William W. Brown, 1873; H. Tubman description: Bradford.
259–60   *I'd go* and *Will Capt. Warfield:* Bradford; *Col. Montgomery* and *Last fall: Commonwealth,* July 10 and July 17, 1863; "She was proud": *Auburn Citizen,* March 11, 1913, quoted in Conrad.
261–63   *I have just: Weekly Anglo-African,* October 19, 1861; M. S. Peake letter: *American Missionary,* December 1861; "still improving" and "She was": DeBoer, pp. 242–43.
263   "I am myself" and "They are socially": S. G. Stanley, AMA Papers; E. G. Jackson letter: AMA Papers.
265–66   S. G. Stanley: AMA Papers; "This is not": DeBoer pp. 227–28; *Your circular:* S. L. Daffin, *I spoke to:* S. G. Stanley, f.: F. L. Cardozo, AMA Papers.
266   L. S. Day letters: AMA Papers.
267–68   "I am prepared": C. C. Duncan, *When I first:* M. L. Magnos, *During the time* and *The interest:* S. L. Daffin, *My labors:* M. E. Watson, *The rear:* M. L. Hoy, AMA Papers; f.: Oberlin Archives.
269   E. G. Jackson and S. G. Stanley, AMA Papers.
270   S. L. Daffin letter: AMA Papers; *Much good:* M. L. Hoy, AMA Papers.
271   *I am in:* E. G. Jackson, AMA Papers; f.1: *New National Era,* May 13, 1873.
272–73   S. G. Stanley letters: AMA Papers.
273–75   E. G. Jackson letters: AMA Papers.
275   S. Iredell letter: Fleetwood Papers; S. Wright: AMA Papers.
276–77   B. Harris, Litts, Wright correspondence: AMA Papers; B. Harris description: Oberlin Archives.

278–79 S. G. Stanley and Shipherd correspondence: AMA Papers; S. G. Stanley description: Lawson and Merrill, Osthaus.

280–82 C. Forten letters: *Liberator*, December 12, 19, 1862; *After the lessons: Atlantic Monthly*, May 1864; "The people" and "When they heard": Rose.

283–84 *After school:* Forten; C. Forten letter: Swint; daily journal: N.E. Freedmen's Aid Papers.

285–86 C. Forten letter: Supt. of Ed. Papers; C. Forten description: N.E. Freedmen's Aid Papers, *New National Era*, July 23, 1873, Forten.

286–94 E. V. Brown letters: Howland Papers; Sumner School: *New National Era*, May 30, 1872, June 14, 1874; H. P. Montgomery: Hutchinson.

294–96 E. Highgate letters: AMA Papers; "deranged . . . wild": C. C. Duncan, AMA Papers; *Miss Highgate: New Orleans Tribune*, October 26, 1864.

297–99 E. Highgate letters: AMA Papers; Louisiana Education Relief Association: *New Orleans Republican*, September 21, 1867.

   300 E. Highgate letter: *American Freedman*, no. 5, 1868.

 301–3 *Even in: National Anti-Slavery Standard*, February 5, 1870; E. Highgate letters: Gerrit Smith Collection and AMA Papers.

   303 "Melancholy and Sudden Death": *Syracuse Daily Courier*, October 17, 1870.

   304 E. Highgate death: *Syracuse Daily Courier*, October 19, 21, 1870, Syracuse *Journal*, October 17, 18, 19, 21, 1870; A. T. Morgan letters: Gerrit Smith Collection.

   305 C. Highgate Morgan: letter from Joseph Logsden, University of New Orleans, August 26, 1981.

Part IV • FREEDWOMEN

   309 "When freedom": Botkin; *I asked* and *Mistress say:* Yetman.

   310 L. Skipwith letter: Cocke Papers, reprinted in Miller.

   311 "They had": De Forest; *After de war:* Rawick, vol. 7, Miss.; *My mother came:* Burton; *One day:* Rawick, vol. 14, N.C.; I. Soustan letter: Singleton Family Papers.

   312 *I had saved:* Veney; "Aged women": *New National Era*, July 20, 1874.

313–14 Advertisements: *Anglo-African*, August 19, 1865, *New National Era*, July 28 and September 29, 1870; letters to Gen. Wallace: [Wallace]; "Not a day": Gutman.

   315 *Mary Smith:* BRFAL, Grenada, Miss. vol. 143; *Harriet Saunders:* BRFAL, Miss., Box 53; *Elizabeth Pollard:* BRFAL, Athens, Ga., vol. 174, February 1867–June, 1868.

   316 W. A. Grey letter: BRFAL, Richmond, Va., Letters Received; F. Smart letter: BRFAL, Miss., Letters Received, 1866.

   317 *Martin Barnwell:* Botume; *Send me some* and *'Twas like:* Swint.

   318 *Today in church:* Towne.

319–20 *Husbands must provide* and *Do not think:* Fisk; *The only furniture:* French; f.: Cooley.

   322 *I seen:* U.S., 1880; "the evil of": De Forest; "My husband never": Fisk University; *I picked:* Rawick, vol. 3, S.C.

   323 *I ain't nebber:* Rawick, vol. 2, S.C.; *I got married:* Rawick, vol. 14, N.C.

   324 *Most of the:* Botume.

325–26 "Inside Southern Cabins": *Harper's Weekly*, November 13, November 27, December 4, 1880.

326–27 Dianna contract: BRFAL, Ga., Box 30; Emmie Gray contract: BRFAL, Anderson Court House, S.C., Box 52 A, 1866–67.

   328 Sarah Nelson contract: Whitehurst Papers.

329–30 *Mariah Baldwin* and *Ellen Latimer:* BRFAL, Dawson, Ga., Box 17.

331 *My contract:* BRFAL, Miss., Box 53; f.: Harper.

332 "I acknowledge her": Litwack, 1979; *Elizabeth Bash:* BRFAL, Darlington, S.C., Box 65; *Rachel Caruth:* BRFAL, Baton Rouge, La., vol. 223½.

333 *Manervia Anderson:* BRFAL, Athens, Ga., vol. 175, April 1867–68; *The Freedwoman:* BRFAL, Ga., vol. 249; *Rhody Ann Hope:* BRFAL, Baton Rouge, La., vol. 222; *Angiline Hollins,:* BRFAL, Aberdeen, Miss., vol. 112.

334 *Hetty Richardson:* BRFAL, Baton Rouge, La., vol. 222; *Helen Palmer:* BRFAL, Athens, Ga., vol. 174; *Amanda, a freedwoman:* BRFAL, Anderson Court House, S.C., Box 52, 1865–67; *Mary Connor:* BRFAL, Miss., vol. 143; *Margaret Martin:* BRFAL, Athens, Ga., vol. 185, April 1867–68.

335 *Emma Cox:* BRFAL, Aberdeen, Miss., vol. 112, August 1867–December 1867; *Bowers, Lucinda:* BRFAL, Gainesville, Ga., vol. 212, 1867–68; *Elisabeth Stingles:* BRFAL, Baton Rouge, La., vol. 223; *Ann Edins:* BRFAL, Gainesville, Ga., Cases Tried, vol. 212, 1867–68.

336 *Matilda Frix:* BRFAL, Calhoun, Ga.; *Rhoda Robinson:* BRFAL, Athens, Ga., vol. 174, February 1867–June 1868.

337 *Viney & Julia:* BRFAL, Calhoun, Ga., vol. 143; *Adaline Smith:* BRFAL, Dallas County, Ala., vol. 180; *Martha Martin:* BRFAL, Athens, Ga., vol. 175, April 1867–68.

338 *Amanda Redmond:* BRFAL, Ga., vol. 212; *After Plaintiff:* BRFAL, La., vol. 222; "connubial bliss": BRFAL, Ga., vol. 186; "a full explanation": BRFAL, Ga., vol. 238; "advised [them]": BRFAL, Miss., vol. 143.

339 *Personally appeared:* BRFAL, Ga., Box 30; *Esther, a freedwoman:* BRFAL, Anderson County Courthouse, S.C., Box 52; *Julia Gibson:* BRFAL, Vicksburg, Miss., vol. 283; *Julia Ray:* BRFAL, Randolph County, Ga., vol. 238.

340 *Black men:* Levine; *I have had:* BRFAL, Catahoula, La., vol. 479; *She urged: Mobile Register,* reprinted in *Semi-Weekly Louisianian,* July 6, 1871; *Brown, Charlotte:* BRFAL, Columbia, S.C., no. 138.

341 *Complainant Betty Ann:* BRFAL, Dalton, Ga., vol. 248; *Harriet Buchanan:* BRFAL, Miss., vol. 121; *Before me came:* BRFAL, Athens, Ga., vol. 176.

342 *Before me came:* BRFAL, Ga., vol. 175; Putative fathers: BRFAL, Ga., vol. 216, 264, 191; *Personally appeared:* BRFAL, Anderson Court House, S.C., Box 52; Harriet Brown and Ann May: BRFAL, Pt. Coupee, La., vol. 396; Isabella Colman: BRFAL, Grenada, Miss. vol. 144.

343 *Mr. L. P. Conner:* BRFAL, La. Journal, vol. 528; Ellen Craft: *Boston Journal,* June 12, 1878; *We have:* Swint.

344 "Our main and fundamental": William P. Randel, *The Ku Klux Klan,* Philadelphia, 1965.

345 *They first came:* U.S., 1872, vol. 9 Ala; *They came:* U.S., 1872, vol. 6, Ga.

346 *They made:* U.S., 1880; *From the moment:* Rawick, vol. 4, Tex.

347 *They went around:* U.S., 1872, vol. 6, Ga.

348 "Your wife": U.S., 1872, vol. 6, Ga.; *They came in:* U.S., 1872, vol. 3, S.C.

349 *They came to* and *I was asleep:* U.S., 1872, vol. 5, S.C.

350 *The colored people:* U.S., 1872, vol. 6, Ga.; *They never had:* U.S., 1872, vol. 4, S.C.

351 *The early part:* U.S., 1872, vol. 9, Ala.; *I was taken:* U.S., 1872, vol. 3, S.C.

352 Mary Elder: U.S., 1872, vol. 6, Ga.; Elizabeth Lyon: U.S., 1872, vol. 9, Ala.; *Just as I:* U.S., 1872, vol. 13, Fla.

353   *McK stopped:* BRFAL, Baton Rouge, La. vol. 222.
354   *Mrs. Richards:* U.S., 1872, vol. 11, Miss.; *Myself and husband:* BRFAL, Ga.,
        vol. 270.
355   *Frances Gilmore:* U.S., 1872, vol. 2, N.C.
356   *Mayor Barrows: Jackson Daily Clarion,* June 24, 1866, reprinted in Foner and
        Lewis, vol. 1; *Monday night: Galveston News,* August 1, 1877, reprinted
        in Foner and Lewis, vol. 2.
357–58 *This year* and *Mr. Jim English: Atlanta Constitution,* July 29, 1881, August
        3, 1881.
360–61 *I can 'member:* Saxon and others; *Bel pam patat* and *Blackberries:* R. Emmet
        Kennedy, *Mellows,* New York, 1926; *Red rose:* Harriette K. Leiding,
        Street Cries of an Old Southern City, Charleston, S.C., 1910; *I live fore
        miles:* William H. Brown, 1880.
361   *In 1867:* S. Taylor; *My idea was:* Burton.
362   Mattie letter: *Louisianian,* September 28, 1871.
363–64 S. Thompson letters: *New National Era,* February 15, 1872, *New National
        Era and Citizen,* January 13, 1873.
365   *Gillem was:* Rawick, vol. 9, Ark.; *Thick carpets:* Avary.
366–68 F. Rollin diary: Rollin diary; f.1: *New York Times,* April 3, 1869; f.3: *Co-
        lumbia Daily Phoenix,* August 4–20, 1868.
369   *You'd laughed:* Harper.
370   *Robert Smalls* and *Women had sticks:* U.S., 1877; f.: Williams.
371   *The white people* and *Thursday night:* U.S., 1876.
372   "The whole South": U.S., 1880.
373   "Tax man make": Haviland; "I don't have": Williams; R. Cunningham
        letter: St. John Papers.
374   Committee of Five Hundred: U.S., 1880 and *Nashville Weekly American,*
        November 8, 1877.
375   *I had some: Topeka Daily Capitol,* August 29, 1939. f.: letter from Kansas
        State Historical Society, October 21, 1981.
376   S. Smith letter: U.S. 1880.
377   J. and M. Evans letter: Olsen.
378–79 Della Hayden: Hayden, Rev. R. Lloyd Heck, *Life, Labors and Tragic Death
        of Mrs. Della Irving Hayden,* n.p.
380   Taliaferro letter: Howland Papers.
381–82 E. Cole, S. Grant, and M. Carnes letters: AMA Papers.
383–85 *I tried, Many a time,* and *The slave songs:* Moore.
386–87 *Poor ignorant me: Fisk University News; We trembled:* Moore; "Their heads
        were not": Marsh; *Last night:* Robinson Papers.
388–92 A. Robinson letters: Robinson Papers.
393   O. Davidson letter: BPL.

Part V • THE POSTWAR NORTH

397–99 *Long 'go:* Holt; H. Tubman description: Conrad; "The audience rose":
        Davis.
399–401 S. Truth quotes and letters: Gilbert and Titus, P.A.S. Papers.
402   H. Jacobs letter: Sophia Smith Collection.
403   In an appeal: *Anti-Slavery Reporter,* March 21, 1868, courtesy Dorothy B.
        Porter; death: Mt. Auburn Cemetery Records; *She impressed me:*
        Grimké Papers.
403–5 F. Harper lectures: *National Anti-Slavery Standard,* January 12, 1867; F.
        Harper letters: Still; *Her voice was: Philadelphia Press,* July 12, 1871,
        reprinted in Still; *Two things:* Dunbar.

406   M.A. Cary description: Bearden and Butler, H.Q. Brown, *New National Era*, July 13, 1871, P.A.S. Papers, *New York Freeman*, April 11, 1885; "Trades for Our Boys": *New National Era*, March 21 and April 11, 1871.

407   Bethel Literary: Cromwell; Association for Advancement of Women: *New York Age*, November 19, 1887; *I first made: New York Age*, November 8, 1890.

408   *I told them:* Coppin.

409   F. Jackson [Coppin] letter: Douglass Papers.

410   "she told the committee": Howland Papers; f.2: Stanton and others and H. Q. Brown.

411   "During my entire life": *New York Age*, November 8, 1890; "I belong" and "Do you really": Conrad; f.1: Shirley Chisholm, *Unbought and Unbossed*, Boston, 1970.

411–12   *I feel that* and *I would like:* Stanton and others, vol. 2; *Battle Creek Journal* reported: Gilbert and Titus; *Women, you forget: New National Era*, November 17, 1870.

413   Colored National Labor Union convention and *The avocations of: Proceedings of the Colored National Labor Convention.*

414–15   Universal Franchise Association and National Woman Suffrage Association: Stanton and others, vol. 3; Colored Woman's Progressive Franchise Association: Cary Papers, M–S; The *Louisianian*, April 9 and April 20, 1871, July 9, 1871; Equal Rights Association, P. Couzins, P. Davis, and F. Harper: Stanton and others, vol. 2.

416–17   *Jacob: New York Freeman*, November 28, 1885.

418–22   R. Douglass Sprague letters: Douglass Papers.

421   "disgraced and scandalized": Foner, vol. 4; sentenced to a year: *Rochester Union and Advertiser*, January 21, 1876; f.: *Rochester Union and Advertiser*, September 22 and October 30, 1876.

422   f.: letter from Ann Teabeau, R. D. Sprague's granddaughter, February 24, 1982.

423   lowest incomes and highest mortality rates: Furstenberg and others; *A Colored Woman* letter: *Philadelphia Post*, November 3, 1871, courtesy American Antiquarian Society.

424   *A—, a dressmaker:* Du Bois, 1899; S. Taliaferro letter: Howland Papers.

425   B. Foule letter: Douglass Papers.

426   *They observe:* Tillman.

427–28   *The tall, graceful* and *The Hall was: Louisianian*, February 21, 1880 and March 19, 1881; "Washington's Colored Society": J. E. Bruce Papers, Schomburg Center.

429   *To be the leader:* sheet music, Moorland-Spingarn; f.1: *New National Era*, February 10, 1870, *New York Freeman*, September 19, 1885, *Voice of the Negro*, July 1904.

430–31   Athenaeum Club, Mignonette Club, Monday Night Literary Club: *Louisianian*, January 2, 1875, December 26, 1874, March 19, 1881; Saturday Evening Club: R. D. Sprague to F. Douglass, February 6, 1890, Douglass Papers; *From the first month:* Fleetwood Papers.

432   *Mr. Grimké was:* Cooper, 1951; Josephine Bruce: B. K. Bruce Papers, Moorland-Spingarn; S. I. Fleetwood: Fleetwood Papers; C. F. Grimké: Cooper, 1951; "it was an": H. Q. Brown; f.: Hutchinson.

434–35   *Oh, you awful: New National Era*, February 22, 1872; *Submission to her: Louisianian*, May 9, 1874; *My mother: New York Freeman*, March 6, 1886; *While our men:* Cooper, 1892.

436–37   F. Douglass letter: Courtesy Dorothy B. Porter; "I am decidedly": John Wesley Cromwell Papers, courtesy Adelaide Cromwell Gulliver; daughters of slaves: James; Mary Eliza Mahoney: Staupers and Thomas; Minnie Hogan: University of Pennsylvania Archives.

438–40   P. Williamson letters: Lyons-Williamson Papers.

440   Dr. Rebecca Cole: Alexander, *New National Era and Citizen,* May 1, 15, 22, and June 5, 1873, *Philadelphia Press,* April 5, 11, and May 23, 1873; f.: James.

441   *On the point: Woman's Era,* October–November 1896.

441–42   Dr. S. S. McKinney Steward description: Alexander, H. Q. Brown; *Fortunate are the:* Steward.

443   Doctors: Med. College, Pa., Majors, H. Q. Brown, Jerrido.

444   M. Evans letter: Med. College, Pa.; f.: James.

445   f.2: Letter from Connie E. McKissack, Archivist Librarian, Meharry Medical College Library, January 20, 1983.

446–47   G. E. L. Patton letter: *Christian Educator,* December to January 1900–1901, courtesy Dr. Leslie Falk; "a coal-black": *Broad-Ax,* October 23, 1897; E. Grier letters: Med. College, Pa.

448   first women: Med. College, Pa. and B. Aptheker.

449   H. Dillon letter: Med. College, Pa.

450   "The College of Medicine" and physicians' statistics: Du Bois, 1906; "the bugbear was": H. Q. Brown; *Everything is new:* Cooper, 1892.

Part VI ⬩ *EPILOGUE: FOUR WOMEN*

454   steamer *Pilot Boy: New York Times,* August 21, 1867; Nell, Hayden, William W. Brown: Logan and Winston; Howards: Majors; f.2: *Boston City Directory,* 1868.

455–61   F. Rollin diary: Rollin diary.

455   f.1: Quarles.

457   f.3: N.E. Freedmen's Aid Papers.

458   f.2: *Boston City Directory,* 1868; f.3 and 4: N.E. Freedmen's Aid Papers.

459   f.1: N.E. Freedmen's Aid Papers.

460   f.1: Farrison.

461   Rollin description: Bovoso; f.3: *New York Times,* July 28, 1975.

462–63   Montgomery family description: Hermann; "a welcome guest" and "Mr. Montgomery": Still.

463–72   M. V. Montgomery diary: Montgomery Papers.

466   f.2: Hermann.

468   f.3: Hermann.

470   f.2: Oberlin Archives, courtesy Ellen Lawson.

472   returned to Mississippi: Hermann; appointed postmistress: letter from National Archives and Records Service, February 17, 1982.

472–79   L. H. Murray diary: Murray Papers.

479–80   I. B. Wells description: Duster and Sterling.

481–95   I. B. Wells diary: Wells Papers.

482   f.2: *Washington Bee,* reprinted in *New York Freeman,* December 12, 1885.

492   f.1: *New York Freeman,* January 15, 1887.

495   I. B. Wells: Duster and Sterling.

Acknowledgments

MY FIRST DEBT is to the historians whose books I read in the 1950s. Herbert Aptheker's *Documentary History of the Negro People*, W. E. B. Du Bois's *Souls of Black Folk* and *Black Reconstruction*, John Hope Franklin's *From Slavery to Freedom*, Philip Foner's *Life and Writings of Frederick Douglass*, Eleanor Flexner's *Century of Struggle*, and Benjamin Quarles's *The Negro in the Civil War* introduced me to black and women's history and taught me much about the historical method.

From among the hundreds of fine scholarly studies published since then the ones that have had the most influence on this book are Herbert Gutman's *The Black Family in Slavery and Freedom* and George P. Rawick's *The American Slave: A Composite Autobiography*. Gutman's magnificent study, which stresses the strength and creativity of black people, reinforced my own observations and pointed to new sources of documents. I had sampled the riches of the WPA interviews with former slaves in Benjamin Botkin's *Lay My Burden Down* and *The Negro in Virginia*, but not until George P. Rawick and Greenwood Press published more than two thousand of the interviews did I appreciate their full importance. It is hard to see how any book on slavery could be written without recourse to this remarkable collection of reports from ex-slaves. Anthropologists, folklorists, poets as well as historians can turn to these volumes for enlightenment and inspiration.

John W. Blassingame's *Slave Testimony*, an impressive compilation of writings and interviews, not only presented fresh material, but also suggested ways to edit and annotate it. Sharing Herbert Gutman's views about the humanity and dignity of slaves, Leon Litwack's *Been in the Storm So Long* provided additional sources and served as a model of fine historical writing. Gerda Lerner's pioneering *Black Women in White America* and *Black Women in Nineteenth-Century American Life*, edited by Bert J. Loewenberg and Ruth Bogin, proved to be valuable references. I have also turned with pleasure to the provocative essays in *The Afro-American Woman,* edited by Sharon Harley and Rosalyn Terborg-Penn.

Other books that were particularly useful include Janet S. Hermann's *The Pursuit of a Dream;* Nell Irvin Painter's *Exodusters;* and Howard N. Rabinowitz's *Race Relations in the Urban South 1865–90.* Clara M. DeBoer's dissertation, "The Role of Afro-Americans in the Origin and Work of the American Missionary Association," available through University Microfilms, deserves publication in book form. It is indispensable to a study of black teachers during and after the Civil War.

Scores of librarians and archivists have been generous with their time and expertise. At the head of my list, as always, is Dorothy B. Porter, curator-emeritus of the Moorland-Spingarn Research Center; Jean Blackwell Hutson, former chief of the Schomburg Center for Research in Black Culture; and Sara Dunlap Jackson of the National Historical Publications and Records Commission. Their profound knowledge of black history is well known; I am also pleased to count them among my friends. Clifton H. Johnson, executive director of the Amistad Research Center, sent me more than 100 letters from black women; then he and Florence E. Borders, Amistad's senior archivist, promptly answered my questions about them. Karl Kabelac of the University of Rochester Library helped to uncover Harriet Jacobs's letters and read old Rochester newspapers for me in his spare time. Elaine G. Everly, of the Military Archives Division, National Archives, gave invaluable assistance when I went through the Freedmen's Bureau papers. Other librarians and archivists who have patiently answered queries include Esme E. Bhan, manuscript research associate at the Moorland-Spingarn Research Center; Sylvia Render, formerly of the Manuscripts Division, Library of Congress; Ann Allen Shockley, Fisk University archivist; W. E. Bigglestone, archivist at Oberlin College; Sandra L. Chaff, director of archives, Margaret Jerrido, archives assistant, and Jill Gates Smith, curator at the Medical College of Pennsylvania; Nancy Dean of the Department of Manuscripts, Cornell University Libraries; Carolyn A. Davis of the George Arents Research Library, Syracuse University; Ellen D. Mark, manuscript librarian, Essex Institute, Salem, Massachusetts; Diane M. Telian of the Historical Society of Pennsylvania, Mary-Elizabeth Murdock, director of Sophia Smith Collection, Smith College; and James L. Murphy, reference librarian, Ohio Historical Society. In a literal sense I could not have completed this book without the help of the librarians of the Wellfleet, Massachusetts Public Library and particularly Claire

Beswick who with great efficiency and good humor borrowed books and microfilm from libraries across the country. Much gratitude is also owed to Jennifer Linton of Eastham, Massachusetts, who typed a bulky, difficult manuscript with intelligence and accuracy.

I am deeply indebted to many historians and researchers. Randall Miller of St. Joseph's College, Philadelphia, introduced me to the letters of Lucy Skipwith in his *"Dear Master" Letters of a Slave Family* and also contributed letters from other slave women. Sally Loomis, biographer of Paul Cuffe, helped me to read and annotate letters from the Cuffe women. Milton Meltzer and Patricia G. Holland, editors of *Lydia Maria Child Selected Letters* provided many letters to and about black women. Louise D. Hutchinson, director of research for the Anacostia Neighborhood Museum, Smithsonian Institution, helped me thread my way through the District of Columbia's maze of records and was of inestimable assistance in locating portraits of black women. Linda Jean Butler and Jim Bearden shared their research on Mary Ann Shadd Cary even before the publication of their biography, *Shadd.*

I am also grateful to Ellen Lawson and Marlene Merrill for their paper, "On the Cutting Edge: Antebellum Educated Black Women Missionaries and Teachers" and for information from Lawson about other Oberlin students; to Amy Swerdlow for her dissertation and paper on the Ladies New York City Anti-Slavery Society; to Clarence Mohr and Richard G. Carlson, editors of the Frederick Douglass Papers, and to Ann Teabeau for information about her grandmother, Rosetta Douglass; to Adelaide Cromwell Gulliver of Boston University's Afro-American Studies Center for a copy of a letter to her father, John W. Cromwell. Harry Henderson, coauthor with Romare Bearden of a soon-to-be published *History of America's Black Artists* and of a biography of Edmonia Lewis, gave me useful insights on Lewis. Marilyn Bailey lent me important letters from Sarah Grimké and helped to identify the black members of the Female Anti-Slavery Societies.

Jean Fagan Yellin of Pace University has worked with me to annotate and date Harriet Jacobs's letters. She has also, in a remarkable piece of historical detective work, uncovered the identities of the people in Jacobs's *Incidents in the Life of a Slave Girl* and has generously shared this information with me. Her detailed report on Jacobs and her circle will soon be published.

I recall with pleasure the hours spent with Alfreda M. Duster as she reminisced about her mother, Ida B. Wells. Leighla Frances Whipper Ford, granddaughter of Frances Rollin, first let me read her grandmother's diary in 1969. Carole Bovoso, Rollin's great granddaughter, has generously given me permission to publish selections from the diary and has exchanged information about her. I am looking forward to Bovoso's book, *Foremothers,* and to "Diary of a Cultured Colored Woman," her television play written with James Lecesne for the American Playhouse's 1984 season.

My deepest gratitude is reserved for members of my family—my niece Dinah Shatz who was always ready for research assignments in the libraries of Boston and Cambridge; my children, Anne Fausto Sterling and Peter Sterling who utilized their university libraries on my behalf; and my husband, Philip Sterling, who read every word of every version of the manuscript, helping to cut, rephrase, and sharpen my ideas. The book owes a great deal to his editorial skills.

Index

Page entries in *italics* refer to illustrations.